Managing Democratic Organizations
Volume II

Classic Research in Management
General Editor: Derek S. Pugh

Titles in the Series

Managing Democratic Organizations
Volume II

Edited by

Frank Heller

The Tavistock Institute, London

Routledge
Taylor & Francis Group

LONDON AND NEW YORK

First published 2000 by Dartmouth and Ashgate Publishing

Reissued 2018 by Routledge
2 Park Square, Milton Park, Abingdon, Oxon OX14 4RN
52 Vanderbilt Avenue, New York, NY 10017

Routledge is an imprint of the Taylor & Francis Group, an informa business

Publisher's Note
The publisher has gone to great lengths to ensure the quality of this reprint but points out that some imperfections in the original copies may be apparent.

Disclaimer
The publisher has made every effort to trace copyright holders and welcomes correspondence from those they have been unable to contact.

A Library of Congress record exists under LC control number:99041125

ISBN 13: 978-1-138-36172-0 (hbk)
ISBN 13: 978-0-429-43251-4 (ebk)

Contents

PART IV   DECISIONS IN ORGANIZATIONS (DIO)

PART V   VALEDICTION AND THE FUTURE

Acknowledgements

The editor and publishers wish to thank the following for permission to use copyright material.

Ashgate Publishing Limited for the essay: Frank Heller (1997), 'The Time Dimension in Organizational Research', in Timothy Clark (ed.), *Advancement in Organizational Behaviour: Essays in Honour of Derek S. Pugh*, Aldershot: Ashgate, pp. 297–312. Copyright © 1997 Timothy Clark.

Blackwell Publishers for the essays: Bernhard Wilpert (1984), 'Participation in Organizations: Evidence from International Comparative Research', *International Social Science Journal*, UNESCO, **XXXVI**, pp. 355–66; Oiva Laaksonen (1984), 'Participation Down and Up the Line: Comparative Industrial Democracy Trend in China and Europe', *International Social Science Journal*, UNESCO, **XXXVI**, pp. 299–318; Velko Rus (1984), 'The Future of Industrial Democracy', *International Social Science Journal*, **XXXVI**, UNESCO Special Issue: Industrial Democracy, pp. 233–54; IDE – Industrial Democracy in Europe International Research Group (1979), 'Participation: Formal Rules, Influence, and Involvement', *Industrial Relations*, **18**, pp. 273–94. Copyright © 1979 the Regents of the University of California; Decisions in Organizations (1979), 'Participative Decision Making: A Comparative Study', *Industrial Relations*, **18**, pp. 295–309. Copyright © 1979 the Regents of the University of California.

The British Psychological Society for the essay: DIO International Research Team (1983), 'A Contingency Model of Participative Decision Making: An Analysis of 56 Decisions in Three Dutch Organizations', *Journal of Occupational Psychology*, **56**, pp. 1–18. Copyright © 1983 The British Psychological Society.

Oxford University Press for the essay: Paul L. Koopman, Pieter J.D. Drenth, Frank A. Heller and Veljko Rus (1993), 'Participation in Complex Organizational Decisions: A Comparative Study of the United Kingdom, The Netherlands and Yugoslavia', in William M. Lafferty and Eliezer Rosenstein (eds), *International Handbook of Participation in Organizations*, **3**, Oxford: Oxford University Press, pp. 113–33. Copyright © 1993 William M. Lafferty and Eliezer Rosenstein. Reprinted from The International Handbook of Participation in Organizations; Volume 3: The Challenge of New Technologies and Macropolitical Change edited by William M. Lafferty and Eliezer Rosenstein (1993) by permission of Oxford University Press.

Plenum Publishing Corporation for the essays: Frank A. Heller, Pieter J.D. Drenth, Paul Koopman and Veljko Rus (1977), 'A Longitudinal Study in Participative Decision-Making', *Human Relations*, **30**, pp. 567–87; Paul L. Koopman, Pieter J.D. Drenth, Frans B.M. Bus, Agaath J. Kruyswijk and André F.M. Wierdsma (1981), 'Content, Process, and Effects of Participative Decision Making on the Shop Floor: Three Cases in the Netherlands', *Human Relations*, **34**, pp. 657–76. Copyright © 1981 Tavistock Institute of Human Relations; Alan

Series Preface

As the history of management and management thought continues to attract greater interest among scholars, the Ashgate/Dartmouth series of collections of articles on the *History of Management Thought* has been successful in making more readily available historically important academic papers in key areas of the subject. *Classic Research in Management* complements the *History of Management Thought* by presenting the contribution of outstanding research programmes whose sustained output of work has had a defining effect on the development of the field of business and management as a discipline.

Classic Research in Management presents, for each research programme, a comprehensive set of papers which have had a major impact on subsequent research and thinking. In many cases these research reports and articles have appeared in books which are now out of print, or are in early issues of journals which are not easily available to libraries. The present series provides a new opportunity for wider access to the research. Each volume has been collected and presented by a scholar who played a leading part in the original research programme. Each chosen article is reproduced in full. The volumes enable a detailed analysis of the distinctive contribution of each research programme in its historical context. The series offers an important resource for use by academics and advanced students in the field of increasing their knowledge and understanding of the historical development of the management discipline.

DEREK S. PUGH
General Editor
Classic Research in Management
Open University Business School, UK

Part III
Industrial Democracy in Europe (IDE)

Part III
Industrial Demand-side Response (DR)

Overview Part III

More than 30 researchers collaborated in this major two-phase study which was spread over more than a decade. The research took place in 12 countries and obtained data, based on questionnaires from 9000 respondents in Phase I when each of the 134 establishments were visited by researchers who administered the enquiry in groups. Phase II, ten years later in the same establishments, used a smaller number of respondents. The project engaged with policy issues which then and now preoccupies the European Union: how to devise an even playing field for democratic organizations among member countries.

Four of the entries in this section, as well as the three books mentioned in 'Further Reading', were published under the title of the research programme rather than under named authors. Publishers are not fond of such gestures to collegiate democracy, and this says much for the way in which the multinational, cross-disciplinary group organized itself.

It is therefore appropriate that the author of the first essay (Chapter 16), which lifts the veil that almost invariably obscures the dynamic of the research process, should be by the person who is *primus inter pares* in our group. Wilpert's description of how such a diverse research team came together and maintained itself over long periods of time, formulated a social contract and rallied around a German as international coordinator makes an unusual and important contribution to our understanding of research.

Chapter 17 is by the same author. He briefly introduces the broad topic of participation and illustrates a variety of approaches through six different cross-national studies on participation and organizational democracy including IDE and the DIO project which forms Part IV of these two volumes.

Chapter 18 introduces the IDE project design, the main variables in the form of a model, the instruments, the set of decisions and the procedures used. The main objective of the research is to see whether formal legal support for organizational democracy leads to *de facto* influence-sharing at lower levels of organizations and whether and how contextual contingency variables affect this relationship. Chapter 19 then presents an overview of the study, the main measures and the model, as well as the first simple descriptive results from the 12-country research and some analytic data in the form of various multiple regression analyses.

The essays presented as Chapters 20 and 21 complement each other by dealing with different theoretical and empirical aspects of the study. Although the introductory comments and description of the model inevitably overlap, the accumulation of results from these chapters present an adequate account of the main achievements of the investigation.

In Chapter 22 Bengt Stymne describes an application of the IDE model and instrumentation to two studies of Swedish industrial relations. One of the studies took place before an industrial democracy law was passed and the second study was carried out five years later when the law had been implemented. The results lend considerable strength to the main findings of the 12-country research.

The essay by Laaksonen which follows (Chapter 23) shows an application of the IDE model and instrumentation to a sample of Chinese enterprises. The study is introduced by an account of history and Chinese culture. The data was collected during two field trips in 1973 and 1978 and makes statistical comparisons between Chinese and European samples. Chapter 32 in Part IV gives another account of a study in China using a different methodology.

Chapter 24 by Heller *et al.* presents aspects of the UK results of the IDE study which were used by the financial sponsor for policy discussions in the then prevailing context of British industrial relations. To check the fieldwork results from 14 UK companies some of the main IDE questions were put to a random national household survey. The survey also contained additional items including three questions, including one on trust, from the well known 1960 Almond and Verber 'Civic Culture' research.

The IDE II replication study took place ten years after IDE I in the same sample of companies and countries, with small exceptions, and is described in Chapter 25. The theoretical and practical value of this longitudinal extension is considerable and the results are briefly analysed from a policy perspective.

Finally, another essay by Bernhard Wilpert (Chapter 26) published in 1989 challenges European industrial leadership with the results of recent social science findings that, over ten years later, still have relevance for organizational governance (economic crises, unemployment, technological change and changing work-related values). The author draws on the outcome of two projects: IDE which is presented in the preceding chapters and a seven-country comparative study of 'The Meaning of Working' (MOW) which also included samples from Japan and the United States. Several members of the IDE team also took part in this study.

Overall, the 12-country two-phase research at all levels of organization comes to a number of policy relevant conclusions. Most important perhaps is the finding that formal policy and legal provisions play a significant part in the degree of influence given to lower levels of employee. However, even with legal backing, the average *de facto* participation of non-managerial staff in all countries is very low and the amount of participation they would like to have, though greater, is still no threat to the managerial prerogative.

Further Reading

The IDE Group (1981), *Industrial Democracy in Europe*, Oxford: Oxford University Press.
The IDE Group (1981), *European Industrial Relations*, Oxford: Oxford University Press.
The IDE Group (1993), *Industrial Democracy in Europe Revisited*, Oxford: Oxford University Press.

[16]

Inside Story: Inside IDE[1]

Bernhard Wilpert

Bernhard Wilpert
Institute of Psychology,
Technical University,
Berlin,
Federal Republic
of Germany

The purpose of publishing inside views is to provide insights otherwise rarely possible. Simultaneously to my writing this inside story, the 'official' IDE story is being distributed intercontinentally through the worldwide channels of Oxford University Press (IDE 1981a, 1981b) as well as through journal articles, including one in this issue of OS (see pp. 113–129).

So, I ask myself, what then is the 'unofficial', and hitherto untold, IDE story? In attempting to answer this question I find myself involved in a peculiar process which can be likened to peeling an onion: the first layer is often easy to peel off, it won't make you cry — in a sense it is the official, outside part of the story (see IDE 1981a, 1981b). With the second layer you usually reach the onion's heart with its pungent smell and your eyes and nose begin to water — you reach the story's emotional dimensions. Finally, with the third layer you start cutting into the heart, your eyes may begin to hurt — you delve into intimate parts of a project history. Not being a masochist, or too much of an exhibitionist, I intend to limit myself to the second layer.

Two inside aspects of the inside IDE story strike me as being particularly important:
— group maintenance over several years, and
— the significance of a German as international coordinator.

Group Maintenance

On the surface, the IDE International Research Group ('the Group') has been remarkably successful in presenting itself as a homogeneous entity. Not only a crucial test but also a symbol of this homogeneity has been final agreement by all members to collectively author all international publications, to waive all personal royalty claims, and to direct all potential royalties to a newly created association, the Industrial Democracy in Europe Fund, to support further research on participation and industrial democracy.

But, of course, nobody could or would claim that 'the Group' displayed total equality among its members throughout its phases of development. After all, there were some 25 members with different national, religious, and cultural heritages; among them were extreme introverts as well as extreme extroverts; engineers, psychologists, sociologists, philosophers; colleagues more than a generation apart in age; colleagues representing politically and methodologi-

Organization Studies
1981, 2/2: 181–184
© 1981 EGOS
0170–8406/81/
0002–0008 $1.00

cally rather diverse outlooks; people who were internationally well known in their field and others who were beginners; some were absolute masters of the English language and others were on a level equivalent to second-year English language students. Hence, any person with a minimum knowledge of group dynamics and organizational behaviour will rightly suspect that such differences would influence the internal role structure of 'the Group'. The research topic itself was power and influence processes in organizations; we were vividly aware that these phenomena were present within our own group. No doubt, we had 'central group members' as well as 'peripheral' ones. At one point in time we even began to objectify this internal structure by means of sociographic techniques.

How then, and this was always a crucial question, could we ensure the basic unity of 'the Group' in spite of existing internal differences, distances covering thousands of miles, and a time period spanning more than seven years? (I do not entertain the hypothesis that unity was possible *because* we were so far apart and only met as a group for limited periods at a time!)

One important factor was certainly that 'the Group' liked and enjoyed itself. There seemed to be no unbridgeable personality clashes. Personal and intellectual styles matched. Without a doubt this was necessary, but certainly not sufficient. In retrospect I can clearly see that we were always aware of the need to make conscious efforts in group maintenance. What do I mean by that?

Five aspects may be distinguished here:

1. Preparation of meetings

One of the responsibilities of the Berlin team was to prepare the agenda of each of the thirteen plenary meetings that were held during the project's life time. I remember that we often spent several sessions planning the sequence of agenda items and discussing the way each item ought to be introduced in order to avoid potentially disruptive reactions from team members. For the same purpose we used subcommittees of the international team as sounding boards to test the likely reaction of the whole team. I believe that this careful planning contributed considerably to smooth plenary sessions. But in the event that a plenary session became stormy anyway, it was a second element that helped to guarantee common purpose and group identification.

2. Conference technique

'The Group' had among its members not only excellent chairmen but also people who had been weathered and seasoned by long years of sometimes strenuous committee work. They knew the 'ins' and 'outs' of when to speed-up the decision-making process, when to slow down and allow an airing of opinions by participants, and when to call for a life-saving break. I distinctly remember one international session in which we risked losing two or three country teams over methodological issues. It was then that expertise in the whole gamut of conference and committee methodology paid off. A break was called, subcommittees went to work, the main antagonists met with a senior colleague to explore constraints and overlaps of their positions. The evening found us united again.

3. After-hours servicing

Our international plenary meetings were deliberately scheduled to last at least four or five days. In other words, the whole international team spent a total of about 2–3 months (not counting the frequent subcommittee contacts and occasional meetings at other international conferences) working together in one location. Almost from the outset we recognized that, beyond professional contact, we needed personal contact in order to steer this giant project to success. The relatively long plenary meetings provided ample opportunity to encounter colleagues as persons. A conversation over a glass of Old Genever or young Slivović must have helped to verify many an opinion; improvised after-dinner speeches, charades, and sketches helped to articulate many pent-up feelings, thus clearing the air for next day's work sessions.

4. Social contract

Apart from such informal means of reducing tensions we also tried to anticipate many possible problems by formally discussing and reaching an agreement on such issues as acknowledgements, data ownership, authorship, and royalties. We even envisioned arbitration procedures in case of conflicts over such issues. We have not yet found it necessary to implement such procedures but the con-sensus reached in our 'social contract' certainly has helped to alleviate many anxieties that frequently undermine similar projects. It has provided the formal normative frame within which work and collaboration could be pursued.

5. The image of the common enemy

Finally, we managed to instil in ourselves a healthy sense of competitiveness with other real or imagined parallel and ongoing projects. I think some of us (occasionally) played up the threat that 'the others will be earlier on the market than we' in order to set time constraints for our own work and to speed up action by the team as a whole. And 'common enemies', whether they be time pressures or real or imagined rival projects, induce group cohesion . . .

The total fabric of these factors, I believe, explains, to a large degree, why, against all odds, we managed to maintain basic unity in 'the Group'.

A German as International Coordinator

Here I may primarily be expressing my own personal feelings or, at best, touching the Group's sub- and unconscious feelings, rather than addressing something that was consciously shared by the whole international team. Never-theless, they seem important enough to report because it is likely that the underlying dynamics characterize any European or international collaboration with German participation.

By the age of nine, at the end of World War II, I had experienced hunger, bombings, evacuation, and flight in horsedrawn carriages through several European countries. Indelible images remain of thousands of Theresien-stadt concentration camp evacuees stumbling and falling along the road to-wards the West. I thought I knew something from my own experience of what that war meant and I believed I could imagine what it still means to other Europeans who had gone through it. Thus, without being burdened by personal guilt I belong to a generation of Germans that appears permanently and inextricably affected by the events caused in the name of Germany.

As a research fellow at the Berlin-based International Institute of Management (IIM) I had been able to muster some internal and external funds to help the development of the IDE project. Given IIM's institutional support and the funds obtained it seemed logical to ask me to continue in an administrative capacity as International Coordinator of the project. In retrospect I realize how naïve I was in taking this action for granted. Only with time did I learn that in addition to our Israeli colleagues the team also included several other colleagues with Jewish backgrounds and emigrant experience. What the German occupation of Holland and Norway must have meant I learned only much later from my Dutch and Norwegian colleagues' evident elation when they told me how they had celebrated the actual day of liberation and how they still commemorate it. Only little by little did I find out some biographic facts of one colleague's life as the son of a national resistance leader in Yugoslavia and what it still must mean to have oneself been a member of the resistance movement as a teenager. Did this unusual constellation in the IDE team manifest itself in any way? I think it did. It showed in jokes (for instance, an urgent request of mine to 'the Group' might be answered by: 'So, the Führer wants . . .'). And I will not forget the sleepless night which followed a session when as chairman I tried to reconvene the participants by saying: 'Let's get back to work' and someone spontaneously responded: 'Ja, Arbeit macht frei'.[2] It was also evident in my own uneasiness when the whole team, spellbound and fascinated, happened to watch Yugoslav liberation day festivities.

Other, maybe less tangible, examples might be given. Some of my IDE colleagues, however, may be totally unaware of such events, not to mention of my own personal reactions. In this sense I present here genuine 'inside' views, which were part and parcel of our collaboration. Inasmuch as we were successful, as an international team, in producing a collective product that will — hopefully — be found by colleagues to constitute an important research contribution, so will we also have shown that such collaboration is possible against all odds of heterogeneity in team composition and historical legacy. However, the final balance sheet should also contain the results of inside learning processes — regardless of how painful they may be at times — which will hopefully provide deeper insights into the European condition.

Notes

1. Industrial Democracy in Europe Study.
2. 'Work liberates' — cynical welcome slogan above the entrance to the Auschwitz concentration camp.

References

IDE International Research Group
1981a *Industrial democracy in Europe.* London: Oxford University Press.

IDE International Research Group
1981b *European industrial relations.* London: Oxford University Press.

[17]

Participation in organizations: evidence from international comparative research

Bernhard Wilpert

The bewildering diversity and sheer number of publications dealing with the topic during the last two decades or so lend credibility to the statement that 'participation is the most vital organizational problem of our time' (Mulder, 1971). These studies have usually been limited to specific national situations. Systematic international comparative research is bedevilled by a host of conceptual, methodological and organizational problems. This may explain why only recently we see more of it directly or indirectly addressing the topic of participation. It is the purpose of this article to review briefly the seven major international comparative research ventures in the area of participation and draw some general conclusions. However, before reviewing them in detail, some theoretical reflections are in order.

Dr Bernhard Wilpert is Professor of Organizational and Work Psychology at the Technical University, Dovest-rasse 1–5, D–1000 West Berlin 10. Among his recent publications are *Competence and Power in Managerial Decision Making* (with F. A. Heller), *Industrial Democracy in Europe* and *European Industrial Relations* (with IDE/International Research Group), *Anspruch und Wirklichkeit der Mitbestimmung* (with J. Rayley), and *Organizational Democracy in International Perspective* (ed., with A. Sorge).

Towards a definition of participation

The great variety of current terms covering participation of employees in their work organizations—industrial democracy, codetermination, self-management, participative leadership (just to name a few more promi-

nent ones)—stress different aspects of the same content. Participation is here understood to denote a linking of decisions to the interests of affected employees by means of organizational conditions, structures and processes. This definition implies that participation is a variable phenomenon which, in the reality of work organizations, is always defined by at least four dimensions and their interaction (Dachler and Wilpert, 1978): (a) the underlying value premisses which guide the different actors and define their goals; (b) the design characteristics of participatory systems; (c) the contextual, environmental (societal) constraints and opportunities for the emergence of participatory processes; (d) the outcomes of participation on an individual, organizational and societal level. Assuming that these broad dimensions constitute, if not exhaustively, the central defining dimensions of participation we may use them as evaluative perspectives in the subsequent review of empirical studies. However, before going into this discussion it seems appropriate to discuss briefly the significance of participation in modern societies.

Significance of participation

We can distinguish at least three different levels on which the question of the significance of participation must be considered: individual, organizational and societal. Although we may analytically treat them separately, it should be clear that in reality they are closely interrelated by virtue of the intricate interrelationship of the defining dimensions referred to above.

The individual significance of participation is most significantly elaborated in various psychological theories that might collectively be subsumed under 'theories of personal growth' (McGregor, 1960; Argyris, 1964; Likert, 1967). Central to them is the postulate of a universally valid human need for self-realization (Maslow, 1954; Alderfer, 1972). Personal growth, though rarely explicitly defined, is seen as individual development towards an active, independent, self-regulated, socially competent personality with long-range goals using available skills (Dachler and Wilpert, 1978). Participation in decisions affecting one's own life space in various segments of reality is here viewed as a central mechanism to stimulate and facilitate such growth for the sake of the ensuing sense of efficacy or competence motivation (White, 1959), a motivation which emerges as a function of the ability to influence and control one's surroundings (Argyris and Schön, 1977). Hence, participation can be conceived as a central factor in personality and identity formation. Given the fact that more than a third of an average person's life is spent in work settings it is clear that participation in work organizations will necessarily have an important impact on such development.

Regarding the significance of participation from an organization perspective we must note that two major lines of reasoning have been adopted in the literature. The first is to look at participation as a fundamental principle of all organizing, the second is to view participation as a means to specific ends, i.e. as a social technology. The former argues that no organization—whether factory, party, cooperative, army, prison, public administration, kibbutz, school, people's commune or whatever—can be conceived without some kind of participation of its members in decision-making processes. The latter concept of participation conceives of it as an instrument to attain particular goals, such as policy acceptance by members, employee satisfaction and involvement in their organization, increased work motivation and ensuing greater aggregate outputs. The distinction between these notions, though rather prevalent in the literature and analytically feasible seems, in practice, to be artificial (Dachler and Wilpert, 1978). No matter what view we take, participation appears as a critical organizational phenomenon.

From a societal point of view participation, finally, is attributed particular importance by two theoretical positions. Democratic theory considers participation to be intrinsically linked to an individual's self-determination, an unalienable human right, thus a value in itself to be realized in all spheres of life. In consequence, the extension of political democracy to working life is demanded. According to Pateman (1970, p. 42):

The existence of representative institutions at national level is not sufficient for democracy: for maximum participation by all the people at that level socialization, or 'social training', for democracy must take place in other spheres in order that the necessary individual attitudes and psychological qualities can be developed. This development takes place through the process of participation itself. The major function of participation in the theory of participatory democracy is therefore an educative one.

For socialistic theorizing participation is a central instrument to allow exploited and alienated workers to become active agents in the process of remodelling society (Vanek, 1975). Both positions clearly reflect the basic value premises that it is ultimately society as a whole that is to be transformed in the general interest—not least by means of participation.

A historical setting for alienated labour: agricultural machinery construction around the turn of the century. H. Roger Viollet.

What, then, can be shown to be the body of knowledge and insight gained about the realities of participation so far from international comparative research?

Comparative studies

Cultural consequences

This research (Hofstede, 1980) was not designed to study participation but attitudes and values defined as 'a broad tendency to prefer certain states of affairs over others'. Data were obtained through questionnaire surveys of employees in a United States-based multinational company with subsidiaries in virtually all countries around the world. Data collection took place at two periods, 1967–69 and 1971–73, on both occasions with about 60,000 respondents using eighteen different languages. The study is based on a data bank which by its sheer size, is unique in the world. Its methodological limitation is that it is exclusively confined to self-reported values.

The value dimension of particular interest in our context is 'power distance' as measured by three fairly broad items: a question relating to how frequently employees are afraid to express disagreement with their superiors and two questions regarding the type of superior an employee actually has and under which type he or she prefers to work. The choices had to be made from ideal, typically described managers who varied in their decision-making behaviour along a continuum from autocratic decision-making, through *ex-post* explanation and consultation with subordinates to group decision-making. Low power distance, then, is an aggregate of not being afraid to disagree with a superior and of his or her use of participatory decision-making methods, as well as the subordinate's preference for such methods. Hofstede finds distinct national differences in power distance which he explains as cultural differences. Low power distance correlates significantly with a measure of gross national product. Furthermore, power distance is seen as separating countries into distinct clusters (more or less developed Latin and Asian, Middle Eastern, Germanic, Anglo and Nordic). However, these same clusters are not replicated in studies that use less attitudinal but more behavioural measures of participation (Heller and Wilpert 1981; IDE, 1981).

Hofstede's research (which he relates to a great variety of similar research findings and of which we here report only the participation-related findings on power distance) focuses on espoused values of employees regarding hierarchical relations in subsidiaries of a large multinational company. His nationally aggregated power-distance index (which may be taken as an index of preferences for participation) shows strong correlations with aggregate economic output measures. Hofstede interprets the causal chain to run from wealth to participation preferences. However, given the fact that this is based mainly on correlational evidence, what is cause and what is effect must be considered moot questions.

Hierarchy in organizations

The study (Tannenbaum et al., 1974) investigates the distribution of perceived influence levels of hierarchical levels in plants in five countries (Israel, Yugoslavia, Austria, Italy, United States). The choice of countries was guided by the aim to include some with higher levels of formal and some with informal participativeness. Formal participativeness is defined 'in terms of legally established decision-making structure' and informal 'in terms of style of management and sharing by superiors of their authority with subordinates'. The study attempts to match ten companies

for each country in terms of size and industrial sector. Data were obtained by way of questionnaires from members of hierarchical chains of linked positions (superior and subordinate) throughout the selected plants. The central measure is the 'control graph', i.e. the slope of perceived 'say' of different hierarchical levels which may vary on a scale from 'much' to 'little'. The gradient of the 'control graph' over hierarchical levels is interpreted as a measure of equality: the steeper the slope, the higher the perceived inequality and vice versa. Tannenbaum et al. find Israeli kibbutzim and Yugoslav plants to be most participative and egalitarian, Italian and American plants lowest on this score. Among the significant correlates of high control scores are higher levels of satisfaction, higher work motivation, lower frequencies of symptoms of peptic ulcers. Participatory behaviour of superiors is correlated with satisfaction of subordinates. Formal schemes of participation, as in Israel and Yugoslavia, are seen to have definite effects on perceived influence while informal participation, as in the United States, works as a functional equivalent to 'mitigate the effect of hierarchy'.

The general nature of the questionnaire items used in this study suggests that the control graph is a measure of general organizational climate rather than of real differences of hierarchical influence. This may also explain the close relationship of perceived control with variables of satisfaction and motivation. Differences in formal participation systems are not measured and related to individual or organizational variables but taken as criteria to choose certain countries. In spite of this conceptual critique the study is rightly considered as a seminal step forward in international comparative organization research.

Competence and power in managerial decision-making

The thematic focus of this research (Heller and Wilpert, 1981) is influence and power-sharing in decision-making among superior

Dials showing various output norms set by central planning to encourage productivity, at Yakutsk, Siberia, *c.* 1928. Snark/Edimedia.

The pause. Henri Cartier-Bresson/Magnum.

and subordinates in senior managerial levels of 129 large and successful companies in eight countries: France, the Federal Republic of Germany, the United Kingdom, Israel, the Netherlands, Spain, Sweden and the United States. Close to 1,600 managers were included in the study, roughly half of whom representing the companies' top executive level, the other half belonging to the level immediately below. The research attempted to study 'dyads' of superior–subordinate (Levels 1–2); 625 such dyads were involved. The use of such dyads served to permit and confront observations of the same phenomena from both levels. The research method employed was 'Group Feedback Analysis', a technique that proceeds in three steps: questionnaire data collection, immediate analysis of responses and feedback to participants, by group discussion of findings (Heller, 1969). The central research interest was to discover the circumstances in which participative decision-making

is used. Participation in the making of specific decisions was measured by the perception of both managerial levels who judged their own behaviour and that of the superior (Level 1), on an 'influence-power-continuum' with the range of: 'own decision without explanation —own decision with explanation—prior consultation—joint decision-making—delegation'. Some of the main findings were:

Managers show a relatively high degree of flexibility in decision-making behaviour which they adjust to situational demands (e.g. uncertainty induces higher levels of participation).

On the whole managers believe that the main function of participation is to improve the technical quality of decision outcomes, i.e. it facilitates better use of competence.

The more objective skills available or perceived, the more participative decision behaviour tends to be.

Significant differences among the various

country samples of managers show up: thus Israeli managers are characterized by rather centralized (autocratic) decision-making behaviour while Swedish managers are the most participative among the various country groups. Managers from the other countries fall between these two extremes. From the fact that American managers do not differ significantly from the European managerial decision-making patterns it is concluded that Servan-Schreiber's thesis of an Atlantic gap in managerial practice (1967) is not supported by these data.

In summary, this research on managerial decision-making centres on behavioural aspects of informal participation, and taps the values of managers regarding participation. It attempts to shed some light on the contextual (organizational and extra-organizational) characteristics that facilitate and inhibit participative behaviour and studies some of the main individual and organizational outcomes of participation.

Models of industrial democracy

The goal˜ of this study (King and van de Vall, 1978) is to compare what the authors term the 'three leading models' of industrial democracy in Europe: the British system of labour management (joint consultation), the Yugoslav system of self- or worker's management, and the system of codetermination in coalmining and the iron-and-steel industry in the Federal Republic of Germany. These three models are compared with reference to eight descriptive dimensions of industrial democracy. The authors distinguish the following organizational dimensions of participation: (a) vertical range (intensity of participation); (b) horizontal span (topics open to participation); (c) timing of participation (access of employees to various decision-making phases); (d) comprehensiveness (social scope in terms of including various system levels); (e) representativeness (ratio of employees to representatives and the linking system among representatives). These are followed by three

institutional context dimensions: (a) education (formal training for participation and learning by 'doing participation'); (b) union attitude towards participation; and (c) conflict regulatory efficiency of participation.

Using these eight dimensions as yardsticks for comparing the formal characteristics of the industrial democracy schemes in the three countries, the British joint-consultation system is found to score relatively low on all dimensions while the systems in Yugoslavia and the Federal Republic of Germany rank moderately high to relatively highest. The study thus accomplishes a major step forward in systematically comparing the formal, normative *(de jure)* participation systems in different countries. This constitutes a major methodological breakthrough. But the volume falls short in comparing the consequences of various normative systems on the emergence of *de facto* (lived) participation. It remains a comparison of blueprints for participation, not of its realities in different countries.

Industrial democracy in Europe

Parallel to King and van de Vall's study this twelve-country comparison (IDE, 1981) was conducted to address the question of the effects of norms for participation on *de facto* participation behaviour. The twelve countries were: Belgium, Denmark, Finland, France, Italy, Israel, Netherlands, Norway, Sweden, the United Kingdom, the Federal Republic of Germany and Yugoslavia. Altogether 134 firms, matched in terms of size and industrial sector participated in the research. The data base consists of interviews with close to 1,000 key respondents and with about 8,000 randomly selected employees, conducted between 1975 and 1977.

Written rules and regulations for participation (laws, collective bargaining agreements, management rules, etc.) were compared in terms of how much participation they prescribed (degree of intensity) for various groups (e.g. workers, worker representatives, management) in the making of sixteen specific decisions (varying from routine to strategic).

The scale of prescribed *(de jure)* participation ranged from 'no regulation' through 'information must be given to the group'/'obligatory consultation'/'joint decision-making with the group (veto)' to 'the group has the final say'. The *de facto* participation was measured by a similar scale by which the respondents described their own involvement in and the various groups' influence on the making of decisions.

The findings based on measuring and comparing formal national norm systems for participation show that Yugoslavia has the most formal rule-making, the United Kingdom and Israel the least. For the majority of countries law is the most important formal base of participation. With respect to the prescribed intensity of participation, countries show certain profiles that are characteristic of their typical distribution of *de jure* participation.

The average amount of *de facto* influence and involvement for country samples was very similar: quite low, with the exception of Yugoslavia where the influence of workers and workers' councils was found to be considerably higher than in the other participating countries. The effect of hierarchy can be observed in all countries, irrespective of their social system and economic order. The strongest predictors of actual involvement and influence were institutional norms *(de jure)* promoting participation. This most important factor contributing to actual *(de facto)* participation is followed by employee mobilization (unionization and 'representativeness' as defined by King and van de Vall).

As to attitudes towards participation the IDE data show significant differences between the country samples. Employees tend to be more positive about representative bodies in those countries where the formal regulations provide bodies with relatively greater powers. Within countries attitudes were most positive in those companies where the actual influence of representative bodies (e.g. works councils, shop-stewards' committees) was greatest. While it was found that individuals who experience themselves as influential are most

satisfied, the same does not hold for whole organizations: it is not true that overall satisfaction is greater in organizations where the influence of workers is higher.

It appears that the IDE study has, for the first time, successfully tackled the difficult problem of relating contextual realities (here norm systems for participation), organizational characteristics (e.g. unionization) and measures at the indivudual level (perceived participation, value judgements about participation) systematically to each other. Relating *de jure* norms to *de facto* behaviour implied the development of new conceptual and methodological tools which may help to advance international comparative research on participation.

Societal differences in organizing manufacturing units

The focus of this research (Maurice et al., 1980) is more on the difference between countries in the 'production of industrial hierarchies' than participation as such. However, inasmuch as it centres on national differences in the division of labour it has an indirect bearing on the issue of participation of various organizational actors. The data base stems from twelve industrial establishments in each of three countries: France, the Federal Republic of Germany, and the United Kingdom. The firms are roughly matched by size, technology and product.

Mainly based on qualitative interviews the findings show convincingly that while similar forces in all countries to rationalize work and to find optimal organizational solutions may exist, the way that this is actually done is rather country-specific. Although the basic form of hierarchical organization of industrial enterprises is found in all three country samples, they differ among countries in terms of their specific characteristics: the proportion of formally qualified workers is highest in companies in the Federal Republic of Germany, followed by French and then by British enterprises.

National differences exist also in the

Testing a Rolls-Royce engine with a stethoscope along a country lane. Peter Marlow/Sygma.

percentage of workers with a craft qualification and a university degree. Decentralization of decision-making to lower levels of the hierarchy in establishments is found to be most accentuated in the Federal Republic of Germany due precisely to such occupational and qualificational differences. Such differences are then linked to national differences in the encompassing educational systems and it can be shown that wider societal structures (here educational and occupational stratification as well as the industrial relations system) correspond to the internal organizational configurations and division of work and decision-making processes.

Similar to the IDE study described above, this research attempts to relate societal structures to organizational characteristics. While the former goes on to include also variables on the individual level, the research by Maurice et al. centres on structural aspects of the organization. Their qualitative structural methodological approach, however, provides rich information on the intricate connection between societies and their typical solutions for organizing industrial establishments. It must be considered to constitute a major step towards international comparisons of organizational phenomena, including participation.

The resurgence of class conflict in Western Europe since 1968

An even broader perspective than any of the aforementioned studies is taken by this attempt (Crouch and Pizzorno, 1978) to compare recent developments in the industrial relations systems (plant-level labour activities, strike frequencies, and government counter-strategies to heightened industrial conflict levels) in six countries: Belgium, France, Italy, Netherlands, the United Kingdom and the Federal Republic of Germany. The two volumes of the study (Vol. 1: 'Country Studies', Vol. 2: 'Comparative Analyses', both edited by Crouch and Pizzorno) are not strictly based on original empirical work but on various analyses of available sources. The

issue of participation is but one aspect of the overall scope of the two volumes.

The topic of participation enters most explicitly when decentralization of industrial relations decisions and the ensuing processes of institutionalizing new bargaining structures are discussed. A new emphasis on plant-level bargaining could be observed during that time which reflects the growing concern for control of the immediate working environment and all aspects of the organization of production of intra-organizational bargaining structures of labour (works councils, shop stewards' committees, etc.) can be seen as enhancing participation potentials of employees. Legal efforts in virtually all the countries under study to institutionalize new structures and to expand the scope of old ones are interpreted by the authors as a more or less direct consequence of the strike waves at the turn of the decade.

The historical and macro-analytical approach of this study raises some fundamental questions about the interdependence of historical events or trends and the functioning and development of participation in European countries. It is in the nature of the approach chosen that the findings are more of an indicative rather than of a conclusive nature. The exclusion of certain countries which at the period studied displayed different characteristics may further somewhat weaken the generalizability of findings (Pool, 1984). Notwithstanding these restrictions, the study represents a valiant attempt to combine historical and structural comparative analysis of industrial relations processes.

Conclusions

The sequence of studies reviewed here does not correspond to the years of their publication. Rather, it was deliberately chosen to reflect a widening perspective, an extension of awareness that it is useful and often necessary to encompass ever higher levels of complexity in the analytic framework if we wish to comprehend the full width of the concept of

Works-council meeting in a Belgrade factory. Vioujard/Gamma.

participation. This is not to say that each and every study of participation must always employ the whole gamut of analytical levels —from the individual through the group and organization to the institutional and societal level, even further complicated by the inclusion of the time axis. This would indeed pose an impossible challenge. What counts is the sensitivity to the possible variety and multiplicity of influencing factors when it comes to analysing participation, particularly from an international, comparative point of view. A second observation can be made in connection with the chosen sequence of presentation: the first three studies focus on aspects of informal participation of employees with their superiors and the influence they have in determining the outcome of given organizational decision-making, irrespective of possibly existing rules and norms regulating participatory processes. The subsequent four studies, on the other hand, explicitly include

formal aspects of written normative systems or formal organizational structures in their analysis. The distinction between informal (immediate face-to-face) and formal (normatively structured) participation is by no means trivial. It characterizes whole societal preoccupations with participation, Anglo-Saxon traditions stressing informal and Germanic traditions favouring formal participation. Furthermore, it coincides with major research strands as is evidenced by the human-relations school of participation (emphasizing the informal) as opposed to studies of structural or normative conditions for participation (e.g. German codetermination).

The notion of informal versus formal participation should not be confused with the conceptual difference between *de jure* and *de facto* participation (IDE, 1981). *De jure* participation, of course, always implies formal participation. But *de facto* participation does not necessarily correspond to its prescriptions; it may not meet the prescribed forms and levels of participation, it may coincide with them or even surpass them. Whether we find a deficit or a surplus in the *de facto/de jure* ratio always remains an empirical question for evaluation research. In policy terms it is, however, important to note that norms (rules and regulations) for participation seem to impact significantly on the emerging *de facto* picture.

These last remarks help to amplify somewhat the rather general definition of participation given in the introductory part of this article. They also illustrate the likelihood that participation in work organizations is going to remain a central topic on the agenda of social policy debate as well as social-scientific inquiry in all industrialized or industrializing nations.

References

ALDERFER, C. P. 1972. *Existence, Relatedness and Growth.* New York, Collier Macmillan.

ARGYRIS, Chris. 1964. *Integrating the Individual and the Organization.* New York, Wiley.

ARGYRIS, Chris; SCHÖN, D. A. 1977. *Theory in Practice-Increasing Professional Effectiveness.* San Francisco, Jossey Bass.

CROUCH, C.; PIZZORNO, A. (eds.). 1978. *The Resurgence of Class Conflict in Western Europe since 1968.* Vols. I and II. London, Macmillan.

DACHLER, H. P.; WILPERT, Bernhard. 1978. Conceptual Dimensions and Boundaries of Participation in Organizations: A Critical Evaluation. *Administrative Science Quarterly,* Vol. 23, March, pp. 1–39.

HELLER, F. A. 1969. Group Feed-Back Analysis: A Method of Field Research. *Psychological Bulletin,* Vol. 72, No. 2, pp. 108–17.

HELLER, F. A.; WILPERT, B. 1981. *Competence and Power in Managerial Decision Making.* Chichester/New York, Wiley.

HOFSTEDE, Geert. 1980. *Culture's Consequences:*

National Differences in Thinking and Organizing. Beverly Hills, Calif., Sage.

IDE (INDUSTRIAL DEMOCRACY IN EUROPE—INTERNATIONAL RESEARCH GROUP). 1981. *Industrial Democracy in Europe.* London, Oxford University Press.

KING, C. D.; VAN DE VALL, Mark. 1978. *Models of Industrial Democracy.* The Hague/Paris/New York, Mouton.

LIKERT, R. 1967. *The Human Organization: Its Management and Value.* New York, McGraw Hill.

MCGREGOR, D. 1960. *The Human Side of Enterprise.* New York, McGraw-Hill.

MASLOW, A. H. 1954. *Motivation and Personality.* New York, Harper & Row.

MAURICE, M.; SORGE, A.; WARNER, M. 1980. Societal Differences in Organizing Manufacturing Units: A Comparison of France, West Germany, and Great Britain. *Organization Studies,* Vol. 1, No. 1, pp. 59–86.

MULDER, M. 1971. Power Equalization through Participation? *Administrative*

Science Quarterly, Vol. 16, pp. 31–8.

PATEMAN, C. 1970. *Participation and Democratic Theory.* London, Cambridge University Press.

POOL, M. 1984. Comparative Approaches to Industrial Conflict—An Assessment of 'The Resurgence of Class Conflict in Western Europe Since 1968'. In: B. Wilpert and A. Sorge (eds.), *International Perspectives on Organizational Democracy. International Yearbook of Organizational Democracy.* Vol. II. Chichester, John Wiley.

SERVAN-SCHREIBER, J.-J. 1967. *Le défi américain.* Paris, Édit. Denoël.

TANNENBAUM, A. S.; KAVCIC, B.; ROSNER, M.; VIANELLO, M.; WIESER, G. 1974. *Hierarchy in Organizations.* San Francisco/Washington/London, Jossey Bass.

VANEK, J. 1975. *Selfmanagement: Economic Liberation of Man.* Harmondsworth, Penguin.

WHITE, R. 1959. Motivation Reconsidered: The Concept of Competence. *Psychological Review,* Vol. 66, No. 5, pp. 297–333.

[18]

IDE — INTERNATIONAL RESEARCH GROUP *

Industrial democracy in Europe (IDE): An international comparative study

Background

The issue of industrial democracy has become a highly significant and at the same time controversial topic in socio-political discussions in most parts of the world today.

Social policy

Pressures of social movements and labor organizations towards a more participative society have been growing. The new developments promised to open up opportunities for a more equitable distribution of influence and power in organizations, thus giving individuals increased self realization and satisfaction. Legislators in industrialized and many developing countries have designed and implemented national frameworks of industrial democracy. Expectations connected with such schemes also cover hopes for an increased democratization of other societal spheres. The problems of participation and industrial democracy will remain one of the key policy issues of industrialized nations.

International coordination

In Europe we observe an unprecedented international labor mobility, a parallel growth of multinational companies and a corresponding drive towards the development of a unified European corporate law. The varying and mostly diverging national schemes of industrial democracy create serious difficulties for all international civil servants and for multinational companies.

Cf. names of researchers and their institutional affiliation in Appendix A. All inquiries should be directed to Dr. Bernhard Wilpert, International Institute of Management, 1 Berlin 33, Griegstrasse 5, West Germany. The whole IDE International Research Group collectively takes the responsibility for this article.

Soc. sci. inform. 15 (1), pp. 177-203.

178 *Comparative research*

Organization theory
The variety of national schemes of industrial democracy and in their consequence the existing multitude of innovative organizational experiments with
self- or participative management present at the same time a fascinating
natural experiment in organizational design and a unique portfolio of comparative research issues. Among them are: conditions of differential organizational efficiency and effectiveness; properties of alternative models of organizational governance; impact of legislation on organizational behavior;
contextual and situational parameters to organizational functioning; effects
of additional incentive schemes on participation.

Research policy
The answer of social science research to these challenges has been predominantly in the area of legal comparativism: considerable knowledge has
been accumulated on differences and similarities of national legal solutions[1].
But little is known about the differential effects of these various national
frameworks on behavior of people and the governance of organizations.
A multinational, comprehensive and comparative social scientific research
effort is still lacking. And yet, we find ourselves in a rare challenge for social
scientists to advance empirical research and organizational theory in the
context of ongoing reforms with remarkable social relevance. On the one
hand one may think of the research methodology of a large scale international comparative study in this field, which both requires and stimulates
specific methods of collection, analysis and interpretation of empirical data.
On the other hand it also refers to procedural and psychodynamic aspects
of a process in which a number of national research teams with their specific
experiences and often idiosyncratic traditions have to get engaged in a co-
operative enterprise trying to achieve a common research objective.

It was from this vantage point that the International Institute of Management (Berlin) took the initiative to invite an international group of social
scientists to a workshop on "Contributions of Social Science Research to
Problems of Participative Management and Industrial Democracy in Europe"
(Berlin, May 1973). This group has since met seven times, it grew and now
comprises renowned scientists and their supporting institutions in twelve
countries (see Appendix). This international, multidisciplinary team of
social scientists decided to carry out a joint research project on industrial
democracy. The pilot stage of this research has already been concluded
on the basis of the collaboratively developed research methodology. The

---

1. A case in point is the formidable work done by the Geneva-based International Institute
of Labour Studies. See also G. Lyon-Caen, *Contribution à l'étude des modes de repré-
sentation des intérêts des travailleurs dans le cadre des sociétés anonymes européennes*, Bru-
xelles, Commission des Communautés Européennes, Série Concurrence-Rapprochement
des Législations N° 10, 1970.

main study is underway: a multi-country comparison of industrial democracy schemes in their impact on organizational functioning.

It is the purpose of this paper to report on the design, intention and instrumentation of this ongoing research project in order to present it to the scientific community in an early stage and to stimulate the possibilities for feedback and discussion. Furthermore we want to encourage other scholars interested in the area to use a similar approach and methodology for comparative purposes.

Research focus

The research proposed here was inspired largely by practical needs of policy makers on national and international levels. In their task of developing policies for legislative actions or international recommendations in the field of participation and industrial democracy[2] they are faced with a considerable lack of systematic and reliable knowledge as to how different models of participative management systems function in real life. The behavioral implications of these systems under varying organizational, political and socioeconomic contexts have not yet been studied systematically. This is why it is proposed to attack the problem on three major fronts.

It is a basic premise of the study that distribution of power and influence in organizations must be considered as the core problem of all attempts to introduce or enlarge participation and industrial democracy in organizations. Therefore, the first research interest is in a comparative analysis of the de facto organizational power distribution as generated by various de jure national industrial democracy schemes (participative structures — PS). The concept of power distribution relates in the context of this research to the relative weight which various organizational bargaining parties can bring to bear on influencing the outcome of decisions.

A second major focus of the research will be a comparison of outcomes and consequences of participation in terms of the organizations and people involved. This comparison will follow dimensions of organizational performance (*e.g.* efficiency, absenteeism, organizational climate) and dimensions of attitudinal and behavioral quality (*e.g.* attitudes towards participation, company and general social involvement of members, satisfaction). This will be studied on the organizational, departmental and industrial level.

Thirdly, a major objective of the research group is to contribute with its scientific findings to the discussion about major issues of social policy. This objective must be accomplished both in the light of ongoing national discus-

2. Examples of particular interest and relevance are the "Proposal for a Council Regulation Embodying a Statute for European Companies", Brussels, Commission of the European Communities, 1970 and the "Proposal for a Fifth Directive on the Structure of Sociétés Anonymes", Brussels, Commission of the European Communities, 1972.

180   *Comparative research*

sions about action programs and legislative proposals for participation as well as in the context of the existing policy recommendations advanced by international bodies.

Research approach (design)

The design of the research is such that it allows for COMMUNALITIES, *i.e.* a common focus for all participating national research teams; for MUTUALITIES, *i.e.* a possible focus that is common only to a subset of national research teams; and for IDIOSYNCRACIES, *i.e.* the treatment of certain aspects that are particular to a given country alone (for illustrative purposes see Figure 1).

Figure 1. *a) Communalities, b) Mutualities, c) Idiosyncracies*

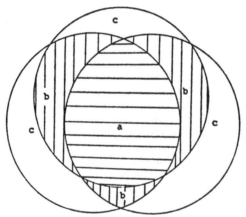

Communalities

The central issue is here to establish whether existing patterns of decision making and influence sharing vary significantly as a consequence of different national arrangements for participative management or to what degree they are due to other intervening factors.

A graphic representation of the main variable sets considered important in the research is provided in Figure 2.

The core variables are "participative structure" (PS) and "power distribution in organizations" (PO). Participative structures are considered

Figure 2. *Sets of variables in the research*

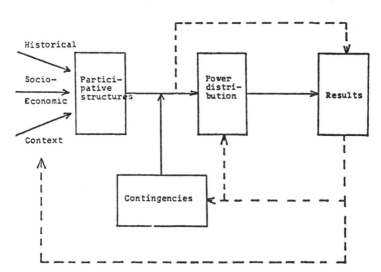

to be all formal (*i.e.* written down) operative rules and regulations that pre-scribe a certain involvement of various groups in intra-organizational decision making. PS may be based on national constitutions or laws, in bargaining contracts or managerial policies. PS thus describes the formal framework of participation. Power distribution in organizations refers to the relative weight that various specific groups can bring to bear on influencing a parti-cular decision outcome. These groups are considered to be workers, first line supervisors (foremen), middle management, top management, super-visory boards, internal representative bodies (works councils, shop steward committees), external groups (*e.g.* banks, unions, communities, governments). The weight of groups may be brought to bear either directly (personal direct involvement and influence) or indirectly (indirect influence through representatives). Thus, PO measures the factual participation and power play in the organization.

Intervening factors are considered to modify the influence of PS on PO. Important moderating factors are assumed to be technological complexity, organizational and professional differentiation, organizational formaliza-tion, general organizational characteristics (size, ownership, growthrate, unionization), level of aspiration and values held by the various groups.

Possible outcomes of certain formal PS and factual PO characteristics are considered to be organizational climate, reactions of people involved (*e.g.* attitudes towards participation and representatives, satisfaction with work role, organizational and societal commitment). The relationship between PS/PO and these outcomes are also considered to be modified by moderating factors, particularly individual characteristics such as age, level of education and need for participation.

Finally, the historical, socio-political, and economic context of the various countries will have to be taken into account in the collection and interpretation of the relevant data.

Exploratory questions and hypotheses

Implicit in the design of the research are a number of exploratory questions and hypotheses of various levels of complexity and generality. The following are examples of such issues:

General comparison between national systems
— Which systems of formal participation lead to the higher level of actual participation in important decisions?
— In which systems of formal participation do we find higher levels of expectation, satisfaction with participation, estimated efficiency of decision making procedures?
— Do the different systems of participation differ with respect to discrepancy between formally stated and actual existing participation?

Relational issues
— Which personal characteristics (educational level, experience with participation, level in hierarchy, etc.) are related to outcome variables like need for participation, level of satisfaction with participation, quality of decisions?
— Which organizational variables (size, industrial sector, complexity of technology, unionization) are related to various outcome-variables?
— To what extent does discrepancy between formal and actual participation lead to lower level involvement, satisfaction, decision quality?

More complex relational patterns
— Are relationships like those mentioned above dependent upon, or moderated by, formal characteristics of the participation system (works council — syndicalistic participation — self-management)?
— Are relationships like those mentioned above dependent upon, or moderated by, specific national characteristics of the system in which participation operates?

These complex patterns can, of course, be broadened to second and third order interaction, for which a more complex analysis of variance design will have to be used.

Furthermore, specific between-country hypotheses and questions will be tested in the mutuality studies (differences between two types of works council representation, between two types of union stands, etc.).

Finally, within one nation with its own idiosyncratic tradition and participation structures specific national issues can be investigated.

At this moment a number of expectations and hypotheses within the different categories have been or are being formulated, based both on the existing literature and on own (pilot-) experiences.

Instruments and procedures

Selection of firms and of respondents
It was agreed that each participating country will choose at least one fairly successful establishment according to the matrix :

| | ——————— Industrial sector ——————— | | |
| | Service | Manufacturing | |
Establishment size	Banking/ insurance	High skill requirements	Low skill requirements
Small < 100 employees			
Medium 200-500 employees			
Large 501-1000 employees			

The manufacturing firms will be taken from metal engineering industries. The skill requirements are assumed to correlate with the level of technological complexity. Firms from the manufacturing sectors would therefore be chosen in harmony with criteria such as

Low level of complexity	*High level of complexity*
1) All types of components (mechanical, electrical, electronics)	1) All types of instruments and tools (mechanical, electrical, electronics)
2) Machine building and construction	2) Computers
3) Metal processing	3) Machine tools

Participating countries are encouraged to expand their firm sample beyond the internationally agreed number of nine and add other sectors (*e.g.* mining, chemical industries, stagnating industries, hospitals, universities, R&D companies). Therefore, substantially more than 100 organizations will

184   *Comparative research*

provide a basis for an adequate international and intranational comparison.

Three types of respondents will be involved in the research: general sample respondents, key person respondents, specialist respondents.

General sample respondents will be selected on a random basis from each establishment with the formula

$$y = .05 \, x + 35$$

Where y = total sample within a given establishment

x = size of establishment (number of employees)

and similarly, on a random basis, from each hierarchical level of the establishment with the formula

$$y' = q\sqrt{x'}$$

Where y' = size of level sample

x' = size of level (number of employees per level)

q = constant 1, 2, 3... (depending on size of x').

These formulae allow for varying sample sizes according to the size of establishments. The grand total of the respondents in each country will therefore be more than 1000, and of the international sample well above 10 000.

The general sample respondents will fill in (usually in small groups with the researcher present) the following forms (see App. B, p. 188 ff.) :

Form 1.1: a Personal Information Form with 12 questions on function, background, age.

Form 1.2: a form on organizational climate with 13 items (5-point Likert-type scale)

Form 1.3: a form on perceived factual and desired personal influence and involvement in 16 different decisions (three questions per decision: 48 items). The set of decisions is a crucial means of standardizing the research focus in all participating countries. The decisions were selected with the help of the paradigm (see page 185).

Form 1.4: a form (10 items) on expected consequences of direct versus indirect participation in decision making.

Form 1.5: a form on experience with and attitudes toward the participative system existing in the company (15 items).

Form 1.6: a form on work role satisfaction (13 items).

Form 1.7: a rank order form on importance of nine job dimensions.

The second category of respondents are key persons. Key persons are considered to be respondents with a particular expertise in the functioning of participation in a firm (*e.g.* top management, shop stewards, works council members, union representatives). They will answer Form 2.1 questions relating to the factual involvement and influence of various groups (workers, supervisors, middle management, top management, supervisory bodies, internal employee representative bodies, external groups) in the making of the 16 decisions (same decision set in Form 1.3).

Decision set paradigm

	Work and social conditions	Personnel	Economic aspects
Routine	Task assignment Tools Work conditions Working hours Holidays	Training Transfer	
Goals	Work study techniques Wage levels	Dismissal Hiring procedures Appointment of department head Appointment of own supervisor	Reorganization
Policies			Major investment New product

Finally, specialist respondents will be individuals with a particular expertise either with regard to the structural and technological aspects of the firm under investigation (they will fill in Form 3.1, a questionnaire on technological level, hierarchical structure, formalization, absenteeism, strike hours lost, unionization — in other words on moderator variables) or with regard to the formal, legal operative participative structures in a given firm. Form 3.2 is a questionnaire which collects data on the legal basis (law, bargaining contract, etc.) and on the mode in which various groups are legally required to participate in the making of the 16 decisions of the decision list (they must be informed, must be asked, can veto, have final and exclusive say in decision). This form will also be answered by specialists such as personnel managers and lawyers together with the researcher himself.

In-depth analysis of decisions

A limited number (two/three) specific contentious decisions (preferably from the decision set) will be studied more intensively in at least two firms. This in-depth technique comprises a historical-genetic approach which studies the origin and development of a contentious issue by way of a tracer technique and a focus on the various bargaining coalitions that emerged in the course of the issue development and its resolution. It will incorporate "objective" data on decision outcomes as much as possible (*e.g.* minutes). This approach resembles very much a case study approach and is believed to yield significant insights into the diachronic dynamics of organizational decision making. Thus this less structured and less instrumented approach complements and

186 *Comparative research*

cross-validates the more survey-type (reputational) techniques described above.

Beyond that, each national research team will develop a more descriptive, qualitative presentation of the national industrial relations system, its main features, trends, political and practical problems, and relevant socio-economic environmental context. This report serves as a frame of reference for interpreting and relating a country's findings. An identical roster will be used by all the participating countries in developing their industrial relations description.

Organization of the research

The collectively developed research is carried out with identical procedures but in a fully decentralized fashion. National teams are responsible for their own data collection, data evaluation, and publication of national results. They also obtain funding for their research independently. The International Institute of Management of the Science Center Berlin performs a certain coordination and clearing-house function for the international research. Standardization and computer analysis of the international data will be done mainly in Berlin. Substantial grants have been obtained from the Thyssen Foundation (Cologne) and the Ford Foundation (New York) to facilitate international cooperation (*e.g.* bi-annual meetings of the international team) and international coordination. Additional contributions were obtained from the Nuffield Foundation (London), the Institute of Organization and Industrial Sociology (Copenhagen), the Boris Kidrič Foundation (Ljubljana), and the Maison des Sciences de l'Homme (Paris).

Thus, the organizational model of the research deviates somewhat from the classical centralized multinational comparative research project where central funding and centralized leadership were the critical features. The decentralized collective nature of this research in fact constitutes a new form of multi-national research cooperation where minimal international overhead funds facilitate a large scale research venture that is mainly based on consensus and commitment rather than centralized resources and guidance.

A formal agreement among the members of the international IDE-team will regulate such matters as collective ownership of all data, rights to materials, publication rights and procedures, acknowledgements, royalties, etc. It is assumed that the main study will last until the end of 1977.

Implications

This research, in concentrating on organizational power distribution, addresses itself to a central issue of Industrial Democracy, an issue which lies at the

core of a great variety of present and future organizational problems and social policy issues. A few may be mentioned:
— What formal schemes of industrial democracy fit what policy intentions? What unintended side effects can be observed?
— Is there an interrelationship between basic types of participation (*i.e.* direct, personal and indirect, representative committee representation) in the sense that they condition each other?
— To what degree is involvement of unions a factor and condition for the functioning of legal prescriptions?
— Is technology a major predictor for organizational decision making and influence sharing patterns?
— To what degree is intra-organizational participation dependent on the comprehensive industrial relations system?
— To what degree are the effects of participation dependent on individual characteristics?
— What are the effects of participative management systems on general political participation (and vice versa)?
— International harmonization policies in the area of industrial democracy: are they possible and/or necessary?

Thus this research purports to contribute to the solution of the problems of the practitioner and policymaker in the field of industrial democracy, as well as to the problems of the organization theorist in understanding the conditions and effects of large scale organizational reform. Colleagues from other countries are invited to use the instruments (see Appendix B) and procedures described in this article for the benefit of wider comparisons and validation.

Appendix A : *IDE International Research Group*

Members of the international research team who were principally responsible for the design of the international study :

BELGIUM : *Dr. Pol Coetsier,* Professor of Psychology, University of Ghent, Ghent.
DENMARK : *Dr. Flemming Agersnap,* Ass. Professor of Organization, Institute of Organization and Industrial Sociology, School of Economics and Social Science, Copenhagen.
FRANCE : *Mr. Dominique Martin,* Centre de Recherches en Sciences Sociales du Travail, Sceaux.
GERMANY : *Dr. Bernhard Wilpert,* Research Fellow, International Institute of Management, Berlin.
GREAT BRITAIN : *Dr. Peter Abell,* Professor of Sociology, University of Birmingham.
— *Dr. Frank Heller,* Senior Staff, Tavistock Institute of Human Relations, London. — *Dr. Malcolm Warner,* Professor of Organizational Behavior, Administrative Staff College, Henley-on-Thames and Brunel University, Middlesex.
ITALY : *Mr. Ricardo Peccei,* Imperial College of Science and Technology, London, Great Britain.

188   *Comparative research*

ISRAEL : *Dr. Eliezer Rosenstein*, Senior Lecturer, Israel Institute of Technology, Haifa.
NETHERLANDS : *Dr. J.H.T.H. Jochum Andriessen*, Senior Staff, Free University, Amsterdam — *Dr. Pieter J.D. Drenth*, Professor of Pschology, Free University, Amsterdam. — *Dr. Cornelis J. Lammers*, Professor of Sociology, State University of Leiden.
NORWAY : *Mr. Thoralf U. Qvale*, Research Fellow, Work Research Institutes, Oslo.
* SWEDEN : *Dr. Walter Goldberg*, Professor of Economics, Director, International Institute of Management, Berlin. — *Mr. Thomas Sandberg*, Research Assistant University of Uppsala, Uppsala — Dr. Bengt Stymne, Ass. Professor of Sociology, Stockholm School of Economics, Stockholm.
YUGOSLAVIA : *Dr. Veljko Rus*, Professor of Sociology, University of Ljubljana.

* FINLAND : *Pr. Oiva Laaksonen*, Professor of Organisation Institute of Organization and Management, Helsinki School of Economics, Helsinki.
* The Finnish team, under Prof. Oiva Laaksonen, joined the Group in January 1976.
  Dr. Bengt Stymne has recently joined the Swedish team as senior coordinator.

Corresponding Members: Prof. Theo Pirker, Germany; Prof. Jean-Daniel Reynaud, France; Prof. Stanley E. Seashore, USA ; Prof. William H. Starbuck, USA.

Associate Researchers: Mr. François Dupuy, France; Ms. Gabriel Freidank, international coordination; Mr. Hendrik Hendrickx, Belgium; Mr. Itzhak Gur-Lavie, Israel; Mr. Wolfgang Potratz, Germany; Ms. Vesna Pusić, Yugoslavia; Ms. Ann Westenholz, Denmark.

Appendix B : *IDE Instruments* [1]

1. *Sample Questionnaires*

    Form 1.1 — PIF
        1.2 — CLIMS [2]
        1.3 — PO2
        1.4 — O — ROC [2]
        1.5 — O — PART
        1.6 — O — SAT [2]
        1.7 — O — RON

    Note : It is proposed to administer the questionnaires in this order.   In any case, O — ROC must be administered before O — PART.

2. *Key Person Questionnaires*

    Form 2.1   PO1
        2.11   PO1 Extension [2]
        2.12   PO1 Optional

3. *Specialist Questionnaires*

    Form 3.1 — CON
        3.2 — PS

---

1. Numbered footnotes have been added by the editor, the asterisk footnotes figure in the questionnaires as administered.
2. The version of these forms presented below is abbreviated.   In the schedule administered, the choice categories appear after each statement or question.

Form 1.1 — PIF

Here are a number of questions about your background. It is understood that your information will be kept strictly confidential by the investigaotrs. Please answer carefully.

1. What is your *main* JOB FUNCTION?
   Enter the appropriate number in the box provided.

   1) production (in manufacturing or service industry)
   2) administration, personnel, general non-specialized management
   3) technical, like : research and development, industrial engineering, quality control, operations research, work study, etc.
   4) sales, marketing, purchasing, stores, etc.
   5) finance, accounting

2. Give your JOB TITLE :
   To which of the four levels do you belong? Enter the appropriate number in the box provided.

   1) Top or senior management (within two levels of the chief executive)*
   2) Middle management
   3) Supervisor (usually first level)
   4) Shop floor

3. How many people are there in your department, section or group (whichever is the smallest)?

4. How old are you?

5. Sex : Male (M)
           Female (F)

6. How long have you been with the company? (In years. If less than one year put "Less". Include mergers or change of name of company, etc.)

7. Level of EDUCATION completed (Enter appropriate number in box)

   1) Primary education
   2) Secondary education
   3) Higher education excluding university
   4) University degree or equivalent

(*Please answer the following three questions by* Yes = 1, No = 2*)*

8. Are you presently a member of a representative (participatory) body?

9. Were you ever a member of a representative (participatory) body? (In this company or previously).

10. Are you a member of a union or similar professional body?

11. Nationality (if not British) [1]

12. If not (British) [1] how many years have you worked in this country?

---

* As not all firms will have a differentiated hierarchy according to these categories, take as top management those who are considered to be at the top of the firm.

1. If not (British, Norwegian, etc.) according to country in which survey is carried out.

190 *Comparative research*

Form 1.2 CLIMS

Here are some statements about your job and the organization you are working in. Your opinion is asked on these statements. Please indicate your response by ticking your choice in the appropriate space[1].

1. Everybody's job in this organization is clearly defined

yes, that is definitely true	that is often true	sometimes true sometimes not	that is often not true	no, that is definitely not true

2. In this organization, it's clear who has the authority to make a decision
3. The policies and structure of this organization are usually clearly explained to us
4. We usually get information from the top very easily
5. Most activities here are planned carefully
6. Work is checked to see if it is done properly and in time
7. There is a lot of wasted time here: few things have been planned right to the minute
8. Everyone in this organization knows exactly what his position and task is
9. Everyone in this organization knows the responsibilities, task and authority of other people
10. We all receive the information we need here
11. In general, I find the situation in this organization relaxed and easy going
12. In this company, management really looks after the workers
13. Management and workers in this organization usually don't get on well together

Form 1.3 PO2

Issue: (Add issues from Decision list PO1/PO2).
Improvement in work conditions of your work group (dust, noise, safety)
In this issue: Please tick here
    1. I am not involved at all   ☐
       I am informed about the matter beforehand   ☐
       I can give my opinion   ☐
       My opinion is taken into account   ☐
       I "take part with equal weight"   ☐
       I decide on my own   ☐

---

1. Abbreviated version. In the schedule administered, the choice categories appear after each question.

2. How would you like it to be?
   I am not interested at all   ☐
   I want to be informed about the matter beforehand   ☐
   I want to be able to give my opinion beforehand   ☐
   I want my opinion to be taken into account   ☐
   I want to "take part with equal weight"   ☐
   I want to decide on my own   ☐
   I don't know, have no opinion   ☐

3. Would you like the main representative body to have a say in this matter?

$$\text{Yes} \quad ☐$$
$$\text{No} \quad ☐$$
$$\text{Don't know} \quad ☐$$

Decision list PO1/PO2

1. Improvements in work conditions of your work group (dust, noise, safety)

2. Appointment of a new department head

3. Establishment of criteria and procedures for hiring and selection of new employees

4. Whether your workers can follow a vocational training course (during work hours)
   for workers: * Whether you can follow a vocational training course (during work hours)

5. Permanent transfer of workers to other jobs within the plant
   for workers: * To be transferred to another job within the plant

6. Major capital investment, *e.g.* an additional production line, a new plant, etc.

7. Whether the company should make a completely new product

8. To establish who will be your immediate superior

9. Changes in how much a certain grade (wage group) shall earn (beyond possible existing collective bargaining agreements)

10. Replacement of personal equipment (hand tools) of your workers (not trivial things like pencils, etc.)
    for workers: Replacement of your personal equipment or handtools (not trivial things like pencils, etc.)

11. Change in the way one or more departments are organized

12. Assignment of tasks to workers
    for workers: Assignment of tasks you have to do

13. Dismissal of one of the workers
    for workers: Dismissal of one of your co-workers

---

* Whenever a separate formulation is used for workers it refers to groups A.

192 *Comparative research*

14. Whether or not work study technique is to be used (e.g. stopwatch, MTM)

15. From when to when you can go on a holiday

16. From when to when working hours are.

Form 1.4 — O — ROC

Industrial democracy and participation can have various consequences irrespective of whether one likes them or not.   Therefore in this questionnaire we have listed some possible consequences and we want you to tick which of these consequences have been brought about by (your system of *representative participation*) in your firm[1].

1. Do people through the work of the (main rep. body) know more about what is going on here?

Definitely	May be	I don't	Definitely
yes	yes	think so	not

2. Do people accept decisions easier because of the work of the (main rep. body)?

3. Has the quality of decisions increased because of the work of the (main rep. body)?

4. Are the interests of employees better represented because of the work of the (main rep. body)?

5. Do employees because of the work of the (main rep. body) have a greater say in what's going on in this firm?

* 6. Has the (main rep. body) led to too slow decision making?

* 7. Has a better mutual understanding and trust developed between management and employees because of the work of the (main rep. body)?

* 8. Do workers through the work of the (main rep. body) just seem to have a say in something but actually they don't?

* 9. Has the work of the (main rep. body) brought about an equalization of power between employees and management?

---

* Optionals.
1. Abbreviated version. In the schedule administered, the choice categories appear after each question.

Again we have listed the same possible consequences but this time we want you to tick which of these consequences have been brought about *by your direct and daily participation* in what is going on in the firm.

1. Do people know more about what's going on here?

Definitely	May be	I don't	Definitely
yes	yes	think so	not

2. Do people accept decisions easier?

3. Has the quality of decisions increased because issues have been discussed widely?

4. Are interests of employees better represented?

5. Do employees have a greater say in what's going on here?

* 6. Have the discussions led to too slow decision-making?

* 7. Has there grown up a better mutual understanding and trust between employees and management?

* 8. Do employees just seem to have a say in something but actually they don't?

* 9. Has an equalization of power been brought about?

Form 1.5 — O - Part

With this form we would like to ask you about your experience with various forms of participation in this company.

Please indicate your response to each question by encircling the appropriate words corresponding most closely to your answer.

A. *Participation through the works council (or the main representative bodies to be selected)*

1. How much do you usually hear about what goes on in the meetings of the Works Council?

Very much	Much	Some	Little	Very little
information	information	information	information	information

2. How interested are you personally in the work of the Works Council?

Very strong	Strong	Some	Little	Very little
interest	interest	interest	interest	interest

3. Do you think that, in this company, the Works Council is given a real chance by management?

Definitely	To a great	To some	To a little	Definitely
yes	extent	extent	extent	no

---

* Optionals.

194   *Comparative research*

*4. If your colleagues ask you to become a candidate for the Works Council in the elections would you be interested in accepting a candidacy?

Definitely	Probably	Perhaps	Probably	Definitely
yes	yes		not	not

5. Do you think that, in this company, the right people are available to represent the interests of the employees?

Definitely	To a little	To some	To a great	Definitely
no	extent	extent	extent	yes

*6. How easily can you get in touch with your representatives in the Works Council?

Very	Quite	Rather	Quite	Very
easily	easily	easily	difficult	difficult

B. *Direct participation*

*7. How often does your superior/boss consult with you and your colleagues before he takes an important decision concerning your department?

(Almost)	Often	Sometimes	Rarely	(Almost)
always				never

*8. If changes in your own work occur, how often does your superior/boss give you the reason why?

(Almost)	Often	Sometimes	Rarely	(Almost)
always				never

*9. To what extent does your superior/boss give you the opportunity to decide on your own?

Not at	To a little	To some	To a great	To a very
all	extent	extent	extent	great extent

*10. If you have an opinion different from your superior/boss, can you say so?

(Almost)	Often	Sometimes	Rarely	(Almost)
always				never

C. *Evaluation of participation*

*11. How satisfied are you with the functioning of direct participation in your department (*i.e.* your taking part in decisions of your superior/boss)?

Very	Fairly	Neither	Somewhat	Very
satisfied	satisfied	satisfied nor	dissatisfied	dissatisfied
		dissatisfied		

12. How satisfied are you with the functioning of the *Works Council*?

Very	Fairly	Neither satisfied	Somewhat	Very
satisfied	satisfied	nor dissatisfied	dissatisfied	dissatisfied

*13. Do you think *your* interests are represented by/in the Works Council?

Yes very	Yes	More or less	Not so well	Not at all
well	somewhat			

---

*Not applicable for respondents from level D (and occasionally not for level C).

14. If you have personal grievances (complaints) what can you do?
☐ I cannot do anything
☐ I ask for support from a superior
☐ I ask for support from a union representative
☐ I ask for support from my colleagues/work mates
☐ I go to court
☐ I shall leave the company

15. In general, how much do you think the following groups have to say about how things are decided?

	Nothing	Some influence	Moderate influence	Much influence	Very much influence
A					
B					
C					
D					
E					
F					
G					

A — Workers   E — Supervisory board
B — Foremen   F — Internal repr. body
C — Middle management   G — External groups
D — Top management   please specify

Optional questions

*16. Do you think you have some influence on decisions in this company through your representatives in the (Works Council)?
Very often   Often   Sometimes   Rarely   Never

*17. How much influence do you think your representatives have upon what goes on in the company?
Very much   Much   Some   A little   Very little

18. Does the Works Council/the system of representatives offer you advantages, which you would otherwise not have?
Not at all   To a little   To some   To a great   To a very
                  extent   extent   extent   great extent

---

* Not applicable for respondents from level C and D.

196   *Comparative research*

19. Do you think the (Works Council) here is a suitable place to reconcile the interests
    of workers and of management?

    | Definitely | To a great | To some | To a little | Definitely |
    | yes. | extent | extent | extent | no |

20. Do you think the (Works Council) here is a suitable place to enforce employee (worker)
    interests against management?

    | Definitely | To a great | To some | To a little | Definitely |
    | yes | extent | extent | extent | no |

21. Do you think the (Works Council) here is a suitable place for discussing problems,
    giving advice and making plans for the whole company?

    | Definitely | To a great | To some | To a little | Definitely |
    | yes | extent | extent | extent | no |

22. In all, who benefits/looses the most from the establishment of the (Works Council) here?

	Benefits			Looses	
	Very much	Some what	No impact	Some what	Very much
Management					
Unions					
Members of the Works Council					
Individual workers					

*23. If your legal or formal rights are offended, what do you do?
   □ I cannot do anything
   □ I ask for support from a superior
   □ I ask for support from a union representative
   □ I ask for support from my colleagues/work mates
   □ I go to court
   □ I shall leave the company

*24. How is your contact with your representatives in the Works Council?
   □ No contact
   □ I am usually informed
   □ I can go to them and give my advice
   □ They often ask my opinion

---

* Not applicable for respondents from level C and D.

*25. Do you think your representative has to take care of the interests of more groups than yours?

| Definitely yes | To a great extent | To some extent | To a little extent | Definitely no |

*26. Do you think your representative thinks too much like management?

| Definitely yes | To a great extent | To some extent | To a little extent | Definitely no |

*27. Do you think your representative is too overloaded with other functions to represent your interests effectively?

| Definitely yes | To a great extent | To some extent | To a little extent | Definitely no |

Form 1.6 — O - SAT

Here are some questions on how you evaluate your work situation at the present moment. Again, the answers are kept strictly confidential and are only accessible to the scientists. Please indicate your response by ticking your choice in the appropriate space[1]

1. Are you doing the job you would really like to do?

Definitely yes	Yes	Don't know/Neither nor	No	Certainly not

2. Does your job give you much opportunity to talk with others?

3. Do you think that the general management of this company is satisfactory?

4. Are you informed regularly about the quality of your work?

5. Does your job give you the feeling of doing something worthwhile?

6. Do you find the working conditions here (time schedule, extra working hours, temperature, etc.) satisfactory?

7. Do you find your colleagues pleasant people?

8. Do you think you should earn more for the job you are doing?

9. Do you find your superior a capable person?

---

1. Abbreviated version. In the schedule administered, the choice categories appear after each statement or question.

198   *Comparative research*

10. Do you think your skills are appropriate for your job?

11. Do you feel that others consider your job as a valuable one?

12. All things considered, are you satisfied presently with *your work?*

13. All things considered, are you satisfied presently with *this company?*

Form. 1.7 — O - RON

Please rank order the following sentences according to what you feel is most important for you in your job.   Mark below the *three most* important and the *three least important* items.

1. To have promotion opportunities

2. To have stability of employment

3. To have the opportunity to influence decisions about my own job

4. To be able to use my capacities in my work

5. To have a nice boss/superior

6. To have a good salary

7. To have effective representatives (*e.g.* in Works Council)

8. To have a clean and safe work environment

9. To have good cooperation with my colleagues

Please fill in the numbers of			Please fill in the numbers of		
□	□	□	□	□	□
the three most important items			the three least important items		

Form 2.1 — PO1

Issue: (Add issues from Decision list PO1/PO2)[1]

Improvement in work conditions of your work group (dust, noise, safety)

1. How much influence do the different groups have over this decision?

	No infl.	Little infl.	Moderate infl.	Much infl.	Very much infl.
A — Workers					
B — First line supervisors					
C — Middle management					
D — Top management					
E — Level above plant					
F — Internal repr. bodies					
G — External groups					

2. Is the decision usually reached through disagreement?
   (No = 1; Yes = 2; Don't know = 3)   □

3. In case of disagreement, who has the final say?
   A   B   C   D   E   F   G

---

1. See above Form 1.3.

200   *Comparative research*

Form 2.11 — PO1 Extension: Negative PO

*4. To what extent can the following groups oppose a change of salaries if this change goes
against their interest?

Groups	Cannot oppose at all	Minimally oppose	To some extent	To large extent	Completely oppose
A					
B					
C					
D					
E					
F					
G					

*5. To what extent can the following groups oppose a dismissal of co-workers if it goes against
their interests?[1]

*6. To what extent can the following groups oppose a new product if it goes against their
interests?

Form 2.12 — PO1 Optional items

7. Is the decision-making in the Works Council subject to severe limitations or is there a wide
range for what decision alternative it can choose?

No limitations	Small limitations	Some limitations	Extensive limitations	Virtually no choice

8. From whom or from what source do the limitations come?

☐ From superiors
☐ From experts, *e.g.* company staff departments
☐ From production technology
☐ From outside the company

---

1. Same answer categories as for question 4 — not reproduced.
* Optional items.

9. Do you normally discuss issues like the previous ones with others, before they are discussed in the Works Council?
   □ With shop stewards/union delegation
   □ With workers who may be affected
   □ With somebody from management

10. Do you think the present level of joint decision making reduces your possibilities for withholding your consent?

Definitely yes	To a great extent	To some extent	To a little extent	Definitely no

11. What is the most frequent way an issue is brought up for discussion in the Works Council? (give rank 1-3)
    □ By initiative from management
    □ By initiative from representatives
    □ It is a regularly recurring issue (*e.g.* yearly)

12. Please rank order the decisions from Decision list PO1/PO2 according to what you feel is most important for the goals of each of the following levels.

    A. *For workers* (please select the *three* most important decisions)

    B. *First line supervision* (idem)

    C. *Middle management* (idem)

    D. *Top management* (idem)

    E. *Level above the plant* (please specify)

    F. *Representations in the plant* (idem)

    G. *External group* (idem)

Form 3.1 — CON (Contextual characteristics) [1]

The questionnaire will be administered to members of the top management or specialists assigned by management for that specific purpose. The questions cover five main categories:

1) Technology of firm under investigation
2) Organizational structure (*e.g.* professional differentiation, number of employees per level) functional specialization and organizational formalization)
3) Personnel policy (*e.g.* payment system, work hour system)
4) Economic data (*e.g.* ownership, turnover, investment dependency on holding company,
5) Managerial philosophy.

Wherever possible, the individual items were carefully chosen from established and standardized research instruments (*e.g.* from the Aston studies).

---

1. This questionnaire, being very long, could not be reproduced here.

202   *Comparative research*

Form 3.2 — PS (Participation structure)

1. This questionnaire [1] is filled in for each establishment by the researcher. Experience from the pilot phase shows that it is helpful and mostly necessary to do this in consultation with
   a) a key informant from the establishment/company (*e.g.* union delegate, Works Council member, top manager), because there may exist participative structures that are company specific such as management policies, bargaining contracts;
   b) an expert in company law/labor law.
2. Definition of participative structures:
   Formal (i.e. written down) *operative (i.e.* still "living" and enforceable — *e.g.* by a labor court) regulations pertaining to the involvement of various groups in company decision making. "Custom and practice" are *not covered* by this definition unless they are enforceable!
3. The groups (and their codes) are identical with the groups in PO1 and PO2:
   A — Workers, white and blue collar, without supervisory functions
   B — First line supervisors (last ones with supervisory functions)
   C — Middle management: according to establishment usage: all hierarchical levels above B and below D
   D — Top management: according to establishment usage all persons considered to belong to the top management of the establishment
   E — Level above the establishment: supervisory body (SB), managerial bodies (*e.g.* conglomerate management — MB), shareholders or owners (OW)
   Note: In this category it will be necessary to indicate specifically the groups that are involved.
   F — Permanent representative bodies at the establishment level, no matter of what origin: works councils, workers councils, union representative bodies (RB)
   Note: Again: Please specify which ones.
   G — Bodies/institutions *outside of company* (not outside establishment!) banks, community councils, regional planning council etc. (BO)
   Note: Again: Please specify which ones.
4. The measurement is done on the basis of the 16 decisions in the Decision list [2]. Two questions have to be answered for each decision, on an ordinal scale regarding the *basis* and a Guttman-type scale regarding the *mode* of the involvement of groups.
5. Basis question and categories (code): "Do (in/for this company) formal (written down) regulations exist which provide an opportunity for one or more of the groups A-G to participate in the making of the respective decision?" Indicate appropriate basis code number:
   1) Constitution
   2) National law
   3) Regional law
   4) National collective bargaining contract
   5) Regional collective bargaining contract
   6) Sectoral collective bargaining contract
   7) Company (anything above plant) collective bargaining contract
   8) Plan/establishment collective bargaining contract
   9) Management policy (defined as written down regulations, otherwise see 10
   10) Other legal bases ("Richterrecht") *e.g.* regulations that are not written down, but are enforceable in court as custom and practice *e.g.* management prerogatives

1. The Answer Sheet for the PS form is not included here.
2. See above Form 1.3.

Note: It may be that there exist several bases for a group's involvement that successively specify the parameters of a group's involvement.   In such cases multiple nominations will have to be registered, *e.g.* 1/3/9.

6. Mode question and categories (code):
   "What kind of participation is provided for different groups by the formal regulations?" Indicate appropriate code number:
   1) No regulation
   2) Information (unspecified) must be given to group
   3) Information ex ante must be given to group
   4) Right of initiative (*i.e.* the group has the right to give an opinion about the issue on its own initiative)
   5) Consultation of group obligatory (*i.e.* group must always be consulted prior to the decisions taken)
   6) Joint decision making with group (*i.e.* group has veto power, must give its approval: the decision outcome is a result of bargaining).
   7) Group itself has the final say
   Note: a) This is a Guttmann-type scale of the increasing degree to which a group must participate and can determine the decision outcome.   Therefore, *only one code nomination* seems theoretically possible per decision (the higher codes presumably imply lower code modes).   However, if we find that different *bases* provide for different *modes* we will make note of that by marking it as follows:

	Basis	Mode
Decision 1:	2	2
	4	2
	9	5

   b) All groups that have no formal basis for participation receive a *mode* code of 1 (= No information.
   c) If a general law (*e.g.* commerce code) states that the directors have the top authority, this is coded 7 for all decisions, unless other rules/laws imply otherwise.

7. The PS-answer sheet has a separate column "Notes on *basis*".   Note down the exact reference of the basis, *e.g.* "constitution § 8 (2)", "coll. barg. contr. January 12, 1966".

[19]

INDUSTRIAL DEMOCRACY IN EUROPE
INTERNATIONAL RESEARCH GROUP*

Participation: Formal Rules, Influence, and Involvement

GROWING RECENT DEMANDS for a greater involvement of employees and their representatives in decision making have provided an impetus for new legislation on industrial democracy and for the introduction of a variety of new participative schemes in Western Europe. In turn, this interest is reflected by a burgeoning literature comparing different national schemes for industrial democracy and reviewing recent legislative developments (Batstone and Davies 1976; von Beyme, 1976; King and van de Vall, 1978). Considerable information is now available about legal frameworks for participation, but relatively little is known about how various national schemes function in practice, especially regarding the impact which different norms and legal systems have on the distribution of power and influence within companies and on the actual involvement of employees in organizational decision making. Clearly, these are critical points particularly since one of the major assumptions underlying current debates is that different norms and regulations do indeed have different behavioral effects.

The present paper gives a brief overview of the findings from an international research project conducted by the Industrial Democracy in Europe Research Group (IDE). Going beyond the legal comparativism that has characterized much recent work, this study focuses on the relationship between *de jure* and *de facto* participation in participative organizations.

The IDE Research

The IDE study is an international collaborative effort involving

*Peter Abell (Great Britain), Flemming Agersnap (Denmark), J. H. T. H. Jochum Andriessen (Netherlands), Pol Coetsier (Belgium), Pieter J. D. Drenth (Netherlands), Frank A. Heller (Great Britain), Oiva Laaksonen (Finland), Cornelis J. Lammers (Netherlands), Dominique Martin (France), Riccardo Peccei (Italy), Vesna Pusic (Yugoslavia), Thoralf U. Ovale (Norway), Jörg Rayley (Germany), Eliezer Rosenstein (Israel), Veljko Rus (Yugoslavia), Marnix Ryckaert (Belgium), Thomas Sandberg (Sweden), Bengt Stymne (Sweden), Malcolm Warner (Great Britain), and Bernhard Wilpert (Germany).

INDUSTRIAL RELATIONS, Vol. 18, No. 3 (Fall 1979). © 1979 by the Regents of the University of California.
0019/8676/79/1025/273/$1.00

274 / IDE

some 25 social scientists from 12 countries (Belgium, Denmark, Finland, France, Germany, Great Britain, Italy, Israel, the Netherlands, Norway, Sweden, and Yugoslavia).[1] The aim of the study is, first, to assess the impact of different formal, legally prescribed systems of participation upon the actual patterns of influence, power, and involvement in organizations, and, secondly, to examine the effects of different patterns of participation upon the attitudes, aspirations, and reactions of employees. The 12 countries covered by the study exhibit a great variety of participation schemes, ranging from the fully fledged self-management concept in Yugoslavia, through codetermination in West Germany, to a variety of participation systems in Scandinavia, France, and Belgium, to the shop-steward movement in the U.K., thus providing an almost ideal experimental setting for such an investigation.

General Research Model

A graphic representation of our general model and major sets of variables is provided below. The core variables are: *de jure* participation structures (PS), patterns of *de facto* participation (PO), and outcomes of participation (O). PS refers to all formal, written operative norms and rules governing the participation of various groups which result from the implementation of national laws, bargaining contracts, or managerial policies. By contrast, *de facto* participation (PO) refers to the actual capacity of various groups to affect decision outcomes. PO includes both the amount of *influence* which different groups are perceived to have over particular decisions (PO1) and the degree of their actual *involvement* in decision making (PO2). Finally, outcome variables (O) include individuals' attitudes and reactions toward participation and representatives, satisfaction with work, organizational commitment, and organizational climate.

At its simplest level, our model postulates that patterns and structures of PS have a systematic determinate effect upon the *de facto* distribution of influence and involvement. PO1 and PO2 are in turn hypothesized as systematically determining outcomes. However, these relationships are affected by a number of other contextual and contingent variables, including techno-

---

[1]The developmental phase of the IDE project lasted from May 1973 to May 1975 and comprised pretesting and a pilot study in eight countries. The main data collection phase started at the beginning of 1976 and lasted through 1977. The data analysis, first on a national and then on an international comparative basis, took place in 1977 and 1978. Two volumes based on the project are currently in preparation for publication by Oxford University Press, London, 1980. The first volume ("Industrial Democracy in Europe") presents the conceptual framework, methods, and findings of the IDE study. The second ("Industrial Relations in Europe") provides a qualitative description of the various legal and socio-economic national contexts that were considered to be relevant in a study of industrial democracy. In that sense the latter publication describes the national background and "couleur locale," the former the systematic international comparison.

Participation: Rules, Influence, and Involvement / 275

FIGURE 1

THE RESEARCH MODEL

| Historical Socioeconomic context | *De jure* patterns and structures of participation (PS) | *De facto* participation
Distribution of influence (PO1) Patterns of involvement (PO2) | Outcomes of participation (O) |

Contextual and contingent variables at organizational and individual level (CON)

logical complexity, organizational differentiation and formalization, size, skill levels, degree of unionization, etc. Such variables are hypothesized as (a) having direct effects upon PO and O respectively and/or (b) modifying the relationships between PS and PO and between PO and O.

The "causal" ordering set forth in the model ignores possible feedback loops. For example, one may conceive of PO gradually feeding back to PS, or of O feeding back to PO and, in turn, to PS. Since the study of such feedback effects requires longitudinal analysis not possible with our data, we elected to exclude such effects from our model.

This Study

The entire model is not addressed here. We seek only to examine the extent to which existing patterns of *de facto* influence and involvement in organizations vary as a consequence of different *de jure* participative arrangements as well as other sets of contextual factors. The analysis will be of the form presented in Figure 2.

In practice, of course, the pattern of relations between the variables is likely to be far more complex. One might argue, for example, that the influence (PO1) exercised by different groups depends in part on their actual involvement in decision making (PO2) which in turn depends on the framework of *de jure* participation (PS). Alternatively, one could argue that patterns of *de facto* participation in organizations partly depend on the existing distribution of influence which, in turn, is affected by formal

FIGURE 2

ANALYTICAL PERSPECTIVES

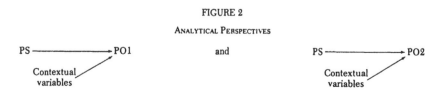

276 / IDE

regulations granting differential access to the decision-making process to different groups.

Similarly, contextual variables could be introduced into the analysis either as (co-)predictors of PO or as moderators of the relationship between PS and PO. Here again, it would be possible to distinguish and explore a number of other possibilities. In the present analysis, however, PS and contextual variables will be treated simply as (co-)determinants of influence and involvement, respectively.

Measures and Sample

Our discussion of measures here will be limited to PS, PO1, and PO2.[2] (The contextual variables relevant for the present discussion are listed in the appendix.)

In other studies of participation, respondents have been asked to rate the perceived amount of influence for different levels in the organization without reference to specific types of decisions (Tannenbaum, 1968). One problem with this approach is that the issues or decisions used as referents might change from one group or organizational level to another, thus resulting in unstandardized responses.

In the present study, unwanted variance has been reduced by selecting for analysis 16 specific decisions covering economic aspects, personnel matters, and working conditions. These 16 were further grouped into four clusters for analytical purposes.

Cluster 1 — holidays;
Cluster 2 — short-term (ST) decisions: work conditions, training, transfers, equipment, task assignment, work hours;
Cluster 3 — medium-term (MT) decisions: appointment of department heads, hiring procedures, appointment of immediate superiors, wage levels, reorganization, dismissals, and work study;
Cluster 4 — long-term (LT) decisions: investments, new products.

These decisions served as the focus for measuring *de jure* participation, the amount of influence, and the degree of involvement of each of seven groups (or levels) in each sample organization. These groups are as follows:

A — Nonsupervisory employees, both white- and blue-collar;
B — First line supervisors;
C — Middle management: levels above B and below D (including staff members at comparable levels);
D — Top management: those considered to be top management by the establishment;
E — Level above the establishment: supervisory, managerial bodies (e.g., conglomerate management), shareholders or owners;
F — Permanent representative bodies at the establishment level, no matter of what origin: works councils, workers' councils, union representative bodies;
G — Bodies/institutions outside of company/establishment: unions, banks, community councils, regional planning councils, etc.

---

[2] A copy of the main IDE questionnaire is published in IDE-International Research Group (1976).

Participation: Rules, Influence, and Involvement / 277

DE JURE *participation.* The prescribed intensity or degree of participation (PS) of a given group was specified for each of the 16 decisions by specialist-expert respondents in each organization. They used a six-point Guttman type scale: 1 = no prescribed regulations; 2 = information (unspecified) must be given to the group; 3 = information *ex ante* must be given to the group; 4 = prior consultation of the group is obligatory; 5 = joint decision making with the group (i.e., group has veto power and must give its approval); 6 = group has the final say.

The expert respondents were also asked to indicate the source of the regulations prescribing each group's participation. Ten possible sources were identified, which can be aggregated into: (a) laws (constitutional, national, and regional laws), (b) collective bargaining contracts (national, regional, sectoral, company, establishment), and (c) managerial policies or other enforceable management prerogatives. Hence, the resulting measures of *de jure* participation (PS) are based on documents regulating the kind of involvement and influence of the seven identified groups (A-G) in each of the 16 decisions.

DE FACTO *participation: influence (PO1).* For each of the 16 decisions, key management and union respondents were asked to rate the amount of influence exercised by each of the seven groups on a five-point Likert-type scale, ranging from "no influence" to "very much influence." Responses were then averaged by level. Since "influence" was undefined in the scale, it is probable that the respondents ascribed different meanings to it. Hence, we shall interpret our influence data as broadly reflecting the different groups' capacity to affect decision outcomes.

DE FACTO *participation: actual involvement (PO2).* The degree of actual involvement in decision making was measured by a six-point scale reflecting different degrees of involvement in decision making. Each individual at levels (groups) A, B, and C was asked to indicate the extent to which he perceives himself to be involved in each of the 16 decisions. The six options were as follows: 1 = I am not involved at all; 2 = I am informed about the matter beforehand; 3 = I can give my opinion; 4 = my opinion is taken into account; 5 = I take part in the decision making with equal weight; 6 = I decide on my own. Individual scores were then averaged for each level.

Sample. The stratification scheme adopted for selecting organizations for study was based on three criteria—size, industrial sector, and skill level. Size categories selected were small (less than 100 employees), medium (100-500), and large (500-1,500). Two sectors were selected: service (either banking or insurance) and manufacturing (limited to metal engineering firms). Manufacturing firms were further divided into high and low skill. Table 1 presents cell frequencies of organizations selected in each country.

Altogether 997 key respondents supplied scale responses for our PO1 measure. The total sample of respondents across all countries and organizations was 7,832. Different proportions of respondents were drawn across organizations, since equal percentages would have resulted in overrepresentation of the larger companies. Our goal was simply to obtain a representative sample from each level in each organization; hence, technically our sample is not "representative" of anything but the organizations from which it was drawn.

278 / IDE

TABLE 1

SMALL ORGANIZATIONS BY COUNTRY, INDUSTRY, AND SIZE

| | Service | | | Manufacturing | | | | | | |
| | | | | High skill | | | Low skill | | | |
Country	Small	Medium	Large	Small	Medium	Large	Small	Medium	Large	Total
Norway	1	1	1	1	1	1	1	2	1	10
Sweden	5	1	1	2	3	2	4	2	2	22
Denmark	1	1	1	1	1	1	1	1	1	9
Finland	2	1	1	2	1	1	2	1	1	12
United Kingdom	2	2	1	2	1	1	1	1	3	14
Germany	1	1	1	1	2	1	1	1	1	10
Netherlands	2	1	1	1	2	1	4	3	1	16
Belgium	1	1	1	1	2	2	1	1	1	11
France	1	1	1	1	1	1	1	1	1	9
Italy	1	—	1	1	1	—	1	1	1	7
Yugoslavia	1	1	1	1	1	1	1	1	1	9
Israel	—	—	—	—	1	1	1	1	1	5
Total	18	11	11	14	17	13	19	16	15	154

De Jure Participation (PS)

It was not known in advance how the 12 countries in our study would differ with respect to the degree of formalization of participation as measured by our methodology. Hence we first consider the degree to which PS is relied on in each country before moving on to identify characteristic PS patterns across hierarchical levels and countries.

Extent of PS. Table 2 shows the average number of decisions for which, in the case of each of our groups, there is some kind of formal rule regulating the group's involvement. The sum total of the average number of decisions with a PS source gives a crude index of a country's overall degree of formalization. Yugoslavia, Italy, Norway, Sweden, Denmark, and Germany have the highest overall scores, followed by Belgium and Finland; Great Britain and Israel have by far the lowest scores.

Within most countries the degree of PS varies considerably across levels. Top management has the highest formalization score of any group in over half of our countries. In the rest, it is the level above top management that has the highest score in the U.K., France, and Norway; in Denmark, the two levels are equal; and in Yugoslavia, it is workers who have the highest score.

In this context, note also that, compared to other countries, Yugoslavia, Norway, and Italy all have relatively high scores for groups and institutions outside the establishment. (For Norway and Italy, these outside groups are mainly union headquarters, state inspectors, or banking institutions; for Yugoslavia, they are mainly community councils or banks.) Whether such scores are evidence of broader attempts to link individual companies more

Participation: Rules, Influence, and Involvement / 279

TABLE 2

EXTENT OF OVERALL FORMALIZATION OF PARTICIPATION BY COUNTRY
(AVERAGE NUMBER OF DECISIONS—OUT OF 16—WITH A PS SOURCE)

	Level or group								
Country	Workers (A)	Supervisors (B)	Middle management (C)	Top management (D)	Level above (E)	Representative bodies (F)	Outside groups (G)	Total	Country rank
Norway	9.0	7.6	7.5	15.9	16.0	6.4	8.9	71.3	3
Sweden	8.2	10.1	10.1	13.6	12.4	12.7	1.7	68.8	4
Denmark	5.9	6.9	8.8	14.8	14.8	9.3	2.2	62.7	5
Finland	10.7	10.7	10.7	16.0	—	4.9	1.7	54.7	8
Great Britain	3.7	3.4	3.3	4.0	4.1	4.0	1.3	23.8	11
Germany	10.0	9.0	9.0	16.0	2.0	14.0	1.3	61.3	6
Netherlands	5.0	—	—	16.0	7.0	13.0	3.0	44.0	10
Belgium	6.4	9.8	10.8	11.8	5.9	10.8	4.5	60.0	7
France	4.7	4.6	4.4	6.9	12.6	11.0	3.0	47.2	9
Italy	11.6	9.4	10.7	14.3	7.9	12.6	7.0	73.5	2
Yugoslavia	15.3	12.6	14.6	14.1	7.2	13.8	8.4	85.6	1
Israel	—	—	—	10.6	2.0	10.2	—	19.6	12

closely with their institutional environments can only be answered through further research and analysis.

Intensity of DE JURE *participation.* There are a number of different ways in which patterns of PS across organizations and countries could be further analyzed. Here we limit ourselves to a description of the relative degree of PS possessed by each group aggregated to the national level. As noted above, the amount of prescribed participation by level was assessed on a six-point scale for each of 16 decisions. The average score of a group in a given firm over all decisions may thus be said to describe its total intensity of *de jure* participation. Similarly, the average score of a group over all organizations within a given country can be seen as an index of that group's total intensity of *de jure* participation within that particular country. These average scores of all groups over the decision set are shown in Table 3.

Four characteristic patterns of PS across countries are apparent: a low profile pattern, a hierarchical one-peaked pattern, a hierarchical two-peaked pattern, and what may be called a "representative peaked" pattern.

The low profile pattern, characteristic of Belgium and Great Britain, is marked by relatively low scores for all groups with only minor peaks for top management and representative bodies. No one group tends to be favored by existing rules. (This interpretation is also supported by the low variance scores for Belgium and Great Britain.)

In the hierarchical one-peaked pattern, represented by France, Norway, and Sweden, the pattern peaks at the level above top management, with top management itself still having a relatively high score. Boards of directors

TABLE 3

INTENSITY OF *De Jure* PARTICIPATION BY LEVEL AND COUNTRY[a]
(AVERAGED OVER 16 DECISIONS AND ALL ORGANIZATIONS)

	Level or group								
Country	Workers (A)	Super-visors (B)	Middle manage-ment (C)	Top manage-ment (D)	Level above (E)	Repre-sentative bodies (F)	Outside groups (G)	Variance[b] A-E	
Norway	2.44	1.88	1.87	4.09	5.71	1.86	1.18	2.36	(2)
Sweden	2.07	2.71	3.17	4.52	4.53	3.29	1.32	1.59	(6)
Denmark	1.74	2.22	2.65	4.75	1.93	2.55	1.32	1.34	(8)
Finland	2.43	2.49	2.68	5.39	1.57	1.92	1.41	2.04	(3)
Great Britain	1.51	1.49	1.46	2.08	1.55	1.82	1.20	0.07	(12)
Germany	2.25	2.16	2.13	5.43	1.63	3.95	1.18	1.89	(5)
Netherlands	1.62	1.00	1.00	5.60	2.00	2.97	1.75	2.97	(1)
Belgium	1.96	2.26	2.55	3.06	2.21	2.58	1.68	0.22	(11)
France	1.79	1.80	1.83	2.90	4.63	3.10	1.38	1.98	(4)
Italy	1.82	2.17	2.81	4.25	1.90	2.31	1.30	0.95	(9)
Yugoslavia	3.40	3.02	3.35	3.36	2.38	4.53	2.50	0.28	(10)
Israel	1.00	1.00	1.00	4.16	1.55	2.59	1.00	1.54	(7)

[a] Correlations of average Mode scores of the total set of 16 decisions for groups A-G with the respective scores of the clusters for short-term and medium-term decisions are in the ranges of .81 to .97 (only exception: short-term decision scores of group G correlate with total set only .75). Correlations with scores for long-term decisions are somewhat lower (.55 to .78) which may be due to the fact that only two decisions (investment and new product) enter this cluster.

[b] Variance in *de jure* participation across hierarchical groups A-E — total set of 16 decisions (country ranks in parentheses).

in these countries apparently enjoy greater prerogatives by law than executive management even over day-to-day operations. This is of considerable methodological importance, since studies of organizational power frequently ignore outside power sources (e.g., Tannenbaum, *et al.*, 1974).

The hierarchical two-peak pattern is most common, being typical of Denmark, Finland, Germany, Italy, the Netherlands, and Israel. Its characteristic feature is a sharp peak for top management with a slump for the next level and another (smaller) peak for representative bodies. Here formal rules regulating intraorganizational decision making clearly favor top management.

The representative peaked pattern is specific to Yugoslavia. It is characterized by an absolute peak for representative bodies and by a relatively small variance in scores across the other six groups. Here formal rules might be seen as promoting an inverse hierarchical ordering since formal power rests much more with representative bodies than with top management.

De Facto Participation: Influence

This section first looks at the distribution of influence across hierarchical levels in our 12 countries as determined by key respondents. We then examine the extent to which existing patterns of influence in organizations are conditioned by formal rules (PS) and contextual variables.

Participation: Rules, Influence, and Involvement / 281

Influence distribution by level and country. Overall patterns of the distribution of influence are presented in Table 4, showing the average amount of influence exercised by each group over the set of 16 decisions in each country. As can be seen, there is considerably less variation in mean scores across countries than across organizational levels. This suggests that the hierarchical ordering within organizations is a much stronger determinant of the distribution of influence than other factors operative at the level of the country.

TABLE 4

DISTRIBUTION OF INFLUENCE (PO1) BY LEVEL AND COUNTRY
AVERAGE KEY RESPONDENT'S SCORES OVER 16 DECISIONS AND ALL ORGANIZATIONS
(SCALE: 1 = NO INFLUENCE, 5 = VERY MUCH INFLUENCE)

Country	Workers (A)	Supervisors (B)	Middle management (C)	Top management (D)	Level above (E)	Representative bodies (F)	Outside groups (G)	Total
Norway	2.3	2.7	3.3	3.7	2.0	2.1	1.3	2.5
Sweden	2.0	2.5	3.1	3.5	2.7	2.8	1.3	2.5
Denmark	2.0	3.0	3.2	3.6	1.9	1.9	1.4	2.4
Finland	2.0	2.6	3.5	4.0	2.3	1.5	1.3	2.4
Great Britain	2.0	2.4	3.2	3.9	2.8	2.2	1.5	2.6
Germany	1.9	2.3	3.0	4.4	1.6	2.6	1.2	2.4
Netherlands	2.1	2.7	2.9	3.7	2.0	2.1	1.2	2.4
Belgium	1.6	2.2	3.1	4.2	2.9	2.4	–	2.3
France	2.1	2.9	3.0	4.7	3.0	2.1	1.5	2.6
Italy	2.1	2.7	3.2	4.1	2.0	2.5	1.6	2.5
Yugoslavia	2.7	2.8	3.1	3.6	2.9	3.9	2.2	3.0
Israel	1.6	2.8	3.1	4.3	2.1	2.4	1.2	2.4

In all 12 countries the distribution of influence (levels A to D) follows an essentially hierarchical pattern, although the pattern does not extend to extraorganizational levels. In all countries, groups at the corporate and societal level have substantially less influence than top management. One explanation is that external groups may not be particularly interested in the kinds of intraorganizational issues represented by our decision set. Another explanation is that external groups may exercise their power indirectly through control over resources and other institutional means rather than through direct involvement in decision making. Even allowing for such possibilities, the difference in influence exercised by top management and by outside groups is sizeable enough to conclude that organizations in all countries (possibly excepting Yugoslavia) tend to be relatively autonomous and closed in relation to their environments.

Table 4 also shows that the influence scores of workers and representative bodies do not vary substantially across countries. With the exception of

282 / IDE

Yugoslavia, workers tend to have little or no influence and representative bodies only a bit more. The scores for top management in all countries are consistently much higher, although the variance across countries is somewhat more pronounced. Hence, one could conclude that, on the whole, there is little industrial democracy in any country.

Our data show that for most countries the influence of workers and representative bodies decreases and that of management increases as one moves from short-term to long-term decisions. Hence, if one attributes greater importance to long-term decisions, the disparity between top management and workers becomes even greater than suggested by the averages.

Here again, Yugoslavia (and perhaps the Scandinavian countries) are exceptions. In Yugoslav organizations, interestingly, the influence of both the workers' council and top management grows as decisions become more important (although the increase is less for top management). This suggests that under certain conditions, representative bodies' influence does not necessarily come at the expense of management's, i.e., it is not a zero-sum game.

The picture overall is of centralized top management control. For example, mean sample-wide influence scores by level show that top management has the highest influence of any group over 13 of the 16 decisions. It controls four decisions almost exclusively — appointment of department heads; major capital investments; introduction of new products; and appointment of immediate superior.

Decisions over which lower and middle management groups exceed the influence of top management and representative bodies were all primarily short-term (e.g., transfers, work assignments). Moderate influence was also exercised over some medium-term decisions (e.g., decisions about work study, dismissals, work conditions, reorganization), but little over long-term decisions. On the whole, therefore, the decentralization of influence in our organizations implies a kind of "programmed participation" oriented towards the execution but not the formulation of goals (Burns, 1967).

As regards democratization, there were only three decisions over which workers and/or representative bodies exercised at least a moderate amount of influence: decisions about the dismissal of employees, holidays, and issues concerning the work environment. These decisions are among those which tend to be most strongly regulated by law in most European countries. External legal regulations, in other words, seem important to support internal democracy.

In sum, except in Yugoslavia most organizations tend to be centralized, closed, and nondemocratic in terms of being management centered. Country-by-country variation from this pattern is slight.

PS and Influence

The most fruitful framework for analyzing the relation between PS and influence would stress their mutual interaction; i.e., a reciprocal process in which legislation promotes structural and behavioral changes
which in turn, over extended periods, affect the development of legislative
activity. As noted, however, our cross-sectional data force us to look simply
at the extent to which legal rules contribute to the development of particular
patterns of influence.

The following discussion deals with the effect of PS on the influence of
only three groups — workers, representative bodies, and top management —
since preliminary analysis indicates but weak effects on other organizational
levels. Also these groups are most critical for understanding how processes
of democratization develop.

Table 5 presents the results of a set of multiple regressions in which the
basic dimensions of PS are taken as predictors and various aspects of
influence are taken as dependent variables. Readily apparent is the considerable impact which PS has. In particular, PS appears to contribute significantly to the development of more egalitarian distributions of influence
(less pronounced differences in influence between top management and
workers and lower variance in influence across levels A-D). Closely related
to this is the fact that PS has a predominantly positive effect on the influence
of workers and representative bodies but tends to have a mixed, if not
predominantly negative, effect on the influence of top management.

The fact that PS has contrasting effects on different levels suggests that
de jure systems have both a direct and an indirect impact. Such systems
appear to operate directly by promoting the influence of workers and representative bodies and indirectly by inhibiting the influence of competing
levels. Thus, for example, the set of rules defining direct participation at the
workers' level enhances not only this particular level's influence but also
that of representative bodies, while at the same time inhibiting the influence
of top management. Formal rules regulating the participation of top management do not appear to inhibit the influence of workers and of representative
bodies.

Finally, the predictive power of PS varies considerably from level to level.
PS explains roughly between 40 and 60 per cent of the variance in the
influence of workers and representative bodies for medium and long-term
decisions. By contrast, only about 10 to 20 per cent of the variance in top
management's influence is accounted for. Note also that PS tends to be a
better predictor of a level's influence over long-term as opposed to short-
term decisions. This is particularly evident with respect to workers, where

TABLE 5

MULTIPLE REGRESSION RESULTS: PS REGRESSED ON DIMENSIONS OF INFLUENCE (POI)[a]

Influence of:

PS	Workers (A)			Top management (D)			Representative bodies (F)		
	ST[b]	MT[b]	LT[b]	ST	MT	LT	ST	MT	LT
Workers (A)									
ST[b]									
MT[b]		.51	.29			-.34			
LT									
Supervisors (B)									
ST	-.47								
MT					-.32				
LT						-.43			
Middle management (C)									
ST				.40					
MT									
LT									
Top management (D)									
ST			.41				-.32		
MT		-.38							
LT			-.61			.43			
Level above (E)									
ST				-.33					
MT			.32						
LT			-.19						
Representative bodies (F)									
ST							.56		
MT					.34			.66	
LT									
Outside groups (G)									
ST			.20			.24		-.25	.37
MT			.21					.22	.14
LT									
Multiple R	.549	.705	.804	.511	.568	.546	.733	.788	.757
Adjusted R²	.17	.40	.58	.12	.19	.16	.45	.55	.49
F	2.3	5.2	9.7	1.8	2.5	2.2	6.2	8.7	7.1
p	.003	.000	.000	.001	.001	.003	.000	.000	.000

[a] Table values are standardized beta coefficients with P ≤ .07.
[b] ST = short-term decisions; MT = medium-term decisions; LT = long-term decisions.

the proportion of explained variance steadily increases as one moves from short-term to long-term decisions.

One conclusion which can be drawn from the above is that democratic decision making can be enhanced best by promoting greater worker participation in medium and long-term decisions and by strengthening the role played by representative bodies in all decisions. However, efforts in this direction should not ignore the impact which changes in the *de jure* positions of other groups can have on the influence of workers and their representatives. The positive side-effects which can be obtained by strengthening the role of external bodies and by restricting top management's prerogatives are particularly important.

Influence and Contextual Variables

In our original study, a separate set of multiple regressions was carried out using our contextual variables alone (see Appendix for definitions) as predictors of actual influence. These results will not be presented here. We found, however, that only about half reached significance for one or more of the groups.

Table 6 presents the results of a set of multiple regressions in which PS and contextual variables are taken as co-predictors of the influence of workers, representative bodies, and top management. The PS variables included in the analysis vary from group to group. They were selected on the basis of the results of the multiple regressions presented in Table 5. The contextual variables, on the other hand, are the same for all three groups and were selected for inclusion based on their having reached significance in the separate analysis referred to above.

Note first that the predictive power of these two sets of variables seems to vary from level to level. PS is a better predictor of the influence of workers and of representative bodies than of the influence of top management. Contextual variables, on the other hand, tend to be better predictors of the influence of top management. This is an important finding, since current research is heavily oriented toward explaining variations in participation and influence in terms of personal attributes and/or structural and technological features of organizations. Our results suggest, however, that while managerial influence may still be primarily conditioned by organizational factors, the influence of workers and representative bodies seems to be more a function of broader social and political factors outside the organization.

In looking at particular levels, it is apparent that workers' influence is enhanced mainly by rules which (a) promote workers' participation in

TABLE 6

MULTIPLE REGRESSION RESULTS: CON AND PS VARIABLES REGRESSED ON INFLUENCE (PO1)[a]

CON and PS	Workers (A)				Top management (D)						Representative bodies (F)			
	ST	MT	LT	Σ	ST	MT	LT	Σ			ST	MT	LT	Σ
Formal independence	.18			.15		-.22								
Political stability	.20													
Sector														
Skill			.24											
Automation			-.16											
Product complexity		.13		.15	.29		.18	.30			.20	.14	.14	.22
Functional differentiation		.17					.17				-.15			-.11
Formalization					-.16	.20	-.29	-.24			-.19	.13	.33	.24
Mobilization		.21			-.21	-.17					-.20			-.13
PSA MT		.59	.63	.48		-.33	-.26	-.21	PSA MT	PSA LT				
PSB ST			.18						PSB ST	PSB MT				
PSB MT			-.18						PSC ST	PSD ST	-.34	-.21		-.29
PSD ST						.22	.35		PSC LT	PSF MT	.64	.73		.67
PSD MT		-.32	-.28	.18	-.22				PSE LT	PSC MT			.41	
PSE MT	.32					.21		-.24	PSF LT					
Multiple R	.513	.753	.752	.637	.583	.586	.653	.594			.744	.768	.754	.824
Adjusted R²	.15	.50	.50	.32	.18	.25	.34	.26			.49	.53	.51	.63
F	2.5	9.1	9.1	4.8	2.8	3.6	5.2	3.8			9.3	10.8	9.9	15.9
p	.003	.000	.000	.000	.001	.000	.000	.000			.000	.000	.000	.000
Df	16,112				16,112						15,113			

The column headers ST, MT, LT refer to short-term, medium-term, and long-term decisions; the three groups are Influence of: Workers (A), Top management (D), Representative bodies (F).

[a] Values in table are adjusted beta coefficients with p ≤ .07; CON predictors are the same for all influence variables, while PS predictors are different for each level. PSA MT means PS score of level A for medium-term decisions, while PSB ST means PS score of level B for short-term decisions, etc. Σ = all 16 decisions.

medium and long-term decisions and (b) facilitate the participation of external bodies in short-term decisions. None of the other contingencies such as skill, mobilization, or sector has a comparable impact on workers' influence. The same could be said for inhibiting factors: rules facilitating top management involvement are the main restriction on workers' influence. Note that these rules play a far more important role than automation or any other contextual variable.

The principal impact of PS is to reduce overall top management influence, as in the case for rules which promote workers' involvement in medium-term decisions. The same tends to be true of contextual variables such as formalization and employee mobilization. Product complexity is the only variable which consistently increases top management's influence.

Among the strongest predictors of the influence of representative bodies are: rules which facilitate their participation in medium-term decisions, employee mobilization, functional differentiation, and rules facilitating top management involvement in short-term decisions. Note that the last variable has a predominantly negative effect.

In summary, the greatest impact on power equalization appears to come from PS which regulates the participation of workers, management, and representative bodies. Rules which enhance the participation of workers and representative bodies tend to have a positive effect on the influence of each while at the same time tending to inhibit the influence of top management. Rules facilitating the participation of top management do not necessarily enhance its influence, but do have a significant negative impact on the influence of both workers and representative bodies. It is also worth noting that institutional rules enhancing the involvement of external bodies tend to have a significant positive effect on the influence of representative bodies. This provides further evidence that formal rules which enhance the participation of external groups help promote a more even distribution of influence within organizations.

At a more general level, the main conclusion to be drawn from our findings is that the distribution of influence is conditioned more by human action than by existing technological, structural, and economic conditions. This suggests, then, that more work should be done on developing theories which take into account the broader socio-political environment in which organizations operate.

De Facto Participation: Involvement

As with influence, we shall first look at patterns of actual involvement across hierarchical levels in the 12 countries and then examine

288 / IDE

TABLE 7

De Facto Participation: Actual Involvement (PO2) Across Levels and Countries

Country	Level			
	Workers (A)	Foremen (B)	Middle management (C)	Mean
Norway	1.8	2.6	3.2	2.5
Sweden	1.8	2.6	2.8	2.4
Denmark	2.0	3.7	3.7	3.2
Finland	1.7	2.6	3.5	2.6
Great Britain	2.1	2.4	3.0	2.5
Germany	1.9	2.5	3.5	2.6
Netherlands	2.1	2.7	3.5	2.8
Belgium	1.8	2.5	2.8	2.3
France	2.0	2.5	3.1	2.6
Italy	1.7	2.5	2.6	2.2
Yugoslavia	2.7	3.1	3.2	3.0
Israel	1.7	2.4	2.9	2.3

the extent to which involvement is conditioned by PS and other contextual variables. Recall that involvement was measured by asking each sampled individual at levels A, B, and C to estimate on a six-point scale the actual amount of involvement he enjoys in each of the decision types.

Patterns of involvement. Table 7 shows the average degree of involvement of the three focal levels — workers, supervisors, and middle management — in the set of 16 decisions in each country. As is evident, average worker involvement, like average worker influence, tends to be quite low in all countries (except Yugoslavia) both in absolute terms and relative to foremen and middle management.

This hierarchical pattern appears in all countries. Such patterns apparently are not conditioned primarily by political, economic, or social characteristics of the environment but by the existing technical division of labor, which is still quite similar in all 12 countries. As noted, the socio-political environment institutionally reflected in *de jure* systems can significantly affect the structure of decision making and modify the nature of hierarchical patterns within organizations. Obviously, however, it cannot dissolve the hierarchy itself as the basic organizational form.

Having said this, however, it is worth noting that there are some differences in patterns of involvement among countries. Thus, differences in involvement between workers and middle management are greater in Finland, Denmark, and Germany than in Yugoslavia, Great Britain, and Italy. More broadly, the differences between the scores of these three levels are not the same in all countries. In Belgium, Denmark, Italy, Israel, Norway, Sweden, and Yugoslavia, there are smaller differences in involvement between supervisors and middle management than between workers and supervisors. In the remaining five countries the relations are reversed. These trends can be important because of their effect on interpersonal relations. In the first seven cases, for instance, we might expect to find a stronger tendency on the part of supervisors to identify with management than with workers and greater worker resistance in the implementation of decisions.

Greater differences emerge among countries if we look at the different clusters of decisions. The 12 countries could be classified into four distinct groups according to differences in the involvement of the three levels across clusters of decisions: (a) actual involvement of the three levels is high in all clusters (Denmark and Yugoslavia); (b) involvement is relatively low in all clusters (Belgium and Israel); (c) involvement is high in short-term and low in long-term decisions (France and the Netherlands); and (d) involvement is low in short-term and high in long-term decisions (Italy and Norway).

Finally, if one excludes Yugoslavia, there is a greater variation in workers' involvement across countries with respect to short rather than long-term decisions. In Yugoslavia, workers' involvement in short-term decisions is only slightly higher than in some of the other countries (and lower than in Denmark), but their involvement in medium and long-term decisions is very much higher than in any other country. These characteristics suggest that while the technical division of labor is the most important factor determining the involvement of workers in short-term decisions, institutional legislation prevails in determining their involvement in medium and long-term decisions.

PS and Worker Involvement

Our discussion of the effect of PS on involvement will be limited to only the most interesting group—the involvement of workers. Table 8 presents multiple regression results in which forms of PS are taken as predictors of worker involvement in short-, medium-, and long-term decisions. Compare this table with Table 5 and note that the proportion of the variance explained by PS is only slightly higher for involvement than for influence. Note too that the extent of workers' involvement is conditioned not only by rules which regulate their own participation but even more by rules which regulate the participation of top management and representative bodies. Here again, rules which enhance top management's involvement, particularly in medium-term decisions, appear to have a consistently negative effect on workers' involvement, while rules aiding representative bodies in medium- and long-term decisions generally have a positive effect on worker involvement.

290 / IDE

TABLE 8

MULTIPLE REGRESSION RESULTS: PS RECRESSED ON DIMENSIONS OF INVOLVEMENT (PO2)[a]
Df = 21,112

PS	Involvement of workers (A)			
	ST[b]	MT	LT	Σ
Workers				
ST	.41			.33
MT		.28	.23	.25
LT				
Supervisors				
ST				−.35
MT				
LT				
Middle management				
ST				
MT				
LT				
Top management				
ST				
MT	−.57	−.37	−.51	−.54
LT				
Level above				
ST	−.40			.37
MT				
LT	.30			
Representative bodies				
ST	−.70			−.46
MT	.54	.30	.32	.58
LT	.29			.25
Outside groups				
ST		.19	.20	
MT			.20	
LT				.16
Multiple R	.604	.763	.808	.760
Adjusted R²	.24	.56	.58	.49
F	3.0	7.4	10.0	7.3
p	.000	.000	.000	.000

[a] Values in table are adjusted beta coefficients with $p \leq .07$.
[b] ST = short-term decisions; MT = medium-term decisions; LT = long-term decisions; Σ = all decisions.

Finally, as with influence, PS tends to be a better predictor of workers' involvement in long-term than in short-term decisions, thus again supporting the notion that worker participation in more strategic issues is explained more by institutional rules than by socio-political factors.

Involvement, Contextual Variables, and Other Factors

In this last part of the analysis, we shall examine the effects of contextual variables on involvement in a different manner than with influence. First, we shall concentrate only on a single level—that of workers. Second, the analysis looks at the joint effects of not only PS and contextual

Participation: Rules, Influence, and Involvement / 291

variables,[3] but three additional variables as well. These are (a) the influence of workers, top management, and representative bodies (PO1), (b) leadership style across all levels in the organization (OPART-D), and (c) organizational climate, defined as the clarity of authority and communications (CLIM-S) and the nature of interpersonal relations (CLIM-R) within the organization.[4] The results appear in Table 9.

TABLE 9

Multiple Regression Results: Actual Involvement (PO2) of Workers (A) Regressed by CON, PS, OPART-D, POL, CLIM[a]
Df = 20,110

Predictors	Involvement of workers (A)			
	ST[b]	MT	LT	Σ
Sector	.15	−.23	−.21	
Automation				
Functional differentiation				
Vertical span				
Mobilization				
PSA ST[c]				
PSA MT			.26	
PSB ST				
PSD MT	−.24	−.21	−.16	−.23
PSF ST				
PSF MT				
PSF LT				
PSE LT		−.15		−.16
OPART-D	.52			.32
Influence level A		.22	.16	.15
Influence level D				
Influence level F				
CLIM-S	−.16		.21	
CLIM-R			−.18	
Multiple R	.767	.757	.779	.755
Adjusted R^2	.51	.49	.53	.49
F	7.8	7.4	8.5	7.3
p	.000	.000	.000	.000

[a] Values in table are adjusted beta coefficients with $p \leq .07$.
[b] ST = short-term decisions; MT = medium-term decisions; LT = long-term decisions; Σ = all decisions.
[c] PSA ST means PS score of level A (workers) for short-term decisions, etc.

[3] As with influence, the overall effects of our contextual variables on worker involvement were quite mixed and will not be discussed here. However, we might briefly summarize their comparative separate effects on both influence and involvement as follows: (a) among all our contextual variables, mobilization is the strongest predictor of both influence and involvement; (b) personal variables, such as skill, are slightly better predictors of workers' involvement than they are of workers' influence; (c) technology (and specifically automation) appears to be a better predictor of involvement than of influence; and (d) economic and environmental contingencies have little effect on either influence or involvement.

[4] The inclusion of these new predictors to some extent involves a modification of our initial research design since influence was not originally treated as a predictor of actual involvement. The same is true for the other two sets of predictors. At the beginning of our investigation, leadership style and organizational climate were treated as outcome variables or as indicators of the possible effects of involvement. Later, however, the members of our research team became increasingly inclined toward the hypothesis that leadership style and climate should be treated as contextual variables or as predictors of actual involvement. Leadership style was measured by an attitude scale consisting of five items relating to direct participation and the superior's decision-making practices. Organizational climate was assessed by two scales of ten (CLIM-S) and three (CLIM-R) items, respectively. For details see IDE (1976).

292 / IDE

While the addition of the new variables makes Table 9 somewhat difficult to compare with Table 6, it does appear that PS tends to be a better predictor than contextual variables of both worker influence and involvement. Table 9 shows that workers' actual involvement in decision making is predicted primarily by: (a) rules regulating the participation of top management and corporate bodies—both have a consistently negative effect on worker involvement, although the latter is less strong; (b) leadership style—this variable is by far the strongest predictor of workers' involvement in short-term decisions; (c) the total amount of influence exercised by workers—this variable has a significant positive effect on workers' involvement in medium and long-term decisions; and (d) sector—a dimension of organizational environment.

What these findings appear to show is that leadership style has strong effects on worker involvement only with respect to short-term, more routine decisions. Involvement in longer-term, more strategic decisions is much more affected by the existing distribution of influence and by PS. But since the distribution of influence is itself strongly affected by institutional rules, one is led to the conclusion that leadership style and institutional provisions for participation are two of the most important factors accounting for the diversity of democratic decision-making patterns across our sample organizations.

Conclusion

Most past participation research has been concerned with either measuring participation as a consequence of different managerial styles or describing and analyzing different national legal frameworks and participation machineries. Neither approach alone seems adequate to describe such a complex phenomenon as industrial democracy in the European context. Rather, our study suggests that high levels of employee participation are a function of an intricate interrelation of internal managerial practices and externally promoted support systems based on formal laws or collective bargaining agreements.

Further, both these variables together do a better job of predicting influence and power distributions than "objective" technological or structural conditions such as organizational size, internal differentiation, or levels of automation. This last finding underscores the "voluntaristic" nature of industrial democracy in the sense of being a system which is more the outcome of socio-political factors than of structural opportunities or constraints.

Appendix

Contextual Variables

The 19 contextual variables included in the analysis are as follows (grouped into basic categories):

A. *Personal variables* (attributes of employees aggregated at the group level):
   Con 5: skill level of employees
   Con 14: stability of workforce (mean age and tenure of employees)
   Con 15: male domination (percentage of male employees)
   Con 16: mobilization of employees (combining the per cent of employees presently members of representative bodies, per cent of employees with past membership in representative bodies, per cent employees belonging to unions)

B. *Technological contingencies*
   Con 6: level of automation of work (combining measures on most typical types of machinery and most automated pieces of equipment)
   Con 7: technological interdependence or work flow continuity (combining measures on multiplicity of outputs and immediacy of effects of breakdowns)
   Con 8: complexity of production (combining measures of product complexity and of predictability and routineness of production)

C. *Structural contingencies*
   Con 19: log size of organization
   Con 9: functional differentiation (number of different specialist functions)
   Con 10: vertical differentiation (number of distinct posts or levels between chief executive and workers)
   Con 11: formalization of organizational roles (number of specific role-defining documents)
   Con 12: span of control of top management
   Con 13: intensity of managerial control (ratio of non-A levels to A levels)

D. Economic contingencies
   Con 17: evaluation of success by top management
   Con 18: growth rate

E. Environmental contingencies
   Con 1: formal independence of organization
   Con 2: strength of market position
   Con 3: instability of political environment
   Con 4: sector in which organization operates

294 / IDE

References

Batstone, Eric, and P. L. Davies. *Industrial Democracy: European Experience.* London: HMSO, 1976.

Beyme, Klaus von. *Gewerkschaften und Arbeitsbefiehungen in kapitalischen Ländern.* Munich: Piper, 1976.

Burns, Tom. "The Comparative Study of Organizations." In Victor Vroom, ed., *Methods of Organizational Research.* Pittsburgh, Pa.: University of Pittsburgh Press, 1967.

IDE International Research Group. "Industrial Democracy in Europe (IDE): An International Comparative Study," *Social Science Information,* XV (February, 1976), 177-203.

King, Charles D. and M. van de Vall. *Models of Industrial Democracy.* New York: Mouton, 1978.

Tannenbaum, Arnold S. *Control in Organizations.* New York: McGraw-Hill, 1968.

_____, et al. *Hierarchy in Organizations.* San Francisco, Ca.: Jossey-Bass, 1974.

[20]

Industrial Democracy in Europe: Differences and Similarities Across Countries and Hierarchies

IDE International Research Group[1]

Abstract

This article attempts to present the focus, methodology, and preliminary results of an international collaborative research project on industrial democracy involving twelve countries in Europe including Yugoslavia and Israel. Rather than explaining variations in participation, power, and influence in terms of contingencies such as personal attributes and characteristics of participants, on the one hand, or structural and technological features of organization, on the other hand, the research looks at both *de jure* and *de facto* participation in terms of participative structure (PS), power distribution (PO), and their outcomes (O).

Initial findings with respect to differences and similarities across countries are presented. One of the main conclusions to be derived from the research is that, whereas all countries reveal a consistent hierarchy in the organizations studied, political and economic environments institutionally reflected in *de jure* participation can, however, significantly modify hierarchical patterns in organizations, but apparently not dissolve them as such. Another finding reported is that workers' satisfaction is unaffected by their own direct influence or that of their works council. But workers value representative participation for its own sake, the more their influence or involvement. Further democratization may require a change in national legal arrangements.

Introduction

The still mounting discussion on how to introduce or improve regulations on industrial democracy in industrialized countries assumes that legislation will have behavioural effects. Political discussion has, however, to date mainly focussed on legal issues and lacks for the most part empirical feedback about the actual consequences of various participative systems (c.f. Walker 1974). Systematic cross-cultural social science efforts on behavioural consequences of industrial democracy relations are, in turn, very rare, although the subject in general now has a burgeoning literature (see Blumberg 1968; Pusić 1973; Bernstein 1976; Rothschild-Whitt 1976, for example). Furthermore, the research to be discussed was inspired at least in part by practical needs of policy makers on national and international levels. In their task of developing policies for legislative action, or international recommendations in the field of participation and industrial democracy, they are indeed faced with a considerable lack of knowledge as to how different models or participative management systems effectively function in real life.

The research we now set out in this article attempts to provide such an

Organization Studies
1981, 2/2: 113–129
© 1981 EGOS
0170–8406/81/
002–0005 $1.00

understanding. It represents an international collaborative effort to study the behavioural concomitants of formal legal structures designed to regulate the interaction patterns of interest groups in business organizations. It takes as given the large variety of national industrial democracy schemes; this provides an almost ideal 'natural experiment' of the treatment variable, 'legal norms' (see IDE 1976: 177–203; IDE 1979a, 1979b).

The research was carried out in twelve countries (Belgium, Denmark, Finland, France, Germany, Great Britain, Italy, Israel, Netherlands, Norway, Sweden, Yugoslavia). Some 30 social scientists from 18 research institutions took part (see 'The Authors', pp. 207–208, this issue). The project development phase lasted from May 1973 through May 1975 and comprised pretesting and a pilot study in eight countries. Field research of the main data collection phase started in the beginning of 1976 and lasted through 1977. Data analysis, first on a national and then on an international comparative basis, took place in 1977 and 1978. The publication of two volumes describing the project and its cross-national results is imminent (IDE 1981a, 1981b).

The basic assumption of the research is that formal rules and regulations on industrial democracy act to bring about mainly (though not exclusively) new processes of participative behaviour. It is assumed that this participation will lead to different patterns of power distribution, which can be demonstrated in the context of organizational decision making. *The central theoretical issue is to establish whether existing patterns of decision making and influence sharing vary significantly as a consequence of different national arrangements for participative management, or to what degree they are due to other intervening factors* (see IDE 1976: 177–180; for the initial theoretical background, IDE 1981a: Ch. II).

The central variables are participative structure (PS) and power distribution in organizations (PO). Of these, the term (PS) is defined as all formal operative rules and regulations that prescribe involvement of various groups in intraorganizational decision making. Correspondingly, (PO) refers to the relative weights that various specific groups can bring to bear to influence a particular decision outcome. The relevant groups examined were: workers, foremen, middle management, top management, supervisory boards, internal employee representative bodies (e.g. works councils) and external groups (e.g. banks, governments). A set of contingencies or moderator variables, we assume, influences the relationship of (PS) - (PO). Furthermore, certain outcomes (O) of participative structures (PS) and processes (PO) are considered of particular significance *vis-à-vis* work satisfaction, attitudes towards participation, organizational climate, economic efficiency and so on (see IDE 1976: 177–203 for details of the methodology). A graphic representation of the theoretical model and main variable sets is provided in Figure 1.

Implicit in the research design are a number of exploratory questions and hypotheses of various levels of complexity and generality. The following are examples of such research questions: which systems of formal participation lead to a higher level of actual participation in important decisions? Do the

Figure 1
Theoretical Model and
Sets of Variables in
the Research*

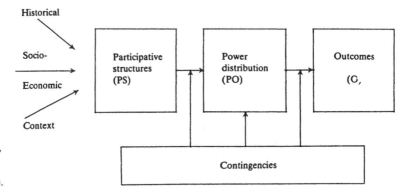

* Feedback loops may,
of course, be
incorporated into this
model (see IDE 1981a).

different systems of participation differ with respect to discrepancy between formally stated and actually existing participation? To what extent does discrepancy between formal and actual participation lead to lower involvement? Are relationships like those mentioned above dependent upon, or moderated by, formal characteristics of the participation system? Are these relationships dependent upon, or moderated by, specific national characteristics of the system in which participation operates?

A target of a minimum of nine companies (chosen according to size and technology) in each country was set. More organizations could be included if national teams were to find this feasible: in Italy and Israel the minimum was not quite attained (see Table 1). Altogether, 134 organizations were investigated involving nearly 9,000 interviews.

Table 1
Number of
Organizations in
Total Sample

	Type of Organization									
	Service			Manufacturing						
				Techn. high			Techn. low			
Countries*	Small	Med.	Large	Small	Med.	Large	Small	Med.	Large	Total
Norway	1	1	1	1	1	1	1	2	1	10
Sweden	5	1	1	2	3	2	4	2	2	22
Denmark	1	1	1	1	1	1	1	1	1	9
Finland	2	1	1	2	1	1	2	1	1	12
Great Britain	2	2	1	2	1	1	1	1	3	14
Germany	1	1	1	1	2	1	1	1	1	10
Netherlands	2	1	1	1	2	1	4	3	1	16
Belgium	1	1	1	1	2	2	1	1	1	11
France	1	1	1	1	1	1	1	1	1	9
Italy	1	—	1	1	1	—	1	1	1	7
Yugoslavia	1	1	1	1	1	1	1	1	1	9
Israel	—	—	—	—	1	1	1	1	1	5
Total	18	11	11	14	17	13	19	16	15	134

* In Tables 1 to 4, countries are ordered geographically, from north to south.

Although the present study has a cross-sectional character, information collected per firm was so elaborate and extensive that it seemed impossible to draw a very large and representative 'sample' of organizations per country. It was felt rather that a careful stratification was needed, so as to provide sufficient relevant variance. Two categories of industries were selected for each industrial sector: manufacturing and service. Within *manufacturing*, metal engineering companies were chosen; within *service*, either banking or insurance companies (94 and 40 from each sector).

Firms (i.e. plants) were also classified into three size categories, less than 100 employees, 100 to 500 employees, and over 500 employees (Table 1). No establishment was included with more than 1500 employees.

A third distinction between *high and low skilled* (Table 1) was only used within the manufacturing organizations, where it was considered to be more relevant than in the service sector. Firms in the 'low skilled' category were producing components (mechanical, electrical, electronics), machine building, and construction, and metal processing. Firms in the 'high skilled' category were making all types of instruments and tools (mechanical, electrical, electronics), computers, machine tools. Where there was a combination of high and low skill requirements in one establishment, the researcher had to decide which was the dominant one. Where there was a discrepancy between technology and skill requirements (they do not always correlate), the latter condition was considered primary.

Standardized interviews were conducted with stratified random 'samples' of the organization's members. General 'sample' respondents were selected on a random basis from each establishment on the basis of $y = .05_x + 35$ where $y =$ total sample within a given establishment; $x =$ size of establishment (number of employees); and similarly on a random basis from each hierarchical level (see IDE 1976). These 'sample interviews' were complemented by 'expert interviews' on aspects such as organizational size, technology, and performance. Strictly speaking, the term 'sample' may be incorrect, since it suggests that national representative samples have been used in the study. The 'sample' respondents were in fact drawn from the organizations participating in the study. They cannot, therefore, be representative of the national work-force as a whole, and probably not even of the work-force in the selected industries. Nonetheless, 'sample' is used as a shorthand term, and the reader should be aware of its restricted meaning.

Unequal percentages of respondents per organization were selected; equal percentages would have resulted in a heavy overrepresentation of the large companies. Within each organization, a representative 'sample' was selected from each hierarchical level (see Table 2). The number of respondents per type of organization is given in Table 3.

A set of 16 specific decisions (drawn from work and social issues, personnel issues, economic issues, and so on) served as an important standardizing device for the measurement of (PS) and (PO) in all participating countries (see Chart 3). Measures were obtained for the degree to which written rules (PS) prescribe

Table 2
Percentages of the
Total Number of
Employees in
the Investigated
Organizations
Belonging to a Certain
Organizational Level.
( ) = Certain
Observations Missing

Countries	Workers (level A)	Supervisors (level B)	Managers (level C + D)
Norway	73	19	8
Sweden	88	6	6
Denmark	83	8	9
Finland	81	12	7
Great Britain	83	10	7
Germany	(78)	(14)	(8)
Netherlands	81	11	8
Belgium	83	10	7
France	83	9	8
Italy	(76)	(17)	(7)
Yugoslavia	90	6	4
Israel	85	13	2
Mean of national samples	82	11	7
Number of countries	12	12	12

Table 3
Number of Respondents
(General 'Sample') per
Type of Organization

	Service			Type of Organization Manufacturing High Skill			Low Skill			
Countries	Small	Med.	Large	Small	Med.	Large	Small	Med.	Large	Total
Norway	42	57	85	21	73	59	33	104	137	611
Sweden	122	77	106	118	201	256	171	136	245	1432
Denmark	58	39	77	36	45	66	35	48	84	468
Finland	208	78	76	114	48	58	90	56	62	790
Great Britain	70	99	85	59	39	63	50	50	186	701
Germany	34	49	62	30	98	89	35	64	85	546
Netherlands	74	60	121	31	72	117	79	102	75	731
Belgium	39	43	58	32	75	179	29	27	106	588
France	65	114	89	40	52	132	34	70	67	663
Italy	38	—	110	36	60	—	34	57	82	417
Yugoslavia	35	43	88	40	52	89	35	61	100	543
Israel	—	—	—	—	53	137	43	42	67	342
Total	765	659	957	557	868	1245	668	817	1296	7832

the roles of various groups in the 16 decisions, and, separately, measures were taken as to the perceived *de facto* and desired involvement of organization members.

Scales of *de jure* participation and *de facto* participation (including both influence and involvement) are set out in Chart 1.

The prescribed *de jure* degree of participation (PS) of a given group was specified across *countries*, with respect to each of the 16 decisions. For each decision, specialist–expert respondents, such as industrial lawyers in each country, selected on an *ad hoc* basis, were asked to indicate the mode of participation prescribed for groups A to E (see Charts 1, 2 and 3). In addition, these specialist respondents were asked for the source of the particular norms prescribing the participation of a given group in decision making. Ten possible sources or *bases* of PS (see Chart 4) were identified and aggregated into: (a) laws (constitution, national, and regional laws), (b) collective bargaining contracts (national, regional, sectoral, company, establishment), and (c) managerial policies and other generally valid and enforceable management prerogatives.

Key management and union respondents in each *firm*, such as the top manager, chief shop steward, and so on, were asked to rate the amount of *influence* (PO1) exercised for each of the 16 decisions by each of the seven groups on a 5-point Likert-type scale, ranging from 'no influence' to 'very much influence'.

Chart 1
Scales Used

For de jure participation

PS: a six-step BEHAVIOURAL scale of prescribed FORMAL participation groups, based on participation in decision making (MODES of participation)*

1 = No information
2 = Information (unspecified) must be given to group
3 = Information must be given to group *ex ante*
4 = Consultation of group obligatory
5 = Joint decision making with group
   (a) Negative sanctioning, i.e. veto
   (b) Positive sanctioning, e.g. agreement by group required
6 = Group itself has final say

For de facto participation
PO1: a five-step INFLUENCE scale**

1 = No influence
2 = Little influence
3 = Moderate influence
4 = Much influence
5 = Very much influence

PO2: a six-step BEHAVIOURAL scale of PERSONAL INVOLVEMENT (actual and designed) decision-specific***

1 = I am not involved at all
2 = I am informed about the matter beforehand
3 = I can give my opinion
4 = My opinion is taken into account
5 = I decide on an equal basis with others
6 = I decide on my own

* Key respondents' group ratings (levels A-E) — 16 decisions	** Key respondents' group ratings (levels A-E) — 16 decisions	*** General sample respondents' (levels A, B and C) individual self-rating — 16 decisions

Chart 2
Bargaining
Groups/Levels

A. Workers/clerks without supervisory function
B. First line supervisors
C. Middle management
D. Top management (within two levels of chief executive within the plant or enterprise)*
E. Level above plant
F. Representative bodies
G. External bodies (institutions such as banks, union headquarters, public agencies)

* For purposes of this study an enterprise was equated with a plant. It was recognized that the situation might be different within a *branch* plant as opposed to the single plant. The data was such that this differentiation could be made.

Chart 3
Decision Set

	Work/Social Conditions	Personnel Decisions	Economic Decisions
Short Term	Work conditions Tools Task assignment Holidays* Working hours	Training Transfer	
Medium Term	Wage levels Work study	Hiring procedures New dept. head Direct superior Dismissal	Reorganization
Long Term			Major investment New product

* Holidays were ultimately analysed as a separate cluster.

The key respondents were supposed to be experts and therefore the differences between ratings have been treated as rating errors and the different ratings for each group have been averaged.

Such key persons were selected from the following groups: top management, works' council members, members of joint productivity councils, union representatives in the company (including shop stewards), personnel department, middle management, direct supervisors, and other activists.

In Table 4 the total numbers of key persons have been listed per country and per type of organization.

Given that with the 5-point PO1 scale, 'influence' was used without any further explanation, it is possible that some key respondents understood this term to mean only behaviourally exercised influence attempts. Others may, in turn, have interpreted it more in terms of the capacity of given groups to resist undesired changes or to prevent certain decisions from being made and implemented. Still others may have understood it more as a latent relationship based on the control over resources. In other words, we believe our PO1 influence question to tap a broad range of influence–power phenomena. As

				Type of Organization						
		Service			Manufacturing					
					High Skill			Low Skill		
Countries	Small	Med.	Large	Small	Med.	Large	Small	Med.	Large	Total
Norway	2	4	15	3	9	5	3	6	12	59
Sweden	31	8	6	16	33	19	24	13	12	162
Denmark	18	11	14	2	14	32	12	17	29	149
Finland	6	3	3	6	3	5	7	6	7	46
Great Britain	8	12	6	7	3	4	5	4	14	63
Germany	4	2	11	2	4	3	3	6	5	45
Netherlands	13	12	16	7	26	27	34	24	13	172
Belgium	3	4	13	1	23	36	6	17	21	124
France	4	5	3	2	5	5	1	3	7	35
Italy	4	—	10	77	8	—	3	12	10	54
Yugoslavia	9	9	9	10	10	8	10	10	5	80
Israel	—	—	—	—	2	1	1	1	1	8
Total	102	70	106	63	145	145	109	121	146	997

Table 4
Number of Key
Respondents per Type
of Organization

such, we shall interpret the PO1 data as broadly as possible, reflecting different groups' capacities to affect decision outcomes.

Next, the degree of actual and desired *involvement* (PO2) in decision making was assessed in terms of a 6-point scale similar to the one used for the PS measure. In this case, however, the question referred to individual involvement and was asked of the general 'sample' of respondents (all workers, supervisors, and middle managers; levels A, B, and C, respectively). More specifically, each respondent was asked to indicate the extent to which were also divided into short-, medium-and long-term decisions after an initial piloting of a longer list of 50 decisions (see Charts 1 and 3). This individual-level data was later aggregated to obtain mean involvement scores for each of the three groups (A, B, and C).

Chart 1 is a schematic classification of the various concepts discussed above and of their corresponding scales.

We shall now attempt to present descriptive data referring to selected aspects of the study covering differences and similarities (across countries and hierarchies) in the following:

1. *participative systems*,
2. *patterns of influence*,
3. *levels of actual and desired involvement of employees*, and
4. *outcomes of participation*.

This by no means covers all the topics investigated and their interrelationships, but it may be suggestive *vis-à-vis* some of the essentials of the approach and initial findings. A fuller analysis is set out in the two volumes of the study (IDE 1981a, 1981b).

Participative Systems (PS) Across Countries

We next tried to measure legalization/formalization in the participative systems studied *vis-à-vis* the normative bases of participation (see Chart 4). A measure was derived by comparing the sum total of formal rules (PS) for participation (all 7 groups, 16 decisions) across the countries. It was found that our firms in Yugoslavia and in Norway ranked the highest; G.B. and Israel ranked the lowest (see Figure 2).

We can now describe the score-levels across countries on the 6-point PS mode scale (see Chart 1 for details):

Hierarchical One-Peak Pattern (Norway, Sweden, France)
   Highest levels of participation found in top management and supervisory bodies (5)
   Other groups near (2)

Hierarchical Two-Peak Pattern (Finland, Denmark, Germany, Netherlands Italy, Israel)
   Highest levels of participation found within top management (5) and representative bodies (3.5)
   All other bargaining groups near (2)

Representative One-Peak Pattern (Yugoslavia)
   Representative bodies (4.5)
   Workers, supervisors, middle and top management (3.3)
   Supervisory bodies and outside groups (2.5)

Both Belgium and Great Britain had what was characterized as a low profile pattern in that there was little variation among bargaining groups, in terms of their participation mode which ranged from levels 2 through 2.7 (further details are presented in IDE 1979: 280, Table 3).

We now turn to a consideration of influence (PO1) as measured by the responses of key respondents, which as we have mentioned earlier attempts to tap a broad range of influence–power phenomena and correspondingly the capacity of their bargaining group (by level) to affect decision outcomes.

Patterns of Influence Distribution (PO1) Across Countries

On the basis of a preliminary analysis, it would appear that hierarchy has a greater impact than country (c.f. Tannenbaum et al. 1974). Table 5 presents patterns of the distribution of influence across these two dimensions. As can be seen, there is greater variation across levels than across countries. The total or average amount of influence per country varies between 2.4 and 2.6, with the exception of Yugoslavia where the average is 3.0 (see bottom row). The inequality of influence across organizational levels, however, is far more

122   IDE International Research Group

Figure 2
Degree of Legalization/
Formalization for
Participation

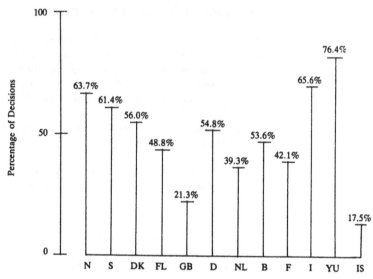

Countries are ordered geographically from north to south.

Percentage of decisions for which formal rules for participation apply (7 groups, 16 decisions)

N	Norway	FL	Finland	NL	Netherlands	I	Italy
S	Sweden	GB	Great Britain	B	Belgium	YU	Yugoslavia
DK	Denmark	D	Germany	F	France	IS	Israel

Chart 4
Normative* Bases of
participation

Law { Constitution
       National law
       Regional law

Collective { National collective bargaining contract
bargaining   Regional collective bargaining contract
              Sectoral collective bargaining contract
              Company (anything above the plant) collective bargaining contract
              Plant/establishment collective bargaining contract

Management { Management policy (defined in written regulation, e.g. self-management
              —otherwise see 10)

Other { Other legal basis (Richterrecht), e.g. regulations, which are not written
         down, but are enforceable in court as custom and practice (management
         prerogatives)

* The term 'normative' is used here to mean formally required.

pronounced. This suggests that the hierarchical ordering of organizations might be a stronger determinant of the distribution of influence than any other factor or difference which may be implicitly operative within any particular country.

Table 5
Distribution of Influence Over Countries — Average Over All Decisions (PO1)

Level	Countries												Means
	Bel	Den	Fin	Fra	Ger	GB	Ita	Isr	Nl	Nor	Swe	Yu	
A Workers	1.6	2.0	2.0	2.1	1.9	2.0	2.1	1.6	2.1	2.3	2.0	2.7	2.3
B Supervisors	2.2	3.0	2.6	2.9	2.3	2.4	2.7	2.8	2.7	2.7	2.5	2.8	2.6
C Middle mgt.	3.1	3.2	3.5	3.0	3.0	3.2	3.2	3.1	2.9	3.3	3.1	3.1	3.1
D Top mgt.	4.2	3.6	4.0	4.7	4.4	3.9	4.1	4.3	3.7	3.7	3.5	3.6	3.8
E Level above plant	2.9	1.9	2.3	3.1	1.6	2.8	2.0	2.1	2.0	2.0	2.7	2.9	2.4
F Rep. bodies	2.4	1.9	1.5	2.1	2.6	2.2	2.5	2.4	2.1	2.1.	2.8	3.9	2.4
G Ext. bodies	—	1.4	1.3	1.5	1.2	1.5	1.6	1.2	1.2	1.3	1.3	2.2	1.4
X	—	2.4	2.4	2.6	2.4	2.6	2.5	2.4	2.4	2.5	2.5	3.0	—

For identification of levels, i.e. bargaining groups, see Chart 2; and for decision-set, see Chart 3.

A second important point concerns the fairly low levels of influence that external societal bodies appear to have in organizational decision making (see Table 5). It is possible that, in reality, the indirect influence of external groups is actually greater than what it is perceived to be. Even taking this possibility into account, however, the difference in the amount of influence exercised by top management and by external groups is such that one is probably justified in concluding that, on the whole, work organizations in the 12 countries are still relatively autonomous in relation to their environment.

Next, the amount of influence of workers' and representative bodies is fairly equally distributed across countries (see Table 5). If we exclude Yugoslavia, workers in all countries have 'little' influence over the set of 16 decisions, and representative bodies have between a 'little' and a 'moderate' amount. In all countries, therefore, the degree of democratization of decision-making processes within work organizations appears to be fairly low. The particular variation for each country does not differ much from the general pattern discussed above. Most organizations in all countries are relatively centralized, and nondemocratic. Yugoslavia is the exception to this general pattern (see also Pusić 1973, for background on the Yugoslav system; and Obradović and Dunn 1978).

Finally, in most countries the amount of influence of workers and of representative bodies decreases from short-term to long-term decisions, while the influence of top management increases. Again, Yugoslavia and, with minor modifications, the Scandinavian countries are exceptions. In Yugoslav organizations, the influence of both the Workers' Council and of top management increases as one moves from less important to more important decisions, although this trend is less pronounced in the case of top management than in the case of the Workers' Council. It appears that the influence of the Workers' Council grows to some extent at the expense of the influence of top management.

Curiously enough on average our respondents in some countries — Yugoslavia, France, and Great Britain — ascribe more influence to various levels than do respondents elsewhere. Does this reflect 'real' international differences in total amount of influence? We doubt it, for on the whole few if any significant correlations were found between average influence per level and other variables which one would expect to be associated with total amount of influence (as an index à la Tannenbaum for the 'energy' of the organization).

Having briefly reported on influence (PO1), we now turn to a second dependent variable, involvement (PO2). This was measured by a behavioural scale (see Chart 1), which was decision-specific, and which looked at levels of involvement.

Actual and Desired Involvement (PO2) of Employees Across Countries

Turning now to such actual and desired involvement (scales in Chart 1), the distribution for *all* countries studied can be seen from Tables 6 and 7. In *all* countries, the data for levels A, B, and C (see Charts 1 and 2) suggest that:

a. workers have the lowest, and middle management the highest, average mode of involvement (overall) in decision making,

b. actual involvement of middle management is also highest within each particular cluster of decisions,

c. middle management desires the highest, and workers the lowest, average mode of direct involvement, and

d. the aspirations for indirect involvement are reversed: aspirations of workers for involvement in representative bodies are the highest in all countries, and aspirations of middle management the lowest.

These four patterns spread across all countries reveal a very consistent hierarchy in all organizations. These patterns exist even in Yugoslavia, although this country has a substantially different political and social environment than do the other countries. It seems that such consistent hierarchical patterns of actual and desired involvement are not conditioned primarily by political, economic, or other social characteristics of the environment, but by the existing technical division of labour, which is still quite similar for all 12 countries, including Yugoslavia. Even if the political and economic environment institutionally reflected in *de jure* participation can significantly modify the hierarchical patterns in organizations, it apparently cannot dissolve the hierarchy itself.

Greater differences among the countries appear if we look more specifically at the differences of actual involvement over decisions and clusters of decisions. Eight of the 12 countries can be classified into four quite distinctive groups,

Table 6	Level	Countries												Means
Involvement (PO2)		Bel	Den	Fin	Fra	Ger	GB	Ita	Isr	Ne	Nor	Swe	Yu	
Over the Countries														
(All Individuals)	*Actual Involvement*													
	Workers A	1.8	2.0	1.7	2.0	1.9	2.1	1.7	1.7	2.1	1.8	1.8	2.7	1.9
	Foremen B	2.5	3.7	2.6	2.5	2.5	2.4	2.5	2.4	2.7	2.6	2.6	3.1	2.7
	Middle mgt. C	2.8	3.7	3.5	3.1	3.5	3.0	2.6	2.9	3.5	3.2	2.8	3.2	3.2
	Total	2.3	3.2	2.6	2.6	2.6	2.5	2.2	2.3	2.8	2.5	2.4	3.0	2.7
	Desired Involvement													
	Workers A	2.9	3.1	2.9	3.1	3.1	2.9	2.7	2.9	3.1	2.7	2.9	3.7	3.0
	Foremen B	3.4	4.0	3.4	3.4	3.5	3.3	2.9	3.5	3.6	3.2	3.4	3.8	3.5
	Middle mgt. C	3.7	4.0	4.0	3.9	4.2	3.7	3.2	4.2	3.7	3.7	3.6	3.9	3.8
	Total	3.1	3.4	3.1	3.2	3.4	3.1	2.8	3.1	3.2	2.9	3.1	3.8	3.2

For identification of levels, i.e. bargaining groups, see Chart 2; and for appropriate scales see Chart 1.

Table 7	Level	Countries												Means
Desired Involvement		Bel	Den	Fin	Fra	Ger	GB	Ita	Isr	Ne	Nor	Swe	Yu	
(PO2) for Representa-														
tive Bodies Over the	Workers A	79	55	66	65	75	60	78	76	66	67	44	79	68
Countries, Over All	Foremen B	62	50	50	53	65	43	66	58	56	48	71	79	58
Decisions	Middle mgt. C	47	49	30	49	55	35	56	41	56	47	73	78	51
	Average X	71	54	60	60	70	51	75	69	63	59	73	79	—

Data contained in this table represent % of yes answers of respondents to the question: 'Would you like the main representative body to have a say in this matter?' (See Chart 3 for a set of decisions appropriate to the question). The percentage refers to the average of responses for the total set of decisions.

according to differences of involvement, across the decisions (for identification of short-, medium- and long-term decisions see Chart 3):

1. countries where actual involvement of the three levels A, B, and C (i.e. workers, foremen, and middle management) is high in all clusters, such as Denmark and Yugoslavia,
2. countries where the actual involvement of three levels is low in all clusters of decisions. such as Belgium and Israel,
3. countries where the actual involvement is relatively high in short-term decisions and low in long-term decisions, such as France and the Netherlands, and
4. countries where the actual involvement of all three levels is relatively low in short- and relatively high in long-term decisions, such as Italy and Norway.

From the wider political point of view, perhaps, the distinction between the first and second group of countries is the most relevant. But from the more specific point of view of industrial democracy, the last two groups are more interesting, since they demonstrate two main strategies of democratization.

The first concerns daily problems of work environment; the second concerns policy issues. It seems that different social forces stand behind such strategies: strong external forces in the case of Italy and Norway, and stronger internal forces in the case of France and the Netherlands.

Participative structures (PS) tended to be a better predictor of the involvement of workers (PO2A) in long-term decisions rather than short-term ones (see IDE 1979: 290). The Multiple R for short-term decisions was .604; for medium-term ones, .763; and for long-term ones, .808, with F levels of respectively 3.0, 7.4, and 10.0 (see 1979: 290 for the relevant table). Indeed, industrial democracy at a strategic level may be seen as more explained by the institutionalization of participation than by other factors.

The Impact of Participation

We now look at the impact of participation on variables indicating workers' evaluation of and their interest in representative participation, and their satisfaction with work and company. The four scales consist of four items in each case (see IDE 1976: 193–198, space here does not allow the details of each scale).

To obtain an evaluation of representative participation (OPART-E) questions were asked about the degree to which works' councils (or similar bodies) represent the respondent's interests and function according to him in a satisfactory manner (IDE 1976: 197–198). Interest in representative participation (OPART-I) was measured by questions referring to people's general interest in the work of the works' council, their willingness to become a candidate, and their level of information with respect to the meetings of the council (1976: 193–197). The satisfaction indices are based on answers to questions concerning the degree to which respondents consider their job worthwhile and attractive (OSAT-W) and have a positive opinion of their management, their working conditions, etc. (OSAT-C) (IDE 1976: 197–198).

As can be seen from the data in Table 8, workers are more positive about — and more interested in — works' councils (and kindred bodies), the more involvement they report (as well as, although slightly less, the degree of PS — see Table 8). This can be due to the impact of workers' involvement in general on their attitudes towards representative participation in their company, and also to the respondents tendencies to exaggerate their degree of involvement more, the more positive their attitudes are towards the representative system.

As to the influence of representative bodies (PO1-F) and of workers in general (PO1-A), these indices are also positively related to evaluation of and interest in representative participation. However, the correlations of PO1-F with OPART-E and OPART-I are higher than the correlations of PO1-A with OPART-E and OPART-I. It stands to reason that people's attitudes towards representative participation are more directly — and thus strongly — related to the specific influence of the works' council in their company than to the general influence of workers. Anyway, it is not without interest to notice that indeed workers value their representation by works' councils (and the like) higher, the more decision making in their company is affected by such bodies (as judged by the key persons).

Turning now to workers' satisfaction with their job and their work organization, there is no evidence that their attitudes in this respect are to any significant degree affected by their own direct influence or by the influence of the works' council. PO1-A and PO1-F do not yield correlations (of sufficient magnitude) with OSAT-W and OSAT-C (see Table 8). Degree of involvement of workers (PO2-A) is to a moderate extent positively associated with satisfaction with work and with company (OSAT-W and OSAT-C). One should realize, however, that these latter two correlations are based upon responses of the same persons. This could mean that workers tend to report more involvement, the more positively they feel disposed towards their jobs and their companies.

It is also relevant in this connection to mention that none of the three measures of participation included in Table 8 exhibits a significant degree of correlation with absenteeism and turnover per company (data not presented here; see IDE 1981a: Ch. VII, Table 18). All in all, therefore, our data indicate that participation, though appreciated by the workers in its own right, contributes next to nothing towards their overall degree of attachment to their work and/or their company.

Table 8
Influence (PO1) and Involvement (PO2) of Workers and of Representative Bodies in Relation to Mean Scores of Attitudes of Workers

	Evaluation of Repr. Part (OPART-E)	Interest in Repr. Part (OPART-I)	Work Satisfaction (OSAT-W)	Satisfaction with Company (OSAT-C)
Influence of workers (Po1-A)	.26	.20	—	—
Influence of representative bodies (PO1-F)	.43	.38	—	—
Involvement of workers (PO2-A)	.44	.44	.23	.27
De jure participation of workers (PS to (A))	.32	.30	—	—
De jure participation of representative bodies (PS to (F))	.42	.40	—	—

Note: Figures are Pearson product moment correlation coefficients calculated over 134 companies. In case of missing values variable means are substituted.
Only coefficients with significance level <.05 are given.

Concluding Remarks

The research findings described above clearly have considerable implications for the study of industrial democracy and participation. What they imply, in fact, is the need for a reorientation of research in this area. Such work has perhaps in the past been too heavily oriented towards explaining variations in participation, power, and influence in terms of contingencies, whether these be personal attributes and characteristics of participants, on the one hand, or structural and technological features of organizations, on the other. In fact, it is hierarchy that is most important.

Second, a circular explanation of relations between *de jure* and *de facto* participation would be the most appropriate framework for the interpretation presented (Nagel 1970). This kind of explanation conceives the institutionalization of participation as a reciprocal process in which legislation promotes structural and behavioural changes and in which these changes retroactively modify and develop legislative activity. However, such an explanation requires a longitudinal type of research design which we have not to date been able to initiate.

Even so, the results of our study as to the impact of participation show that workers more highly value representative participation for its own sake, the higher their influence or involvement. However, their satisfaction with their work or with the organization in which they are employed does not appear to be noticeably influenced by the degree to which they either directly or indirectly have a say in the decision making of their companies.

It is possible that increasing participation improves workers' chances to promote their interests, and so contributes towards better communication and understanding in the company. In fact, other results of our study (see IDE 1981a: 145ff) indicate that most employees of all ranks believe that participation in general has these kinds of positive consequences both for their own interests and for the functioning of their company. Nonetheless, claims sometimes used by social scientists or consultants to 'sell' participation to managers, i.e. that participation makes workers more committed to their jobs and their companies and thus reduces the costs of turnover and absenteeism, are not supported by the outcome of our analysis.

Having asked initially whether existing patterns of decision making and influence sharing vary significantly as a consequence of different national arrangements for participative management, we can argue that they do. The research has cross-analysed the effects of PS on the other variables thus far investigated (space does not permit a detailed elaboration of this here). The PS scores were fed into multiple correlational analysis and the findings reported above regarding PO1 (Influence), for example, thus take into account what we called the 'country' effect, which was the second-best predictor. As this means, of course, the kind of *de jure* system as measured by PS, an important implication follows. The more democratic, legal participative systems do appear to make a difference, for example by modifying the impact of hierarchy. In addition, the effect of PS on evaluation of and interest in participation has also been noted. There is convincing support that the national participative system (PS) does make a difference, although its effect is uneven over the wide range of variables and levels examined in the study (for further details, see IDE

1981a). The bold inference to make is that further democratization may require a change in such national legal arrangements.

We have tried in this article to explore the initial findings of the project, although we have only attempted to describe a limited amount of the data which has been analysed. It is hoped that the aspects discussed (participative systems, influence and involvement, as well as outcomes) may give the reader an insight into some of the problems raised in the research endeavour. The initial findings can only stimulate further debate regarding the significance of the results in the study, and bring further possible rival explanations to those hinted at here, to which we would hope to be able to respond.

Note

1. See 'The Authors', pp. 207–208, this issue.

References

Bernstein, P.
1976 'Worker participation in decision-making'. *Journal of Economic Issues*. 10:490–523.

Blumberg, P.
1968 *Industrial democracy*. London: Constable.

IDE International Research Group
1976 'Industrial democracy in Europe (IDE): an international comparative study'. *Social Science Information* 15:177–203.

IDE International Research Group
1979a 'Participation: formal rules, influence and involvement'. *Industrial Relations* 18:273–294.

IDE International Research Group
1979b 'Die Messung von Mitbestimmungsnormen—Darstellung eines international vergleichenden Forschungsansatzes' in *Jahrbuch der Rechtssoziologie und Rechtstheorie*. Erhard Blankenburg and Klaus Lenk (eds.). Opladen: Westdeutscher Verlag.

IDE International Research Group
1981a *Industrial democracy in Europe*. London: Oxford University Press.

IDE International Research Group
1981b *European industrial relations*. London: Oxford University Press.

Nagel, S.
1970 'Law and social change'. *American Behavioural Scientist*, Special Issue 13.

Obradović, J. and W. Dunn
1978 *Workers' self-management and organizational power in Yugoslavia*. Pittsburgh: University of Pittsburgh Press.

Pusić, E., *editor*
1973 *First international conference on participation and self-management, Dubrovnik* (6 vols.). Zagreb: Institute of Social Research.

Rothschild-Whitt, J.
1976 'Conditions facilitating participatory-democratic organizations'. *Sociological Inquiry* 46:75–86.

Tannenbaum, A. S., B. Kavcić, M. Rosner, M. Vianello, and G. Weiser
1974 *Hierarchy in organizations*. San Francisco: Jossey-Bass.

Walker, K. F.
1974 'Workers' participation in management: problems, practices and prospect'. *International Institute for Labour Studies Bulletin* 10:3–35.

[21]

Industrial democracy in Europe: Cross national comparisons[1][2]

Pieter J.D. Drenth & Bernhard Wilpert

Introduction

The study of laws, social norms, rules and regulations has traditionally been a domain of the sociology of law (Koenig, 1971; Blankenberg, 1977). Although the behavioural implications of such norms clearly fall also into the area of psychological analysis, it is a rather recent development that systematic analyses of this topic have been carried out from psychological perspectives. This contribution is based on such research efforts. However, quite apart from the relative novelty of the theme being taken up by psychologists, the research shows various additional characteristics, worth noting. They concern the research as being
- international comparative,
- interdisciplinary,
- longitudinal,
- rather unique in its organization.

a) International comparison
In the mid-70's a group of some 25 social scientists from 12 European countries (incl. Israel) conducted a study of the impacts of formal rules for participation (laws, collective agreements, formal managerial policies) on the factual participation behaviour in 134 establishments, matched according to size and technology (IDE, 1981a, b). The national contexts of the twelve countries were considered as a natural experimental setting in which the effects of norms on behaviour could be investigated. Data were collected from about 1000 key respondents (from management, unions) and close to 8000 randomly selected employees from the establishments. Judging from the size of the sample alone the research thus represents one of the largest organization studies hitherto conducted. The single most important findings of this IDE-study was that the best predictor of *de facto*

participation are hierarchical level and the intensity of prescribed norms for participation (*de jure* participation).

b) Interdisciplinary nature

The very problem under study required a multi-disciplinary approach. First, the assessment of existing formal rules called for juridical competence. The analysis of the socio-historical national contexts of given rules required philosophical, industrial relations, and sociological expertise. The analysis of organizational context factors (economic efficiency, technological level) suggested the involvement of engineers and experts in business administration. Hence, psychologists cooperated in this research with colleagues from half a dozen different disciplines.

c) Longitudinal character

In 1983 the international IDE-team decided to carry out a replication of the original study in the very same companies '10 years after'. This decision was, among others, motivated by the realization that replication studies, particularly international comparative ones, are extremely rare in the social sciences. But only longitudinal (diachronic) approaches will help to put assumptions about causal relationships on firmer grounds than can be expected from cross-sectional (synchronic) studies. This implies that only longitudinal research will help to clarify the differential role of 'natural maturation' processes over time as against changing environmental impacts (e.g. value, changes, technological developments, labour market conditions). The replication (now a panel study) was conducted in 1987. Basically the same theoretical model and the same methods (slightly simplified) were employed. However, the notorious mortality effect of panel research affected also IDE II: Only 10 countries of the original 12 could participate, and only 96 of the original 134 companies formed the data base. (Note: Quasi as a compensation: a Japanese and a Polish team joined in the 1987 research with 15 additional companies).

d) Organizational uniqueness

IDE in both its study phases I (1977) and II (1987) employed a research organization that can be called 'collective-decentralized' (Wilpert, 1989). This meant joint development of theoretical framework, methodological approach, data analysis strategy and data ownership (collective aspects) as well as decentralized responsibility for data collection, funding, national data interpretation for each national team. A 'social contract' among the team members made certain stipulations regarding publication and data ownership rights, acknowledgements etc. (Drenth and Wilpert, 1980).

In this paper we will pay some detailed attention to the differences between the countries which participated in the study. The main emphasis will be put on the differences as they appear in the second measurement phase (IDE II), although some references will be made to the national differences with respect to the changes in scores or score patterns over the period '77 - '87 (IDE I - II).

The present paper will present the results of the '87 cross national comparisons with respect to a) the formal participative systems (PS), b) the actual involvement practices and distribution of power in the organizations (PO) and c) the relationships between the two (PS-PO). A separate section will devoted to each of these three themes. (A more comprehensive report on the combined findings of IDE I and II is forthcoming).

Formal norms and participation

In Table 1 the total de jure participation scores of all groups in the organization are represented. These scores may range from 1 (no information given) through 2 (information ex post) 3 (information ex ante and advice given) 4 advice taken into consideration) 5 (joint decision making) to 6 (decision delegated to the group). For each group an average mode score over all 16 decisions is established, thus describing its overall participative potential, the total *de jure* participation in the organization. The data in Table 1 refer to the averages of these company de jure participation mode scores for each country for each group.

Looking at the separate scores for the various groups the following conclusions can be made:

For the level of *workers* the formal, de jure participation is quite low. With the exception of Yugoslavia, where the score exceeds slightly the level 3, all countries score below the level 3, which is 'information ex ante must be given'. As far as the other countries are concerned only in Norway and Germany level A scores higher then level 2 (information (unspecified) must be given to the group). The scores in all other countries are even lower than level 2; the lowest scores being found in Belgium (1.36) and Japan (1.35).

The formal participation power for the level of the *first line supervisor* is not much higher than that for the workers' level. Again with the exception of Yugoslavia all scores fall below level 3, the majority in this case between level 2 and 3. For Belgium, Great Britain and the Netherlands the average scores for level B are below level 2.

Table 1. Total de jure participation of all groups in the whole
         organization (1978 data).

	Level	A	B	C	D	E	F	G
Country								
Belg.	M²	1.36¹	1.81	2.37	3.67	2.08	2.09	1.09
Denm.	M	1.68	2.11	2.50	4.80	1.88	2.45	1.36
Germ.	M	2.22	2.14	2.14	5.36	1.27	3.99	1.35
UK	M	1.99	1.69	1.21	1.19	1.19	1.43	1.19
Isr.	M	1.75	2.56	2.50	5.19	3.25	2.69	1.06
Neth.	M	1.89	1.00	1.00	5.38	1.29	3.06	2.31
Norw.	M	2.72	2.50	2.31	5.90	5.90	3.69	5.11
Sweden	M	1.78	2.57	3.63	4.90	5.68	4.19	1.88
Yugosl.	M	3.22	3.53	3.76	3.85	-	4.79	1.48
Finland	M	2.88	2.36	4.46	5.01	1.59	1.06	1.15
Japan	M	1.35	2.01	3.39	3.89	3.97	1.63	-
Poland	M	1.67	2.95	3.41	5.47	1.45	3.70	2.27

A = Workers; B = Supervisors; C = Middle Management; D = Top Management;
E = Level above company; F = Works Council; G = Institutions outside the company

¹ Average mode of participation scores for groups and countries (total
  set). Scale from 1 - 6 (1 = no prescribed involvement, 6 = the group
  has final say over decision).
² Average mode score over organizations.

As far as the *middle management* level is concerned, the data show
quite some variety. A low score is found in Great Britain and the
Netherlands, a score between level 2 and 3 in Denmark, Germany,
Israel and Norway. In Sweden, Yugoslavia, Japan and Poland the
score exceeds the level 3, and in Finland even level 4 (obligatory
consultation).
In most countries the real formal power is still in the hands of top
management. With the exception of UK, where apparently little
formalization and regulation of participative power exist for any
level, including top management, most countries display a score for
the formal power of top management which exceeds level 3 or even
level 4. In Germany, Israel, the Netherlands, Norway, Finland and
Poland the average score is even higher then 5, which indicates that
top management must give its approval and, therefore, has veto-
power over the decision concerned.
The greatest differences are to be seen at *the level above the company*,
level E. One finds on the one hand very low formal power (below

level 2) in the countries   Denmark, Germany, Great Britain, the Netherlands, Finland and Poland, on the other hand moderate scores (between level 3 and 4) in Israel and Japan and very high scores (above 5.5) in the Scandinavian countries Norway and Sweden.

It is interesting to analyze the score distribution for level F, the *Works' Council* or other representative organs within the company. As expected from the nature of the self management systems which exists in Yugoslavia, in this country the formal power of the Works' Council is the highest (4.79) and approaching the level of veto-right. On the other hand in three West-European countries (Norway, Sweden and Germany) and one East-European country (Poland) the formal influence is substantial as well (approaching level 4).

In countries like the Netherlands and Israel its score is about 3 (consultative power), whereas for the other countries the formal participative power of the representative body varies from rather moderate to minimal.

The level G, institutions *outside the company* such as national or local government, unions etc. generally have a modest formal influence on the decisions made within the company. The exception is Norway where the formal rules seem to give governmental forces an often decisive formal authority over such decision making.

Various types of profiles which are characteristic for the patterns of distribution of formal power in organizations can be distinguished.

First of all there are two unique patterns. Firstly the 'low profile patterns', marked by a relatively low score for all groups involved, which was discerned in Great Britain (Fig. 1). In this country there is little formal regulation of participation, and it is pretty much left to the informal developments and interactions. Second, the representative one peak pattern characteristic of Yugoslavia (Fig. 1). In the latter the highest score is found for the representative organs and the differences in scores between the other groups are rather small. This system calls for a strong formalized control of the decision making by the workers, but indirectly through the representative organ.

Then there are clear 'one peak patterns'(Fig. 2), to be found in Belgium, Israel, Norway and Sweden. The profiles peak in either the top management within the company (top dominance without much control), or the level above the establishment's top management, such as the Board of Commissioners, or in both (joint control of top management and supervisory bodies). The power, at least according to the law or formal rules and regulations is firmly concentrated in the top or the responsible organ above the top of the companies. This one peak pattern can thus be characterised as hierarchical.

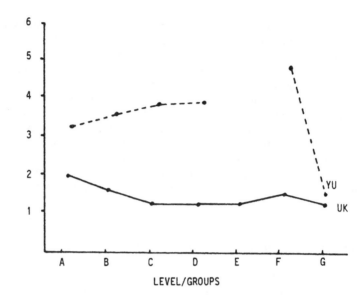

FIG. 1.   YU = Yugoslavia; UK = United Kingdom

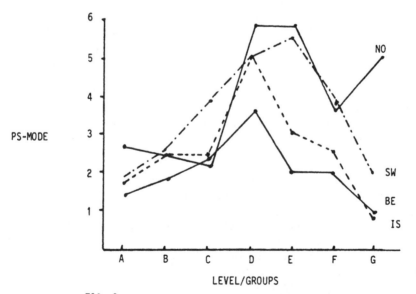

FIG. 2.   NO = Norway; SW = Sweden; BE = Belgium; IS = Israel

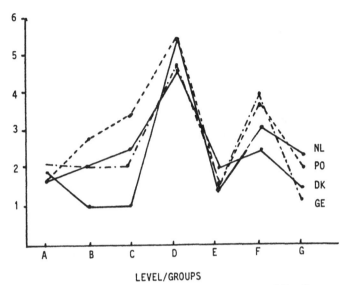

NL = Netherlands; PO = Poland; DK = Denmark; GE = Germany
FIG. 3.

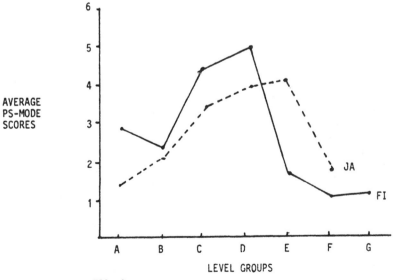

FIG. 4.

JA = Japan; FI = Finland

In the third place there is the 'two-peak pattern' (Fig. 3) to be found in the countries Denmark, Germany, the Netherlands and Poland. Without exception the highest formal participation score is obtained by the top management (reason why this pattern can also be named hierarchical), but a moderately high score, indicating the 'second in command' is found for the representative bodies. According to the law and/or formal regulations there should be some balance of power between these two groups or at least some control of top management through the workers representation.

Finally there is the 'one peak pattern', but with a reasonable sharing of the power by middle management (Fig. 4). This pattern is found in Finland. The formal (de jure) control of top management decisions in Finland seems not to be attributed to workers representation, nor to a supervisory control organ, but by a rather powerful middle-management jointly with top-management. The PS-score for the latter in Finland was the highest in all the countries under study.
In Japan (Fig. 4) also an almost equal balance of formal power between the middle and top management is found, but in contrast with Finland the highest formal power in this country is acquired by the supervisory body, whereas the control power for the workers representation is very low.

A comparison of the country profiles for the de jure participation distribution with those obtained in the 70's (IDE, 1981a, p.135) shows great similarity for a number of countries. Great Britain has the same low profile pattern (with a somewhat higher score for the level of workers in the 1987 data). Yugoslavia still has the representative one-peak pattern, with an even slight increase for level F (representative organ). However, it appears that in 1987 the score for workers (A) is somewhat lower, whereas the score for all three supervisory and management levels has increased. Apparently the change in legislation on participation has caused a (small) shift towards the classical hierarchical power distribution. At the same time, the Workers Council remains the organ with the highest level of de jure participative power.
The profile of Belgium generally is still rather low, but some differentiation seems to have taken place. A lower score for level A, B, C and F is coupled with a higher score for level D, top management. A shift towards the hierarchical one peak pattern is noticeable.
The profiles for Denmark, Germany and the Netherlands, all three representatives of the two peak hierarchical patterns, have remained almost identical over the past 10 years with an exception of the increase in de jure participation for top management (level D) in Denmark.

In Israel change in legislation or bargaining rules have caused quite noticeable changes, both in the profile as such, and in the level of de jure participation in general. With the exception of level F (workers council) and G (outside bodies) all levels display a substantial raise in formal participation, the strongest increase being seen in the supervisory and management levels and within the board of commissionaires.

A similar augmentation of formal participative power can be observed in Norway and Sweden. Here again, the change in legislation and formal regulations has affected the absolute de jure participative power level of all parties rather than the pattern of distribution of power over the various levels.

A further interesting indication of the balance of power between management and workers maybe the differences in PS-scores between management (level D) and workers (level A). Of course this is not the only and sometimes not even a correct indication of formal attempts to 'power equalization'. In addition to the workers a workers council may exercise considerable influence, and next to the top management other supervisory levels within (middle management) or above (supervisory board) the company can exercise power. Nevertheless the difference score just mentioned may provide some illustration of the democratization processes in organizations, at least as far as formal prescriptions and legislation (i.e. political intentions) are concerned.

In Table 2 the difference scores are presented for the short term, medium term and long term decisions, respectively. In the last column the score for the total decision set is presented. Between brackets the rankorder from large (=1) to small differences (=12) is given.

In Table 2 one sees in general a fair amount of difference in formal power over all types of decisions between worker and management levels. The low level of formalization in the U.K. and the strong democratic control in the legal system in Yugoslavia reveal themselves again. It is striking that the largest differences in formal power between top management and the workers are found in Poland, closely followed by the Netherlands and Israel. Only in the countries U.K., the Netherlands, Yugoslavia, Finland and Japan there is (some) increase in the differences if one goes from short time to long term decisions.

In a number of cases, such as Belgium, Germany, Israel, Sweden and Poland the biggest differences are found with respect to the medium term decisions. In a number of cases this may be due to the influence which the supervisory bodies exercise and will particularly pertain to the strategic decisions.

Table 2. Topmanagement-worker differences in de jure participation
          (1987 data).

Country	Short t.	Med.t.	Long t.	Total IDE II	Total IDE I	(Rank) IDE II
Belgium	1.93	2.81	2.33	2.30	1.11	(8)
Denmark	3.71	3.06	3.50	3.13	3.01	(5,6,7)
Germany	2.55	4.08	2.14	3.13	3.18	(5,6,7)
Great Britain	-1.07	-.91	0	-.18	.56	(12)
Israel	2.67	4.43	3.00	3.44	3.16	(3)
Netherlands	3.35	3.68	4.00	3.49	3.98	(2)
Norway	3.28	2.92	3.11	3.17	1.65	(4)
Sweden	2.85	3.50	3.03	3.13	2.45	(5,6,7)
Yugoslavia	.22	.86	1.28	.63	-.04	(11)
Finland	1.87	2.32	3.20	2.13	2.96	(9)
Japan	1.60	1.84	2.21	1.81		(10)
Poland	3.40	4.21	3.89	3.80		(1)

In the last column the difference-scores for the total set in the first
IDE-study are presented (IDE, 1981a, p.139). One sees no or only
slight differences for the countries Denmark, Germany, Israel, and
the Netherlands, a moderate decrease in the U.K. and Finland, a
moderate increase in Sweden and Yugoslavia and a substantial
increase in Belgium and Norway. It seems that the change in
legislation or regulation of participative practices in the latter two
countries has led to a relative weakening of the workers de jure
influence vis à vis top management.

Actual distribution of influence

De facto participation was measured in relation to the groups
(levels) and not to individuals. The data in this section (PO1) are
based upon a rating by experts. Key respondents were asked to rate
the amount of influence which the different groups/levels have on a
five-point scale ranging from 'no influence' (1) to 'very much
influence' (5). In Table 3 an overview of the average actual influence
scores per country for the levels A through G is presented. The
following observations can be made on the basis of the data in Table
3.

Table 3. The distribution of influence by country, based on experts
judgements (1987, data).

Level Country	A	B	C	D	E	F	G	‖ All.
Belgium	1.75	2.48	3.22	4.00	2.48	2.53	2.01	‖ 2.64
Denmark	2.10	2.75	3.09	3.50	1.58	1.63	1.13	‖ 2.25
Germany	1.88	2.24	3.41	3.42	1.18	2.69	.099	‖ 2.26
U.K.	2.01	2.70	3.19	3.48	1.98	2.00	1.36	‖ 2.40
Israel	1.82	2.65	3.11	4.71	2.71	3.28	2.13	‖ 2.92
Neth.	2.06	2.79	3.20	3.55	1.78	1.95	1.33	‖ 2.38
Norway	2.26	2.62	3.40	3.43	1.80	2.22	1.16	‖ 2.41
Sweden*	2.28	2.78	3.18	3.16	2.63	3.13	1.04	‖ 2.60
Yugosl.	2.44	2.60	3.03	3.64	-	3.44	1.56	‖ 2.78
Finland	1.89	2.70	3.78	4.06	1.73	1.43	1.35	‖ 2.42
Japan	1.67	2.30	3.07	3.86	3.94	2.19	1.28	‖ 2.62
Poland	1.96	3.05	3.72	4.38	1.52	2.95	1.29	‖ 2.70
Average	2.01	2.64	3.28	3.77	1.90	2.21	1.39	‖

* Average score for the two subsamples (Stymne and Sandberg).

(1) It can be concluded that variation across hierarchical levels is
much stronger than across countries. The average amount of influence
per country varies from 2.25 (Denmark) to 2.92 (Israel), and for
levels *within* the company the scores vary from 2.01 (level of workers)
to 3.77 (top management). It appears that the hierarchical ordering is
a much stronger determinant of differences in influence than any
factor or differences which are operative in or limited to the national
country characteristics.

(2) The rather moderate average scores for the level of workers (A)
and representative bodies (level F) (scores of 2.01 and 2.21
respectively) indicate that the power distribution is still traditional
hierarchical, the highest level of influence being located at the level
of management and the lowest at the level of the (representatives of
the) workers. Yugoslavia is the only exception to the general pattern
in which workers and their representatives have between little and
moderate influence on decisions. The degree of democratization or
delegation to the lower levels seems to be still fairly low in all
countries, except Yugoslavia, but including the Eastern European
country Poland.

With respect to the differences of the influence distribution within the specific countries between 1987 and 1977 the following observations may be made (for the exact data we refer to the forthcoming publication IDE II).

Belgium shows a rather similar pattern of influence distribution with a slight decrease in influence for level D (top management). The only noticeable difference refers to level G (level outside the company).

For Denmark no substantial differences are noteworthy; just an slight decrease of influence for level E and G (above and outside the company).

In Germany some increase in influence for the supervisory and middle management positions, and some decreased influence on the part of top management may indicate a tendency towards decentralization of actual influence.

In the U.K. only a slight decrease of influence for top management and the supervisory level above the company can be observed. For the rest a similar pattern as was found in the first IDE-study emerges.

In Israel the power distribution for the four hierarchical levels within the company have remained more or less at the same level. For the levels E (above the company), F (workers council) and G (outside forces) an increase in influence can be observed.

The Netherlands and Norway the level and distribution of influence has remained unchanged. Both show also a rather similar classical hierarchical pattern with a moderate influence for the Works' Council.

In Sweden only minor changes in influence distribution have taken place over the past 10 years. These slight changes point to a somewhat increased influence for the workers and Works' council and a decrease of influence at the top management level. But, as said, the magnitude of these changes is small.

In Yugoslavia the general picture is not much different as compared to 10 years ago either. If an observation is to be made one could mention a small but consistent decrease in influence for all levels except for top management.

The comparison of the two measurement points in Finland does not reveal any note worthy differences as far as the influence level and influence distribution are concerned.

For Japan and Poland the two new countries in the 1987 sample, we see a pattern of influence distribution which is quite similar to the patterns of de jure participation (Fig. 5). In Japan a one peak hierarchical pattern, with the highest score for the supervisory level above the plant, and in Poland the hierarchical two peak pattern with a moderate influence for the workers' representation.

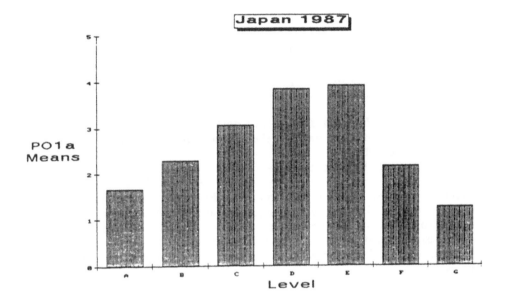

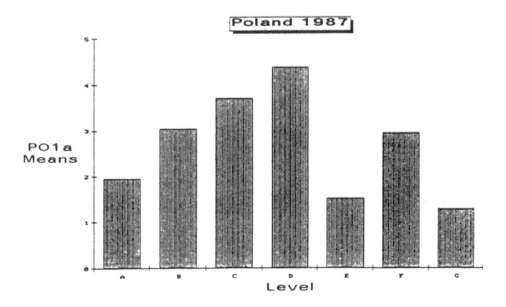

Fig. 5. Influence distribution in Japan and Poland (1987 data).

128   PIETER J.D. DRENTH & BERNHARD WILPERT

As a general conclusion it can be said that the actual patterns of power distribution in organizations have remained strikingly similar over the 10 years period, in spite of sometimes significant changes in the political or economic environment. In fact these changes seem to be reflected more in de jure power distribution of patterns and levels than of actual influence and power.

(3) *Relationships between de jure and de facto participation.*
Finally we present some data on the relationship between de jure and de facto participation.
It should be noted that the scores as such can not be compared in an absolute way, since they represent different scale positions and different ranges. The scores on the PS–scale run from 1 (no information) to 6 (complete delegation) and the scores on the PO–scale from 1 (no influence) to 5 (very much influence). The comparison, therefore, should be made only in a relative way, so as to indicate the different ranking positions of the countries on both scales.

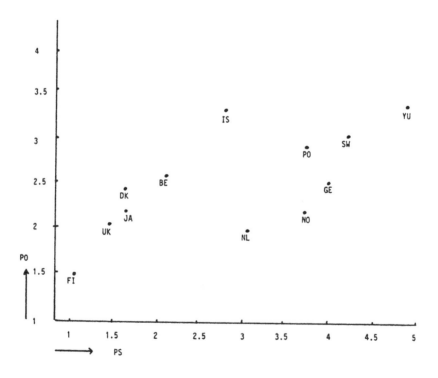

Fig. 6. Formal participation and influence of representative bodies.

In Fig. 6 the various positions of the countries in the PO-PS matrix (for representative organs) are indicated. In general we see a reasonably strong relationship between PO and PS. A group of countries (Finland, Great Britain, Japan, Denmark and Belgium) show a relatively low to moderate score for both participation dimensions. In other countries (Poland, Sweden and Yugoslavia) both de jure and de facto participation are relatively strong (although still moderate in an absolute sense, with the exception of Yugoslavia).
In four countries the combination of scores deviates from the covariance pattern. In Israel there seems to be a relatively stronger emphasis on actual influence of the representative bodies than on their formal, prescribed participation. In the countries the Netherlands, Norway and Germany the situation is reversed. The score for formal participation seems to be relatively higher than that for actual influence, thus indicating a possible under utilization of the room provided by legal and formal conditions.

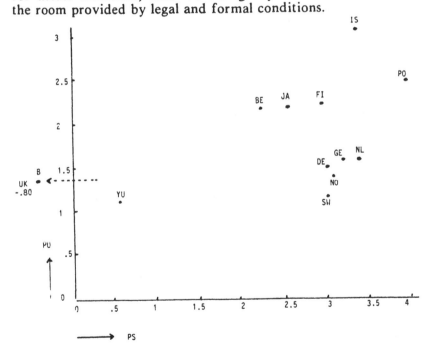

Fig. 7. Differences in formal participation and actual influence between top management (level D) and workers (level A), total score.

In Fig. 7 the patterns of relationships between differences in formal and actual influence between levels D and A (top management and workers) are represented. It can be seen that in a group of countries: (Sweden, Norway, Denmark, Germany and the Netherlands) the formal and legal regulations allow for more differences in participation and influence between the highest and lowest level in the company than the differences in actual influence reflect. Exactly the opposite is true in Great Britain and Yugoslavia. In the latter two countries the (moderate) differences in actual influence between the two levels exceed those for the formal and legal regulations, in which hardly any difference in influence is presented. In the other countries, Belgium, Japan and particularly Poland and Israel a fair amount of difference in influence and power between the highest and lowest levels in the company can be discerned both in legal provisions and norms and in actual practice.

Conclusion

IDE, without originally intending it, turned into a replication study. Such replications may be considered intermediary steps towards more comprehensive longitude. After all, a replication is nothing more (and nothing less) than a second cross-sectional study based on the same panel or target sample. As pointed out above, longitudinal research is important for a better theoretical comprehension of dynamic interactions of the variables under study. However, longitudinal research is rare (as a case in point see the IDE-spin-off research on 'Decision Making in Organizations - DIO, Heller et al., 1980). This is so for good reasons: their cost demands are considerable and usually surpass the possibilities or inclinations of existing research support organizations. Hence, replications appear as feasible options, in spite of their relative costliness as well.

Notes

1. The international cooperation for this research was supported by the Maison des Sciences de l'Homme (Paris) and a grant from the Stiftung Volkswagenwerk (FRG).

2. This paper is based on the research by the International Research Group Industrial Democracy in Europe (IDE). Members participating in the replication study were: P. Coetsier, R. Spoelders-Claes (BE), F. Agersnap, B. Pedersen (DK), O. Laaksonen (FI), P. Abell, F. Heller, R. Peccei, M. Warner (GB), B. Wilpert, P. Bott, J. Rayley (GE), E. Rosenstein (IS), A. Ishikawa, R. Suzuki (JA), P. Drenth, P. Koopman, C. Lammers, J. Pool (NL), R. Kalleberg, B. Lafferty, Th. Qvale (NO), A. Peretiakowicz (PO), Th. Sandberg, B. Stymne (SW), V. Pusic, V. Rus, D. Vrecko (YU).

References

Blankenberg, E. (1977). Uber die Unwirksamkeit von Gesetzen, Archiv für Rechts- und Sozialphilosophie, 63.

Drenth, P.J.D. & Wilpert, B. (1980). The role of 'social contracts' in cross-cultural research. *Int. Review of Applied Psychology, 29*, 293-305.

Heller, F.A., Drenth, P.J.D., Koopman, P.L. & Rus, V. (1988). *Decisions in Organizations*. London: Sage.

IDE-International Research Group (1981a). *Industrial Democracy in Europe*. Oxford: Oxford University Press.

IDE-International Research Group (1981b). *Industrial Relations in Europe*. Oxford University Press.

Koenig, R. (1971). Das Recht im zusammenhang der sozialen Normensysteme. *Kölner Zeitschrift für Soziologie und Sozialpsychologie, 11*.

Wilpert, B. (1989). Mitbestimmung. In: S. Greif, H. Holling & N. Nicholson (Eds.), *Europäisches Handbuch der Arbeit und Organisations Psychologie*. Weinheim: Psychologische Verlag Union.

[22]

Bengt Stymne
Stockholm School of Economics

Industrial democracy and the worker

Establishment and breakdown of consensus

Labour unrest used to be a rather common phenomenon in Swedish industrial relations during the 1920s and 1930s. Strikes were more common in Sweden than they were in most other countries (Korpi, 1978). But a meeting at the Stockholm summer resort of Saltsjöbaden in 1938 marked the advent of a new era of understanding between labour and employers. The Saltsjöbaden spirit prevailed for three decades, the labour market exhibited very little conflict and the economy grew steadily, thereby providing the population with an unprecedented improvement in income and living standards. A wildcat strike at the state-owned mines in the northern part of the country in 1969 brutally signalled an end to the era of consensus (Dahlström et al., 1971). It also set in motion a debate concerning worker dissatisfaction, sources of dissatisfaction and possible remedies.

The miners' strike and a number of other wildcat strikes, increasing levels of labour turnover, difficulties in recruiting skilled labour and absenteeism were interpreted as signs of growing worker dissatisfaction. A number of reports which indicated unsatisfactory working conditions appeared and were cited in critical analyses of management ideology and the role of industrial psychology (Christiansson et al., 1969).

One interpretation of the miners' strike was that management had treated the workers in an authoritarian way and had not really regarded them as human beings. In other instances, such as the automobile industry, dull work and a lack of intrinsic motivation were seen as likely causes of labour alienation. From a sociological perspective, industrial relations problems were interpreted as erosion of the legitimacy of the prevailing industrial order. It was

International Review of Applied Psychology (SAGE, London, Beverly Hills and New Delhi), Vol. 35 (1986), 101–120

pointed out that workers were no longer willing to accept a clause known as clause 32, which stipulates employers' exclusive right to organize and direct work and which has been included in all collective agreements in the Swedish labour market, at the insistence of the Swedish Employers' Confederation. Labour's challenge to managerial authority could be understood on the basis of the very high degree of unionization – approaching 100 percent in many industries. Thus unions began to demand a say in what used to be managerial decision-making.

Events in Sweden were merely a reflection of circumstances in Europe which erupted in May 1968. Students and workers demanded that existing authority structures be dismantled and that power be given to the people. There was also unrest in the US which spread to the labour market, including both passive forms of worker protest such as absenteeism and low product quality and active protests such as sabotage and wildcat strikes (*Work in America*, 1972).

Contributions from behavioural science

Problems between management and workers – especially with regard to productivity – were investigated in the famous study at Western Electric during the 1930s (Roethlisberger and Dickson, 1939). The problem was formulated in psychological terms, i.e., worker morale was low because the way people in industry were treated by supervisors and the way work was organized left essential human needs unfulfilled. The human relations school suggested that workers should be treated more as human beings and that work should be organized in a more intrinsically rewarding way (McGregor, 1960). The human relations school gave impetus to the work on supervisory behaviour in Ohio (Kerr et al., 1974) and on socio-psychological aspects of organization in Michigan (Likert, 1961). In Sweden the 'human relations' concepts inspired Westerlund (1952) to carry out an experiment using two forms of supervisory behaviour at the Stockholm Telephone Exchange.

When worker dissatisfaction seemed to reach new heights at the end of the 1960s, the proponents of the human relations school analysed the extent to which industry left needs unfulfilled and how work enlargement could alleviate the situation (Herzberg, 1976). Such ideas were also implemented in US industry, e.g. in the General

Foods pet-food plant in Topeka (Walton, 1977). The European branch of human relations was conceptually developed at the Tavistock Institute in London (Emery and Trist, 1969). The Tavistock school formulated its sociotechnical design theory in an attempt to understand why a new method − the long-wall method of coal extraction − did not function well. These design concepts say that work should not be allocated so that one work group becomes specialized in a single task, and that work must not be organized according to a rigid plan. Instead work groups should be flexible so that members can carry out different tasks and the group itself should be allowed to adjust the division of tasks according to the needs of the situation. During the 1960s these ideas were put to a field test in Norway, in which Thorsrud and Emery (1969) claimed that their solution should increase the possibilities of fulfilling human needs from a whole rather than a fragmented task, with the worker learning new tasks and interacting with others. Similar ideas were applied on a larger scale in Swedish industry through the mediation of the Technical Department of the Swedish Employers' Confederation (Lindholm, 1975) and the Swedish Development Council (Stymne, 1980). They even involved experimentation with radical new factory design, as at the Volvo plant in Kalmar (Gyllenhammar, 1977).

Attempts by management and behavioural scientists to organize work in a more humane way have been partially successful in the sense that worker satisfaction has been shown to increase as a consequence of job enlargement and socio-technical design and that absenteeism and labour turnover have decreased (Srivastva et al., 1975). However, redesign of work did not curtail the demands for legal action in support of labour on the part of unions and politicians.

Industrial democracy

In Europe, the quest for more employee participation in decision-making at the workplace and a greater union say in management by establishing legal norms has been termed industrial democracy. An early example of industrial democracy was the *Mitbestimmungsgesetz* which prescribes workers' representation on supervisory boards. This law was introduced in the West German mining and metal industries after the war. The ideas were initiated by the

occupying powers to prevent owners and managers from transforming these industries back into machines for producing war
materials. The *Betriebsverfassungsgesetz* was introduced somewhat
later and has been expanded to provide rights for employee participation in a wide range of matters. The Yugoslavian system of *self-
management* introduced by Tito after the break with Stalin was also
an early attempt to use legislation and formal norms to guarantee
employees a good deal of say in the management of production and
administration. Like *Mitbestimmung, self-management* was motivated by wider political goals. Yugoslav society needed an ideology
which could serve as a common ground and unite that disparate
country which consists of different nationalities and religions.

The problem of industrial democracy was also raised within the
European Community. A new, all-European corporate law was
envisaged which would facilitate achievement of the Community's
goal of overcoming trade barriers and furthering economic
integration between the different countries. But it was asked whether
industrial democracy should be included in the law, in which case
legislation would have had to incorporate clauses about employee
participation in decision-making.

This question led to the formation of a research project on
industrial democracy in Europe – IDE – at Dubrovnik in 1972. The
occasion was the First International Sociological Conference on
Participation and Self-management. A great number of papers were
presented on new forms of authority relationships that could comprise
a basis for solutions to the crucial industrial relations problems which
had arisen towards the end of the 1960s (*Participation and Self-
management*, 1973).

The role of legal norms

The IDE project posed its main research question in the context of
contemplated European corporate law: could the establishment of
formal norms such as legislation and written agreements between
labour market parties lead to more employee participation (IDE,
1981a)? This question can be formulated even more bluntly: is it
possible to enact a law which will change authority relations at work?
If this question could be answered affirmatively, legislators would
have at their disposal a mechanism for meeting the challenges posed
by increasing labour discontent and workers' demands for a greater
say.

In Sweden, unions and politicians pressed hard for such legislative measures in the mid-1970s. The proposed legislation was regarded not only as providing the unions with a further means of improving working conditions, but also as a way of making company activities more efficient through the use of joint instead of purely managerial decision-making. Swedish employers opposed the proposed legislation. Their spokesmen stressed that both efficiency and worker satisfaction were related to leadership, work organization and qualitative aspects of relations at the workplace. Since legislation is an external factor, it could not be expected to improve the quality of management at the workplace. On the contrary, legislation could introduce external and disturbing elements into the organization and thereby decrease efficiency (Kling and Stymne, 1981: 63–65). Despite this opposition, the proposed legislation about codetermination went into effect.

The difficulties participants in the discussion about industrial democracy have in communicating with one another can be explained to some extent by arguments on two theoretical levels. One set of arguments is derived from a sociological analysis and states that the established societal structure, including laws and labour market relationships, reflects the domination of the 'worse off' by the 'better off'. According to this view, changes in the structure and patterns of domination are the only way to move towards a just society. The effect on people's feelings about their work situation is not the main focus of this line of reasoning (Björkman and Lundqvist, 1981). More important for this view is that a change towards industrial democracy could have effects for the legitimacy of the authority relationships inherent in the industrial production system.

The second set of arguments is based on psychology rather than sociology. According to this line of reasoning, people's psychological state is important and affected by their immediate situation. Factors emphasized by psychological theories include an interesting job, some independence on the job and good relations with the boss and workmates. The question of legitimacy does not figure prominently in psychological theories; instead, need fulfilment is more conspicuous.

Different European legislative measures in the area of industrial democracy may be used to study whether there is a relation between the sociological and psychological levels. Do changes in formal norms in society penetrate the psycho-sphere of individual citizens and change the quality of their work situation? And if such a connection can be detected, what mechanisms are involved? Do laws in themselves constitute a stimulus with *direct* consequences for the individual or do they lead to changes in the work environment which in turn affect the individual's psychological state?

If new formal norms make people believe that they live in a more just world when nothing has really changed, legislation and norm-setting can be used to propagate ideology or for political propaganda. This in turn would involve an ethical problem for legislators; they have to consider whether the instrumental functions of new norms match the degree to which people's beliefs are changed.

On the other hand, if formal norms mainly have an instrumental function, for example by restricting powerful groups from exploiting weaker strata, there is a problem of efficiency rather than an ethical problem in norm-setting. In this case the legislator runs the risk of creating an ineffectual law which causes disappointment among the public and eventually erodes confidence in legislators.

Questions for research

One of the tasks that the research group on industrial democracy set for itself was to determine the extent to which legal norms in different countries varied in their stipulations about the right of workers and their representatives to be involved in corporate decision-making. If such variations could be established, they could subsequently be used to analyse different types of legislative effects. Legal norms were defined as including laws, collective bargaining contracts, legally enforceable customs and practices and management policy. The following scale was used to determine the degree to which such formal norms prescribed the rights of labour to be involved in decision-making:

1. No right;
2. Labour must be informed;
3. Labour must be informed before a decision is taken and/or has the right to initiate consultations;
4. Labour must be consulted in advance;
5. Labour has the right to joint decision-making, i.e. has veto power, must give approval or can bargain with management about what the decision should be;
6. Labour has the final say.

FIGURE 1
Workers' legal rights in 1976

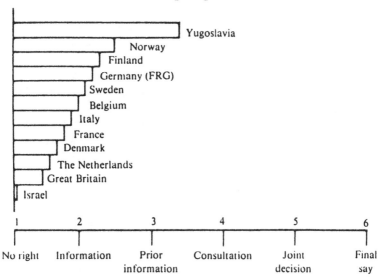

Source: IDE, 1981a.

FIGURE 2
Legal rights of representative bodies in 1976

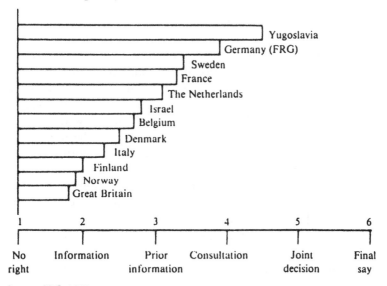

Source: IDE, 1981a.

Figures 1 and 2 show the right to participate in decision-making ascribed to workers and the body which represents workers in twelve countries. The figures show the average right to participate in 16 specified decisions varying from daily, routine decisions such as 'assignment of tasks to workers' to longer-range decisions such as 'major capital investment'. The figures were arrived at by scrutinizing laws and agreements, interviewing experts on both the labour and employer side about company policy and consulting legal experts.

Figure 1 shows that workers in most countries seem to have the right to be informed, with two exceptions. One is Israel where formal norms do not grant workers any right of participation and the other is Yugoslavia where workers have to be informed or consulted before decisions can be taken. The legal foundations on which the workers' right is based are in most cases management policy (which is, of course, a rather weak legal basis) or some kind of collective bargaining contract.

Figure 2 shows the rights to participate for those who represent the workers. In Britain and the Nordic countries these representatives are the unions, in Yugoslavia it is the workers' council, while in the other countries it is a works council or similar body to which the employees elect representatives and which is supposed to represent the workers' interests in relation to management. In some instances, like the German *Betriebsrat*, only employees are represented in these bodies, while others are bodies for joint consultation, for example the Israeli 'joint productivity councils' (IDE, 1981b).

We now turn to the question of whether industrial democracy in terms of formal norms affects the way people perceive themselves as being involved in decision-making. A random sample of 7,832 employees from a total of 134 establishments (firms) in metal engineering and financial services (banks and insurance companies) were asked how they judged the degree to which they were involved in the 16 decisions for which their legal rights had been assessed. With slight modifications, the scale set up to evaluate norms was also used in the questionnaires.

The correlations in Table 1 demonstrate a relationship between legal rights and the way people experience their involvement in questions other than daily work. A regression analysis was performed to find out the extent to which formal norms could predict employee involvement. For workers, the formal norms could predict 24 percent of the variations in workers' involvement in short-

TABLE 1
Correlation between workers' legal rights to participate and workers' reported degree of involvement

Type of decision	r
Decisions affecting daily work	0.10
Medium-range decisions	0.45
Long-term decisions	0.41
All decisions	0.32

Source: IDE, 1981a.

N = 134 establishments in 12 countries.

term decisions, 50 percent in medium-range decisions and 58 percent in long-term decisions (IDE, 1981a). With respect to short-term decisions, formal norms that gave workers a right to participate had a positive effect on their actual involvement, while a formal right for unions and other representatives to participate in such decisions had a negative effect on actual worker involvement. As for worker involvement in medium- and long-term decisions, a right for both workers and their representatives had a positive effect. The degree of variance in involvement which could be explained by legal norms was much higher than what could be achieved by variables describing the situation in the company such as technology, organization structure and market conditions.

The degree to which workers and their representatives had a right to participate in decision-making also showed positive correlations with the following attitudinal measures (IDE, 1981a): workers' attitudes towards representative bodies; workers' attitudes towards direct participation.

The results give some support for the hypothesis that legal norms affect the way workers view their situation. However, when it comes to the most personal part of one's work situation, i.e. daily routine decisions, the relationship is rather weak. The fact that legal norms can, at least to some extent, explain workers' involvement in routine decisions is mainly due to the sizeable *negative* effect of legal rights for workers' representatives to participate in daily routine matters on workers' involvement. A further sign that formal norms do not penetrate the personal sphere too deeply is that there is no relationship between legal norms and workers' satisfaction with their job or company.

For medium- and long-term decisions, the percentage of variation in worker involvement that can be explained by legal norms is quite high. Moreover, workers evaluate the system of participation more highly and are more interested in it when legal norms prescribe a high degree of participation for workers and their representatives. Legal norms thus seem to be capable of lending some degree of legitimacy at least to the aspects of the decision-making system which deal with *work conditions* rather than with *work itself*.

A certain relationship between legal rights and workers' involvement in decision-making has thus been established. The next question we would like to ask is whether norms actually cause people to see themselves as more involved. Or do legal norms affect structure and processes in the company which in turn affect people's opportunity to participate? In order to study this question, the actual distribution of influence over different groups was used to operationalize structure and processes.

The actual distribution of influence was assessed by interviewing a number of key persons in each company about decision-making processes for the 16 specified decisions. Each category of employees and managers was assigned a score ranging from 1 ('no influence') to 5 ('large influence') on every decision issue by applying a Tannenbaum-type response scale (Tannenbaum, 1968). Rather than reflecting individual attitudes, the influence measure is intended to describe the social organization in the company.

Actual influence of workers correlates with legal norms. The first-order correlations between legal norms and influence are actually somewhat stronger than the correlations between legal norms and worker involvement. According to the regression analyses, however, the power of legal norms to explain influence is somewhat less than for involvement. Legal norms provide the least explanatory power for workers' influence in day-to-day decision-making and better explanatory power for medium- and long-term decisions, as was the case for the degree of involvement the workers reported in various types of decisions (IDE, 1981a). The influence of bodies which represent the workers may to a large extent be explained by the stipulations of legal norms.

We then went on to consider the extent to which actual influence can explain involvement experienced. As shown in Table 2 influence contributes substantially to the explanation of involvement experienced even when the effects of legal norms are partialled out. There are also correlations between the workers' attitudes in terms of evaluation of and interest in the system for participation and influence. As was the case for legal norms, a high degree of influence for representative bodies is associated with positive evaluations of the system for participation.

TABLE 2
Partial correlations between workers' influence and workers' reported level of involvement — the effects of legal norms held constant

Type of decision	r
Short-term decisions	0.28
Medium-term decisions	0.49
Long-term decisions	0.61
All decisions	0.37

Source: IDE, 1981a.

The results we have arrived at are consistent with the following interpretation. Legal norms in the firm affect the degree to which people perceive themselves to be involved in decisions that affect work conditions and their attitudes to the decision-making system. However, there is little support for the hypothesis that legal norms can explain the way in which workers perceive their daily work. Also the social organization in the company, operationalized by the distribution of influence, is strongly affected by legal norms. However, the influence distribution has to be considered over and above the effects of legal norms when explaining workers' involvement. These interpretations of the results are illustrated by Figure 3.

FIGURE 3
Interpretation of the relationships found in the international comparison

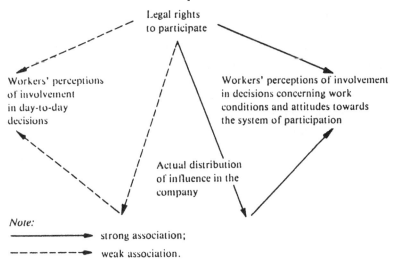

Note:

——————▶ strong association;

— — — — —▶ weak association.

A Swedish experiment

Swedish legislation concerning industrial democracy was changed in 1977. The main change was that unions representing workers were given the right to consult with management on most issues. The situation in Swedish companies was assessed before (1976) and after (1981) the change, using the same methods as those used in the international study described above. The study was carried out in seven metal-engineering companies and three companies from the financial sector — one bank and two insurance companies. A total of 142 key informants were interviewed in 1976 and 92 in 1981 about distribution of influence in the companies. Questionnaires about involvement and other aspects of their work situation were filled in by 1,050 employees in 1976 and 1,069 in 1981, sampled randomly from different groups in the companies.

The intention of the Swedish Codetermination Act, as the new law is called, was that employers and employees should agree on collective bargaining contracts which stipulate more detailed rules for decision-making in companies. These rules could, for example, give some rights of participation to workers at the workplace. When our follow-up of the effects of the legislation was carried out, such contracts had been signed only for the financial sector. Even in these cases the agreements were of such recent date that there had been little time to adapt them to the local situation in the companies. Therefore, the legal change at the time of measurement was confined to granting unions more rights to participate in all types of decisions. The law did not assign any new rights to workers individually. There were even those involved in bargaining on the employers' side who said that the new law had perhaps eroded workers' rights to participate which they had previously been given by traditional management policy.

TABLE 3
Change in actual level of influence (five-point scale) of workers and their unions, five years after the Swedish Codetermination Act

Type of decision	Blue-collar workers	Blue-collar unions	White-collar workers	White-collar unions
Short-term decisions	+ 0.355*	+ 0.313*	0.316*	0.328*
Medium-term decisions	+ 0.127*	+ 0.602*	0.255**	0.716*
Long-term decisions	− 0.147*	+ 0.464*	0.077	0.744*

*$p < 0.01$; ** $p < 0.02$ (two-tailed t-test).

The changes in distribution of influence according to key informants in the companies are summarized in Table 3. The legal change had clearly resulted in more influence for unions, especially in medium- and long-term decision-making, i.e. the kind of decisions that affect work conditions rather than daily work itself. The typical change for long-term decisions is from about 'little influence' (2) halfway to 'moderate influence' (2.5). For medium-term decisions, the change is from halfway between 'little' and 'moderate influence' (2.5) to just above 'moderate influence' (3). Top management was still seen to have much more influence than the unions in long-term decisions, but only slightly higher influence than unions for medium-term decisions. Workers' actual influence had changed for short-term decisions, but not for long-term decisions. Blue-collar workers actually had less influence over long-term decisions after the legal change than they had before.

The pattern of change points to a causal relationship between the legal change and the increase in union influence. Since the law did not give any more rights to workers themselves, the change in influence for workers must have been mediated. Perhaps the increased influence for unions did rub off on their members through the contacts union representatives have with members before they consult with managers. The figures for short- and medium-term decisions point in the direction of such an interpretation. On the other hand, worker influence increased the most in areas where union influence increased the least. Worker influence increased the least, or even decreased, in areas where union influence increased the most. Thus, it seems that the changes in union influence triggered by the new law cannot fully explain changes in the social organization of companies that led to the changed pattern of influence for workers.

TABLE 4
Change in workers' perceived involvement (six-point scale), five years after the Swedish Codetermination Act

Type of decision	Blue-collar workers	White-collar workers
Short-term decisions	+ 0.274*	+ 0.226*
Medium-term decisions	+ 0.074*	+ 0.231*
Long-term decisions	+ 0.028	+ 0.211*

*$p < 0.01$ (two-tailed t-test).

The changes in the degree of involvement reported by the workers themselves are shown in Table 4. Generally, the degree of involvement has increased. However, this pattern does not follow the pattern of new rights that the law gave to unions – blue-collar workers' involvement increased the most for short-term decisions in spite of the fact that union influence increased the most for medium-term decisions. The pattern of change in workers' involvement follows more closely the pattern of change in worker influence. But the small change in influence in long-term decisions for white-collar workers cannot fully explain the relatively large increase in involvement in the same type of decisions that they reported.

When we turn from worker involvement to worker attitudes, we find an interesting difference between the cross-sectional international data and the Swedish longitudinal results. In the international study, a positive correlation was found between rights to participate and workers' attitudes towards representative bodies. However, the Swedish Codetermination Act was followed by a marked decrease in workers' evaluation of and interest in the 'system for joint decision-making' (see Table 5). Thus, it seems as if the law achieved its purpose in changing influence distribution and workers' involvement, but it is doubtful whether this can be said to have increased the degree of legitimacy or worker acceptance of the system for decision-making. In fact, the system was held in greater respect and workers were more eager to become union representatives *before* the legislation was passed.

TABLE 5
Change in workers' attitudes towards the formal system for participation in ten Swedish companies, five years after the Codetermination Act

	Change in blue-collar workers' attitudes	Change in white-collar workers' attitudes
Evaluation of the system for participation	−0.301*	−0.142
Interest in the system for participation	−0.347*	−0.365*

*$p < 0.01$ (two-tailed t-test).

The longitudinal data from the Swedish study support the inferences from the international study that changed industrial democracy which implies more rights for union representatives to participate in decision-making leads to increased influence and involvement for workers. However, the Swedish data strongly suggest that the mechanisms of change are not simple. The law did not merely give people the feeling that they had become more involved; the greater involvement workers felt was accompanied by more influence for them in day-to-day decisions. This greater influence cannot simply be explained as an outcome of increased union influence because unions became influential in different areas from those in which workers increased their influence. Industrial democracy may have set other events in motion in companies which have to be considered when giving a more detailed account of the effects of the Codetermination Act. We considered supervisory behaviour as such an additional explanation.

Supervisory behaviour

One of the reasons for introducing legal rights for workers and their representatives allowing them to participate in decision-making is that workers have traditionally been treated in an overly authoritarian way by their bosses. The way in which people on different levels in the international study evaluated their immediate superiors' behaviour is compared in Table 6, according to the following items:

(i) superior consults you before taking a decision
(ii) superior gives you reason for a change
(iii) superior gives you an opportunity to decide on your own
(iv) you can tell your superior if you have a different opinion

TABLE 6
How people on different levels rate their immediate supervisor's behaviour on a five-point scale where 5 = perfectly democratic

Group	Evaluation of supervisor's style
Workers	3.18
Foremen	3.82
Middle managers	4.07

Source: IDE, 1981a.

Figures are average mean evaluations from 134 companies in 12 countries.

Changes in the behaviour of supervisors and other important aspects of workplace organization have been suggested, especially in the US, as alternative means of achieving industrial democracy and creating a more humane work environment for workers. Analysis of the international study, however, indicates that changes in supervisory behaviour and industrial democracy are not necessarily mutually exclusive. Firms where formal norms prescribe more worker participation and firms where workers have more actual influence also tend to have more democratic supervisors than do other companies. This relationship clearly received further support in the Swedish study. Workers reported that their supervisors had become more democratic after introduction of the legislation. The same clear shift in *their* bosses' behaviour was not reported by foremen and managers (see Table 7).

TABLE 7
Change in ratings of immediate supervisor's behaviour on a five-point scale, five years after the Swedish Codetermination Act

Group	N (1981)	Value (1981)	Change between 1976 and 1981	p (two-tailed t-test)
Blue-collar workers	345	3.06	0.30	< 0.01
White-collar workers	379	3.64	0.29	< 0.01
Supervisors	196	4.03	0.02	
Managers	134	4.30	0.04	

Although we do not have any independent observational data to confirm whether supervisory behaviour really changed, the data provided by the respondents are suggestive. What they suggest is that supervisors met the challenge from changed formal norms and greater union power by changing their behaviour so as to involve workers to a greater extent in the way the workplace is run. The result is that the authority system within the firm has gained in legitimacy and in the confidence workers have in it, while the representative system has lost in acceptance.

Figure 4 is an attempt to illustrate our interpretation of the Swedish study. The dotted lines denote preliminary findings which await a more thorough analysis of the material in order to gain more confidence. There are two main differences between the interpret-

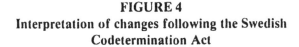

FIGURE 4
Interpretation of changes following the Swedish Codetermination Act

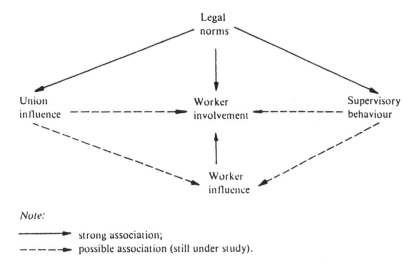

Note:

⎯⎯⎯⎯► strong association;

⎯ ⎯ ⎯ ⎯► possible association (still under study).

ations of the Swedish and the international material. First, the analysis of the Swedish material has led to the introduction of supervisory behaviour as an additional factor for explaining both worker influence and worker involvement. Second, worker attitudes that reflect the legitimacy of union and managerial authority cannot be regarded as identical. Nor does legitimacy of the authority systems increase automatically as an outcome of more industrial democracy. In the Swedish case, workers' attitudes towards the system for participation became more negative. There may be many explanations for this fact. One is that workers may have become disappointed because employers and unions could not sit down and agree on a decision-making procedure in companies which would have given workers themselves a greater say. Instead, there were increased signs of tension between managers and union representatives − at least at the national level. Another reason is that the Swedish economy was in poor shape between 1976 and 1981. Workers could have felt increasingly insecure as unemployment figures rose and they realized that increased rights for unions to participate in decision-making did not really alleviate their anxiety regarding the future.

Discussion

Industrial democracy has been regarded as a means of changing the actual pattern of influence in companies and the degree to which workers see themselves as involved in decision-making. Comparative cross-sectional data and longitudinal Swedish data support the notion that industrial democracy has indeed had these two desired effects. Industrial democracy has thus been effective in better integrating workers into the decision-making apparatus of companies and could therefore be assumed to have contributed to improving the legitimacy of authority in industry.

Unions and representative bodies such as works councils play a mediating role between legal norms and the workers' situation in the company. The Swedish data in particular indicate that this role may be ungratifying and that the representative system can lose support through industrial democracy.

The association found between legal norms and the increased involvement reported by workers can be seen as a psychological effect of industrial democracy. But neither the international nor the Swedish data lend much support to the notion that legal norms have more profound effects in terms of greater satisfaction with one's work or one's company. However, the psychological effects of industrial democracy may have been more consequential for supervisors than for workers. The changes in legal norms may have induced Swedish foremen to adjust their leadership style towards a more participatory attitude. The workers in our sample reported that such a change had actually taken place. Since supervisory behaviour is an important source of worker satisfaction, the indirect effects mediated by changed supervisory behaviour may well be the most important social-psychological consequences of industrial democracy. However, more rigid testing of the relationship between legal norms and supervisory behaviour requires that researchers use not only reputational data but, as Westerlund did, obtain observational data of supervisors at work.

References

Björkman, T. and Lundqvist, K. (1981). *Fran MAX till PIA. Reformstrategier inom Arbetsmiljoormradet.* Lund: Arkiv.

Christiansson, L., Fahlén, T., Flordh, C., Grosin, L., Hedlund, R., Hofsten, A.-M., Thernlund, G., Thorell, G. and Agren, G. (1969). *Konsten att Dressera Människor.*

Mental Hälsa – Arbete – Ideologi. Stockholm: Prisma.

Dahlström, E., Eriksson, K., Gardell, B., Hammarström, O. and Hammarström, R. (1971). *LKAB och Demokratin. Rapport om en Strejk och ett Forskningsprojekt*. Stockholm: Wahlström and Widstrand.

Emery, F.E. and Trist, E.L. (1969). 'Socio-technical Systems'. In F.E. Emery (ed.), *Systems Thinking*. Harmondsworth, Middlesex: Penguin.

Gyllenhammar, P.G. (1977). *People at Work*. Reading, Mass.: Addison-Wesley.

Herzberg, F. (1976). *The Managerial Choice*. Homewood, Ill.: Dow Jones Irwin.

IDE (Industrial Democracy in Europe International Research Group). (1981a). *Industrial Democracy in Europe*. Oxford: Clarendon Press.

IDE (Industrial Democracy in Europe International Research Group). (1981b). *European Industrial Relations*. Oxford: Clarendon Press.

Kerr, S., Schriesheim, A., Murphy, C.J. and Stogdill, R.M. (1974). 'Toward a Contingency Theory of Leadership Based upon the Consideration and Initiating Structure Literature'. *Organizational Behavior and Human Performance*, 18: 62–82.

Kling, M. and Stymne, B. (1981). *Spelet Mellan Facket och Företagsledningen. Sociala Strategier for Medbestämmande*. Malmö: Liber.

Korpi, W. (1978). *Arbetarklassen i Välfärdskapitalismen*. Stockholm: Prisma.

Likert, R. (1961). *New Patterns of Management*. New York: McGraw-Hill.

Lindholm, R. (1975). *Job Reform in Sweden*. Stockholm: Swedish Employers' Confederation.

McGregor, D. (1960). *The Human Side of Enterprise*. New York: McGraw-Hill.

Participation and Self-management. (1973). Vols. 1–6. Zagreb. Institute for Social Research.

Roethlisberger, F.J. and Dickson, W.J. (1939). *Management and the Worker*. Cambridge, Mass.: Harvard University Press.

Srivastva, S., Salipante, P., Cummings, T., Notz, W., Bigelow, J. and Waters, J. (1975). *Job Satisfaction and Productivity*. Cleveland: Case Western University.

Stymne, B. (1980). 'Design Principles for a Participative Organization of Work. Some Conclusions from the URAF Experiments'. *Economic and Industrial Democracy*, 1: 197–224.

Tannenbaum, A. (1968). *Control in Organizations*. New York: McGraw-Hill.

Thorsrud, E. and Emery, F.E. (1969). *Mot en ny Bedriftsorganisasjon*. Oslo: Tanum.

Walton, R.E. (1977). 'Work Innovations at Topeka: After Six Years'. *Journal of Applied Behavioural Science*, 13: 422–433.

Westerlund, G. (1952). *Group Leadership. A Field Experiment*. Stockholm Nordisk Rotorgravyr.

Work in America (1972). Cambridge, Mass.: Massachusetts Institute of Technology.

[23]

FOCUS

Participation down and up the line: comparative industrial democracy trends in China and Europe

Oiva Laaksonen

Introduction

From the beginning of the so-called Cultural Revolution in 1966 there have been many changes in enterprise management in China which have included different 'experiments' in the area of participation. Our aim here is to describe and analyse these systems. The article is divided into three main parts: first, we examine the different participation systems practised during the Cultural Revolution; second, we describe the new participation systems created after Chairman Mao Zedong's death and, third, we examine the influences of different personnel and interest groups in enterprises compared with European empirical data.

The data were collected by myself during two visits to China, the first in 1973 when I visited eleven industrial enterprises in Guangzhou (Canton), Hangzhou (Hongchow), Beijing and Shanghai. The second journey was made in 1980, when the new rulers had already established their positions after Mao Zedong's death. Then I interviewed managers in fourteen organizations located in Beijing, Guangzhou, Chongqing, Yichang, Shanghai and Wuhan. The enterprises rep-resented the metallurgical and engineering industry, the textile industry, construction firms and porcelain factories. The size categories according to number of employees were very much the same during both visits: one-fifth of the enterprises had between 200 and 600 employees, one-fifth between 1,000 and 2,000, two-fifths between 2,000 and 10,000 and one-fifth over 10,000 employees. Two of the enterprises included in 1973 were also included in 1980.

I conducted the interviews in English with the help of an interpreter. Each interview took place in a group situation consisting of two to four persons, the main person interviewed usually representing top line management and/or personnel administration.

Oiva Laaksonen is Professor of Business Administration and Organizational Behaviour at the Helsinki School of Economics, Runeberginkatu 22-24, SF-00100 Helsinki 10, Finland. He is also the Chairman of the Finnish Society for Management Research. His main research interest is in comparing capitalist and socialist organizations in Western and Eastern cultures.

Power and resistance as analytical concepts

One of the main concepts used here is power. In examining it the so-called control-of resources approach is used (French and Raven, 1959), because we are comparing capitalist and socialist organizations. One of the main differences between capitalist and socialist systems is in the ownership and

Not a battle scene but an aspect of mobilization during China's Cultural Revolution: digging a vast trench to control the Haiho River in Hopei Province. Camera Press.

control of the means of production and of other resources.

Blau (1964) states that the resources an actor or actors can use in exchange processes create power relations. According to Burt (1977), power is defined as an individual's or another system's ability to transform resources in order to influence the relations between individuals or other systems.

In power relations there are at least two parties. Party A can offer commodities to Party B which he needs and cannot get as advantageously from elsewhere. Party B therefore becomes dependent on Party A (Emerson, 1962, pp. 282–98). Party B often tries to free himself from this dependence relationship. This can create direct or covert resistance. Rus (1980, p. 3) sees these relationships as a power cycle with two closely related poles: 'Positive power (induction), as an ability to initiate activity, and negative power (resistance), as an ability to stop some activity.'

In the research literature only positive power is usually handled, but from the point of view of efficient leadership, reducing resistance is of vital importance (Kotter, 1979). Participation is in most cases conceived as a negation of resistance, and not as a negation of power (Rus, 1980, p. 11). It depends from whose point of view one is analysing participation. Management can use it as a tool for activating the knowledge resources and initiative (motivation) of subordinates; workers

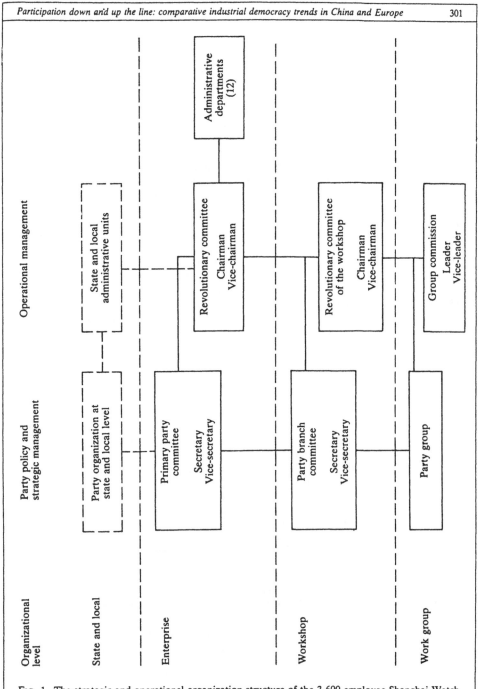

FIG. 1. The strategic and operational organization structure of the 3,600-employee Shanghai Watch Factory in 1973 (Laaksonen, 1977, p. 88).

can see it as a negation of the power of management by dividing its decision-making power to lower levels of the organizational hierarchy.

Participation during the Cultural Revolution

After the failure of the development programme known as 'The Great Leap Forward' (1958–60), the Chinese created a limited free-market system for agriculture and a profit-making system for enterprises to stimulate production. Mao Zedong then became afraid that this direction would lead China along the capitalist road. He stressed that the Chinese should not forget the class struggle. The country would always need a new 'revolution' after a certain time. There was also a deep ideological conflict between the thinking of Mao Zedong and the Soviet Communist Party, the ideology of which was represented in China by the then President, Liu Sao-tŝi. Last but not least, the Cultural Revolution was associated with the power struggle for Mao's succession.

During the period of Soviet influence in China, which ended abruptly in 1958, the one-man management system developed, with managing directors holding considerable power in enterprises. During the Cultural Revolution, revolutionary committees were created to represent collective management. As in the party organization structure, there were usually several revolutionary committees at different levels of organization (Fig. 1). Every large workshop usually had one committee, which was responsible for the operational management of the firm.

The revolutionary committee of the enterprise consisted of twenty to fifty members, depending on the size of the firm. Usually the leaders of the largest and most important organizational units—such as workshops and administrative departments—belonged to the revolutionary committee of the firm. As in the party organization, it was also recommended in the revolutionary committees that a third of the members should represent the elderly, a third the middle-aged, and a third the younger employees. In this way the Chinese tried to overcome generation gaps, which often create serious personnel conflicts.

During my interviews in the enterprises I also discovered that women were well represented on the revolutionary committees. As the shop-floor workers were also well represented on the committees, it is evident that the Chinese tried to extend participation in enterprise management to many different groups, taking into account the different hierarchical levels, different age-groups and both sexes. The party's dominant role created a problem with respect to the principle of participatory equality, since the most important decisions were in any case in its hands.

The Chinese attempted to reduce hierarchy and to increase participation and innovational ability during the Cultural Revolution by establishing what were known as 'three-factor project groups' to solve various technical and other problems. In principle, these project groups included: administrators, technical experts and shop-floor workers. It was also clear that the Chinese tried to avoid emphasizing the status of for example technicians or other experts. The political motive was to avoid creating a new élite or social class, but there was also a motivational reason. Highlighting expert groups would have destroyed the spirit of initiative among the ordinary workers in enterprises, 'the participation of the masses', on whose contribution the Maoist model greatly relied.

Efforts were made to ensure the participation of shop-floor workers by trying to activate those in subordinate positions through unofficial social groupings. These were based on the work-group and discussion groups formed for ideological training and discussion, etc. These groups, which usually consisted of six to a dozen members, chose their own officials and arranged leisure-time activities, held political study meetings outside working hours and carried out self-criticism and group criticism.

Portraits of workers rewarded for their conduct (with some gaps) at a factory entrance in China.
Marc Riboud/Magnum.

I would like to mention especially the Chinese system of criticism because one can discern in it a link between direct and indirect participation—a control mechanism exercised by the electorate. Through criticism the electorate was in principle able to carry out constant, direct evaluation of the leadership of their representatives and obtain immediate feedback. Leader accountability is an important dimension of participatory democracy. Criticism functions also as a conflict-regulating mechanism, and can thus be used as an instrument in reducing resistance among subordinates.

Participation generally means that subordinates take part in higher-level decision-making, an activity traditionally reserved for their superiors. We more rarely conceive of participation in other directions: horizontally or vertically downward. The latter was generally ignored until the Cultural Revolution. In the throes of it, the Chinese created a system in which managers, experts and other office workers—the cadres—worked part of the time alongside their subordinates, performing the same tasks, according to the 'mass-line

principle'. In the industrial and commercial enterprises (fourteen altogether) where my interviews in 1973 took place, the rule was that cadres usually did physical work one day a week.

Down-the-line participation can vary in depth; for instance, it may cut across one or more levels in the organization's hierarchy. It may also vary according to whether it travels in a straight line or diagonally, that is, whether the head of marketing takes part in production-line work. It may also vary in duration, ranging from a short visit at the lower level to a longer period of work, or even to a complete exchange of tasks.

Organizational advantages of down-the-line participation

Certain people in China soon noticed that the system originally created to level out class differences also frequently produced certain purely organizational advantages. I will deal below both with the positive experience, and with the advantages which down-the-line participation can theoretically provide to firms according to organizational studies:

Communication upward is improved. The inadequate upward flow of information in organizations is frequently regarded as one of the most serious problems of communication and efficiency. The Chinese discovered that their new system opened new direct channels for the upward flow of information.

Management learns in practice about the really important problems (personnel and other) of the lower levels of the hierarchy. Korpi (1974) has shown that more than half of all strikes in Sweden are caused by shop-floor grievances.

Managers have a unique opportunity to examine their own working routines from 'outside'.

There is better hierarchical cohesion throughout the organization. Numerous studies show that personal contact reduces prejudice and conflict, and increases positive attitudes (Etzioni, 1961).

The managers of organizations are often quite old and have lost most of the energy and innovativeness of their youth. Often they have become a burden on their organization. An approved system for moving 'down' to less demanding tasks could be a relief both to a manager and his firm. However, the contemporary worldwide value system focusing on continuous growth and higher status does not 'allow' for down-the-line participation in such cases, at least not in the same organization. There is a grave danger of 'losing face'.

Many studies concerning managers' actual use of their time show that a very small part of their working time is devoted to important managerial tasks like strategic planning, etc. (Stewart, 1967). Managers waste a great deal of their time on routine tasks of secondary importance for the efficiency of the enterprise. It can be argued that the time a manager invests in down-the-line participation can yield a many-sided positive return to an enterprise and its employees.

We must remember that the continual rise in prominence of senior managers, or at least the permanence of their positions, is mainly the creation of a historically relatively young industrial society. In earlier agricultural and other societies, older people shifted gradually to less demanding tasks with age and decreasing efficiency. There are also many other developments in contemporary society that seem to support down-the-line participation, or at least recommend its serious study. Some of these are as follows:

Value systems are moving way from goals of power, status and material wealth towards a higher 'quality of life', based more on equality and non-material satisfaction.

The constant rise in training levels has led to a situation in which increasingly more people are prepared for demanding supervisory positions in terms of both knowledge and personal traits.

The number of those prepared to do monotonous physical work is declining constantly. A call may arise for a more equitable distribution of hard and unpleasant tasks and not only of 'easy' and rewarding ones.

Outside of work, managers in industrial societies are already doing jobs performed by the lowest hierarchy of workers in their organization. Examples include housework, home repairs, shopping in supermarkets, filling up their own petrol tanks.

Wage differences between those at the highest and the lowest levels of the hierarchy have been decreasing constantly. There has also been a trend towards wage parity, even altering the differences between professions.

Sharply rising progressive taxation means that work at the higher hierarchical level is no longer rewarded with net earnings very much above the average level.

Unemployment, especially among young people, is one of the greatest problems all over the world. Some forms of down-the-line participation could be worth experimenting with, in order to make the labour market more flexible.

Generally accepted goals of democracy include equality, the possibility of replacing management, and joint responsibility. As far as the first is concerned, down-the-line participation implements equality downward from above, and not merely upward from below. Despite the development of official democracy in many societies, the implementation of the second goal, the replacement of management, is a questionable practice in both political and other systems. When leaders remain firmly in their positions, joint responsibility is also rarely achieved in practice.

Large-scale implementation of down-the-line participation would, at the extreme, require considerable rearrangement throughout society. However, contemporary societies are everywhere struggling with what seem to be impossible problems with respect to employees and employment: old remedies have most often proved useless in solving them. In this sense down-the-line participation is worth investigation and experimentation.

The present Chinese leadership looks back at the Cultural Revolution as a decade of chaos during which the economic, cultural and social development of the country was practically brought to a halt. Yet, in the area of participation, many novel ideas were tried, which could have resulted in high motivation and efficient performance among employees. What, then, went wrong?

First, the many-sided participation system was to a great extent a sham because enterprises had very little effective decision-making power of their own; they had to follow plans and orders from the top of the social pyramid. A small group of party officials at different levels in fact made the really important decisions. Thus the participation systems did not activate positive power but probably rather covert negative power, i.e. resistance, in the form of low performance. Second, if the official ideology and decisions were not followed, resistance was often overcome by physical force, which created fear, alienation and covert resistance in the form

of decreasing motivation and efficiency (Etzioni, 1961).

Some of the measures taken during the Cultural Revolution were enthusiastic but counter-productive, and were often adapted in the wrong place and at the wrong time in relation to the development phase of Chinese society and enterprises. For example, the sudden substitution of party ideology for economic rewards (bonus systems) could not succeed in a developing country with a low standard of living.

All this means that we should study carefully Chinese experiences during that time, because the country then resembled a huge human laboratory in which interesting and partly novel experiments were being conducted in a natural environment.

Participation in Chinese enterprises after 1976

After the death of Mao Zedong in September 1976, the new leadership took many measures to reduce resistance to its policies. It also radically changed both the power structure and the value system: guiding society and organizations, and setting the goals to aim for and the measures to use.

To reduce resistance (negative power), the new leadership changed the occupancy of important positions in the Communist Party and in enterprises. According to the decisions of the Central Committee of the Communist Party in October 1983 to purge the party organizations, special groups active in the Cultural Revolution are to be expelled from the party (Central Committee of CPC, 1983, p. 6). Most of the revolutionary committees were abolished by 1978, and a one-management system was re-created in enterprises. In nearly all the enterprises I visited at the end of 1980, there were new top managers mostly nominated in 1978.

Hua Guofeng, the then First Secretary of the Communist Party, said in a speech on economic reform (reported in the *Beijing Review* of 22 September 1980):

The general orientation for this reform is to transform over-centralized management by the state (central and local authorities included), extend the decision-making power of the enterprises and the power of their workers and staff to participate in management, transform regulation through planning alone into regulation by the market, and transform management relying mainly on administrative organs and methods into management relying mainly on economic organs as well as on economic and legal methods.

These ideas meant profound changes in Chinese society at many levels. The content of industrial democracy changed radically from the time of the Cultural Revolution. The move towards a freer market system with much greater independence and responsibility for enterprises and their managers also altered the significance of the new enterprise-level participation systems. They could now exercise real decision-making power concerning important matters.

The new Constitution of China (4 December 1982) specifies that:

State enterprises practise democratic management through congresses of workers and staff and in other ways in accordance with the law [Article 16]. . . . Collective economic organizations have decision-making power in conducting independent economic activities, on condition that they accept the guidance of the state plan and abide by the relevant laws. Collective economic organizations practise democratic management in accordance with the law, with the entire body of their workers electing or removing their managerial personnel and deciding on major issues concerning operation and management [Article 17].

These citations date from the end of 1982. However, the provisional regulations concerning workers' congresses of June 1981 specify in Article 3 that workers' congresses exercise their functions and powers 'under the leadership of the party committee' (Provisional Regulations, 1981). Only eighteen months later, the party was no longer mentioned in the constitution in connection with the functioning of the workers' congresses. This was probably a sign of the divorce of

the party from operative enterprise management, a divorce which represents a very profound change in a socialist country.

According to information supplied to me by a government official at the end of 1983 there were then workers' congresses in 200,000 enterprises, and the employees had elected the top management and factory directors in about 15,000 enterprises.

Representatives to workers' congresses are directly elected by employees, with work groups, work sections or workshops (offices) as the electoral units. Every full-time employee of an enterprise who enjoys citizenship rights may be elected as a representative for a renewable term of two years.

In workers' congresses appropriate representation is to be guaranteed to scientific, technical and administrative personnel, young employees and female workers. Workers should account for no less than 60 per cent of the total number of representatives (*Provisional Regulations*, 1981, Chapter III, Article 8).

In the composition of the new workers' congresses, traces of the participation systems of the Cultural Revolution remain, such as that different kinds of personnel groups are to be represented according to profession, sex, age, etc. The crucial difference is that the new participative systems have more real power, because of the greater independence of the enterprises in decision-making and because of the reduced power of the party.

The new participative systems were first created in so-called Special Economic Zones, where novel strategies of economic reform were tested. But the system of workers' congresses had already spread all over China by 1983).

According to Chen (1982, pp. 6–7), most of the established workers' congresses now follow these directions:

1. To be involved in the public election of the Factory Manager or Director and Assistant or Deputy Factory Manager or Director. To submit to the higher authority the results of the election as a proposal for approval.

Director of a truck factory in his office in 1965. Slogans on the wall read 'A resolute and fighting spirit—an ardent class sentiment—an unflinching scientific attitude'. Marc Riboud (*L'empire du bureau*, p. 28).

2. To elect the heads of workshops, departments, sections or units.
3. To appraise the performance of the officers, managerial or supervisory personnel of the enterprise and to decide whether such personnel deserve awards, praise, promotion, demotion, transfer or other appropriate action. Such decision will also be submitted to the higher level authorities for approval and implementation.
4. To examine and approve proposals concerning the management and organization of the enterprise, the wage system, the training of workers and regulations and methods for performance appraisal.
5. To examine and approve collective contracts signed between the management and the trade union.
6. To examine and approve financial plans and budgets for the enterprise.
7. To examine and approve proposals for trade-union fees.
8. To examine and approve schemes for workers' welfare and benefits, profit retaining and profit sharing, award system and labour security.
9. To examine and approve reports and plan proposals made by the Factory Manager [see also *Provisional Regulations,* 1981, Chapter II, Article 5]

Since Mao Zedong the Chinese have thus created formal and informal participation systems at different levels of the organization hierarchy. They display some continuity with earlier practices. At the management level there are special management representatives' meetings, at the workshop level there are the worker representatives' assembly and so-called democratic life meetings, where workshop heads meet with their workers and trade-union shop stewards on welfare, problems of daily life and so on, usually once a month (Chen, 1982, p. 4).

Coal-miners in Shantung Province reporting their recent achievements to the party committee.
James Andanson/Sygma.

At the end of 1983 the Tenth National Congress of Chinese Trade Unions met in Beijing to elect new leaders and revise its constitution. By the end of 1982 there were 430,000 grass-roots trade-union organizations with 73.31 million members.

We have not mentioned trade unions in relation to participation in enterprises earlier because of their limited power and their mostly social and ideological activities. According to the new constitution also (see *Beijing Review,* 31 October 1983, pp. 5–6) Chinese trade unions differ greatly from their counterparts in Western capitalist countries, where they are employees/ interest organizations negotiating with employers, and figthing for better wages andother benefits for their members.

However, if we recall the tasks of workers' congresses mentioned above, such as the approval of wage and bonus systems, and collective contracts signed between management and trade unions, one can predict that the trade unions may well be involved in the future in promoting employees' interests as they do in capitalist countries. Given the close contact between workers' congresses and trade unions, the latter may in the future become an important element of the participation system in Chinese enterprises.

The influence of interest groups in decision-making

To obtain a comparative picture of the participation and influence of different interest groups in the decision-making process in enterprises, I used the same measure in China as was adopted by the Industrial Democracy in Europe (IDE) International Research Group, reported below in the article by Bernhard Wilpert on page 355. The present author was the leader of the Finnish IDE research group.

The influence measure used was a mixture of the so-called reputational approach and the decision-making approach for

TABLE 1. The distribution of influence across levels and decision type in European countries (IDE)[1] and in China (C)[2]; and differences between means of top management (D) and workers (A) (in means)[3]

Decision type	A Workers		B Foremen		C Middle managers		D Top management		E[7] Representative bodies	E[8] Party committee	F Trade union	G[9] Level above plant	G[10] Government body	Differences D:A	
	IDE	C	IDE	C	IDE	C	IDE	C	IDE	C	C	IDE	C	IDE	C
Short-term[4]	2.5	1.4	3.2	2.3	3.5	3.1	3.6	3.8	2.5	2.1	1.4	1.8	1.9	1.1	2.4
Medium-term[5]	1.6	1.8	2.2	1.8	3.0	2.4	4.1	3.9	2.4	2.7	1.3	2.5	2.5	2.5	2.1
Long-term[6]	1.3	1.2	1.8	1.3	2.7	2.1	4.3	4.2	1.9	2.5	1.3	4.2	3.8	3.0	3.0
All 16 decisions	2.0	1.6	2.6	2.0	3.2	2.6	3.8	3.9	2.4	2.4	1.4	2.4	2.4	1.8	2.3

1. 12 countries, 134 enterprises.
2. 9 industrial enterprises.
3. Values are means of means: means of appraisers → enterprise means → national means (China) → means of 12 countries (IDE).
   Scale: 1 = no influence; 2 = little influence; 3 = moderate influence; 4 = great influence; 5 = very great influence.
4. Short-term decisions = decision Nos. 1, 4, 5, 10, 12 and 16 in Table 2.
5. Medium-term decisions = decision Nos. 2, 3, 8, 9, 11, 13 and 14 in Table 2.
6. Long-term decisions = decision Nos. 6 and 7 in Table 2.
7. For example 'workers' councils.
8. Party committee of the enterprise (see F'g. 1).
9. Advisory board and equivalent.
10. Government body immediately above the enterprise, e.g. local industrial bureau.

Sources: IDE (1981, p. 148), Laaksonen (1964), and author's interviews in China, 1980.

measuring influence (Bachrach and Baratz, 1970; Tannenbaum, 1968). In the IDE study the researchers interviewed experts selected from among managers and union representatives about the influence which organizational groups had in sixteen specified decisions. In the analysis the decisions were grouped according to time perspective into short-term, medium-term and long-term decisions (the decisions appear in Table 2). The IDE material was collected during 1976.

The gathering of the data from China in 1980 differed from the IDE study in so far as the nine Chinese enterprises represent industry as a whole and not just the metallurgical and engineering industry. The second difference was that I did not have an opportunity of interviewing representatives of managers and unions separately. The measure concerning influence in decision-making of different interest groups was written out both in Chinese and English. Those interviewed filled in the Chinese form by putting a cross in the relevant place, representing their evaluation of a group's influence under each of the sixteen questions asked, under my own guidance, without interpreter or other mediation. More detailed information concerning the collection, reliability and validity of the data is given in IDE International Research Group (1981) and Laaksonen (1984).

Participation in decision-making among various groups

In Table 1 the influence of different interest groups in different types of decision is compared as between China and twelve European countries (IDE). All the sixteen decisions are listed in Table 2.

The means in Table 1 show that, on the average, Chinese workers, foremen and middle managers (department heads, etc.) have less influence than their European counterparts in nearly all types of decision, these being aggregate variables. The only exceptions are medium-term decisions, where Chi-

nese workers seem to have more influence than Europeans. This derives from the fact that some of the Chinese enterprises studied had already moved to the new participative system, where the workers (through the workers' congress) could elect their own superior and new department heads, and examine and approve proposals concerning wages.

Since the means of top management do not differ very much according to decision types and to the means of all sixteen decisions, they can be retained as a point of comparison. If we examine the differences between means of managers and workers we notice that the greatest difference between China and European countries lies in short-term decisions, which most closely concern workers and their conditions. This may be a result of the traditional patriarchal Chinese culture in which the older men played a dominant role, controlling everything. This result can also be a sign of differences in production technology; the less mechanized and automated Chinese production process needs more control, but perhaps not only from top management.

As can be seen from Table 2, the only decisions over which Chinese workers had more influence than their European counterparts were: Decision 2 (C = 1.6, IDE = 1.2); Decision 8 (C = 3.6, IDE = 1.3); and Decision 9 (C = 2.1, IDE = 2.0). These results are reflections of the new Chinese participative system. The reform was planned for stepwise implementation: certain areas or provinces, and certain enterprises in them were selected as test units and the application of the reforms advanced gradually. The participation of workers was first applied in less strategic decisions, for example the right to elect their immediate superior, or foreman (Mean 3.6). Next come decisions concerning wages (Mean 2.1), and last appointment of a new department head (Mean 1.6).

One of the measures most used for reducing resistance to guiding organizations is the selection of personnel. The dominant role of top managers in China and Europe in

TABLE 2. The distribution of influence across levels and decisions in European countries (IDE)[1] and in China (C)[2] (in means)

Decisions	Workers		Foremen		Middle managers		Top management		Representative bodies	Party committee of the firm	Government body
	IDE	C	IDE	C	IDE	C	IDE	C	IDE	C	C
1. Improvements in immediate working conditions	2.7	2.0	3.1	2.2	3.5	3.2	4.1	4.8	3.4	3.0	3.9
2. Appointment of new department head	1.2	1.6	1.6	1.7	2.5	2.2	4.5	4.4	1.9	3.7	2.9
3. Establishment of criteria and procedures for hiring and selection of new employees	1.4	1.1	2.5	1.1	3.3	1.2	4.0	3.6	2.3	2.7	4.6
4. Whether a vocational training course can be followed	2.2	1.2	2.7	2.1	3.5	3.1	3.9	4.2	2.3	3.7	3.1
5. Transfer to another job within the plant	2.5	1.3	3.1	1.4	3.7	3.7	3.7	4.2	2.5	2.6	1.4
6. Major capital investment, e.g. an additional production line, a new plant, etc.	1.3	1.1	1.8	1.3	2.7	2.0	4.3	4.2	2.0	2.6	4.6
7. Whether a completely new product is to be made	1.3	1.5	1.7	1.5	2.8	2.5	4.3	4.6	1.9	2.9	3.4
8. Establishment of one's immediate superior	1.3	3.6	1.5	2.0	2.0	2.1	3.6	2.3	2.0	2.0	1.7
9. Changes in how much a certain wage bracket earns	2.0	2.1	2.4	2.1	3.1	2.8	4.2	4.3	2.9	3.9	3.2
10. Replacement of personal equipment or tools	2.8	1.9	3.5	2.9	3.6	3.8	3.2	3.2	2.0	1.0	1.2
11. Change in the way one or more departments are organized	1.7	1.1	2.4	1.1	3.4	1.8	4.4	4.6	2.4	2.9	2.2
12. Assignment of tasks to be performed	2.2	1.3	3.9	3.6	3.6	3.2	2.7	2.4	1.7	1.7	1.2
13. Dismissal of a colleague	1.7	1.6	2.9	1.7	3.4	2.7	4.1	4.3	3.2	3.3	2.8
14. Whether work-study techniques are to be used	2.0	1.4	2.8	2.8	3.5	3.9	3.9	3.4	2.7	1.6	1.6
15. Timing of holidays	3.2	1.2	2.9	2.8	3.1	2.8	3.1	3.1	2.2	1.0	1.0
16. Determination of working hours	2.8	1.1	2.4	1.2	2.7	1.8	3.8	4.7	3.2	1.6	1.2
All 16 decisions	2.0	1.6	2.6	2.0	3.2	2.6	3.8	3.9	2.4	2.4	2.4

1. 12 countries, 134 enterprises.
2. 9 industrial enterprises.
Source: IDE (1981, p. 148) and author's interviews in China, 1980.

Urban transport, Beijing. Patrick Zachmann/Rush.

relation to workers and middle managers emerges especially in decisions concerning personnel and organizational matters.

From Table 2 we can see how tight is top management's control of personnel and organizational matters (Decisions 2, 3, 5, 13, 16 and 11). The latter nearly always involve personnel also. Top management's dominance, for example, over middle management is even more accentuated in China than in Europe. It is interesting that 'top management's tight control over personnel policy is not usually mentioned in the management science literature' (IDE, 1981, pp. 151–2).

What do these results signify for the use of positive, and the lessening of negative, power, or for the guidance of enterprises and reducing resistance? First, the Chinese have replaced ideological power markedly by economic power (reward) in guiding organizations. They now apply a multi-sided bonus system, which had been altogether abol-ished during the Cultural Revolution. Second, to motivate employees and to reduce resistance, Chinese leaders have placed the power of selection of foremen and managers into the hands of personnel. This can have positive results if the employees also exercise influence in deciding where the enterprise is going and how. In giving more independence to enterprises and their managers, China's top leadership has put the fate of enterprises and their employees into their own hands. Most of the participating systems in the rest of the world have failed in this matter: participation in decision-making exists without the real power to make decisions.

It is interesting to note that all those decisions where the influence of the party committee was greatest at the end of 1980 were related to personnel matters and could be used as instruments controlling the allocation of ideological resources (power) in enterprises, to reward, train and promote those

In a radio factory, 1982. Patrick Zachmann/Rush.

who were ideologically 'pure'. The four decisions in which the party enterprise committee was most influential compared with top managers can be seen in Table 3.

In evaluating the leeway of top managers we must remember that, in a way, managers mediate party power, since in the nine Chinese enterprises studied the top manager was either the first secretary (in three firms) or the second secretary (in six firms) of the powerful party enterprise committee.

We can conclude from these results that actors who wish to retain dominant power in a society or organization will first of all seek to control personnel resources. In a socialist country like China it has been the party that has controlled these resources, partly directly and partly through top managers originally selected by the party. In European countries top management also tightly controls personnel decisions. In capitalist countries top management represents the owners, their capital

TABLE 3. Decisions in which party committee was most influential, 1980

Decision (see Table 2)	Means	
	Party committee	Top manager
Appointment of new department head (Decision 2)	3.7	4.4
Whether a vocational training course can be followed (during working hours) (Decision 4)	3.7	4.2
Changes in how much a certain wage bracket earns (Decision 9)	3.9	4.3
Dismissal of a colleague (Decision 13)	3.3	4.3
All 16 decisions	2.4	3.9

Independent workers in a Shanghai lane. Patrick Zachmann/Rush.

Advertising Chinese high technology. Patrick Zachmann/Rush.

and ideology. In a socialist country top managers represent not only the party (ideological resources), but also government bodies (economic resources), which are in turn subordinated to the party. From this analysis an interesting conclusion emerges: major strategic decisions concerning, for example, capital investment, turn out not to be the most important, especially from the power-play angle. People come first because they make, and will continue to make, all decisions (Laaksonen, 1984).

Against this background we can say that the Chinese have made bold and far-reaching decisions by giving the power of selecting personnel for important posts to the workers' congresses, and by divorcing the party from the strategic and operative decision-making of enterprises. In terms of a socialist system they have leaped into the great unknown.

One may reflect on how the power structure of Chinese enterprises will change in the future under the new participation system. From Table 1 and the foregoing analysis, we have learned that three influence centres exist in Chinese enterprises: top management, the party committee and the government body supervising the enterprise. The latter are especially important in strategic (long-term) matters. In what relation has their influence stood to each other and other interest groups of enterprises? Has the influence of one group been positively related to that of another group, so that the influence of both has either grown or decreased jointly, or has a variable-sum game been played? The alternative is the zero-sum game, whereby any increase in the power of one actor is made at the expense of another. Behind this type of game may lie the idea that aggregate power resources available to both parties represent a cake; if one gets a larger slice, less remains for the other.

Theories derived from Marxist ideas of class antagonisms would suggest a zero-sum

TABLE 4. Inter-level correlations of influence for all decisions in nine Chinese industrial enterprises (C) and in European countries (IDE) (product moment correlation)

Decisions		A C	A IDE	B C	B IDE	C C	C IDE	D C	D IDE	E C	E IDE	F IDE
Workers	A											
Foremen	B	0.58	0.44									
Middle management	C	0.20	0.17	0.31	0.37							
Top management	D	0.23	−0.32	0.17	−0.02	−0.11	0.02					
Party committee	E	0.37		−0.06		0.17		0.08				
Representative bodies	E		−0.37		−0.07		0.59		−0.05			
Trade union	F	0.09		−0.28		0.14		−0.07		−0.01		
Government body	G	0.18		−0.24		0.13		−0.08		−0.08		
Level above plant	G		0.06		−0.04		−0.08		0.18		0.26	0.06

Sources: IDE (1981, p. 159) and Laaksonen (1984).

game in capitalist organizations, especially between those organizational levels which represent the interests of labour and capital or workers and top management (IDE, 1981, pp. 30, 157–8). The inter-level correlations in Table 4 seem to support this hypothesis. In capitalist European countries (IDE) the correlation between the influence of top management and workers is negative (−0.32): the greater the influence of top management, the less that of workers. In socialist China it is positive (0.23). One of the crucial differences between the influence structures in European capitalist countries and socialist China then, lies in the position of top management. In both systems a tendency towards the formation of two main power coalitions can be observed. In European countries (IDE, 1981, p. 158):

One at the bottom of the organization where alliances between workers and supervisors are more or less supported by middle management, and another coalition at the top of the organization where alliances between representative bodies and external groups are partly supported by bodies at the corporate level. Top management lies between these two power coalitions, partly isolated, partly in opposition to them.

In China a similar power coalition exists at the base of the organization hierarchy; between workers, foremen and middle management in that order. Corresponding correlations are: 0.58 and 0.31. But the coalition at the top is different from that of European countries, in which all the correlations of top management with other groups were negative except one with middle management (0.2). In China all the coefficients of top management are positive with the same exception—middle management—but a slightly negative direction (−0.11). In interpreting the results we must, however, remember that the number of Chinese enterprises is merely nine, so only the highest correlations can statistically be meaningful.

As earlier analysis showed, a very strong power coalition between the party, top management and supervisory government bodies exists in China. The correlation between the influence of the party committee and of top management is the highest in Table 4 (0.59). The main source of power in this coalition has been the party, because general managers were appointed through it. Further, government bodies supervising enterprises were also subordinated to the party. In China top management has therefore represented and mediated the power of the party, the influence of which originated from the highest national organ, the Central Committee of the Communist Party and its First Secretary or equivalent.

Chinese plans to divorce party administration from that of government and enterprises are really far-reaching in a socialist country. Whence is 'new' Chinese top management to derive its power? Probably from independence in the guidance and control of the various resources of enterprises. However, very much will depend on how the new participation systems with workers' congresses and others, which are to share the right to elect the managers and other enterprise supervisors is implemented. Will elections be conducted according to the principle of the best person for the job or the most politically suitable for the most powerful position? This will be a crucial question for the development of China.

References

BACHRACH, P.; BARATZ, M. S. 1970. *Power and Poverty: Theory and Practice.* New York/Oxford, Oxford University Press.

BLAU, P. M. 1964. *Exchange and Power in Social Life.* New York, John Wiley.

BURT, R. S. 1977. Power in a Social Typology. In: R. J. Liebert and A. W. Imerschein (eds.), *Power, Paradigms and Community Research.* Beverly Hills, Sage.

CENTRAL COMMITTEE OF CPC 1983. Decision on Party Consolidation. Second Plenary Session of the 12th Central Committee of the Communist Party of China (11–12 October 1983). Beijing, Xinhua News Agency, 14 October.

CHEN, P. K. 1982. *Industrial Relations and Participation in China.* The Chinese University of Hong Kong, Department of General Business Management and Personnel Management. (Mimeo.)

CONSTITUTION OF THE COMMUNIST PARTY OF CHINA. 1982. *Twelfth National Congress of the CPC.* Beijing, Foreign Languages Press.

EMERSON, R. M. 1962. Power-dependence Relations. *American Sociological Review,* Vol..27, pp. 31–41.

ETZIONI, A. 1961. *A Comparative Analysis of Complex Organizations.* New York, The Free Press.

FRENCH, J. R. R.; RAVEN, B.

1959. The Bases of Social Power. In: D. Cartwright (ed.), *Studies in Social Power.* Ann Arbor, University of Michigan Press.

IDE International Research Group. 1981. *Industrial Democracy in Europe.* Oxford, Clarendon Press.

KORPI, W. 1974. Conflict and the Balance of Power. *Acta Sociologica*, Vol. 17, No. 2.

KOTTER, J. P. 1979. *Power in Management. How to Understand, Acquire and Use It.* New York, AMACOM.

LAAKSONEN, O. 1977. The Power Structure of Chinese Enterprises. *International Studies of Management and Organization* (White Plains, N.Y., Sharpe), Vol. 7, No. 1, pp. 71–90. M.E.

LAAKSONEN, O. 1984. The Management and Power Structure of Chinese Enterprises during and after the Cultural Revolution. *Organization Studies*, Vol. 5, No. 1.

Main Documents of the Third Session of the Fifth National People's Congress of the People's Republic of China. 1980. Beijing, Foreign Languages Press.

PAN, C. 1980. Experimentation on Reforming the Economic Management System in the People's Republic of China. Beijing, State Economic Commission, PRC. (Unpublished report.)

Provisional Regulations Concerning Congresses of Workers and Staff Members in State-owned Industrial Enterprises. 15 June 1981, Beijing.

RUS, V. 1980. Positive and Negative Power. *Organization Studies*, Vol. 1, No. 1.

STEWART, R. 1967. *Managers and Their Jobs: A Study of Similarities and Differences in the Ways Managers Spend Their Time.* London, Macmillan.

TANNENBAUM, A. S. 1968. *Control in Organizations.* New York, McGraw-Hill.

ZHAO ZIYANG. 1981. *China's Economy and Development Principles.* Beijing, Foreign Languages Press.

[24]

WHAT DO THE BRITISH WANT FROM

PARTICIPATION AND INDUSTRIAL DEMOCRACY?
PREFACE

This project undertaken by Frank Heller, Malcolm Wilders (both of the Tavistock Institute), Peter Abell (Birmingham University) and Malcolm Warner (Administrative Staff College Henley; and Brunel University), financed by the Anglo-German Foundation, has been part of a wider study of Industrial Democracy in Europe. The Thyssen and Ford Foundations contributed to the international costs, but each autonomous country team obtained separate financial support. Bernhard Wilpert (International Institute of Management, Berlin West), acted as co-ordinator: for further details see Appendix I.

This report was the joint responsibility of the British team involved in the U.K. investigation, who formulated the research strategy and its direction. The U.K. field-investigation was co-ordinated by Frank Heller; both parts of the report and the technical appendices were drafted by Malcolm Wilders, (in collaboration with the other members of the team, Heller, Abell and Warner). The team would particularly like to thank the sponsoring institutions involved (Tavistock Institute, Birmingham University and the Administrative Staff College, Henley) for their assistance and encouragement in supporting the project. We would also like to thank Bob Mays and Mike James for their help in data-analysis and Wendy Jackson and Sue Parkin-Moore for their secretarial support. The findings presented here have been set out as far as has been feasible for the non-specialist reader:—the more technical details have been placed in further appendices.

1. INTRODUCTION

Since in Britain, the major political parties as well as the employers' organisations and trade unions are in favour of re-examining the present system of industrial relations, the real question to be answered over the next few years is not whether something should be done, but *what* can be done.

Moreover, it is widely agreed that what is now called employee participation has to be different from the schemes of joint consultation that sprang up in large numbers during the 1950s and often petered out a decade or so later. What should the difference be? The growth of plant based collective bargaining during the last twenty years has been extended to some subjects which could be handled either through the traditional systems of negotiation i.e. collective bargaining, or by a representative system of participation. There are now advocates for merging these two systems, while others prefer to keep them separate. Are there soundly based facts that could help people to make this decision and deepen the public debate?

1

The first problem associated with the development of the public discussion on participation over the last couple of years is an over-emphasis on legal, historical and political issues relating to it. This over-emphasis has tended to exclude consideration of factual findings based on empirical research.

Even when discussion has been based on practical experience, it has almost invariably been confined to journalistically interesting but unrepresentative case studies of enterprises like Scott Bader Commonwealth or the Fairfield experiment of Upper Clyde Shipbuilders or the John Lewis Partnership. Such case studies are useful to students of industrial relations but few managers or trade unionists would seriously credit them with any chance of a really wide application to British industry. The Scott Bader Commonwealth, for instance, depended on the emergence of a very unusual man, and the John Lewis Partnership methods are probably only applicable to an aspect of the retail trade.

In addition, the harsher economic climate, among other things, has led to several experiments such as the Kirkby, and more recently the Meriden cases being pushed closer to outright failure or contraction. The advent of a Conservative Government has also meant that such worker cooperative experiments can no longer expect state-suupprt in the form of subsidies.

As far as the attempt to 'harmonize' company legislation with that of our EEC partners is concerned, the very fact of late entry into the Community may have put the case for 'European' arrangements for worker representation at a disadvantage.

'Participation' has also become a rather emotive term in many quarters; both positively and negatively often meaning many things to many persons. The ideological intensity of the issue has been without parallel for many years, at least in many management, and some union, circles. Is it a question of the inherent conservatism of British managers, and indeed trade union officials? Is the *status quo* as firmly gelled in industrial attitudes as many imagine? Is a cooler, more clinical examination of these questions possible? This study tried to look beneath cliches and sloganizing. There is little evidence that the problem will simply go away whatever the composition of the Government.

Another reason why public discussion on this subject has been very inconclusive and impracticable is the preference for fashionable labels to cover an unmanageable mixture of different ingredients. Umbrella terms like industrial democracy and, to some extent, participation, have been used to describe everything from schemes of workers' control advocated by a minute section

2

of the work force, to schemes like 'flexitime', which have become very popular in many countries. It is, of course, true that all these schemes contain some element of 'involvement' but one has to stretch the meaning of democracy and participation very considerably to accommodate such diversity.

2.   RECENT BRITISH DEVELOPMENTS

Although recent legislation has formalized and consolidated the influence and position of unions (e.g. Employment Protection Act, 1975, Health and Safety Act, 1974, Trade Union and Labour Relations Act, 1974), there remains no 'main' legal basis for participation in British companies, unlike their European counterparts.[1] Apart from Whitleyism, some developments in consultation, British workers have seen little that compares with the German arrangements, for example as far as formal, legally prescribed procedures are concerned. However, recent legislation would seem to indicate a growing tendency towards establishing legal rights for participative procedures.

It is hard to predict the outcomes of the debate, as the polemic is conducted in rather different terms. Those in favour of an extension of industrial democracy argue that the worker should be more involved in decision-making in the workplace and through this in the broader economy and society. Many Labour Party politicians and union leaders back this, although a minority are sceptical either about the ends or the means to achieve this. It would be true to say that trade union activists are probably also divided in their attitudes. The Conservatives may be formulating their own proposals in this area, emphasizing company autonomy in the implementation of such schemes. Similar views are held by the main employers' body, the C.B.I.

Apart from a limited number of isolated experiments in industrial democracy, Britain has experienced relatively little development of formal participation schemes. The growing interest in industrial democracy may be seen as one at attempt to improve British economic performance by fostering better industrial relations. Others would go further and advocate the development of formal participation as the 'right' of labour to be involved in decisions affecting their place of work. Whichever view one takes, it is probably true to say that improvements in education have lead to people wanting a greater say in their destiny and this includes the workplace. It is claimed, on the basis of repeated survey evidence, that workers want a greater control over what affects them in the immediate work context.

Recent discussions concerning the extension of industrial democracy have been heavily dominated by the Bullock Report[2] on industrial democracy. The *Majority Report* recommended that employees should have the right to

3

elect trade union based worker directors in companies employing more than 2,000 employees on a 2X + Y basis, i.e. an equal number of worker and share-holder representatives, plus a quota of independent directors. The three employer members of the Committee issued a *Minority Report* dissenting from these main recommendations.

The original T.U.C. proposal had echoed the German D.G.B. in advocating 50% union representation on Supervisory Boards.[3] The Employers have also argued for representation on such a top board, rather than on a single, main Board, but for only one-third representation of all employees (including management) and they also favour direct election by the employees not through trade union channels. In addition, some employers see the 50% worker representation as a 'rubicon' of power, the crossing of which is tantamount to 'back-door nationalisation'.

The question of industrial democracy in public corporations had also been reviewed by another committee running in parallel to the Bullock deliber-ations, and envisaged trade unionists from those industries being elected to their boards. In addition, there is also a debate about whether employees of local councils should have representation on these democratically elected bodies, as opposed to domination by the citizens' representatives.

Other bodies, leaning towards the political centre, such as the Industrial Society, the Industrial Participation Association and similar groups, lead the debate for more employee consultation, even participation. Many con-ferences, both business-oriented as well as academic, have been held on the topic. Few social science journals, political reviews and management magazines have been without their quota of articles on the topic.

Although there was considerable delay between the publication of the Bullock Report and the appearance of legislative proposals, the recent Govern-ment issued a White Paper[4] on Industrial Democracy in May 1978 carrying a firm commitment to introducing legislation on a fallback basis. Essentially, the document followed the general proposals of Bullock concerning workers directors, but differs in favouring a two-tier company structure. In addition, the document places on companies employing more than 500 people, an obligation to discuss with employee representatives policy issues affecting 'employees of the business before decisions are made'. However, the new Conservative Government seems unlikely to pursue this approach to employee participation.

Whether the present public debate in Britain will lead to significant changes in the industrial relations system, is difficult to anticipate. The gentle pres-sures of the European Economic Community may exert some influence and

4

trade unions may increasingly see advantages in having a "foot in the door" of the decision making process other than through collective bargaining and shop steward influence. The attitudes of bodies representing managers and the industrial establishment are not yet clearly focussed on particular partici- pation solutions and are likely to undergo various changes in the future.[5]

We have now entered a crucial stage in the important process of reaching decisions concerning industrial democracy on a national and/or industrial level; even a decision *not* to introduce any structural changes would be an important one. The future of our industrial relations system is likely to be decisively influenced by the policies currently emerging from the public debate, and we believe that results of carefully carried-out empirical research have a role to play in this debate.

WHAT DO THE BRITISH WANT FROM PARTICIPATION AND INDUSTRIAL DEMOCRACY?

PART I

A Field-Study in 14 Companies selected from the Metal Working Industry, Banking and Insurance

3.   INTRODUCTION

The first part of this report on participation and industrial democracy is based on a far-ranging research project involving twelve countries[6]. Such a comparative study has rarely been undertaken on such a scale. Since these topics are currently receiving a great deal of attention from industrialists, trade unions and the government, we hope the findings will make a useful contribution to the public debate.

The research deliberately concentrated on two very different sectors of the economy: manufacturing (metal) and service (banking and insurance). One hundred and thirty four companies and nearly 10,000 people took part in the twelve countries. In Britain, we worked with over 700 respondents from 14 companies[7]. The present report will deal only with the British data.

There are three main questions to which the present report is addressed. First, how much and what kind of participation (that is to say involvement in decision making) do people experience in their work? Second, how much do they want? Third, what other industrial relations type factors are relevant to matters of participation; for instance, incentives and job satisfaction?

The findings have policy implications for those concerned with establishing or running schemes of employee participation as well as for government legislators.

4.   RESULTS[8]

4.1.   The extent of participation[9]

How much influence do people at various levels of organisation have over decisions? How much influence would they like to have?

We have assessed the answers on a scale from 1 to 6 as follows:
1 = not involved at all
2 = informed beforehand
3 = can give opinion
4 = opinion taken into account

8

5 = take part with equal weight
6 = decide on my own

Each person described how much influence he had over 16 carefully chosen decisions (for a list see Appendix One). These 16 decisions fall into three broad categories:

Personal decisions: includes assignment of tasks, transfer of workers and hours of work etc.

Goal or tactical decisions: includes departmental organisation, dismissals, use of work study etc.

Policy decisions: includes new products or services and major capital investment.

4.1.1. **The actual involvement** of workers, foremen and managers in these three types of decision is shown in Figure 1.

Overall, it is clear that the amount of influence available to our respondents is very small. This is true even at managerial level.[10] It will be seen that on personal decisions managers can give their opinions and these are sometimes taken into account. These results are based on averages so that some managers have more and others less than this amount of influence. The average manager has substantially less influence on goal oriented decisions and less still on policy decisions. On policy decisions he is informed beforehand, but he rarely has an opportunity to give an opinion.

As we move to foremen and workers, we see that their involvement in the decisions process is, as expected, noticeably lower than managers.

On personal decisions like work conditions, workers are frequently. informed but do not often get an opportunity to give an opinion. On goal and policy decisions they are sometimes given information but are usually not involved at all.[11]

4.1.2. The amount of participation varies very startlingly with the nature of decisions. It is possible to illustrate this by referring to individual decisions. Forty percent of our total sample, for instance, can make their own decision about holidays, but only 2% have this amount of autonomy over changes in departmental organisation; and only 6% can make a decision on their own about being transferred to another job. At the other extreme, only 7% are not at all involved in work study decisions; while 21% report that they are not at all involved in

9

FIGURE 1 ACTUAL AND DESIRED INVOLVEMENT (MEAN SCORES)
IN DIFFERENT TYPES OF DECISION

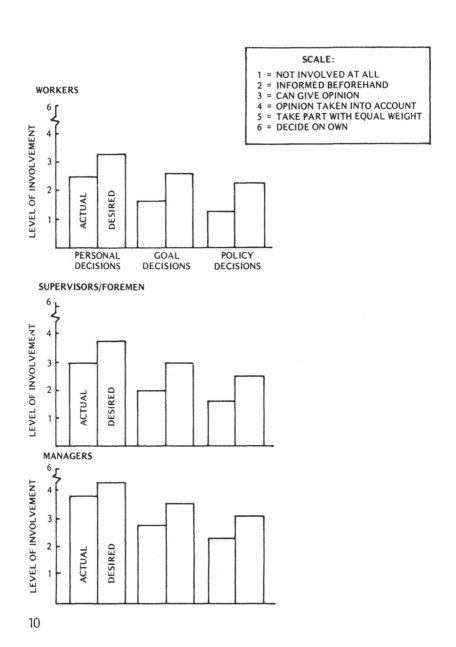

10

decisions relating to improvements in working conditions of their group.

While the last two findings are more unexpected than the previous ones, the important fact, to which we will return in our conclusions, is that one cannot usefully generalise about participative practices without considering specific decisions.

4.1.3. Examination of the *desired level of involvement* indicated a similar hierarchical pattern to that of actual involvement (see Figure 1). Furthermore, the different patterns of influence exercised over personal, goal and policy decisions are maintained. At the same time, it appears that the desire for greater involvement in all types of decisions is very moderate. On average, people seem to want only a single step increment in their involvement. For example, workers want to increase their influence over personal decisions from "being informed beforehand" to "giving their opinions", but they do not go so far as asking that these opinions are taken into account. A similar progression is indicated by supervisors on policy decisions. They want to increase their influence from generally "not being involved at all" to "being informed beforehand". This would seem to indicate an evolutionary process to the wider involvement of all job levels in decision-making. The suggestion, that increasing employee involvement in decision-making will open the floodgates of demands for greater involvement, would seem unfounded.

4.1.4. The two sectors (metal manufacture and service) differ in actual and desired involvement.[12] This is a reflection of the type and organisation of the work being performed. For instance, service workers experience higher levels of involvement over decisions relating to hours of work; this relates to the operation of flexible hours in this sector. In contrast, hours of work in the metal sector are generally tied to the technology of production. Another example is the higher involvement of management in the metal sector concerning major capital expenditure, which probably reflects the greater autonomy many of the plants are able to exercise. Plants in the service sector tend to be linked to a centralised policy making unit covering most decision areas, whilst the main control over metal plants is by way of approval of overall budget submissions.

4.2 **The importance of hierarchy**

What are the differences in influence between the various groups inside a plant?

11

It was of course expected that perceived differences in influence between workers, foremen and managers would reflect their position in the organisational pyramid and would be similar to the self assessment of influence shown in Figure 1. All the people interviewed asked to assess the overall distribution of influence various groups within their plant and outside exercised over plant matters.

4.2.1.   The difference in influence from one level to the next is moderate (see Figure 2). However, the difference between workers and management is considerable.

4.2.2.   It was interesting that boards of directors are seen as having extremely high level of influence over plant decisions. This was unexpected and when we followed this up and confronted our respondents with this finding, we were given evidence that this perception was incorrect. Boards do not concern themselves with the majority of plant level decisions in our sample of companies. This kind of mistaken perception is important, since it is likely to affect demands for board room representation; and is almost certainly reflected in the current debate on industrial democracy.

4.3   **Trade Union involvement in Decisions**

To what extent do people want trade unions involved in decisions? Are there decisions considered more suitable for direct personal participation by managers and workers? Are there major differences as to the decision areas considered suitable for trade union involvement by managers and workers?

Trade unions are, in general, seen to be more influential through the representative systems than workers through informal channels of participation. This is unlikely to be simply a reflection of greater trade union militancy, since there was little evidence of this in our sample of companies. Furthermore, recent legislative developments for extending participation like the Health & Safety at Work Act 1974 have tended to be based on union representation. Therefore, in terms of extending participation, it is of considerable importance to assess the potential for expanding the range of issues trade unions are currently involved in. Individuals were asked to assess over the 16 decision areas whether or not they would like the trade union(s), through the shop steward or negotiating machinery, to have a say in the particular decision.

4.3.1.   As might be expected, in general, managers were considerably less positive in their desire for trade union involvement in personal, goal

12

and policy types of decisions than were workers. However, although managers and supervisors in both sectors (particularly the service sector) are strongly against trade union involvement in policy matters, their opposition is more variable with regard to personal and goal decisions.   In particular, substantially over half of all managers and supervisors were in favour of trade union involvement in matters concerning working conditions and hours of work (personal decisions) and changes in the earnings of a wage group, dismissals and the use of work study (goal decisions).   Other personal decisions, such as training, permanent transfer of workers, task assignments, and goal decisions such as the establishment of hiring procecures, and departmental reorganisation were not seen as areas for trade union involvement.

FIGURE 2 OVERALL INFLUENCE OF SPECIFIED GROUPS (MEAN
SCORES) WITHIN THE PLANTS

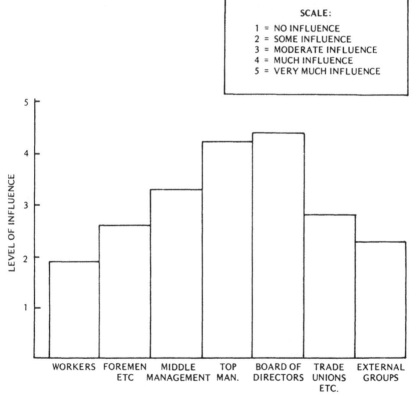

SCALE:
1 = NO INFLUENCE
2 = SOME INFLUENCE
3 = MODERATE INFLUENCE
4 = MUCH INFLUENCE
5 = VERY MUCH INFLUENCE

The role of trade unions in the metal sector would seem to be clearly indicated by the desire of the majority of workers in this sector for trade union involvement on *all* 16 decisions[13].   In particular, workers in the metal sector indicated matters concerning working conditions (79%), transfer of workers (60%), changes in earnings of a wage group (70%), departmental reorganisation (61%), dismissals (73%), the use of work study (68%), and hours of work (68%) had high priority in terms of union involvement.   Workers in the service sector displayed a more restricted range of issues considered suitable for trade union involvement, being concerned mainly with working conditions (70%), hours of work (56%), changes in the earnings of a wage group (80%), dismissals (74%), and the use of work study or equivalent techniques (69%).   Interestingly, these are the same issues on which managers and supervisors favour trade union involvement in decision making.

There was some indication that workers in the service sector desired trade union involvement in policy matters such as major capital investment (47%) and new products or services (47%). Metal workers were slightly more favourable to such involvement, with 50% and 53% respectively indicating a desired trade union involvement in such policy issues. As stated earlier, little support was found among managers and supervisors for such involvement, particularly in the service sector.

It should be noted that on a number of decision areas, particularly high levels of uncertainty (i.e. don't know, no opinion) were recorded[14]. This type of response was largely restricted to workers' replies (particularly in the service sector) and tended to concentrate on issues such as the appointment of a department head, capital investment, new products and the appointment of a superior. The high levels of uncertainty are probably reflections of the lack of familiarity with decision-making in such areas[15].

4.4.   Disagreements over Decisions

What is the level of disagreement experienced by companies? Are there particular decision areas which give rise to particularly high levels of disagreement?

We asked people to indicate which of the 16 decisions cocvered were usually reached through disagreement.   The research further identified who (i.e. workers, supervisors, managers, unions, etc.) finally resolves those issues which are subject to disagreement.

14

4.4.1. Over all sixteen decisions, respondents indicated a relatively low level of disagreement. Less than a third said that such decisions were usually reached through disagreement. However, a number of specific decision areas did appear more likely to involve at least moderate levels of disagreement.[16] For both sectors, the main areas of disagreement were changes in how much a certain grade (wage group) shall earn (beyond existing collective bargaining agreements) and the use of work study or equivalent technique. Other areas of moderate disagreement were the permanent transfer of workers and dismissals in the metal sector, and major capital investment in the service sector. Departmental reorganisation and the replacement of personal equipment in the service sector, and assignment of tasks in the metal sector also appeared to be potential problem areas.

In situations where disagreements did occur, the majority of the 16 decisions were resolved at the *level above the plant* (i.e. Headquarters, Board of Directors) in the service sector and by *top management* in the metal sector. The main exception to this procedure were decisions concerning dismissals which was seen in the main as the province of middle management.

5. THE CONSEQUENCES OF PARTICIPATION

What are the consequences of participation for increasing people's knowledge of plant activities? Do people accept decisions more readily? Is the quality of the decisions improved? Are the interests of employees better represented? Do employees have a greater say in plant decisions? To what extent do representative forms of participation (e.g. trade unions, works consultative councils etc.) conflict with direct (possibly daily) participation in plant decisions?

5.1. Representative Participation

The following analysis concerns eleven plants in which the main channel of participation was via the trade union machinery. The remaining three metal plants had developed some form of works consultative council, and will be dealt with at a later stage.[17]

Most people saw the consequences of trade union participation positively. Over three-quarters of all respondents stated that employees' interests were better represented *via* the trade union machinery. Furthermore, approximately two-thirds also felt that people knew more about plant activities and accepted decisions more readily as a result of trade union involvement. However, views about the role of trade union representation in improving the quality

15

of decisions, and in giving people a greater say in plant decisions, were less positive. Just over half of all respondents gave positive replies to these two questions. There did not appear to be major differences between the two sectors (service and metal manufacturing), although there was some indication that service sector representatives were more likely to feel people knew more about plant activities due to the work of the trade unions.

Although there was a fairly high level of agreement about the positive consequences of trade union participation, job level appeared to influence certain replies. Managers were less inclined than other levels to indicate that the work of the trade unions had improved the quality of decisions, or that decisons were accepted more easily (Table 1). On the other hand, a higher percentage of managers than lower levels thought that employee interests are better represented through a combination of trade union and direct involvement.

These findings should be seen against the views that in general respondents *did not* feel particularly strongly that trade union

TABLE 1   Consequences of Trade Union and Personal Participation in Plant Decisions, by job level.

	Managers		Supervisors		Workers	
	Repres-entative	Per-sonal	Repres-entative	Per-sonal	Repres-entative	Per-sonal
	%	%	%	%	%	%
People know more about what is going on in the plant	60	89	69	79	68	50
People accept decisions more easily	58	76	61	69	71	53
The quality of decisions has improved	42	78	50	64	61	56
The interests of employees are better represented	79	80	76	72	76	57
Employees have a greater say in plant activities	53	65	56	50	56	38
(% base)	(107)	(143)	(159)	(193)	(313)	(357)

16

negotiating procedures were given a real chance by management in their company. Approximately a third of both supervisors and workers felt such procedures were given a real chance, with a further 46% stating they were to some extent.

5.2   **Personal Participation**

Approximately two-thirds of all respondents felt that personal participation in plant decisions increased people's knowledge of plant activities, enabled decisions to be more readily accepted, improved the quality of decisions and provided a "better" represent-ation of employee interests. Slightly less than half took the view that employees had a greater say in plant decisions as a consequence of their personal involvement. People in the service sector were more positive than those from the metal sector on all questions relating to the consequences of their personal involvement in plant decisions. For instance, 69% of the service sector compared to 58% from the metal sector gave a positive reply to the question whether or not decisions were more readily accepted. The sector differences were particularly noticeable on the question of whether employees had a greater say in plant decisions — 58% and 41% respectively gave positive replies.

Results show that workers have a less positive view of direct partici-pation than those at higher levels in organisations. In addition, it would appear that there were occasions when no information was provided through the channel of personal participation. Just under a quarter of all informants (and slightly more for workers) indicated information was rarely or never forthcoming in change situations. On the positive side, the results show that the majority felt that where they had an opinion different from their superior/boss con-cerning their work, they could often or always say so (64%). Clearly, managers and supervisors (74%) felt they could more freely express their opinions than did workers (57%).

5.3.   **Relative Importance of Participation**

When one considers the overall consequences derived from the two forms of participation, managers and supervisors tended to favour their own personal participation as increasing employees' knowledge of plant activities, improving the quality of decisions etc. Workers thought that more positive results were achieved via the trade union machinery than by their personal involvement. However, these two forms of participation were not really alternatives. They had the appearance of being complementary. This is interesting because it

17

suggests that this issue which has preoccupied people in public discussion is not based on an irreconcilable conflict. There is almost certainly room for both.

6.   EVALUATION OF PARTICIPATION

How satisfied are people with the functioning of direct participation in their department? How satisfied are people with trade union procedures? Do people feel their interests are represented by the trade unions? A number of questions concerning the functioning of the two systems were asked, some of which have already been referred to in the previous section.[18]

6.1   Approximately half the answers we obtained showed that people were satisfied with the functioning of direct participation in their department (53%). A similar proportion were satisfied with the functioning of trade union negotiating procedures (49%). However, a further 28% were dissatisfied with direct participation and 21% with trade union procedures.

6.2   As might be expected from earlier findings, there is a differential satisfaction with the two systems of participation according to job level (Table 2). In general, however, there was a significant association between higher degrees of involvement and higher job satisfaction.

TABLE 2   Satisfaction with Direct Participation and Trade Union Negotiating Procedures.

	Managers		Supervisors		Workers	
Satisfied with direct participation	63%		57%		47%	
Satisfied with trade union negotiating procedures		43%		47%		52%
(% base)	(46)	(138)	(124)	(190)	(269)	(359)

7.   SOME SECTOR RELATIVITIES

Difference between the two sectors were expected, but are nevertheless of value in understanding the industrial relations climate in the U.K. We have already shown that it is not easy to generalise about participation, without

18

taking account of level in organisation and type of decision. The following brief details of the two sectors are given to further emphasise the importance of relativities (i.e. findings that apply only under certain conditions) [19].

7.1   The metal sector's tendency to conflict and strained relations at work is well known, particularly in Britain, and this is confirmed by our findings. The causes of the discontent and why it should differ from the service sector are not well understood, and our research makes a contribution towards a better understanding of these factors so that remedial action can be taken.

7.2   The findings suggest that the stresses and strains of the metal manufacturing sector have some connection with its relatively poor flow of information, low levels of forward planning and a lack of clear job descriptions. Furthermore, the metal sector compared with services has not managed to transmit a clear picture of its company policies, its organisational structure or the critical issue of who has the authority to make decisions, nor are people regularly informed about the quality of their work. It is likely that the metal sector's problem is not simply one of communication, although the findings would seem to be relevant to discussions on the disclosure of information.

7.3   In addition to the problems of communication, the metal sector experiences a more marked physical separation of senior management from the work place, and less stability in organisational structure. The metal sector has a long history and this may account for a reduced willingness on the part of management to adopt modern methods of adminstration. This interpretation is supported by the startling finding that 72% of the service sector sample say that plant management is satisfactory, compared with 40% who are prepared to say as much for the metal sector. There are similar though smaller differences in the two sectors' judgement on the capability of the immediate superior.

7.4   Further findings suggest that contrasting management-worker relations in the two sectors may reflect different motivational patterns and differences in the ability of organizations to cope with changes in aspirations. Whilst salary and stability of employment were seen to be of great importance to everybody, opportunities for promotion and opportunities for utilising one's skill were rated considerably higher by the service sector sample. Since the service sector gives high scores to satisfaction with their job and their

19

organization, it would seem that their aspirations are not frustrated by inadequate organizational measures.

7.5   In addition, the difference in the perceived role of the trade union in the two sectors needs to be assessed. Certain differences have already emerged in the text. Further support is given by analysis of situations where respondents have personal grievances (complaints). The majority of service workers sought the support of their superiors (76%), with only 10% seeking union support. In contrast, metal workers were more likely to seek union support (47%), with only 39% stating they would approach their superiors.

8.   CONCLUSIONS FROM PART I

The results can be summarised in five main conclusions which are briefly described. In the final section of this report, we will discuss the implications of these results for British organisations and policy makers.

8.1   The total amount of involvement in decision making at work is astonishingly low. There is evidence that our results are typical of the population in middle sized organisations in the manufacturing and service sector of British industry.

8.2   At the same time, there is *little evidence* that workers (or any other level of organisation) want to have a *radically* different degree of influence or control over decisions. While people want more say over personal decisions close to their daily job than over the more distant goal and policy decisions, even the demand for influence over personal decisions is fairly moderate. Nevertheless, the gap between actual and desired participation shows that there is scope for substantial improvement.

8.3   The consequences of greater involvement are *positive*. Our findings show that one can expect better knowledge by employees of what goes on in the organisation, a more ready acceptance of decisions, a higher satisfaction with work, and, above all, a better quality of decision.

8.4   While managers prefer direct person to person participation and workers prefer representative participation, the two methods are complementary rather than opposed to each other.

20

8.5 Finally, several of our findings are dependent on certain specified circumstances. That is to say, generalisation about participation covering all levels, types of industry and types of decisions must be avoided; they can be very misleading. The difference due to personal goal and policy decisions mentioned in 8.2 above, is an example.

8.6 In addition to these five main conclusions, there are other interesting findings which we describe in the Appendix 1 to this report.

WHAT DO THE BRITISH WANT FROM PARTICIPATION AND INDUSTRIAL DEMOCRACY?

PART II

A National Random Household Survey

9.　INTRODUCTION

The second part of this report deals with a parallel study of industrial democracy using a large national random household survey of people in full-time employment. As with Part I, the present research has been developed from an extensive project involving twelve countries[20]. The topics covered in Part II are of equal importance to those dealt with in Part I and we hope the findings will also make a useful contribution to the public debate and the development of policy on employee participation at both company and government level.[21]

The problem of industrial democracy is one which has faced both social scientists and practitioners for sometime. In Part I, we set out some of the issues associated with the question of employee participation in general as well as in the British context. To refresh the readers' memory, we may refer to the following characterization of the issue:

> "Apart from a limited number of isolated experiments in industrial democracy, Britain has experienced relatively little development of formal participation schemes. The growing interest in industrial democracy may be seen as one attempt to improve British economic performance by fostering better industrial relations. Others would go further and advocate the development of formal participation as the 'right' of labour to be involved in decisions affecting their place of work. Whichever view one takes, it is probably true to say that improvements in education have lead to people wanting a greater say in their destiny and this includes the workplace".[22]

As with Part I, three main questions are posed. How much and what kind of participation (that is to say involvement in decision making) do people experience in their work? How much do they want? What other industrial relations type factors are relevant to matters of participation for instance skill utilisation and incentives.

24

More specifically the national survey was undertaken with two objectives:—

(i) to provide a matching for the in-depth field work data collected on a sample of companies (see Part I)
(ii) to shed light on some current controversial issues in industrial relations.

In addition, information was collected on recent developments with regard to worker directors and consumer representation on the Board of Directors of large companies. A section of the survey also re-tested parts of an earlier well-known international study dealing with social trust, adolescent partici- pation and school participation, which had highlighted substantial differences between Germany and Britain.[23]

10   RESULTS[24]

10.1   Involvement in Decision-Making

In the in-depth study of 14 companies already described,[25] respon- dents' involvement in 16 decision areas were investigated; they ranged from personal decisions (e.g. improvements in work condi- tions, replacement of personal equipment or tools, etc.) through goal decisions (e.g. appointment of a new department head, use of work study, etc.) to policy decisions (e.g. major capital investment and new products or services). In the National Survey, *three* major decision areas were selected for further study,[26] namely those concerning:—

(i)   improvements in work conditions
(ii) permanent transfer within the plant
      and
(iii) major capital investment.

As in the previous study, both the respondents' *present* (or actual) involvement and *desired* involvement in the respective decision areas were investigated.[27] Two further questions were also asked, firstly one concerning the extent to which the respondents' super- visors/bosses give them the opportunity to *decide on their own* matters concerning the organisation and planning of their work, and secondly, whether they *take part* in decisions *with* their superior/ boss concerning their own work.[28]

10.2   Actual and Desired Involvement in Decision-Making

How much influence do people have over decisions? How much influence would they like to have?

25

In contrast to the actual level of involvement in the respective decisions, there was a clear indication of a desire for greater involvement in each of the decision areas that present practice actually provides. Although there remained a substantial proportion of respondents *not wanting* involvement in captial investment decisions (53%), only 10% of all respondents did *not want* to be involved in decisions concerning work conditions (Table 3).

TABLE 3. Actual and Desired Involvement in Respective Decisions

	Working Conditions		Permanent Transfer		Major Capital Investment	
	Actual	Desired	Actual	Desired	Actual	Desired
	%	%	%	%	%	%
No involvement	25	10	41	21	77	53
Some involvement[29]	52	52	41	48	15	31
'Power' involvement	23	38	18	32	9	16
(% base)[30]	(1,667)	(1,592)	(1,483)	(1,399)	(1,606)	(1,468)

However, the contents of Table 3 do seem to indicate a fairly persuasive·desire for greater levels of involvement, at least in the decision areas studied. The results in the table need to be interpreted with some caution though as they refer to all respondents whatever their occupation or 'level' in their place of work. So let us now see how the 'job level' of the respondent completes the picture.

10.3   Actual Involvement in Decision Making by 'Job Level'

How much influence do people at various levels of organisation have over decisions? Are there differences in influence according to the type of work people do?

Consistent with the hierarchical nature of decision-making in most British companies, 'job level'[31] was quite strongly associated with the actual level of involvement (working conditions decisions r = 0.35; permanent transfer r = 0.19; major capital investment r = 0.54).[32] Top managers are clearly very heavily involved in all decision-making areas. In particular, substantially more than half (73% in the case of decisions concerning work conditions) of the top managers exercised joint or personal decision-making powers ('Power' involvement) in all decision areas. Middle-management and

26

supervisors appeared to share a relatively low level of involvement compared to top-management. Shop floor respondents are even further removed from the decision-making process, with involvement in decisions concerning major capital investment being extremely restricted (Table 4). There would appear to be a substantial involvement gap between, on the one hand, supervisory and middle-management, and on the other top-management positions.

TABLE 4. Actual Involvement in Decision Making by 'Job Level'

	Total %	Top Mgt. %	Middle Mgt. %	Sup. %	Shop Floor Clerical %	Manual %
Working Conditions:						
No involvement	25	5	12	15	36	32
Some involvement	52	22	55	58	53	54
'Power' involvement	23	73	33	28	11	14
(% base)	(1,600)	(122)	(300)	(213)	(255)	(710)
Permanent Transfer:						
No involvement	38	22	47	43	26	40
Some involvement	43	12	34	34	59	49
'Power' involvement	19	66	19	23	15	10
(% base)	(1,306)	(99)	(261)	(163)	(208)	(575)
Major Capital Investment:						
No involvement	77	16	53	74	91	92
Some involvement	15	25	34	18	8	7
'Power' involvement	9	59	13	8	2	1
(% base)	(1.548)	(117)	(290)	(204)	(241)	(696)

In addition to the examination of 'Job level', the research also investigated the relationship of 'job function' (i.e. production, technical, professional jobs) to involvement. With the exception of involvement in decisions concerning permanent transfer, respondents in production jobs consistently displayed low levels of involvement in all decision areas, compared with other job functions. For example, over three quarters of those respondents in production compared with two-thirds or less in professional, sales and technical jobs indicated they had no involvement in major capital investment decisions. However, closer analysis of the data indicates these results are as much reflections of *job level* as *job function*, i.e.

27

production jobs being heavily dominated by manual shop floor
workers. Furthermore, although differences were observed in the
distribution of influence between manual and non-manual occupations as well as between members of a trade union or a professional
body; these differences were again largely accounted for by the
importance of job level.

10.4   Desired Involvement in Decision Making by 'Job Level'

How much influence would people at various levels of organisation
like to have?

The hierarchical nature of involvement in decision-making was
also maintained across the respondents' desired levels of involvement. 'Job level' correlated with working condition decisions with a
value of $r = 0.27$; major capital investment $r = 0.40$ but for perma-

TABLE 5.   Desired Involvement in Decision Making by 'Job Level'

	Total %	Top Man. %	Mid. Man. %	Sup. %	Shop Floor Clerical %	Manual %
Working Conditions:						
No involvement	10	3	9	5	12	13
Some involvement	52	16	42	53	62	58
'Power' involvement	38	80	50	41	26	29
(% base)	(1,531)	(117)	(293)	(208)	(237)	(676)
Permanent Transfer:						
No involvement	19	12	30	29	10	16
Some involvement	49	14	44	41	60	55
'Power' involvement	32	75	27	30	31	29
(% base)	(1,239)	(94)	(239)	(153)	(199)	(554)
Major Capital Investment:						
No involvement	53	13	31	52	68	65
Some involvement	31	21	46	33	24	28
'Power' involvement	16	66	23	16	8	7
(% base)[33]	(1,418)	(114)	(270)	(192)	(208)	(634)

nent transfer decisions where the correlation was negative (r = −0.11). Shop floor workers indicated a strong desire for at least some involvement in decisions concerning permanent transfer within the plant. Only 14% of the shop floor respondents (both clerical and manual) indicated they did not want any involvement in such decisions. Supervisors and middle managers appear to desire less involvement in transfer decisions than do the shop-floor (Table 5).

It is instructive to compare Tables 4 and 5; for every job level and each decision making area the proportion of respondents desiring 'power involvement' outstrips the proportion actually having this level of involvement. This again confirms our earlier impression that there is some fairly persuasive desire for more involvement at all levels. However, a comparison of Tables 4 and 5 does not enable us to identify, for instance, which of 23% of respondents with 'power involvement' in working conditions are included in the 38% who *desire* this level. We now turn to this issue.

10.5   Relationships between actual and desired involvement

Do people want more influence over decisions than they have? Do people want only a moderate increase in their influence over decisions or a more substantial change?

Table 6 gives the actual against the desired level of involvement for all levels of respondent. The actual involvement in each decision area was considerably below the desired level. Of those respondents with no involvement in decisions concerning working conditions, 59% indicated a desire for a greater involvement. In the case of capital investment decisions, the percentage was 29%.

Although the difference between actual and desired involvement was less for those with 'some involvement', there remains a substantial proportion who desired further involvement. Of those with some involvement in work conditions decisions and permanent transfer (shopfloor only), 29% and 23% respectively indicated a desire either for joint or personal decision-making ('Power' involvement). There was some indication that those respondents in positions of 'power involvement', particularly with regard to work conditions, desired less involvement than they actually exercised.

29

TABLE 6.   Desired Involvement by actual involvement in decision-making.

| | | ACTUAL INVOLVEMENT | | |
	Total %	No involve- ment %	Some involve- ment %	'Power' involve- ment %
DESIRED INVOLVEMENT IN				
Working Conditions:				
No involvement	10	41	*	*
Some involvement	52	49	71	13
'Power' involvement	38	10	29	87
(% base)	(1,570)	(371)	(824)	(275)
Permanent Transfer:				
No involvement	12	38	1	1
Some involvement	53	46	77	6
'Power' involvement	35	16	22	93
(% base)	(1,140)	(353)	(548)	(239)
Major Capital Investment:				
No involvement	53	70	1	–
Some involvement	31	24	81	2
'Power' involvement	16	5	18	99
(% base)	(1,465)	(1,105)	(228)	(132)

*less than 0.5%

Table 6 demonstrates a relationship between actual involvement and desired involvement. (Working conditions $r = 0.63$; permanent transfer $r = 0.66$; major capital investment $r = 0.70$).[34] Further analysis of the data indicates a fairly consistent pattern across all decisions as to the proportions of respondents wanting more involvement than they actually have. Slightly over a quarter of all respondents want more involvement in decision making; whilst the substantial majority, nearly three quarters of all respondents, appeared to be satisfied with their present level of involvement (Table 7).

TABLE 7. Level of desired involvement compared with actual involvement.

	Working Conditions %	Permanent Transfer %	Major Capital Investment %
Wanting less involvement	4	2	*
Satisfied with involvement	67	71	75
Wanting more involvement	29	28	25
(% base)	(1586)	(1240)	(1465)

* less than 0.5%

The picture, therefore, is not one of unbridled aspirations for more involvement. We should, therefore, bear in mind that those results are aggregated from a cross-sectional study; it may be that the numbers wanting more involvement than they have at present is increasing (or more unlikely, decreasing) over time. We are unable to comment directly on this issue, though it should be noted that our findings concerning satisfaction with the level of involvement of a large majority is consistent with similar studies carried out earlier.

Furthermore, an examination of Table 6 shows that those respondents wanting more involvement are more likely to actually have no involvement, and seek 'some' than have 'some', and seek 'power involvement'.

10.6   Involvement and the Size of Plant

Does the size of plant affect how much influence people have? Are there differences in how much influence people would like, according to the size of plant?

Plant size was found to be associated with levels of actual and desired involvement only at the extremities of the size scale i.e. plants employing under 10 or over 10,000 employees. Plants employing between 10 and 10,000 employees displayed very similar patterns of actual and desired involvement. Substantially more respondents in plants employing under 10 employees were in joint or personal decision-making ('Power' involvement) positions than in plants employing between 10 - 10,000. Plants employing over 10,000 had higher levels of no involvement than all other size categories. Although a lower proportion of all respondents indicated they were not involved or did not want to be involved in decisions concerning work conditions, the remaining decisions (i.e. transfers and investment) revealed similar variations in the distribution of actual and desired involvement within the size groups.

31

10.7 **Actual and Desired Involvement and 'Tenure'**

Does the number of years worked at a plant affect how much influence people have or want?

Tenure was found to show some relationship to the actual level of involvement in decisions concerning work conditions ($r = 0.14$). Respondents who had completed less than one year's tenure with their particular plant were least likely to have involvement in decisions concerning work conditions. There appeared to be a steady increase of involvement in such decisions, with increasing tenure. Those respondents with less than one year's tenure, 38% compared with 20% of those with ten years' tenure, indicated they had no involvement in work conditions decisions. These differences in involvement may reflect a lack of familiarity with the appropriate procedural arrangements by relatively new recruits. Those respondents with less than one year's tenure aged 15-20 tend to account for the main involvement differences. Insignificant relationships were found between tenure and involvement for permanent transfer and major capital investment decisions.

The relationship between tenure and desired involvement tended to be very weak. In other words, there is no evidence that the longer a person has been in employment in a particular place of work, the more he will desire involvement in the sorts of decision studied. This finding seems to run counter to some previous studies which have suggested such a relationship.

10.8 **Actual and Desired Involvement and Income/Education**

Do people with higher incomes have and want more influence than others?

Is education related to how much influence people have or want?

Education and income were found to be related to both the actual and desired level of involvement in decision making. Those respondents who had attained some form of tertiary education and those that earned income in excess of £6,500 displayed higher levels of actual and desired involvement, particularly in major capital investment decisions. This would seem to reflect the hierarchical nature of decision making as well as the association of particular skill levels to such decisions.

In general, the relationship between income and actual involvement was fairly weak. The same was the case with desired involvement. Furthermore, a similar weak pattern of relations was found between

32

education attained and actual involvement, as well as with eduction and desired involvement.

10.9   **Decision-Making Opportunities**

What sort of opportunities do people have to make decisions on their own? Do people regularly take part in decisions concerning their work?

Approximately half of all respondents stated they were given either great or very great opportunities by their superior/boss to *decide their own* matters concerning the organisation and planning of their work. In response to a separate question, a more substantial proportion (74%) stated they had opportunities to *take part* in decisions concerning their work.

The relationships established in the previous sections were also of significance to the decision-making opportunties available to respondents. Job level was again the dominant factor in the different opportunity patterns. Only 4% of managers, compared to 40% of shop floor workers (clerical and manual), indicated they had little or no opportunities *to decide* how to organise and plan their work. Although a high proportion of all respondents *took part* in work decisions, the influence of job level was still apparent. Under two-thirds (60%) of shop floor workers (manual) indicated they *took part* in such decisions, whilst 90% of both managers and supervisors had similar involvement.

11.   **THE EFFECTS OF INVOLVEMENT IN WORK SITUATIONS**

What are the consequences of people taking part in work decisions on production? Are there effects on the quality of work? Are people better able to use their skills?

Further analysis was undertaken to ascertain the estimated effects, if any, of taking part in work decisions on[35] :—
  (i)   increases in production
  (ii) the quality of work
  (iii) better use of the respondents' skill.

76% of respondents who took part in 'work decisions' felt production had been increased as a result of taking part in such decisions, 79% that the quality of work had improved, and 89% that their skills were better used. Again, job level was of significance to respondents' assessments of the effects on production quality and use of skills of their involvement in work decisions. In particular, 63% shop floor (clerical) workers, compared with 87% of managers, and 82% of supervisors, indicated their involvement in work

33

decisions had increased production. Similar results were obtained for the effects on the quality of work. However, the importance of job level diminishes substantially concerning the better use of skills as a result of involvement in work decisions, with over 80% of all levels giving positive replies.

As the age of respondents increases, there was a tendency for him to be more positive in assessing the effects of involvement in decisions on production and the quality of work. Just over half of the respondents aged under 21 compared with over three-quarters of those over 45 indicated their involvement in work decisions increased production. Similarly, with an increase in the length of tenure, respondents were more likely to indicate positive effects on production and quality i.e. 62% of those with less than 1 year's tenure compared with 83% for those with 10 or more years tenure indicated an increase in production. However, closer examination indicated that these differences are more related to age than tenure, with the 15-20 year-olds with less than 1 year's tenure accounting for the more negative views of the effects on production and quality of their involvement in work decisions.

In situations where respondents were more positive as to the management-worker relationship there was an indication of greater impact on production and quality as a result of their involvement in work decisions. Over three-quarters of those respondents considering that management-workers got on well together compared with approximately two-thirds who negatively assessed this relationship felt production had increased and the quality of work had improved as a result of their involvement.

There was some indication that respondents' assessment of the effects of their taking part in work decisions was related to certain wider involvement issues. Respondents with low levels of involvement in decisions concerning work conditions were less likely to indicate increases in production or quality as a result of their part in work decisions. Of those respondents with no involvement in improvements in work conditions of their work group, 60% felt their *taking part* in work decisions increased production. In contrast, 87% of those with "power involvement" concerning work conditions indicated such increases. Similarly, those respondents who had great or very great opportunities to decide on their own organisational and planning matters were found to view the effects of involvement on production, quality and the use of skill more positively.

12.   WORKING CLIMATE

How well do managers and workers get on in British industry? Do people at various levels of organisation view this relationship differently? Is the size of the plant important?

34

In an attempt to examine the working climate of plants, respondents were asked to assess how well managers and workers got on at their place of work. Just under half (47%) of respondents indicated they got on well. A further 31% stated the relationship was more variable (i.e. sometimes getting on, sometimes not) whilst 22% felt managers and workers did *not* get on well.

As before, job level was found to be a critical factor in respondents' assessments of working climate. Three quarters of top management respondents compared with less than half of all shopfloor respondents (clerical and manual) considered management and workers got on well at their place of work.

In plants where respondents considered their skills were underutilised, there was a slight tendency for management-worker relationships to be more strained. Only 20% of those respondents in situations where they felt their skills were well utilised, compared to 35% in underutilised skill situations, indicated strained management-worker relationships.

There was also evidence that, in plants employing less than 50 people, respondents were more likely to feel management and workers got on well than in larger sized plants. Approximately two-thirds of those respondents in plants employing less than 50 people, compared with substantially less than half in larger plants, indicated a positive management-worker relationship.

13.   JOB INCENTIVES

What are the important aspects of work to people at various levels of the organisation? Do older people have different priorities?

Respondents were asked to choose from a list of nine job characteristics those three which they considered most important to them in their job. Predictably, stability of employment (58%) and having a good salary (53%) were most frequently chosen. A further item considered important was having good cooperation with colleagues (51%). Items least frequently chosen were having a nice boss (15%) and having effective representatives (9%) i.e. shop stewards, etc.

The priorities placed on various aspects of job incentives were strongly related to job level. Two items which appear particularly related to job level were, the importance of having opportunities to use their skills, and to influence decisions concerning their work (Table 8). Shopfloor workers were more concerned with the more general aspects of employment, (i.e. stability of employment and pay) whilst top managers gave priority more to aspects of job content (i.e. skill use and influence over work). However, approximately

35

half of all managers also place considerable importance on pay and stability of employment.

TABLE 8. Importance of work items

	Total %	Top Man. %	Mid. Man. %	Sup. %	Shop-floor Clerical %	Manual %
Stability of Employment	58	47	51	64	59	60
Good Salary	53	43	48	51	55	57
Good cooperation etc.	51	39	48	52	55	52
Opportunity to use skills	34	58	49	35	24	27
Clean/safe work environ.	28	15	11	26	23	39
Influence on decisions	23	41	39	26	17	14
Promotion opportunities	21	13	29	21	28	16
Nice boss	15	5	9	12	19	19
Effective representatives	9	16	8	9	11	8
(% base)	(1,640)	(127)	(308)	(216)	(258)	(731)

A number of other variables found to be of significance in predicting the rating of the nine job items such as job function, education level, income, trade union membership as well as actual involvement in the respective decisions were found to be highly dominated by the job level relationship.

Certain job items ratings were found to be related to age, although these are generally of an expected nature. Respondents aged 45-64 were more likely to place a higher priority on stability of employment (61%) and a lower priority on promotion (10%) than those aged under 21, where the figures were 44% and 37% respectively. Furthermore, there was some indication that older respondents (35-64) saw having influence on decisions concerning their own job as being of importance compared to the younger elements (under 21). Only 12% of the under 21's, compared with 25% of those over 35, indicated influence on job decisions was most important.

14.   SKILL UTILISATION

Do people feel they use their skills and experience in their job? Do people who are involved in decisions feel they use their skills more fully?

36

Respondents were asked how well they felt their skill and experience were used in their job. Substantially over three quarters (83%) of all respondents indicated their skills and experience were either fairly well or fully utilised.

There was some indication that those who indicated their skills were under-utilised were less likely to have involvement in decisions concerning work conditions and capital investment. Of those who felt their skills were under-utilised, 44% had no involvement in work condition decisions whilst only 3% of those in power positions indicated such an underutilisation of their skills. A similar pattern existed for capital investment decisions. Similarly, those with opportunities to make decisions on *their own* were more likely to feel their skills were being used (87%) than those lacking such opportunities (4%).

Although less pronounced than in other data, job level was seen to be of importance to respondents' assessment of skill use. 94% of top managers, compared with 80% of shop floor workers, indicated their skills were fairly well or fully utilised.

Interestingly, respondents' assessments of their skill and experience progressively increased with the length of tenure. Approximately 70% of those with less than one year's tenure compared with 88% of those with ten years' tenure, indicated their skills were being fairly well or fully used. This relationship was unaffected by controlling for age.

15.   THE CIVIC CULTURE – A RETEST

Do people trust one another less now than used to? Do people have more influence on family and educational matters?

In the early 1960's Almond and Verba published a detailed comparative study of 'the civic culture' in five countries, including the U.K.[36] The following analysis was conducted in order to replicate nearly twenty years later that part of the study dealing with the degree of trust people have in one another and the level of participation experienced in the family and school.

Examination of the results reveals a marked movement towards a more distrustful society (Table 9). In the Almond and Verba study nearly half of their respondents felt most people could be trusted, with only a marginal number regarding people generally untrustworthy. Our own research clearly shows that approaching half of our respondents now generally distrust people. Has this movement in trust levels been a major factor in many of the industrial problems facing Britain?

37

TABLE 9. Extent of Trust People Have in Others

	1958 U.K. Survey (Almond and Verba) %	1978 National Household Survey %
Most people can be trusted	49	38
You can't be too careful	9	42
It depends	39	19
Others	2	*
(% base)	(959)	(1,678)

* less than 0.5

The extent of respondents' influence in family decisions affecting them when they were about sixteen did not appear to have radically changed. However, it is of interest that the slight movement in influence since the 1960's is at the extremities of the influence scale i.e. there is a slight increase in those with much influence as well as those with no influence (Table 10). In the case of opportunities at school to discuss political and social issues and to make up their own minds, such opportunities had increased but possibly not to the extent that might be expected from the educational developments of recent years.

TABLE 10. Influence on Family Issues

	U.K. Survey (Almond and Verba) %	National Household Survey %
Much influence	21	26
Some influence	51	42
None	28	32
(% base)	(917)	(1,647)

TABLE 11. Opportunities to Discuss Political and Social Issues at School

	U.K. Survey (Almond and Verba) %	National Household Survey %
A lot	5	10
Some	22	26
None at all	73	64
(% base)	(908)	(1,643)

38

16. WORKER DIRECTORS: THE ISSUES

Although certain companies had prior to the sixties already developed some form of worker directors scheme, the most significant development in this respect is generally regarded as the British Steel Corporation introduction of worker directors in the mid-sixties.[37] The main outlines of this scheme were developed by April 1967 but only a few other companies were subsequently to follow the Corporation's example. In Europe, a number of worker director schemes have been introduced, but they also have had little or no impact on the British industrial relations. Since 1970, a number of new or amended schemes have been established in Europe.[38]

In December 1975, the Bullock Committee of Inquiry was set up by the Government to consider how 'the extension of industrial democracy in the control of companies by means of representation on boards of directors and accepting the essential role of trade union organisations in this process' can be achieved. A year later a *Majority Report* was issued by the Committee with the recommendations that employees should have the right to elect trade union based worker directors in companies employing more than 2,000 employees on a $2X + Y$ basis.[39] Although the Bullock Committee received a number of submissions from individuals, and institutions, there were relatively few contributions based upon scientific research findings concerning the attitudes in the population at large towards 'worker directors'. Furthermore, surprisingly little account was taken of the British Steel Corporation's experiences with the worker directors.[40]

In May 1978, the Government issued a *White Paper* on industrial democracy[41] containing a firm commitment to introduce legislation on a fallback basis. The document follows in most respects Bullock's proposals concerning worker directors, but differs in favouring a two-tier company structure. Possibly because of the uncertainty over the timing of the General Election and the lack of Parliamentary time, this document seems to have stimulated remarkably little debate. The Election of May, 1979 sealed its fate.

Six controversial issues have emerged from the debate surrounding these publications.

1. The actual desirability of giving workers representation on Company Boards.

2. Whether or not worker representation is better handled by establishing consultative committees 'lower down' the company rather than at Board level (i.e. Works Councils)

3. Which issues actually affect the interests of workers most directly. And (related to Item 2) are these likely to be on the agenda of most Company Boards.

39

4. Granted that worker directors are desirable, what should the composition of the Board be? The 2X + Y formula advocated by Bullock allows for an equal group of top executives and worker directors, with the balance of power being held by outside independent directors chosen by both sides. It is thus not clear how the interests of the shareholders are to be served.

5. The most controversial feature of the Board structure concerns the basis of selection/election of the 'X' worker to the board. The *Majority Report* of Bullock recommended the setting up of a Joint Representation Committee of all unions in a company to nominate worker directors, who would then be elected by the full labour force of the Company. Thus, worker directors would be elected by the labour force exclusively from trade union members. This invites the question about the representation of non-unionists in the labour force. There is a suggestion in the *White Paper* that homogeneous groups of employees numbering at least 100, whether or not they are members of trade unions, might be able to nominate candidates following a successful appeal against the working of the trade union representative system.[42] However, the main proposals of the *White Paper* follow those of the Bullock Report.

6. Finally, an issue which has received increasing attention is the desirability of consumers being able to directly influence decisions undertaken by large corporations. The National Consumer Council (NCC) made representation to the Bullock Committee concerning the need to protect consumer interests.[43] Whilst not supporting the notion of worker directors, the NCC indicated that some form of consumer representation would be necessary to protect their interests if worker directors were introduced onto Boards. The Bullock Committee (*Majority Report*) rejected any consumer representation, partly on the grounds that they didn't accept the thesis that Board level representation of employees would damage the consumer interests.[44] And partly because of considerable difficulties in establishing any 'recognisable consumer constituency equivalent to that of employees and shareholders'.[45]

16.1 The Desirability of Introducing Worker Directors

National surveys conducted prior to and immediately after the publication of the Bullock Report have in general indicated a majority in favour of introducing employee representatives to Boards of Directors. For example, a MORI survey indicated 69% of all respondents (and 74% of the trade union members) thought employees should be represented on the Boards of large British companies.[46]

40

Despite claims of declining interest in the worker director issue since the Bullock Report, the following national survey conducted in fact well after the publication of the Bullock Report proper, would seem to suggest a continuing of interest by the general working population.

In response to a question asking respondents whether or not they thought some representation of workers on the Boards of large companies were desirable, 72% of the sample gave a positive answer. Only 28% stated they did not think such representation was desirable. There thus seems to be considerable general support for the introduction of workers on Boards, but as shall be seen, this observation is subject to a number of reservations.

Shop-floor workers (clerical and manual) were substantially more inclined to see such developments as desirable, compared to top management (Table 12).

TABLE 12. Desirability of Board Level Representation of Workers in Large Companies, by Job Level

	Total %	Top Management %	Middle Management %	Supervisors/ Foremen %	Shop-Floor Clerical %	Manual %
Yes, desirable	72	56	64	67	77	78
No, not desirable	28	44	36	33	23	22
(% base)	(1,508)	(118)	(294)	(203)	(239)	(654)

However, it should be noted that although there is a difference in the magnitude of support for the notion of worker directors, over half of the sample of top-managers and nearly two-thirds of the middle-managers sample regarded the representation of workers on Boards as desirable. This result would seem to be of particular importance in view of the widespread belief that managers are largely opposed to the worker director developments.

41

Particularly high levels of support for worker directors on Boards was found among women and young respondents (under 21). Although all age groups were in favour of worker directors, there appeared to be a steady decline in support with increasing age. Of those respondents under the age of 21, 87% were in favour, but this figure declined to 63% for the 43-64 age group. A similar decline was found with increasing length of employment at the respondents' place of work. 86% of women, compared with 67% of men, indicated support for worker directors on Boards.

Our results indicate that union members, members of professional bodies and non-members have roughly equal likelihood of supporting worker directors. However, over two thirds of each category of informant were positively disposed to the introduction of worker directors. Similarly, neither the industrial sector nor the size of plant at which the respondent worked significantly affected the likelihood of a favourable or unfavourable attitude.

TABLE 13. The Desirability of Introducing Worker Directors, by Union/ Professional Membership

	Total %	Union Member %	Professional Body Member %	Non-Member of either %
Yes, desirable	72	73	67	72
No, not desirable	28	27	33	28
(% base)	(1,541)	(816)	(149)	(576)

16.2   Choosing Worker Directors

If worker representatives were to have seats on Boards, who should be responsible for choosing them? Two-thirds of the sample indicated the workers themselves should be involved in choosing the worker directors, with 40% stating *only* workers should be involved, and 35% wanting some combination of workers with trade unions or management. Only 15% of the sample excluded workers from the choice of worker directors, favouring selection by management only.

42

This latter view was more likely to be held by certain top-management and non-unionists.

TABLE 14. Who should be responsible for choosing worker directors, by job level.

	Total %	Top Manage- ment %	Middle Manage- ment %	Superiors/ Foremen %	Shop Floor Clerical %	Shop Floor Manual %
Workers	40	30	35	40	44	43
Management	15	32	18	16	12	10
Trade Unions	5	3	3	5	4	6
Workers and Management	20	24	27	20	23	15
Trade Unions and Workers	3	2	3	4	4	3
Trade Unions and Management	3	2	3	2	2	4
Workers, Trade Unions and Management	12	4	9	12	10	16
Other Answers	2	3	3	1	1	3
(% base)	(1,479)	(116)	(283)	(202)	(235)	(643)

16.3 Importance of Issues to Worker Directors

Examination of the sort of issues respondents felt would be of importance to worker directors indicates wage rates, working conditions and dismissals are most often mentioned. Over two-thirds of the respondents felt each of the issues would be very important to worker representatives. Issues such as working hours and training were also considered to be of prime importance. Of the issues examined, least importance was placed on matters such as capital investment and new products. Only just over a third of all respondents stated such issues would be very important to worker directors (Table 15).

43

TABLE 15. Importance of Issues to Worker Directors

		Very Important	Fairly Important	Neither Important Nor Unimportant	Fairly Unimportant	Very Unimportant	Don't Know	(% base)
Capital Investment/ New Products	%	36	35	7	8	3	12	(1,700)
Wage Rates, Working Conditions, Dismissals	%	69	23	1	1	*	6	(1,700)
Working Hours, Holidays	%	56	33	3	2	*	6	(1,700)
Training of Staff	%	55	30	4	4	1	7	(1,700)

*Less than 0.5%

44

To some extent, it would seem that the level of importance placed on certain issues reflect misunderstandings of the function of the Board of Directors. Although there is relatively little detailed analysis of the working of Boards, the available evidence suggests a heavier concentration on strategic policy such as capital investment, long term planning rather than more localised issues such as wage rates, etc. Thus, the sort of issues articulated as having high priority to worker directors are not among those currently involving Board Meetings. Thus misunderstanding concerning Boards probably stems from the lack of visibility to many employers of the decision-making process at their place of work. Thus, all managers were as likely as shop-floor workers to indicate wage rates, working hours, training, etc. would be of high importance to worker directors. Furthermore, union members displayed similar priority patterns on the respective issues. There was some indication that respondents who had received tertiary education or beyond and older respondents (35 or more years old) gave higher priority ratings to all issues.

16.4   **Worker Directors or Consultative Committees?**

The respondents were asked to choose between having workers' representatives on the Board *or* consultative committees at lower levels of the organisation. The results do not suggest any dominant preference in the total sample, 51% preferred worker directors, whilst 49% preferred consultative committees.

Job level was again found to be major predictor of the direction of the preference between worker directors or consultative
Approximately two-thirds of all managers preferred the development of consultative committees rather than worker directors, whilst these figures were effectively reversed for the shop floor.

The relatively low percentage of shop-floor (manual) workers opting for consultative committees may perhaps be explained by a general disenchantment with such developments as a means of extending participation.

45

TABLE 16. Preference for Workers' Representatives on the Board or Consultative Committees at Lower Levels of the Organisation, by Job Level.

PREFERENCE FOR:	Total %	Top Manage- ment %	Middle Manage- ment %	Super- visors %	Shop-Floor Clerical %	Shop-Floor Manual %
Worker Directors	51	32	36	44	50	62
Consultative Committees	49	68	64	56	50	38
(% base)	(1,170)	(71)	(215)	(162)	(175)	(547)

Other factors influencing respondents' preferences revealed a strong relationship between being a member of a professional body and favouring consultative committees (70%). Membership of such a body is, of course, strongly linked with a managerial position. In contrast, just under one half of those who were members of a trade union indicated such committees would be of importance to themselves (57% favouring worker directors). This would seem to indicate a considerable mixture of views among union members concerning the best way of increasing worker participation. Non-union/non-professional body members indicated a slight preference for consultative committees (53%).

Additional data indicated that the low income groups (less than £3,500) saw worker director developments as more important than consultative committees. Similarly, respondents who finished their full-time education at secondary level or earlier also preferred to have worker representation on Boards. Again, these variables would seem closely linked to job level.

Of particular importance in understanding the preference of respondents was the degree to which they have opportunities to decide on their own matters concerning the organisation and planning of their work. In situations where there were little or no such opportunities, respondents indicated a preference for worker representatives on Boards. Slightly less than half of those who felt they had great or very great opportunities to decide matters on their own showed a similar preference (Table 17).

46

TABLE 17. Preference between Workers' Representatives on the Board of Consultative Committees at Lower Levels of the Organisation, by extent to which Superior/Boss gave Opportunities to Decide on their Own Matters Concerning Organisation/Planning of Work.

EXTENT OF OPPORTUNITIES

PREFERENCE FOR:	Total %	None/Little Extent %	Some Extent %	Great/Very Great Extent %
Worker Directors	51	60	60	43
Consultative Committees	49	40	40	58
(% base)	(1,143)	(298)	(269)	(576)

16.5   The Desirability of Introducing Consumer Directors?[47]

Over half (62%) of all respondents felt that there should be some representation of consumer interests on Boards if workers were to be represented.   Only 38% were opposed to such representation. Just two factors appeared to be of significance in explaining the strength of support given to consumer representation on Boards. Shop-floor workers and women indicated particularly high levels of support.   Over two-thirds of the shop-floor sample (manual and clerical), compared with half of the managers sample felt some form of consumer representation on Boards was desirable if workers gained representation (Table 18).   Similarly, 75% of women, compared to 61% of men indicated such support.

TABLE 18. Desirability of Board Representation of Consumers if Workers were Represented, by Job Level.

	Total %	Managers %	Supervisors %	Shop-Floor %
Yes, desirable	62	50	57	70
No, not desirable	38	50	43	30
(% base)	(704)	(189)	(100)	(415)

16.6   Composition of Consumer Representation?

On a Board of ten (assuming three worker directors), 46% of the respondents favoured one or two representatives.   A further 34%

47

favoured an equal representation of consumers to worker directors of three. Slightly higher levels of desired representation were found among respondents in manual occupations, with 58% compared with 42% of non-manual respondents requiring more than a minimum representation of one or two consumers.

The method most favoured by respondents for the selection of such consumer representatives was selection by an independent consumer organisation (47%). The main alternative suggested was to advertise for such representatives, like any other job (30%).

16.7   **Some Political Differences**

Interestingly, a number of the key differences in response to the worker director questions were closely related to the intended voting behaviour of respondents. This would seem in keeping with the different proposals generally advocated by the various political parties for the extension of industrial democracy in organisations.

As we have seen, a substantial majority, indicated that some representation of workers on the Boards of large companies was desirable. However, those who intended to vote Conservative were less positive (61%) than those with Liberal (79%) or Labour (79%) voting intentions.

A major difference occurs concerning the preference for worker directors or consultative committees at lower levels of the organisation. Only 37% of those intending to vote Conservative favoured the worker director developments compared to 61% Labour. Those intending to vote Liberal were fairly evenly divided between the two lines of development.[48]

17.   CONCLUSIONS FROM PART II

The main conclusions of this report may be summarised as consisting of:

17.1   A confirmation of the results reported in Part I. In particular the low levels of involvement in decision making on all topics and the very moderate demands for more involvement at all levels were confirmed.

17.2   Involvement in decision making is clearly related to job level. The biggest difference in involvement exists between top and middle management. This gives factual support to substantiate the very unsatisfactory position of middle management in British industry today.

17.3 The consequences of greater involvement are positive. Our findings suggest that involvement in decision making is seen as leading to increased production, an improvement in the quality of work and a better use of skills.

17.4 The importance of size of plant to the industrial relations issues studied only operates at the extremities of the size scale i.e. plants employing under 10 or over 10,000 employees.

17.5 Our findings indicate a marked decline over the last decade in the degree of trust people have in each other. A factor that may have important implications for industrial relations.

17.6 There is considerable support for the idea of workers' representatives on company boards chosen by the workers themselves. Contrary to popular belief over half of the managers in the sample saw such a development as desirable. There is also wide support for consumer directors selected by an independent consumer organisation.

17.7 The position is less clear as to the preference between having workers' representatives either on the Board, or consultative committees at lower levels of the organisation. Where differences in preference for these alternatives occur, they tend to be strongly related to job level.

17.8 As with the earlier report several of our findings are dependent on specific circumstances. In examining issues concerned with participation it is necessary to take account of both individual, task, and organisational characteristics such as the type of decision, and job level.

18. DISCUSSION RELATING TO PARTS I and II OF THIS REPORT

18.1 There has recently been extensive public discussion concerning employee participation and industrial democracy in Britain. In continental countries, a similar debate has developed since the end of the second world war and has led to a substantial amount of legislation and the introduction of formal schemes.

18.2   Up to now, little relevant evidence has been made available to help us to make reasonable and practical judgements. Every bit of information helps. The data we have presented and the conclusions based on it should be able to make a small but positive contribution.

18.3   Many people think that, as we approach the end of the twentieth century, it is desirable to involve people more in the making of decisions about circumstances that affect them. Is this sentiment simply a fashion or are there sound reasons for it? Is there more scope for such an involvement and are there risks in going too far?

18.4   To begin with, our research suggests that there is plenty of scope for increasing the amount of participation of all levels of workers and staff in our sample of industry. It is clear that only a very small number of people are involved in decision making, even of the smallest kind. Furthermore, the extent of influence exerted is very limited. These conclusions apply to the average middle managers as much as to the lower levels of employees.

The average middle manager cannot usually do more than give an opinion, even on routine decisions like assignments of tasks or improving working conditions. He does not usually feel his opinions are taken into account and he certainly does not get involved in joint decision making. He has even less say on what we call "goal oriented" decisions like department organisation or staff redundancies. In relation to such matters, the average manager gets informed beforehand and can sometimes give an opinion, that is all. This is further supported by the substantial difference in involvement in decision making between top and middle management.

At foreman and worker level the amount of involvement is, of course, substantially lower still. We expected a low involvement on "policy" decisions, but it is now clear that even "personal" and "goal oriented" decisions appear to be taken at the very top of our organisations, or even above plant level.

18.5   The advocacy of increased participation is often related to the knowledge that modern methods of schooling as well as current child-rearing practices accustom us to participate in daily events more than in the past. Do these expectations carry over into people's working life? The answer is a guarded 'yes'. Our sample of workers, foremen and managers want to have a greater say in decision making, but these demands are by no means extreme. We find that workers, for instance, are informed before "personal"

50

decisions are taken and they can sometimes give their opinion. How much say would they like to have? Would they like to make decisions jointly with higher levels or would they even want to make these decisions entirely by themselves?

The answer is that, on average, they are content with an opportunity to give their opinion and, whenever possible, to have their opinion taken into account when the decision is taken. This result is quite typical. Expectations are lower for "goal" oriented decisions and lower still for "policy" decisions.

18.6   We can generalise and say that the aspirations for involvement is above the actual involvement but not very much. These moderate shifts apply to shop floor workers as well as foremen and managers. Consequently, it is clear that there is no danger of exploding expectations which the ordinary factory or office could not contain. This is quite an important conclusion because of the often expressed fear that "give an inch, take a mile" could apply. It is said that organisations are pyramids and this implies a hierarchy with some degree of centralisation. Our findings do not suggest that the existence or even desirability of the hierarchy is seriously challenged by our samples of workers, foremen and managers. But they do want to have more say.

18.7   Arguments for greater participation are sometimes put forward on ideological grounds, but our research questions were more concerned with practical consequences. Among these, three stand out. Managers, supervisors and workers believe that increased involvement in decision making leads to an easier acceptance of decision, it gives people more knowledge about what is going on in the plant, and it improves the quality of the decisions made. Furthermore, our findings also suggest that involvement in decision making is seen as leading to increased production, an improvement in the quality of work and a better use of skills.

18.8   There is some further supporting evidence to suggest that appropriate involvement can improve the quality of decisions. When people were asked what they considered to be the most important aspects of their job, they gave a high score to "to be able to use my capacities in my work". It makes sense to conclude that when circumstances make it possible to make better use of experience and skill, and when people are motivated to use their capacities, better quality is a consequence. Participation seems to provide an important link in this chain of events.

51

18.9 Over the last decade, there appears to have been a substantial decline in the degree of trust people have in each other. The positive aspects of increased involvement in decision making we have mentioned, are likely to contribute to an improvement in the trust position, and in turn to the management-worker relationship.

18.10 It is often said that participation is easy and makes sense in small organisations, but becomes increasingly problematic as they get larger. Our findings show that within the range of 10-10,000 employees, size does not make a very substantial difference.

18.11 Most of the public discussion, on industrial democracy and participation, has revolved around formal schemes which require the election of representatives. However, there is also direct person to person (informal) participation which requires no changes in law or structure.

Predictably, managers prefer direct participation, while workers opt for the representative system, but there are indications that these two approaches are complementary rather than in conflict.

It is important to go back to our first observation that, in any case, the total amount of involvement under whatever system our sample of companies use, is remarkably small. This means that there is plenty of scope for increasing the use of the direct as well as the representative system. Our findings concerning the worker director development are particularly relevant to any increased usage of either system.

18.12 When we look at our findings carefully, we realise that, as we have already seen, conclusions rarely apply right across the board. They are usually related to specific conditions, that is to say, they are dependent on circumstances.

The most important contingent circumstances or conditions are level in the organisation (manager, supervisor or worker), type of organisational task (metal sector, engineering or banking-insurance, service sector) and type of decision (personal, goal or policy).

18.13 In some respects the metal and service sectors are very similar; for instance, management in both sectors has almost exactly the same amount of influence over a wide range of different decisions and the same is true for the amount of influence they would like to have. Similar patterns apply to foremen and workers.

52

18.14   However, the two sectors differ in several important respects. We will concentrate on three differences.

In the first place, the supply of information available to the metal sector is very poor; second, jobs are not well defined or planned, nor do people get a clear picture of company policies, organisation-structure and who holds authority. Third, management and workers do not get on well together and job satisfaction is low.

On each of these dimensions, the service sector is significantly better and this is likely to be related to its superior industrial relations record.

18.15   It is reasonable to ask whether any of these findings are relevant to policy makers at the micro-level of organisations, and at the macro-level of government and institutions representing interest groups like trade unions and employers. We can assume that our findings are reasonably representative of a broad spectrum of British industry. In such a case, we are prepared to argue that our main conclusions have substantial relevance to policy makers.

19   SOME MAJOR POLICY IMPLICATIONS

The following are the main implications of the research:

19.1   The consequences of giving British employees more say in industrial decisions are likely to be *positive*, rather than negative. The fear that the pent-up demand for more influence is so great that an increase in participation will change the whole fabric of society, appears to be unfounded.

19.2   Very little is now happening, apart from a few important but un-representative examples of leadership, as a natural development or as a result of exhortation. It may therefore be appropriate to try to change the situation more quickly through deliberate, and probably *formal* measures.

19.3   Employees' needs and wishes for greater participation are very different in different circumstances: they depend on the type of decision, the hierarchical level, the industry, and the established practices of the enterprise. Sweeping legislation, which does not take this fact into account, is likely to be ineffective or even counter-productive.

19.4   Existing European schemes, which appear to work well, are based on carefully designed constitutional arrangements in which rights to participation in decisions are defined for specified issues and circumstances. Both law and practice arise from the historical and cultural background in the countries concerned, and hence complete systems could *not* be transferred to the British environment as they stand.

19.5   Whilst it would be inappropriate to make very specific policy recommendation, our research suggests two principal items for the agenda of the discussion, leading up to possible legislation for Britain. Consideration should be given:

— to the structure of a workable system in terms of the extent of participation at different levels of decision, i.e. those affecting the individual (personal level), those affecting current business and technical practice (tactical level), and those affecting the general policy of the enterprise (strategic level); and

— to the structure of participation at each level in terms of its practical form, i.e. whether direct or through representatives or by an agreed combination of both.

54

Footnotes

1 Batstone, Eric, and Davis, P.L., Industrial Democracy: European Experience, London: HMSO, 1976.

2 Bullock, Lord, (Chairman) Report of the Committee of Inquiry on Industrial Democracy, London: HMSO, 1977.

3 T.U.C. Report on Industrial Democracy, 1974.

4 Dept. of Trade, Industrial Democracy (White Paper) London: HMSO, 1978

5 A recent book by the Industrial Editor of the Financial Times (Elliott, John, The Growth of Industrial Democracy, London, Kogan Page, 1978) is a forthright attempt to persuade the various parties to re-examine the Bullock Report in the light of history and the de facto balance of power in industry.

6 See Preface and Appendix 1. The research has been carried out in twelve countries (Belgium, Denmark, Finland, France, Germany, Great Britain, Italy, Israel, Netherlands, Norway, Sweden, Yugoslavia). Some 30 special scientists from 18 major research institutions were involved. In Part I we will not give any findings about worker-directors; this will follow in Part II. The British research was in fact carried out between mid-1976 and late 1977, with further analysis in the subsequent year and a half.

7 Part II deals with a national random sample of over 1,700 people in Britain.

8 The methods used in this research to obtain the answers we present are described in Appendix 1 and 2. In non-technical language we also give some more details relating to statistical findings.

9 We use the terms participation, influence and involvement interchangeably for the purposes of this report.

10 The sample consists mainly of middle managers.

11 56-59% are not involved at all in any of the three categories of decisions.

12 However the overall distribution of actual and desired involvement in the two sectors reveals similar patterns. See Appendix 1.

99

[13] A further indication of the importance of trade unions to workers was that over three-quarters of the workers' sample stated their interests were generally represented by their trade unions.

[14] Levels of uncertainty as high as 24% were recorded. All percentages presented in this section are based on all replies, including don't knows/no opinion responses.

[15] It must be remembered that this is part of a 12 country study and issues of this kind may be easier to answer elsewhere.

[16] Moderate disagreement refers to situations where between 30-60% of respondents stated the decision was usually reached through disagreement. No decision area revealed a high disagreement level 60%+.

[17] Preliminary indications suggest respondents were less positive about the consequences of having a works consultative council than trade union representation.

[18] Other details are provided in the Appendix 1.

[19] See Appendix 1 for detailed tables.

[20] See preface and Appendix I

[21] Of the 12 countries, only Britain and Germany are conducting the random household survey as described in Part II. The field-work was carried out for us by N.O.P.

[22] "What do the British want from Participation and Industrial Democracy?" Part I, p 3.

[23] Almond. Gabriel, and Verba, Sidney, The Civic Culture, Princeton Univ. Press 1963.

[24] Results are significant at the .01 level.

[25] What do the British want from Participation and Industrial Democracy? Part I.

[26] These decisions were chosen because they span all three types of decisions, i.e. personal, goal and policy decisions.

100

[27] The same scale of 1 to 6 was used in Part I as follows: 1 = not involved at all, 2 = informed beforehand, 3 = can give opinion, 4 = opinion taken into account, 5 = takes part with equal weight, and 6 = decide on my own.

[28] The first question was investigated in the Part 1 study, whilst the latter question was an extension of the previous work. For details of the questionnaire, see Appendix 3.

[29] Some involvement includes scale items 2-4, i.e. informed beforehand, can give opinion, and opinion taken into account; 'power' involvement includes scale items 5 and 6, i.e. take part with equal weight and decide on own.

[30] % bases on this and other tables are less than the total sample due mainly to non-response. Don't know categories have also been omitted for calculations.

[31] 'Job level' includes the following categories: Top management, Middle management, Full-time Supervisors or Foremen, Clerical Shopfloor and Manual Shop floor.

[32] 'Job level' was scored 1 to 5 from Manual Shop Floor to Top management respectively; actual level of involvement was scored 1 = no involvement, 2 = some involvement and 3 = 'power' involvement.

[33] Base figures differ from Table 4 because of non-response.

[34] Actual involvement was scored 1 = no involvement, 2 = 'some' involvement, and 3 = 'power involvement'. Desired involvement was scored on the same basis, prefixed by wanting.

[35] The replies to (i), (ii) and (iii) are the respondents' estimates of the effects of their taking part in work decisions.

[36] Almond, Gabriel A. and Verba, Sidney *The Civic Culture*, Princeton University Press, 1963.

[37] Brannen, Peter. et al *The Worker Directors: A Sociology of Participation.* London: Hutchinson, 1976.

[38] Batstone, Eric, and Davies, P.L. *Industrial Democracy: European Experience.* London: HMSO, 1976.

[39] Bullock, Lord. (Chairman) *Report of the Committee on Inquiry on Industrial Democracy.* London: HMSO, 1977.

[40] Banks, John. and Jones, Ken, *Worker Directors Speak.* London, Gower Press 1977.

[41] Dept. of Trade, Industrial Democracy. (White Paper). London, HMSO, 1978.

[42] Dept. of Trade, Op cit. p.9.

[43] National Consumer Council, *Industrial Democracy and Consumer Democracy. Seven Reasons the TUC is Wrong!* London, NCC 1976.

[44] Bullock, Op cit. p.53.

[45] Ibid.

[46] Worcester, Robert. *Public Attitudes Towards Employee Representation.* London, Market and Opinion Research International, January 1977.

[47] Questions on consumer representation were jointly undertaken with the National Consumer Council.

[48] Political affiliation (on the basis of right, left, centre right etc. orientation) was found to be a major factor in managers' attitudes to worker director developments in Clegg, C. et al, Managers' Attitudes to Industrial Democracy, *Industrial Relations Journal,* Vol. 9 No. 3 Autumn 1978, pp. 4-17.

[49] The data given in Appendix 1 and 2 form part of a twelve country study carried out by an autonomous team in each country and co-ordinated by Bernhard Wilpert in Berlin. The design is described in IDE International Research Group Industrial Democracy in Europe, *Social Science Information,* Vol. 15, 1976, pp. 177-203.

[50] An additional plant was included for the British sample but does not fall within the sector specification of the international comparison. The 15th plant gave results from 24 respondents in the service sector of the Aerospace industry.

[51] Of this total, 63 were key respondents according to our research specification (see p. 16) the remaining 698 answered all questionnaires.

[52] For the purpose of the present research, service sector means insurance and banking.

102

[53] This finding does not contradict the results described in relation to Figure 1A where people in the metal sector had greater influence on direct (person to person) participation.

[54] Labour Party; *Banking and Finance,* London, August 1976.

[55] Yao-Su Ho, *National Attitudes and the Financing of Industry;* London, PEP Vol. XLI, Broadsheet 55-9.

[56] *Department of Employment Gazette,* June 1977, pp. 579-586.

[57] The sample was a two-stage stratified random sample, names being drawn at random from the Electoral Register. The resulting sample is supplemented by a random sample of non-electors drawn from the households of the selected electors. The survey was conducted on a "two-shot" basis on the NOP Omnibus Survey.

[58] The sample was extended for the purpose of investigating questions concerning consumer directors. Only 'one-shot' was attempted on the consumer questions, but the sample was extended to include part-timers and the non-working population. A sample of 1,871 informants was obtained.

[25]

IDE — International Research Group

Industrial democracy in Europe revisited: summary and conclusions

At the congress on Participation and Self-Management in Dubrovnik (then Yugoslavia), a group of some 25 social scientists from a dozen countries decided to conduct jointly an international comparative study on the impacts of rules and regulations on participation in companies. This international, interdisciplinary network: "Industrial Democracy in Europe (IDE) — International Research Group" has now cooperated in joint research for two decades. A first major study was conducted in 1975–7 (IDE, 1981). The following report covers a replication of that research "ten years on". Some 80 publications resulted from the work of the IDE team (see IDE, 1992, in press). The first collective IDE report on theory, design and methods was published in this journal (IDE, 1976). Hence, with its present paper, the IDE group reaches the termination of a long-standing research cooperation.

Objectives

The present study had a number of objectives. The overall and primary aim was to have another opportunity to look at the same organizations in the same countries in Europe ten years after the first survey, and learn about any changes that might have occurred. More specifically, we wanted to see whether the external and formal influence and power structures and the extent of participative behaviour inside organizations had changed and whether the previous finding of a positive relationship between formal power structures and de facto participation was still true in the 1980s.

The most ambitious and most difficult aim was to see whether a longitudinal link between the two cross-sectional studies might give

This paper was drafted by Malcom Warner, Cambridge University, on behalf of the IDE-International Research Group.

Social Science Information (SAGE, London, Newbury Park and New Delhi), 31, 4 (1992), pp. 773–785.

us some insight into possible causal relationships over time. To do justice to this ambitious endeavour, we had to try to select a group of contingencies which could be hypothesized as strengthening or weakening the relationships between our major dimensions and, in addition, assess the impact of selected economic and technological changes (in particular the rate of unemployment) over the intervening period, up to 1987. Not all our aims could be accomplished. The downturn in economic conditions which affected our sample of companies also reduced the availability of research funding and, consequently, we had to be content with a less complete schema than we would have wanted to use. However, the replication study benefited from our analysis of the 1977 results (see IDE, 1981), where we found that some aspects of the enquiry were relatively unimportant and could be dispensed with. At the same time, although we had to economize our resources, we wanted to introduce a few variables that had gained salience in the intervening years.

In this summary, we report selectively on a number of findings that are thought to have strategic relevance for future research as well as for industrial relations policy.

The value of replication

In spite of the limitation of resources available to carry out the 1987 study, we are convinced that replication studies are of considerable scientific and practical value. We can, however, understand why the vast majority of industrial relations and organizational studies use a cross-sectional design without wishing that this state of affairs should continue indefinitely or is considered adequate for scientific or policy purposes. A replication study with only two measurement points may not be as interesting as one that has three, or even more, and for the purpose of understanding behavioural dynamics, longitudinal studies have to use methods of tracing structural, social and psychological processes over prolonged periods of time (Heller, 1984).

Nevertheless, the results from the present replication study show very clearly that, while some findings from 1977 were confirmed and can consequently be considered more secure, other conclusions have to be modified in the light of the evidence from an analysis of the available 1977–87 data. This possibility undoubtedly enriches our understanding of the interaction between aspects of organizational behaviour and the economic–political environment. We were also fortunate that after such a long interval of time the majority of researchers who had taken part in the earlier study were still available to carry out the second study, and that most of the companies had survived and agreed to work with us again.

While a decade is always a long time in an organization's life, the period 1977–87 was in some respects unusually turbulent. It included a major oil crisis which precipitated a significant downturn in economic activity, an increase in competition – particularly from Japan – and a noticeable increase in unemployment, which affected all countries in our sample, but some much more severely than others. In addition, the decade was characterized by very substantial changes in technology in manufacturing as well as in service industries.

In most countries the political balance had moved to the right, attitudes towards trade unions had become less favourable, and the role of employers was more dominant. These and other factors have, of course, varied somewhat from country to country.

Outline of the studies

The principal focus of both research studies was the distribution of influence at all levels of organization, its antecedents and consequences (IDE, 1976). Both studies were based on an examination of sixteen decisions covering short-term operational, mainly shopfloor issues, as well as longer term strategic decisions. The respondents were key senior management and trade union respondents within each of the 72 companies that were involved in 1977 as well as in 1987. The replication study included ten out of the original twelve countries: *Belgium, Denmark, Finland, Germany, Britain, Israel, Netherlands, Norway, Sweden* and *Yugoslavia.* In addition, the 1987 study included *Poland* and *Japan.*

In each organization, respondents were interviewed and filled in a number of questionnaires. The answers to the set of sixteen standardized decisions covered an influence-distribution continuum on a scale from 1 (no influence); 2 (little influence); 3 (moderate influence); 4 (much influence); 5 (very much influence). This distribution of influence (abbreviated PO) was assessed for all levels of the organization (worker, first-line supervisor, middle management, top management, and representative bodies: works councils or joint consultative committees plus some which will not be reviewed here).

The major antecedent variable was *participative structure* (PS). This was a measure of formal prescribed participation based on laws or recognized collective agreements, measured on a scale from 1 to 6.

Findings from country data

- The overall pattern and distribution of *influence* (PO) in the 72 organizations from ten countries did not change very much over the decade. Some changes in influence at the lowest level of organization were found in four countries. Worker influence increased slightly in Israel, Sweden and Finland, but declined in Yugoslavia.
- There were more substantial changes for *representative bodies* (PO). In Britain and Yugoslavia their influence declined, while in other countries, particularly in Israel and Sweden, and to a lesser extent in Finland, it increased.
- At the level of top management, the *influence scores* (PO) between 1977 and 1987 were identical for Yugoslavia and Finland. They declined very slightly in Belgium, Britain, Denmark, Netherlands, Norway and Sweden, and increased slightly in Israel. In Germany the drop in top management influence was fairly large.
- The changes in formal *participative structures* (abbreviated PS) over the same period showed substantially more variability. Most movements were in an upward direction (see Table 1). Participative structures supporting senior management registered consistent increases in every country except Britain, where it declined slightly. The increase was very large for Israel; substantial for Denmark and Norway; moderate in the Netherlands, Sweden and Finland; and small in Yugoslavia.
- At the lowest level of organization, there were increases in formal participative structures (PS) in Britain, the Netherlands, Israel, Norway and Finland. In Yugoslavia and Belgium, such formal support declined and there was no change in Denmark and Germany.
- An important objective of the present research is to test the assumption, derived from the 1977 study, *that participative*

structures (PS) could have a determining influence on participative behaviour at the lowest level of organization measured by our Influence-Power-Continuum (PO). It is therefore interesting to look at the difference in participative structure scores between top management and workers over the ten-year period. This difference has increased in six out of the ten countries (Belgium, Denmark, Israel, Norway, Sweden, Yugoslavia), most noticeably in Belgium and Norway. In four countries, the difference has decreased (Germany, Britain, Netherlands and Finland).

- If we examine the changes in participative structures (PS) and de facto participation (PO) over the ten years, country by country, we find *no* consistent relationship in the pattern of changes. Two explanations may spring to mind. One is that participative structures (PS) do not determine the amount of influence (PO) available at the level of workers. Alternatively, it is possible that changes in formal participative structures (PS) take a long time to work through the system and affect shopfloor behaviour. Our data do not tell us when in the decade 1977–87 the structural changes took place. If, for instance, many of the changes took place in the mid-1980s, then one would not expect the consequences to have cascaded down to behavioural changes at the lowest level of organization by 1987. In other words, there may have been a time-lag in the system.

TABLE 1

Changes over the decade 1977–87 in participative structures (PS) and de facto influence (PO) for workers and top management

| | *Worker level* | | *Top management* | |
	PS 1977–87	*PO* 1977–87	*PS* 1977–87	*PO* 1977–87
Belgium	−	+	−	+
Denmark	0	+	+ +	−
Germany	0	0	+	− −
Britain	+	0	−	−
Netherlands	+	0	+	−
Israel	+	+	+ +	+
Norway	+	−	+ +	−
Sweden	0	+	+	−
Yugoslavia	−	−	+	0
Finland	+	−	+	0

− = less; + = more; + + = much more; 0 = unchanged.

- In each country, the highest level of prescribed formal influence (PS) is given to senior management, except in Britain. Britain is unusual in this sample for having very few well-defined formal or legal rules relating to participation. Nevertheless the de facto power of senior management in Britain is substantial and about the same as in other countries. From another research project which followed up the 1977 Industrial Democracy research, we also know that in addition to externally prescribed formal structures (PS), there are company-level prescribed or sanctioned norms (which we call status power) that have a strong determining influence on the de facto distribution of influence (DIO, 1979).

Aggregate analysis

We now come to report on the more global analysis for which country data are aggregated, in order to explore the extent to which patterns of de facto influence distribution (PO) are affected by formal power structures (PS). The calculations were carried out separately for the 1987 data, as well as for the strictly comparable variables from 1977. Finally, a longitudinal analysis was carried out to trace the relationship of formal power structures (PS) on the distribution of de facto influence between 1977 and 1987. The only macro-economic factor in these analyses is the annual average percentage of unemployment between 1985–7 and 1975–7.

Some important policy-relevant conclusions are reported below:

1. To make the two time-periods comparable, it was necessary to re-analyse the 1977 data by leaving out variables not covered in 1987 and removing France and Italy because they did not take part in the replication, largely because of the unavailability of research funding.

(a) This new 1977 analysis re-confirmed the earlier conclusion that formal power structures (PS) predict the overall influence distribution (PO) between management and labour. This prediction was particularly strong for the impact of PS on the influence (PO) of representative bodies.

(b) A high rate of unemployment is usually assumed to reduce the influence of labour and this was confirmed for nine countries. However, it is of some interest to report that, under certain circumstances, a high degree of unemployment does not have this negative effect on workers, which in fact was the case with Yugoslavia. It is very likely that the robustness of that participative system was a function of its having been very firmly embedded in the socio-political system at that time, although this may now be changing (Warner, 1990).

(c) If we leave Yugoslavia out of the 1977 re-analysis, unemployment is a stronger predictor of worker influence (PO) than formal power structures (PS). Workers in the service sector have more influence than in manufacturing, but other contingency factors, like size of organization or product complexity, made no impact.

(d) The 1977 statistical analysis provides a fairly clear picture of the *de facto* influence of top managers and worker representative bodies. In both cases, the impact of formal power structures (PS) and unemployment are strong predictors. In the case of representative bodies, the unemployment rate has a negative effect, but in predicting the influence (PO) of top managers, it has a positive effect.

2. Analysis of the 1987 data has to be approached with caution, but a number of conclusions and comparisons with 1977 can be made.

(a) In spite of the substantial economic and social changes over the decade separating the two measurement periods, there are important similarities in the overall results.

(b) In particular, the apparently causal impact of formal participative structures (PS) on the pattern of influence (PO) for workers and representative bodies is repeated in 1987. In both time-periods, we can observe a similar prediction between participative structures (PS) and the difference in the extent of influence (PO) between top management and labour.

(c) Unemployment strengthened the position of management in 1977 as well as, more weakly, in 1987. Unemployment weakened the influence of labour in 1977 and, to a lesser extent, also in 1987.

Findings from longitudinal analysis

Thus far we have confined ourselves to a somewhat static analysis of the results of the two periods of research and a comparison between them. Finally, it is important to make use of the longitudinal data in an attempt to introduce a dynamic pattern of relationships into the discussion of industrial relations over the decade

780   *Trends and developments*   *IDE*

1977–87. This was achieved by combining the statistics from the two
periods and conducting various analyses with this new two-period
data set.

One objective was to see whether the pattern of influence (PO)
at the end of the decade was conditioned by factors derived from
the material collected ten years previously. Furthermore, the two-
period data could also be used to study changes in patterns of
influence distribution (PO) between 1977 and 1987 and related to
three factors: (i) changes in formal participative structures (PS);
(ii) changes in the general rate of unemployment over the decade;
and (iii) the extent to which different groups in the organizations
exercised influence (PO) at the beginning of the decade in 1977.

The procedures for carrying out these analyses are complex and
again we report only the most important, policy-relevant findings.

- Perhaps the most important result of the longitudinal analysis is
  to demonstrate that it leads, in one or two important respects, to
  different conclusions from the cross-sectional analysis.
- In particular, it shows that formal participative structures (PS)
  are less important predictors for the pattern of influence distribution than the indices of unemployment. This conclusion substantially amends the conclusion derived from the 1977 study
  alone (IDE, 1981). It is, of course, important to bear in mind
  that the 1977–87 period was fairly exceptionally turbulent, in that
  its turbulence combined a major oil price-generated economic
  recession, with substantially increased economic competition and
  changes in technological sophistication. One consequence of
  these indicators of turbulence was the increase of unemployment
  in each of the ten countries. It would be important to repeat such
  a longitudinal analysis during a less turbulent decade, when the
  impact of participative structures (PS) on the de facto distribution of influence (PO) may very well turn out to be dominant.
- An important refinement was introduced into the longitudinal
  analysis by testing two alternative models of accounting for
  changing patterns of influence between the different organizational groups over time. A system "inertia model" would predict
  that groups that were powerful in 1977 would be able to survive well even under unfavourable conditions, while groups that
  started off weakly would lose ground. An alternative "management strategy model" assumes that, during a recession, management would actively seek to reduce the power of the influential

groups which could appear to threaten the managerial prerogative, while they would not be concerned to take steps against
weaker groups.

- In both models, the strategy would also have to take account
  of changes in the rate of unemployment and the strength of participative structures (PS).
- The statistical analysis strongly supports the management
  strategy model. Over the ten-year period, labour tended to lose
  ground in organizations where it had been strong in the 1970s,
  rather than where it started off without posing a threat to
  management. The management strategy of reducing the strength
  of labour, which it might have seen as a threat to its own position,
  was facilitated in places where unemployment was high.
- Where unemployment was not high and labour was not particularly strong in the 1977 research, the influence (PO) of workers
  did not change very much. In these circumstances it is quite likely
  that management initiated quasi-participative human resources
  measures, like briefing groups and various employee involvement
  programmes, including quality circles.

Interpretation and discussion

The arguments in favour of measures to support organizational
democracy or in opposition to it have been prominent over several
decades. In the United States, the argument in favour of participation of employees is sometimes advocated as a way of increasing the
competitiveness of American industry vis-a-vis Japan (Cole, 1979;
Lawler, 1986: 10). In Europe the arguments against participation by
some managements, particularly in Britain, are the reverse: namely,
that companies would lose competitiveness. However, in general,
the debate in Europe is conducted as much on the political as on the
economic level (Foundation for the Improvement of Living and
Working Conditions, 1989).

The academic and research literature is very extensive (see for
instance the series of *Yearbooks* and *Handbooks*: Crouch and
Heller, 1983; Wilpert and Sorge, 1984; Stern and McCarthy, 1986;
Lammers and Szell, 1989; Russell and Rus, 1991).

There is no agreement about what increases in organizational
democracy should achieve (Wagner and Gooding, 1987). Employers
and some academics would like to see increases in profitability or

a reduction of conflict, while political scientists see organizational democracy as a 20th-century extension of political democracy and therefore as something worthwhile in itself. Some trade unions are concerned that through co-optation, successful participative practices would undermine the power of collective bargaining and managers are concerned that organizational democracy will usurp their right to manage.

Against the background of these controversies, our research produces some useful evidence, which is relevant for the formulation of policy. To begin with, the research in the ten countries separated by ten years shows that, on average, neither de jure participative structures (PS) nor de facto participative behaviour (PO) are very highly developed in the majority of our studied countries or organizations. In the 5-point influence and power continuum (PO), the highest score for workers is 2.44 for Yugoslavia. This signifies a position half-way between "little" and "moderate" influence. Most scores are much closer to "little influence" and six are between "no influence" and "little influence".

Is this amount of influence-sharing a matter of concern? Could this evidence give objective support to management's fear of usurpation or trade unions' anxiety of weakening an adversarial policy? Furthermore, given such a very low level of participation, even in Germany where legally supported codetermination has existed since the early 1950s, is it reasonable to expect participation to produce measurable improvement in an organization's profitability or a reduction in conflict? Of course, the figures we cite are means and our sample did not include the most advanced companies in terms of participation policy.

The figure for the influence (PO) of representative bodies, for example, is higher; in Yugoslavia it reaches 3.44, that is to say, half-way between "moderate" and "much" influence, but in Germany, with its forty-year tradition of Works Councils, it is only 2.69 (between "little" and "moderate" influence).

The formal, often legal prescription (PS) to induce participative behaviour shows a wide variation between countries. The 1987 data give the representative bodies in Yugoslavia an average score of 4.79 (on a 6-point scale). This result signifies that they are close to achieving joint decision-making rights with management. In the case of Germany, with 3.99, it almost reaches the obligatory right of a group to be consulted before a decision is taken. The legal prescription for Poland almost reaches such a position, but in Japan,

Finland and Britain, the formal structures fail to provide even the right to receive information. This finding of the very low average level of de facto participation (PO) and the moderate but very varying formal supportive structures (PS) must be borne in mind when drawing policy-relevant conclusions about the current and future role of participative behaviour in organizations.

The European Economic Commission has tried to achieve a common policy on information sharing and consultative rights since 1972, but progress has been very slow in the face of heavy opposition from management. The original proposals, which were based on the German system, have been very considerably scaled down. One of the practical problems facing the European Commission is the great variety of participative structures (PS) and practices in its member countries.

Our finding, that there are very few contingencies that affect the relationship between participative structures (PS) and influence-sharing behaviour (PO), may turn out to be a useful support in the formulation of national or cross-national policies. In 1977, as well as in 1987, factors like size of organization, level of automation, skill requirements, product complexity, perceived market dominance and political instability were of little significance in understanding the dynamics of participative behaviour. This result would suggest that a single framework of requirements within a European Company Law structure could be applied to information disclosure and participation in organizations of different sizes (though our sample extends only from 100 to 2000 employees), skill requirements, and so on.

Similar considerations apply to policy at the level of organizations. Findings in support of the "management strategy model" suggest that under the umbrella of an economic recession and high unemployment, companies may deliberately have reduced the influence of labour where it had previously been relatively strong. It is possible that such a strategy was based on an emotional rather than a factual interpretation of the strength of labour's real influence in the decision-making process. In support of this is the finding from the 1977 research that when respondents are asked how much influence they would like to have, compared with what they currently have, the increase is very moderate (IDE, 1981; 191–4). Other research has reported similar findings (Wall and Lischeron, 1977). In looking at the overall result of the longitudinal replication study reported here, it is reassuring that over a turbulent ten-year period, the basic pattern of results shows substantial stability.

It would seem that some formal prescriptive or legally supported participative structures (PS) lend support to participative behaviour (PO) reaching down to the lowest level of organization. The very high unemployment rate in the decade 1977–87 undoubtedly made its own major impact on reducing the influence of labour during this period, and it is therefore necessary to look at these relationships again during a less turbulent decade. It would also be important to explore the length of time it takes in the different countries for structures to affect behaviour.

In this connection, it is worth reporting briefly on a longitudinal research following the 1977 field work. Three countries from the Industrial Democracy in Europe team (IDE, 1981) were able to carry out a five-year in-depth study in seven organizations using the same influence–power measuring instruments, but adding several output measures and refinements which can only be tackled in a continuous-monitoring type of longitudinal research. The study, called "Decisions in Organizations" (DIO) took place in *Britain*, *The Netherlands* and *Yugoslavia* (DIO, 1979; Heller et al., 1988).

Several findings from the DIO research are relevant for the replication study. In the first place, once again the overall distribution of Influence (PO) over the different levels of organization was similar to the results reported here and did not differ significantly over the five years of the research. The DIO study followed 217 tactical and strategic decisions from start-up to implementation. Instead of measuring formal participative structures (PS) at the national level, it used a structural measure called status power (SP), which assessed the formal authority of each group or committee in each organization. The measure was based on written evidence or long-established policy. The predictive potential of status power on de facto participation of top management and workers was very substantial and significant.

The finding reinforces the evidence on the importance of structures in the decision-making processes of the 1977–87 replication study. Taken together with the DIO results, it seems that a reasonable amount of influence distribution (PO), down to the lowest level of organization, probably requires formal structural support, either at the national or organizational level, or at both. It has important policy implications and weakens the argument in favour of voluntaristic ad hoc arrangements in support of participation. It may also add to our knowledge of organizational behaviour by emphasizing the importance of formal structures as a key variable in attempting not only internal but also societal change. We may also generalize these findings with respect to predicting longitudinal shifts in behaviour over time and the difficulties in achieving this.

References

Cole, R. (1979) *Work, Mobility and Participation*. Berkeley, CA: University of California Press.

Crouch, C. and Heller, F., eds (1983) *Internationol Yearbook of Organizational Democracy*, Vol. 1. Chichester: Wiley.

DIO (Decisions in Organizations) (1979) "Participative Decision Making: a Comparative Study", *Industrial Relations* 18: 295–309.

Foundation for the Improvement of Living and Working Conditions (1989) *New Information Technology ond Participation in Europe*. Shankill, Eire: Loughlinstown House.

Heller, F.A. (1984) "The Role of Longitudinal Method in Management Decision Making", in J.G. Hunt, D. Hosking, C. Schriesheim and R. Stewart (eds) *Leaders and Managers: International Perspectives on Managerial Behaviour and Leadership*. New York: Pergamon Press.

Heller, F.A., Drenth, P.J.D., Koopman, P. and Rus, V. (1988) *Decisions in Organisations: A Longitudinal Study of Routine, Tactical ond Strategic Decisions*. London: Sage.

IDE — International Research Group (1976) "Industrial Democracy in Europe (IDE) — An International Comparative Study", *Sociol Science Information* 15: 177–203.

IDE — International Research Group (1981) *Industrial Democracy in Europe*. London: Oxford University Press.

IDE — International Research Group (1992) *Industrial Democracy in Europe Revisited*. London: Oxford University Press.

Lammers, C. and Szell, G. (1989) *International Handbook of Participation in Organizations*, Vol. 1. London: Oxford University Press.

Lawler, E.E. (1986) *High Involvement Management: Participative Strategies for Improving Organizational Performance*. San Francisco, CA: Jossey-Bass.

Russell, R. and Rus, V. (1991) *International Handbook of Participation in Organizations*, Vol. 2. London: Oxford University Press.

Stern, R.M. and McCarthy, S. (1986) *International Yearbook of Organizational Democrocy*, Vol. 3. Chichester: Wiley.

Wagner, J.A. and Gooding, R. (1987) "Effects of Societal Trends on Participation Research", *Administrative Science Quarterly* 32: 241–62.

Wall, T.D. and Lischeron, J.A. (1977) *Worker Participation: A Critique of the Literature and Some Fresh Evidence*. London: McGraw-Hill.

Warner, M. (1990) "Management Versus Self-Management in Yugoslavia", *Journal of General Management* 16: 20–38.

Wilpert, B. and Sorge, A. (1984) *International Yearbook of Organizational Democracy*, Vol. 2. Chichester: Wiley.

[26]

Advances in Industrial Organizational Psychology
B.J. Fallon, H.P. Pfister, J. Brebner (eds.)
© *Elsevier Science Publishers B.V. (North-Holland), 1989*   125

INDUSTRIAL DEMOCRACY - A CHALLENGE TO LEADERSHIP IN EUROPEAN WORK ORGANIZATIONS

Bernhard Wilpert

Institute of School, Berlin University of Technology, Berlin, F.R.G.

Three important features characterize the context of European work organizations, each of them with a significant impact on participation and industrial democracy in their role within the organizational governance: economic crisis and unemployment, technological change, and changing work related values. This paper links the major findings to two large scale international comparative studies that explicitly address some of the ensuing challenges to organizational leadership: (1) An eight country comparison on the Meaning of Working with close to 15,000 respondents, and (2) a twelve country comparison on Industrial Democracy in Europe investigating de facto levels of participation in 134 matching companies in the mid-70's and mid-80's. The research findings are evaluated in terms of their relevance to shed light onto present dynamics European work organizations.

INTRODUCTION

The central issue that we are addressing here is organisational governance. The focus in this paper is on industrial democracy which - in its modern understanding can be considered a genuinely European topic. However, even within Europe alone the term denotes a bewildering variety of concepts, structures and processes (IDE, 1981b). It refers

- to notions such as worker self management in Yugoslav enterprises,
- to co-determination of employee representatives on supervisory boards of companies or of elected works councils in German companies,
- to union-management agreements about the form and content of interest articulation in French work organisations,
- to institutionalized consultation patterns between Dutch supervisors and their work groups on day-to-day activities,
- to joint management and labour safety committees in Sweden, just to name a few examples.

Yet there is a uniting link for all these diverse forms: they all are characterised by their quasi-statutory nature based on legal or collective bargaining norms with an intent to facilitate a bottom-up participation of employees in the governance of their work organisations. Such statutes constitute rights vis-a-vis traditional top-down management and thus transform employee participation in organisational decision making into a totally different phenomenon than is meant by 'participative management' under human relations auspices. Human relations induced participation is a consequence of environmental impacts upon work organisations, a consequence of deliberate, externally induced organisational change.

But since factors other than statutory norms for participation may as well impact on intra-organisational processes and moderate the participative behaviour in organisations we must employ an open socio-technical systems perspective which has been so elegantly and seminally developed by some of our eminent Australian colleagues (Emery, 1969; Emery and Trist, 1960).

Based on two international comparative studies which we conducted ourselves I would like to show some empirical evidence which might shed some light onto the following questions:

(1) What special features characterise work meanings held by the working population in European countries, especially with reference to work distribution strategies?

(2) Can we indeed speak of a demise of traditional work ethics in Europe?

(3) What do we know about increased demands for participation in European work organisations?

(4) Do statutory rules for participation make a difference in terms of participative behaviour?

The Meaning of Working (MOW) Study

In a comprehensive study of work meanings in eight countries (MOW 1981, 1987) we interviewed in 1982-83 close to 15,000 respondents. This alone puts the study in the category of one of the largest systematic international comparisons of work related values. In our sampling procedures we used both a representative sample from the national labour force and a choice of 10 target groups per country, the latter ones chosen according to criteria of the target group's centrality/marginality to the labour market (e.g. engineers, part time employees, retired). "Meaning of Working" was understood to denote a concept that refers to complex and relatively stable cognitive-evaluative structures regarding working (Ruiz Quintanilla and Wilpert, 1988). More specifically, the concept was understood to comprise at least three major components:

the general importance of working and its relative weight attributed as a life role

Industrial democracy in Europe   127

in comparison to others (Work Centrality)
- internalized social norms about working relating to specific entitlements or duties connected with working (Social Norms)
- work goals and preferences relating to work settings (Work Goals).

I am using here only a very minor part of the data collected in order to give at least a partial answer to the first question posed above regarding specific features of work meanings in Europe. On a scale ranging from 2 to 10 there are some striking similarities and differences:

Britain 6.36, Germany 6.67, Netherlands 6.69, Belgium 6.81, U.S.A. 6.94, Israel 7.10, Yugoslavia 7.30, Japan 7.78.

Two observations seem in order here:

(1) The mean work centrality of all national samples is well above the mid-point of the scale (6.0). This indicates that working in all our countries is still an important life role.

(2) In comparison to all other country samples the labour forces of the EC-countries have significantly lower mean work centrality scores.

Let us add to these findings our results regarding work time preferences (Table 1):

Table 1
Work Time Preferences (national representative samples), n = 8,661.

Question:	"Suppose people were able to work less hours for the same pay in the future; which alternative would be most preferable to you?" (percentage distribution)							
	B	UK	D	IS	JAP	NL	US	YU
more holidays	24	17	23	20	36	20	12	14
less work hrs daily	17	18	19	37	28	21	19	32
free aft. weekly	17	9	10	9	11	14	15	3
more prework educ.	4	3	2	5	3	2	8	1
sabbatical every 10 yrs	7	6	3	11	5	4	16	3
less work hrs. f. older	10	10	10	5	11	15	7	10
earlier retirement	22	34	32	10	1	24	23	37

Here we note that the two alternatives that imply a reduction of weekly work time (options 2+3 combined) represents the most preferred solution in five of the eight countries, the exception being the UK, Germany and Yugoslavia where earlier retirement is the option preferred by a relative majority. In other words working remains a very important life role for all our national work forces. I leave aside the difficult question of how to explain the relatively lower centrality of working in our EC-countries. (It could be a consequence of general socio-economic conditions based on historic and cultural factors such as the length of experience with industrialization, cf. MOW, 1987. But it could also be that the work forces in these unemployment marked EC-countries are developing something like a psychological anticipatory coping strategy: "if it becomes so hard to get/keep a job one shouldn't put too much value on it"). However, when it comes to strategic choices on how to create conditions of distributing work anew by means of work time reduction our politicians and unions would be well advised to consider existing preferences.

My second question related to the presumed demise of traditional work ethics. Our findings on social norms may provide some partial answer. Internationalisation of social norms regarding work was measured by agreement/disagreement with 10 statements concerning obligations and duties (e.g. "A worker should value the work he or she does even if it is boring, dirty or unskilled") and concerning entitlements connected with work (e.g. "Every person in our society should be entitled to interesting and meaningful work").

Generally speaking we find no support in our data that young workers are more entitlement oriented than older ones. But the agreement with the duty norm increases with age in all our countries. Only longitudinal cohort studies can decide whether this is a life cyclical effect ("the older we get the more we feel the duty to work") or whether this finding reflects an intergenerational change. In any case, our data suggests that it is dangerous to sweepingly claim a wholesale deterioration of work ethics. Things may change in relation to duty norms while they remain stable in relation to entitlement norms. On the whole, however, our data also show that our EC-countries are all barely on or below the grand mean score when it comes to obligation norms, while three of them (Germany, Belgium and Netherlands) find themselves clearly above the grand mean of entitlement norms. This, I believe, says something also in connection with likely demands to be put forward within work organisations.

The Industrial Democracy in Europe (IDE) Study

This is the question I will address next by using data from a comparative 12-country (West European and Israel) study on industrial democracy in Europe. This is research we have been conducting since 1973 with two measurement points, the first in 1975/7 and the second in 1986/7. The study used close to 9,000 respondents from 134 establishments, matched in terms of size and technology. Its central concern is to measure the impact of formal rules and regulations for employee participation (de jure participation) and of organisational contingencies (size, technology, unionization etc) on actual (de facto) participation of employees in organisational decision making. To answer the question as to what we know about participation demands in

Table 2
Actual and desired involvement in decision making (N = 7,832 from 12 countries, 134 establishments). The six decisions with actual (desired) involvement

	Workers	Foremen	Middle mgt
Working conditions	2.4(3.4)	3.3(3.8)	3.6(4.2)
Training courses	2.2(-)	2.9(3.6)	3.6(4.1)
Transfers	2.3(3.4)	3.1(3.6)	3.6(4.1)
Personal equipment	2.6(3.6)	3.5(4.1)	4.0(4.4)
Task assignment	2.5(3.5)	4.2(4.6)	4.6(4.8)
Holidays	3.5(4.3)	3.9(4.4)	4.2(4.7)
Working Hours	- (4.3)		
Dismissals	- (3.6)		

Scale: 1 = no involvement
        2 = informed beforehand
        3 = informed beforehand and can give opinio
        4 = opinion taken into account
        5 = take part with equal weight
        6 = decide on my own

European work organisations I again will only use a small part of our huge data bank, namely only data concerning the actual and the desired involvement of our respondents in the making of 16 decisions which we studied. Actual and desired involvement was measured by the Influence-Power-Continuum (IPC)-scale with six steps. Table 2 gives the results on the six (out of 16) decisions where workers, foremen and middle level managers have the highest actual and desired involvement scores.

The data are striking in various respects:

(1) All three groups have their highest actual and desired level of involvement in the same five/six decisions.
(2) These decision are all related to the immediate job environment; department or investment decisions are not among them.
(3) There exists a clear-cut slope of involvement intensity as one ascends hierarchical levels.
(4) The overall level of involvement is rather modest ranging from information beforehand to opinion being taken into account.
(5) Desired participation exceeds actual participation in all decisions and for all hierarchical levels.
(6) Working hours, although not among the six decisions where workers are most involved, ranks, however, third for them when it comes to desired involvement.

If we ask ourselves how actual participation is related to desired participation and look at the intercorrelation of the two measures we make an astonishing discovery: the correlation coefficients range from .58 to .74. In other words: the more people participate the more they want to. What seems to loom behind that and other corroborating findings is an apparent dynamic spiraling effect which implies that once people have experienced some form and degree of participation their desire for more participation is likely to increase with the level of actual participation they enjoy. Evidently, participation is not a phenomenon which management is likely to be able to turn on and off arbitrarily.

Since, as we have seen, all European countries have some form of statutory industrial democracy scheme, we can now turn to our last question - whether such statutory rules and regulations make any difference in terms of actual participation.

Again we use evidence from our IDE-study. Probably the single most important finding of our first round of IDE research in the mid 70's was that the most important predictor of actual participation was formally prescribed intensity of participation (de jure participation), followed by a variable which we called "employee mobilisation" (a combined index of a company's unionization and the percentage of employees who are or had been elected employee representatives). In our recent replication study where we went back to the original establishments studied in the mid 70's, apart from conducting a test of robustness of the findings 10 years before, we were able to add to our design a set of macrovariables such as average GNP over 10 years, average unemployment rates and national R&D efforts as an indicator of technical change. Our preliminary analyses show: we were indeed able to replicate basically the same results as in IDE I, i.e. low overall participation remains in most countries, hierarchical effects play a major role irrespective of the given national or societal context, and, in particular, the overriding importance of statutory rules as predictors of actual participation. Furthermore, we could show that macro-variables of the kind I described on the national aggregate level do also serve as significant predictors of actual participation, however to a lesser degree than formal prescriptions of participation. With these findings we believe to have empirically demonstrated that an open socio-technical systems approach which has to include environmental factors is necessary if we want to study a phenomenon adequately such as industrial democracy.

Implications for Work and Organisational Psychology

I have approached my topic in a somewhat roundabout way. I have addressed the problem of the present economic and unemployment crisis in Europe and the national counterstrategies of work time reduction which attempt to cope with that crisis; I have reflected upon the technical change in our industries and the apparent concomitant managerial options to favour more decentralised authority distributions; I have discussed some problems of work related value changes in European work forces and respective expectations regarding work; finally, I have pointed at some trends of internationalisation or rather Europeanization of national economies in Europe and the prospective importance of harmonizing industrial democracy schemes within the EC.

What does all this have to do with our topic of industrial democracy and leadership in European enterprises? The answer is simple: all these intimately intertwined factors that form significant aspects of the European context of work organisations operate as forces towards higher levels of worker involvement in the making of decisions within their work organisations. Participation may thus turn out to be a hinge problem for future development.

CONCLUSION

In the advance of Work and Organisational Pychology as reflected by the research reported here I see, in an aspect which I claim to be at least a partial success, progress in the direction of including variables and factors of a meso and macro level order in the systematic study of participation, which traditionally has always been conceptualized and studied exclusively on an individual or at best an organisational level.

And the challenge to business leaders in Europe? I see it in the need to understand the significance of these environmental conditions and changes which have to be taken into account when it comes to structuring work places, work time allocations and decision making procedures.

CORRESPONDENCE

Address all correspondence to Dr. Bernhard Wilpert, Institute of School, Berlin University of Technology, Berlin, FRG.

REFERENCES

Emery, F.E. (1969). Systems Thinking. Harmondworth: Penguin.

Emery, F.E., & Trist, E. (1960). Socio-Technical Systems. In C.W. Churchman, M. Verhulst (Eds.), Management Science: Models and Techniques, New York: Pergamon.

IDE-International Research Group (1981a). Industrial Democracy in Europe. Oxford: Claredon Press.

IDE-International Research Group (1981b). European Industrial Relations. Oxford: Claredon Press.

MOW-International Research Team (1981). The Meaning of Working. In C. Dlugos, K. Weiermair (Eds.), Management under Differing Value Systems - Managerial Philosophies and Strategies in a Changing World. Berlin/New York: W. de Gruyter.

MOW-International Research Team (1987). The Meaning of Working. London: Academic Press.

Ruiz Quintanilla, S.A., & Wilpert, B. (1988). The Meaning of Working Scientific Status of a Concept. In V. de Keyser, T. Qvale, B. Wilpert, & S.A. Ruiz Quintanilla, (Eds.), The Meaning of Working and Technological Options. Chichester: Wiley.

Part IV
Decisions in Organizations (DIO)

Overview Part IV

The nine chapters in Part IV describe an in-depth five-year longitudinal study in three countries covering seven medium-sized organizations. This project is a natural continuation of the three preceding studies (TMDM and IDE I and II). The top management study described in Part II (Volume I), although cross-sectional in design, gained a moderate degree of insight into the dynamics of power distribution in large-scale organizations through the use of Group Feedback Analysis (GFA) in some countries (see Chapter 10, Volume I). The two-phase longitudinal comparison of IDE I and IDE II involved a replication in the same organizations after an interval of ten years. This gives us the unusual advantage of linking up two cross-sectional studies with a longitudinal dimension and an interpretation covering a slice of history. The DIO project took longitudinality one step further by following the whole cycle of decision-making over its various phases from 'start-up' to 'implementation'. It also made use of a variety of methodologies, including GFA, to add a processual longitudinal dimension to our understanding of decision-making, the distribution of influence and the utilization of employee competence.

The opening essay (Chapter 27) describes the design, the main instruments and the theoretical framework covering routine short-term, medium duration tactical and long-term strategic issues.

The first part of Chapter 28 describes the three-country sample, the operationalization of the variables and the four-phase decision process model. Some data analysis is presented for the routine decision process based on 12 specific decision areas and five outcome variables including satisfaction, effectiveness and skill utilization. The second part presents some analysis of long-term strategic decisions, their relation to the Influence–Power Continuum and, in particular, to Status Power (SP) which assesses variations in formal rules, policies and regulations relating to power in organizations. In the DIO research, Status Power is similar to the formal legally backed power structure (PS), used as an independent variable in the IDE project, and achieves similar results.

Chapter 29 gives a more complete review of the relevant literature in relation to the longitudinal space–time dimension. The fieldwork focuses attention on 217 tactical and strategic decisions and the amount of influence brought to bear by different levels of organization during the four phases of the decision cycle in relation to four outcome variables. Descriptive data on the distribution of influence by level and decision phase is shown for the three countries. Multiple regression results based on a reduction of variables from factor analysis are explained. The multiple regression relates seven predictor variables to four outcomes including skill utilization of managers and lower-level employees.

The next two chapters apply the model and method to three organizations in the Netherlands. Chapter 30 concentrates on 12 short-term routine decisions within the European framework of Works Councils and the Dutch system of work consultation between supervisors and lower-level employees (a formalized approach to direct participation). In addition to questionnaires, the study used direct observation and an analysis of work consultation minutes over two years.

Chapter 31 concentrates on 56 strategic and tactical decisions to determine under what circumstances, different leadership methods (described by the Influence–Power Continuum [IPC]) affect outcomes such as efficiency, achievement and skill utilization. The model includes contingency variables which, like meta-power, decision phase and hierarchical level can act directly on the IPC or on the relation between the IPC and outcomes.

The essay by Wang and Heller (Chapter 32) applies aspects of the DIO and IDE model to a comparison between matched samples of Chinese and British companies in manufacturing and service industries. The information came from 40 managers and 20 trade union leaders who described short-, medium- and long-term decisions at all organizational levels. The procedure obtained quantitative and qualitative data from questionnaires as well as interviews, although only the statistical results are shown in this chapter.

Chapter 33 makes a strong theoretical and practical argument for longitudinal research designs. Most organizational events have a beginning, a process, and an outcome. This is particularly true of decision-making. However, more generally, most socio-psychological assessments could benefit from a phase analysis, for instance, job satisfaction measures may differ between Monday morning and Friday afternoon. Although longitudinal research requires more resources than cross-sectional research, the gain in realism and validity is considerable. Two of the research projects described in these two volumes are used as examples of the utility of longitudinal design.

Chapters 34 and 35 present the Group Feedback Analysis methodology in two British medium-sized companies. In Chapter 34 the method is applied to two phases of questionnaire administration (separated by 12 months) with routine short-term decisions and, in Chapter 35, to the processual longitudinal work with tactical and strategic issues. The utility of GFA which had previously been used mainly with cross-sectional designs (as in Part II) is shown to have similar, as well as enhanced, functions in processual longitudinal research. GFA achieves three objectives: (1) it helps to validate the data; (ii) it obtains additional historical and/or ethnographic information; and (iii) the people who provided the data (usually called subjects) are able to help with interpreting the results, jointly with the researcher, and thus contribute to organizational learning.

Overall, the DIO research, while usefully confirming many of the findings of the preceding studies also extends them significantly and increases the probability of justifying causal assumptions. It is now possible to show that leadershp decision-making styles (as measured by the IPC) change significantly over the phases of the longitudinal decision cycle, as does conflict, the expenditure of time, satisfaction and efficiency. Furthermore, different levels of the hierarchy exert influence during the four phases and this is functionally justified by the distribution of competence. The role of skill as an antecedent to influence on the one hand, and the role of skill utilization as an outcome of influence, can now be incorporated in an extension of the Human Resources Model (see Chapter 7).

Further Reading

Heller, F.A., Drenth, P.J.D., Koopman, Paul and Rus, Veljko (1988), *Decisions in Organizations: A Longitudinal Study of Routine, Tactical and Strategic Decisions*, London and Beverly Hills: Sage Publications.

[27]

Human Relations, Volume 30, Number 7, 1977, pp. 567–587

A Longitudinal Study in Participative Decision-Making[1,2]

Frank A. Heller[3]
Tavistock Institute of Human Relations

Pieter J. D. Drenth and Paul Koopman
Free University of Amsterdam

Veljko Rus
Sociological Institute, Ljubljana

A framework and method of a three-country comparative study on the process of participative decision-making is described. Research methods, models, and instruments are developed in the context of a longitudinal design. The major hypotheses relate to the situationally determined relation between power decentralization, skill utilization, and effectiveness. The four-year study hopes to provide at least partial answers to some theoretical as well as practical questions in a field of considerable current controversy in Europe.

INTRODUCTION

It is reasonable that most social science research starts with a "snapshot" or cross-sectional approach. This means that, at least for the time

[1]Besides the senior authors, Erik Andriessen, Miro Odar, Andre Wierdsma, Alan Brown, and Franz Bus have all made substantial contributions. The research is supported in the Netherlands by the Dutch Organization for Pure Research (ZWO), in Yugoslavia by the Research Community of Slovenia (previously the Boris Kidric Foundation), and in Britain by the Social Science Research Council. The Social Science Research Council is also making a small contribution to the joint UK-Yugoslavia project. The Chemical Industry Training Board is co-sponsoring the project in Britain.

[2]The editor believes that the research design and methods to be used in this longitudinal study will be of interest to those working in this developing field. It is anticipated that the first data article will be available in 9-12 months.

[3]Requests for reprints should be addressed to Dr. Frank A. Heller, Tavistock Institute of Human Relations, Tavistock Centre, 120 Belsize Lane, London NW3 5BA, U.K.

being, one assumes that the "snapshot" is representative of reality, although events take place over time. Further encouragement for continuing with cross-sectional research occurs if a number of such studies at different times and in different places produce similar results. The sophistication of modern survey techniques based on carefully assembled samples adds to the reluctance to use other methods, quite apart from the apparent cost effectiveness of such an approach.

There are at least two major reasons, however, why these arguments are inadequate in the case of many subjects of social science research. One is the high percentage of variance of a phenomenon that is frequently not accounted for by the cross-sectional data. This is particularly true of correlational analyses, in which the coefficients may be highly significant but often account for less than 25% of the total variance. Error or omitted variables often "explain" more of the research topic than the results. We have gotten used to living with this difficulty, but the possibility has to be faced that some of the unexplained variance is due to sampling errors and other measuring problems inherent in the dynamic nature of the phenomenon under investigation (Manning & Dubois, 1958; Ghiselli & Haire, 1960; Bass, 1962).

Second, there are social phenomena in which the sequence of events over time constitutes an essential element. One thinks of subjects like the introduction of payment systems in work organizations. Using a static design to measure a dynamic phenomenon is in itself unsatisfactory and "before-after" assessments are in some danger of missing out on the critical aspect of the "in between" process.

Problems of this kind justify longitudinal studies. Without raising unrealistic expectations about sudden improvements to the explanatory power of the results, it is realistic to take the conclusions from a cross-sectional study and retest some of the major hypotheses in a longitudinal setting. Such studies can also be used to lay out the topography of a dynamic process and to test dynamic hypotheses about change; this cannot be adequately done by the usual questionnaire or interview method in a cross-sectional design.

Two major difficulties probably inhibit researchers from planning longitudinal research; one is its cost and the other a relative paucity of adequate methodology. We do not wish to enter the complex and controversial arguments about "hard" and "soft" methodologies; they are well documented in innumerable texts. See, for instance, Festinger and Katz (1953), de Groot (1962), Churchman (1968), Drenth (1975). It is an undeniable fact, however, that longitudinal studies have tended to use less measurement than cross-sectional research. It is quite possible, of course, to take cross-sectional measurements at several points of a longitudinal process, but the "in between" process has to be approached by other means.

By its very nature, the results of a longitudinal study take a considerable time to accumulate and write up. This article is therefore designed to serve as a preliminary communication to scientific colleagues who are working in a similar subject area or using longitudinal research methods. While we have already spent two years in planning and piloting this research, we expect that our continuing field work will lead us to adopt further changes and, we hope, refinements to the formulations we now present.

The research to be described in this article addresses itself to several of the problems just mentioned. The main objective of the project is to study, in depth and over time, certain defined aspects of the process of decision-making and participation in organizations.

Antecedents

In the past, studies in decision-making and participation have made a number of assumptions that the present research sets out to question. Laboratory as well as cross-sectional field studies tend to assume that decisions are made by one person and that the choices available can be adequately described by a series of binary alternatives leading to a decision tree model. One major hypothesis of innumerable studies on leadership and participation associates a single method or style with successful behavior. Many research studies assumed that participative behavior is most appropriate in nearly all circumstances and that this leads to higher job satisfaction.

Recent research has tended to question these assumptions. The relationship between participation and job satisfaction has frequently been called into question (Vroom, 1964; Lischeron & Wall, 1975; Payne, Fineman, & Wall, 1976). It seems that successful managers use a wide variety of quite different decision styles with the same subordinates (Heller, 1971; Vroom & Yetton, 1973); two people collaborating in a given decision process will describe it differently; a substantial number of people are usually involved in decisions and a "go-no go" choice does not allow for the complexity of the process in which people from different levels and with different skills are involved (Simon, 1960; Friend & Jessop, 1969; Mintzberg, 1973, Mintzberg et al., 1976; Pettigrew, 1973; Braybrooke, 1974).

The present project is in some respects a new phase in a series of research projects that started in the 1960s and in which one of the present authors was the principal investigator (Heller, 1968, 1971, 1973, 1976; Heller & Yukl, 1969). The model described in Figure 1 is an extension and refinement of the original contingency model. In most important respects, however, the present project stands on its own for two reasons. In the first place, this is a longitudinal study, while the previous work was cross-sec-

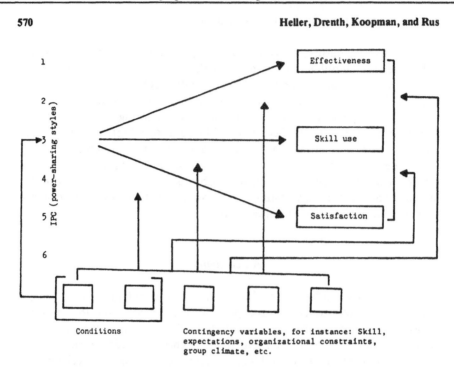

Fig. 1. Contingency model for the analysis of participation and decision-making.

tional. Second, and most important, new research questions were developed. At the end of the previous phase it had become clear that a substantial variety of decision styles were used by managers in every sample investigated. The decision styles varied with level of organization, type of decision, skills and qualifications of staff, etc. (Heller, 1973, 1976). However, the research questions were not directed towards the effectiveness of the various leadership styles under the different circumstances, nor very specifically towards their consequences in terms of the quality of decision implementation and reactions of subordinates. It is one of the major objectives of the present research to study the effectiveness and consequences of the various participatory methods in more detail. The research model had to be extended and those changes are the result of a two-year collaboration between the Dutch, Yugoslav, and British investigators who constitute the present team and are joint authors of this article.

The present project and its previous phase are also related to current research on industrial democracy in Europe that is taking place in ten countries.[4] The industrial democracy project will study the relationship between

---

[4] An article on this project is published in *Social Science Information*, the journal of the UNESCO-sponsored International Social Science Council (March-April 1976). The research will cover at least 10 organizations in each of the 10 countries but not longitudinally. The authors of the present article are involved in both research projects, as is Erik Andriessen.

formal and legal structures prescribing participatory arrangements on the one hand and the actual amount of leadership and power exercised at different levels of organizations on the other. The two projects are complementary.

The Model

The postulated interaction of our main variables is described in a contingency-type model as illustrated in Figure 1. Our objective is to describe and explain the interaction between influence and power sharing in organizations and three groups of outcome variables: (i) skill utilization, (ii) effectiveness, (iii) a number of satisfaction variables, including an index of general satisfaction and a more specific index of satisfaction with participative methods of decision-making.

The independent variable is called the Influence and Power Continuum (IPC); it has six alternative positions, which are briefly described in Figure 2. Two versions have been developed. The one in Figure 2 applies to decisions taken in a normal hierarchical group of two or more people. The second IPC is an adaptation that is used in analyzing the decision process in committees, works councils, and similar management-worker forums.[5]

The model (see Figure 1) describes a number of situations that affect the interaction between independent and dependent variables. We call these situations contingencies and arrange them into four groups:[6]

1. Personal variables, such as age, education, expectations, etc.
2. Situational variables close to the person such as job characteristics, job constraints.
3. Microstructural variables, such as span of control, size of department, group climate.
4. Macrostructural variables like the size of the total organization, attitude to top management and its rules, uncertainty of the environment.

In addition there are some contingency-type variables that influence or limit the amount of influence and power that is excercised in a given situation, for instance, policy or legal regulations. We call these variables "conditions" if they act directly on the independent variable rather than on the interaction between the independent and dependent variables. One of the national teams has worked with the notion of "meta power." While this concept is still evolving within the framework of this research, it is currently seen as a form of constraint exercised by somebody outside the organization (Buckley & Burns, 1974). More specifically, meta power can be described as

---

[5]For further information please apply to the authors.
[6]These groups are derived from the alpha-to-omega hierarchy (Heller, 1973, p. 109).

1. NO INFORMATION
No detailed information about the decision is made available.

2. INFORMATION
Fairly detailed information about the decision is made available.

3. OPPORTUNITY TO GIVE ADVICE
Before the decision is made, the superior explains the problem and asks advice. The superior then makes the decision by himself.

4. ADVICE IS TAKEN INTO CONSIDERATION
As above, but your superior's final choice usually reflects the advice he has received.

5. JOINT DECISION-MAKING
Your superior and his subordinate(s) together analyze the problem and come to a decision. Your superior usually has as much influence over the final choice as his subordinate(s). In fact, one could say everybody in principle has equal influence (one man, one vote).

6. COMPLETE CONTROL
You or members of your work group are given the authority to deal with this decision on your own. Superiors would intervene only in exceptional circumstances. Naturally, every now and then you or the group are expected to account for the action taken.

Fig. 2. The influence power continuum (IPC).

a predetermined and indirect set of constraints exercised by an outside group of individuals or organizations that limits the freedom of decision-making for any particular group or individual. The term "outside" has to be defined in a systems framework.

The objective of our contingency model is to document and, if possible, measure the circumstances under which influence and power sharing lead to one or more of the outcomes (skill utilization, etc.). An example may be useful. For instance, we can take as a contingency a personal variable like education. It can then be postulated that a high degree of influence and power sharing (i.e., method 3, 4, or 5) will be associated with an efficient decision outcome, *if* the people involved in the decision have a requisite amount of education or training. If this condition is not met, we would expect no association between our independent and dependent variables.

Sample and Decisions

Cost limitations usually prevent longitudinal in-depth studies from being carried out in a large number of companies. This often leads to the use of case studies and the avoidance of measurement. The design used in the present research overcomes some of the negative features of case studies by taking decisions as a main unit of analysis for certain purposes. In theory one can choose as large a number of decisions as one normally chooses organizations, so that most of the usual techniques of statistical analysis can be applied. Sampling by decisions is particularly appropriate for long-term issues (see Table I) or for studying processes in management-worker committees. On the other hand, when it comes to short-term decisions (Table I) we are particularly interested in the strategy of decision-making in different groups. Consequently, the group becomes the main unit of analysis. This means that we use the variance in IPC as the independent variable. For medium-term decisions these two lines of approach meet and overlap; sampling by decisions as well as groups becomes important.

Our design aims at studying six companies in three countries matched by size and decision set but not necessarily by sector or product. We would also have liked to specify the product, but it has to be accepted that longitudinal research lasting 3-4 years has to give preference to companies that are willing to provide a supportive climate for research over such a time span. Willingness to collaborate is therefore the decisive variable; the other aspects of the deisgn will be matched as far as practicable.

We have chosen three ranges of decisions to make up our sample. They can be identified in Table I.

In each company, there will be at least one example of decisions described under 1, 2, and 3 in Table I. There will be two cycles of budget forecasting and several work conditions decisions (decisions 4 and 5). Finally, a set of questionnaires relating to the 12 short-duration decisions described in the Appendix will be administered twice, separated by about 18 months.

Table I. Description of Decision Set

Decisions or issues	Duration[a]	Frequency[b]	Organization level
1. Setting up a consultative procedure	Long	Low	Top[c]
2. Initiating a new product or service	Long	Low	Top
3. Deciding on a medium-size capital investment	Long	Low	Top
4. Budget forecasting	Medium	Low	Top and medium
5. Work conditions (safety, environmental conditions, etc.)	Medium	Medium	Medium and low
6. 12 specified short duration decisions.	Short	High	Low

[a] Low = less than 1 a year; medium = 3-5 a year; high = more than 5 a year.
[b] Long = more than 6 months; medium = 2-3 months; short = about one month.
[c] The initiative can come from any level but requires top management sanction.

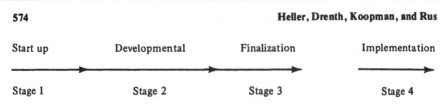

Fig. 3. Stages in decision process.

The word "decision" has been used so far because this term is well established in the organization literature, but we will now speak of an "issue" when we wish to describe the process by which a problem goes through several stages of transformation before it ends up as a decision (Braybrook, 1974). We distinguish four phases in the (decision) process, as illustrated in Figure 3, although it is recognized that mergers and overlap can occur, particularly between stages 1, 2, and 3.

METHODS OF RESEARCH

A variety of methods are being used to cover different requirements of the research design. To begin with we take the medium- and long-term issues (Nos. 1, 2, 3, 4, and 5 in Table I) and trace their process *backwards* through document analysis, including committee minutes, and/or interviews with key people who were involved in it. We call this "retrospective tracing." At the same time we document the *present* state of the process by observation in committees and interviews. Whenever possible we interview people before a committee to ascertain how they feel about the issue and what they expect to happen. We interview them again afterwards to get reactions about what happened during the meeting, at which we are also present.

As a result of our analysis of committee meetings, observations of behavior, and interviews, the range of variables given in Table II are coded. Definitions of variables and coding instructions are available on request. The analysis subsequent to retrospective tracing is called "process registration." The sequence can be seen in Figure 4. Whenever a reasonable amount of information about an ongoing process has been documented in the categories described in Table II, it is assembled and fed back to the respondents who gave us the information. We call this method "Group Feedback Analysis" (GFA) since the information feedback is usually carried out in groups (Heller, 1969).

Group Feedback Analysis, in the present study, is a development from previous phases of research where it was used in a cross-sectional con-

Table II. Examples of Major Variables
Coded During Observation of Meetings
and Interviews

Stages of decision
Time structure of decision
Status power of committees and
   decisions
Trust between the people involved
Decision method (see Figure 2)
Clarity of goal
Conflict
     Intensity
     Type of conflict
     Method of resoltuion
Achievement feasibility
Acceptability
Satisfaction
     With the outcome of the decision
     With the decision process
Skill utilization
Implementation
Achievement
Resistance
Outside influence (meta power)

---

text or as an agent of change (Heller, 1971). In our longitudinal study, GFA has the following objectives:

1. To provide an opportunity for mutual learning to the client organization (our respondents) as well as the research team.

2. To enable us to verify the findings up to the point where feedback occurs, or to amend our findings in the light of the new information obtained during the feedback session.

3. To use the partial results on some of the variables under investigation to serve as a stimulus for assessing aspirations or expectations of future

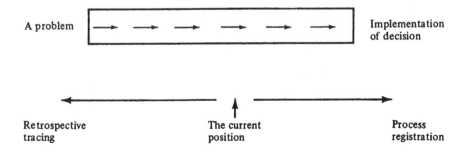

Fig. 4. Documentation of a decision issue over time. "The current position" is shown in the middle of the cycle but, of course, it could come at any point from the very beginning of problem formulation to implementation.

Table III. Questionnaires for Short-Duration Decision
Issues

Variable	Abbreviation of questionnaire
Personal identification form	PIF
Influence-power continuum[a]	IPC
Methods of decision-making defined	Definitions
Importance of decision-tasks	IMP-D
Skill utilization	SU
Importance of skills	IMP-S
Reasons for underutilization	R-UU
Effects of consultation	EFF-CONS
Expectations of consultation	EXP-CONS
Satisfaction in general	SAT-G
Satisfaction with participation	SAT-P
Group characteristics	GR-CH
Job characteristics	JOB-CH
Organization climate	CLIM-P

[a] Two versions are used. One applies to decisions made in
a normal (hierarchical) work group. The other is used
for decisions arrived at in committees, works councils,
etc.

events. It is to be hoped that this use of GFA will introduce a dynamic element into the longitudinal methodology by assessing the strength and
direction of motives and their changing pattern over the process of decision-
making.

We are aware that the "dynamic" property of GFA can be criticized
for its possible effect on the "objectivity" of the research information. To
some extent this problem is unavoidable and is inherent in any intensive
field study where an observer tries to make unbiased analyses of phenomena
and processes while at the same time being concerned with ongoing changes
(Landsberger, 1958; Webb, Campbell, Schwartz, & Sechrest, 1966). Other
social scientists have put forward the claim that the introduction of relevant
and apparently objective information, with the subsequent action adjustment to it, can itself be considered as a check on the validity of the research
results (Argyris, 1970, 1976; Clark, 1976).

Even without this argument, however, it can be claimed that a longitudinal study is always concerned with ongoing changes based on innumerable inputs of information. These inputs cannot usually be assessed by the
researchers and this constitutes an unavoidable hazard. GFA is one such
input, but it has the advantage of being known. The greater the relative
impact of GFA to other inputs, the more rather than the less control does
the research team exercise over ongoing events.

So far the method has been described in relation to the long- and medium-term issues of Table I. Equally important for the research design are the short-term issues that occur with reasonable frequency in most organizations; 12 of these form our "decision set." While questionnaires constitute a small part of our data gathering for medium- and long-term issues, they are the major method for measuring the variables of our model on the more repetitive and probably more routine decision-issues. For this purpose, a complete set of questionnaires was developed and pretested in the three countries.[7] These questionnaires are briefly described in the Appendix. A list of the questionnaires can be seen in Table III.

It will be seen that our measurements cover all aspects of the contingency model shown in Figure 1. A variety of multivariate statistical methods will be used to test the main assumptions implicit in our model.

COMPARISON OF THE THREE COUNTRIES

The three countries represented in this study were selected because they have different legal and administrative provisions for sharing power and influence inside organizations.

The system of self-management was introduced in Yugoslavia as an alternative to a state bureaucratic system typical of East European countries. Extensive documentation of the system and several substantial research projects designed to assess its effectiveness have been published (see, for example, Pusic, 1972-3; Rus, 1970, 1972; Obradovic, 1970; Kavic, Rus, & Tannenbaum, 1971). It was also an extension of the revolutionary populist movement into the field of work organizations.

By the first law of 1950 Workers Councils were established at enterprise level with the right to decide about some crucial matters of enterprise policy. During the next 10 years the rights of Workers Councils were enlarged and new committees of Workers Councils were established. At the same time a large decentralization of state power occurred; directive planning was replaced by indicative planning, which meant there was far less control from the government and an increased role for the market.

In 1963 the new Constitution established almost complete autonomy for work organizations. All work organizations (economic and social services like hospitals, schools, etc.) had a right to decide about profit allocation, internal organizational structure, and personnel policy. However, this external autonomy of work organizations did not coincide with a sub-

---

[7]In pilot studies, alpha coefficients of .75 to .87 for the dependent variables have been obtained.

stantial power redistribution within organizations. Despite a highly developed representative self-management structure at the enterprise level, top management still remain the most influential group, and workers themselves the least influential group. At the top of the enterprise some kind of more or less equal power sharing between top management, Workers Councils, and staff was established, while at the other levels of organization the amount of power remained substantially lower. This type of power structure within work organizations was labeled polyarchic centralism.

On the other hand, high external autonomy of work organizations increased responsibility for effectiveness and competitiveness between organizations. Rapid economic development was one consequence of such an environmental dynamic. At the same time this liberalization of the economy provoked higher social differentiation among employees and greater economic differences between local communities and regions. The lack of coordination and the increased differentiation of value orientation were also consequences of the above-mentioned environmental changes.

The new Constitution of 1974 was a response to these phenomena. However, this response did not mean the substitution of the market economy by the previous state economy. Instead a new system of social contracts and self-management agreements has been developing. By this system coordination between all organizations at all levels of society has to be achieved through bargaining and mutual agreement.

Administrative coordination of the state and competitive regulation of markets will be substituted by contractual agreements between work organizations. Within work organizations the following two changes should be achieved: (1) greater direct participation of workers through local bodies of self-management at lower levels of work organizations, and (2) greater control upon all executive and representative bodies, based on new structures of workers' control. Both changes are methods of trying to achieve higher equality among all employees within work organizations. Greater activity of political organizations should guarantee the accomplishment of this goal.

In the Netherlands there are two interesting developments in the field of industrial relations. In the first place the legal and social changes with respect to the works' council. In the first Works' Council Act (May 1950) the council has been described as a consultative body concerned not primarily with the interests of either the employee or the employer, but with the common interests of the undertaking. In 1971 a new act was passed by the parliament in which a number of changes have been realized. One of the changes increases the competence of the works' council (right of codecision in a number of social matters and the obligation of management to ask advice relating to vital organizations and economic measures). The second major change acknowledges the interrelation between joint consultation and the promotion of workers' interest. Further changes have more recently been proposed by the Dutch government in which the council's influence and power increases and in which the idea of cooperation is questioned to a still greater extent. This last development certainly parallels a change of attitudes in one of the major labor unions in the Netherlands (see also Alberda, 1976).

Second, the direct supervisor-subordinate relationship has become subject to formal regulations in a great many enterprises, although no legislation in this field has materialized up to now. Many organizations have installed the so-called werkoverleg procedure, which is a formalized, regular meeting of the superior with the subordinate(s) to discuss matters of work content, work conditions, and work organization.

The problems with both the works' council and werkoverleg types of participative structures are manifold. The works' council has not been able to find a balance between the opposition role with the objective "promotion of interests of the workers" on the one hand, and the constructive, responsible role with the objective "well-being of the total firm" on the other (see also Drenth, 1969, 1973).

Werkoverleg suffers from the fact that in the opinion of some unions this "participation" may function as a means of reducing workers' aspirations. They feel that such a scheme cannot be supported, since it distracts attention from the desired more fundamental and structural changes in the power structure of the enterprise (Ramondt, 1974).

It will be understood from this description why, next to the major long-term decisions, short-term and very frequent decisions (subject to werkoverleg) will also be investigated in the Dutch part of the study. A study of both types of decisions and the interaction between the two participative systems will raise some very interesting questions.

Collective bargaining is the central method of joint regulation in the United Kingdom. The British system of collective bargaining is more highly developed in terms of the range of issues and the number of people it covers than elsewhere in Europe (Commission of Industrial Relations, 1974). However, there are wide variations in the scope of collective bargaining between industries and even between firms within the same industry. While in the most advanced cases there are already substantive negotiations on manpower planning, job and income security, and disclosure of information, frequently these are regarded as areas of "managerial prerogative." Indeed, some writers (e.g., Flanders, 1970) have questioned the regulative impact of collective bargaining, considering that "internal" regulation was often unilateral (whether by management or workgroup). The development of plant-level organizations (documented by the Royal Commission on Trade

Unions and Employers' Associations, 1968; Government Social Survey, 1968; Office of Population Census and Surveys, 1974) and any subsequent extension of collective bargaining represents a de facto participation in managerial decision-making. This is still seen by the Trades Union Congress as the "main way forward in extending collective control at local level" (Trades Union Congress, 1974).

However, some subjects are not well suited to formal negotiations (e.g., investment, development plans, etc.). Voluntary joint consultative committees that operated separately from trade-union-based negotiating machinery flourished in the 1940s and early 1950s but subsequently declined in importance. This was because they either inhibited the development of local negotiating machinery or were reduced to discussing trivial matters. Even where there are long-established works' councils these have tended to become integrated into the trade-union machinery.

This failure of joint consultation has led to a search for other ways to extend "participation." There has been much recent debate and, gradually, formal provisions are being introduced that require some participative structures. A Government Committee of Inquiry on Industrial Democracy is, at present, taking evidence from "interested parties" and is due to report early in 1977. The Trades Union Congress has recently committed itself to an approach to industrial democracy favoring a 50% representation of trade unions at the top tier of a two-tier board structure similar to the German system operating in the coal, iron, and steel industry since 1952 (Trades Union Congress, 1974).

A recent investigation into an attempt by the British Steel Corporation to introduce a measure of democracy by inserting a small number of workers as directors at divisional board level points to many weaknesses in the particular form this experiment took (Brannen, Batstone, Fatchett, & White, 1976). At the same time, this study shows that independent research can play a practical role in developing improved work organizations based on a greater understanding of social dynamic forces in specified situations.

It can be seen that there is currently much debate about the appropriate degree and forms of "participation." This has resulted in legislation being introduced or at least proposed in each country designed to change the existing distribution of power within organizations. However, findings from both the Netherlands and Yugoslavia indicate that the setting up of formal participative structures at company level does not necessarily increase the power of lower levels, although there may be a wider horizontal dispersal of power at the top. Furthermore, in the Netherlands and the United Kingdom some major unions have reservations about this type of participation, since they believe that it may compromise the traditional trade-union "oppositional" role. Other unions consider these dangers to be outweighed by the advantages to be gained directly from having a greater influence on major decisions and indirectly from the increased "well-being of the total firm."

Because of these problems with representative participation, attempts are being made in both Yugoslavia and the Netherlands to introduce greater direct participation of the workers. This type of participation is again viewed by some unions in the Netherlands and the U.K. as a "double-edged sword." These unions welcome the idea of a genuine redistribution of power to the workers on the shop-floor. However, they suspect that the introduction of "participation" may be manipulative and that, far from leading to a sharing of power, it is intended to consolidate those already in control.

It can be seen that the three countries have adopted a variety of arrangements and in each case account has to be taken of very recent developments that have not yet been investigated by social science research. The longitudinal design of the present project should enable us to gain some useful insights into the ongoing change processes although our small sample of companies (notwithstanding a reasonable sample of decisions and decision groups) will severely limit generalizations on the more global issues affecting power sharing. It has to be remembered, however, that our research is designed to be complementary to the large sample study on industrial democracy (IDE, 1976). The reciprocity of information between these two research projects should be of considerable value.

Our research questions and assumptions follow from the model illustrated in Figure 1. We are investigating the nature of the relationships between different degrees of influence and power sharing (IPC) and our groups of outcomes variables (effectiveness, skill utilization, and satisfaction). We expect this relationship to be affected by a number of contingency variables, for instance, expectations, job constraints, group climate, established rules, etc. Furthermore, we expect conditions like the nature of the task to determine or limit the type of influence and power sharing used. These assumptions can be tested by the use of multivariate statistical procedures as long as a sufficient number of observations are available. Many of the specific hypotheses used for this part of our research would be developments of the hypotheses from previous stages of the research (Heller, 1971, 1976) and the related literature (Vroom & Yetton, 1973).

A second group of questions and assumptions depends quite specifically on the longitudinal process of decision-making, which has been divided into three gross stages (see Figure 3). We put forward the view that our variables (see Table II) will be distributed differently during these stages. Trust, for instance, can be expected to be low during the start-up phase, to improve up to finalization, but to fall back again during implementation. We would expect the decision method to follow a similar cycle: More power sharing in the middle phases than at the beginning or end.

Some of the hypothesized relations may seem obvious but have to be confirmed nevertheless, for instance, the idea that the overall time cycle is shortest for the least complex decision. One of Parkinson's so-called laws would suggest the opposite.

The research operates with a number of quite distinct decision tasks (Table I) and it has already been said that, according to our model, we expect a different amount of power sharing and consequently different outcome variables to result. The longitudinal research process will want to question whether these interrelations are true of different stages of the time cycle.

Finally, it is worth drawing attention to the committee aspect of the decision-making process. Many of our decisions are brought up and processed through works committees or other participative structures. But the decision process also goes on outside the committees. Some issues are not normally brought before committees for various reasons; for instance, the budget-forecasting exercise, though the results or arguments about budgeting may well come to the committee. The research is in a position to explore the relationship between decision-making inside and outside employee participation committees. We also expect to be able to relate the formal structure of the committee and its changing policy over the three-year period of investigation to some of our decision variables (Table II), for instance, trust, conflict, acceptability, and satisfaction.

REFERENCES

ALBERDA, W. *Arbeidsverhoudingen in Nederland.* Alphen a.d. Rijn: Samson, 1976.

ARGYRIS, C. *Intervention theory and method: A behavioural science view,* Reading, Mass.: Addison-Wesley, 1970.

ARGYRIS, C. Problems and new directions in industrial psychology. In M. D. Donnette, (Ed.), *Handbook of Industrial and Organizational Psychology.* Chicago: Rand-McNally, 1976.

BASS, B. M. Further evidence on the dynamic character of criteria. *Personnel Psychology,* 1962, *15,* 93-97.

BRANNEN, P., BATSTONE, E., FATCHETT, D., & WHITE, P. *The worker directors: A sociology of participation.* London: Hutchinson, 1976.

BRAYBROOKE, D. *Traffic congestion goes through the issue machine.* London: Routledge & Kegan Paul, 1974.

BUCKLEY, W., & BURNS, T. Power and meta power. Relational control and the development of hierarchical control systems. Paper presented at the 8th World Congress of Sociology, Toronto, 1974.

CHURCHMAN, C. W. *Challenge to reason.* New York: McGraw-Hill, 1968.

CLARK, A. W. (Ed.). *Experimenting with organizational life: The action research approach.* New York: Plenum, 1976.

COMMISSION ON INDUSTRIAL RELATIONS. *Worker participation and collective bargaining in Europe* (Study 4). London: Her Majesty's Stationery Office, 1974.

DRENTH, P. J. D. The works' council in the Netherlands. In P. J. D. Drenth (Ed.), *Industrial democracy in the Netherlands.* Meppell: Boom, 1969.

Longitudinal Study in Participative Decision-Making **583**

DRENTH, P. J. D. The works' council in the Netherlands: An experiment in participation. In *Participation and self-management* (Ie nat. soc. conference on participation and self-management). Zagreb, 1973, pp. 67-75.

DRENTH, P. J. D. *Inleiding in de testtheorie.* Deventer: Van Loghum Slaterus, 1975.

FESTINGER, L., & KATZ, D. (Eds.). *Research methods in the social sciences.* New York: Dryden Press, 1953.

FLANDERS, A. *Management and unions.* London: Faber, 1970.

FRIEND, J. K., & JESSOP, W. N. *Local government and strategic choice.* London: Tavistock Publications, 1969.

GHISELLI, E. E., & HAIRE, M. The validation of selection tests in the light of the dynamic character of criteria. *Personnel Psychology,* 1960, *13,* 225-231.

GOVERNMENT SOCIAL SURVEY. *Workplace industrial relations.* London: Her Majesty's Stationery Office, 1968.

DE GROOT, A. D. *Methodologie.* The Hague: Mouton, 1962.

HELLER, F. A. Power sharing as a style of leadership and its relation to situational variables. Paper presented to the British Psychological Society London Conference, December 1968 (published in Proceedings).

HELLER, F. A. Group feedback analysis: A method of field research. *Psychological Bulletin,* 1969, *72,* 108-117.

HELLER, F. A. *Managerial decision-making: A study of leadership styles and power sharing among senior managers.* London: Tavistock Publications, 1971.

HELLER, F. A. Leadership and the process of decision-making: A contingency approach. *Industrial Relations,* 1973, *12,* 183-199.

HELLER, F. A. The decision process: An analysis of power sharing at senior organizational levels. In R. Dubin (Ed.), *Handbook of Work, Organisation and Society.* Chicago: Rand-McNally, 1976.

HELLER, F. A., & YUKL, G. Participation, managerial decision-making and situational variables. *Organisational Behaviour and Human Performance,* 1969, *4,* 227-241.

IDE-INTERNATIONAL RESEARCH GROUP. Industrial democracy in Europe, an international comparative study. *Social Science Information.* April, 1976, *15,* 177-203.

KAVIC, B., RUS, V., & TANNENBAUM, A. Control, participation and effectiveness. *Administrative Science Quarterly,* 1971, *16,* 74-86.

LANDSBERGER, H. *Hawthorne revisited.* Ithaca, New York: Cornell Univ., 1958.

LISCHERON, J. A., & WALL, T. D. Employee participation: An experimental field study. *Human Relations,* 1975, *28,* 863-884.

MANNING, W. H., & DUBOIS, P. H. Gain in proficiency as a criterion in test validation. *Journal of Applied Psychology,* 1958, *42,* 191-194.

MINTZBERG, H. *The nature of managerial work.* New York: Harper and Row, 1973.

MINTZBERG, H., RAISINGHAM, D., & THEORET, A. The structure of "unstructured" decision processes. *Administrative Science Quarterly,* 1976, *21,* 246-275.

OBRADOVIC, J. Participation and work attitudes in Yugoslavia. *Industrial Relations,* 1970, *9,* 161-169.

OFFICE OF POPULATION CENSUS AND SURVEYS. *Workplace industrial relations, 1972.* London: Her Majesty's Stationery Office, 1974.

PAYNE, R. L., FINEMAN, S., & WALL, T. D. Organizational climate and job satisfaction: A conceptual synthesis. *Organisational Behaviour and Human Performance,* 1976, *16,* 45-62.

PETTIGREW, A. The politics of organizational decision-making. London: Tavistock Publications, 1973.

PUGH, D. S., & HICKSON, D. J. *Organisational structure in its context. The Aston programme 1.* Farnborough: Saxon House-Lexington Books, 1976.

PUSIC, E. (Ed.). *Participation and self-management* (5 vols.). Zagreb: Institute for Social Research, University of Zagreb, 1972-73.

RAMONDT, J. J. *Bedrijfsdemocratisering zonder arbeiders.* Alphen a.d. Rijn: Samson, 1974.

ROYAL COMMISSION ON TRADE UNIONS AND EMPLOYERS' REPORT: 1965-68. Cmnd. 3623. London: Her Majesty's Stationery Office, 1968.

RUS, V. Influence structure in Yugoslav enterprise. *Industrial Relations,* 1970, *9,* 148-160.
RUS, V. The limits of organized participation. In Pusic, E. (Ed.), *Participation and Self-Management* (Vol. 2). Zagreb: University of Zagreb, 1972.
SIMON, H. *Models of Man.* New York: Harper, 1960.
TRADES UNION CONGRESS. *Industrial democracy.* London, author, 1974.
VROOM, V. *Work and motivation.* New York: Wiley, 1964.
VROOM, V., & YETTON, P. *Leadership and decision-making.* Pittsburgh, Pa.: University of Pittsburgh Press, 1973.
WEBB, E. J., CAMPBELL, D. T., SCHWARTZ, R. D., & SECHREST, L. *Unobtrusive measures: Nonreactive research in the social sciences.* Chicago. Rand-McNally, 1966.

BIOGRAPHICAL NOTES

FRANK A. HELLER joined the Tavistock Institute of Human Relations in 1969, after two years as Visiting Professor of Psychology and Organizational Behavior at the University of California at Berkeley and the engineering department of Stanford University. Previously he had been Head of the Department of Management at The Polytechnic, London, and consultant for the International Labour Office and the United Nations in Argentina and Chile. In recent years his major research interests have been in the area of decision-making and power sharing using a contingency and action framework.

PIETER J. D. DRENTH has been, since 1967, Professor of Industrial and Organisational Psychology at the Free University of Amsterdam, where he graduated and took his doctorate. Before becoming a lecturer in 1963 he worked as an industrial psychologist in the Royal Dutch Navy, and in the Social Science Research Division of Standard Oil. His main interest is in cross-cultural research; he is involved in a number of international comparative projects in organizational psychology, test development, and educational measurement. The latter studies are carried out primarily in developing countries.

VELJKO RUS is Professor in the Institute of Sociology and Philosophy at Ljubljana. He is a graduate in philosophy from Belgrade and took his doctorate in Zagreb. For many years he was Professor of Sociology of Work at the Faculty of Sociology at Ljubljana University, and is a pioneer of research on the Yugoslav Self Management System. He has studied at the Sorbonne, was Visiting Professor at the University of California at Berkeley, and collaborated with the University of Michigan on a research project. He is now a senior Visiting Research Fellow at the Swedish Institute for Social Research and at the International Institute of Management in Berlin.

PAUL L. KOOPMAN is Research Fellow in the Department of Industrial and Organizational Psychology of the Free University of Amsterdam, from which he graduated in 1972. His interests are in the field of organizational theory and organizational development, and at present he is preparing a PhD thesis on the effects of direct participation in the work situation.

APPENDIX

ABBREVIATED DESCRIPTION OF QUESTIONNAIRES[1]

For each questionnaire, a few examples are given.

IPC   *Below is a list of activities or events. Please indicate how you and your work group participate in them.*
1. Arranging the layout of your work place (position of machinery, desks and the like).
2. How to arrange and plan the work *within your group.*
.
.
.

9. Recommending a group member for promotion.

12 decisions. Scale: the 6 alternatives described in Fig. 2.

SU   *Please think of your own job as it is at the moment. The following is a list of skills, abilities, and so on. Please indicate whether you find that your job gives you the opportunity to use them.*
1. Initiative
3. Practical work experience
.
.
.

13. Capacity to look ahead.

16 skills. Scale: Seldom, occasionally, usually, almost invariably.

SAT-G   *How satisfied are you?*
1. All in all, how satisfied are you with the people you work with closely?
5. Considering your skills and the effort you put into the work, how satisfied are you with your pay?
7. How satisfied do you feel with your chances for getting ahead in this organization in the future?

7 questions. Scale: Very dissatisfied, somewhat dissatisfied, neither satisfied nor dissatisfied, fairly satisfied, very satisfied.

SAT-P   *How frequently, do you feel, does the following occur?*
1. My superior asks me for my opinion on matters related to my work.

[1]See Table 8 for identification of abbreviations of the questionnaire titles.

5. When changes occur in my work, I am consulted by my superior.

5 questions. Scale: Almost invariably, usually, occasionally, seldom.

EFF-CONS   *Consultation may have all sorts of consequences. We would like you to look back on your experience with consultation in your department and to state below what consequences it has had up till now.*

1. People know better what is going on in the company.
3. People accept decisions more easily.
11. There is a better atmosphere in the department.

14 questions as above and two open questions. Scale: Yes, definitely; Yes, I tend to think so; I don't think so; definitely not.

EXP-
CONS   *Could you state below what consequences you expect will happen in the next two or three years in your department as a result of your consultative procedure?*

The questions are identical with Form EFF-CONS. Scale: Yes, definitely; Yes, probably; No, probably not; No, definitely not.

IMP-D   *The following is a list of 12 activities or events. Please indicate how important you think each is for your productivity or that of your work group.*

Questions are identical with Form IPC. Scale: very great, moderate, small.

IMP-S   *Please think of your subordinates' job as they are at the moment. The following is a list of skills, abilities, and so on. Please indicate how far their jobs give them the opportunity to use the following.*

The 16 skills are identical with Form SU. Scale: identical with SU.

R-UU   *To what extent do you agree or disagree with the following statements:*

My present experience and capacities would be better used if:
2. There were fewer company regulations.
6. I had more chance of organizing my own work.

8 questions. Scale: Strongly agree, agree, disagree, strongly disagree.

JOB-CH   *How would you describe your present job?*
1. In terms of the amount of pressure on you (pressure of time and quantity of work).

     5. To what extent is your work group organized formally with definite roles assigned to members.

7 questions. Scale: A range of 10 with two verbal anchoring points, e.g., low, high.

GR-CH   *Would you answer the following questions?*
1. Does a friendly atmosphere prevail among the people in your group?
9. Does your group work as a real team?

10 questions. Scale: Yes, definitely; Yes, I tend to think so; I don't think so; definitely not.

CLIM-P   *To what extent are the following statements true in your organization?*
1. Suggestions from the bottom have little chance in this company.
9. In general relations between management and unions are very good.

9 questions. Scale: definitely true, mostly true, undecided, mostly false, definitely false.

[28]

DECISIONS IN ORGANIZATIONS°

Participative Decision Making: A Comparative Study

THIS ARTICLE DISCUSSES some preliminary findings of a comparative study of different forms of participative decision making carried out in three countries: England (by the Tavistock Institute), Yugoslavia (University of Ljubljana), and the Netherlands (Free University of Amsterdam).[1] The study is to some extent a natural complement to the research carried out by the Industrial Democracy in Europe Research Group (IDE), which is also reported in this issue. The IDE study is a cross-sectional, large sample research effort which makes generalizations across countries. Our project— Decisions in Organizations (DIO)—is a longitudinal, in-depth study of a large number of decisions in a small number of organizations. Our intent is to generate findings which are generalizable across decision-making groups for a considerable variety of decision types.

The DIO project is in some respects a new phase in a research project which started in the sixties (Heller and Yukl, 1969; Heller, 1973). The present study stands on its own, however, for two important reasons. First, it is an extension of the earlier model and research questions, and secondly, it is longitudinal, while previous work was mainly cross-sectional. Having ascertained that managers differed substantially in decision styles, according to the level of organization, the type of decision, and the skills and qualifications of the staff (Heller, 1976), we are now investigating the consequences and effectiveness of these participatory decision-making styles in detail. Additionally, by using a longitudinal approach, we hope to achieve the kinds of insights into how medium- and long-term decisions are made that cannot be obtained by the snapshot procedure. Our selective focus on those organi-

°Pieter J. D. Drenth and Paul L. Koopman, Free University, Amsterdam, Netherlands; Veljko Rus and Miro Odar, Institute of Sociology, Ljubljana, Yugoslavia; and Frank Heller and Alan Brown, Tavistock Institute, London, England.

[1]The study is sponsored by the Netherlands Organization for the Advancement of Pure Research (ZWO), the Social Science Research Council in the U.K., and the Research Community of Slovenia in Yugoslavia. For a full description, see Heller, Drenth, Koopman, and Rus (1977).

INDUSTRIAL RELATIONS, Vol. 18, No. 3 (Fall 1979). © 1979 by the Regents of the University of California.
0019/8676/79/1025/295/$1.00

296 / DIO

zations where changes took place during the period of study enables us to assess the effects and outcomes of these changes in relation to participative style.

The broad scope of the DIO project makes it impractical to attempt to report here the full range of our results thus far. Instead, we discuss two important aspects of the research, using data from seven medium-sized companies. The first part of the article investigates short-term "operational" decision making. Here, the decision style is taken as the independent variable. We analyze its effect on skill utilization and work satisfaction, among other dependent variables. Later, we shift the focus to long-term "strategic" decisions and to discrete phases of the decision-making cycle. We investigate certain variations in power and influence which occur at each step of the decision-making process. Here decision style is the dependent variable, shaped by a variety of internal and external organizational factors. Our evidence supports and extends the theory that decision making is a complex process in which people from different levels with different skills and power are involved (Simon, 1960; Mintzberg, Raisinghani, and Theoret, 1976; Pettigrew, 1973).

The Influence Power Continuum

Decision methods are measured in terms of the Influence Power Continuum (IPC), a key concept throughout our research. IPC refers to the way decisions are made (i.e., the extent of participativeness or control) in normal hierarchical groups. The continuum ranges over six decision-making alternatives which extends the previous options (Heller, 1971):

1. No information — subordinates have no detailed information about the decision being made.

2. Information — fairly detailed information is made available.

3. Opportunities to give advice — before the decision is made, the superior explains the problem and asks advice.

4. Advice is taken into consideration: as with No. 3, but here the superior's final choice usually reflects the advice he has received.

5. Joint decision making: superior and subordinate analyze the problem together and come to a decision. Influence over the final choice is, in principle, shared equally.

6. Complete control: subordinates are given the authority to make the final decision (and are potentially accountable for their choices). Superiors intervene only in exceptional circumstances.

The point of the continuum indicating the method by which any given decision or set of decisions is made can be determined by a variety of methods, among others by questionnaires directed to participants (subordinates, superiors, or both), by observing how actual decisions are made, and by reviewing the documents relating to a decision already made.

Or analysis is concerned with a variety of types of decisions, which we categorized under three headings.[2]

Strategic decisions. Long-term (i.e., taking longer than six months from initial discussion to implementation), low frequency (occurring less than once a year) decisions made mostly at the top level of the organization. Examples include: introducing a new product or service, deciding on medium-size capital investment; and budget forecasting.

Tactical decisions. Medium-term (two to three months), low-to-medium frequency (occurring three to five times per year) decisions made somewhere between the highest and lowest organizational levels. For example, decisions over changes in methods of operation; job grading procedures; training methods, and safety procedures.

Operational decisions. Short-term (about one month), high-frequency (occurring more than five times per year) decisions made at the lower organizational levels. These include arranging the layout of one's own workplace (positioning the desk, machinery, etc.); changing the amount to be produced by one's work group; deciding who works which shift; and deciding who gets overtime work and how much.

Sample

Data were collected in seven companies; three in the Netherlands; two in the U.K., and two in Yugoslavia. All are medium-sized and all are engaged in introducing or developing participatory schemes of one kind or another.[3] In the Netherlands the following companies have been studied: a municipal transport organization, one of the geographical areas of the Dutch Railways, and a plant belonging to a large steel concern (here referred to as companies 1, 2, and 3, respectively). In the U.K. the two companies were a paint producing firm and a firm manufacturing cosmetic products (companies 4 and 5). In Yugoslavia we selected a paper producing factory (company 6) and a medium-size steel products firm (company 7). In each company we collected samples of strategic, tactical, and operational decisions.[4] However, in this section, we are concerned only with the last type.

The Impact of Participative Decision Making

In this section our independent variable consists of measures

---

[2]A full description of each of the three decision sets is available from the authors upon request. In this report we only cover the first and the third category.

[3]The attempt to ensure strict comparability among the seven companies in terms of technology and size was not successful. Priority had to be given to obtaining long-term cooperation from participating companies. Consequently, the possibility of specific company factors being responsible for certain differences or similarities rather than the independent factors under study cannot be ruled out.

[4]Table 1 indicates the number of respondents from each site.

of various forms of short-term, operational decisions. The dependent variable includes measures of effectiveness, skill utilization of group members/subordinates, and two satisfaction indices. Two waves of questionnaires were administered to collect the relevant data; only one set of results is reported here.

To determine perceived decision-making methods, questionnaires were administered asking respondents to indicate how decisions were made with regard to each of 12 specific areas, for example, "deciding on who works on what shift," "safety procedures," and "changing the amount to be produced by your work group." For our purposes here, these topics may be merged into two clusters — one task-oriented (designated "AB") and the other people-oriented (designated "CD").[5]

TABLE 1

INFLUENCE POWER CONTINUUM SCORES FOR OPERATIONAL DECISIONS, BY COMPANY AND SUBJECT MATTER

Companies		Number of respondents	Influence power continuum scores					
			Task oriented		People oriented		Total	
			M	SD	M	SD	M	SD
Netherlands	1	191	2.44	.87	2.65	.82	2.53	.72
	2	156	2.08	.95	2.47	.87	2.26	.85
	3	160	2.21	.75	2.59	.91	2.36	.69
Britain	4	116	1.74	1.13	1.80	1.03	1.77	1.16
	5	69	2.88	1.14	2.74	1.27	2.80	1.51
Yugoslavia	6	135	3.01	1.14	3.11	1.13	3.02	1.35
	7	161	3.24	.99	3.44	.97	3.33	.88

Note: Higher score indicates more participative decision making on a six-point scale as described above.

Table 1 reports the average IPC scores by company for the total set of 12 operational decisions and for the two clusters.

Intercountry differences in IPC. The highest IPC scores are received by the two Yugoslav companies. This would seem to suggest that in addition to *representative* participation, through their works councils, Yugoslav workers also enjoy a good deal of *direct*, face-to-face participation in their relationships with their own superiors. Alternatively, the high scores could mean that the works council itself gives workers more influence over day-to-day operational decisions, just as it gives them more with regard to strategic, company-wide decisions. Or it may mean that respondents simply don't distinguish between direct and representative influence, and that the perception of workers' power in general, as a function of the self-management system, is incorporated into their judgments on the extent of direct participation they enjoy. In any case, in Yugoslavia the IPC average score indicates

---

[5]The alpha coefficients for the AB and CD clusters are .75 and .67, respectively.

a degree of influence slightly above the level of "opportunity to give advice."

The three Dutch firms have a consistent pattern, even though they have different technologies, organizational structures, and ownership. The IPC score falls, on average, between the level of "presenting information" and "opportunity to give advice," and the standard deviation is fairly low in all three cases. The two U.K. companies vary considerably, although neither IPC score reaches level 3, "opportunity to give advice." There is also substantial variance within the companies (company 5 has the highest standard deviation of the sample).

We can say that in this study the average influence level of subordinates in decisions relating to their own immediate work and work conditions is low. In certain specific cases, subordinates experience joint decision making or even control, but the majority of these decisions are made by the supervisor, without prior consultation of the subordinates.

Task-oriented vs. people decisions. Table 2 seems to indicate a higher level of worker influence (IPC) with respect to decisions that are related to personnel problems and worker conditions (CD), than to decisions that deal with the task and the setting of norms and standards. Possibly personnel decisions give subordinates more freedom to exert influence than does the often rather structured task itself.

TABLE 2

CORRELATIONS BETWEEN THE INFLUENCE POWER CONTINUUM AND OUTCOME VARIABLES[a]

	Companies						
	Netherlands			United Kingdom		Yugoslavia	
	1	2	3	4	5	6	7
Satisfaction with participation							
Total	44	57	35	59	47	25	41
AB[b]	37	57	28	58	53	27	43
CD	42	43	31	52	37	20	30
General satisfaction							
Total	14	19	31	−31	11	30	28
AB	05	19	25	−31	15	27	29
CD	19	10	29	−28	08	29	24
Participative effectiveness							
Total	42	38	10	36	39	26	22
AB	34	40	05	37	41	28	27
CD	31	27	09	29	27	22	16
Skill utilization							
Total	38	08	24	57	32	41	27
AB	28	08	21	56	40	43	28
CD	33	03	18	53	22	35	19
Number of respondents							
	175	154	153	110	59	131	153

[a] Coefficients are multiplied by 100. Significance levels: 5 per cent, 15 and above; 1 per cent, 23 and above.
[b] AB = task-oriented decisions; CD = people-oriented decisions.

300 / DIO

The impact of different decision styles. To assess this impact, we examined the effects of IPC on four dependent variables: skill utilization (SU), general satisfaction (SAT-G), satisfaction with regard to participation (SAT-P), and the effectiveness of participation (EFF). To operationalize SU, the respondent was asked to indicate on a four-point scale (varying from "hardly ever" to "almost invariably") the extent to which his job afforded the opportunity to use initiative, verbal ability, practical work experience, the capacity to develop new ideas, and the like. We used a general "satisfaction with work" type scale (Taylor and Bowers, 1972), consisting of seven items, to measure SAT-G; SAT-P was assessed separately, using a five-item questionnaire. The effectiveness of direct participation on factors like wasting time, quality of decisions, and diffusion of information (EFF) was determined by responses to 14 items included on the questionnaire.[6]

Table 2 presents the correlations between IPC and these dependent (or outcome) variables. Not surprisingly, the highest and most consistent correlations are with satisfaction with participation. Apparently, workers appreciate participative leadership and become more satisfied with participation the more influence they have. This pattern occurs in all three countries. A fairly similar and strong relationship exists between participation and rating of participation effectiveness (EFF). More influence is not only more satisfying, but is also considered to lead to better decisions, better mutual understanding, a better atmosphere, a better acceptance of the decisions, and the like. This relationship, too, is independent of differences between countries. Strong positive correlations exist between IPC and skill utilization (SU). In all three countries, the more participation and influence in decisions, the more respondents indicate that their capacities and skills are being utilized — thus supporting the view that one of the great advantages of participative management is that it makes more effective use of subordinates' skills (Heller, 1976).

As in other studies (Wall and Licheron, 1976), we found a weaker and less consistent relationship between IPC and general satisfaction. Conceptually, this is not surprising. General satisfaction has more determinants than participative climate, and the contribution of influence, therefore, will be relatively smaller. Company 4 provides an interesting but extreme case: it shows a significant negative correlation between participation and general satisfaction. It is probably not accidental that this negative relationship exists within the firm with the lowest average IPC score. This suggests that workers may view very low scores on the IPC (up to "information is avail-

---

[6]Alpha coefficients for these four scales are as follows: SU = .87; EFF = .87; SAT-G = .77; and SAT-P = .65. (The IPC coefficient is .85.) Note that the homogeneities for the various scales are sufficiently high for further use.

able") as pseudo-participation. Thus, slight increases in participation, from very low levels, may lead only to frustration.

Finally, Table 2 also indicates a general trend towards higher correlations between IPC and the AB cluster than between IPC and the CD unit. Task-oriented decision issues tend to yield higher returns in skill utilization, effectiveness, and satisfaction for any given amount of influence sharing behavior than do personnel-oriented decisions.

Long-term Decision Making

We now shift our focus to the process of making strategic decisions. Unlike other research, which has been mainly concerned with descriptive categorization (Mintzberg, Raisinghani, and Theoret, 1976), we are interested in the cognitive structure of decision making. Following Abell (1975), we see long-term strategic decision making as a mechanism for the distribution of organizational power and influence, rather than as "problem solving" or "choice behavior" (Ebert and Micehaell, 1975). We assume, with March, that "influence is to the study of decision making what force is to the study of motion—a generic explanation of the basic observable phenomenon" (1955, p. 432).

In this section, the decisions themselves (N = 103) are the unit of analysis. The sample represents major choices made by our seven companies during 1976-1977. These decisions include budget forecasting (17 decisions), major investments (70 decisions), new products (18 decisions), and the introduction of new participation structures like staff or works committees (19 decisions). The data were collected by interviews heavily supplemented by observations made during committee meetings, record analysis, and tracer methods[7] as a way of validating the results of our interview schedule. The impact of the strategic decisions was assessed at each of seven organizational levels: workers, foremen, middle management, top management, staff specialists, representative bodies (like works committees), and the head office of the parent body. Since the sequencing of events is a major consideration when analyzing long-term strategic decision making, we traced the sample decisions retrospectively, as well as through continuous observations and interviews as the decision process unfolded.

Variations in influence over the decision cycle. We are interested in determining whether influence and power sharing vary over what we identify as the four phases of the decision cycle. These are: (1) initiation;

---

[7]Tracer or "snowballing" methods start with a question on who else is involved in a given decision and then follow up each of these contacts with further interviews.

302 / DIO

(2) development; (3) finalization; and (4) implementation.[8] Table 3 gives the IPC scores for the seven organizations and each of the four phases. We see that in some cases there are substantial variations over the time cycle. This becomes particularly clear when we use the power difference score (PDS) (see last column Table 3). This is a measure of the inequality of influence between top managers and workers (computed by subtracting the latter's score from the former's). In both Yugoslav organizations (companies 6 and 7), as well as in the Dutch Railways (company 2), there exists a wide measure of power sharing. In companies 6 and 7, we find that the concentration of influence varies by phase of the decision cycle, as follows: in phase 1 (initiation) it is greatest for top management; in phase 2 (development) for staff; in phase 3 (finalization) for workers; and in phase 4 (implementation) for staff and top management.

Although a hierarchical distribution exists across the decision cycle as a whole, a different but equally interesting pattern emerges when we examine the distribution of influence within phases of the cycle. In some cases the variation between phases is very considerable, though this is masked by averaging scores for all levels. In the Yugoslav organizations, for instance, there are strong variations according to phase in IPC at the worker level. In company 6 there are also substantial variations for middle and top management, but much less for staff and representative bodies. In general, variations of the IPC between decision phases appear to be greater at middle and top management levels than at worker or foreman level. With the exception of Yugoslav companies, the IPC variation between phases is particularly low for representative bodies.

Variations in IPC over phases are important for a number of reasons. For instance, under certain schemes of participation or industrial democracy, greater influence sharing might be encouraged at the initiation stage of the cycle (phase 1) or during finalization (phase 3). Such increases in variation between phases point to the possibility of transforming or at least mitigating the traditional effect of hierarchy.

We suggest two interpretations of the observed differences in the profiles of influence distribution for decision phases. First, if we make the assumption that the cognitive structure of decision making is rational, it follows that the first phase of decision making is the most important, since it is here that the goals of the decision are defined, while in the following phases only means for implementation are sought.[9] Rationality further dictates that the

---

[8]This formulation differs from Mintzberg, *et al.'s* (1976). We use fewer categories for the process up to finalization (authorization), but add implementation, which we consider an important aspect of the long-term cycle.

[9]A detailed discussion of this assumption and its implications is provided in Rus, *et al.* (1978).

TABLE 3

INFLUENCE POWER CONTINUUM SCORES BY ORGANIZATION, ORGANIZATIONAL LEVEL, AND DECISION PHASE

	Worker	Foreman	Middle management	Top management	Staff	Representative body	Mean score	Power differential score
Netherlands								
Company 1								
Phase 1	1.3	1.3	1.6	2.7	2.0	1.3	1.7	1.4
Phase 2	1.3	1.3	2.0	3.0	2.6	1.6	2.5	1.8
Phase 3	1.0	1.0	1.3	2.4	2.0	1.6	1.6	1.4
Phase 4	1.7	1.7	2.3	3.0	2.8	1.7	2.2	1.3
Company 2								
Phase 1	1.6	1.5	2.5	2.0	2.4	1.3	1.9	1.4
Phase 2	1.5	1.8	2.8	2.3	2.6	1.5	2.1	0.8
Phase 3	1.3	1.8	2.8	2.0	2.6	1.3	2.0	0.7
Phase 4	1.5	2.0	2.0	2.0	3.0	1.5	2.0	0.5
Company 3								
Phase 1	1.2	1.3	2.2	2.7	1.9	1.3	1.6	1.5
Phase 2	1.4	1.5	2.1	2.5	2.3	1.3	1.9	1.1
Phase 3	1.2	1.1	1.4	2.9	1.5	1.3	1.5	1.7
Phase 4	1.8	1.8	2.4	1.4	1.6	1.2	1.7	0.4
United Kingdom								
Company 4								
Phase 1	1.0	1.1	1.9	1.9	1.7	1.1	1.5	0.9
Phase 2	1.0	1.4	2.3	2.2	1.7	1.1	1.6	1.2
Phase 3	1.0	1.3	2.0	3.0	1.6	1.0	1.8	2.0
Phase 4	1.1	1.5	2.1	2.4	1.6	1.5	1.7	2.3
Company 5								
Phase 1	1.0	1.1	1.5	2.6	1.6	1.0	1.5	1.6
Phase 2	1.1	1.1	2.2	2.6	1.4	1.0	1.5	1.5
Phase 3	1.0	1.0	1.5	2.5	1.3	1.0	1.4	1.5
Phase 4	1.3	1.3	2.1	2.8	1.1	1.0	1.6	1.5
Yugoslavia								
Company 6								
Phase 1	1.1	1.1	2.3	2.9	2.7	1.4	1.9	1.8
Phase 2	1.6	1.3	1.9	2.4	2.7	1.3	1.9	0.8
Phase 3	2.2	1.2	1.9	1.9	2.1	1.6	1.8	-0.2
Phase 4	1.2	1.3	1.6	2.1	2.7	1.0	1.7	0.9
Company 7								
Phase 1	2.2	1.5	1.6	2.5	2.0	1.8	1.9	0.3
Phase 2	1.4	1.3	1.7	2.8	2.8	2.0	2.0	1.4
Phase 3	2.3	1.4	1.7	2.1	2.0	1.3	1.8	-0.2
Phase 4	1.3	1.4	1.9	3.0	2.9	1.4	2.0	1.7

Note: All figures in this table, with the exception of the power differential score, are IPC scores. The four phases of the decision-making cycle are: (1) initiation; (2) development; (3) finalization; and (4) implementation.

group which controls the first step actually controls the other three phases even in the case when this group does not have the highest IPC score in these later phases. If we accept this criterion, top management in both Yugoslav organizations still dominates, although it shares power with other groups to a greater degree than in English or Dutch organizations (with the exception of the Dutch Railways). The second interpretation involves adopting a definition of the decision process as an integration of "pouvoir et savoir" (Sfez, 1978). We can then define the first and third phases of the decision cycle as power phases and the second and fourth stages as knowledge phases. According to this assumption, the dominant position will be held by that organizational group which has the greatest influence in the first and third phases.

The Relationship Between Influence and Status Power

When the IPC is taken as the dependent variable, an important predictor of its distribution is a factor we call "status power" (SP). This variable encompasses the variation in formal rules, policies, regulations, or legally backed influence pertaining to decision making at each of the seven organizational levels (i.e., from workers through the head office of the parent company) by company and country. Each work group's SP was assessed for each strategic decision along a continuum similar to the IPC.[10] A score of 1 = no status power; 2 = unspecified information must be given; 3 = specified information must be given; 4 = consultation is obligatory; 5 = joint decision making is necessary or prescribed (this includes situations where a group has veto power); and 6 = group has final say.

Table 4 reports the relationships between IPC and SP for long-term strategic decisions, by country. Average SP scores are lower than IPC scores in Great Britain, equal in the Netherlands, and greater in Yugoslavia. This could mean that existent SP discourages or has no effect on democratization of long-term decision making in England, supports it or is congruent in the Netherlands, and encourages it in Yugoslavia. These findings were expected, and they are supported by the IDE findings. The operationalization of SP at the micro level of decisions and groups bears some relation to the measure of formal legal power structures assessed at the macro level of organizations and country-specific legal norms in the IDE study. Where legal norms exist, SP would measure their specific impact on different forms of organizational behavior. Where few legal norms exist, as in the case of Britain or the United States, SP alone may be a particularly useful predictor of variations in de

---

[10] In the absence of legal regulations, as in the U.K., self-evident patterns checked by Group Feedback Analysis were used to assess Status Power.

TABLE 4

AVERAGE INFLUENCE POWER CONTINUUM AND STATUS POWER SCORES
BY COUNTRY AND ORGANIZATIONAL LEVEL

	Netherlands		United Kingdom		Yugoslavia		Average	
	IPC	SP	IPC	SP	IPC	SP	IPC	SP
Workers	1.4	1.2	1.0	1.0	1.6	2.2	1.3	1.7
Foremen	1.5	1.3	1.3	1.0	1.3	1.2	1.3	1.2
Middle management	2.1	1.6	1.9	1.2	1.8	1.3	1.9	1.3
Top management	2.5	2.5	2.4	2.4	2.5	2.0	2.5	2.2
Staff	2.3	n.a.	1.6	n.a.	2.5	n.a.	2.1	n.a.
Representative bodies	1.4	1.5	1.1	1.1	1.5	2.5	1.4	1.9
External bodies	n.a.	2.7	n.a.	2.3	n.a.	1.5	n.a.	1.9
Average	1.8	1.8	1.6	1.5	1.9	2.0	1.7	1.7

Note: IPC = influence; SP = status power. The figures are means on a six-point scale as in Tables 1 and 3. Higher scores indicate more participative decision making.

facto participation. Thus, in view of the results we report below, it seems that if one wanted to increase participative behavior, perhaps one should consider strengthening SP.

Note also that all *managerial* levels (i.e., foremen, middle and top management) have greater IPC than SP, which means that they have at their disposal some kind of "illegitimate power."[11] The amount of this illegitimate power is relatively low for top management and foremen but quite high for middle management. It seems that middle management absorbs the greatest amount of free floating power. The greater de facto over de jure influence of middle management is congruent with a previous finding. Substantial samples of American, British, and German middle managers reported that they had more influence (as measured on the IPC) than their senior managers were aware of (Heller, 1971; Wilpert, 1977). This suggests that senior managers judge their subordinates' influence in terms of formal rules or conventions, while middle levels are prepared to act outside these formal requirements. Thus, the gap between the two levels, though still considerable, is smaller on the IPC than on SP. We are not yet able to say why and how this illegitimate power accumulates at certain levels. One could look to the effect of communication processes for a possible explanation. For example, sometimes middle management holds a very strategic position in relation to upward as well as downward communications. Being a modal point in the communication network could lead to an accumulation of influence. Secondly, there is "Meta Power" (Baumgartner, 1976). While our study uses Meta Power as a variable, it is beyond the scope of this paper to develop its significance or to demonstrate its statistical impact on other

---

[11]The term "illegitimate" is used here to signify a surplus over the formally sanctioned amount described by SP.

variables. It can be briefly defined as an assessment of intervention by powerful external groups acting on the IPC. These groups include head office, banks, government agencies, trade unions, political parties, etc. Meta Power exercised by such groups may be seen as an explanation for the accumulation of illegitimate power insofar as it can be conceived of as the historic events, including the growth of legislation and formal policies, which have led to the formulation of SP norms.

For instance, in some countries banks take an unfavorable view of industrial democracy practices by cooperative producer organizations. This would substantially lower the SP of employees at middle levels concerned with decisions about design, working conditions, or new products and increase the SP of the financial controller. To the extent that such tactical decisions continue to be made by middle level employees in defiance of the external influence of banks, illegitimate IPC may accumulate.

In addition to suggesting that some groups are able to accumulate power, the data in Table 4 indicate that it may be possible to "lose" power as well. The IPC scores for workers and representative bodies are lower than their SP scores which means that these two levels appear to be "deprived" of some legitimate power. The reason for this deprivation is not yet clear, but could be similar to the historically conditioned Meta Power explanation advanced above.

A cross-country comparison of IPC scores with SP scores by organizational level demonstrates that in Great Britain no level is "deprived" (i.e., none has a lower IPC than a SP score), in the Netherlands only representative bodies are slightly deprived, while in Yugoslavia workers as well as representative bodies are significantly deprived. At the same time, it is important to be aware that in Yugoslavia these two levels have higher IPC scores than in the other two countries. This gives further support to the suggestion that SP acts as an incentive for greater power distribution. In all three countries, the higher the SP, the greater the IPC for the corresponding level. This conclusion is particularly true of representative bodies in the U.K. and the Netherlands. In both, SP scores are almost exactly the same as IPC scores. The high SP score for Yugoslavia is not, however, matched by an equally high IPC score. Note also that the SP for external bodies like head office or parent company is substantially lower in Yugoslavia than in the other two countries. This is likely to be a consequence of the extensive legal backing which the company-based self-management system has received since 1950 through several constitutional provisions (*The Associated Labour Act*, 1977).

Table 5 shows correlations between Status Power and IPC scores. In some cases the correlations are substantial. It seems that, after hierarchy, SP is one of the strongest predictors of the IPC in organizations. SP increases workers' influence (IPC) in all phases of decision making, most of all in phases 1 and 2 (see Table 5). The SP of foremen has a less consistent impact on the IPC, but is substantial in the second and fourth phases. This could be a typical symptom of the problems experienced by the lowest level of the managerial chain. Middle management influence is even less well supported by SP in the important initiation (phase 1) and finalization (phase 4) stages of the decision cycle. SP supports them only in the execution of policies and initiatives that were already taken at higher levels. We know that top management's de facto influence is very considerable (see Tables 3 and 4), but SP is no help at this level. In fact, as we saw earlier, top management enjoys a higher de facto than de jure influence. It seems, therefore, that the relatively small amount of influence exerted by the lower levels in the organizational hierarchy is due in no small measure to the existence of SP norms for these levels.

TABLE 5

INTERCORRELATIONS BETWEEN INFLUENCE POWER CONTINUUM AND STATUS POWER SCORES
FOR PHASES OF THE DECISION CYCLE

Status power scores	IPC scores, phases of decision cycle:				IPC total scores
	Initiation	Development	Finalization	Implementation	
Workers	66	63	48	49	70
Foremen	35	67	32	81	44
Middle management	05	43	13	61	10
Top management	02	03	08	27	07
Representative bodies	59	36	62	−01	52
External bodies	−58	−31	−48	−02	−59
Total	50	43	26	27	38

Note: Figures are gamma values. A correlation of 33 is significant at the 5 per cent level. Coefficients are multiplied by 100.

The moderate amount of influence enjoyed by representative bodies seems to be due to the existence of SP, particularly at the initiation and finalization decision stages. Lastly, the external bodies' (head office and parent company) SP has, as expected, a negative effect on the IPC within companies, especially in the first and fourth phases.

Conclusions

While the evidence shows that workers exercise very little influence on any topic and particularly little over matters related to tasks, norms, and standards, they nevertheless like participation and believe it leads to more effectiveness. Such a belief in the practical value of participation is reinforced by strong positive correlations between influence sharing and skill utilization.

308 / DIO

The longitudinal analysis of a large number of strategic decisions makes clear the importance of assessing the four phases of the decision cycle separately. It is now evident that influence sharing is not equally distributed over the cycle. In general, the lower the level of organization, the less influence people have over the most important phases, namely the goal-setting initial phase and the decisive finalization phase. This finding alone justifies a careful assessment of events over time because cross-sectional findings from one segment of a long cycle could be quite unrepresentative of the total decision process.

A second important finding relates to the distinction between formal normative aspects of power (SP) and the actual exercise of power measured by the IPC. The relationship between SP and IPC varies with the level of organization. At the top, actual power is greater than SP and at lower levels this is reversed. Moreover, there are strong indicators that the relatively small amounts of influence enjoyed by lower levels, particularly at the critical stages of the cycle, are buttressed by SP. This suggests the possibility that changes in the distribution of influence in organizations can be facilitated by changing legal, formal, or policy norms, such as those we measure by Status Power. Further study of the relationships between SP and the IPC promises to be interesting.

Participative Decision Making / 309

References

Abell, P. *Organization as Bargaining and Influence System.* London: Heinemann, 1975.

Baumgartner, T. "Meta Power and the Structuring of Social Hierarchies." In Tom Burns and Walter Buckley, *Power and Control.* London: Sage, 1976.

Ebert, E. and T. Micehaell. *Organizational Decision Process.* New York: Crane and Russak, 1975.

Heller, Frank. "Decision Process: An Analysis of Power Sharing at Senior Organization Levels." In Robert Dubin, ed., *Handbook of Work, Organization and Society.* Chicago, Ill.: Rand McNally, 1976, pp. 687-711.

―――. "Leadership, Decision Making and Contingency Theory," *Industrial Relations,* XII (May, 1973), 183-199.

―――. *Managerial Decision Making.* London: Tavistock Publications, 1971 .

―――, Pieter J. D. Drenth, Paul L. Koopman, and Veljko Rus. "A Longitudinal Study in Participative Decision Making," *Human Relations,* XXX (July, 1977), 567-587.

―――, and Gary Yukl. "Participation and Managerial Decision Making as a Function of Situational Variables," *Organizational Behavior and Human Performance,* IV (August, 1969), 227-241.

March, James G. "An Introduction to the Theory and Management of Influence," *American Political Science Review,* XLIX (June, 1955), 431-451.

Mintzberg, Henry, D. Raisinghani, and A. Theoret. *The Structure of "Unstructured" Decision Processes.* Montreal, Canada: McGill University Press, 1976.

Pettigrew, A. M. *The Politics of Organizational Decision-Making.* London: Tavistock, 1973.

Rus, Vjelko, M. Odar, F. A. Heller, A. Brown, P. J. D. Drenth, and P. L. Koopman. "Status Power and Meta Power." Paper presented at the Ninth World Congress of Sociology, Uppsala, Sweden, August, 1978.

Sfez, Lucien. "Existe-t-il des decisions democratiques?" *Dialectiques,* XXII (1978), 59-72.

Simon, Herbert A. *The New Science of Management Decision.* New York: Harper and Row, 1960.

Taylor, J. C. and David G. Bowers. *Survey of Organizations: A Machine Scored Standardized Questionnaire Instrument.* Ann Arbor, Mich.: Institute for Social Research, 1972.

The Associated Labour Act. Dopisna DeLavska, Univerza, Ljubljana; D. Durovic, Ed., 1977.

Wall, T. D. and T. A. Licheron. *Worker Participation.* London: McGraw-Hill, 1976.

Wilpert, Bernhard. *Fuhrung in Deutschen Unternehmen.* Berlin: Walter de Gruyter, 1977.

[29]

Participation in Complex Organizational Decisions: A Comparative Study of the United Kingdom, The Netherlands, and Yugoslavia

PAUL L. KOOPMAN, PIETER J. D. DRENTH,
FRANK A. HELLER AND VELJKO RUS

Introduction

In contrast to most of the organizational psychologists, sociologists and political scientists have developed arguments in favour of a political analysis of decision-making (Lammers and Széll, 1989; Koopman and Pool, 1990). Pettigrew, for instance, seeks to emphasize the essentially 'political character of organizational life' (Pettigrew, 1975: 204) and in the same tradition is the analysis of power games (Crozier and Friedberg, 1977).

Benson (1977) argues that rational assumptions about people and organizations still dominate theory but that several non-rational theories are now evolving. Interestingly, sociologists and political scientists have failed to notice the extensive psychological evidence on non-rational decision-making (for instance Kahneman et al., 1982) which has been frequently quoted by Simon (1984: 52). One of these theories demonstrates the importance of the external economic-social environment. Another describes organizational events as games and strategies which are played out as rituals within diversified work cultures. The goal of rationality itself becomes a ritual. It is conceivable that within such a framework 'the most potent type of power is that which is rarely exercised' (Clegg and Dunkerley, 1977). Power then becomes the submerged part of the iceberg, it 'maintains its effectiveness not so much through overt action, as through its ability to appear to be the natural convention. It is only when this taken-for-grantedness fails, . . . that the overt exercise of power is necessary' (ibid.: 35).

The power game can also be played more deliberately as a way of stopping latent demands for change from reaching the agenda of decision-making. For instance, 'demands for change in the existing allocation of benefits and privileges . . . can be suffocated before they can even be voiced' (Bacharach and Baratz, 1970: 44). An even more submerged part of the iceberg has been

114   *Paul L. Koopman* et al.

analysed by Lukes (1974) who calls it the third dimension. The most insidious
use of power, he believes, is 'to prevent people ... from having grievances by
shaping their perceptions, cognitions and preferences in such a way that they
accept their role in the existing order of things...' without conflict (ibid.:
24). The position of the French philosopher Foucault has developed along
similar lines. He has argued that control over people in modern times has
shifted from its earlier emphasis on physical measures through organs of
State like the army and police to subtler measures which embed and control
social behaviour through schools, psychiatric clinics, and work organizations
(Foucault, 1977; Sheridan, 1980). Such theories are, however, not easily
applied to organizational analysis through empirical data.

Slightly more operational is the concept of meta-power. Meta-power is
seen as an outside force exercising control over social relationships and social
structures. It is a higher-order power operating outside a given sub-system,
exercising relational control and thereby imposing limitations on lower-order
power (Baumgartner *et al.*, 1976). There are three control aspects to be
considered. Meta-power controls action opportunities, differential pay-offs
and ideology (Baumgartner *et al.*, 1975). This last category links up with
Lukes' third power dimension. We will see later that in the present research
we attempt an operationalization of the first meta-power category, namely
that concerned with the relational control from outside a sub-system over
action opportunities within it.

The space dimension

The concept of space in the analysis of organizational life has two facets;
intra-organizational space is bounded by the area of the triangle which we
normally use to symbolize a unit or company while extra-organizational space
covers the area between triangles and this can include governments, banks,
and influences from the economic-social environment.

Galbraith's description of decision-making in large modern corporations
using complex technology requires a consideration of intra-organizational
space. He argues that embedded in the bowels of these organizations there is
a technostructure which absorbs problems, converts them into solutions, and
then sends them up the hierarchy for scrutiny, costing, and seals of approval
(Galbraith, 1967: 65–70). This is a fairly rational approach, but similar space
considerations apply to models that stress the haphazardness of decision-
making or the art of muddling through (Lindblom, 1959). Here the emphasis
is on tracing the tentative or disjointed steps which move problems from one
position to another, up or down or sideways in search for some reasonably
acceptable solution. Disjointed incrementalism is characterized by a search
process with inadequately formulated values, strained cognitive abilities, dis-
organized information and difficult cost analyses (Braybrooke and Lindblom,
1963). This unflattering description of organizational meandering has at-

tracted much attention in recent years. Researchers have caricatured the older more static models of rational behaviour by descriptions of cases which resemble 'organized anarchy'. Decision-makers move about like animals in a maze, using trial and error procedures, learning through accidents, imitation, and invention resulting from crises (Cohen and March, 1974). A 'garbage can model' has been used to describe decisions by oversight or by running away from the problem (Cohen *et al.*, 1972).

While organizations have always existed in an external environment, theorists have made use of this aspect of organizational space only recently (Burns and Stalker, 1961; Lawrence and Lorsch, 1967; Thompson, 1967). As so often happens, the pendulum has swung from having largely ignored the external dimension, to recent attempts to give it primacy over most others (Pfeffer and Salancik, 1978; Aldrich, 1979). A special aspect of environmental space is the recent recognition that strategic decision-making takes place between as well as within organizations. Friend and Jessop (1969) looking at the local government planning process, developed a theory of strategic choice which relate different organizations to each other. This was later expanded into what is now a new field of analysis called inter-organizational decision-making.

The time-dimension

In some studies, the longitudinal dimension becomes a major tool for understanding power and other relationships. The three-year field-study of the worker-director experiment in British Steel is a good case in point (Brannen *et al.*, 1976). The gradual changes in sentiment by top management from hostility to fairly enthusiastic acceptance of the worker-director idea are traced through to the structural provisions for such a scheme. The values and political philosophies of the planner are seen to play a major part in the decision to reject the main British Steel Board and Management Committees as suitable locations for power-sharing (ibid.: 90–5). The research then follows through the evaluation of the scheme, for instance by showing how the uncertain role and power attributions of worker-directors led to formal job descriptions which may have helped them gradually to infiltrate a number of committees that were previously considered to be out of bounds (ibid.: 145–7).

A different use of the time–space–power dimensions in the analysis of industrial democracy is made through a detailed historical account of the industrial relations system in the period preceding and immediately following the British 1976 enquiry into industrial democracy under the chairmanship of Lord Bullock (Elliot, 1978). Elliott shows how trade union attitudes have gradually shifted towards an acceptance of such schemes from earlier positions of scepticism.

The work on decision behaviour developed by the Bradford group

116　　　　　　　　*Paul L. Koopman* et al.

(Hickson *et al.*, 1986) concentrated on analyses between units and sub-units of organization rather than on individuals. Power was seen as residing in social relationships, not in actors. Coping with uncertainty and the control of contingencies were critical and these were gradually conceived as varying over time. The difference between short-term and long-term influence of variables became important in studying the speed and severity with which the flow of work of sub-units affects the final output of the organization. The timing consequences of cash forecast and the variations in predicting degrees of uncertainty became clearer and, in relation to participation, four decision stages were postulated: initiation, information provision, choice, and implementation (Hinings *et al.*, 1974). However, little use was made of the longitudinal dimension although its theoretical importance received substantial further attention (Butler *et al.*, 1979).

A much more specific use of time stages is the basis of a field study of complex decision processes undertaken in tracing 233 decisions dealing with data-processing equipment (Witte, 1972). Witte uses five sequential phases: problem recognition, gathering information, development of alternatives, evaluation of alternatives, and choice. To test his sequential assumption of time phases, he divided the decision process into ten equal time intervals and then noted the level and type of activity in each of these. His findings do not support the sequential hypothesis. Communication activity reached peaks at the beginning and end of the cycle and the number of choices increases at the end of the process. His information about the cycle came from four companies selling the equipment and he did not check with the purchasers; moreover the equal interval assumption is likely to have distorted the findings since subsequent research by Mintzberg and ourselves would suggest that such a division is highly unrealistic.

A different phase approach was used in the study of decision-making of a Scandinavian university. Enderud (1977) based his work on the Cohen *et al.* (1972) 'garbage can model'. He puts forward four phases: an initial unstructured 'bull session'; a bargaining–coalition negotiating phase; a persuasion sequence; and a final bureaucratic phase using an 'administrative man model'. Enderud concludes that although in a broad general sense, the model of an organized anarchy applies to the total process, there is a definite movement towards greater clarification and reduced ambiguity as the decision moves from phase 1 to phase 4.

The most detailed processual analysis up to now comes from a study of twenty-five strategic decisions assembled by fifty teams of four or five students taking courses for a Masters' degree under the direction of Mintzberg and colleagues. The longitudinal dimension was now the major consideration. The decision process was defined as 'a set of actions and dynamic factors that begins with the identification of the stimulus for action and ends up with a specific commitment to action' (Mintzberg *et al.*, 1976: 246). The authors describe three main phases of the decision cycle: identification, development, and selection. In addition, Mintzberg's study draws attention to a considerable number of subdivisions and elements, most of which have a space-time implication. A category called 'decision communication', for instance, is designed to capture an active stream of communication throughout a decision process, like scanning the environment for alternatives. Several categories highlight interruptions and delays of various kinds. Decision processes are thought to be circular rather than linear, requiring movements between phases and subdivisions; this dynamic is called comprehension cycles and was discovered in each one of the twenty-five decision processes described in this research. One element, called 'failure re-cycles' identifies blockages due to rejections of proposals during the evaluation and choice stages. The authors conclude that although strategic decision processes are 'immensely complex and dynamic...yet... they are amenable to conceptual structuring'. At the same time they accept that the study has barely 'scratched the surface of organizational decision-making' and that the literature still lacks 'a single acceptable theory to describe how decision processes flow through organizational structures' (Mintzberg *et al.*, 1976: 274).

Method

Designing a longitudinal study

The present project, 'Decisions in Organizations' (DIO, see Heller *et al.*, 1988), is the result of a desire to extend the cross-sectional analysis of decision-making and participation by obtaining a greater depth of under-standing of the dynamics of the process than had been possible by previous research (IDE, 1981*a*, 1981*b*). At the same time we wanted to keep some of the same variables like the influence-power continuum (IPC) for which a lot of interesting data had already become available. The main requirement for such an extension was to engage in a longitudinal study and a minimum of four years was thought to be appropriate for moving from the cross-sectional study of routine operational issues to long-term decisions.

The term 'longitudinal' can be applied to at least three fairly distinct approaches. The most widely used longitudinal method, the 'time-interval method', makes two or more assessments separated by interval of days, months, or years. This includes measurements of a variable like attitude to violence 'before' and 'after' showing a war film, or economic time-series measurements. It also includes follow-up studies of individuals or age cohorts over their lifetime. A second quite distinct longitudinal method is continuous assessment by participant observation or other methods of living with the ongoing events. We call this method 'processual'. For obvious reasons of cost and effort it is not often used. For the third variety of longitudinal method we use the term 'diachronic'. Diachronic analysis is less continuous than processual methods but attempts, by a variety of means, to link up the intervals between assessments in order to obtain a fairly reliable picture of events or change.

Medium- to long-term decisions as defined in our study take at least two months and upwards of two years to move from the start-up to the implementation phase and usually involve at least two levels of the organization. When the researcher first starts the investigation he is likely to find that several of the decisions he would like to study—such as budget forecasting—have already begun and will not start up again for some time. It is therefore important to develop methods of retrospective tracing through written evidence and interviewing which allow one to make a realistic and valid assessment of the major characteristics of the early part of the decision process. The diachronic analysis after the researcher's entry into the organization is called 'process registration'. However, since diachronic analysis is not continuous but takes place at intervals, the size of which depends on the nature of the events being traced and the availability of the researcher, there will often be a need to fill the gap between observations by retrospective tracing.

The model and variables

The overall model with the variables and their postulated interactions are represented in Fig. 6.1. The research is directed towards the interactions between three sets of variables. On the one hand as independent variable the

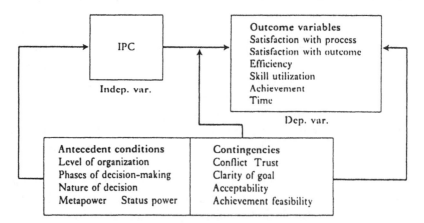

Fig. 6.1 Overview of interview-schedule variables in model used for medium- and long-term decision-making

influence–power continuum (IPC), ranging from 1 (no or minimal information) to 6 (complete control). A number of indices were derived from the IPC: power difference (PD) is the difference between the IPC of top management and workers. Locus of power (LP) is the assessment of which organizational level has the highest score in each phase of the decision cycle. On the other hand there are dependent variables like achievement, efficiency, utilization of skills, and a number of satisfaction variables. Scores are: high, medium, low. A third set are antecedent and contingency variables. Some can be seen as primarily determining the IPC score; they are called 'antecedents'. For example, meta-power (MP): influences from outside the company (for instance, head office, banks, government) and status power (SP): this is a measurement of the formal or constitutional power possessed by committees or groups, ranging from 1 (no rule for influence of the group) to 6 (the group has the final say). Contingent variables act as intervening variables influencing the relationship between the dependent and the independent variables (for example, conflict and clarity of goal).

Research questions were:

- Do we find differences in various relevant aspects of decision-making (time, amount of conflict, power distribution) between various phases of complex decision-making?
- Is the extent of participative decision-making related to the results of the decision-making process as a whole?
- Do the 'antecedents' have any influence upon the decision-making style?
- Do the contingencies have any influence upon the relationship between IPC and outcome variables?

Three countries, seven organizations, 217 decisions

Yugoslavia, the United Kingdom, and The Netherlands, were chosen because they were involved in an interesting debate about the most appropriate form and degree of 'participation' in industrial organizations. In each country this has led either to the introduction of, or to proposals for, new forms of legislation, aiming to change the existing distribution of power within organizations. The three countries have clearly different legal and administrative provisions for the distribution and sharing of power within organizations and the various proposals and plans are far from similar. It was thought to be interesting to find out to what extent the relationships among the various types of variables from the model are comparable or different in the three countries. For further details on the historic background see Heller *et al.* (1988).

In Yugoslavia the system of self-management was introduced as an alternative to the capitalistic system from the West and the state bureaucratic system typical in the Eastern European countries. The constitution of 1963 gave almost complete autonomy to work organizations (both economic and social organizations). However, despite a highly developed representative self-management system at the level of the enterprise, substantial differences in influence and power between top management, Workers' Council members, staff members, and workers remained. In Yugoslavia (Slovenia) the research took place in two companies. One was a metal-manufacturing place concentrating on making chains, screws, and anchors for naval craft. The company employed 1,118 people. The second enterprise was a company producing cardboards, packages, and various paper products as well as coloured printing processes. It employed 1,700 employees.

Essential to the methods of joint regulation in the United Kingdom is collective bargaining. In addition to the formal bargaining procedures, informal negotiations may also play a significant part in the determination of *de facto* conditions. The trade union movement's consistent and continuing commitment is to an extension of collective bargaining, as offering the greatest possibility of increasing workers' influence over decisions which affect them. Two organizations took part in the British study. One manufactured a variety of pharmaceutical products and was part of a multinational company. The factory employed 460 people. The second company was a manufacturer of paints, also part of a multinational company, making a variety of products connected with the building trade. It employed about 450 people.

In The Netherlands two interesting developments in the field of industrial relations and participation in work organizations may be mentioned. First is the legal and social changes with respect to the works council. A new Act (1979) increased the right of initiative and the right of advice of the works council (right for co-decision in a number of social matters, and the obligation of management to ask advice relating to vital organizational and economic measures). Secondly, the direct supervisor–subordinate relations has become the subject of formal regulations in a great number of enterprises. Many organizations have taken the initiative to develop 'work consultation', which is a formalized, regular meeting of the superior with the subordinates to discuss matters of work content, work conditions, and work organizations at all levels of the organization. In The Netherlands three companies composed the sample. The first was a municipal transport organization, with approximately 4,000 employees. The second organization was an area of the Dutch railways. The area contained approximately 750 employees. The third organization was a large steel plant, employing 250 production personnel.

The *selection* of the medium- and long-term *decisions* was based on earlier studies of Heller (1973) and Vroom and Yetton (1973). For the final selection the following consideration has been relevant: some balance should

Participation: A Comparative Study 121

be reached between decisions which are more directly important for the continuity and growth of the whole organization (Steiner 1970; Child 1972) and decisions which are more directed towards the control system, being relevant for continuity of personnel management as well as an adequate execution of the tasks. The first type of decisions are called 'strategic' and the control decisions 'tactical'.

Strategic decisions are characterized by a relatively long duration and low frequency, and are usually initiated and dominated by the top of the organization. Tactical decisions occur more frequently and can be found at lower levels of the organization as well. The distinction relates more to impact on the organization than to actual duration. Table 6.1 gives the numbers of decisions for each category and country.

Various methods were employed to detect the dynamics of the complex decision-making process. The main emphasis was put on the use of an interview schedule to be used as a guideline for interviews with key figures. The interview schedule has not been used in a 'mechanistic' way. For instance, extensive use was made of group feedback and individual feedback procedures so as to validate the information collected and to deepen insight in the processes by qualitative enrichment of the information.

The interview was supplemented in various ways. First, use has been made of document analysis, including memoranda and particularly minutes of

Table 6.1. *Numbers of medium- and long-term decisions in the UK, The Netherlands, and Yugoslavia*

	Number of decisions studied in each country		
	UK	Netherlands	Yugoslavia
Tactical			
Task orientated	15	17	17
People orientated	34	10	22
Total number of tactical or medium-term decisions	49	27	39
Strategic			
Budgeting	4	3	5
Capital investment	15	16	26
New product	4	5	4
Consultative procedures	8	5	8
Total number of strategic or long-term decisions	31	29	43
Total number of strategic and tactical decisions	80	55	82

meetings in which decisions were made. Secondly, because of the longitudinal character and the more prolonged stay of the researcher in each of the companies it was possible to attend meetings and to observe directly the way the decisions were made. In fact, in a number of cases the decisions were selected with an eye on the possibility of making such direct process registration. In most cases this information has been treated as additional to the interview information.

Results

Participation in different countries

In Table 6.2 mean scores of participation are presented for countries and decision types. The first three columns contain the scores for countries; they suggest as the most general conclusion that stable hierarchical patterns exist in all three countries: top management has the highest score for participation in medium- and long-term decisions, workers and foremen the lowest. While this hierarchical pattern is understandable for the United Kingdom and for The Netherlands, it is less understandable for Yugoslavia where the self-management system has been established for a long term. However, the hierarchical patterns are not equally steep: power equality is greater in Yugoslavia than in the other two countries. The reason for this is not a lower index of participation of top management, but a relatively high score of workers' participation in the Yugoslav enterprises. This means that demo-

Table 6.2. *Mean IPC-scores of hierarchical groups across countries and decision types (long and medium)*

Group	Country				Decisions	
	Level	UK	NL	YU	Long	Medium
Workers	A	1.8	1.9	2.6	2.1	2.2
Foremen	B	1.7	2.3	2.2	2.1	2.0
Middle management	C	3.5	3.4	3.4	3.4	3.5
Top management	D	3.8	4.2	4.2	4.4	3.7
Staff advisers	P	1.7	2.9	3.9	3.6	2.2
Representative bodies	Q	2.5	1.9	2.4	2.1	2.5
Locus of power (LP)[a]		1.6	1.8	1.6	1.5	1.8
Power difference (PD)[b]		2.0	2.3	1.6	2.3	1.5
Total power (Σ)[c]		57.7	62.7	74.9	67.2	63.9

[a] LP indicates the level in the hierarchy at which power is strongest; scores of 1 (high-level locus) to 3 (low-level locus).
[b] PD is the IPC score of top management (D) minus the IPC of workers (A).
[c] Total power is the sum of the IPC scores for all levels of the organization (Σ A + B + C + D + P + Q).

cratization does not follow an anarchic pattern based on overall low participation across hierarchical levels. Instead it follows a multiple-level pattern based on overall intensive participation of hierarchical groups in the decision-making activity. This statement is also confirmed by the scores in the last row of the first three columns where we can find that the total amount of participativeness is considerably greater in the Yugoslav enterprise than in enterprises of the other two countries.

According to the scores presented in Table 6.2, the total amount of participativeness does not result only from higher power equality but also from higher decentralization in enterprises. The overall decentralization is indicated by the locus of power score. The score of locus is the highest (i.e. decentralization) in the Dutch enterprises which have also an above average total amount of participativeness.

The two British enterprises demonstrate the lowest overall participativeness. In addition to this, the scores of participativeness for UK staff are substantially lower than in other enterprises while the scores of participativeness for middle management are the highest. One can see that the British enterprises retain traditional bureaucratic structures, for which domination of line management over staff is typical. Considerable variation of participativeness exists between organizations, although the total amount of participation is mostly determined by the country context.

Participation in different phases

One of the most interesting parts of our study is the analysis of participation for each separate phase of medium- and long-term decisions. In relation to the existent literature, we would like to develop the following three interpretative models:

1. *Rational model*. This model postulates that the first phase of decision-making is the most important since within this phase goals are defined, while in the following three phases only means for goal achievement are considered. According to this hypothesis, the first step has strategic function while all other steps are to some extent dependent on it or even programmed by it (Burns, 1967). According to the rational model of interpretation, the group which controls the first step exerts a strong control also on other steps of decision-making activity. Such an interpretation is implicitly accepted by Mintzberg who says that 'diagnosis is probably the single most important routine since it determines in large part, however implicitly, the subsequent course of action' (Mintzberg *et al.*, 1976: 274).

2. *Power-information model*. Some theorists try to define decision-making as a process of integration between information and power. Such for instance is the theory of Sfez (1978) who tries to see the process of decision-making as an integration 'de pouvoir et de savoir'. Similar are suggestions of Bass

124   *Paul L. Koopman* et al.

and Valenzi (1974) who treat leadership decision-making as a distribution of information and power between managers and subordinates (also Strauss 1963).

Following these definitions we would like to describe the first and the third phase of decision activity as power phases while the second and the fourth phases are more dependent on information. According to this assumption, domination over decisions will be achieved by that organizational group which has the highest score on participation in the first and the third phases.

The replication of Mintzberg's investigation made by Shapiro and Dunbar (1977) demonstrated that the ten managerial roles described by Mintzberg, actually created only two clusters: (*a*) cluster of informational roles which contains technical or expert-like functions, and (*b*) decisional roles which generate power through reallocation of resources within organizations.

3. *Relativistic model.* A third model of interpretation can be called relativistic. It tends to define as strategically most important those decisional phases in which the most powerful group within a particular organization has the highest score of involvement. The consequence of such a model is to recognize that each organization or even each decision issue could have its own key phase of decision-making. The relativistic model therefore offers more complex information, but at the same time lends itself less to comparisons.

Since there is no experience with phase analyses of participation in decision-making activity, we will try to assess all three interpretative models in our findings.

The findings about participation through particular phases of decision-making are presented in Table 6.3. This table contains aggregate scales of IPC scores across countries. Locus of power, which indicates the levels of decentralization, is fairly similar for all three countries and for the first, second, and fourth phase of decision-making activity. However, it is different for the third phase where decentralization of decision-making has the highest score in Yugoslav enterprises and the lowest in British and Dutch enterprises. The same could be said for the power inequality index: in the third phase, it is highest for the British and Dutch enterprises and the lowest for the Yugoslav enterprises.

In line with the relativistic model of interpretation, we are inclined to treat the first and the third phase as the most strategic, at least in the case of the organizations studied in this research. The third phase occupies an important role, since in the British and Dutch enterprises power is most concentrated in the hands of top management, while in the Yugoslav enterprises it is shared by the other groups. It means that in both cases this phase is treated as a key for control over decision-making: control by managers in the case of the UK and The Netherlands, and control by workers or workers' representative bodies in the case of Yugoslavia.

Table 6.3. *Mean IPC-scores for particular phases of decision-making across countries*

Power indicator/phase[a]	Country		
	UK	NL	YU
LP_1	1.8	1.7	1.8
LP_2	1.8	1.7	1.7
LP_3	1.6	1.5	2.1
LP_4	1.7	1.9	1.7
PD_1	1.3	2.5	1.7
PD_2	2.2	1.9	2.2
PD_3	2.9	3.0	0.5
PD_4	1.4	1.0	2.0
Σ_1	13.5	15.5	19.1
Σ_2	15.4	18.1	18.7
Σ_3	15.4	15.7	19.1
Σ_4	15.8	18.3	18.0

[a] LP (locus of power); PD (power difference); Σ (total power) in phases 1 to 4.

In relation to the amount of participation, the Dutch and British enterprises show different patterns. Organizations differ across countries in the following way:

- In the British enterprises the total amount of power is the lowest in the first and the highest in the last phase of decision-making activity. Since phase 1 is one of the two strategic phases, we think that such a distribution of participation does not contribute significantly to power-sharing in the total decision process.
- Dutch enterprises have a similar distribution. The lowest amount of participation exists in the first and third phases, and the highest in the second and fourth phases. We conclude that participation is lower in the power than in the information phases of decision-making.
- In the Yugoslav enterprises, patterns of participation are distinctly different. They amount to a reversal of the Dutch pattern: the greatest amount of participation exists in the first and third phases of decision-making and the lowest in the second and fourth phases. It seems that this pattern expresses, at least to some extent, the Yugoslav self-management philosophy.

If we try to summarize these patterns of participation in hierarchical groups, we can see that the second and the third model of interpretation can be applied to our findings, while the first—that is to say, the rational model

126 *Paul L. Koopman* et al.

of interpretation—seems to be less applicable. None of the hierarchical groups concentrated their participation on the first phase, which suggests that the strategic value of the first step stressed by the rational model may not be recognized in our samples. It seems that the third phase of decision-making is actually perceived as the most strategic one.

Another explanation of our findings is possible if we take into account the non-decision-making theory of Bacharach and Baratz (1970). According to this theory, it is possible that the dominant group eliminates all issues which could distort the existing power distribution before they appear in the first step of the decision-making process. If this is so, the first step of decision-making activity is strategically less important.

Consequences of participation

In order to reduce the complicated patterns of interactions that occur in organizational decision-making and increase our understanding of salient features as well as causal relationships, multiple regression has been employed.

Before using multiple regression we had to reduce the number of variables by grouping them through factor analysis and by taking out nominal variables like type of decision. Details of the methods used and the factor structure that emerged are shown in Heller *et al.* (1988: 161).

The results of the multiple regressions computed for all decisions are presented in Table 6.4. Factor scores of four groups of outcome variables are regressed by predictors as status power, influence-power-sharing, meta-power, conflicts, and a factor combining trust and clarity of goals. It can be seen that all outcomes are significantly explained by certain predictors of SP, IPC, and contingencies. The following results can be emphasized:

- Status power of all groups is a strong predictor of skill utilization—as long as management participation is absent. Conflicts (that is to say disagreement) also makes a small contribution to this prediction. It seems that moderate amounts of conflict or disagreements enhance skill utilization, particularly with medium-term decisions.
- Strong management influence has negative consequences for outcomes. Its inhibition on skill utilization is strong and has important theoretical implications. Strong management influence on the decision process also has a negative effect on achievement and on satisfaction with outcomes. The negative effect on achievement was unexpected. Achievement, it will be remembered, is scored on the extent to which the overall decision objectives are fulfilled. The finding suggests that concentration of power at the top may lead to changes in objectives away from their original focus.
- Finally a particularly important finding is that decision outcomes—our

Table 6.4. *Multiple regressions where outcome-factor scores are dependent variables while status power (SP), influence-power continuum (IPC), metapower (MP), and contingencies are independent variables (medium- and long-term decisions)*

Predictors	Abbreviation	FSAT[a]	FACH[b]	FSKILL[c]	SFOUT[d]
Status power all levels except top management	SP/ALL	—	—	0.39	—
Status power of top management	SP/D	—	—	0.12	—
IPC (workers and foremen)	IPC/W	—	—	—	—
IPC (top management and professionals)	IPC/M	—	−0.21	−0.33	(−0.11)
Metapower (frequency × intensity)	MPO	—	0.14	—	—
Conflicts (frequency × intensity)	OD	−0.15	(−0.11)	0.14	−0.13
Factor combining trust and clarity of goals	CON 1	0.53	0.36	—	0.51
Multiple regression	R^2	0.61	0.49	0.61	0.60
Adjusted	R	0.35	0.22	0.36	0.34
Probability beyond 1% level		0.00	0.00	0.00	0.00

[a] FSAT = factor score of efficiency, satisfaction with outcomes and satisfaction with process.
[b] FACH = factor score of achievement and satisfaction with outcomes.
[c] FSKILL = factor score of skill utilization of workers and managers.
[d] SFOUT = factor score of efficiency, achievement, satisfaction with process, and satisfaction with outcome.

dependent variables—are more powerfully predicted by contingencies (trust, clearness of goal, feasibility, and satisfaction with outcome) than by status or behavioural power. Only skill utilization as an output variable is not predicted by contingencies.

Conclusions

We will start with a summary of some findings.

1. The importance of hierarchy in organizational life in general and in decision-making in particular is fully confirmed.

2. There is apparently no one method and no one superior way of making decisions. The distribution of influence varies (i) with the type of decision (it is different for medium- and long-term decisions); (ii) with the organization (there is something like an organizational culture which leads to more or less centralization); and (iii) it seems to vary also by country (the country variations seem to be influenced by differences in legal structures like laws on employee participation).

3. Employees exert more influence over tactical than over strategic decisions.

4. In general, the amount of influence exerted by the lower levels of organizations and by works councils is very limited. On average it lies somewhere between being informed and being consulted. This means that in practice for most decisions there is no regular practice of prior consultation. The highest influence scores are achieved by the Yugoslav companies in all three categories of the decisions process.

5. Contrary to some previous research, we find that a moderate degree of conflict (perhaps better called disagreement) is consistently associated with more participative behaviour. This should not have been unexpected; after all, it is only through sharing information and consultation that potential or hidden disagreements can come to the surface. However, this finding does not fit in with the frequent assumptions in the literature which supports employee participation as a way of encouraging consensus and conformity. Rather its seems reasonable to explore the possibility that a combination of participation and moderate amounts of disagreement are compatible with accepting and implementing decisions reached by this means.

6. Skill underutilization is high if top management exercises considerable power or when the difference in influence between top management and the lowest levels is great.

7. Our assumption that the longitudinal process of decision-making can be divided into distinct phases which will show different patterns of behaviour has been substantiated. In theory and in practice power is not handled in the same way and is not distributed between organizational levels equally in start-up, development, finalization, and implementation.

Garbage?

There is one further outcome of this research which departs from much of the literature on organizational behaviour. Since Cohen *et al.* (1972) coined the phrase 'garbage can model' to describe a form of decision-making within 'organized anarchies', these terms have found much favour with social scientists. The stimulus for these designations of decision-making came from analyses of what happens in universities and it may also have relevance elsewhere, for instance in descriptions of the research process (Martin, 1982: 17–39). The model suggests that 'as members of the organization generate problems and solutions, they dump these into the garbage-can' (Martin, 1982: 21). It is alleged that organizations can be conceptualized as 'a collection of choices looking for problems, issues and feelings looking for decision situations in which they might be aired, solutions looking for issues to which they might be answers, and decision-makers looking for work' (Cohen *et al.*, 1972: 2).

Since the traditional decision literature usually makes dull reading, such racy inversions of accepted wisdom immediately created strong rapport among academics who see themselves struggling against anarchy. However, our own research does not support such a model and others have also voiced concern (Janis and Mann, 1977: 423; Padgett, 1980; Hickson *et al.*, 1986). In the very detailed Bradford study of 150 strategic decision processes in thirty organizations covering both the public and the private sectors, they found plenty of examples of complexity, uncertainty, discontinuity, and power politics. Nevertheless, they conclude that 'whilst the image of rollicking in a dented dustbin is fun, the wide differences in decision-making belie it as a general model' (Hickson *et al.*, 1986: 251).

National differences?

Since the research took place in three countries, some comments on similarities or differences between them may be expected. However, the reader will be aware that our sample in each country was small and may not be adequately representative. Furthermore, our main concern has been with the decision process itself and the different tasks investigated in handling tactical and strategic issues. In these areas, our samples are adequate in size and are matched between countries.

Quite apart from the representativeness of the national samples, the evidence on country differences is not always very clear. In the preceding research into industrial democracy in twelve countries (IDE, 1981*b*) we obtained much larger samples and country differences certainly emerged, but did not establish any clear trend and certainly did not follow the kind of 'culture pattern' claimed by some authors (Hofstede, 1980). Over a wide range of comparative research, the most important findings that can be usefully explained relate to differences *between* organizations or *within* organizations. This is certainly the case in the present DIO research, as the reader will have noticed.

Recent years have in fact seen a re-emergence of interest in the concept of organizational culture since the early work of Jaques (1951). Our data clearly support the need to consider differences in organizations within the same country to be due to certain unique historic and/or situational characteristics (Heller *et al.*, 1988). The concept 'organizational culture' seems justified in relation to these between-company differences (see also Frost *et al.*, 1985; Schein, 1985).

In spite of these caveats, which suggest the need for caution, there is one country difference that stands out. The British companies consistently show the lowest level of participation in decision-making and the Yugoslav companies the highest. This applies to tactical decisions as well as to strategic decisions. The Dutch companies are in between. Since the various measures of influence and power (IPC) are central to our model, this could be an

130   *Paul L. Koopman* et al.

important finding, because it supports and repeats the results in the twelve-country IDE research which used the same IPC measurement in a different and much larger sample of organizations. The main explanation for the country differences in the IDE study was the existence of formal and/or legal support structures. These were very strong in Yugoslavia, strong in The Netherlands, and weak in Britain (IDE, 1981*b*, ch. 6). We believe that the DIO findings can be explained in the same way.

Policy implications

Our evidence confirms that even the most democratically run organizations have a hierarchy. It follows that major policy changes will originate at the top, although works councils can, on occasions, play an important role.

If we assume that those responsible for organizational policy are concerned with the effective use of all available resources, then our findings on skill utilization have immediate practical implications. We have argued, on the basis of past and present evidence, that managers as well as lower-level employees who have experience and skill which they want to use, are often prevented from doing so. There are three obstacles: one is the rigidity of the decision-making process, which concentrates power at a higher level than the operation justifies. A second is the lack of recognition of distinct phases in decision-making. It is not necessary for senior levels to dominate all phases equally, and we saw that experience and skill can be introduced at different points of the decision cycle and improve its effectiveness. The third obstacle is the widely held but mistaken belief that the practice of influence-sharing is a slippery slope and sooner or later leads to a lack of control.

Our own findings show that participative decision-making has a range of alternative practices, from sharing information via different kinds of consultation to joint decision-making and, ultimately, the delegation of power. These alternative methods (described as the influence-power continuum) are not equally applicable to all situations. There is also no reason why the same decision approach should be used at the various phases of the cycle—from 'start-up' via 'development' and 'finalization' to 'implementation' of the decisions.

The available flexibility of varying decision methods for different types of issue and different phases come out very strongly in our research. They give managers and works councils a considerable range of choice to match their approach to varying conditions.

References

Aldrich, H. E. (1979), *Organizations and Environments* (Englewood Cliffs, NJ, Prentice-Hall).

Bacharach, P., and Baratz, M. S. (1970), *Power and Poverty: Theory and Practice* (New York, Oxford Univ. Press).

Bass, B. M., and Valenzi, E. R. (1974), 'Contingent Aspects of Effective Management Styles', in J. G. Junt and L. L. Larson (eds.), *Contingency Approaches to Leadership* (Carbondale, Ill., Southern Illinois Univ. Press).

Baumgartner, T., Buckley, W., and Burns, T. (1975), 'Meta Power and Relational Control in Social Life', *Social Science Information*, 14: 49–78.

―― ―― ―― and Schuster, P. (1976), 'Meta Power and the Structuring of Social Hierarchies', in T. Burns and W. Buckley (eds.), *Power and Control* (Beverly Hills, Calif., Sage).

Benson, K. (1977), 'Organizations: A Dialectial View', *Administrative Science Quarterly*, 12: 1–21.

Brannen, P., Batstone, E., Fatchett, D., and White, P. (1976), *The Worker Directors: A Sociology of Participation* (London, Hutchinson).

Braybrooke, D., and Lindblom, C. E. (1963), *A Strategy of Decision: Policy Evaluation as a Social Process* (New York, Free Press).

Burns, T. (1967), 'The Comparative Study of Organizations', in V. Vroom (ed.), *Methods of Organizational Research* (Pittsburgh: Univ. of Pittsburgh Press).

―― and Stalker, G. M. (1961), *The Management of Innovation* (London, Tavistock).

Butler, R. J., Astley, W. G., Hickson, D. J., Mallory, G., and Wilson, D. C. (1979), 'Strategic Decision-Making in Organizations: Concepts of Content and Process', *International Studies of Management and Organization*, 9: 5–36.

Child, J. (1972), 'Organization Structure, Environment and Performance: The Role of Strategic Choice', *Sociology*, 6: 1–22.

Clegg, S., and Dunkerley, D. (1977), *Critical Issues in Organizations* (London, Routledge and Kegan Paul).

Cohen, M. D., and March, J. G. (1974), *Leadership and Ambiguity* (New York, McGraw-Hill).

―― ―― and Olsen, J. P. (1972), 'A Garbage Can Model of Organizational Choice', *Administrative Science Quarterly*, 17: 1–25.

Crozier, M., and Friedberg, E. (1977), 'Organization as Means and Constraints of Collective Action', in M. Warren (ed.), *Organizational Choice and Constraint* (Farnborough, Saxon House).

Elliot J. (1978), *Conflict and Cooperation: The Growth of Industrial Democracy* (London, Kogan Page).

Enderud, H. (1977), *Two Views on Participation in Organizational Decision-making* (Copenhagen, Institute for Organization and Industrial Sociology).

Foucault, M. (1977), *Discipline and Punish: The Birth of the Prison* (London, Allen Lane).

Friend, J. K., and Jessop, W. N. (1969), *Local Government and Strategic Choice* (London, Tavistock).

―― Power, J. M., and Yewlett, C. J. (1974), *Public Planning: The Inter-corporate Dimension* (London, Tavistock).

Frost, P. J., Moore, L. F., Louis, M. R., Lundberg, C. C., and Martin, J. (1985), *Organizational Culture* (Beverly Hills, Calif., Sage).

132   *Paul L. Koopman* et al.

Galbraith, J. K. (1967), *The New Industrial State* (Boston, Houghton Mifflin).
Heller, F. A. (1973), 'Leadership, Decision-Making and Contingency Theory', *Industrial Relations*, 12: 183–99.
—— Drenth, P. J. D., Koopman, P. L., and Rus, V. (1988), *Decisions in Organizations: A Three-Country Comparative Study* (London, Sage).
Hickson, D., Butler, R., Gray, D., Mallory, G., and Wilson, D. (1986), *Top Decisions: Strategic Decision-Making in Organizations* (Oxford, Blackwell).
Hinings, C. R., Hickson, D. J., Pennings, J. M., and Schneck, R. E. (1974), 'Structural Conditions of Intraorganizational Power', *Administrative Science Quarterly*, 19: 22–44.
Hofstede, G. (1980), *Culture's Consequences: International Differences in Work-Related Values* (London, Sage).
IDE (1981*a*), *European Industrial Relations* (London, Oxford Univ. Press).
—— (1981*b*), *Industrial Democracy in Europe* (London, Oxford Univ. Press).
Janis, I. L., and Mann, L. (1977), *Decision-making: A Psychological Analysis of Conflict, Choice and Commitment* (New York, Free Press).
Jaques, E. (1951), *The Changing Culture of a Factory* (London, Tavistock).
Kahneman, D., Slovic, P., and Tversky, A. (1982), *Judgment under uncertainty heuristics and biases* (Cambridge, Cambridge Univ. Press).
Koopman, P. L., and Pool, J. (1990), 'Decision-making in Organizations', in C. L. Cooper and I. T. Robertson (eds.), *International Review of Industrial and Organizational Psychology*, v (London, Wiley): 101–48.
—— and Wierdsma, A. F. M. (1984), 'Work Consultation as a Channel of Communication and as a Consultative Framework', in P. J. D. Drenth, H. Thierry, P. J. Willems, and C. J. de Wolff (eds.), *Handbook of Work and Organizational Psychology* (Chichester, Wiley).
Lammers, C. J., and Széll, G. (1989), 'Organizational Democracy: Taking Stock', in C. J. Lammers and G. Széll, G. (eds.), *International Handbook of Participation in Organizations*, i (Oxford, Oxford Univ. Press).
Lawrence, P. R., and Lorsch, J. W. (1967), *Organizations and Environment: Managing Differentiation and Integration* (Boston, Harvard Graduate School of Business Administration).
Lindblom, Ch. E. (1959), 'The Science of "muddling through" ', *Public Administrative Review*, 19: 79–99.
Lukes, S. (1974), *Power: A Radical View* (London, Macmillan Press).
Martin, J. (1982), 'A Garbage Can Model of the Research Process', in J. McGarth, J. Martin, and R. Kulka (eds.), *Judgment Calls in Research* (Beverly Hills, Calif., Sage).
Mintzberg, H., Raisinghani, D., and Théorêt, A. (1976), 'The Structure of "Unstructured" Decision Processes', *Administrative Science Quarterly*, 21: 246–75.
Padgett, J. F. (1980), 'Managing Garbage Can Hierarchies', *Administrative Science Quarterly*, 25: 583–604.
Pettigrew, A. M. (1975), 'Towards Political Theory of Organizational Intervention', *Human Relations*, 28: 191–208.
Pfeffer, J., and Salancik, G. R. (1978), *The External Control of Organizations* (New York, Harper & Row).

Schein, E. (1985), *Organizational Culture and Leadership* (San Francisco, Jossey-Bass).

Sfez, L. (1978), 'Existe-t-il des décisions démocratiques?' *Dialectiques*, 22: 59–72.

Shapiro, Z., and Dunbar, R. L. M. (1977), *Testing Minzberg's Managerial Roles* (Berlin, International Institute of Management).

Sheridan, A. (1980), *Foucault: The Will to Truth* (London, Tavistock).

Simon, H. A. (1984), 'On the Behavioral and Rational Foundations of Economic Dynamics', *Journal of Economic Behavior and Organizations*, 5: 35–55.

Steiner, G. A. (1970), 'Strategic Factors in Business Success', *Tijdschrift voor Efficiency en Documentatie*, 40: 434–41.

Strauss, G. (1963), 'Some Notes on Power Equalization', in J. H. Leavitt (ed.), *The Social Science of Organizations* (Englewood Cliffs, NJ, Prentice-Hall).

Thompson, J. D. (1967), *Organizations in Action* (New York, McGraw-Hill).

Vroom, V. H., and Yetton, P. W. (1973), *Leadership and Decision-Making* (Pittsburgh, Univ. of Pittsburgh Press).

Witte, E. (1972), 'Field Research on Complex Decision-Making Processes: The Phase Theorem'. *International Studies of Management and Organization*, 2: 156–82.

[30]

Human Relations, Volume 34, Number 8, 1981, pp. 657–676

Content, Process, and Effects of Participative Decision Making on the Shop Floor: Three Cases in the Netherlands[1]

Paul L. Koopman[2], Pieter J. D. Drenth, Frans B. M. Bus, Agaath J. Kruyswijk, and André F. M. Wierdsma

Free University of Amsterdam

This article discusses the experiences with participative decision making on the shop floor ("work consultation") in three Dutch organizations. Work consultation is characterized in terms of content, process, and effects. Besides the moderating effect of a number of contingency variables on the relation between participation and outcome variables is researched. The results lead to questioning the usefulness of a contingency model in research on the effects of participation.

INTRODUCTION

A longitudinal study of participative decision making in organizations (DIO, see footnote 1) was started in late 1974 (Heller, Drenth, Koopman, & Rus, 1977). Research teams from three countries (Great Britain, Yugoslavia, and the Netherlands) were involved in this project. Results of the field work have been reported at several intervals (Rus, Odar, Heller, Brown,

[1]This article is based on an international research project on Decision Making in Organizations (DIO) in Great Britain, Yugoslavia, and the Netherlands. The authors are members of the Dutch group. The other members of the international team are: Frank A. Heller, Alan Brown (UK), Veljko Rus, and Miro Odar (Yugoslavia). The Dutch part of this study was financially supported by the Netherlands Organization for the Advancement of Pure Research.
[2]Requests for reprints should be addressed to Dr. Paul L. Koopman, Department of Industrial and Organizational Psychology, Free University, De Boelelaan 1081, 1081 HV Amsterdam, The Netherlands.

Drenth, Koopman, Wierdsma, Bus, & Kruyswijk, 1977; Drenth, Koopman, Rus, Odar, Heller, & Brown, 1979). The present article discusses some findings from the research carried out in the Netherlands. The complete results of the Dutch study have been published in Koopman (1980).

The most important hypotheses of the DIO project concern situationally determined relationships between the manner of decision making and variables such as effectiveness, skill utilization, and satisfaction (see Fig. 1 and Appendix B). It is assumed that an increase of participation does not lead to consistent effects in all situations, and it is seen as a task of the social sciences to identify the inhibiting and stimulating conditions. In this respect we are in line with the theories and research results of Fiedler (1967), Lowin (1968), Heller (1971), and Vroom and Yetton (1973).

The DIO project has studied decision-making processes of varying degrees of complexity and at different levels of the organization. In the present article we will confine ourselves to decision making on the shop floor. Participation in matters relating to one's own work situation has taken on an institutionalized form in the Netherlands known as work consultation (*werkoverleg*). Before discussing the methods and results of the research, we will briefly describe the position of work consultation in the organization in the Netherlands and the functions it may fulfil.

THE SITUATION IN THE NETHERLANDS

In order to explain how work consultation presently operates, it is necessary to present a picture of the industrial relations system at the organizational level and some recent developments in this field (for a more extensive discussion see Andriessen, 1976; Windmuller & De Galan, 1977; IDE-International Research Group, 1980, Vol. II).

It should be emphasized that industrial relations in the Netherlands have always had a centralized nature. Consultation and negotiations used

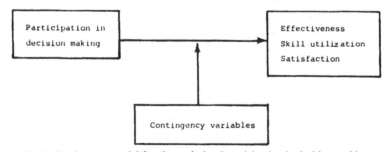

Fig. 1. Contingency model for the analysis of participation in decision making.

to take place at the national or sectorial level: the organizational level was scarcely represented. Only more recently (since the late 1960s) has emphasis shifted somewhat from consultation and agreements at a central level to the level of the individual organization.

The four main institutional forms of workers' participation at the organizational level are: the works council, the board of directors, the system of union representatives on the shop floor, and work consultation.

The Works Council

In the Netherlands, every enterprise with at least 100 employees must have a works council. This body has from 7 to 25 elected members, depending on the size of the company. Candidates may be nominated by trade unions and by groups of employees.

The first Works Council Act (1950) described it as a consultative body whose primary concern was the general interest of the firm. An objective such as this was fully in line with the post-war industrial climate, which was harmonious and cooperative. But industrial relations gradually became strained, and it was apparent that the objectives and interests of the management and the workers were at variance, especially in that the unions felt the original character of the works council did not leave enough room for promotion of the workers' interests.

The second act, in 1971, designated as objectives "joint consultation" and "representation of the interests of employees." It also extended the council's formal powers: it got a say in several matters concerning personnel and social policy, and it had to be consulted in decisions on vital organizational and economic matters (Drenth, 1973). Soon after the 1971 act came into effect, a political discussion arose on whether the works council's powers should be further increased. Some of the trade unions felt that the works council should represent employees only, rather than be a consultative body with the firm director as chairman.

In 1979, after heated political debates, a third act was passed which is a compromise between two seemingly opposed objectives: joint consultation for the entire organization, and representation of the workers and promotion of their interests. The works council has now primarily become an "employees' council" in which management takes no part. But at least six times per year consultative meetings with the firm director must take place. At these meetings, the council's advice is discussed, or some kind of agreement has to be reached on issues requiring the council's approval. The council's powers have been further extended: more decisions require its opinion or its approval.

The Board of Directors

In 1971 a board of directors became compulsory in companies with at least 100 employees or one million guilders in capital. The board was then also given more power. For instance, it has the right to appoint and to dismiss managing directors, and its consent is needed for important decisions such as mergers, the issue of shares, large scale dismissal, etc. Neither employees nor union representatives can be board members. Appointment takes place through cooptation, and the works council, the shareholders, and the managing directors have the right to nominate candidates. The works council may also veto an appointment, as may the shareholders, but not the managing directors. As a result of this arrangement, many large firms have an employee representative on the board who can sometimes (informally) exert quite a bit of influence. Unlike the German system of codetermination, workers' representatives in the executive board (*Arbeitsdirektor*) has not been introduced in the Netherlands.

The System of Union Representatives on the Shop Floor

Since the late 1960s, attempts have been made by the trade unions to introduce a system of union representatives in companies. This is entirely different from past union policy and activities, which were concentrated on bargaining at the national or sectorial level, outside the individual firm. The union representatives' chairman represents the union within the company, and leads union members among the workers in conflictual issues and actions. This system has been implemented in a small but growing number of companies, particularly in the metal industry.

The objectives of the system of union representatives are: (1) Improving communication within the trade union and increasing active participation by the members; and (2) promoting interests of trade union members in the company and achieving greater influence on the general management of the company. Trade unions in the Netherlands are not at all in agreement on how this greater influence should be exerted: in the form of a larger say in the formulation of management policy, implying greater responsibility, or in the form of monitoring decisions after they have been made.

Work Consultation

Work consultation can be defined as (1) a regular and organized form of consultation (2) between a supervisor and his co-workers as a group or representatives of the group (3) in which the prime objective is participating in and exerting influence on decision making (4) in the first instance concerning the work and working conditions.

Work consultation is subject to *rules and regulations* which govern certain matters. Some kind of regularity is also a requirement in the above definition. So the ordinary day-to-day consultation between a supervisor and one of his subordinates cannot be considered work consultation. The *group nature* of work consultation gives it an entirely different character and opens up new possibilities. The collective element requires a different attitude on the part of both the supervisor and the group members. The third element in our definition—*influence* on decision making—implies that the purpose of work consultation is more than giving instructions, improving the atmosphere, etc. The issue of changing the apportionment of participation in the organization definitely does fall under the heading of work consultation. The *content* and radius of work consultation may also change with time. The definition focuses on the content aspect of work consultation in the start-up phase. How much one succeeds in the long run to include matters of broader range in the discussions will determine to a large extent the integration of work consultation in the existing information and decision-making structure, which is of essential importance for the continuity of work consultation (Ramondt, 1974).

A fairly large number of companies in the Netherlands have some form of work consultation (apart from the works council). The works council is required by law; work consultation is not. But it is a task of the works council to stimulate work consultation (Works Council Act, 1971). The new Works Council Act (1979) requires the works council's approval of any arrangements covering work consultation.

It is not easy to pinpoint the beginning of formal work consultation in the Netherlands. The first publications which mention the concept of work consultation date from the early 1960s. Of course, before that time, in the Netherlands as well as in other countries, experiments had taken place with some form of participation in the work situation. But it has only been in the past ten years that much attention has been given to the systematically organized and formal systems of work consultation in the Netherlands.

A more elaborate discussion on the points of view of the Dutch government and employers' and employees' organizations on work consultation can be found in Koopman and Drenth (1977) and Koopman (1980). Briefly summarized, the expectations and motives these parties have with respect to work consultation may be put into three categories as suggested by Dachler and Wilpert (1978).

    (1) *Democratization.* This perspective is particularly found among the trade unions, the chief objective being a more equal distribution of power.

(2) *Humanization.* Here the objective is to make the work situation more attractive, more human, and more decent—through job enrichment, for example.

(3) *Effectiveness and organization.* This includes many factors that improve the manageability of the organization, such as better coordination, communications, and so on. Lammers (1975) has termed it "functional democratization." It is particularly from this perspective that management seems to value work consultation.

Needless to say, elements from each of these viewpoints are generally encountered in each party's stance on work consultation.

METHOD

Phases of Data Collection

The main research in the Netherlands took about two years to complete and can be divided into five phases. The most important goals, research activities, and methods will be indicated for each phase.

1. *Orientation phase.* The objectives of this phase were a definitive organization of the study, an acquaintance and orientation period within the company (including history, organization, characteristics, and origins of work consultation). The activities included discussions with management, personnel representatives and specialists, document analyses (notes, minutes, etc.), and adaptation of the questionnaires to the specific company. This phase took approximately two months.

2. *Inventory phase.* The objective of the inventory phase was to gain an overall view of the present situation, particularly of how work consultation and decision making operated, and of the wishes and expectations for the future. Activities included administering questionnaires to members of 12 to 15 work-consultation groups. This was followed by feedback and discussion of the results [Group Feedback Analysis (see Heller, 1969)], and subsequent reporting and discussion at the company level. This took approximately three months.

3. *Process phase.* In this phase the objective was to study developments in work consultation and its relationship to other forms of decision making in the organization. Activities involved attending consultation meetings (observation) and an extensive analysis of a number of issues, some of them "serious management issues." The way in which these decision-making processes took place was examined through document analysis and supplementary interviews. This took a little over one year.

4. *Evaluation phase.* The objective here was to find out what changes had taken place since the beginning of the study. The activities were largely similar to those of the second phase and resulted in around three months' work.

5. *Feedback.* This involved tying up any loose ends and discussing the results with people and groups at all levels. The possibilities for follow-up study were also investigated. The final phase took about two months.

Description of Sample Organizations

Three companies were involved in the Dutch portion of the project. Below are short descriptions of each company.

Organization A is a municipal transport organization in the western part of the country. It has approximately 4,000 employees, 2,500 of whom are drivers and 1,000 technical employees. The organization has a centralized functional structure. The large geographical area covered by the work is characteristic. A situation of conflict in one of the technical departments in 1968 was the first inducement to start work consultation. Initially it took on a *representative* form and was introduced in the technical section only. In 1972 representative work consultation was set up throughout the company. Because there was too little communication between representatives and those who had elected them, in 1972-1973 *direct* work consultation was introduced.

Organization B is one of the regional divisions of the Dutch railways, with some 750 employees. The work load is largely determined by the train schedules and the number of passengers. Nearly all employees are on rotating shifts. The tasks, duties, and responsibilities are generally planned or defined in advance. The central and district levels have a great deal of influence on the area activities to keep regulations and tasks uniform throughout the company. Around 1970, the idea of team management was promoted by the central personnel office. To this end, organization B offered training to management employees in 1970-1971. This led to regular and well-conducted consultation at the area and sectional levels. At the lower levels of the organization, work consultation has evolved in only a very limited sense.

Organization C is one plant of a steel works. In C, steel slabs are heated in furnaces and molded into sheets. The plant employs 250 production workers divided into four shifts (continuously operating factory). Another 200 employees work in supportive and complementary departments. The direct cause which led to the introduction of work consultation was a strike in March 1973. The company management developed plans which, after discussion with employee representatives

Table I. Research Methods in Main Phases

Method	Inventory	Process registration	Evaluation
Interview	X	X	X
Questionnaires	X		X
Group feedback analysis	X	X	X
Observation		X	
Analysis of minutes		X	

and other persons, resulted in the introduction of work consultation at the end of 1973.

Instruments for Data Collection

At the outset of the project, a "multimethod approach" was deliberately chosen. Table I shows which methods were used in the various phases.

In the present article we will confine our discussion to the methods and instruments used for the results which will be presented here. Table II gives a summary of the most important questionnaires, with an indication of their reliabiity. For a more detailed description see Appendix B.

In addition to information derived from the questionnaires, we made use of information obtained by meeting observation and a content analysis of minutes. The observation categories utilized can be differentiated into content and process categories. The observation scheme has been included in the Appendix A. Table III contains indications of reliability of information obtained through observation and minutes analysis. The reliability of questionnaires and the observation scheme is clearly satisfactory.

Table II. Main Questionnaires and Reliability

Code	Content (see Appendix B)	Internal consistency[a]: Organization		
		A	B	C
IPC	Influence-power continuum	.75	.84	.77
EFF-C	Effects of consultation	.87	.87	.82
SU	Skill utilization	.84	.85	.87
SAT-G	Satisfaction in general	.73	.65	.83
SAT-P	Satisfaction with participation	.68	.74	.68

[a] Cronbach's alpha coefficient.

Table III. Interobserver Agreement for Observation and Analysis of Minutes (two observers)

Category	Observation	Analysis of minutes	
		Inter	Intra
Content	78%[a]	79%	77%
Presentation	82	81	84
Initiative	93	72	89
DM style	72	59	75
Settlement	77	84	74
Time	70	–	–
Number of issues	90	160	125

[a] Percentages of issues scored in the same way.

RESULTS

Content

Most of the subjects discussed in work consultation relate to the work itself and the immediate working environment. Figure 2 shows the results, based on observation and analysis of the work consultation minutes, in the three organizations over a period of approximately two years.

Between 50 and 60% of all issues discussed deal with the "work itself." Issues such as arrangement of daily work, improving work methods,

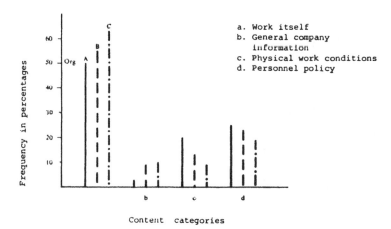

a. Work itself
b. General company information
c. Physical work conditions
d. Personnel policy

Fig. 2. Frequency distribution of topics discussed during work consultation (data based on observation and analysis of minutes).

acquisition of materials, etc., come under this heading. Approximately 20% to 25% of the topics covered concern "personnel policy." Examples would be: understaffing, absenteeism, evaluation, reward, leadership style. Another 10% to 20% of the topics can be placed under the heading of physical work conditions. This would include safety, noise, sanitation and hygiene, etc. Category (b) has a lower frequency (2% to 10%): issues relating to production standards, departmental budgets, costs, and departmental results, and more general company information on financial results, long-term planning, etc. are seldom discussed in work consultation. This is true as well of profit-making organization C.

Process

Figure 3 shows the frequency with which different decision-making styles are utilized during work consultation in the three organizations. It is apparent that, as far as the process itself is concerned, work consultation can be characterized as providing information and consultation. In only 5% to 11% of all cases do decisions take place *during* the meeting. In at least 40% retrospective information only is given, after the decision has been made.

The style of decision making is affected by the initiator and the presentation of the topic. If the initiative comes from management, then in about two-thirds of all cases only retrospective information is given,

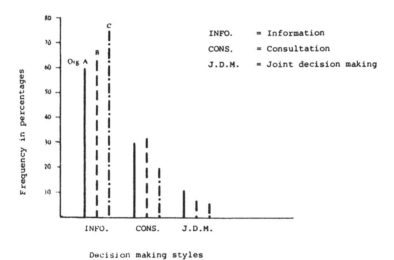

Fig. 3. Frequency of decision-making styles in work consultation (data from observation and analysis of minutes).

usually as one of the "announcements." If the initiative comes from the side of the workers (generally through questions before closure of the meeting), then the chances that serious consultation will result are increased. The chance of influence on management by the participants is also clearly greater in the separate items on the agenda, which are usually the most serious issues.

In addition to information from the minutes analysis and participative observation, the opinions of the participants were asked. Figure 4 shows the replies to questionnaire IPC (see Appendix A) for each organization. In this questionnaire, participants are asked to indicate how they participate in 12 specific issues.

The results show that the style of decision making is partially determined by the content of the issue. Participants in work consultation are involved the most in improving work conditions and in safety procedures

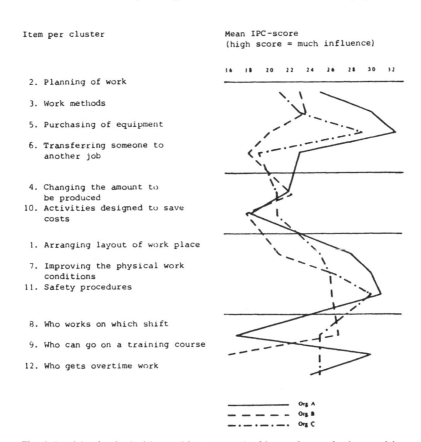

Fig. 4. Participation in decision making, as perceived by work consultation participants (questionnaire data).

(items 7 and 11), and in purchasing equipment needed for the work (item 5). They are the least involved in cost saving activities (10), transferring someone to another job (6), and changing the amount to be produced by the group (4). Apart from a few peaks per organization (for example, item 8 for organization A and items 5 and 9 for organization B), the profiles show a certain amount of consistency. This is true not only for the two transport organizations (A and B) but also for the steel processing organization C.

The extent to which participants are involved in a given issue during work consultation partially depends on the chairman's judgment of the import of the issue for the group or departmental productivity. In two of the three organizations (A and B) there is a positive relationship between the amount of participation per item (IPC) and the chairman's evaluation of the importance of the subject (IMP-D). The Spearman correlations are .43 and .70, respectively. In the third company no such relationship was found.

Effects

What are the most notable effects of work consultation as perceived by the participants? Figure 5 shows the replies of group members to the EFF-C questionnaire. This shows that they see work consultation primarily as an instrument to improve the information flow from lower levels to the top (item 10), a finding corroborated by other studies (Van der Bruggen & Den Hertog, 1976). To a somewhat lesser degree, they feel that people know better what is going on (1) and that workers' interests are better looked after (5). Results such as better decisions (8) and greater acceptance of decisions (3) are mentioned fairly often. They do not feel work consultation is a waste of time (7). Few effects are found in an increased influence on departmental policy (9), or even on day-to-day matters (4). Increased job satisfaction (2) and a better utilization of the group's abilities (12) are mentioned by only a handful.

Evaluation of the effects by work-consultation chairmen runs largely along the same lines; the greatest difference is one of degree. On nearly all points, the chairmen are more positive in their evaluation than the group members. But relatively speaking there is a consensus (Spearman rho = .81). The most important difference is that chairmen feel the group members have more influence on daily routine than the group members themselves do.

Although there are differences between the companies in absolute terms, there is a fair amount of profile consistency in terms of effects. Work consultation appears to be fairly constant, despite the highly diverse contexts.

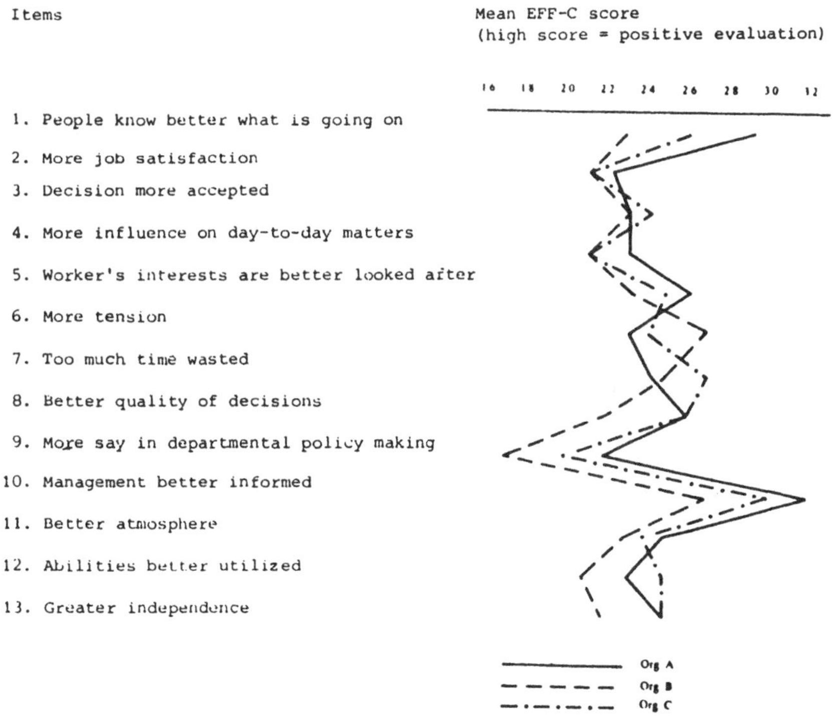

Decision Making on the Shop Floor 669

Items

Mean EFF-C score
(high score = positive evaluation)

```
                        16   18   20   22   24   26   28   30   32
```

1. People know better what is going on

2. More job satisfaction

3. Decision more accepted

4. More influence on day-to-day matters

5. Worker's interests are better looked after

6. More tension

7. Too much time wasted

8. Better quality of decisions

9. More say in departmental policy making

10. Management better informed

11. Better atmosphere

12. Abilities better utilized

13. Greater independence

Org A

Org B

Org C

Fig. 5. Effects of work consultation, as perceived by participants (questionnaire data).

To assess further the impact of the different decision styles, we examined the effects of participation (IPC) on four independent variables: skill utilization (SU), general satisfaction (SAT-G), satisfaction with participation (SAT-P), and the effectiveness of participation (EFF-C). To operationalize SU, the respondent was asked to indicate on a 4-point scale (varying from "hardly ever" to "almost invariably") the extent to which his job afforded him the opportunity to use initiative, verbal ability, practical work experience, the capacity to develop new ideas, and so on. We used a general "satisfaction with work" type scale (Taylor & Bowers, 1972), consisting of seven items, to measure SAT-G; SAT-P was assessed separately, using a 5-item questionnaire (Koopman & Werkman, 1973). The effectiveness of participation on factors like wasting time, quality of decision, and diffusion of information (EFF-C) was determined by responses to 14 items on the questionnaire (see Appendix A).

Table IV presents the correlations between IPC and the dependent (or outcome) variables. Not surprisingly, the highest and most consistent correlations are with satisfaction with participation. Apparently, workers

Table IV. Pearson Correlations Among Participation (IPC) and Outcome
Variables

Outcome variables	Organization A	Organization B	Organization C
SU	.38[b]	.08	.24[b]
EFF-C	.42[b]	.38[b]	.10
SAT-G	.14[a]	.19[a]	.31[b]
SAT-P	.44[b]	.57[b]	.35[b]
$N >$	175	154	153

[a] $p < .05$.
[b] $p < .01$.

appreciate participative leadership and become more satisfied with
participation the more influence they have. This pattern occurs in all three
companies. A fairly similar and strong relationship exists between participation and rating of participation effectiveness (EFF-C). More influence is
not only more satisfying, but is also considered to lead to better decisions,
better mutual understanding, a better atmosphere, a better acceptance of
the decision, and the like. This relationship is much weaker in one company (C).

As in other studies (Wall & Lischeron, 1977), a weaker and less
consistent relationship between IPC and general satisfaction was found.
Conceptually, this is not surprising. General satisfaction has more determinants than the participative climate, and the contribution of influence
to general satisfaction will thus be relatively small. We will discuss these
results later in more detail. Rather weak correlations exist between IPC
and skill utilization. There seems to be only partial support for the view
that one of the great advantages of participative management is that it
makes more effective use of subordinates' skills (Heller, 1976).

Effect of Contingencies

A possible moderating effect on the relationship between participation and the outcome variables was studied for the following contingency
variables: duration of employment, length of time in present job, age,
education, group size, frequency of work consultation, rating of the importance of issues, union membership, expectations from the consultation
system, perception of reasons for under-utilization of skills, group atmosphere, and organizational climate. The results of subgroup analysis and
multiple regression analysis show that such a moderating effect hardly
exists: for none of the contingency variables a consistently significant
effect over three organizations could be established. If specific effects

occur they vary greatly over organizations, sometimes even in direction (Koopman, 1980). These results are clearly inconsistent with the basic concept behind our contingency model, and partially disagree with data reported elsewhere.

It may be pointed out that the lack of support for the contingency model was found only for the *short-term* operational decisions, which are being discussed in this article. As was demonstrated elsewhere (Koopman & Drenth, 1980) there is substantial evidence from this study for the contingency model of decision making with respect to the more *tactical* and *strategic* decisions.

DISCUSSION

Many publications assume or discover a generally positive relationship between participation and satisfaction (e.g., Blumberg, 1968; Filley, House, & Kerr, 1976). A more elaborate picture is sketched by Locke & Schweiger (1979). These authors discuss the results of 43 studies on the relationship between participation and satisfaction. In around 40% of the studies, no such positive relationship was found. The evaluation of results in this field by Wall & Lischeron (1977) is even more critical. These authors mention a number of methodological imperfections, particularly in correlational studies. The present study has attempted to avoid such objections. Participation and satisfaction were operationalized as clearly independent of each other. The items for participation were formulated in descriptive rather than evaluative terms. Furthermore, the measure of participation is not an "overall score," as in so many studies, but is composed of questions on participation in regard to various concrete subjects.

The results of this study show a positive, but rather weak, relationship between participation and general satisfaction. In only one of the three organizations could we speak of a more substantial relationship. The results seem to fit in well with the contention of Wall & Lischeron that the "participation-satisfaction thesis" is definitely not so prominent and generalizable as it is generally thought to be.

According to the literature (Locke & Schweiger, 1979), the relationship between participation and effectiveness of the decision-making process is inconsistent. In the present study, effectiveness of the decision-making process was operationalized as the sum score of a number of possible effects of work consultation (for instance, better quality, greater acceptance of decisions). In two companies a stronger positive correlation was found between the extent to which an employee indicates to participate in operational decisions and his judgment as to the effectiveness of work consultation. The relationship between participation and skill utilization was also positive, though slightly weaker.

In the light of the discussion in the literature on "human relations" versus "human resources" (Miles, 1965), indications were sought in support of the hypothesis that the relationships participation-satisfaction and participation-effectiveness would be mediated by the concept skill utilization. In both cases the partial correlations, when controlled for the variable skill utilization, were lower than the zero-order correlations, and this was consistent in all organizations. The differences, however, were nowhere significant. This means that no clear evidence was obtained for the theory that skill utilization plays a crucial role in explaining the relationship of participation to satisfaction and effectiveness of work consultation.

We would like to conclude with a few remarks on the import of the results for theory and practice. For decision making as it takes place in work consultation, the relationship between participation and the outcome variables turned out to be only slightly, if at all, moderated by the various contingency variables (which are considered relevant in the literature). In concrete terms, this means that the relationship between participation and outcome variables per firm is apparently quite stable, and not very dependent on situational factors. In other words, the results do not justify the conclusion that a (large) number of conditions must be satisfied before participation will lead to certain effects. For further theoretical developments on the effects of direct participation, these results imply that the usefulness of the contingency model, at least with respect to operational decisions, must be sharply questioned.

APPENDIX A

Scheme for Observation and Minutes Analysis

Content categories:

    a. Issues on the *work itself:* arrangement of the daily work, improving of work methods, purchasing of tools and equipment, layout of work place, internal transport.

    b. Topics relating to *production and standards* (departmental budget, production standards, costs and results of department). Also more *general company information* (financial results, order-book, sale, long-term planning).

    c. Issues on *physical work conditions:* work place, noise, dirty work, ventilation, safety, hygiene, temperature, illumination.

d. Issues relating to *personnel policy:* personnel strength, absenteeism, illness, turnover, appraisal system, wage system, career planning and development, communication, leadership, work consultation.

Process categories:

Presentation	1. Reactions on minutes
	2. Announcements
	3. Separate item on agenda
	4. Questions before closure of meeting
Initiative	1. Chairman
	2. Group member
	3. Outsider
Decision style (Influence-Power Continuum)	1. Information (after decision)
	2. Information (before decision)
	3. Consultation (opportunity to give advice)
	4. Consultation (advice taken into consideration)
	5. Joint decision making
Settlement	1. Postponed
	2. Sent to . . . (under consideration)
	3. Concluded
(Time)	

APPENDIX B

Abbreviated Description of Questionnaires[3]

For each questionnaire, a few examples are given.

IPC   Below is a list of activities or events. Please indicate how you and your work group participate in them.

1. Arranging the layout of your work place (position of machinery, desks and the like).
2. How to arange and plan the work within your group.

---

[3]See Table II for identification of abbreviations of the questionnaire titles.

.

.

.

9. Recommending a group member for promotion.

12 decisions. Scale: no information, information, opportunity to give advice, advice is taken into consideration, joint decision making.

SU   Please think of your own job as it is at the moment. The following is a list of skills, abilities, and so on. Please indicate whether you find that your job gives you the opportunity to use them.

1. Initiative
3. Practical work experience

.

.

.

13. Capacity to look ahead.
16 skills. Scale: Seldom, occasionally, usually, almost invariably.

SAT-G   How satisfied are you?
1. All in all, how satisfied are you with the people you work with closely?
5. Considering your skills and the effort you put into the work, how satisfied are you with your pay?
7. How satisfied do you feel with your chances for getting ahead in this organization in the future?

7 questions. Scale: Very dissatisfied, somewhat dissatisfied, neither satisfied nor dissatisfied, fairly satisfied, very satisfied.

SAT-P   How frequently, do you feel, does the following occur?
1. My superior asks me for my opinion on matters related to my work.
5. When changes occur in my work, I am consulted by my superior.

5 questions. Scale: Almost invariably, usually, occasionally, seldom.

EFF-C   Consultation may have all sorts of consequences. We would like you to look back on your experience with consultation in your department and to state below what consequences it has had up till now.

1. People know better what is going on in the company.
3. People accept decisions more easily.
11. There is a better atmosphere in the department.

14 questions as above and two open questions. Scale: Yes, definitely; Yes, I tend to think so; I don't think so; definitely not.

REFERENCES

ANDRIESSEN, J. H. T. H. Developments in the Dutch industrial relations system. *Industrial Relations Journal*, 1976, *7*, 49-59.

BLUMBERG, P. *Industrial democracy*. London: Constable, 1968.

BRUGGEN, A. L. A. VAN DER, & HERTOG, J. F. DEN Werkoverleg op afdelingsniveau. *Mens en Onderneming*, 1976, *30*, 334-353.

DACHLER, H. P., & WILPERT, B. Conceptual dimensions and boundaries of participation in organizations: A critical evaluation. *Administrative Science Quarterly*, 1978, *23*, 1-39.

DRENTH, P. J. D. The works council in the Netherlands: An experiment in participation. In E. Pusic et al. (Eds.), *Participation and self-management* (Vol. 5), Zagreb, 1973.

DRENTH, P. J. D., KOOPMAN, P. L., RUS, V., ODAR, M., HELLER, F. A., & BROWN, A. Participative decision making: A comparative study. *Industrial Relations*, 1979, *18*, 295-309.

FIEDLER, F. E. *A theory of leadership effectiveness*. New York: McGraw-Hill, 1967.

FILLEY, A. C., HOUSE, R. J., & KERR, S. *Managerial process and organizational behavior*. Glenview, Ill.: Scott, Foresman and Company, 1976.

HELLER, F. A. Group feedback analysis: a method of field research. *Psychological Bulletin*, 1969, *72*, 108-117.

HELLER, F. A. *Managerial decision-making: A study of leadership styles and power sharing among senior managers*. London: Tavistock Publications, 1971.

HELLER, F. A. The decision process: An analysis of power sharing at senior organizational levels. In R. Dubin (Ed.), *Handbook of work, organization and society*. Chicago: Rand-McNally, 1976.

HELLER, F. A., DRENTH, P. J. D., KOOPMAN, P. L., & RUS, V. A longitudinal study in participative decision-making. *Human Relations*, 1977, *30*, 567-587.

IDE-INTERNATIONAL RESEARCH GROUP. *Industrial democracy in Europe*. London: Oxford University Press, 1980.

KOOPMAN, P. L. *Besluitvorming in organisaties. Een onderzoek naar de effekten van participatie in operationele en komplexe beslissingen*. Assen: Van Gorcum, 1980.

KOOPMAN, P. L., & DRENTH, P. J. D. "Werkoverleg", experiments in participative decision making on the shop floor. *Second international conference on participation, workers' control and self-management*. Paris, 1977.

KOOPMAN, P. L., & DRENTH, P. J. D. Een contingentiemodel voor participatie in complexe besluitvorming. *Tijdschrift voor organisatiekunde en sociaal beleid (M&O)*, 1980, *34*, 464-478.

KOOPMAN, P. L., & WERKMAN, B. Het verhoudingsmodel bij de meting van satisfaktie. In P. J. D. Drenth, P. J. Willems, & Ch. J. de Wolff (Eds.), *Arbeids- en organisatie-psychologie*. Deventer: Kluwer, 1973.

LAMMERS, C. J. Self-managment and participation: two concepts of democratization in organizations. *Organization and Administrative Sciences*, 1975, *5*, 17-33.

LOCKE, E. A., & SCHWEIGER, D. M. Participation in decision-making: one more look. In B. Staw (Ed.), *Research in organizational behavior*. Greenwich, Conn.: Jai Press, 1979.

LOWIN, A. Participatory decision-making: A model, literature critique and prescription for research. *Organizational Behavior and Human Performance*, 1968, *3*, 68-106.

MILES, R. E. Human relations or human resources. *Harvard Business Review*, 1965, *43*, 148-163.

RAMONDT, J. J. *Bedrijfsdemocratisering zonder arbeiders. Een evaluatie van ervaringen met werkoverleg en werkstructurering.* Alphen a.d. Rijn: Samsom, 1974.

RUS, V., ODAR, M., HELLER, F., BROWN, A., DRENTH, P. J. D., KOOPMAN, P. L., WIERDSMA, A. F. M., BUS, F. B. M., & KRUYSWIJK, A. J. Participative decision making under conditions of uncertainty. *Second international conference on participation, workers' control and self-management.* Paris, 1977.

TAYLOR, J. C., & BOWERS, D. G. *Survey of organizations: A machine scored standardized questionnaire instrument.* Ann Arbor, Mich.: Institute for Social Research, 1972.

VROOM, V. H., & YETTON, P. W. *Leadership and decision-making.* Pittsburgh: Pittsburh University Press, 1973.

WALL, T. D., & LISCHERON, J. A. *Worker participation.* London: McGraw-Hill, 1977.

WINDMULLER, J. P. & GALAN, C. DE *Arbeidsverhoudingen in Nederland.* Utrecht: Het Spectrum, 1977.

BIOGRAPHICAL NOTES

PAUL L. KOOPMAN is a lecturer in Industrial and Organizational Psychology at the Free University of Amsterdam, from which he graduated in 1972. His main interests are in the field of organization theory and organization development. In 1980 he obtained his PhD degree for a thesis on the influence of participation on the quality and effectiveness of decision making.

PIETER J. D. DRENTH has been, since 1967, Professor of Industrial and Organizational Psychology at the Free University of Amsterdam, from which he graduated and received his doctorate. Before becoming a lecturer in 1963 he worked as an industrial psychologist in the Royal Dutch Navy and in the Social Science Research Division of Standard Oil. His main interests is in research in organizational psychology, in particular from a cross-cultural perspective. He is presently involved in cross-national studies in industrial relations, participation and decision making, and meaning of working.

FRANS B. M. BUS, AGAATH J. KRUYSWIJK, and ANDRE F. M. WIERDSMA were research assistants at the time of the project. At this moment F. Bus is management consultant of the Transport Company of Amsterdam, A. Kruyswijk is social researcher on the Ministry of Home Affairs, and A. Wierdsma is lecturer in Organizational Communication at the Netherlands School of Business.

[31]

Journal of Occupational Psychology, 1983, **56**, 1–18. Printed in Great Britain

A contingency model of participative decision making: An analysis of 56 decisions in three Dutch organizations

DIO INTERNATIONAL RESEARCH TEAM*

This article presents and discusses some results from a study of different forms of participative decision making. The report describes the model used in the study as related to the relevant literature. Decision making is seen as a longitudinal process in which several phases can be distinguished. Moreover, even within complex decisions, which have been studied in this research, a further distinction between medium-term/tactical and long-term/strategic decisions seemed fruitful. The model underlying the decision-making research is a 'contingent model', implying that there is no one best way of decision making.

The independent variable in the model is the participative style of decision making. A number of outcome variables, including efficiency, achievement, satisfaction with the process and with the outcome, have been selected as dependent variables. Nature of the decision, phase of the decision-making process and a number of factors such as clarity of goal, conflict and meta power, have served as contingent factors.

The study shows that the phase of the decision-making process in an important contingency variable. Phase-specific analysis gave better insight into the nature and effects of participative decision making. Moreover, the other contingency variables also proved quite effective. A number of interesting relations could be found within subgroups classified on the basis of the contingent factors, whereas in the total group very few relationships could be established. Effectiveness and satisfaction with process and outcome resulting from participative decision making were found only for tactical and for strategic decisions. A similar contingency was found under conditions of low clarity of goal, and high level of conflict.

Research on decision making has been approached by several disciplines. Most have used a social psychological perspective, even if the framework within which it is analysed is broader (Simon, 1957; Cyert *et al.*, 1958; Newell & Simon, 1972; MacCrimmon & Taylor, 1976). While individual choice models remain important (Audley, 1970; Huber. 1980), individual attributes, particularly personality variables, are of limited value in explaining decision behaviour (Taylor & Dunnette, 1974). Decisions require anticipations and judgements in a social context (Hogarth, 1980) and, in most cases, a socio-psychological dimension of power (French & Raven, 1959; Vroom & Yetton, 1973). This is the tradition within which the present research has been developed.

The present study on participation in complex decision-making processes forms a part of the international research project 'Decision Making in Organizations' (DIO), in which

*A three-country research team: Dr F. A. Heller, Tavistock Institute of Human Relations, London, UK, Dr P. J. D. Drenth & Dr P. L. Koopman, Free University, Amsterdam, The Netherlands; Dr V. Rus, University of Ljubljana, Yugoslavia. The first draft of this article has been prepared by Dr P. L. Koopman.
Requests for reprints should be addressed to Dr P. L. Koopman, Department of Industrial and Organizational Psychology, Free University, De Boelelaan 1081, 1081 HV Amsterdam, The Netherlands.

0305–8107/83/010001–18 $02.00/0

2   DIO INTERNATIONAL RESEARCH TEAM

research teams from England (Tavistock Institute, London), Yugoslavia (the University of Ljubljana), and the Netherlands (the Free University of Amsterdam) collaborated. The research has two roots: one is a development of a series of projects on decision making and power sharing among two levels of senior management (Heller, 1971; Heller & Wilpert, 1981); the other is a multi-level comparative study of the antecedents and consequences of organizational power sharing in 12 countries (IDE, 1979, 1981). Both previous studies, however, used concurrent validity measures and a synchronic research design, while the present research is longitudinal and measures variables separated by time in an attempt to obtain some predictive validity. In several other respects it refines and extends both the contingency model and the research methodology used in the previous studies (Heller *et al.*, 1977; Rus *et al.*, 1977; Drenth *et al.*, 1979).

This article describes the DIO model, relates it to some of the relevant literature and reports findings from an analysis of three organizations in the Netherlands. Other details from the Dutch study and its findings have been reported elsewhere (Koopman & Drenth, 1977; Koopman, 1980; Koopman *et al.*, 1981); and a few preliminary findings from the Yugoslav, Dutch and British samples were reported in Drenth *et al.* (1979).

In the literature, decision-making processes are often set out as a continuum variously termed ' programmed vs. non-programmed ' or ' routine vs. non-routine ' (March & Simon, 1958; Simon, 1960, 1977), and ' structured vs. unstructured ' (Mintzberg *et al.*, 1976). In general, the decisions studied in this project are located on the unstructured side of the continuum—uncertainty, complexity and conflict are the most important factors contributing to the unstructured character of decision making (MacCrimmon & Taylor, 1976).

RESEARCH ON COMPLEX DECISION-MAKING PROCESSES ON THE ORGANIZATIONAL LEVEL

Two themes have played a central role in research on complex decision making; rationality of the decision process, and power and conflict (Hickson *et al.*, 1978; Astley *et al.*, 1981).

Simon (1947, 1957) was one of the first to point out that complex decision-making processes usually do not follow the logical order attributed to them in classical decision-making models. Such models view decision making as a *rational* process in which the decision maker is aware of all possible alternatives and, on the basis of a conscious preference, comes to a decision which yields a maximum profit (Shubik, 1958). But Simon's work calls into question such premises as profit maximization through exploring all the alternatives and assessing the consequences of each one. In general, the participants in complex decisions have access only to a small part of the relevant information; and decision makers, due to the limitations of human information-processing capacities, tend to form a subjective and simplified model of reality. The exploration is often confined to only one, or a small number of alternatives, and it ceases altogether when a ' satisficing ' solution has been found. In short, behaviour in these situations is characterized by a ' bounded rationality ', a highly restricted view of reality, and by the goal of satisfactory, instead of optimal, alternatives.

Support is to be found for Simon's theory in a number of case studies published in the late 1950s and early 1960s (Cyert *et al.*, 1958; Cyert & March, 1963). Braybrook & Lundblom (1963) describe complex decision making as a long succession of small steps, an uncertain and irregular process of ' muddling through '. The choices which participants make during this process are mainly strategy-oriented; again and again ' successive limited comparisons ' are made between various alternatives.

With these publications the rising interest in the variables *power* and *conflict* becomes evident. Decision-making processes are viewed more and more as political processes, and organizations as coalitions. It turns out that not all conflicts are solvable (the authors speak of ' quasi-resolutions of conflict '); indeed, conflicts need not always be dysfunctional. This line of thought is further elaborated by Pettigrew (1973), MacMillan (1978), Pfeffer (1978, 1981), and Bacharach & Lawler (1980).

Irrationality in decision making is the central theme of the ' garbage can ' model (Cohen *et al.*, 1972). In this model, organizations are seen as ' organized anarchies ', characterized by inconsistent and ill-defined goals, an unclear technology, and fluid participation by its members. The university is the prototype of this model (Cohen & March, 1974; March & Olsen, 1976). In the authors' view, organizations can be regarded as collections of (1) problems, (2) solutions, (3) participants, and (4) decision opportunities. These four elements are mixed together more or less arbitrarily in the garbage can, giving rise to unpredictable combinations. There is no *a priori* time sequence. Solutions can come before problems, or problems and solutions can wait for a suitable opportunity for a decision.

It will be obvious that the order which was long taken for granted—' identification and definition of the problem, seeking solutions, considering the alternatives, and selection ' (Simon, 1947; Witte, 1972; Harrison, 1981)—is turned topsyturvy here. But the question remains: how far can these results be generalized to other kinds of organizations? The labels ' organized anarchies ', collections of free and autonomous interest groups, ' loosely coupled systems ' (Glasman, 1973; Weick, 1976), which are bound only by a common budget, may have some accuracy for universities, but seem unfair for many other organizations (Baldridge, 1971; Blau, 1973; Pfeffer & Salancik, 1974; Butler *et al.*, 1978).

The conclusions reached by Mintzberg *et al.* (1976) are completely different. On the basis of a study of 25 strategic decisions, they designed a phase model, shown in Fig. 1 in simplified form. Contrary to Cohen *et al.* (1972), Mintzerg *et al.* do encounter the long-theorized three steps of ' identification—development—selection ' in most complex decision-making processes, albeit with frequent feedback, delays and interruptions.

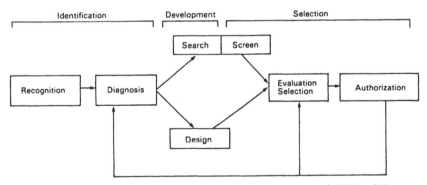

Fig. 1. Simplified phase model of decision making (after Mintzberg *et al.*, 1976, p. 266).

The *identification phase* consists of two main activities: the recognition of a problem situation, and a tentative diagnosis of it. A decision-making process usually begins when a discrepancy between an actual and a desired situation is observed. Whether this observation will also lead to the resolve to do something about it depends partly on the estimated likelihood of finding a satisfactory solution. Then follows the diagnosis of the problem, which begins with an exploration of the usual information channels within the organization. The diagnosis is by no means always explicit—in a number of cases no mention is made of it in official documents. Other sources (Larson, 1962; Pfeffer, 1981) attach considerable importance to this phase for the further course of the decision-making process.

4   DIO INTERNATIONAL RESEARCH TEAM

An essential question at this point is whether the issue should be viewed primarily as a 'logical' or 'political' problem (Thompson & Tuden, 1959; Shull *et al.*, 1970) in connection with the decision-making strategy to be followed. Some authors emphasize the value commitment inherent in a definition of the issue (March & Simon, 1958); others demonstrate how the identification phase itself can form a political process (Koopman *et al.*, 1980).

The *developmental phase*, which takes up the most time, is described in terms of two basic processes: 'search' and 'design'. 'Search' applies to an exploration of already existing solutions; 'design' refers to designing new solutions, or at least adapting existing alternatives. The search is conducted along hierarchical lines. First, the most obvious, commonly recognized alternatives are considered. If they yield no satisfactory result, more inaccessible alternatives are explored. This confirms what Cyert & March (1963, pp. 120–122) have hypothesized concerning the 'simple-mindedness' of the search process. If there are no solutions available, alternatives must be generated, and this is approached in a very prosaic manner. Mintzberg *et al.* (1976, p. 256) report that usually only one solution is elaborated, which would agree with the results of Snyder & Paige (1958).

The *selection phase* in this model has three steps: 'screen', 'evaluation/choice', and 'authorization'. 'Screening' is important if a large number of options are available. It is a rather superficial process whose main purpose is to rule out less acceptable alternatives. Later, after a more thorough evaluation, the most satisfactory one will be chosen. A similar step procedure is also described by Soelberg (1967). A good example is the procedure usually followed in personnel selection. The definitive choice is postponed as long as possible (Cyert & MacCrimmon, 1968, p. 580), but all kinds of subdecisions are taken. The 'evaluation/choice' step itself can take three different forms: 'judgement', that is, a choice made by one person; 'bargaining', where a group of people with conflicting goals make the choice; and 'analysis', evaluation, by specialists, on the basis of strictly factual information.

According to the study by Mintzberg *et al.*, there is a general preference for 'judgement', probably because this is the quickest, easiest, and most relaxed way. The authors find little support for the analytical approach so lauded in normative decision-making literature (utility functions are drawn up on the grounds of pre-formulated criteria, maximum profitability determines the choice). The empirical studies of Soelberg (1967) and Carter (1971) have also borne out this gap between theory and practice. The final step in the decision-making process is official endorsement of the decision. With strategic decisions, this usually takes place at the top of the organization.

A number of supportive processes run parallel to the three main phases of decision making: decision-making control processes, communication processes, and political processes (Mintzberg *et al.*, 1976, pp. 260–263). We mention them but cannot go into them here. The picture sketched so far is further complicated by a number of 'dynamic factors' —interruptions, delays, and feedback circuits regularly crop up in complex decision-making processes.

DIO PROJECT: MODEL AND VARIABLES

The DIO project addressed itself primarily to the following question: 'what circumstances influence different decision-making methods and how do these circumstances and methods affect decision outcomes?' A few remarks will serve to clarify this. First of all, the wording makes it clear that we are concerned not only with a description of complex decision-making processes, but with focusing attention on the relationship between the method of decision making and a number of criteria, and in this respect, the study goes one step further than most previous research in this field. The relationships between decision-making methods and criteria are studied through a *contingency model*; in other words, we do not assume that there is one best method of decision making, but that a method must be adapted to the particular circumstances at hand (contingencies) in order to bring about an optimal result.

Partly following Mintzberg *et al.* (1976), four phases were distinguished in this project: start-up, developmental, finalization, and implementation. For each phase a listing was made of the groups and organizational levels involved, how the decision-making process took place, in how far there were conflicts and/or outside interventions, etc.

The study was carried out during the period 1976–1979 in three organizations in the Netherlands, two of them in the transport sector and one in the steel industry. Organization A is a municipal transport organization in the western part of the country, with approximately 4000 employees, of whom 2500 are drivers and 1000 technical employees. Organization B is one of the regional divisions of the Dutch railways, with some 750 employees, nearly all of whom are on rotating shifts. Organization C is one plant of a steelworks, where steel slabs are heated in furnaces and moulded into sheets. The plant employs 250 production workers divided into four shifts with continuous production, while another 200 employees work in supportive and complementary departments.

In all, 56 decision-making processes were analysed, using two different methods. *Tracing:* after the decision-making process was finished, an attempt was made to reconstruct or 'trace' a number of aspects of the process through interviews with key persons and by studying relevant documents (minutes, memoranda). *Process registration:* in this case the analysis did not take place after but during the decision-making process. Direct observation provided additional information alongside data obtained through interviews.

Figure 2 shows the model with the most important variables. All these variables, discussed in more detail below, have been rated for each of the 56 cases.

Independent variable (IPC)

The influence–power continuum (IPC; top left of Fig. 2) acts primarily as an independent variable. The IPC is measured on a six-point scale: at one end is the qualification 'entirely uninvolved in the decision making', and at the other end 'complete control of

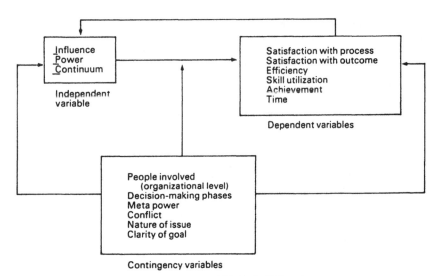

Fig. 2. Model and variables in the DIO project.

6   DIO INTERNATIONAL RESEARCH TEAM

the decision-making process by the participants'. Various levels of involvement and influence made up the scale. For each decision an IPC score was determined for four organizational levels, as well as for professional staff groups and the works' council. This was done for each of the four phases in the decision-making process.

Dependent variables

The dependent or outcome variables have in common that they were measured only once, when the 'outcome' of the decision-making process was known. The questions, indicated in brief below, were presented to the selected informants, whose responses were registered on a simple three-point scale (high, medium, low):

(i) Satisfaction with the decision-making process: that is, with the way in which the problem was tackled.

(ii) Satisfaction with the outcome: here a distinction is made between satisfaction with the 'solution chosen' (scoring after phase 3) and with the outcome after implementation of the solution chosen (scoring after completion of phase 4).

(iii) Efficiency: a general judgement of the input–output ratio, the amount of time and energy spent in proportion to the final results.

(iv) Skill utilization: are the competent persons and/or groups involved in the decision-making process?

(v) Achievement: judgement of the extent to which the expected goals and objectives set were reached.

(vi) Time: the amount of time spent on the entire decision-making process (number of weeks for each of the four phases).

Contingency variables

In this study four *organizational levels* were used: lowest level workers (A), first level supervisors (B), middle management (C), and top management (D). Besides these four levels the professional staff groups (P) and the works' council (Q) were distinguished.

One of the difficulties in an analysis of complex decision-making processes is to pinpoint the *phases* in time. In this study, we chose to set the beginning of the decision-making process at the moment that people in the organization became aware of a problem and expressed their intention of doing something about it. In the start-up phase, an exploration and tentative diagnosis of the problem takes place. During the developmental phase the issue is further explored in a number of aspects. The transition between the developmental phase and the finalization phase is formed by judgement and/or bargaining processes by means of which the number of potential solutions is reduced. The final selection and/or authorization take place in the finalization phase. Departing from Mintzberg *et al.* (1976), this study also looks at aspects of participation and decision making during the implementation phase. The decision-making process is considered to be finished when implementation has been completed; for example, when the machine has been installed and is in operation, or the new consulting committee is meeting.

A third contingency variable in this study is *meta power*. The concept is derived from Buckley & Burns (1974). In our study meta power is defined as a set of external interventions which become visible during the decision-making process, but which originate outside of the work unit (firm or part of a firm) under study (Rus *et al.*, 1977). According to studies by Rus (1974), Pennings (1975), and Wilpert (1977), external power is one of the few environmental variables with a rather large influence on intra-organizational structures and on leadership behaviour.

One characteristic of many complex, non-routine decision-making processes is the existence of tensions or *conflict*. The type of conflicts that occur, and the way in which they are treated, can be of great importance for the effectiveness of the decision-making process and for the probability that a chosen solution will indeed be implemented without

CONTINGENCY MODEL OF PARTICIPATIVE DECISION MAKING   7

Table 1. *Summary of decisions analysed in the three Dutch organizations*

Decision or issue	Org. A	Org. B	Org. C	Total
Strategic				
1. Setting up a consultative procedure	2	1	2	5
2. Initiating a new product or service	3	1	1	5
3. Deciding on medium-size capital investment	10	3	3	16
4. Budget forecasting	1	1	1	3
Tactical ('task')				
5. Changes in methods of operation	4	2	3	9
6. Disclosure of information	—	—	1	1
7. Cost-saving methods	—	—	—	—
8. Appointment department head	1	4	2	7
Tactical ('people')				
9. Job grading procedures	2	—	1	3
10. Training methods	—	—	1	1
11. General work conditions	2	—	2	4
12. Safety procedures	—	—	2	2
Total number	*n*=25	*n*=12	*n*=19	*n*=56

too much delay and resistance. On the analogy of Coser (1956) we distinguish between conflicts with respect to:

(a) operations and procedures (' operational '): this is an issue both of setting norms (' how *should* it be performed? ') and of testing them empirically (' does actual performance conform to the norm? ');

(b) division of the ' profit ' (' distributive '): not only in a material sense, but also in terms of power, status, and privileges;

(c) differences in perception (' perceptual '): differences in manner of looking at a problem, for example as a result of differences in professional orientation.

The *nature of issue* (type of decision) is also considered an important contingency variable; this has been discussed by several authors (e.g. Vroom & Yetton, 1973; Heller & Wilpert, 1981).

Table 1 gives a summary of decisional areas examined in this study. An attempt has been made to reach a balance between ' strategic decisions ' which are of direct importance to the survival and continuity of the organization (Steiner, 1970; Child, 1972), and ' tactical decisions ', which are more directed towards control systems, both with respect to the personnel policy and to an adequate work performance. Strategic decisions generally take a relatively long time, are comparatively infrequent, and are mostly initiated and dominated by the top of the organization. Tactical decisions take less time, occur more often, and also take place at lower levels within the organization.

Three response categories are distinguished with regard to the *clarity of goal* of the decision-making process; very clear (one dominant goal); several equally ranked (coordinate) goals; opposite or very unclear goals.

Collection of data

Tracing complex decision-making processes usually began with a general *analysis of documents,* such as minutes of top management, works' council, and consulting committee meetings. On the basis of these, plus a few conversations, a choice could be made of which subjects to consider for analysis. This exploration was necessary to obtain a corresponding list of subjects per firm. The minutes gave a first impression of objective variables such as time taken for the decision-making process, and also assisted in the choice of the informants with whom to discuss the decision-making processes.

8　　　　　　　DIO INTERNATIONAL RESEARCH TEAM

The *informants* had to be experts and at the same time should be unprejudiced. Obviously, these two criteria are not entirely compatible, especially in situations involving conflicts; those directly involved are a party to the conflict, and will tend to colour the picture to their own advantage. To offset this tendency, it was decided that 'both sides' must be heard. The operational guideline here was: at least one, but preferably two, respondents from the side of the management, and from the side of the employees as well. For some decision-making processes, a large number of people were interviewed. If a professional staff group was involved in a conflict, an attempt was also made to obtain information from them.

Most information was collected through interviews with these informants. For a number of decision-making processes, additional information was collected through *observation* by the researchers during meetings of top management, departments, and works' councils. This procedure, of course, could be used only in cases which were analysed through 'process registration', or following the decision-making process in time. Most decisions were studied through 'tracing', or looking back in time to a process that had already been completed.

After aggregation of the scores, a description was made of each decision-making process and sent to the individual informants for comments. In this step, each informant was confronted with a description of the decision-making process which usually did not tally completely with his own account; it was, after all, based on information from several sources. The informant was asked to check the account and ratings for accuracy and to make corrections (written or oral) where necessary. The amendments which thus came to light were usually incorporated into a new version of the report. This version was once again checked for accuracy by two groups—the top management and the works' council. In these meetings everyone agreed (apart from a few small details) on the descriptions and ratings in the revised version.

RESULTS

In this context, only a proportion of the results of this study can be touched on. In making this selection, we have allowed ourselves to be led primarily by the question of what indications are found that a contingency model, as used here, offers a fruitful approach to this field of research. The question is also raised of what extra insights a phase-specific analysis offers beyond an overall analysis.

The phase demarcation of the decision-making process

We distinguish four phases in complex decision-making processes: start-up, developmental, finalization, and implementation. This section examines whether there are differences between these four phases in time taken, degree of conflict, and influence distribution: if yes, what are these differences?

We first consider the *length of time* of the various phases. An analysis of variance carried out for all 56 decisions indicated a significant difference ($P = 0.01$) in length of time between the phases. Further testing between the phases showed that the developmental phase lasts significantly longer than the other three (t test, see Table 2). This is in agreement with the findings of Mintzberg *et al.* (1976). Although the finalization phase, on average, is shorter than the start-up and implementation phases, these differences are not significant due to the amount of variance among the decision-making processes within each phase.

Are certain phases of the decision-making process more prone to *conflicts* than other phases? This question is hardly mentioned in the literature. Mintzberg *et al.* say that postponing problems often leads to conflicts in the finalization ('selection') phase. But they say nothing about the extent to which the other phases are marked by conflicts (Mintzberg *et al.*, 1976, p. 263).

CONTINGENCY MODEL OF PARTICIPATIVE DECISION MAKING 9

Table 2. *Differences between the phases in time taken (means in weeks)*

Phase		Mean	n	Differences between means		
				S	D	F
Start-up	(S)	20·55	56	S	D	F
Developmental	(D)	40·70	56	D	20·14**	—	—
Finalization	(F)	9·23	56	F	11·32	31·46**	—
Implementation	(I)	21·92	50	I	1·37	18·78**	12·69

**$P < 0.01$.

Table 3. *Differences between the phases in the amount of conflict (frequency × intensity)*

		Mean	n	Differences between means		
				S	D	F
Start-up	(S)	0·46	56	S	D	F
Developmental	(D)	1·48	56	D	1·01**	— **	—
Finalization	(F)	0·39	56	F	0·07	1·09*	—
Implementation	(I)	0·71	56	I	0·25	0·77	0·32

*$P < 0.05$; **$P < 0.01$.

The analysis of variance showed that there is, indeed, a significant difference ($P < 0.01$) in the amount of conflict. Conflict in the developmental phase was found to be significantly higher than in the other phases (*t* test, see Table 3). The differences between the other phases are small. Postponement of conflicts to the finalization phase is not confirmed by our data.

A relatively large number of conflicts in the developmental phase occur in both strategic and tactical decisions. Comparing the three organizations, it is striking that in one organization the implementation phase shows almost as many conflicts as the developmental phase. Surprisingly enough, this proves to be the organization with the lowest overall number of conflicts—a possible explanation for this can be sought in the nature of the conflicts, which are generally of an operational or perceptual, rather than distributive, nature.

Two comments can be made on these results. The greater amount of conflict in the developmental phase in general can perhaps be explained by the fact that this phase also takes the most time. Conversely, it would seem at least as plausible that the occurrence of conflicts protracts the decision-making process. We would once again point out that an important activity during the developmental phase is to formulate or design alternatives. If we see decision making partly as a political process (Cyert & March, 1963; Pettigrew, 1973; Pfeffer, 1981), then it is not so surprising that a lot of conflicts occur in this phase.

The second comment relates to the conspicuously small number of conflicts in the start-up phase, which includes the diagnosis of the issues (cf. Mintzberg *et al.,* 1976; Rus *et al.,* 1977). This indicates that the diagnosis is implicit and involves a limited number of participants (for example, top management and professional staff). An alternative explanation could be that in most of the decision-making processes studied there was relatively little difference of opinion over the primary goal. In 37 of the 56 cases there was one clear, dominant goal at the start of the decision-making process. In such a situation it would seem less likely for conflicts to crop up as early as the start-up phase.

Two topics fall under the heading *influence distribution*: the influence distribution

10   DIO INTERNATIONAL RESEARCH TEAM

within the organization, and the influence exerted on the organization from outside. To begin with the latter, there is a big difference between the implementation phase and the other phases as regards meta power or outside influence. This pattern of strong external influences during the first three phases is apparent in each of the three organizations separately. These results are not so surprising, considering the nature of the organizations which we studied; two of them form part of a larger concern, and the third is dependent on local governmnent for approval of important decisions. It is only in the implementation phase that the three organizations can be completely autonomous. This is true of both strategic and tactical decisions.

Do the four phases differ in influence distribution between the internal participants? In order to answer this question, we compared the participation profiles for each phase and recorded which group or groups dominated each of the four phases (see Fig. 3).

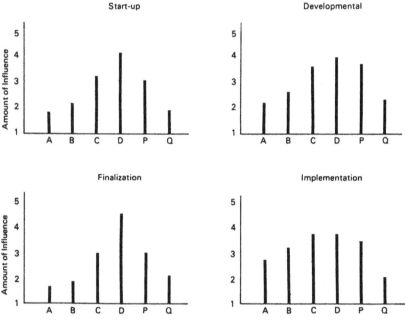

Fig. 3. Influence of internal participants (groups A, B, C, D, P and Q) in each decision-making phase. Groups are as follows: A, workers; B, first-level supervisors; C, middle management; D, top management; P, professional staff; Q, works' council.

The start-up phase is dominated by top management (D); to a lesser extent, middle management (C) and professional staff groups (P) are also involved. The developmental phase shows a spread of influence over a broader 'top layer', namely top management, middle management, and staff. The differences in influence between these three groups are not significant; the differences from each of the other groups are. The finalization phase is again strongly dominated by top management. This means that both the initiative (plus diagnosis) and the selection are dominated by the top. During the implementation phase, the contribution of each group is more equal. The lower levels in an organization are generally actively involved only in this phase of decision making. The influence of the works' council (Q), however, is here also very slight. This general pattern is found in all three organizations, and, with small deviations, in both strategic and tactical decisions.

The relationship between the method of decision making (per phase) and the outcome variables

This section discusses the relationship between the method of decision making in each phase and the outcome variables. The start-up phase needs only a brief mention: it showed no systematic relationship whatsoever. As we show later, this sets it quite apart from the other phases in this respect.

Table 4 gives the Kendall tau correlations for the other three phases. Participation in the *developmental phase* (2) by those who implement the decisions (group A) seems to increase the chance for satisfaction, both with the outcome (see also group B) and with the decision-making process itself. Too much influence by the top (group D) in this phase seems to have a frustrating effect: it decreases both the chance for achievement and the chance for satisfaction with process and outcome. The participation of middle management (C), staff (P), and works' council (Q) shows no systematic relationship with the outcome variables in phase 2.

More influence of supervisory level and middle management (B and C) and professional staff (P) in the *finalization phase* (3), means less efficiency of the decision-making process. There is also a negative correlation between the influence of staff groups in this phase and the variables achievement, satisfaction with the decision-making process, and utilization of available skills of employees. This may suggest a compensation mechanism: under-utilization of the available knowledge in the decision-making process makes the use of ' experts ' necessary in the finalization phase.

The most striking aspect of the results in the *implementation phase* is that influence by top management or works' council goes together with lowered achievement and decreased satisfaction with the outcome, both before and after implementation. The most plausible interpretation of the negative correlation is that the works' council is either chiefly involved once problems have arisen, or is only called in to assist at that point. In that case, the top management is itself more active in the implementation phase of the decision making.

An interesting fact is that the patterns described above are almost all removed if the participation scores are summed over the phases. Apparently a number of effects are phase-specific, illustrating again the need for phase-by-phase analyses.

Effect of other contingency variables on the relationship between IPC and outcome variables

In this section we examine the moderating effect of the other contingency variables through subgroup analysis. However, a practical problem arises in connection with the very many IPC measures in this study. Combining groups and phases alone yields 24 indices, and a number of ' derived measures ' have been employed as well. In view of this, two primary IPC measures were chosen for this part of the analysis:

IPC-A, that is, the average participation score for level A (workers) over the four phases;

PE, an indicator of ' power equalization ' (or the even distribution of power) within the organization, which was operationalized as the difference in average IPC score for top management (D), middle management (C), and staff (P) on the one hand, and for workers (A), supervisors (B), and works' council (Q) on the other.

The choice of IPC-A is a natural development from our special interest in participation by workers. The choice of the other measure is chiefly based on theoretical grounds and results found elsewhere (Pennings, 1976; Mulder, 1977).

Table 5 shows the general relationships between the two IPC measures and the outcome variables. Significant predictions are found for IPC-A only in respect of satisfaction

Table 4. *Kendall tau correlations* between participation per decision-making phase and outcome variables (n = 56)*

	Group A			Group B			Group C			Group D			Group P			Group Q		
	2	3	4	2	3	4	2	3	4	2	3	4	2	3	4	2	3	4
Achievement					−0.35			−0.30		−0.26		−0.41		−0.25				−0.37
Efficiency														−0.27				
Satisfaction with process	0.25									−0.32				−0.22				
Satisfaction with outcome	0.25									−0.31	−0.21	−0.34						−0.39
Satisfaction after implementation	0.26			0.28						−0.27		−0.41						−0.31
Utilization of skills								−0.21						−0.34				
Time					−0.20													−0.33

Participation scores for groups A, B, C, D, P and Q[a] in phases 2, 3 and 4[b]

*Only significant correlations (P < 0·05) are reported. Correction formula for ties was used.
[a]Groups are as follows: A, workers; B, first-level supervisors; C, middle management; D, top management; P, professional staff; Q, works' council.
[b]Phases are as follows: 2, developmental; 3, finalization; 4, implementation.

Table 5. *Kendall tau correlations between IPC scores (average over four phases) and outcome variables (n = 56)*

Outcomes	IPC-A	PE
Achievement	−0·02	0·02
Efficiency	−0·08	0·10
Satisfaction with process	0·12	0·19*
Satisfaction with outcome	0·14	0·07
Satisfaction after implementation	0·21*	0·28*
Utilization of skills	0·08	0·21*
Time	0·09	0·00

*P<0·05.

after implementation, and for PE in respect of satisfaction with the process and satisfaction after implementation and of utilization of skills.

Next we look at the relationships between these two participation measures and the outcome variables within subgroups, classified on the basis of the contingency variables, nature of decision, clarity of goals and amount of conflict.

Nature of decision. In Table 6 the relationship between IPC-A, PE and outcome variables is presented separately for tactical and strategic decisions. In tactical decisions participation by workers would seem functional: it increases the possibility of satisfaction with the outcome both before and after implementation and the chance of achievement as well. Equalization of power is associated with more satisfaction and better utilization of skills. For strategic decisions such relationships do not exist. In fact, a number of correlations (with achievement and efficiency) are negative, that between IPC for the workers and achievement reaching a significant level.

Clarity of goal. Where there is a lack of clarity or agreement on goals, participation by the workers or power equalization go together with satisfaction with the process, utilization of skills, and efficiency. With clear goals, increased participation by the lower levels apparently has little or no influence on the result, except for the level of satisfaction after implementation of the decisions (Table 7).

Table 6. *Kendall tau correlations between IPC-A and PE and outcome variables, separately for tactical and strategic decisions*

	Tactical (n=27)		Strategic (n=29)	
	IPC-A	PE	IPC-A	PE
Achievement	0·31*	0·22	−0·35*	−0·18
Efficiency	0·07	0·27	−0·18	−0·01
Satisfaction with process	0·09	0·19	0·17	0·19
Satisfaction with outcome	0·31*	0·26	0·04	−0·11
Satisfaction after implementation	0·34*	0·40**	0·08	0·13
Utilization of skills	0·20	0·46**	0·01	0·02
Time	0·06	0·08	0·26	−0·02

*P<0·05; **P<0·01.

Table 7. *Kendall tau correlations between IPC-A and PE and outcome variables, separately for high and low clarity of goal*

	Low/medium clarity of goal (n=19)		High clarity of goal (n=37)	
	IPC-A	PE	IPC-A	PE
Achievement	−0·03	0·03	0·04	0·05
Efficiency	0·23	0·35*	−0·20	0·05
Satisfaction with process	0·36*	0·20	0·04	0·19
Satisfaction with outcome	0·30	0·11	0·13	0·11
Satisfaction after implementation	0·22	0·21	0·25*	0·36*
Utilization of skills	0·37*	0·40*	−0·15	0·00
Time	0·08	0·19	0·07	−0·16

*$P < 0.05$.

Table 8. *Kendall tau correlations between IPC-A and PE and outcome variables, separately for high and low levels of conflict*

	High conflict (n=42)		Low conflict (n=14)	
	IPC-A	PE	IPC-A	PE
Achievement	−0·05	0·00	−0·03	0·14
Efficiency	0·03	0·06	−0·34	0·21
Satisfaction with process	0·27*	0·14	−0·38	0·31
Satisfaction with outcome	0·21	0·03	−0·13	0·08
Satisfaction with implementation	0·27*	0·27*	0·00	0·32
Utilization of skills	0·24*	0·18	−0·31	0·31
Time	0·11	0·07	0·16	−0·42*

*$P < 0.05$.

Conflicts. Particularly in a situation with many or very severe conflicts, participation by workers (level A) has a positive association with satisfaction with the decision-making process. Under this condition, participation by the workers also goes together with greater utilization of knowledge and experience. This is in agreement with the results found earlier under the condition 'low clarity of goal'. The tendency towards greater satisfaction with the outcome, both before and after implementation, is further enhanced when level A participates in decision-making processes with a high proportion of conflicts. Under the condition 'low conflict', worker participation does not correlate with the outcome. The only significant correlation in the right-hand column indicates that more equal distribution of power does have a time-saving effect on decision making (Table 8).

DISCUSSION AND CONCLUSIONS

The phases in the decision-making process distinguished by Mintzberg *et al.* proved to be rather easily identifiable in the decisions we studied. This was particularly true of the primary activities which take place in the various phases according to this model. On this point our experiences are more consistent with those of Mintzberg *et al.* than with those of Cohen *et al.* The use of the phase model has, we feel, two limitations. First, it is not always possible to demarcate the phases precisely: there is sometimes a transitionary zone. Second, many decision-making processes show a high degree of 'feedback' to earlier phases. Mintzberg *et al.* also encountered many examples of 'recycling' in their study. In spite of these reservations, it was fairly simple in most cases to indicate how the various groups in the organization were involved in the decision-making process at each phase, what conflicts there were, etc. In view of the aims of our study, the phase model was quite useful in these respects.

The results provide further confirmation of the importance of phase-specific analysis. This is especially clear in the results on the relationship between the method of participation and the outcome variables, but classifying the phases as to time taken, amount of conflict, and influence distribution also reveals interesting differences between the phases. The most important points are recapitulated below.

The developmental phase, encompassing the generation and preliminary 'screening' of available alternatives, takes the most time. In this phase the largest number of conflicts also occur. Strong outside influences were observed, particularly during the first three phases. As regards internal power distribution, it was found that the first and, more conspicuously, the third phase were management dominated. During the developmental phase, middle management and professional staff groups exerted great influence on the decision-making process. Participation by the lowest levels turned out to be almost entirely limited to the implementation phase. The influence of the works' council was very small throughout the entire decision-making process.

Several interesting differences were observed in the correlations between the method of decision making in the four phases and the outcome variables. The method of decision making in the *development phase* (the longest phase and the one with the most conflicts) seems to be of crucial importance for satisfaction with the decision-making process and with the outcome. Participation by the workers particularly increases the chance of satisfaction. Domination of this phase by top management decreases the chance of satisfaction. The method of decision making in the *finalization phase* seems particularly decisive for the efficiency of the decision-making process. More participation by lower and middle management (levels B and C) and the staff groups (P) in this phase means less efficiency.

It is quite remarkable that, in the *implementation phase,* more participation by both top management and works' council goes together with lower achievement and satisfaction with the outcome. Our interpretation of these data was that the works' council is either chiefly involved once problems have arisen, or is only called in to assist at that point. In that case top management is itself more active in the implementation phase of the decision-making process.

Another striking point is that not a single phase showed a systematic relationship between the method of decision making and the length of the decision-making process, while the variance was certainly great enough. Apparently, participation does not automatically entail great delays.

We feel that these results sufficiently demonstrate that the phase of the decision-making process is an important contingency variable, and that a phase-specific analysis of complex decision-making processes can lead to testable hypotheses. Further, the interacting effect of a number of other contingency variables on the relationship between the method of decision making and a few outcome variables was established.

In particular, the variables nature of issue, clarity of goals, and conflict had a moderating effect on the relationship between the method of decision making and the outcome variables. Statistically significant relations between participation and outcome measures primarily existed for tactical decisions and were virtually non-existent for strategic decisions. Futhermore, participation and power equalization is more efficient and satisfactory, under conditions of low clarity of goals and a high level of conflict.

16 DIO INTERNATIONAL RESEARCH TEAM

ACKNOWLEDGEMENTS

The Dutch study was financed by the Netherlands Organization for the Advancement of Pure Research (ZWO), the British study was supported by the Social Science Research Council, and the Yugoslav research received its funds from the Research Community in Slovenia.

The Dutch team is glad to acknowledge the contribution of the following researchers: F. B. M. Bus, A. J. Kruyswijk and A. F. M. Wierdsma.

REFERENCES

ASTLEY, W. G., AXELSSON, R., BUTLER, R. J., HICKSON, D. J. & WILSON, D. C. (1981). An arena theory of organizational decision processes. Pre-publication draft. University of Bradford.

AUDLEY, R. (1970). Choosing. *Bulletin of The British Psychological Society,* **23,** 177–191.

BACHARACH, S. B. & LAWLER, E. J. (1980). *Power and Politics in Organizations.* San Francisco: Jossey-Bass.

BALDRIDGE, J. V. (1971). *Power and Conflict in the University.* New York: Wiley.

BLAU, P. M. (1973). *The Organization of Academic Work.* New York: Wiley.

BRAYBROOKE, D. & LINDBLOM, C. (1963). *A Strategy of Decision: Policy Evaluation as a Social Process.* New York: Free Press.

BUCKLEY, W. & BURNS, T. R. (1974). Power and meta power. Relational control and the development of hierarchical control systems. Paper given at VIIIth World Congress of Sociology, Toronto.

BUTLER, R. J., HICKSON, D. J., WILSON, D. C. & AXELSSON, R. (1978). Organizational power, politicking, and paralysis. *Organization and Administrative Sciences,* **8,** 45–59.

CARTER, E. E. (1971). The behavioural theory of the firm and top level corporate decisions. *Administrative Science Quarterly,* **16,** 413–428.

CHILD, J. (1972). Organization structure and strategies of control: A replication of the Aston study. *Administrative Science Quarterly,* **17,** 163–177.

COHEN, M. D. & MARCH, J. G. (1974). *Leadership and Ambiguity: The American College President.* New York: McGraw-Hill.

COHEN, M. D., MARCH, J. G. & OLSEN, J. P. (1972). A garbage can model of organizational choice. *Administrative Science Quarterly,* **17,** 1–25.

COSER, L. (1956). *Functions of Social Conflict.* New York: Free Press.

CYERT, R. M., DILL, W. R. & MARCH, J. G. (1958). The role of expectations in business decision making. *Administrative Science Quarterly,* **3,** 307–340.

CYERT, R. M. & MACCRIMMON, K. R. (1968). Organizations. In G. Lindzey & E. Aronson (eds), *The Handbook of Social Psychology,* vol. 1. Reading, MA: Addison-Wesley.

CYERT, R. M. & MARCH, J. G. (1963). *A Behavioral Theory of the Firm.* Englewood Cliffs, NJ: Prentice-Hall.

DRENTH, P. J. D., KOOPMAN, P. L., RUS, V., ODAR, M., HELLER, F. A. & BROWN, A. (1979). Participative decision making: A comparative study. *Industrial Relations,* **18,** 295–309.

FRENCH, J. R. P. & RAVEN, B. (1959). The bases of social power. In D. Cartwright (ed.), *Studies in Social Power.* Ann Arbor, MI: Institute for Social Research.

GLASMAN, R. B. (1973). Persistence and loose coupling in living systems. *Behavioral Science,* **18,** 83–98.

HARRISON, E. F. (1981). *The Managerial Decision-Making Process.* Boston, MA: Houghton Mifflin.

HELLER, F. A. (1971). *Managerial Decision Making.* London: Tavistock.

HELLER, F. A., DRENTH, P. J. D., KOOPMAN, P. L. & RUS, V. (1977). A longitudinal study in participative decision-making. *Human Relations,* **30,** 567–587.

HELLER, F. A. & WILPERT, B. (1981). *Competence and Power in Managerial Decision Making.* New York: Wiley.

HICKSON, D. J., BUTLER, R. J., AXELSSON, R. & WILSON, D. (1978). Decisive coalitions. In B. T. King, S. Streufert & F. E. Fiedler (eds), *Managerial Control and Organizational Democracy.* Washington: Winston, Wiley.

HOGARTH, R. (1980). *Judgement and Choice: The Psychology of Decision.* London: Wiley.

HUBER, G. P. (1980). *Managerial Decision Making.* Glenview: Scott, Foresman.

IDE—International Research Group (1979). Participation: Formal rules, influence and involvement. *Industrial Relations*, **18**, 273–294.

IDE—International Research Group (1981). *Industrial Democracy in Europe*. Oxford: Oxford University Press.

KOOPMAN, P. L. (1980). *Besluitvorming in Organisaties*. Assen: Van Gorcum.

KOOPMAN, P. L., BROEKHUYSEN, J. W. & MEIJN, M. O. (1980). Complexe besluitvorming op het niveau van de organisatie. In P. J. D. Drenth, Hk. Thierry, P. J. Willems & Ch. J. de Wolff (eds), *Handboek Arbeids- en Organisatiepsychologie*. Deventer: Van Loghum Slaterus.

KOOPMAN, P. L. & DRENTH, P. J. D. (1977). 'Werkoverleg': experiments in participative decision making on the shop floor. Paper given at Second International Conference on Participation, Workers' Control and Self-Management, Paris.

KOOPMAN, P. L., DRENTH, P. J. D., BUS, F. B. M., KRUYSWIJK, A. J. & WIERDSMA, A. F. M. (1981). Content, process, and effects of participative decision making on the shop floor: Three cases in the Netherlands. *Human Relations*, **34**, 657–676.

LARSON, R. L. (1962). How to define administrative problems. *Harvard Business Review*, **40**, 68–80.

MACCRIMMON, K. R. & TAYLOR, R. N. (1976). Decision making and problem solving. In M. D. Dunnette (ed.). *Handbook of Industrial and Organizational Psychology*. Chicago: Rand McNally.

MACMILLAN, I. C. (1978). *Strategy Formulation: Political Concepts*. New York: West Publishing.

MARCH, J. G. & OLSEN, J. P. (1976). *Ambiguity and Choice in Organizations*. Bergen, Norway: Universitetsforlaget.

MARCH, J. G. & SIMON, H. A. (1958). *Organizations*. New York: Wiley.

MINTZBERG, H., RAISINGHANI, D. & THÉORÊT, A. (1976). The structure of 'unstructured' decision processes. *Administrative Science Quarterly*, **21**, 246–275.

MULDER, M. (1977). *Omgaan met Macht*. Amsterdam/Brussels: Elsevier.

NEWELL, A. & SIMON, H. A. (1972). *Human Problem Solving*. Englewood Cliffs, NJ: Prentice-Hall.

PENNINGS, J. M. (1975). The relevance of the structural-contingency model for organizational effectiveness. *Administrative Science Quarterly*, **20**, 393–410.

PENNINGS, J. M. (1976). Dimensions of organizational influence and their effectiveness correlates. *Administrative Science Quarterly*, **21**, 688–699.

PETTIGREW, A. M. (1973). *The Politics of Organizational Decision Making*. London: Tavistock.

PFEFFER, J. (1978). *Organizational Design*. Arlington Heights, IL, AHM.

PFEFFER, J. (1981). *Power in Organizations*. Boston: Pitman.

PFEFFER, J. &. SALANCIK, G. R. (1974). Organizational decision making as a political process: The case of the university budget. *Administrative Science Quarterly*, **19**, 135–151.

RUS, V. (1974). Power relationship between territorial and work organizations. Paper given at VIIIth World Congress of Sociology, Toronto.

RUS, V., ODAR, M., HELLER, F., BROWN, A., DRENTH, P. J. D., KOOPMAN, P. L., WIERDSMA, A. F. M., BUS, F. B. M. & KRUYSWIJK, A. J. (1977). Participative decision making under conditions of uncertainty. Paper given at Second International Conference on Participation. Workers' Control and Self-Management, Paris.

SHUBIK, M. (1958). Studies and theories of decision making. *American Science Quarterly*, **3**, 289–306.

SHULL, F. A., DELBECQ, A. L. & CUMMINGS, L. L. (1970). *Organizational Decision Making*. New York: McGraw-Hill.

SIMON, H. A. (1947). *Administrative Behavior*. New York: Free Press.

SIMON, H. A. (1957). *Models of Man*. New York: Wiley.

SIMON, H. A. (1960). *The New Science of Management Decision*. New York: Harper & Row (2nd ed., 1977, Englewood Cliffs, NJ: Prentice-Hall).

SNYDER, R. C. & PAIGE, G. D. (1958). The United States decision to resist aggression in Korea: The application of an analytical scheme. *Administrative Science Quarterly*, **3**, 341–378.

SOELBERG, P. O. (1967). Unprogrammed decision making. *Industrial Management Review*, 19–29.

STEINER, G. A. (1970). Strategic factors in business success. *Tijdschrift voor Efficient Directiebeleid*, **40**, 434–441.

TAYLOR, R. N. & DUNNETTE, M. D. (1974). Relative contributions of decision-maker attributes to decision process. *Organizational Behavior and Human Performance*, **12**, 286–298.

THOMPSON, J. D. & TUDEN, A. (1959). Strategies, structures, and processes of organizational decision. In J. D. Thompson, P. B. Hammond, R. W. Hawkes, B. H. Junker & A. Tuden (eds), *Comparative Studies in Administration*. Pittsburgh: University of Pittsburgh Press.

18 DIO INTERNATIONAL RESEARCH TEAM

VROOM, V. H. & YETTON, P. W. (1973). *Leadership and Decision Making.* Pittsburgh: University of Pittsburgh Press.

WEICK, K. E. (1976). Educational organizations as loosely coupled systems. *Administrative Science Quarterly,* **12,** 1–19.

WILPERT, B. (1977). *Führung in Deutschen Unternehmen.* Berlin: De Gruyter.

WITTE, E. (1972). Field research on complex decision-making processes: The phase theorem. *International Studies of Management and Organization,* **2,** 156–182.

Received 3 November 1981; revised version received 24 February 1982

[32]

The International Journal of Human Resource Management 4:1 February 1993

Patterns of power distribution in managerial decision making in Chinese and British industrial organizations

Zhong-Ming Wang and Frank A. Heller

Abstract

This article is one of three reports about the results of a Sino-British joint research project on managerial decision making in eleven Chinese companies and ten British companies. Forty managers and twenty trade union leaders from both manufacturing and service industries participated in the study. Data about decision-making patterns in eighteen different decision tasks in the organizations were collected. The results showed that there were interesting organizational and cultural differences in decision-making patterns in the two countries between manufacturing and service industries, between management and trade union groups, among short-, medium- and long-term decisions and across organizational levels. There were clear shifts of the decision-making power across organizational levels depending upon the type of decision tasks. A model of decision power shift was proposed in terms of the effects of organizational and cultural factors on patterns of organizational decision making. The implications of the decision power shift model to the management practice in the international context were highlighted.

Introduction

Since China adopted an open-to-the-world policy and launched its economic reform programme in the early 1980s, a nation-wide managerial and organizational reform has been carried out in relation to compensation systems, personnel systems and the management system as a whole. From the mid-1980s, ten aspects of management power have been delegated to the enterprises: production planning, pricing, marketing, purchase of materials, use of funds, handling of assets, organizational structure, personnel and labour, wage and bonus, and inter-company operation. As a result, managerial psychology, a name for industrial and organizational psychology in China, has become an active area of research and a popular subject in management training and practice (Chen, 1983; Chen, 1987; Xu and Wang, 1991; Wang,

Zhong-Ming Wang and Frank A. Heller 114

1991). Especially, there has been an urgent need for a more scientific and democratic decision-making procedure for enhancing Chinese management systems (Wan, 1986). Some psychologists studied participation and decision making in Chinese enterprises and demonstrated the importance of participation in managerial decision making (e.g., Wang, G., 1984; Lockett, 1983; Laaksonen, 1988; Wang, 1989). In 1986, a joint research project on organizational decision making and new technology was developed by psychologists at Hangzhou University, China, and at the Tavistock Institute of Human Relations, UK, sponsored by the British Council. Part of this project was to study and compare eleven Chinese companies with ten British ones and to research decision-making patterns and power structures in companies of both countries, so as to formulate some kind of cross-cultural model of organizational decision making and propose effective decision-making procedures and management strategies. This article reports the results from the first part of the joint project.

Before reviewing some previous literature in this area, we would like to mention some important differences and similarities in management structures and practices between Chinese and British companies, which have a significant impact upon management behaviour. In most of the Chinese industrial organizations, there are three systems: (1) the Communist Party organization; (2) the management responsibility system; (3) the trade union and Workers' Congress. According to the Chinese Enterprise Law, the role of the Party organization is to guarantee and supervise the implementation of the guiding principles and policies of the Party; the director of the management responsibility system shall be the legal representative of the enterprise and assume overall responsibility in production, operation and management; and the trade union and Workers' Congress shall represent and safeguard the interests of the staff and workers and organize for participation in democratic management and supervision (Wang, 1991). Whereas in British companies there are basically two systems: the management system and the trade unions. The hierarchical levels of organizational structures in the two countries are quite similar: (1) ordinary worker; (2) first-line supervisor; (3) middle manager; (4) top management; (5) level above plant (industrial bureau in China). There are also trade unions in the companies and external groups such as banks or other governmental agencies who may have an influence on organizational decision making. For the purpose of comparison, management and trade unions in both countries were sampled in this study. The focus of the study was on the perceptions of management and trade unions about the decision-making power across organizational levels.

Organizational decision making and participation have been an active area in industrial and organizational psychology (e.g., Heller and Wilpert, 1980; Jain, 1980; Hickson *et al.*, 1986; Chen, 1986; Wang, 1989). In a series

115   *Decision making in Chinese and British industrial organizations*

of early studies involving twelve countries (Heller *et al.*, 1979; IDE research group, 1981), it was found that in the medium-sized organizations of the manufacturing and service sector of British industry, the total amount of involvement in decision making at work was astonishingly low and there was little evidence that workers wanted to have more influence over decisions. But participative decision making did have some positive effects on job satisfaction and decision quality (Heller and Wilpert, 1981). In China, studies showed that, while the level of participation was still not satisfactory, workers generally had high needs for participation in organizational decision making (e.g., Wang, G., 1984). Further research indicated that participative decision making had very positive effects upon management practice and that the average evaluation of participative decision making was higher than that from similar studies abroad (e.g., Wang, 1989).

Studies in China as well as those abroad also showed that the participative decision-making style was related to the type of decision tasks concerning the department and employees, whereas decisions related to subordinates were more centralized (IDE research group, 1981; Wang, 1989). In general, decision tasks could be classified into three categories: (1) long-term decisions, concerning long-term development of the organization, e.g., large investment; (2) medium-term decisions, relating to actions or changes at the departmental level, e.g., personnel selection and placement, wage and bonus systems, and production procedures; (3) short-term decisions, concerning daily tasks of the employees. So far, there is little systematic evidence about the general decision-making patterns under different types of decision tasks in the organization. It was also not clear whether managers and trade union leaders perceived participation and decision-making patterns differently. Since the relationship between management and trade unions is crucial to the effectiveness of the leadership in the organization and the differences in perceptions may affect the co-ordination between the two groups, it would be useful and important to find out and compare their views about decision-making patterns and power structures in relation to different types of decision tasks, i.e., long-, medium- and short-term decisions.

Some previous studies show that intra-organizational decision power associates with the organizational structure and processes (e.g., Lachman, 1989). Several studies have tried to integrate a variety of proposed power sources into more general frameworks of intra-organizational power (e.g., Hickson *et al.*, 1971; Astley and Sachdeva, 1984; Lachman, 1989). However, the dynamics of managerial decision power is not just limited within the organization. It could also be influenced by more macro-organizational and cultural factors. In discussing influence and power sharing in organizational decision making, Heller and Wilpert (1981) differentiated three levels of analysis: (1) macro-level analysis, concerning the country context; (2) meso-level analysis, dealing with industrial sectors and dominant

Zhong-Ming Wang and Frank A. Heller   116

technology; (3) micro-level analysis, examining individual, tasks and organizational features. This provides a general framework for analysing the patterns of organizational decision making. Further study is needed to investigate how decision-making power changes or shifts across intra-organizational and outside-organizational levels and to find out the underlying mechanism of those changes. Moreover, it would be very interesting to find out the differences and similarities in decision-making patterns across different cultures, i.e., between Chinese and British enterprises.

Several hypotheses were derived from previous research (IDE research group, 1981; Heller et al. 1979) about the patterns of decision making power in the Chinese and British industries:

(1) There will be a difference in decision-making power between manufacturing and service industries. The decision-making power would be less centralized in Chinese manufacturing industry and British service industry.

(2) In general, the differences of perceptions between management and trade unions would be larger in Britain than in China. Chinese trade unions would be more powerful in decision making in relation to management than British trade unions.

(3) Decision-making power would be more centralized at middle- and top-management levels in Chinese than in British companies; the level above the plant is expected to have more power in China than that in Britain.

(4) Decision-making patterns will vary with different types of decision tasks. Specifically, British management influence would be more decentralized in short-term decisions, but more centralized in long- and medium-term decisions than in equivalent Chinese companies. There would be a kind of 'power shift' in decision making across organizational levels depending on the types of decision tasks, (i.e. the highest power shifted from middle management towards top management level while decision tasks changed from short term to medium and long term decisions).

Methods

Subjects

This study involved eleven Chinese companies (seven companies in manufacturing industry and four from service industry) and ten British companies (six from manufacturing and four from service industry). Both managers and trade union leaders from these companies participated in the study. The management sample included forty executive managers and personnel managers (thirty Chinese and ten British managers), whereas the trade union sample consisted of eleven Chinese trade union leaders and ten British ones. Table 1 presents background information of the subjects from both countries.

117   *Decision making in Chinese and British industrial organizations*

Table 1 *Background information of the Chinese and British samples*

	Chinese sample		British sample	
	management	*trade union*	*management*	*trade union*
manufacture	21	7	6	6
service	9	4	4	4

Note
Number: number of subjects

Instruments

The questionnaire instrument included eighteen items of decision tasks, of which sixteen items were adapted from a previous twelve-country study (IDE research group, 1981). Among these items, seven were short-term decisions, seven medium-term decisions and four long-term ones. One of the four long-term decisions, 'decision on dismissing substantial number of employees', was not applicable and suitable to the present Chinese management situation. It was replaced in the Chinese version of the instrument with a decision on important welfare issues such as assigning housing. Housing was apparently a very significant aspect of the work life in Chinese organizations (Wang, 1993). Table 2 presents the list of three categories of decision tasks.

The eighteen decision tasks were randomly presented in the questionnaire and all measured by 5-point scales. A typical item was as follows:

Decision on improvement in work conditions of your work group (dust, noise, safety): how much influence do the different groups have over this decision?

	No influence	*Little influence*	*Moderate influence*	*Much influence*	*Very much influence*
A. Workers					
B. First-line supervisors					
C. Middle management					
D. Top management					
E. Level above plant					
F. Internal representative body					
G. External groups					

Zhong-Ming Wang and Frank A. Heller 118

Table 2 *Three categories of decision tasks*

Category	Content of decision tasks
Short-term decisions	Improving working conditions
	Assigning vocational training
	Transferring jobs within departments
	Replacing small equipment
	Assigning daily tasks
	Approving extra holidays
	Adopting flexible working time
Medium-term decisions	Selecting new head of a department
	Adopting selection procedures/methods
	Selecting supervisors
	Changing wage systems
	Changing departmental organizations
	Dismissing one employee
	Conducting a work study
Long-term decisions	Allocating large investment
	Producing new products
	Introducing new technology
	Deciding important issues (dismissing large number of employees, assigning houses, etc.)

The English version of the questionnaire was translated into Chinese through a parallel translation-checking procedure in which two translators (researchers) independently translated the questionnaire and a third translator (also a researcher) checked the translation. A working meeting was then held by the joint research team to discuss and check the translation of each item of the instrument in terms of wording, meaning and structure. Therefore, both equivalence and compatibility of the instrument were ensured.

Procedures

To obtain both quantitative and qualitative information about decision-making patterns in the organizations, a procedure combining questionnaire with interview methods was adopted. The questionnaire was distributed to respondents during an individual interview session conducted by two

119   *Decision making in Chinese and British industrial organizations*

researchers. The respondent was asked to describe his or her opinion and perception about managerial decision making and power structure in the organizations. They could explain their ideas or reasons about the responses while filling in the questionnaires. In many cases, more detailed information was obtained concerning the ideas behind the responses. The qualitative data will be presented in another paper.

The Chinese and British researchers joined in the field work carried out in each other's country. After some preliminary analysis of the data from the questionnaire and interview, a group feedback session was held in each company using the group feedback analysis techniques (GFA) (Heller, 1969). Both researchers and respondents (including top and middle managers and worker representatives) joined in the session to discuss the results and plan for further actions. The results of the group feedback session are reported in a separate article.

Analysis

The comparisons of the decision-making patterns were made between Chinese and British samples in terms of (1) types of industry (manufacturing industry vs. service industry), (2) sample groups (management vs. trade unions), (3) organizational levels (workers, first-line supervisors, middle management, top management, level above the plant, internal representative body and external groups) and (4) different types of decision tasks. The emphasis here was put upon the quantitative comparisons of the decision-making patterns and the shift of decision-making power between management and trade union groups and across organizational levels.

Results

Decision-making power in manufacturing and service industries

A comparison was made in decision-making power between manufacturing and service industries. Table 3 presents the comparison in decision-making power for three categories of eighteen decision tasks across sample groups in two industries in both Chinese and British companies.

Decision-making power was perceived as more decentralized in both medium- and long-term decisions in the Chinese manufacturing industry than in the service one, whereas an opposite tendency was found in the British sample, i.e., more decentralized decision-making power in the service industry than the manufacturing industry. This repeats the finding in previous British research (Heller et al. 1979). Manufacturing industry has a longer history dating back to the time when organizations were more cen-

Zhong-Ming Wang and Frank A. Heller 120

Table 3 *Average scores of decision power in three categories of decision tasks between manufacturing and service industries in Chinese and British companies*

Decision tasks	Manufacturing industry		Service industry	
	China	UK	China	UK
Short-term decisions	2.48	2.44	2.50	2.47
Medium-term decisions	2.51	2.22*	2.30	2.31
Long-term decisions	2.90	2.50*	2.54	2.75*

Notes
Scores on 5-point scale: 1 = no influence; 3 = moderate influence; 5 = very much influence. * significant difference by t-test.

tralized. It seemed that, on average, decision-making power was less centralized in the Chinese manufacturing industry than in the British one.

Decision-making patterns between management and trade unions

Table 4 presents the results of the perceptions of management and trade unions concerning their decision-making power in different decisions.

Table 4 *Decision-making power perceived by management and trade unions in different decision tasks*

Decision tasks	Management		Trade Unions	
	China	UK	China	UK
Short-term decisions	2.43	2.54*	2.57	2.45*
Medium-term decisions	2.46	2.35*	2.45	2.21*
Long-term decisions	2.78	2.56*	2.76	2.71

Notes
Scores on 5-point scale: 1 = no influence; 3 = moderate influence; 5 = very much influence. * significant difference by t-test.

Table 4 showed that Chinese subjects in general had stronger perceptions of decision-making power than the British subjects. It was found that, when compared with the Chinese sample, there were larger differences in percep-

121   *Decision making in Chinese and British industrial organizations*

tions of decision-making power in the British sample. It is also very interesting to note that there were large differences between the UK samples with regard to the power to make medium-term decisions involving such personnel matters as employee selection, wages and employment. Apparently, this could be attributed to the big differences in labour and personnel systems between Chinese and British organizations.

Decision-making patterns across organizational levels

The influence in decision-making across organizational levels characterizes the decision-making pattern in the organization. Table 5 presents the results of the perceptions by both Chinese and British managers concerning decision-making power in three kinds of decision tasks across organizational levels. Table 6 shows the results of the perceptions of decision-making patterns by trade union samples.

Table 5 *Decision-making patterns in three categories of decision tasks across organizational levels between Chinese and British manager samples*

Decisions	WK	FS	MM	TM	LA	TU	EG
Short-term	Chinese	2.02	2.79	3.82	3.60	1.79	1.63	1.35
decisions	British	2.79	3.76	3.37	2.78	1.72	2.06	1.30
t-test		**	**	*	**	ns	*	ns
Medium-term	Chinese	1.79	1.98	3.49	4.38	2.37	1.94	1.26
decisions	British	1.53	2.22	3.59	3.88	1.78	2.06	1.36
t-test		*	*	ns	**	**	ns	ns
Long-term	Chinese	1.54	1.50	3.14	4.64	3.61	2.41	2.62
decisions	British	1.33	1.63	2.48	4.42	4.13	1.73	2.22
t-test		ns	ns	**	*	**	**	**

Notes
WK = workers; FS = first-line supervisors; MM = middle management; TM = top management; LA = level above the plant; TU = trade union/representative body; EG = external groups.
Scores on 5-point scale: 1 = no influence, 3 = moderate influence; 5 = very much influence. * $p < .05$; ** $p < .01$; ns: non-significant

Tables 5 and 6 reveal some interesting patterns of decision-making power across organizational levels in both Chinese and British companies. As perceived by the management samples, the decision-making power distribution

Zhong-Ming Wang and Frank A. Heller 122

Table 6 *Decision-making patterns in three categories of decision tasks across organizational levels between Chinese and British trade union samples*

Decisions		WK	FS	MM	TM	LA	TU	EG
Short-term	Chinese	2.32	3.04	3.95	3.63	1.71	2.16	1.29
decisions	British	3.00	3.48	3.35	2.51	1.32	2.10	1.08
t-test		**	*	*	**	*	ns	ns
Medium-term	Chinese	1.75	1.93	3.51	4.41	2.17	2.16	1.23
decisions	British	1.44	1.96	3.11	4.00	1.81	1.93	1.21
t-test		ns	ns	*	*	*	ns	ns
Long-term	Chinese	1.66	1.85	2.93	4.54	3.38	2.77	2.30
decisions	British	1.31	1.56	2.25	4.81	4.76	2.43	2.60
t-test		ns	ns	**	ns	**	*	ns

Notes
WK = workers; FS = first-line supervisors; MM = middle management; TM = top management; LA = level above the plant; TU = trade union/representative body; EG = external groups.
Scores on 5-point scale: 1 = no influence, 3 = moderate influence; 5 = very much influence. * p< .05; ** p < .01; ns: non-significant

of short-term decision tasks was located more at middle- and top-management levels in China while it was more decentralized towards the bottom levels (workers and first-line supervisors) in Britain. For the medium-term decisions, the decision-making power remained in a similar pattern in Chinese industries while there was a power shift from bottom levels to the middle- and top-management levels in British industries. Therefore, the two countries had similar patterns in organizational decision making. For the long-term decision tasks, it is worth noting that, in both countries, the level above the plant became much more powerful than in short- and medium-term decisions while external groups also possessed more power. In U.K., the level above plant organizations was banks which had to support capital investment, etc., whereas in China, the level above plant organizations was industrial bureaus.

The decision-making power as perceived by the trade union samples was somewhat different as perceived by the management groups. Compared with the management groups, trade union representatives in both countries had relatively similar perceptions of decision-making power in the companies. Trade unions believed they had more influence upon long-term deci-

123 *Decision making in Chinese and British industrial organizations*

sions than short- and medium-term decisions. There was a power shift to a more centralized pattern in medium- and long-term decisions. Table 6 shows a clearer picture of the decision power shift from an inconsistent lower-level pattern (inconsistent between the two countries), to a consistent medium-level pattern (consistent between the two countries), and then to an inconsistent higher-level pattern.

Discussion

Differences and similarities in decision-making patterns in Chinese and British industries

The results of this research largely verified the general hypotheses about patterns of decision-making power in Chinese and British industries. First of all, as was expected, there were interesting differences in power distribution between manufacturing and service industries. In Chinese industries, decision-making power was perceived to be less hierarchical in the manufacturing industry than in the service one (Table 3). This result seems to relate to some external factors such as government influence and legal prescriptions and structures. In China, in the last fourteen years of economic reform as a result of government intervention, the management structure has been more decentralized and the decision-making procedure more formalized in the manufacturing industry than in the service industry. In fact, the service sector as an industry is still new in China. In the UK, however, the service industry is a well-developed and prosperous sector which has more decentralized decision-making procedures. Notice that there were no large differences between the two industries in the short-term decision tasks. The main differences were found among medium- and long-term decisions, namely more significant decisions concerning personnel management and organizational changes. Those decisions were apparently more affected by higher-level organizational changes.

Second, there was a larger amount of disagreement in perceptions of decision-making power between the British managers and trade union representatives than in the equivalent Chinese samples, in medium- and long-term decisions (Tables 5 and 6). This may be partly due to the fact that Chinese management and trade unions have more common objectives and interests in achieving organizational effectiveness. They work closely with each other and both are parts of the management responsibility systems (*China Daily Business Weekly*, 1988).

Third, as was hypothesized, decision-making power was in general more centralized at middle- and top-levels in Chinese enterprises than in British ones. Interestingly, the management at level above plant in China had a stronger influence on the medium-term decision making but was less powerful in long-term decision making than in Britain (Table 5). The latter finding was somewhat surprising. There were clear shifts of decision-making power across organizational levels among different decision tasks. In the Chinese organizations, there was a shift of decision-making power from the middle- and top-management levels in short-term decisions towards the level-above-the-plant in medium-term decisions and towards the trade union and the external groups in long-term decisions. In the British organizations, there were larger shifts of decision-making power from the bottom level (workers and supervisors) in short-term decisions towards middle- and top-management levels in medium-term decisions and towards the level-above-plant, the trade union and the external group. These findings were largely verified by the subjects during the group feedback sessions and explained their experience in decision-making

A model of decision power shift in organizational decision making

One of the important results of this research is that decision-making power is contingent upon several organizational factors, such as the types of the decision tasks, the management systems and the industry. The decision-making power pattern is dynamic rather than static. While decision tasks and management systems can be conceptualized in terms of micro- and meso-organizational factors, type of industry and ownership are more macro-organizational factors. With short-term decisions concerning daily management activities, task uncertainty is relatively low so that micro- and meso-organizational factors may play a more important role. The patterns of decision making were affected by the task itself and the company management systems in each country. Here, task uncertainty refers to a lack of information about future events so that decisions and their outcomes are unpredictable. In this study, decision-making power for short-term decisions was located at middle- and top-levels in the Chinese companies, but more at supervision levels in the British companies (Table 5). As the decision tasks become more uncertain in tactical, and, strategic in medium-term and long-term decisions, macro-organizational factors may exert more influence upon the decision making and change the decision power pattern. The higher level groups then share more power in the organizational decision making, which causes the decision power shift towards higher organizational levels. Therefore, while there was a larger difference in decision power location between Chinese and British companies in the short-term decisions characterizing the cultural differences in the management systems, there appeared a similar pattern of decision-making power in both countries in the medium-term decisions and a little different pattern in long-term decisions (Table 5). Figure 1 presents a model of decision power shift in the organizations, sum-

125   *Decision making in Chinese and British industrial organizations*

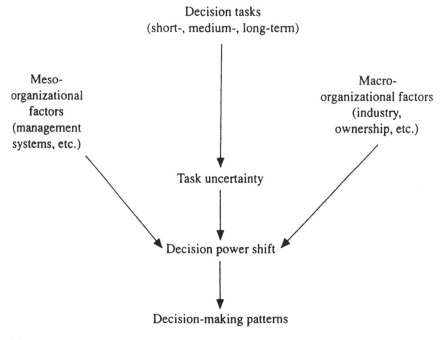

Figure 1 *A model of decision power shift in the organizations*

marizing the effects of decision task characteristics and both meso- and macro-organizational factors upon decision power shift and in turn the decision-making patterns.

Hinings *et al.* (974) carried out an exploratory empirical study and found that coping with uncertainty was critical to power distribution in organizations. They proposed a strategic-contingencies theory of intra-organizational power, hypothesizing that the power of sub-units resulted from contingent dependence among them created by coping with uncertainty and work flow centrality within the organization. The present study tries to look at the decision power patterns and their dynamics, linking power at intra- and inter-organizational levels from a cross-national perspective, and explains how and why decision-making power shifts across organizational levels along with decision tasks in different countries.

Notice that the nature of decision power shifts was different in the two countries. In Chinese industries, the power shift was relatively moderate: while top and middle management retained their high power in decision making, the level above plant and other groups gained more decision power. To some extent, it was a 'non-zero-sum game' in which the increment of one group's decision power didn't result in decrements of another group's

Zhong-Ming Wang and Frank A. Heller   126

power (IDE research group, 1981). However, in the British industries, while the decision power was shifting towards the level above plant in the long-term decisions, lower levels lost certain decision power. This appeared to be a kind of 'zero-sum game' in which the increments of decision power at a higher organizational level were associated with decrements of some low-level decision-making power. We may assume that the macro-organizational factors (e.g., state or private ownership) have affected the nature of decision power shift in the organizations.

The present study has some implications for management in the international context. It shows that there are interesting interactions among factors such as ownership, industrial sectors, management structures, decision tasks and organizational levels, which largely determine the decision power patterns in various organizations. An important factor here seems to be the degree of uncertainty relating to different kinds of decision tasks. The higher the degree of uncertainty the decision situation has, the higher the level the power influence. Since there may be larger differences in macro-organizational factors between countries, the same decision power patterns may lead to different decision actions. Therefore, it would be important to take the effects of decision power shift into consideration in managing industrial organizations, especially in joint ventures where there are more interactions among different cultural factors and managerial styles. Proper decision support should be provided for groups at higher organizational levels in making medium- and long-term decisions. Further studies should be carried out to find out the organizational consequences of the decision power shift in the different countries. In the second report of this joint research, we will compare and discuss the impact of different decision-making patterns, especially upon technological changes in Chinese and British companies.

Zhong-Ming Wang
Department of Psychology
Hangzhou University
PRC
Frank A. Heller
Tavistock Institute of Human Relations
UK

Acknowledgements

We wish to express our thanks to Professor Li Chen, Honorary President of Hangzhou University, for his most valuable encouragement of this research project. We would also like to express our great appreciation to the British

127   *Decision making in Chinese and British industrial organizations*

Council for the support to the joint research project, especially the support for joint research activities in both countries. The Chinese part of the research was supported by a grant from the Chinese State Education Commission to the first author. G. Wang, Q.Q. Zheng, J.H. Ma, B. Zhang, X.L. Pan and H. Ying from the psychology department of Hangzhou University participated in the data collection. The first author also wishes to express his appreciations to the Council for International Exchange of Scholars, USA, for the support of a Fulbright Scholarship at Old Dominion University, Norfolk, where the first draft of this article was written.

References

Astley, W.G. and Sachdeva, P.S. (1984) 'Structural Sources of Intra-organizational Power: A Theoretical Synthesis', *Academy of Management Review*, 9: 104–13.

Chen, L. (1983) *Prospectus of Industrial Psychology* (in Chinese). Hangzhou: Zhejiang People's Press.

Chen, L. (1986) 'New Directions in Managerial Psychology', *Chinese Journal of Applied Psychology*, 1, 1.

Chen, L. (1987) 'Recent Research on Organizational Psychology in China', paper presented at the Sixth Annual Conference of Chinese Psychology Society, Hangzhou.

China Daily Business Weekly (1988) 'The Law of the People's Republic of China on Industrial Enterprises Owned by the Whole People', 15 May.

Heller, F.A. (1969) 'Group Feedback Analysis: A Method of Field Research', *Psychological Bulletin*, 72: 108–17.

Heller, F.A. and Wilpert, B. (1981) *Competence and Power in Managerial Decision Making*. New York: Wiley.

Heller, F.A., Wilder, M., Abell, P. and Warner, M. (1979) *What Do the British Want from Participation and Industrial Democracy*. Anglo-German Foundation: David Green Printers.

Hickson, D.J., Butler, R.J., Cray, D., Mallory, G.R. and Wilson, D.C. (1986) *Top Decisions: Strategic Decision-Making in Organizations*. San Francisco: Jossey-Bass.

Hickson, D.J., Hinings, C.R., Lee, C.A., Scheck, R.E. and Penings, J.M. (1971) 'A Strategic Contingencies' Theory of Intra-organizational Power', *Administrative Science Quarterly*, 16: 216–29.

Hinings, C.R., Hickson, D.J., Pennings, J.M. and Schenk, R.E. (1974) 'Structural Conditions of Intra-Organizational Power', *Administrative Science Quarterly*, 19: 22–44.

IDE research group (1981) *Industrial Democracy in Europe*. Oxford: Clarendon Press.

Jain, H.C. (1980) *Worker Participation: Success and Problems*. New York: Praeger.

Laaksonen, O. (1988) *Management in China: During and After Mao*. Berlin: de Gruyter.

Lachman, R. (1989) 'Power from What? A Re-examination of its Relationships with Structural Conditions', *Administrative Science Quarterly*, 34: 231–51.

Lockett, M. (1983) 'Organizational Democracy and Politics in China'. In Crouch, C. and Heller, F.A. (eds) *International Yearbook of Organizational Democracy*, Vol. 1. *Organizational Democracy and Political Processes*. London: Wiley.

Wan, L. (1986) 'An Important Topic in Political System Reform: Democratic and Scientific Decision Making', *People's Daily*, 15 August; Beijing (in Chinese).

Wang, G. (1984) 'The Necessity and Feasibility of Participative Management in Chinese Companies', unpublished master's thesis, Hangzhou University (in Chinese).

Zhong-Ming Wang and Frank A. Heller 128

Wang, Z.M. (1989) 'Participation and Skill Utilization in Organizational Decision Making in Chinese Enterprise'. In Fallon, B.J., Pfister, H.P. and Brebner, J. (eds) *Advances in Industrial Organizational Psychology.* Amsterdam: Elsevier Science, pp. 19–26.

Wang, Z.M. (1991) 'Recent Developments in Industrial and Organizational Psychology in People's Republic of China'. In Cooper, C. and Robertson, I.T. (eds) *International Review of Industrial and Organizational Psychology.* Chichester: Wiley, pp. 1–15.

Wang, Z.M. (1993) 'Culture, Economic Reform and the Role of Industrial and Organizational Psychology in China'. In Dunnette, M.D and Hough, L.M. (eds) *Handbook of Industrial and Organizational Psychology*, Vol. 4. Palo Alto: Consulting Psychologist.

Xu, L.C. and Wang, Z.M. (1991) 'New Development in Organizational Psychology in China', *Applied Psychology: An International Review*, 40, 1: 3–14.

[33]

The Time Dimension in Organizational Research

FRANK HELLER, *The Tavistock Institute*

Introduction

The seminal Aston Studies initiated by Derek Pugh and his colleagues in the 1960s have had considerable impact on the behaviour and organizational science literature. Inevitably, people have appreciated them for different reasons. For me, one important aspect of this work is its systemic theoretical framework developed from the orientation of a psychologist building bridges towards other disciplines (Heller, 1976). Such a psychological orientation was shown most clearly in the methodological approach of the Aston Studies and the choice of statistical methods. Perhaps the most important bridge was its connectedness with sociology and later with administrative and management science (Pugh *et al.*, 1963).

Why is this important? First of all, the social sciences still operate in a very narrow and compartmentalized constituency following the tramlines laid out by the historic development of university departments and, while this helps to develop the intellectual credentials of a discipline, it does little to test its validity on the wider campus of a complex world. This is not a denigration of disciplines, since it is obvious that they have to be developed and show their strength before a cross-disciplinary approach can be expected to yield results. A discipline grows and develops to a state of isolated maturity beyond which it is difficult to achieve further growth without venturing outside the self-imposed boundaries of a given field. I believe that applied psychology reached this stage several decades ago, for instance in the study of leadership, decision making and other facets of organizational life. Moving across disciplinary boundaries requires ingenuity, confidence and perseverance. Kurt Lewin was an early transgressor of boundaries (Lewin, 1936) and he inspired Eric Trist and Fred Emery to venture further into the undercharted territories of technological and organizational life (Trist *et al.*, 1963; Emery, 1982; Emery and Trist, 1973). Another great bridge builder using psychology and economics to explore the limits of rationality in organizations was Herbert Simon (Simon, 1982).

The Aston Studies were from the beginning based on an interdisciplinary group of scholars, bringing together psychology, sociology and anthropology in a conceptual scheme of organizational analysis (Pugh *et al.*, 1963). Rather than continuing the tradition of studying organizational processes, they set out to discover basic structural characteristics and the context in which they occur. Structure and context tend to be fairly stable over time and their cross-sectional design yielded very significant results, explaining often up to 50 per cent of the variance between the variables under investigation. Another reason for the considerable success of their programme of research was their use of a carefully validated interview schedule rather than the more popular and less reliable distributed questionnaire. However, when later they came to look at the interaction between structure, context and individual roles and group behaviour, the statistical relationships were very much weaker (Pugh and Payne, 1977). Such results are not unusual and it is likely that the greater variability of individual and group behaviour, compared with structural dimensions, is a part of the explanation.

In research dealing with structure as well as processes of individual and group behaviour, a strong case can be made out for a longitudinal research design. Even when variances are relatively low, if they are found to be stable over time, the explanatory power is enhanced. If, however, significant differences are found over time, then this has to be considered within an appropriate process-oriented theoretical framework.

In the subsequent discussion I will describe four distinct approaches to longitudinal design and relevant methodological considerations. This is followed by a brief description of two pieces of organizational research – Industrial Democracy in Europe (IDE) and Decisions in Organizations (DIO) – which used different longitudinal methods with some success.

The Case for Longitudinality

In a 1973 symposium on leadership, Ed Fleishman identified the urgent need for longitudinal studies and for a time dimension in research design (Fleishman and Hunt, 1973, pp. 183–4). The logical case for longitudinal research is very strong. Everybody and everything has a history and a future, except at the point of death. So even in selection testing one could make out a case for differentiating results achieved on a Monday morning – maybe after a hectic Sunday – from a Friday afternoon, which may combine signs of fatigue with euphoria anticipating the pleasures of the coming weekend.

The case becomes stronger when we deal with characteristics which clearly vary over time, so the assessment of a manager who has just moved into a job may be substantially different from the same person's attitudes and behaviour after six months, and two years later. A representative and valid leadership profile probably requires a time dimension, particularly if we want to match leader characteristics to success or failure. There is no shortage of examples from the last 10 years or so to show that people who were considered eminently successful suddenly failed. Only a longitudinal study would make it possible to discover the antecedents to success or failure.

The need for longitudinality becomes irresistible when one investigates the activities employees undertake in a working day or in the process of decision making or participation. If we carry out cross-sectional studies on events which occur over time, we make assumptions about representativeness which may not be justifiable. For instance, most research on participation and decision making is carried out cross-sectionally although we know that issues involved in participation take days, weeks or months from beginning to end. The assumption we make is either that the time chosen to solicit an answer to our question is representative of the universe of events we attempt to cover or that the respondent is capable of calculating his/her own average or mode for a representative sample of events. A moment's reflection will suggest that these are risky assumptions to make and we might then fall back on the hope that differences over time do not have any theoretically justifiable pattern or are randomly distributed.

Variations of Longitudinal Design

Having made out the theoretical case and the policy relevance of a longitudinal research design for certain topics of investigation in organizational psychology, I want briefly to discuss a few issues of methodology. In general, a longitudinal approach is more costly than cross-sectional design, but different longitudinal designs incur different costs and probably also yield commensurately different benefits. I will describe four different ways of achieving time-sensitive data collection. In each case the data can be collected through interviews, questionnaires, observation or analysis of available documents.

300   *Advancement in Organizational Behaviour*

1   A *two-stage before-and-after longitudinal* design is the most widely used. It is particularly appropriate if the research itself introduces a new factor or wishes to monitor the effect of a given change event. It is also the least costly. The IDE study described below uses this design.

2   *Segmental longitudinal* design consists of more than two cross-sectional stages and is therefore an extension of method (1) above. It covers longer periods and is more suitable for establishing trends.

3   *Processual studies* are designed to create continuity over time. They can take many forms, from participant observation, via case studies, to diachronic research which resembles segmental longitudinal research in method (2) above, but finds some way to establish a degree of continuity between visits and observations. A researcher's visit may occur while a process is going on but, to get continuity, it is possible to link up with past events through what we call retrospective tracing (using interviews or available documents and so on) and from then on carry out process analysis followed later by further retrospective tracing, and so on. Standardized questionnaires can only play a limited role in extensive longitudinal field studies because people soon get tired of filling in forms. We have found a method called Group Feedback Analysis useful in establishing reliable data over time (Brown and Heller, 1981; Heller and Brown, 1995). The method systematically feeds back interview and other material to the people who provided it or are involved in the activity under discussion. This group (or individuals) are asked to verify the data and help interpret them in the light of their experience. The DIO study to be described below uses this method. Processual studies can clearly use a considerable variety of methods. This is a point in their favour.

4   Finally, there is what I call a *simulated longitudinal study*. It uses the conventional cross-sectional design but asks people to focus on specific time periods and describe what happens in each (see, for instance, Fröhlich *et al.*, 1991, pp. 65–71).

Industrial Democracy in Europe (IDE) Research

This project was jointly designed and executed by 16 social scientists from 12 mainly European countries covering a number of disciplines including economics, philosophy, sociology, industrial relations and psychology. It adopted an open systems framework starting with formal, mainly legal, structural variables which are assumed to have an impact on individual and group behaviour and ultimately on individual and group outcomes moderated by a variety of contextual variables. (IDE, 1981a).

The Time Dimension in Organizational Research   301

The research design was derived from prevailing policy preoccupations relating to organizational democracy, leadership, conflict, organizational climate and individual satisfaction. An important preoccupation in individual countries as well as in the European Commission was to discover the necessary antecedents for successful participative or influence-sharing behaviour at various organizational levels. Was it useful or even necessary to support changes in behaviour at company level, by legal or other formal schemas? More specifically, is influence sharing at various organizational levels dependent on or facilitated by formal structures like the German codetermination scheme?

The research design was complex and I will only describe in outline the basic theoretical model and the main variables (see Figure 17.1). Box 1 was based on a detailed assessment by each of the 12-country teams of four specified context conditions. This descriptive account is contained in a separate book and was consulted in the final assessment of the results (IDE, 1981b). Box 2 contains formal legally prescribed participative measures (such as German codetermination) which were the main dependent measures and varied

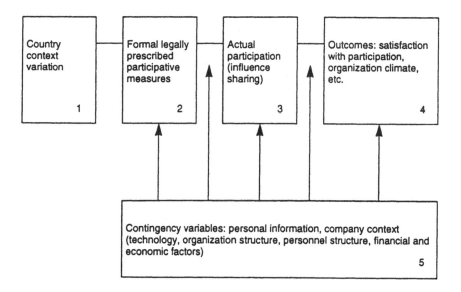

Figure 17.1   The IDE I theoretical model

substantially in the 12 countries. Box 3 describes a measure of actual participation, that is to say, influence and power sharing at all organizational levels. Box 4 describes five outcomes, including satisfaction with participation, satisfaction in general and organizational climate. Finally, box 5 used two types of contingencies which were hypothesized to intervene or moderate the assumed chain of causal relationships. They included several variables derived from the Aston Studies and were based on interviews with managers (IDE, 1981a, ch. 4).

Ten years later, the same international research group carried out a replication study in the same organizations in the same countries.[1] The objective was to test the validity of the previous research conclusions, at the same time extending the design to include some of the most likely variables that had become critical in the intervening 10 years. There are, of course, many methodological and practical problems in carrying out such a large-scale replication study and these are freely acknowledged. The most difficult objective was to see whether a longitudinal link between two cross-sectional studies (we have called this method 'two-stage longitudinal') might give us some insight into possible causal relationships over time (IDE, 1993).

To attempt such an assessment, we had to select a group of contingencies which could be hypothesized to strengthen or weaken the major relationship we had found in the previous study and assess the impact of selected economic and technical changes over the intervening period – in particular the rate of unemployment, which had gone up very substantially.

The theoretical model for the IDE II study is shown in Figure 17.2. The macro variables in box 1 contain the descriptive data on the major political, economic and industrial relations factors which characterize the 1977–87 period. Boxes 2 and 3 are the same as in IDE I but now include comparisons over the 10 years. Outcomes were not considered to be central for the replication study. Box 4 measures a number of contingencies and, in particular, the rate of unemployment and changes in unemployment over the 10-year period.

The replication design allowed us to describe and evaluate the data of the two studies from a cross-sectional as well as longitudinal perspective. It became clear that the longitudinal analysis was more policy-relevant than the conclusions from the cross-sectional material alone. The major conclusion of the replication study is that the relationship between macro variables of formal and legal structure and micro dimensions of influence sharing at the lowest organizational level remains valid. However, in the replication study, the macro variable (formal, legal, participative structure) was less predictive than the indices of unemployment. The 1977–87 period was very turbulent; it included the oil crisis, the subsequent economic

The Time Dimension in Organizational Research   303

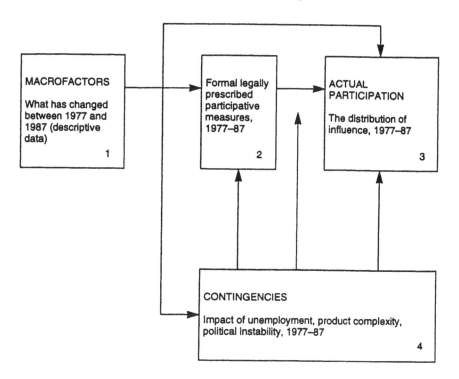

Figure 17.2   The IDE II theoretical model

recession, greatly increased competition and changes in technological sophistication. Our data show that, over the 10-year period, labour
lost ground in organizations, particularly where it had previously
been strong. It seems that, under the umbrella of an economic recession and high unemployment, companies deliberately reduced the
influence of labour where it had previously been strong. Using the
1977 data, it was also possible to conclude that management policy
to reduce the influence of employees by reducing the strength of the
unions was based more on an emotional than a factual interpretation
of employee influence in the decision-making process. We had asked
all employees how much influence they would like to have compared with the influence they currently had and the difference was
very moderate (see also similar evidence from Wall and Lischeron,
1977).

More generally, it was reassuring that, in the two studies separated
by 10 turbulent years, the overall pattern of relationships remained
substantially stable.

Decisions in Organizations (DIO) Research

The two-stage before and after longitudinal IDE research described above was followed up by a subgroup of the original group of researchers in three countries using what we have called a processual longitudinal study. The research lasted five years, four of them on field work. A similar open system theoretical framework was adopted and many of the variables, particularly those measuring the distribution of influence (the influence–power continuum) remained the same. As before, we assessed influence at all organizational levels and in this case in relation to a set of 217 specific tactical and strategic decision issues. Our structural variable was not the country's formal legal provision, but the nearest equivalent at the organizational level, namely formal, usually written, policy on organizational democracy (the structure and function of works councils in particular). This variable was called 'status power'. Since the study covered only seven organizations, the in-depth design over the four years could include a number of additional variables such as three important outcome variables: skill utilization, the efficiency of the decision process and achievement of the decision.

The research methodology was based on interviews, participant observation, access to written records, a detailed interview schedule and frequent use of group feedback analysis (GFA) as a way of validating our interview schedule assessment and exploring the meaning of our data with employees at all levels (Heller, 1969; Brown and Heller 1981; Heller and Brown, 1995). A feature of the processual design was to obtain quantitative as well as ethnographic material relating to the same decision process (Heller *et al.*, 1988).

Our method of following the sample of decisions over time is illustrated in Figure 17.3. Although we visited each company frequently, there was always the possibility that something important had happened between visits. To catch up we used 'retrospective tracing' through interviews and documentation. While we were in the company we observed, talked to various people engaged in the decision and took part in meetings, particularly of the joint consultative procedure (works councils) and safety committees, as well as budget forecasting meetings. This is called 'process registration'. In asking questions to cover the data for the interview schedule it was frequently suggested that we should check with some other people who could tell us more about the issue with which we were concerned. This is called 'snowballing' and covered a variety of levels and functions.

During the pilot investigation we decided to divide the decision process into distinct phases and for the purposes of this chapter we will confine ourselves to a brief description of the phase model used

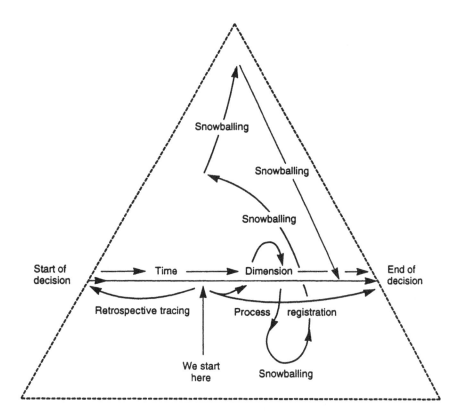

Note: The dotted triangle is used to draw attention to the analysis at different levels of the organization; the diagram illustrates the need to operate in two dimensions: organizational level and time.

Source: Heller *et al.* (1988).

Figure 17.3   The decision process through retrospective tracing, process registration and snowballing

in this research and some of the results achieved. Using the 217 medium- and long-term tactical and strategic decisions as our unit of analysis, we traced each decision over its life cycle of four phases:

1   *start-up*, which contains recognition of issue and definition of goals;
2   *development*, which contains search for responses, investigation of alternatives and creation of possible solutions;

3   *finalization*, which contains evaluation of alternatives, a choice
     among them and ratification of decision; and
4   *implementation* of decision, which contains implementation and
     modification of the decision made in the previous phases.[2]

The degree of participation measured by the influence–power continuum (IPC) had six alternatives: (1) no or minimal information, (2)
information only, (3) opportunity to give advice, (4) advice taken into
consideration, (5) joint decision making and (6) complete control.
These six degrees of influence sharing in the decision process were
scored separately for each of the four phases of our sample of decisions. Previous research on the distribution of power in organizations
had led us to hypothesize that perhaps substantial differences might
result from custom and practice, motivation and variability in competence. The results fully supported these expectations. The
distribution of influence and power over the four phases was significantly different for all levels of organization and in relation to most
decisions. Furthermore, there were significant and consistent differences in the amount of time taken up in each phase. The finalization
phase was nearly always the shortest and the implementation phase
the longest.

A typical distribution of the IPC over the four phases is shown in
Figure 17.4. The lowest level of employee has no real influence over
new product decisions; the difference in scores between phases reflects the amount of information received. Only in the finalization
phase are workers fully informed on new product decisions. When it
comes to consultative procedures, there are substantial differences
over the four phases, rising from very little influence in start-up and
development to considerable influence during finalization and somewhat less in implementation. Managers, of course, have considerably
more influence in all phases. The difference between the four phases
is smaller than for workers but nevertheless statistically significant.
Moreover, the pattern of distribution is reversed between these two
types of decisions.

This distribution is not unexpected, but it does suggest that a
description of the amount of influence a shopfloor worker or manager has cannot usefully be described by a single word or figure. A
number of consequences follow from such a conclusion at the level
of theory as well as of practice.

First of all, it calls into question many of the policy recommendations from the existing literature on participation. In particular, it would
seem necessary to adjust the models used for training managers in
using participative styles of leadership in certain contingencies (for
instance, Vroom and Yetton, 1973). In leadership training, phase should
be considered a contingency. For instance we find that the amount of

The Time Dimension in Organizational Research

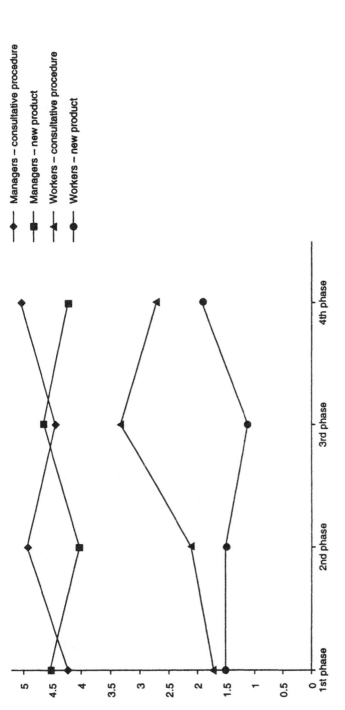

Note: The vertical axis is the influence–power continuum as described in the text. Phase 1 = start-up; 2 = development; 3 = finalization; 4 = implementation.

Source: Heller *et al.* (1988).

Figure 17.4 Differences in influence sharing between workers and managers on two lon

308   *Advancement in Organizational Behaviour*

participation varies significantly between the phases of the decision cycle (see Figure 17.4) and these variations seem to make sense in relation to the experience of the employees engaged in the process. This result of the longitudinal analysis should be used in leadership training and replace the more usual exhortation to use the same method irrespective of the differential conditions characterizing the four phases.

At the theoretical level, it is possible to discern several distinct patterns; we have described six.

1   Dominance without responsibility describes a pattern of participation in which a group has the highest score of involvement in the first phase of decision-making activity and a relatively low score of involvement in the other three phases. The rationale behind this pattern is that the control established through the first stage is not legitimized in the third stage, or elsewhere. This means that another group takes responsibility for the decision.
2   Dominance with responsibility describes a situation where a group has the highest score of involvement in the first and third stage of decision-making activity, and a relatively low score in the second and fourth stages.
3   Overcommitment is the pattern of a group that has a high score of involvement in all four stages of decision-making activity.
4   Controlled participation is created in circumstances where a group is highly involved in the second and third phases, but relatively little involved in the other two phases. In this case the activity of some group or groups is controlled by whoever dominates the first and third phases.
5   Dependent participation appears in cases where a group participates only in the implementation phase and has no great influence on the previous phases of decision-making activity.
6   Zero participation applies to situations where one or more groups have very low involvement scores in all four phases of decision making. This pattern sometimes applies to workers and to representative bodies.

In the seven organizations of the DIO study we found examples of each of these patterns. We believe that this type of analysis could be helpful for policy making as well as for training to the extent that it imposes an obligation to explain and possibly justify a certain distribution of influence. It would be particularly useful if the analysis were to lead to an attempt to match influence sharing with the distribution of experience and skill in the organization, thus pinpointing the need for further training.

Another important phase variation applies to 'skill utilization', described in the interview schedule as a rating of the extent to which capacities and experiences of competent people and groups involved in a given process have been utilized. It is a difficult variable to assess accurately and we therefore specified that these assessments must always be checked through group feedback analysis. We considered skill utilization to be a somewhat neglected variable in organizational analysis and in particular in its relation with influence sharing. This was borne out by our findings, which showed very clearly that, in each of the four phases, skill utilization depended on two antecedent conditions: one was the amount of influence sharing practised by management and the other was what we called 'status power', that is to say the amount of formal, usually written, influence assigned to participative bodies like works councils, safety committees and so on.[3] Our ethnographic data from one of the companies provided a number of useful illustrations. In budget forecasting, for instance, the frequent inaccuracies of this procedure could usually be traced back to a lack of consultation with those levels who had the relevant information, for instance the salesperson who knew why customers were not interested in buying the product at certain times of the year. The sequence of events was clear: a lack of participation led to underutilization of the sales staff's experience and this in turn resulted in grossly inaccurate budget forecasts. Looking at this procedure over the four phases, we saw that the lack of consultation was particularly important during the search process of phase 2 and to some extent in finalization during phase 3. It was unimportant in phases 1 and 4. However, in the implementation phase there was a noticeable increase in dissatisfaction for both the sales staff and management since the finance officer held them responsible for not achieving their forecasts and therefore attributed the inappropriate investments in capital equipment to their failure. The other causal factor was status power, which affected the accuracy of the budget decisions because these decisions were not part of the agenda of existing consultative committees; they had their own separate and ad hoc procedure.

There were two ways of improving the situation and both were discussed in our feedback sessions. One was to persuade the senior marketing staff to consult their salesmen regularly, particularly at certain times of the budget forecasting process, the other was to include budget forecasting in the formal joint consultative procedure, particularly in phases 2 and 3. The managing director thought that changing what we called 'status power' was preferable, since he had little confidence in affecting the somewhat autocratic management style of the marketing manager; moreover, he thought that it was easier to confine the sales staffs input during the development and finalization phases within a formal committee procedure. To save embarrassment for the marketing manager, one could, he thought, start off by bringing the sales staff only into the pre-finaliz-ation phase. These findings illustrate the policy relevance of the phase model. We know from previous research and other investigations that management frequently resists participation on the grounds that it invades their prerogative. It is likely that this argument has less force if it can be shown that consultation taps into relevant experi-ences and skills and therefore improves the quality of decisions and, furthermore, can be confined to certain phases of the decision cycle.

The utility of a longitudinal design is of course accepted by people who use the case study method which usually eschews quantifica-tion. Even so, our experience with DIO would suggest that a clearly defined phase structure would produce useful additional descriptive results. Furthermore, there are issues, particularly in comparative cross-national research, were some quantification is advantageous and there is really no reason, except cost, why substantial ethno-graphic material should not be collected at the same time to extend the data and deepen our insight into causality and the complexity of organizational life.

We have seen that there are a number of results that provide links between the two projects described in this paper. One is the finding that a formal organization structure at company level (called 'status power' in DIO) has a very similar effect of increasing the influence of lower levels to the effect that legal structures at national level had in the IDE research. The longitudinal dimension adds a refinement by suggesting that the relationship between structure and behaviour is more significant and has more useful outcomes in some phases of the decision cycle than in others.

The Argument

Modern organizations are complex entities and benefit from being studied from a multidisciplinary perspective and an appropriate var-iety of methods. It is interesting to see that similar considerations apply in the physical sciences and that there, too, a multidisciplinary approach is often resisted. Hawkes (1995) tells us that 'traditional methods of supporting science do not usually favour interdisciplin-ary research'. Sir William Mitchell, chairman of the Science and Engineering Research Council in the 1980s, recalls that, when appli-cations for research grants for projects involving both chemistry and physics arrived, they would be sent separately to both the chemistry and physics committees. Each would do their own scoring and then the Council would take an average. This, he argued, completely neglected the possibility of cross-fertilization between the two disci-plines. Following these experiences, Sir William Mitchell managed to build up an interdisciplinary research centre in the face of very strong opposition from subject specialists.

Starting with the interdisciplinary and well known Aston Studies on organization structure and context, we have described two other pieces of research (IDE and DIO) which used Aston-like variables of structure and added individual and group dimensions in an attempt to assess the impact of structure on behaviour. Since some of the behaviour variables were processual, it was thought appropriate to use a longitudinal method. Four longitudinal methods were described and two different ones were used in the IDE and DIO projects.

The desirability of tailoring methods to the nature of the research task is widely accepted but not easily practised because of the attitude of funding bodies and the need to limit costs. In some countries, particularly in the United States, the need for frequent publications also mitigates against processual studies like DIO; this pressure is now experienced in many European countries. In these circumstances it becomes important to demonstrate the value added by longitudinality in terms of its relevance for policy and practice as well as theory.[4]

Notes

1   There were some changes in personnel and two additional countries.
2   Mintzberg *et al.* (1976), using students doing a master's degree, had previously used a three-phase model which excluded implementation. In the event, we found this final phase was particularly important.
3   LISREL was the statistical method used for most of the longitudinal analysis. In addition, we collected extensive ethnographic material (see Heller *et al.*, 1988, ch. VI).
4   In this context it may be useful to compare the studies described here with a continuing stream of mechanistic cross-sectional studies on participative decision making that concentrate on psychological variables (see, for instance, Sagie and Koslowsky, 1966).

References

Brown, A.J. and Heller, F.A. (1981), 'Usefulness of group feedback analysis as a research method: its application to a questionnaire study', *Human Relations*, **34**, pp. 141–56.

Emery, F.E. (1982), 'New perspectives on the world of work: sociotechnical foundations for a new social order?', *Human Relations*, **35**, 1095–1122.

Emery, F.E. and Trist, E.L. (1973), *Towards a Social Ecology*. London: Plenum Press.

Fleishman, E. and Hunt, J. (1973), *Current Developments in the Study of Leadership*, Carbondale, Ill.: Southern Illinois University Press.

Fröhlich, Dieter, Gill, Colin and Krieger, Hubert (1991), 'Roads to participation in the European Community: Increasing prospects of employee representatives in

312   *Advancement in Organizational Behaviour*

technological change', European Foundation for the Improvement of Living and
Working Conditions, Loughlinstown House, Shankill, Dublin.

Hawkes, N. (1995), 'Making the right connections', *The Times*, 29 November 1995, p.
39.

Heller, F.A. (1969), 'Group feedback analysis: a method of field research', *Psychological Bulletin*, **72**, 108–17; reprinted 1973 in D. Graves (ed.), *Management Research: A Cross-Cultural Perspective*, London: Elsevier Scientific Publishing Co., pp. 49–69.

Heller, F.A. (1976), 'Towards a practical psychology of work', *Journal of Occupational Psychology*, **49**, 45–54.

Heller, F. and Brown, A. (1995), 'Group feed-back analysis applied to longitudinal monitoring of the decision making process', *Human Relations*, **48**.

Heller, F.A., Drenth, P.J.D., Koopman, P. and Veljko, R. (1988), *Decisions in Organizations: A Longitudinal Study of Routine, Tactical and Strategic Decisions*, London/ Beverly Hills: Sage.

IDE (Industrial Democracy in Europe) (1981a), *European Industrial Relations*, Oxford: Oxford University Press.

IDE (Industrial Democracy in Europe) (1981b), *Industrial Relations in Europe*, Oxford: Oxford University Press.

IDE (Industrial Democracy in Europe) (1993), *Industrial Democracy in Europe Revisited*, Oxford: Oxford University Press.

Lewin, Kurt (1936), *Principles of Topological Psychology*, New York: McGraw-Hill.

Mintzberg, H., Raisingham, D. and Theoret, A. (1976) 'The structure of "unstructured" decision processes', *Administrative Science Quarterly*, **21**, 246–75.

Pugh, D.S. and Payne, R. (eds) (1977), *Organization Behaviour in its Context. The Aston Programme III*, Aldershot: Dartmouth.

Pugh, D.S., Hickson, D.J., Hinings, C.R., Macdonald, K.M., Turner, C. and Lupton, T. (1963), 'A conceptual scheme for organizational analysis', *Administrative Science Quarterly*, **8**, 289–315.

Sagie, A. and Koslowsky (1996), 'Decision type, organizational control and acceptance of change: an integrative approach to participative decision making', *Applied Psychology*, **45**, 85–92.

Simon, H.A. (1982), 'Rational decision-making in business organization', in H. Simon (ed.), *Models of Bounded Rationality*, Vol. 2, Cambridge, Mass.: MIT Press, pp. 474–94.

Trist, E.L., Higgin, G.W., Murray, H. and Pollock, A.B. (1963), *Organizational Choice*, London: Tavistock.

Vroom, V. and Yetton, P. (1973), *Leadership and decision-making*, Pittsburg: University of Pittsburgh Press.

Wall, T.D. and Lischeron, J.A. (1977), *Worker Participation: A Critique of the Literature and Some Fresh Evidence*, London: McGraw-Hill.

[34]

Human Relations, Volume 34, Number 2, 1981, pp. 141–156

Usefulness of Group Feedback Analysis as a Research Method: Its Application to a Questionnaire Study[1]

Alan Brown and Frank Heller[2]
Tavistock Institute of Human Relations

This paper describes the use of a field research method called group feed-back analysis (GFA) applied in two British companies. The study used two phases of questionnaire administration separated by over 12 months. Three major functions of GFA are elaborated and analyzed with examples based, in part, on tape-recorded sessions: (1) validation of the results; (2) producing a deeper understanding of the data; and (3) providing an opportunity for mutual learning.

INTRODUCTION

This paper will concentrate on one of the key research methods used in a study of decision making. The method is called group feedback analysis (GFA) and was applied to a questionnaire study concerned with operational decisions at the workplace level.

The research project as a whole investigated the situationally determined relationships between decision-making style and outcome, such as effectiveness, skill utilization, and satisfaction. Certain defined aspects of the process of decision-making and participation in organizations were

---

[1]This represents a small part of a much wider project: Decision-Making in Organizations (DIO), a three-country comparative study in which three semiautonomous research teams share responsibility equally. In the Netherlands, Professor Pieter Drenth and Paul Koopman; in Yugoslavia, Professor Veljko Rus and Miro Odar. The British part of the research was financed by two grants from the Social Science Research Council, the Dutch research from the Dutch Organization for Pure Research, and the Republic of Slovenia Research Community financed the Yugoslav part of the study.
[2]Requests for reprints should be sent to Dr. F. A. Heller, The Tavistock Institute of Human Relations, Tavistock Centre, Belsize Lane, London NW3 5BA, England.

monitored in depth and over time, using a variety of research methods. The research framework and the detailed results are described elsewhere (Heller, Drenth, Rus, & Koopman, 1977; Drenth, Koopman, Rus, Odar, Heller, & Brown, 1979). However, to illustrate the usefulness of GFA as a research tool, in this paper the study is best regarded as a self-contained investigation into shop-floor decision-making in two British companies.[3] A brief description of the underlying theoretical model, the questionnaires, the sample, and the results of the questionnaire study are necessary to sustain the main aim of the paper, which is to examine the functions and usefulness of GFA.

BACKGROUND

Model

The most important variables and their postulated interactions are represented in the model given in Fig. 1. The research is directed towards interactions between three sets of variables. The independent variable, the extent of participation in decision-making, reflects one of six positions on an influence-power continuum (IPC) given in the Appendix (Exhibit A).

The dependent variables are effectiveness of decision-making, utilization of skills, and satisfaction. The third set of variables are "CON variables." These could be *condition* variables, if they primarily determine the IPC score. For example, various "outside influences" could effectively limit the freedom of choice work groups have in making certain decisions. Other "CON variables" are treated primarily as *contingent* or intervening variables, if they influence the relationship between the dependent and independent variables. Contingent variables can be arranged in three groups:

1. Personal variables—such as age, education, etc.
2. Group variables—such as job characteristics, group climate, etc.
3. Organizational variables—such as attitude of top management, span of control, etc.

It is possible for some of these variables to fall into both the condition and contingency categories.

The adequacy of this model for looking at relatively simple, short-term, *operational* decisions, which are primarily made at the lower

---

[3]It should be stressed that the responsibility for the development and utilisation of the questionnaires and GFA procedures was shared by the whole team.

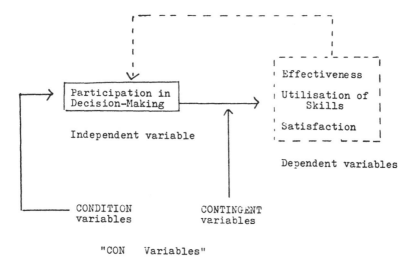

Fig. 2. Model of decisions in organizations.

levels of organizations, was tested by using the set of questionnaires described in the Appendix (Exhibit B).

Sample

Two British companies took part in the research, giving 185 respondents to the British questionnaire inquiry.[*] The set of questionnaires was given to status-homogeneous groups. The sample of 185 respondents was drawn from 40 work groups. These consisted of 16 production, 2 supervisory (production), 7 technical (computing and laboratory), 9 blue-collar support, and 6 lower-level administrative work groups. The work groups were taken to be the "natural" ones (i.e. those working together on a particular line or department), rather than those working under a non-co-working supervisor. (The latter groups were much larger, as a supervisor might be in charge of several "natural" work groups.) The size of the "natural" work groups varied between 3 and 30, while the number under a single supervisor went up to 80. We will see later that both figures have significance for the interpretation of the questionnaire results. The supervisor of each work group was interviewed to find out general and any

---

[*]The Yugoslavs and the Dutch contributed 5 more companies, giving a total of 988 respondents.

special characteristics of the work group. The results of each question were aggregated for each work group, then they were ready for the feedback sessions.

Results of the Questionnaire Study

For the purpose of providing some background information, some of the results of the questionnaire study are given:

1. There is a significant positive relation between participation (IPC) and utilization of skills.
2. There is a significant positive relation between participation (IPC) and education.
3. There is a significant positive relation between participation (IPC) and satisfaction.
4. The method of decision-making varies with the nature of the task.
5. Only very rarely do workers in the sample exercise any considerable amount of influence in any of the task situations we observed. Joint decision-making was rare, and even "advice taken into consideration" did not occur often.
6. There is a negative relation between group size (i.e., the number working under a single supervisor) and participation.

So far, all this could have been obtained by a straightforward questionnaire study. What additional contribution can GFA make? This is the question we propose to deal with in the forthcoming sections of the paper.

METHOD

The method to be described is a form of group feedback analysis (Heller, 1969) which had previously been adapted to multinational research (Graves, 1973, pp. 49-69; Wilpert, 1977).

The method has three principal stages. In the first stage the questionnaires are administered in groups with a researcher present to explain the objective of the inquiry and help with any questions respondents may have. The results are then analyzed in Stage 2. Stage 3 presents this analysis to the groups who originally provided the answers.[5] This third stage is called the feedback session and was usually held within a few days of the questionnaire administration. However, in this study this basis process was

---

[5]On occasion some members of the original group were unavoidably absent. Occasionally two groups were merged for feedback sessions.

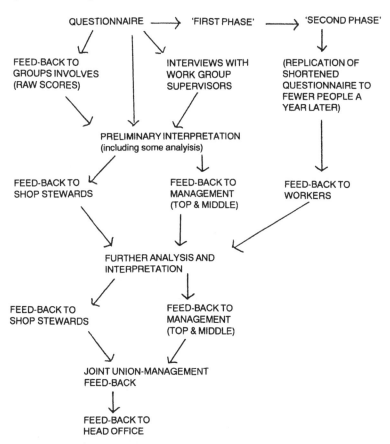

Fig. 2. The process of feedback and sources of information in Company A.

supplemented by the use of additional feedback sessions to discuss the findings with other interested parties.[6] The various stages of GFA meetings in one of the companies are shown diagramatically in Fig. 2. The meetings were with various union and management groups separately and together, and information from the second phase questionnaire administration was fed into later sessions. The exact series of stages and cycles was tailored to the particular requirements of each company,[7] but the overall design of re-

---

[6] All feedback data was presented in a form that made it impossible to identify individuals. However, each group was still asked if it would sanction discussion about the overall results at subsequent levels. Similarly, factory management and union representatives had to sanction our sessions with head office before we felt justified having meetings there.

[7] For example, the feedback cycle for company B was slightly different and less intensive.

peated loops of group feedback meetings remains a central feature of the method.

The experience, interpretation, and understanding of the feedback sessions constitute the rest of this paper. It was part of our method to tape record feedback sessions and to use the transscript for the objectives we describe below.[*] We have never had any difficulty getting permission to tape record sessions. In our experience respondents like their testimony to be taken seriously. Anonymity is safeguarded, though each group would have access to its own recording if it wanted. The method ensures that if there is any dispute about the data or its interpretation, we can go back to the evidence and reexamine it. This has in fact been necessary on a number of occasions during the study.

OBJECTIVES AND RESULTS

In the present study, group feedback analysis has three objectives. In the first place, it helps to validate results; secondly, it facilitates a deeper understanding of the date (clarification of ambivalent findings and collection of additional information triggered off by the stimulus of the data feedback). In both companies, the early sessions concentrated on validation. Once confidence in the results was established, the second objective was achieved. In the third place, GFA may be used as an opportunity for mutual learning or as a tool for change (Heller, 1970). However, this is dependent on the researcher's relationship with the company, and it is not always possible to use GFA in the same way. Indeed, we believe that it should be tailored to be relevant to each company. This would ensure that each organization gets some benefit from its expenditure of time and effort. With both British companies there was prior agreement that the overall results would be discussed with senior management in a systematic way. Our experience with each of these objectives will now be examined in greater detail.

Validation

Validation was the prime function of GFA in this research. Respondents gave reasons why they produced certain answers; they had an opportunity to vent their doubts about parts of the questionnaire and/or

---

[*]Complete transcripts are expensive. We have used highly skilled administrative assistants who learn about our research and transcribe summaries interspersed with verbatim quotations when dealing with critical issues.

answers and their overall reaction to issues raised by the inquiry. The feedback comments were, therefore, extremely useful in putting questionnaire responses in context.[9]

This can be illustrated with some specific examples.

Explanation of Results

One worker explained that he had answered a question about how much influence he had over decisions relating to the layout of his work place by saying that he had "complete control." To explain this, he volunteered the information that ". . . in our department, the garage, the machinery is very light, we can move it around to ,wherever we can work best! Another person had answered the same question by indicating that he had no influence at all over this decision. He explained: "(we have) heavy machinery and obviously you work around that machinery." These two contrasting answers were not untypical responses, and this entitles us to hypothesize that an important factor in the range of influence workers have over decisions relating to their work place is technology. In this way GFA validates the results, while at the same time giving additional insight into the variations around a given mean score.

One should also add a note of caution that in marginal[10] cases it is quite possible that an individual does not remember what his reply to a particular question was. In such a case people are inclined to look for explanations of the modal behavior, as demonstrated by the range of scores presented during feedback. However, this is not necessarily a weakness since the discussion invariably centers on those questions on which there is a difference in score. Some indication of validity is then obtained by examining the extent to which these differences represent "real" differences of perception or experience, rather than merely different interpretations of the question. Indeed, it would be possible to analyze intragroup differences according to type, degree and cause. For example:

Type: Whether a given difference was reconcilable/intransigent and systematic/casual.

Degree: Whether it was due to differing perceptions of the same process.

Causes: Whether it was due to different criteria, different experiences or different needs, goals, aspirations, interests, or values.

[9]All questionnaires had been carefully pretested.
[10]That is, where he was undecided as to which category applied to his case.

Questioning the Questionnaire

Although the questionnaires had been carefully pretested, some respondents had difficulty when the question related to very rare events, for instance, sending someone on a training course or transferring them to another job. Alternatively, a respondent may have lacked knowledge about a procedure about which he was asked to provide an answer (e.g., direct consultation). This could constitute useful additional information.

Overall Reactions to Issues Raised by the Questionnaires

This was often considered to be the most important part of the feedback session by the respondents themselves. For example, one group of supervisors explaining their low involvement in work-related decisions, as measured by the influence-power-continuum (IPC) (see Exhibit A in the Appendix) made the point that "often [they] did not receive prior information, so it was impossible [for them] to tell the girls on the lines anything." They agreed that this was sometimes unavoidable, given time constraints and so on. However, they thought that even in such a case, the reason why they lacked information could and should be communicated. This kind of reaction leads us into the second function of GFA, namely providing additional information and understanding of the data.

Producing a Deeper Understanding of the Data

In addition to the respondents' reactions to their particular set of results, they often wanted to talk about their work as a whole, their realationship with superiors, systems of communication, and any grievances they had. They wanted to make sure "you had the picture" and were at pains to point out what was and was not important to them. Discussion, therefore, often went beyond the data to cover not only the existing situation but also what happened in the past, what was expected to happen in the future and even what they would like to happen.

For example, an engineer talked about the irritating circumstance that during an average day he may have four or five "bosses" giving him different instructions. He contrasted this with what happens during overtime:

> Talking of responsibility, take working on a Sunday—no supervision, the men run the plant, same every evening from 5:00—10:00 p.m.; there's nobody here, only a fitter who is solely responsible for keeping the lines and machines running.

Another example concerns the mixed feelings with which one group of engineers viewed direct consultation (discussions with their immediate superior):

> The engineering department has regular meetings and seem to be better informed than other departments, but we aren't told things from outside the department; and even if we brought things up which the engineering department was prepared to act on, we are told that they couldn't take action because of wider implications for other groups.

Discussion about the data during feedback sessions acted as a stimulus to explanation. For example, in Company A the majority of workers had little involvement in work place decisions, and only a moderate opportunity for utilization of their skills. The system of direct consultation was poorly developed or nonexistent. However, in general they were satisfied with their jobs. During the feedback sessions, the point was made over and over again that the "good spirit" and companionship of the "natural" work groups was what made all else bearable. Indeed, they explained that from time to time they came to expect supervision and management to act in a bizarre or incompetent manner, and the best thing to do was a to respond with humorous resignation. The "good spirit" explanation would appear to be substantiated by the statistical results (Drenth et al., 1979). These indicated that group characteristics (as measured by questionnaire GR-CH) was the major determinant of general satisfaction (SAT-G) (see Appendix Exhibit B). Further corroboration came from later stages of the feedback cycle, where this explanation was readily accepted as valid.

The feedback discussions, as has been seen, have supported the statistical findings but they have also extended and deepened them. What our respondents meant to stress when they answered the questionnaire on group characteristics was the pleasant climate associated with interpersonal relations in a "natural" work group. But what is a "natural" work group? As we said earlier, they are people who work closely together on a task. Such a group would have one of its workers as a "leading hand" with very limited authority. By contrast, the supervisor would be in charge of a number of "natural" work groups. These larger groups have neither task similarity nor physical proximity.

This explanation enabled us to unravel a seeming paradox in our results. The statistical findings showed a positive relationship between general satisfaction and group size (the number of people working under a single supervisor). This meant the larger the group, the greater the satisfaction. This apparently contradicted previous research and the results obtained in the other six companies in the DIO study, which all indicated a negative relationship between group size and satisfaction. Indeed, it appeared in sharp contrast to other statistical findings *in the same company,* that there was a strong negative relationship between group size and the other major variables, especially participation (IPC) and skill utilization (SU). This means that as the number of workers under a supervisor increases, so people are less involved in decision-making, fewer of thier skills are utilized, their satisfaction with participation decreases, as does their expectations about the possible benefits of participation. Why then should their general satisfaction increase? The answer becomes apparent from the feedback discussions: *while the number of people working under a single supervisor* has an important influence on the possibility and the extent of participation and peoples' reactions to this, this number has little significance for other elements associated with their work, such as their general satisfaction. This is, as we have previously seen, was primarily influenced by the relations in the smaller "natural" workgroups (*those people who work closely together on a particular task*).

Therefore, to summarize, the apparent paradox is solved by the existence of two meanings for workgroup size: the organizational or hierarchical one (which may comprise the members of several natural work groups). These figures then have differing significance for separate aspects of the respondents' attitudes and behavior. The smaller the natural work group, the greater was the degree of group cohesiveness and general satisfaction (the groups were happy and united, even in otherwise adverse circumstances), whereas the larger the organizational work group (which in this company were associated with large numbers of *small* natural work groups) the less opportunity the members had to participate, use their skills, etc. It also illustrates that for these groups the positive advantages of small work groups held together by task and proximity were considered to outweigh the negative consequences of large organizational work groups held together by a supervisor with line responsibility. This example demonstrates the value of GFA in picking up and explaining apparently contradictory results.

Overall then, one can see that GFA helps to produce a deeper understanding of the data. In particular, the rolling process of group feedback meetings described in Fig. 2 enables ideas, understandings, and explanations to be floated at several levels of an organization. At the same time the discussions could always return to a "hard" data base for testing. This painstaking approach meant that our analysis was eventually accepted by all parties, although, needless to say, the various groups stressed different elements which were important or significant to them.

Opportunity for Mutual Learning: A Facilitator of Change?

The process of repeated cycles and feedback loops using relatively objective information provides a fertile setting for learning. We have just seen that in both British companies the data and the conclusions to which it gave rise, were accepted as valid. Some of the conclusions were drawn by the groups themselves. However, acceptance of facts and reasonable inferences from them do not necessarily lead to action. At the same time we can assume that such a learning process is a stimulus or even a facilitator for action.[11]

In the case of the two British companies, participants felt that feedback sessions were a worthwhile learning experience and there was also wide agreement that the results would seem to require certain changes.[12] The work groups were content to release their (anonymous) results to management, making comments like: "it is a pity we're telling all this to you and not to the plant manager." At the same time they did not believe that any lasting and worthwhile changes would result. This skepticism proved to be prophetic, at least for GFA applied to the first phase of questionnaires.

Management agreed that the results of the research implied that "action should be taken to improve a number of aspects of our operation," in particular the system of direct consultation. Action was promised, but none was forthcoming. The results of the second phase questionnaires confirmed this position and showed there had been no change.

In company B there was an interesting incident when, as a direct consequence of a feedback session to management, the factory and

[11]The research project did not have change as a major objective, but we know from previous experience that GFA produces a favorable climate for reevaluation of current practices. Any change based on such a reevaluation could be treated as other ongoing change in any longitudinal research with organizations. We do not think that our conclusions from the research data would be falsified by such a process. Furthermore, it can be argued that any change produced by a stimulus introduced by the research itself is more easily taken account of in the interpretation of data than the many economic and other changes that occur over a three-year period. The researcher as well as the respondents may be unaware of the impact of the non-researcher-induced changes. Extraneous changes do not affect all groups or departments equally. This is one reason, but there are others, why "control" group methodology is often not appropriate in field research. Deliberate attempts by "change agents" to produce action or new behavior patterns is not covered by the arguments we have adduced. While the deliberate introduction of change was not the major objective in the present project, more intensive forms of GFA can be used for such a purpose and have been successful (Heller, in Graves, 1976).

[12]For a validation of this, refering to the tape transcript is particularly important.

personnel managers decided to change the system of representtion and participation. GFA had shown that the works committee did not function well and that there was a great deal of apathy among the workers as well as their representatives. The data suggested that some way to strengthen the participation system was desirable. The researchers were present when the two senior managers reached this conclusion. To increase interest and bring communication closer to the work force, the managers decided to introduce a two-tier method of representation. The lower tier committee would be closer to the shop floor and free the higher tier to deal with the less immediate issues. A questionnaire was sent out asking for agreement or alternative views. Twenty-seven questionnaires were returned out of a constituency of over 150. Thirteen were for the change, thirteen were against and one made a different proposal. In addition, the present representatives on the works committee were hostile to the suggested change.[13] This finished the initiative. No attempt to deal with the problem by some other means was tried.

DISCUSSION AND CONCLUSION

Feedback methods are a well-established approach among researchers who are interested in organizational change (Mann, 1957; Argyris, 1970; Clark, 1976); they are more frequently used with large-scale surveys than with small groups and a considerable variety of methods have developed (Bouchard, 1976). They are not, however, used for research purposes in most cases.

The present research had as one of its stated objectives the development of field methods sutiable for longitudinal projects. In this article we have briefly described how group feedback analysis was used in combination with questionnaires in two British companies. Similar experiments with GFA were made in the two other contries in which this research was carried out.[14] Moreover, other adaptations of GFA have been used on the non-questionnaire part of the longitudinal study. This too is reported elsewhere (Heller & Brown, 1978).

---

[13]It should however, be noted that they were not consulted about the management initiative and could have regarded the move as a way of undermining their authority.

[14]Their experience will be described in a book which will cover the work of the three country research and should be completed during 1981.

For the moment we conclude that GFA can play a useful part in validating and extending the data base of questionnaires. It also enables potential users of social science research to learn from their experience with the research process. This should facilitate the application of findings even if no immediate or drastic changes are introduced.

APPENDIX

Exhibit A

The Influence-Power Continuum (IPC)

Style 1. No Information

No detailed information about the decision is made available.

Style 2. Information

Fairly detailed information about the decision is made available.

Style 3. Opportunity to Give Advice

Before the decision is made, the superior explains the problem and asks advice. The superior then makes the decision by himself.

Style 4. Advice is Taken Into Consideration

As above, but superior's final choice usually reflects the advice he has received.

Style 5. Joint Decision-Making

Superior and subordinate(s) together analyse the problem and come to a joint decision.

Style 6. Complete Control

Members of the work group are given the authority to deal with this decision on their own.

Exhibit B

Abbreviated Description of Questionnaires

For each questionnaire, a few examples are given.

IPC Influence-Power Continuum

Below is a list of activities or events. Please indicate how you and your work group participate in them.

1. Arranging the layout of your work place.
 :
 :
12. Deciding on who gets overtime and how much.
Scale: six alternatives described in Fig. 2.

SU Skills Utilization

Please think of your own job as it is at the moment. The following is a list of skills, abilities and so on. Please indicate whether you find that your job gives you the opportunity to use them.

1. Initiative
 :
 :
16. Understanding of people
Scale: Seldom, occasionally, usually, almost invariably.

SAT-P Satisfaction with Participation

How frequently, do you feel, does the following occur?

1. My superior asks me for my opinion on matters related to my work
 :
 :
5. When changes occur in my work, I am consulted by my superior

Scale: Almost invariably, usually, occasionally, seldom.

EFF-CONS Effects of Consultation

Consultation may have all sorts of consequences. We would like you to look back on your experience with consultation in your department and to state below what consequences it has had up until now.

1. People know better what is going on in the company.
.
.
.
13. People have gained greater independence and responsibility.

Scale: Yes, definitely; Yes, I tend to think so; I don't think so; definitely not.

EXP-CONS Expectations of Consultation

Could you state below what consequences you expect will happen in the next two or three years in your department as a result of your consultative procedure? Questions and scale are identical with Form EFF-CONS.

R-UU Reasons for Under-Utilization of Skills

My present experience and capacities would be better used if:

1. My work was more challenging.
.
.
.
8. I had the chance of extra schooling and/or training.

Scale: Strongly agree, agree, disagree, strongly disagree.

GR-CH Characteristics of Work-Group

Would you answer the following questions?

1. Does a friendly atmosphere prevail among the people in your group?
.
.
.
10. Does your group produce good and fast results?

Scale: yes, definitely; Yes, I tend to think so; I don't think so; definitely not.

PIF Personal Information Form

This questionnaire asked a series of personal questions about age, sex, education length of service, etc.

REFERENCES

ARGYRIS, C. *Intervention theory and method: A behavioral science view.* Reading: Addison Wesley, 1970.

BOUCHARD, T. J. Field Research Methods: Interviewing, Questionnaires, Participant Observation, Unobtrusive Measures. In M. D. Dunnette (Ed.), *Handbook of industrial and organizational psychololgy.* Chicago: Rand McNally, 1976.

CLARK, A. (Ed.). *Experimenting with organizational life: The action research approach.* New York: Plenum Press, 1976.

DRENTH, P. J. D., KOOPMAN, P. L., RUS, V., ODAR, M., HELLER, F. A., & BROWN, A. Participative decision-making: A comparative study. *Industrial Relations,* 1979, *18,* 295-309.

GRAVES, D. (Ed.), *Management Research: A cross-cultural perspective.* London: Elsevier Scientific Pub. Co., 1973.

HELLER, F. A. Group feed-back analysis: A method of field research, *Psychological Bulletin,* 1969, 72, 2, 1098-117.

HELLER, F. A. Group feed-back analysis as a change agent, *Human Relations,* 1970, *23,* 319-333.

HELLER, F. A., DRENTH, P. J. D., RUS, V., & KOOPMAN, P. L., A Longitudinal study in participative decision-making. *Human Relations,* 1977, *30,* 567-587.

HELLER, F. A., & BROWN, A. Group feed-back analysis applied to longitudinal monitoring of the decision making process. Tavistock Institute Paper, 1978.

MANN, F. C. Studying and Creating Change: A Means to Understanding Social Organization. *Research in Industrial Human Relations,* Industrial Relations Research Association, No. 17, 1957.

WILPERT, B. *Führung in deutschen unternehmen,* Berlin and New York. Walter de Gruyter, 1977.

BIOGRAPHICAL NOTES

ALAN BROWN received a BSc with distinction in the physical sciences, took a diploma in Business Studies and an MSc (Economics) in Industrial Relations before taking up a research position on an Engineering Industry Training Board project. He joined the Tavistock Institute of Human Relations as Research Fellow on the four-year longitudinal study of Decisions in Organizations which is the basis of the present article. He is a part-time tutor at the Open University.

FRANK A. HELLER qualified as a motor car engineer with an advanced City and Guilds Diploma, took an honors BSc in Economics and a PhD in Social Psychology. he was Head of the Department of Management Studies, the Polytechnic of Central London, Consultant to the International Labour Office in Argentina and Chief of Mission, United Nations project on small-scale industry, Visiting Professor at Berkeley and Stanford Universities. At the Tavistock Institute of Human Relations since 1969, he is now Director of its Center for Decision Making Studies.

[35]

Human Relations, Vol. 48, No. 7, 1995

Group Feedback Analysis Applied to Longitudinal Monitoring of the Decision Making Process

Frank Heller[1,3] and Alan Brown[2]

The paper describes the application to longitudinal research of a method of data collection which combines quantitative and qualitative material. It is claimed that Group Feedback Analysis (GFA) helps to validate data collected by various methods and produces additional ethnographic material and insight into the process under investigation. When the people who supply the data are experienced in the subject matter, as is the case with managers and other employees in organizational research, GFA makes it possible for them to help with the interpretation of the data instead of leaving it entirely to the researcher. The method, which has previously been used in cross-sectional research, is shown to have utility in a longitudinal design where it can facilitate organizational learning. It can also contribute to the refinement of a theoretical model.

KEY WORDS: decision making; longitudinal design; multi-method design; field method; group feedback analysis; motivated competence model.

INTRODUCTION

Organizational analysis takes many different forms and employs a range of methodologies. One widely used approach is through distributed questionnaires in a cross-sectional design reaching fairly large but rarely representative samples of people involved in the phenomenon under investigation. A contrasting approach is to rely on in-depth case studies of a necessarily very small number of organizations, often without quantification.

As Bryman (1992) has pointed out, the debate about the superiority of positivistic or nonpositivistic methods of research seems to have in-

[1]30 Tabernacle Street, London EC2A 4DE.
[2]Department of Education Studies, University of Surrey.
[3]Requests for reprints should be addressed to Frank Heller, 30 Tabernacle Street, London EC2A 4DE.

0018–7267/95/0700–0815$07.50/1 © 1995 The Tavistock Institute

tensified since the 1960s. While triangulation through the application of different methods to the same problem has been advocated from time to time there are "a number of barriers to the integration of quantitative and qualitative research. One barrier . . .(is the) view that (they) are based upon fundamentally incompatible epistemological positions" (Bryman, 1992, p. 153). Perhaps as a consequence, different university departments favor one approach and directly, or by implication, criticize the other.

The polarization of research designs is more easily sustained where research is carried out within a single social science discipline or where application to practical problems or policy relevant solutions is not the primary objective. We are prepared to argue that where research outcomes can be tested in the field, or where they are seen primarily as solving specific problems, some form of triangulation or combined methodologies would be advantageous. Such a situation exists in organizational and management research which has to combine a number of different attributes, but principally quality and relevance.

The point has been stressed in a recent assessment and evaluation of management research by the British Economic and Social Research Council (1994). In the section which deals with the need for relevance in organization research, the Report of the Commission on Management Research argues for an improvement in quality by "increasing the stakeholding that users have at various stages of the research process . . ." (p. 27). One way of interpreting this is to allow the experienced managers and other employees who supply organization researchers with data to help with this interpretation. This can be achieved by a feedback method to be described in this article. The method, which is called Group Feedback Analysis (GFA), gives managers and other employees the opportunity to check on validity, omissions, and possible misunderstandings as well as to help with interpretation (Heller, 1969; Brown & Heller, 1981). Traditional methods, particularly surveys, but to some extent also nonquantitative methods rely entirely on the judgment of the researcher for the interpretation of results. It is likely that this reduces the richness and utility of the conclusions and the likelihood that they will be applied.

A previous paper has described GFA applied to short-term operational decisions and found that it was able to correct important misconstructions of data interpretation (Brown & Heller, 1981). Longitudinal research is, of course, much more demanding of the participating organizations than the more conventional cross-sectional "snapshot" research. But for certain social science topics, for instance decision making, an investigation of the total process which can extend over months and years may be necessary. In such situations, continuous process monitoring

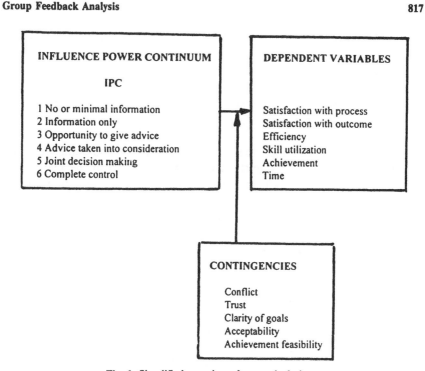

Fig. 1. Simplified overview of research design.

as in participant observation is rarely possible, but a diachronic[4] longitudinal method can use GFA as a way of validating and extending data collected by a variety of different methods. The additional ethnographic material includes explanations and probable causal relationships by drawing on the judgment and experience of employees at various levels. By feeding back research-based material and encouraging the participating groups to explain this through their own diverse experiences, the researcher obtains a deeper understanding of interpersonal and organizational events. This understanding can, under favorable circumstances, produce organizational learning and may precipitate change.

THE DIO RESEARCH PROJECT

The present analysis is derived from a 4-year project in three countries. Large parts of it have been described (DIO, 1979; DIO, 1983; Heller

[4]Diachronic, in the context of this research, is a method of following longitudinal processes by a variety of means (documentary evidence, interviewing, attendance at meetings, etc.) at sufficiently regular intervals to obtain a reliable picture of all critical events.

et al., (1988) but the volume and diversity of the data allows us to extract further useful material in relation to organizational issues which remain similar over time.

The Decisions in Organizations (DIO) project set out to investigate the relationship between six distinct methods of making decisions[5] and a variety of contingency and dependent variables briefly summarized in Fig. 1.

This article draws upon the extensive qualitative and some quantitative field data collected during the 4-year DIO research in the two British companies. The study produced a very considerable amount of evidence which was not fully analyzed at the time. From more recent research on similar decisions (IDE, 1993) we conclude that the decision issues analyzed here remain valid.

Betacomb was an only moderately profitable, medium-sized paint manufacturer, employing about 300 people, and operating in South East England. The production process was semi-batch, and much of the equipment and machinery was old. Only the technical staff of the factory were unionized.

The other company, which we will call Recup, was a highly profitable, medium-sized pharmaceuticals manufacturer operating in a new purpose-built factory in the northwest of England with just over 400 employees. Much of its technology was semi-automatic and over 90% of the workers belonged to one of three unions.

Both companies are multinationals. Betacomb is British based, while Recup is American owned. The longitudinal processes observed involved sets of strategic and tactical decisions described in Appendix A.

The diachronic research method divided the decision-making process into four phases: (1) start up phase; (2) development phase; (3) finalization phase, and (4) implementation phase.

While a phase design is still unusual (Mintzberg *et al.,* 1976), it has been shown to have utility (Fröhlich, Gill, & Krieger, 1991).

GROUP FEEDBACK ANALYSIS

GFA bears a limited resemblance to survey feed-back methods which have been used fairly extensively since the 1950s (Jenkins, 1948; Mann, 1957; Baumgartel, 1959; Chase, 1978; Brown, 1972; Greller & Herold, 1975; Nadler, 1976; Meijer & Roe, 1993), but there are important differences. Survey feedback tends to be used with large groups and usually one of its

---

[5]Called the Influence-Power-Continuum (IPC) which had been used in several previous projects (Heller & Wilpert, 1981; IDE, 1981).

objectives is periodically to assess the morale or job satisfaction of departments or organizations. The feedback can then be a tool of evaluation or control or an assessment of leadership. While it has also been used to create favorable conditions for improving performance and/or the facilitation of change (Heller, 1970), the original use of GFA was as a method of research. The objective was to work with small to medium-size groups to improve the quality of the research data and to add qualitative material to statistical information (Heller, 1969). It is the extension of these original aims with which we are concerned in the present article.

GFA has three phases:

(i) Data collection which can be by questionnaire but in the present case came from a variety of sources, including interviews (based on a schedule), minutes of meetings, and observation of committees.

(ii) Data analysis. All quantitative information was transferred to summary charts, often presented in simple frequency distributions and/or averages (as in Table 1). Ethnographic descriptive information was based on field diaries.

(iii) Feedback meetings. The collected material, be it quantitative or ethnographic, is fed back to the people who provided it in the first place. Table 1 shows one kind of data used in small group presentations. The horizontal axis is made up of scores describing the decision behavior of five levels of organization during the four phases of the decision cycle. The vertical dimension covers seven longitudinal decisions. The figures in each cell describe the amount of influence which each level of the organization has within the four decision phases for each task. The measure of influence is described in the Table.

Table I is a summary of several feedback sessions; each would deal with only one decision issue and sometime with only one phase. Feedback meetings and some committee meetings were tape recorded and transcribed for content analysis.[6]

OBJECTIVES OF GFA

There are three objectives: one is to assess the validity of the information by asking the people who provided the raw data (by what they said or what they did), to check on its accuracy. Second, we use the feedback information as a trigger to obtain in-depth descriptive accounts of the often complex decision process, hidden agendas, conflicts and fuller explanations of motives or antecedent circumstances. Third, we believe that people who have sanctioned the research and spent time and effort responding to ques-

---

[6]For fuller details of the transcripts, see Heller *et al.*, 1988, Appendix VI, pp. 192-203.

Table I. Example of the Material Provided During a Group Feedback Analysis Meeting with Middle Level Managers

	Involvement in capital investment decisions																			
	Start up					Development					Finalization					Implementation				
	A	B	C	D	E	A	B	C	D	E	A	B	C	D	E	A	B	C	D	E
1. Factory Reorganization	1	2	5	5	1	1	3	4	6	1	2	3	4	4	2			NOT YET		
2. Attritor	1	2	4	6	1	1	5	5	2	1	1	1	2	6	2	2	5	5	1	2
3. Dynamill	1	1	6	2	1	1	3	6	2	1	2	4	5	5	2	3	4	5	5	1
4. Cavitator	1	1	6	2	1	1	2	6	3	1	1	2	5	5	2			NOT YET		
5. New can store	1	2	6	4	1	1	4	6	4	2	1	2	4	5	2	2	4	6	2	2
6. Warehouse reorganization	1	4	6	4	1	1	4	6	4	1	1	2	4	6	1	2	4	6	2	2
7. Modification to filling dep.	1	4	6	4	1	1	4	6	4	1	1	3	4	6	1			NOT YET		
Average involvement per phase of each group	1	2.3	5.6	3.3	1	1.1	3.6	5.6	3.6	1.1	1.3	2.4	4	5.3	1.7	2.3	4.3	5.5	2.5	1.8

[a]Workers = A; Supervisors = B; Middle management = C; Top management = D; Works committee = E.

[b]Overall average involvement (on the IPC scale of 1–6); Workers = 1.3, supervisors = 3, middle management = 5.1, top management = 3.8, works committee = 1.4.

[c]Influence-power continuum (IPC) 1 = no or minimal information, 2 = information only, 3 = opportunity to give advice, 4 = advice taken into consideration, 5 = joint decision-making, 6 = complete control.

tions, have a right to know what we make of the material and to add their own interpretation. In this way, the participants gain an understanding of organizational dynamic processes and can use this in adjusting their behavior if that seems appropriate. Feedback material can be ethnographic rather than quantitative. We found that the information provided in these feedback meetings was appreciated and helped to sustain the research momentum during the 4 years of field work. Our full interpretation of the data was only made available at the end of the project and it included our own learning from the GFA process.

USING GFA OVER SPACE-TIME

Most tactical and strategic decisions are handled by more than one person, at more than one level and may take weeks, months, and sometimes years from the first discussions to final implementation. Any monitoring of these events has to take account of this space–time dimension and any new key respondents have to be introduced to the GFA process. Whenever the research starts, several decisions will already be in progress; for instance budget forecasting may start in August, while the first visit to Betacomb took place in October. To avoid waiting until the beginning of the next cycle, we used retrospective tracing through selected interviews and any available documentary evidence, like committee minutes. When this material was assembled, we held a GFA session with those involved with the objectives described earlier. Since the researcher was in the factory only once a week or even less frequently, some *retrospective tracing* was necessary if events between visits had moved quickly on an important issue under investigation.

As decision processes are traced backward and their complexity is revealed, there is a tendency for the number of "key persons" involved to grow. This *snowballing effect* tends to spread the enquiry through the organization, across departments and hierarchical levels. The current processes are investigated through observation of committees, meetings and through interviews. This *process registration* ascertains how people felt about the issue and what they expected to happen at different stages in the decision cycle. In this way, the researchers could build a profile of the decision process for each key participant. The categories used to analyze the process are given in Appendix B.

The number of people interviewed varied with the nature of the decision. If different hierarchical levels or groups were involved, then at least one from each group would be in our sample. If the picture being built up revealed significant differences of interpretation, we would interview a greater number of those involved. When we had gathered comprehensive

SEQUENCE OF EVENTS OF A TYPICAL DECISION PROCESS
USING GROUP FEEDBACK ANALYSIS

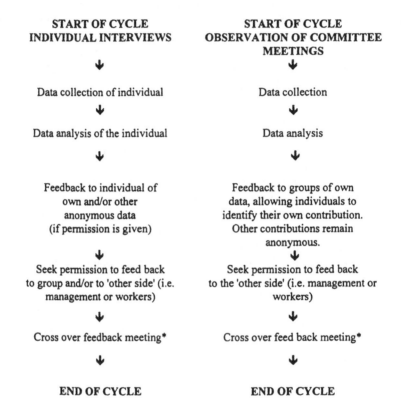

START OF CYCLE	**START OF CYCLE**
INDIVIDUAL INTERVIEWS	OBSERVATION OF COMMITTEE
	MEETINGS
↓	↓
Data collection of individual	Data collection
↓	↓
Data analysis of the individual	Data analysis
↓	↓
Feedback to individual of own and/or other anonymous data (if permission is given)	Feedback to groups of own data, allowing individuals to identify their own contribution. Other contributions remain anonymous.
↓	↓
Seek permission to feed back to group and/or to 'other side' (i.e. management or workers)	Seek permission to feed back to the 'other side' (i.e. management or workers)
↓	↓
Cross over feedback meeting*	Cross over feed back meeting*
↓	↓
END OF CYCLE	**END OF CYCLE**

* Cross over meeting crosses over anonymous information from one level to another (middle to senior management) or from workers to management or *vice versa* or from one union to another.

Fig. 2.

and verified accounts from the individuals involved, the information was ready to be used at GFA sessions.

It is important to stress that all interview material was guaranteed anonymity. Individuals could not be identified when data was fed back for discussion. Furthermore, a group had to give permission before its own data (though without personal identification) could be shared with another group for GFA.

The initial GFA sessions would attempt to obtain an agreed profile of the decision issue. The sessions would focus upon and seek to resolve any differences in interpretation, although the discussion itself could be used by the researchers to contextualize further the understanding of the decision process.

The search for agreement in homogeneous groups was important in that, after permission, profiles could be exchanged with other groups at joint GFA sessions. At joint sessions between different levels or between management and unions, less emphasis was put on reaching agreement since some conflicts of interest and interpretation was legitimate. Instead, the discussion opened out to broader issues, with the data acting as a starting point and a base to which to return. These GFA sessions were a very rich source of information for the researchers. The sequence of events in the use of GFA is represented in Fig. 2, which shows that the cycle is slightly different for individual interviews or group meetings.

PRODUCING A DEEPER UNDERSTANDING OF THE DECISION PROCESS

One example of this emerged in discussions with worker representatives on the works and safety committees in Betacomb. They agreed that they had been given every opportunity to become involved in a number of issues; nevertheless they were deeply dissatisfied with the decision-making process (Appendix B, Item 9). This result is the reverse of that reported from most previous research, which finds high involvement in decision-making to correlate with high satisfaction (for instance Likert, 1961; Wall & Lischeron, 1977; IDE, 1981). Left alone, the researcher would find it impossible to explain such a counterintuitive relationship. However, during the later stages of a GFA session, the representatives pinpointed the lack of training as a key explanatory factor in their dissatisfaction. Subsequently, when the researchers asked several managers for their views on the involvement of workers in the newly formed committees, they said they were satisfied and did not see the necessity for training. In subsequent months, evidence accumulated that representatives often felt they could not participate effectively because they lacked skills or knowledge and were sometimes unclear about their roles and responsibilities, especially as safety representatives.

Eventually at a joint GFA session almost a year later, management did accept the need for representatives to receive more training. However, the importance for the researchers' understanding of the decision processes was the way that GFA highlighted the significance of the training issue, and how this could then be monitored as an undercurrent in management's thinking before it surfaced as a major issue months later.

The feedback evidence of a relationship between knowledge and participation reinforced statistical findings from the total sample of decision issues (Heller *et al.*, 1988, pp. 9, 220). The GFA data drew attention to a relatively neglected aspect of participation research, that is to say, the importance of competence in effective influence-sharing behavior. Further evidence from various studies has now led to an adaptation of the Human Resources model described by Miles (1965). The adaptation has been called the "Motivated Competence Model" and stresses the role of competence as a requisite antecedent of effective participate behavior (Heller, 1992). Other recent evidence from Sweden has given further support to the need for developing experience and skill before semi-autonomous groups can function effectively (Ellegard, 1992). It took time to develop this knowledge, although to some extent it was already apparent in the early Tavistock studies in British coal boards (Trist *et al.*, 1963).

GFA sessions at Recup uncovered another important issue relating to safety. Long delays had been evidenced over a number of issues and a comment was made that "there is a feeling that the minimum possible is being done about safety . . .and when issues are brought up, there are long delays in implementation" (for example, on Item 17, Appendix A). After some initial attempts to shift the blame, discussion focused upon attitudes that treated safety as an expense item. It was possible to follow this line of reasoning, in committee discussion and at subsequent interviews. Factory management at Recup were much readier than at Betacomb to incur direct costs on safety issues. Here the "safety as an expense" attitude operated in a more indirect way, in that there were insufficient engineers on site to carry out the required modifications. Factory management believed that the size of the indirect labor budget was one of the criteria on which management efficiency was judged.

In such circumstances, maintenance engineering was kept short-staffed and priority was given to crisis maintenance to keep production going. As a consequence, it was relatively rare for engineers to have sufficient spare capacity to deal with urgent safety issues unless these had an immediate effect on production.

The deepened understanding of safety issues generated in the GFA sessions also informed the understanding of other issues. Thus the approach to engineering permeated other processes, such as those related to capital investment. All those involved in capital investment decisions seemed well satisfied up to and including the finalization phase, yet problems continually arose during implementation. Indeed, these problems were so commonplace that they were built into the expectations of top management, who regarded them as inevitable teething problems. They even made allowance for extensive delay in implementation and initial under-performance in their budget forecasts.

Looked at from the perspective of those middle managers and supervisors charged with installing and using the new machinery, the picture appeared somewhat confused. With the insights gained from the GFA safety discussions, it was possible to tease out the relationship between particular cases and more fundamental cases. Through discussion of specific instances, it became clear that middle management considered there was nothing inevitable about the teething problems. They identified three more basic causes. First, their lack of involvement at earlier stages of the decision meant that middle management lacked the direct experience to enable them to anticipate and overcome potential problems. Second, there was no active review of previous capital investment implementation to see if lessons could be learned about the process itself. The final factor, as in the previous example, was the use of engineers primarily to respond to crises in production. They found it dispiriting that they had continually "to make do and mend," even with new equipment.

The problems did not stop there, however. The engineers' work was made doubly frustrating in that, unlike in some other factories when the temporary demise of some machinery might give operators a respite, here, operators had to work much harder on other tasks if machines on the line were not operating smoothly. Hence there was a tendency for mutual recrimination between operators and engineers, with each group seeing the inadequacies of the other as the cause of their problems. This surfaced in our analysis of several other decisions, where a clear chain of events could be established between conflicts over particular shop floor issues and failures in more strategic decision-making. Such connections were not made in judging the effectiveness of those decisions so that management was unaware of the sequence and occasionally thought it operated in reverse.

The irony of the crisis maintenance approach was that overriding concern with immediate issues of production exacerbated problems over the long term. Staff from the engineering department could not spare the time to be involved in earlier stages of the decision process when deliberations about the acquisition and installation of new equipment took place, because of the more pressing problems associated with the implementation of the previous installation. Thus a classic vicious circle was set up.

This analysis, although challenged initially, was accepted as accurate by these most closely involved after further corroboration at a joint GFA session. Since top management was present, and capital investment decisions were considered of prime importance, the question arises whether the disclosure of this information through GFA would elicit some commitment to change. This brings us to the third function of GFA, namely as an opportunity for mutual learning.

OPPORTUNITY FOR MUTUAL LEARNING

The process of repeated cycles and feedback loops using relatively objective information, provides a fertile setting for learning. It allows the data and any inferences from it to be carefully examined and accepted as valid, since the evidence is drawn from the respondents themselves during preceding interviews or at earlier GFA sessions. This process has been called Research-Action (Heller, 1986).[7]

While individuals may well learn more about decision-making processes as a result of GFA, in an organizational setting it is perhaps more appropriate to look at the position of particular groups and see whether it is possible to institutionalize some of the lessons learned from a reflection on the decision processes.

Representatives and shop stewards were forthright in welcoming the opportunity to discuss issues and were nearly always ready to exchange their opinions with management in joint GFA sessions. There was a variety of reasons for this: first, in both companies, representatives felt management deliberately procrastinated and this would be highlighted through feedback sessions. Secondly, there were many issues on which they were unhappy with the outcome, and this would be an opportunity to register their views or perhaps continue the dialogue through GFA. Third, it often provided an interesting break from their work. However, although they were generally glad of another opportunity to "tell management exactly what we think of them," they did not believe that the research would necessarily result in any lasting change. They felt that the intervention through GFA was capable of challenging the *status quo* by generating discussion on alternatives and this could lead to requests for change.

In general, management, too, were highly cooperative, and keen to discuss a wide range of issues. They were frank about some of the problems and questioned the value of certain procedures and methods of operation. However, group feedback sessions with managers from different levels or departments were sometimes less open. It seemed that some managers felt

[7]Research-Action differs from Action Research in putting more resources into the scientific fact-finding phase before attempts are made to implement the results. Research-Action is therefore appropriate when our knowledge of the phenomenon in question, organizational decision-making for instance, is fairly rudimentary. When a scientific paradigm is fairly well established, as for instance in the case of the socio-technical model, much less prior investigation may be necessary and the method is then appropriately called Action Research.

their position was threatened and consequently attempted to defend their present or past actions. At the same time, some of the most interesting discussions occurred when there was conflict of opinion among managers over current practices.

There was, for instance, considerable debate about the value of budget forecasting. Middle managers often complained of its distorting effect on day-to-day operations, while top management and the finance departments saw it as an invaluable tool for planning and action. Feedback meetings drew attention to the cost of Budget Forecasting (BF) as well as to its limited accuracy. The need for BF was not doubted by any of the senior managers interviewed in both companies. However, middle managers who had to provide the raw material for the forecast and who bore the brunt of responsibility for adhering to the budget once it was agreed, saw the cost of this procedure more clearly than the benefits. By contrast, the senior managers, and particularly the Financial Controllers, were convinced that the company could not operate without BF and were less willing than lower levels to countenance the possibility that the system was more elaborate and costly than the benefits would seem to justify.

It should not be thought that the researchers believed that BF is an unnecessary procedure, but instead of being made more complex, it could have been simplified and made less demanding in manpower. This was also the privately expressed view of the Chief Accountant at one company (Heller *et al.*, 1988, p. 168). We raised the cost and low accuracy issue several times during feedback sessions but our comments were met with blank stares and incredulity. It became clear that existing financial processes were thought to be beyond challenge.

Budget forecasting is one of the medium-term decisions which we traced for 3 years but here it is used only as an example of the opportunity provided by repeated GFA sessions for mutual learning and insight into the complexities of the decision process. However, it would be unrealistic to expect an organization to change its BF system solely on the basis of the evidence we provided; its function and structure is much too firmly established. We have seen that top management tends to regard BF as a managerial control mechanism (Argyris, 1952; Lowe & Shaw, 1968; Berry & Otley, 1975; Hopwood, 1976). From this point of view, any increase in flexibility and lower level inputs to decision making, could be seen as a reduction in top management power and in particular as a challenge to the position of the Finance Department.[8] Middle-level managers were able to learn from GFA and received some satisfaction from the knowledge

[8]In both companies the head office finance department, and in Betacomb the Financial Controller, were more powerful than their equivalents in production.

that this issue had been raised and was almost unanimously accepted by departmental and functional managers, including the chief accountant.

DISCUSSION

GFA provides opportunities for managers and other employees as well as researchers to learn about individual and group attitudes, values, and organizational processes. When managers and employees become aware of problems and possible improvements, they may, under favorable circumstances, decide to act on the basis of the new knowledge. This is the approach taken by Action Research or its variant Research Action (Heller, 1986, pp. 4-5). Both methods are designed to bridge the gap between research findings and action, but this kind of bridge-building is not always successful. Reviews of the literature on the utilization of social science findings, show that there are many obstacles (Karapin, 1986; Bulmer, 1982; Nowotony & Lambiri-Dimaki, 1985). Argyris had faced the challenge of converting theoretical knowledge into action for several decades (Argyris, 1970, 1974, 1985). However, success may more easily be achieved if pressures external to the organization, like unfavorable economic conditions or new technology, coincide with internally generated organizational learning (Dunphy, 1990).

Since GFA facilitates organizational learning, any change resulting from this process is voluntary and not induced through the hierarchy or based on the interpretation or recommendation of consultants. As we have seen, organizational learning has utility even if, at least in the short term, it does not always lead to observable change.

From the research point of view and quite independent of facilitating change, we have show that GFA verifies, enlarges and deepens our knowledge of interpersonal and organizational processes. Conventional methods, like questionnaires or formal interviews based on prepared schedules, may yield a wealth of data but leave the interpretation of the evidence, and particularly its internal causal connectedness to the judgment of the researcher.

Under GFA, the researcher's interpretation is augmented or even superseded by the experience and judgments of the people who provided the data in the first place. These experience-based interpretations often suggest causal connections that strengthen or correct conclusions made by traditional analysis methods.

The principal objective of this report on the use of GFA is to give some examples of the insight into organizational decision-making processes which complement evidence from questionnaires, interviews, attendance at meetings, and company documents.

There are two requirements for insight and learning; first, validation of data, and second, enlargement of knowledge. Validation takes place in the opening GFA question: "This is what we think happened, is this correct?" The second question is "OK. So what do you make of it?" or "How do you explain it?"[9]

GFA sessions have to be conducted in an atmosphere of trust and in a spirit of enquiry. After an initial pause and sometimes helped by a little prompting, the analysis rapidly gathered momentum and was sometimes difficult to bring to an end. We have reviewed some of the results of decisions relating to safety issues to illustrate two ways in which GFA enriches our understanding of organizational events. Once the validity of the data has been accepted by our respondents, the first results may give a preliminary explanation, almost like a "presenting problem." Betacomb worker representatives faced with evidence of extensive opportunities for participative involvement during safety committee meetings but high levels of dissatisfaction agreed that this was a correct interpretation of results and confirmed their experience. Only toward the end of the GFA session did they venture the explanation that lack of technical knowledge prevented them from using the participative opening to their satisfaction. This led to more evidence of a similar kind and a demand for more training which was eventually accepted by management after several GFA sessions.

The initial response to the ineffectiveness of the safety committee at Recup was to highlight the inordinate delay before a satisfactory technical solution was achieved. Starting with this "presenting problem," GFA discussion moved on to blame middle management's reluctance to increase indirect labor cost by not hiring staff with sufficient engineering skills to handle the safety issues. While this was accepted as the cause of the slow progress in the implementation phase and employee dissatisfaction, a deeper problem emerged during GFA with head office management. It seems that despite efforts by senior management, middle management perseverated the stereotype that their own success would be judged by the indirect to direct cost ratio and this is why they cut down on preventive maintenance. However, senior management had adopted quite different ways of judging efficiency but had not communicated this effectively to operational levels.

---

[9]These openings and follow-up questions have to adjust themselves to the exact issue under discussion. The only requirement is that the question is neutral and does not suggest that the researcher has a preference.

GFA can therefore be a valuable way for generating additional insight and deepening understanding of longitudinal decision processes. It can do this because the methodology mirrors the decision process in its dynamic and developmental nature. Finally, it is suggested that an understanding of causal relationships between interpersonal or organizational events derived from GFA may also improve the theoretical models with which social scientists work. Models tend to be based on cross-sectional data although arrows suggest causal relationships and a sequence of events. We used the example of the Human Resources Model (see Fig. 3) to suggest a causal relationship between participation, an improved decision making capability and improved satisfaction. It is questionable, however, whether this Model can be used to explain other findings on decision-making, for instance the limited success of legislative provision for employee participation in organizational decision-making in some European countries (see IDE, 1993; Schienstock, 1989). Evidence generated by GFA, as well as from other sources, was used to consider a modification and extension of the model by specifying relevant competence as a necessary antecedent for effective participative decision-making (Heller *et al.*, 1988, pp. 145-147, 151-152, 216-217; O'Brien, 1979; Rus, 1984; Heller, 1991).

Consequently, following a review of other research findings in support of such an extension, a new model was formulated (Heller, 1992). It is called the "Motivated Competence Model" on the assumption that providing opportunities for participation alone—for instance in the consultative meetings at Betacomb dealing with safety issues—without giving participants the relevant experience and skill, is unlikely to be motivating (Fig. 4). Competence derived from experience and training is now considered to be an essential precondition for effective participation.

CONCLUSIONS

Field research studies in organizations use a very limited range of methods. In cross-sectional investigations, questionnaires are most fre-

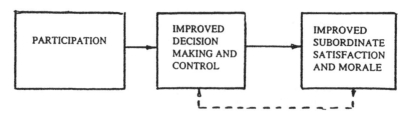

Fig. 3. The human resources model (from Miles, 1965)

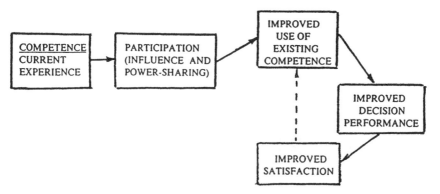

Fig. 4. The Motivated Competence Model (a modified version)

quently used while longitudinal research tends to concentrate on case studies. The former approach is almost exclusively statistical and the latter descriptive.

Relatively few research techniques explore the middle ground between quantification and description. Interview data is sometimes quantified or reported descriptively and occasionally more than one method is used in the same study. Group Feedback Analysis is a middle ground method designed to use questionnaire or interview data (quantitative or descriptive) as a trigger for further exploration and validation in which the views of managers and other employees can be incorporated. Previous reports of GFA were based on cross-sectional data, while the present article describes how the method was applied to a diachronic study lasting 4 years.

APPENDIX A

Recup company

1. Set-up of safety committee
2. Recognition of union to represent staff employees
3. Line extension 1
4. Line extension 2
5. New filler and capper
6. New compounding tanks
7. Cookroom refurbishing
8. Warehouse extension
9. Tableting extension
10. Budget forecasting: Cycle 1.
11. Budget forecasting: Cycle 2.

Betacomb Company

1. Set-up of works committee

2. Set-up of safety committee
3. First reorganization of safety committee
4. Second reorganization of safety committee
5. Set-up of staff committee
6. Set-up of supervisors committee
7. Factory reorganization
8. Attritor improvements
9. Dynamill improvements
10. Cavitator improvements
11. New can store
12. Warehouse reorganization
13. Modification to filling department
14. Shrink-wrapper
15. Budget forecasting: Cycle 1
16. Budget forecasting: Cycle 2
17. Retail wood preservative - Expansion of capacity
18. Trade wood preservative - Expansion of capacity
19. Hand cleaner - Expansion of capacity
20. White spirit - Expansion of capacity

APPENDIX B.
THE CATEGORIES USED TO ANALYZE THE DECISION PROCESS

1. The influence-power continuum (IPC)
2. Stages in the decision cycle
3. Skill under-utilization
4. Trust
5. Conflict
6. Status power
7. Meta power (outside influence)
8. Satisfaction with process
9. Satisfaction with outcome
10. Achievement feasibility
11. Clarity of goals
12. Non-implementation
13. Achievement
14. Acceptability
15. Who is involved
16. Time structure

REFERENCES

ARGYRIS, C. *The impact of budgets on people.* New York: Controllership Institute, 1952.
ARGYRIS, C. *Intervention theory and method: A behavioral science view.* Reading, MA: Addison-Wesley, 1970.
ARGYRIS, C., & SCHON, D. *Theory in practice: Increasing professional effectiveness.* San Francisco: Jossey-Bass, 1974.
ARGYRIS, C. *Strategy change and defensive routines.* Boston: Pitman, 1985.

Group Feedback Analysis   **833**

BAUMGARTEL, H. Using employee questionnaire results for improving organizations. *Kansas Business Review*, 1959, *12*, 2-6.

BERRY, A. J., & OTLEY, D. T. The aggregation of estimates in hierarchical organizations. *Journal of Management Studies*, (1975), *12*, 175-193.

BROWN, L. D. Research action: Organizational feedback and change. *Journal of Applied Behavioral Science*, 1972, *8*, 697-674.

BROWN, A. J., & HELLER, F. A. The application of Group Feedback Analysis to questionnaire data in a longitudinal study. *Human Relations*, 1981, *34*(2), 141-156.

BRYMAN, A. *Quantity and quality in social science research*. London: Routledge, 1992.

BULMER, M. *The use of social research: Social investigation in public policy making*. London: Allen & Unwin, 1982.

CHASE, P. A survey feedback approach to organization development. *Proceedings of the Executive Study Conference*. Educ. Test Service, Princeton, 1968.

DIO (Decisions in Organizations research group), Decisions in organizations: A comparative study. *Industrial Relations*, 1979, *18*, 295-309.

DIO, A contingency model of participative decision making: An analysis of 56 decisions in three Dutch organizations. *Journal of Occupational Psychology*, 1983, *56*, 1-18.

DUNPHY, D. *Under new management: Australian organizations in transition*. Sydney: McGraw-Hill, 1990.

ECONOMIC AND SOCIAL RESEARCH COUNCIL, *Building Partnerships: Enhancing the Quality of Management Research*. The Report of the Commission on Management Research, Economic and Social Research Council, Swindon, UK, 1994.

ELLEGARD. K., ENGSTROM, T., & NILSSON, L. *reforming industrial work: principles and realities*. Swedish Work Environment Fund Pamphlet 64, Vol. 19, 1992, p. 307.

FRÖHLICH, D., GILL, C. & KRIEGER H. *Roads to participation in the European community*—Increasing prospects of employee representatives in technological change. Dublin: European Foundation for the Improvement of Living and Working Conditions, 1991.

GRELLER, M. & HEROLD, D. Sources of feed-back: A preliminary investigation. Organizational Behavior and Human Performance, 1975, 13, 244-256.

HELLER, F. A. Group feed-back analysis: A method of field research. *Psychological Bulletin*, 1969, 72, 108-117.

HELLER, F. A. Group feed-back analysis as a change agent. *Human Relations*, 1970, *23*, 319-333.

HELLER, F. A. (Ed.). *The use and abuse of social science*. London and Beverly Hills: Sage Publications, 1986.

HELLER, F. A., DRENTH, P., KOOPMAN, P. & RUS, V. *Decisions in organizations: A longitudinal study of routine, tactical and strategic decisions*. London and Beverly Hills: Sage Publications, 1988.

HELLER, F. A. Participation and competence: A necessary relationship. In W. Lafferty and E. Rosenstein (Eds.), *International Handbook of participation in organizations* (Vol. 2). Oxford University Press, 1991.

HELLER, F. A. Decision making and the under-utilization of competence. In F. Heller (Ed.), *Decision making and leadership*. Cambridge: Cambridge University Press, 1992.

HELLER, F. A. & WILPERT, B. *Competence and power in managerial decision making: A study of senior levels of organization in eight countries*. Chichester: John Wiley & Sons, 1981.

HELLER, F. A., DRENTH, P. J. D., KOOPMAN, P., & RUS, V. *Decision in organizations: A longitudinal study of routine, tactical and strategic decisions*. London and Beverly Hills: Sage Publications, 1988.

HOPWOOD, A. *Accounting and human behavior*. New Jersey: Prentice-Hall, 1976.

IDE (Industrial Democracy in Europe research group). *Industrial democracy in Europe*. Oxford: Oxford University Press, 1981.

IDE (Industrial Democracy in Europe research group). *Industrial democracy in Europe revisited*. Oxford: Oxford University Press, 1993.

JENKINS, D. H. Feedback and group evaluations. *Journal of Social issues*, 1948, *4*(2), 50-60.

KARAPIN, R. S. A review of the literature. In F. A. Heller (Ed.), *The use and abuse of social science*. London: Sage, 1986.

LIKERT, R. *New patterns of management*. New York: McGraw-Hill, 1961.

LOWE, E. A. & SHAW, R. W. An analysis of managerial biasing: Evidence from a company's budgeting process. *Journal of Management Studies*, 1968.

MANN, F. C. Studying or creating change: A means to understanding social organization. *Research in Industrial Human Relations*, Industrial Relations Research Association, No. 17, 1957.

MEIJER, T. & ROE, R. A. The Analysis and Design of Mental Information Work: A Method Based on the Action Facilitation Approach. WORC Paper 93.01.002/3, *Paper presented at the Sixth European Congress on Work and Organizational psychology*, Alicante, April 14–17, 1993.

MILES, R. E. Human relations or human resources? *Harvard Business Review*, 1965, *43*, 148-163.

MINTZBERG, H., RAISINGHAM, D., & THEORET, A. The structure of "unstructured" decision processes. *Administrative Science Quarterly*, 1976, *21*, 246-275.

NADLER, D. The use of feed-back for organizational change. *Group and Organization Studies*, 1976, *1*, 177-186.

NOWOTNY, H. LAMBIRI-DIMAKI, J. (Eds.), *The difficult dialogue between producers and users of social science research*. Vienna: European Center for Social Welfare Training and Research, 1985.

O'BRIEN, G. E. The Centrality of Skill Utilization for Job Design. *Bedford Park, The Flinders University of South Australia, Working Paper Series No. 37*, 1979.

RUS, V. Yugoslav Self-Management: 30 years later. In B. Wilpert and A. Sorge (Eds.), *International yearbook of organizational democracy* (Vol. II), Chichester: John Wiley & Sons, 1984.

SCHIENSTOCK, G. Industrial relations theory and employee participation. In C. Lammers and G. Szell (Eds.), *International handbook of participation in organizations* (Vol. 1). Oxford: Oxford University Press, 1989.

TRIST, E. L., HIGGIN, G. W., MURRAY, H., & POLLOCK, A. B. *Organizational choice*. London: Tavistock Publications, 1963.

WALL, T. D., & LISCHERON, J. A. *Worker participation: A critique of the literature and some fresh evidence*. London: McGraw-Hill, 1977.

BIOGRAPHICAL NOTES

FRANK HELLER is the Director of the Center for Decision Making Studies at the Tavistock Institute in London. Over the last 20 years his work has covered studies on leadership, decision-making practices at all levels of organization, trade union and industrial relations, the utilization of competence, communication procedures, organization development, training, and the impact of new technologies. Among research projects, seven have been comparative and cross-national, working with teams in 14 countries. Recent projects have included two on the impact of technology and one on the gap between available and required skills as well as comparative studies in China and Chile on management decision making. A project on energy consciousness in British schools and another on the consequences of privatization in Hungary are presently in progress, supported by the European Community. He has published numerous articles, books, and chapters in books.

Group Feedback Analysis   **835**

ALAN BROWN is a researcher in education, training, and employment. He is a Senior Research Fellow at the Department of Education Studies, University of Surrey. He previously worked at the Tavistock Institute of Human Relations.

Part V
Valediction and the Future

Part V
Valuation and the Future

Overview Part V

The three chapters in Part V produce a reasonable balance between optimism and pessimism about the democratic management of modern organizations.

Chapter 36 is by far the most positive and optimistic. Thoralf Qvale, the author of the essay, was the main Norwegian researcher in the two IDE studies (see Part III), has been closely associated with four generations of research and action programmes on organizational democracy in Norway and is well informed about similar work in Sweden. He and a number of co-workers in the Oslo Work Research Institute have come to believe that participative forms of management are necessary for organizational competitiveness in the modern world because it is only through participation that human resources can be adequately utilized. The Scandinavian programmes are the most well resourced and extensive in the world.

The essay goes through the history of theoretical and practical developments since 1964 and ends with a brief anticipation of a follow-up programme which will not finish until the new millennium. Although the author has no doubt about the economic importance of democratic management, he admits that achievement has always been lower than expectations and that progress, both at national as well as organizational level, has been agonisingly slow. Diffusion even of successful practices is rarely achieved, and managerial fears of losing prerogatives continues to obstruct progress.

Chapter 37 by Frank Heller also provides a historic perspective, being based on extensive work in North and South America as well as Europe, including the three programmes described in these volumes. The chapter shows that power differentials at work can be traced back to prehistoric times and have changed remarkably slowly over the millennia. From this perspective, the author argues that it may be appropriate to lower expectations. At the same time, the conjunction of an ever-increasing average standard of education and the impact of decentralization of decision-making through modern technology may support an increased degree of influence distribution. However, even these democratizing trends will be neutralized if participative structures are introduced piecemeal instead of holistically.

The final essay by Veljko Rus (Chapter 38) champions the need for anticipating the future as a necessary discipline for understanding social realities. Understanding the trend in democratization of organizational life is facilitated by drawing a distinction between *professionalization* and *industrialization*. Industrialization, based on a technical division of labour, derives from Frederick W. Taylor's mechanistic approach. Professionalization, on the other hand, is a more complex entity including investment in education and skill creation combined with a display of socialization and ethics (or values) associated with non-routine, non-competitive work and universalistic cosmopolitan relationships.

Management embraces industrialization values and this inevitably conflicts with professional aspirations. However, modern technology requires professional competence and hence management has to share some power with expertise based professionalism. This dual hierarchy is not the same as democracy which would include all employees. Such an aspiration is unrealistic since even legislation seems unable to create equality of influence when expertise is lacking. The author therefore argues that workplace democracy will have to be confined to the micro-level – that is, job-related decisions for which employees have the appropriate experience and skill.

[36]

Thoralf U. Qvale

2. Local development and institutional change: Experience from a 'fifth generation' national programme for the democratization of working life

Abstract

This article deals with employees' participation in decision-making in their work roles. It briefly reviews four 'generations' of programs for developing participative democracy in Norwegian working life over the last three decades and uses this as a background for discussing the context and experience from the fifth and most recent program, SBA (Senter for Bedre Arbeidsliv-program), which was concluded in 1993. A main premise of the article is that nowadays participative forms of management and organizations are prerequisites for the development and utilization of human resources and hence for organizational competitiveness. The experience from SBA's involvement in leading, innovative enterprises supports this view. The challenge of SBA was to design and implement an efficient, participative strategy through which the utilization of limited resources would have the largest positive impact on the country's economy. Experience showed that this strategy was demanding, but worked well at the enterprise, regional and industrial sector level, but that time, resources and passiveness of the national stakeholders limited the national impact. However, SBA also shows that aspects of the industrial relations heritage that are linked to democratization efforts may represent a hindrance, and that future efforts need to be linked to industrial policies. Several spin-offs and follow ups of SBA have such linkages. SBA could, however, also signal the demise of industrial democracy and industrial relations as the point of departure for increased participation in organizational decision-making.

Introduction[1]

In Norway the first practical project to help promote the democratization of working life through research started in 1964 with collaboration between the Tavistock Institute of Human Relations and professor Einar Thorsrud, who at the same time created a new social science research institute at the Norwegian Technical University in Trondheim. (Thorsrud and Emery 1970; Emery and Thorsrud 1976). The socio-technical systems ideas, developed through Tavistock's coal mine studies, formed the basis (Trist and Bamforth 1951; Emery 1959; Emery and Trist 1969). In this *first generation* of programs two main innovations were introduced: 1) The Tavistock ideas about social and psychological consequences of work were linked to the upcoming debate about industrial democracy in Norway, and suggested an alternative to the traditional board level workers' representation model (Emery and Thorsrud, 1969). 2) The ideas about a 'better fit' between social and technical systems needed to tried out in real life under the auspices, financing and joint support of the two dominant labour market organizations at the time.

Researchers and top managers agreed that if experience from local, plant level 'field experiments' was positive, the Two dominant labour market organizations would be actively involved in the diffusion process across working life later. The criteria according to which the results should be evaluated were: increased direct participation and learning, local commitment to the new organizational solutions, and long term productivity development to remain within the average for the industry in question.

A main conclusion of the coal mine studies

---

[1] The article builds on published books, reports and articles related to the Work Research Institute through its 25 years' research in industrial democracy and participation, as well as on unpublished material from the author's own involvement as researcher and programme director at the institute during this period.

was that technology was very important for organizational design or organizational choice (Trist et al. 1963). When transferred to Norway it was therefore believed that it was necessary to demonstrate the feasibility of new and, from a humane point of view, better forms of organization of work (e.g. autonomous work groups instead of tayloristic job design) in typical, and different industries. Other companies utilizing the same basic production technology could then learn from the 'experiments' and implement similar ideas. The legitimacy of and trust in the joint leadership of the programme would make it possible to get it started. The model for diffusion had been developed in studies of innovation in Australian sheep farming (Emery and Oeser, 1958).

In that period, four advanced manufacturing companies (a steel plant (Marek et al. 1964), a paper and pulp plant (Engelstad 1970), a small batch producer in the mechanical industry sector (Ødegaard, 1967; Qvale, 1969) and a chemical process plant (Gulowsen, 1967; Qvale, 1974a). joined the project. In practice the 'field experiments' were started sequentially over 3 years. The *methods* applied were modified from one stage to the next as the researchers learnt more. The *scope* of individual projects could also be expanded following increasing interest in the approach in industry.

The main lessons from these pioneering 'experiments' can be summarized as follows:

1. It was possible to create better jobs[2] through socio-technical redesign of existing industries. Commitment among the involved workers and supervisors also emerged as they gained experience in working under a 'new system'. (Emery and Thorsrud, 1976). The particular basic technology utilized in the individual plant was not the determining factor for the possibilities to improve. However, the special features of each plant, enterprise,

[2] The 'psychological criteria for job design' (Emery and Thorsrud, 1969) were used as guidelines in the first 'experiments'. The participating workers' own evalutation of and commitment to the new way of working, however, was the decisive factor in deciding whether jobs had indeed improved.

management and local union would call for differences in change strategy (Qvale, 1972, 1974a, 1974b, 1976). The experiments highlighted the systemic properties of the enterprises. Shop floor changes (e.g. from the scientific management model of organization of work to autonomous work groups) required several changes in administrative systems and functions (Qvale, 1971). In some of the companies, top management became interested and willing to endorse such changes, and a general transformation process in the company was started.

However, the understanding that redesigning the organization of work towards participative forms, such as autonomous work groups, and participation in the planning and implementation of change, could actually be seen as a constructive supplement or alternative to representative forms for participation in decision-making did not spread outside the involved enterprises (Qvale, 1978).

2. The productivity requirements, to stay within the general trend of the sector of industry, were *not* difficult to meet, rather the opposite (Gulowsen, 1975). The large productivity increases following the work redesign, however, tended to embarrass top and middle management and central union leadership, and counterstrategies prevailed. Or the local project became 'encapsulated', which meant that there was no diffusion to the rest of the enterprise (Herbst, 1976). Management often found the productivity increases and the new demands for further changes to sustain these increases difficult to deal with. The obtained productivity improvements were also often seen as a strong criticism of the ordinary way of managing, the use of 'scientific management' methods etc. Central union leaders were traditionally sceptical of productivity increases which they saw as expressions of a stronger exploitation of workers.

3. No diffusion took place along the technological dimension, i.e. within the same sector of industry during the 1960's. There

were a large number of local attempts to 'introduce autonomous work groups' in industry in the period 1968–74, but they generally failed. The main reason for this failure was the lack of *'system'* in the approach. The diffusion that did occur, generally took place through networks of leaders and enterprises, and tended to go across industrial sectors, e.g. from the pulp mill to a hotel in the neighbourhood. Action researchers were invited to participate in most of these.

4. The expert domination in the first 'field experiment' was necessary in order to demonstrate something to the national stakeholders and researchers. For sustained, enterprise level development it was detrimental. (Thorsrud, 1972; Emery and Thorsrud, 1976). Therefore in the third and fourth 'field experiment' a shift in research strategy took place. Researchers concentrated their efforts on setting up enterprise level joint bodies for the planning of change, and helping these bodies with change concepts and methods. The focus, however, was still on socio-technical redesign, but emphasising action research and participative design rather than new organizational structures.

5. After several years of 'field experiments' it became clear to the researchers that promoting participatory industrial democracy was not only a fight against 'scientific management', it was a more general fight against the domination of the bureaucratic organizational paradigm (Thorsrud, 1972). Scientific management methods and techniques were only applications of basic bureaucratic principles of management (the individual and the single job as the basic building blocks, maximum job fragmentation, hierarchic control etc. (Emery, 1978)). It appeared that the main obstacles to change were not the workers, local unions and first line supervisors, but the higher level line-managers, union leaders and university educated staff-experts. These groups tended to feel a loss of control or to feel that their expertise was challenged or becoming obsolete or unneeded.

Some clearly felt that their belief system was being questioned, e.g. production engineers with expertise in time and motion studies. Unless there was top management commitment linking internal organizational change to the general strategy of the enterprise, there was not enough energy to work through such obstacles. (Qvale, 1995). It also became clear that the fact that the educational system was built on the same bureaucratic paradigm, created a large impediment to the development of new, participative, roles in working life (Herbst, 1971).

6. There had been considerable confusion among the stakeholders about the values implied and the purpose of promoting participative democracy in working life. Workers and managers who had personally been involved in projects, gradually learnt that it was not a question of creating a comfortable, placid work situation, but to take responsibility, to be active, to become involved even in difficult and sometimes unpleasant tasks, to learn and to work hard, and, to participate in continuous change. It was not a question of *replacing* management and leadership with participation or 'workers' control', but of managers and staff experts taking new, supportive, more demanding roles, to acquire new expertise, and to develop new enterprise strategies (Thorsrud, 1978). In practice, most projects that stagnated, did so because of lack of top management support and ability/willingness to sort out new strategies and make changes at middle management levels. Projects which developed and became company policy did so because top management saw participative organizational forms as necessary for the utilization of the company's human resources and hence its ability to compete on the market. There were few cases where the workers were in the way of the development. Provided that top management was consistent, trust developed and the workers' support and commitment followed. This support from the workers tended to be based on the belief that it was the 'right

thing to do', on feeling rewarded by doing a useful job and on seeing this as a way of securing their own future (Emery and Thorsrud, 1976; Qvale, 1974, 1976, 1994).

Such understanding, however, did not quickly spread through working life to policy makers who had no personal exposure to new ways of working. By them participative democracy was seen as being solely concerned with workers rights and welfare and perhaps with the psycho-social work environment. Thus in the 1970's parallell initiatives for board level representation, for representation in management committees and works' councils and in work environment committees were taken by the same stakeholder organizations as those promoting programs for direct participation (IDE 1981). The main problem, however, was that management in general tended to belief that in order to promote productivity and competitiveness methods were needed that were completely different from those involving the employees in new ways.

In view of this, the action researchers with a commitment to the democratization of work in the following decades chose to work simultaneously with both enterprises *and* their institutional environment (including education at different levels). So, *the second generation* of programs built on this *ecological approach* to organizational change (Trist, 1976, 1983). The basic assumption from 1964 (Thorsrud and Emery, 1970; Emery and Thorsrud, 1976), that the private sector industry would represent the most dynamic force in the transformation of organizations and institutions towards more participative forms, was upheld. Further, working with the leading enterprises within this segment was expected to have the largest general impact. The reasons for these assumptions were the following:

– Technological development, implying the automation of simple, repetitive tasks, and the development of information processing technology, was eroding the basis for scientific management. This trend was clearly visible in the process industry as it was exposed to international competition

as early as 1960, e.g. in oil refineries. In shipping, automatic control of the engine room was a fact in the early 1970's. Competitiveness in advanced shipping became closely related to the ability to utilize these new technological opportunities.

The rising level of education in the working population and related expectations for autonomy in work ask in principle for the design of jobs and forms of organization of work which utilize emplyees' intellectual capacity. Commitment to work will not grow among highly educated employees unless their tasks are challenging and the organization in general is participative. However, the educational system had been developing in a way dissassociated from working life developments. National educational reforms were instituted with relatively short intervals, but seemed to fail in changing the basic way of working in the schools. There was a need for new methods to promote 'school reform' and hence obtain coordinated development across these sectors (Herbst, 1976).

– Public service agencies, educational institutions and other parts of the general infrastructure of industry were expected to be able to change in the same direction, only if they were partners in joint projects with innovative industrial enterprises in combination with a more general decentralization of the public sector. In the long term perspective the democratization of *work organizations and directly connected institutions* was expected to have a more general spill over effect on families and the political system. Thus a vision of participative democracy in society (Pateman, 1970) was the background.

The first of the second generation programmes was started in Norwegian shipping in 1967 (Roggema and Thorsrud, 1974; Walton, 1987). It involved simultaneous redesign of ships' superstructure (architecture) (Rogne, 1974), developing new types of integrated organization of work on board, redesigning educational system for sailors/officers, efforts to change the shipowners' central administration, new career paths for sailors, and new legislation. The last factor was important because manning norms, working hours, education and training requirements, and certificates for seamen were controlled through laws.

A remarkable fact, which was often overlooked later (see e.g. Gustavsen, 1992), was that the diffusion of experience and change within this sector actually did follow the lines expected but not found in the first generation. Once one leading shipowner started participative redesign of ships and ship organization, the others tended to follow suit and to involve systematically larger parts of the ecology of shipping. Cultural differences between the sectors may be a first part of the explanation of this remarkable fact, the international orientation and flexibility of shipowners, their organizations and the sailors may be another part.

Later, research projects were started which were targeting changes in the management and organization of schools more directly (Blichfeldt, 1992; Herbst, 1976). Some only covered the students and teachers, others involved external stakeholders e.g. a set of enterprises interested in the quality of vocational or professional training for their future recruits or in further education of their employees.

The last in this second generation of programmes took place during the period 1978 – 88 in the emerging offshore oil industry. Ultimately this large effort, which was a part of a national technology programme, aimed at utilizing the 'green field site' design opportunities in this new sector (Qvale, 1985, 1990, 1993), in order to promote productivity, safety and new industrial policies in connection with this new national resource.

As indicated above, the labour market organizations themselves were expected to take the main responsibility for the 'horizontal diffusion' of experience from the first series of 'field experiments.' Parallel to the action research projects, which were linked to the more dynamic parts of industry and associated institutions, the labour market organizations, – notably, the workers' trade union federation (LO) and its counterpart, the employers confederation (NHO) – were running a series of 'horizontal diffusion of experience' programmes and

systematically improving the efficiency of these programmes. These efforts constitute the third generation of democratization programmes. Joint training courses and seminars, job redesign workshops and information diffusion mechanisms were set up throughout the early 1970's to disseminate the experience from the first 'field experiments' to the rest of industry. The efforts had some effect in several participating enterprises, but again the national significance seemed negligible at the time. The most successful attempt, the job design workshops, had a high 'success rate' among participating enterprises, but weakening central union commitment to the program, caused the NHO to be concerned about the risk for imbalance in the national industrial relations systems and to stop the program.

Several years later an extension of the main national collective agreement that was reached around 1980 (HABUT) was the start of the fourth generation. NHO accepted the trade unions' demand for a formal basis for the participatory enterprise development efforts. The new provisions in the basic agreement were to take care of this demand. Joint planning and implementation of organizational change was encouraged, and financial resources for an enterprise level search conference, and for internal fellowships and some guidelines were provided centrally. The inherent value of participation was still the target. The local management/union representatives, however, had to rely mostly on their own ability and competence to make use of external resources. Only around 1990 was 'productivity' written into the agreement as an objective.

The effects of the new agreement on industrial relations have probably been positive, but until recently there were few cases of significant productivity increases. Participative democracy was kept within an industrial relations frame of reference by the national stakeholders, while locally, the concern for competitiveness and the securing of jobs became strong in the late 1980's. This coincided with the outcome of a long planning process preparing for the fifth generation of democratization programmes.

In 1983 a national initiative to bring together the various stakeholders and experiences in a new, comprehensive, national programme was taken. A broadly composed 'Royal Commission' on the further development of industrial democracy reported its recommendations in 1985 (NOU, 1985:1), and at the Einar Thorsrud Memorial Symposium in 1987 the Prime Minister announced the start of the new programme (Harlem Brundtland, 1989). In the following section, the context, strategy and some of the results of this program will be discussed.

The fifth generation; participative democracy in a new context

In principle the shift in Norway from seeing participation in decision-making as a part of the Human Relations Model to seeing it as a condition for competitiveness (the Human Resources Model) (Miles, 1965; Heller, 1992) took place through the work of the 'Royal Commission' on industrial democracy. There was oral and written consensus among the leaders of labour market organizations and the government that there was a strong need to change the work organizations towards participative forms, and to modernize their institutional context to become more open for direct cooperation across sectors and institutions in order to regain international competitiveness. Resources had to be mobilized in order to help the enterprises. Hence the new program needed to cover both the private and the public sectors and involve the white collar and academic union federations as well. A 'search conference' (Emery and Emery, 1976) within the commission itself, hearings with advanced enterprises and local unions, visits abroad, were methods used to develop this understanding within the commission and to outline the strategy of the program. Behind the consensus was a shared fear for mass unemployment from the late 1980's unless drastic changes took place. But undoubtedly, the formal support from some of the leaders on the employers' side, was based only on its role in keeping at bay demands for other, more threatening solutions to the industrial democracy issue.

As one would expect, agreement in principle at the top, was not a sufficient condition for consistent and systematic support from the stakeholders at all levels and stages. It was, however, sufficient to obtain financing for 5 years and to establish well staffed governing bodies for the program which was to be linked to the new Work Life Centre (SBA)[3]. An international council for the program was also set up with the purpose of helping with planning and evaluation. A major challenge for the program was to involve the stakeholders to the degree that their support and commitment would be strengthened. It was understood from the start that 5 years would be too short to have a significant impact on a large number of enterprises not to mention on the country's international competitiveness. It was assumed, however, that after 5 years, the stakeholders would have a basis for joint decisions of how to follow up. If experiences were positive, the program would be continued under the auspices of the country's ordinary budgets and institutions.

SBA's strategy mainly built on experience with the multilevel ecological approach to organizational change, developed through the shipping and oil research programs. The idea was to work with relatively advanced enterprises in various sectors, and to establish direct cooperation between these enterprises and several institutions with a permanent role in the sector, so that these institutions could play a key role in the diffusion process later. At least, these (changed) institutions would facilitate the process of changing the internal organization for other enterprizes later. SBA assumed it was mainly a question of speeding up a development process that was already on its way. In the mid-80's advanced enterprises were already in the process of leaving the traditional bureaucratic/tayloristic organizational paradigm, frequently assisted by management consultants. In this process SBA made its unique contribution in the area of institutional change and the

---

[3] SBA; Senter for Bedre Arbeidsliv, was set up as a new independent foundation to be financed through a fixed, yearly contribution from the stakeholder organizations, and governed through a board of directors and a council. In the latter, all top leaders of all major national labour market organizations and the government were represented. From the start it was agreed that SBA should be disbanded after 5 years.

development of new, supportive, national policies. This is a field where neither individual enterprises nor management consultants seem to get involved, partly because they lack legitimacy. SBA had legitimacy from its stakeholders and the status as a national program. Also, working with advanced, powerful, enterprises was expected to increase chances of having impact on the enterprises' infrastructure ('the demanding customer').

SBA was not formally a research program, as opposed to the slightly older Swedish LOM-program (Gustavsen, 1992)[4]. For that reason the goal was not to test out one specific method or hypothesis, but to obtain widespread change in working life through strategic use of limited resources and with a certain value basis: Direct, broad participation to improve productivity and, hence, also secure employment. The increasing use of action research based institutes by SBA was in part motivated pragmatically: Action researchers were more familiar with participative methods of organizational development. In part, the involvement of researchers at universities was motivated from the need to open channels for diffusion of experience via education and setting up collaborative relationships between work and education.

SBA became involved in 516 enterprises (both in the private and public sector) through 98 projects. There were documented changes according to the set criteria in 133 of the enterprises by the end of the program in June 1993. 64% of the enterprises continued the ideas and methods introduced through cooperating with SBA. (SBA, 1993). The latter is probably the most significant indicator of positive results at the enterprise level. From the perspective of diffusion of experience, the fact that 19 projects

linked to permanent institutions were defined, financed, and continued after SBA stopped is probably most significant.

SBA was evaluated by a team consisting of four social scientists. Three of these were drawn from the international council, and four persons were nominated by the main stakeholder organizations. One of the key conclusions from the evaluation report may be quoted here:

'SBA in many senses marks the end of an era in which industrial relations policy has been the generative force in determining the imperatives for Norwegian working life. In the new era modernized industrial policy will be the major determinant shaping Norwegian working life as it will be in all advanced economies. The legacy of SBA is the distinctive contribution it has made to herald this change and develop a strategy that directively linked the micro environment of the workplace and the enterprise to industry policy which is being driven by the need to be internationally competitive. In the more turbulent worldwide economic environment there is a need to be able to compete on the basis of technology and capital inseparably linked to an intelligent, involved, committed, flexible, and informed workforce delivering productivity, quality, flexibility and continuous improvement. To do this many factors may apply including direct participation, wages and conditions tied to sustained increases in productivity, quality flexibility and smartness.' (Davies et al. 1993, p. ix).

Hence the evaluating team endorsed the basic assumption that increased direct participation was an economic necessity. They also agreed that the strategy and methods were basically well chosen, but pointed to the disparity between the ambitions of the program and the resources made available. They found there had not been very much diffusion of change beyond the focal organizations where the projects took place and indicated that this was mainly due to the lack of active support from SBA's stakeholder organizations. Especially the fact that the labour market organizations themselves had not incorporated learning from SBA in their own behavior, was seen as detrimental to diffusion. In practice these organizations treated SBA as an exercise in industrial relations.

---

[4] LOM, which is the acronym for Ledelse, Organisation och Medbestammande (leadership, organization and co-determination) also had a 5 year duration and was terminated in 1990. Its purpose, support and resources were similar to those of SBA, but its approach was almost entirely process oriented (Naschold, 1992).

What did we learn through SBA?

Several of the other general assumptions about future developments upon which the program built, turned out to be fairly accurate. The economic situation of the country deteriorated, for the first time since the 1930's there was mass unemployment, demands for a strengthened board level and similar forms for representative democracy in working life had temporarily disappeared, dissatisfaction with quality and cost efficiency of public services had risen, and the leading, internationally oriented, competence based, enterprises had started adopting new organizational concepts which frequently imply enhanced direct participation (flat, lean organization, total quality management, time based management, just-in-time management, business process reengineering, matrix organization etc.). Although such concepts, with a socio-technical perspective in their focus on the core production process or value-added chain, can give good starting points, working through all other necessary changes in the whole enterprise organization was almost as demanding and time consuming as in the early democratization projects in the late 1960's. In spite of formal spoken and written support for the new ideas at top management and union levels, the concrete working out of new solutions and their acceptance have always been felt like an uphill struggle.

In practice SBA's projects proceeded as a combination of top-down, bottom-up and center-out processes with large conferences where all participated at critical stages. Once the fruitfulness of the strategy was demonstrated in a single enterprise, commitment to continue with this new methods tended to arise. The point that the new concepts are parts of a different organizational paradigm, and hence require a total systems change in order fully to succeed, has been amply demonstrated. The popular belief that the unionized workers would be the most important obstacle to changes in the work organization, did not find general support. The main problem in this generation of programs was, to overcome what could be named 'resistance to change' at the intermediate levels, – line management and staff

experts, – whose roles, tasks and competencies were no longer adequate or sometimes no longer necessary. The need to upgrade the competence of staff experts and their need to learn new work roles is almost limitless and can only be covered through more direct and continuous cooperation with the educational system. To deal with inertia or lack of ability to change at intermediate levels, top management understanding, support and willingness to use its power to enforce needed changes, is decisive. Although the use of 'search conferences' (Emery and Emery, 1976) and similar methods tends to bring forth the needs and direction for change, there is still a lack of top managers able to lead the change process. Their willingness and ability to do this therefore, has to be built up gradually. Therefore, the time needed to enforce such turnarounds becomes lengthy.

The need to change or develop the infrastructure of working life (at municipal, regional and national levels), which was one of SBA's explicit objectives, has also been amply demonstrated through SBA's interventions. There is e.g. little doubt that the work roles students learn during their long initial period are at odds with the realities of modern working life. Students learn to work individually in a hierarchical system with single discipline based, predefined problems which have a well defined solution. In a participative work organization they would often have to work with the definition and solution of problems in a multidisciplinary, cross functional team together with the 'clients'. Sometimes they would find that the problem needs to be redefined before it can be solved. New pedagogic ideas such as 'Problem Based Learning' used in direct cooperation with industry are being tried out through some of SBA's continuing projects and may provide some answers to this need.

An industrial structure largely composed of small enterprises, represents a challenge of its own. To have national significance, any program must be able to deal with groups of enterprises simultanuously. Furthermore, with the ambition of developing the enterprises' infrastructure in order to make new (public) resources available to them, common interests across enterprises should be identified and promoted vis-a-vis the infrastructure. It is impossible for any municipal, county based or state agency to adjust or change the organization according to the specific wishes of anyone single, small enterprise.

Through SBA we also found that the individual enterprise, whether small or large. normally did not make their needs clear to the extent that any external body could adjust to them. The most common attitude in the enterprises was: 'It (the school, the county's or government's support programs for industry etc) is useless and it is impossible to change it'.

Normally national industry policy based programs were directed towards a specific *industrial sector* (steel, transport, electronics, food, paper/pulp etc). SBA also helped start several projects based on collaboration between union and employers in industrial sectors. A number of these are continuing and show interesting developments. It may still be argued that industrial sector as an organizing principle is of diminishing importance. Both from economic and organization theory perspectives other principles for organizing probably are more central. Methods for the development of *regional networks of enterprises* may be the most important innovation in the SBA program. These networks cross industrial sector and traditional center/district distinctions which dominate industry policies and industrial relations. They have showed their potential for helping the individual enterprise with new resources and flexibility. In the more advanced networks the members are identifying specific common interests which they can communicate to their external environment. Thus they can affect institutions and regional and national policies.

The largest network in which SBA was involved links more than 70 enterprises, some of which are large and internationally competitive. In another SBA-project an old integrated enterprise was devided into a set of independent enterprises working together trough a network.

Existing industrial networks have been studied quite extensively, while there is less knowledge about the conditions and methods for network development. There are assumptions about the interrelationships between the internal structure of the individual network participant, stages or phases of development etc. and its ability to benefit it, but this is still a new field of research (Hanssen-Bauer and Borgen, 1992; Hanssen-Bauer and Snow, 1994). For instance, we assume that, in order to participate in a mature network, all employees of the individual enterprise have to share, to some degree, an understanding of what this implies. Such common understanding is unlikely to develop unless *all* employees are involved in the change process, i.e. participative strategies are required for this reason as well. SBA's experience from working with the creation of four networks supports this notion.

In the public sector (municipal agencies, government services, railway, post, road-building, tax office, hospitals etc) the driving forces were the need to provide better quality customer service, and the need to improve the working environment and productivity within shrinking budgets. Several organizations have been, and still are, under the threat of privatization and want to demonstrate that a 'bottom-up'-customer-oriented strategy is a better alternative. Strategies and results are similar to those in the private sector.

The limiting factors for SBA's penetration in worklife became time, and the availability of competent consultants/action researchers who could assist in the processes. Therefore, during the last two years of SBA's period more emphasis was placed on initiating and supporting more long term R/D projects in cooperation between working life and universities. As mentioned there are approximately 20 of such projects. The largest will be 'Bedriftsutvikling 2000' (Gustavsen and Mikkelsen, 1994)[5] and may represent the *sixth generation* in the series. It has been planned to be a 7 year program initiated by the two largest labour market organizations in Norway, the national science foundation and SBA. Hence, it will represent a 'merger' of the two lines of development originating in the first 'field experiments'; the action research and the industrial-relations line. A number of SBA's

[5] Bedriftsutvikling 2000 (BU 2000) in English: Enterprise Development 2000.

projects and programs may find further support through this initiative, but the majority of the participating enterprises are expected to build on the collective agreement about 'enterprise development'. The Norwegian universities are all expected to participate in the programme and provide professional support.

The exclusion of the public sector and the other union federations (the white collar staff association and the confederation for academic workers) from the new program may, however, limit its scope and resources, and shows that the broad alliance created for SBA has not survived. 'BU 2000's' vulnerability to industrial action and conflicts will therefore probably be higher than in the case of SBA.

In some respects, however, the new initiative represents a considerable expansion both in scope and resources as compared with SBA, or indeed any predecessor in this field. The expansion is only possible because the understanding that participation in decision-making is an economic necessity, is slowly penetrating at national policy making levels. However, if broad, direct participation becomes established as a common element in organizational development and as a basic principle for organizational design, it will also become redundant as an issue in itself. This is a concern the trade unions who feel something is disappearing and seem to find it hard to reconceptualize the issue and develop new policies.

Concluding comments

In a Lewinian tradition, change is necessary in order to understand a social system. The real structures are revealed through change. If we see as SBA as an intervention at different levels in Norwegian working life, we can draw a number of conclusions about the relevance of SBA for the understanding of organizational decision-making under different economic and political conditions.

SBA's basic values – increasing participation in decision-making in connection with own job – is commonly accepted. At this level Taylor's, or the general bureaucratic principles of maximum task fragmentation, external control etc.

are dead. The preconditions for, and consequences of, abolishing these principles, however, are less well understood and accepted. Although ideas about 'empowerment', motivation, total quality management, just-in-time management, technological innovation, service development, customer orientation etc, are quickly spreading and give ample opportunities for riding 'piggy back', their opportunities for triggering more profound changes are not often utilized in practice. Most enterprises still try to install such ideas without changing the hierarchy, work organization, administrative systems etc. There is fear of loss of control, infringement on managerial prerogatives and certainly a fair amount of personal insecurity and fear among managers and staff experts. 'One step at a time' seems safer than a comprehensive and committing strategy for systematic change. Hence, the potential for productivity increases inherent to the new ideas is not being fully utilized.

Although SBA (and other projects in other countries) demonstrated that the more *radical* (in terms of the degree to which all employees are involved and the scope of the participation) and *systematic* the participation is, the more successful the project is from a business point of view, managers and owners initially tend not to believe this. In advanced, innovative organizations which depend on the utilization of highly competent employees, for example engineering companies, such understanding is emerging and is enforced by management, sometimes opposed by employees who feel their individual autonomy is being reduced (Qvale and Hanssen-Bauer, 1990; Qvale 1993).

There is little doubt that SBA's relatively large success (compared with earlier programs of the same kind) in reaching many enterprises and promoting far reaching changes in these, is largely due to economic pressure and political shifts, i.e. contextual changes. Interest among workers and managers in further participation in decision-making in working life is declining unless participation contributes to productivity. On the other hand, once the link between participative methods and productivity has been established, the need for democratization as legitimation goes down.

The methods used in SBA reflected the experiences from earlier generations of action research programs. Rather than encouraging the introduction of specific solutions (e.g. autonomous work groups), methods for participative planning and strategy development were used. Emphasis was placed on helping the client organizations to manage the change themselves and to take over the functions of the external consultant/researcher as soon as possible.

Also, in Norway there is a trend towards liberalization. Frequently it is supported by the social-democratic government. Its emergence is, to a large extent, due to the failure of national policies/programs and institutions to provide good services at an acceptable price. Although privatization has been limited so far, there are clear signs there will be more of it unless public enterprises and institutions change. Finding alternative strategies to the crude and frequently unsuccessful privatization is a burning issue for unions, employees and many citizens.

In public services, involving the clients/customers in interaction with 'empowered' employees, is a method for developing new policies, linking the micro and macro levels; learning from the customer and converting these experience into new policies. SBA's assumption, however, that the labour market organizations could take active roles in promoting such processes, seemed somewhat optimistic. So far it seems that the changes needed in these organizations to enable them to maintain their central roles in the future, are beyond what can be achieved in 5 years. In the future one might expect that further diffusion of methods for democratization of decision-making in organizations will follow from implementation of new technology and intertwined organizational concepts, or from general organizational development/productivity drives, rather than from specific democratization programs. If this indeed will be the future, 'horizontal diffusion' of new practices across working life may quickly erode the basis for central union and employer federation power.

The recently started joint program; 'Enterprise Development 2000', is a clear sign of a certain reorientation among leaders of the labour market organizations, and it may be the last test of the fruitfulness of a national labour/management program for action research in the field. One weakness of the program, however, is that it fails to involve the core activity of the labour market organizations, the bargaining and designing of collective agreements. Also this program may find that diffusion of change will have to take place without the active involvement of the stakeholders' main functions. It may be argued that the inertia of these large, central organizations is such that they can hardly profit from 30 years of quite systematic sponsorship of participative working life research and development. While the development towards flexible, participative forms at the enterprise and regional levels is accelerating, the central labour market organizations in Norway seem unchanged. A recent study even seems to indicate that sister-organizations in other European countries may have come further in the process of developing new policies and actions (Kester and Pinaud, 1994). Action researchers, who want to promote participative democracy in Norway, and who believe trade unions are important safeguards for democracy, may therefore be facing formidable challenges.

References

Blichfeldt, J.F. What did you learn at school today? *Cybernetics and Human Knowing.* Vol 1. No 2-3, 1992.

Brundtland, G.H. The Scandinavian challenge: Strategies for work and learning. In C.J. Lammers and G. Szell (Eds.), *International handbook of participation in organizations.* Oxford: University Press, 1989.

Davies, A., F. Naschold, W. Pritchard and T. Reve. *Evaluation report commissioned by the board of the SBA programme.* Oslo: Work Research Institute, 1993.

Emery, F.E. *Characteristics of socio-technical systems.* London: Tavistock Institute, 1959.

Emery, F.E. (Ed.). *The emergence of a new paradigm of work.* Canberra: The Centre for

Continuing Education: Australian National University, 1978.

Emery, F.E. and M. Emery. *A choice of futures. To enlighten or inform.* Leiden: Nijhof, 1976.

Emery, F.E. and O.A. Oeser. *Information, decision and action.* Melbourne: Cambridge University Press, 1958.

Emery, F.E. and E. Thorsrud. *Form and content in industrial democracy.* Leiden: Nijhoff, 1969.

Emery F.E. and E. Thorsrud. *Democracy at work.* Leiden: Nijhoff, 1976.

Emery, F.E. and E. Trist. Socio-technical systems. In F.E. Emery (Ed.), *Systems thinking: Selected readings.* Harmondsworth: Penguin Books, 1969.

Engelstad, P.H. *Teknologi og sosial forandring på arbeidsplassen.* Oslo: Tanum, (1970).

Gulowsen, J. *Arbeidervilkår.* Oslo: Tanum, 1975.

Gulowsen, J. *Norsk hydros samarbeidsforsok i fullgjødselfabrikken.* Oslo: Work Research Institutes, 1968.

Gustavsen, B. and L. Mikkelsen. *Enterprise development 2000; Concept driven productivity development and organizational renewal in working life.* Oslo: Work Research Institute, 1994.

Gustavsen, B. *Dialogue and development.* Assen: Van Gorcum, 1992.

Hanssen-Bauer, J. and S.O. Borgen. Industriutvikling gjennom regionale klynger. *Bedre Bedrift* No. 4, 1992.

Hanssen-Bauer, J. and C.C. Snow. *Responding to hypercompetition; The structure and processes of a regional learning network organization.* Oslo/University Park: Work Research Institute/Penn State University, 1994.

Heller, F. Decision-making and the utilization of competence. In F. Heller (Ed.), *Decision-making and leadership.* Cambridge: Cambridge University Press, 1992.

Herbst, P.G. *Demokratiseringsprosessen i arbeidslivet.* Oslo: Universitetsforlaget, 1971.

Herbst, P.G. *Alternatives to hierarchies.* Leiden: Nijhoff, 1976.

IDE-International Research Group. *European industrial relations.* Oxford: Clarendon Press, 1981.

Kester, G. and H. Pinaud (Eds.). *'Scenario 21'.*

Trade unions and democratic participation. Paris: L'Harmattan, 1994.

Marek, J., K. Lange and P.H. Engelstad. *The wire drawing mill of christiania spigerverk.* Trondheim: Institutt for Industriell Miljøforskning, 1964.

Miles, R.E. Human relations or human resources? *Harvard Business Review.* p. 43, 148–163, 1965.

NOU. *Videreutviklingen av bedriftsdemokratiet, 2.* Oslo: NOU, 1985.

Pateman, C. *Participation and democratic theory.* London: Cambridge University Press, 1970.

Qvale, T.U. *Samarbeidsprosjektets fase B: Etterstudie ved nobø fabrikker A/S.* Trondheim: Institutt for Industriell Miljøforskning, NTH, 1968.

Qvale, T.U. Organisasjonsprinsipper. En komparativ studie. In P.G. Herbst (Ed.), *Demokratiseringsprosessen i arbeidslivet.* Oslo: Universitetsforlaget, 1971.

Qvale, T.U. *Rapport fra samarbeidsprosjektet i Norsk hydros magnesiumfabrikk., Herøya.* Oslo: Work Research Institutes, 1974a.

Qvale, T.U. Berichte aus der praxis – partizipation und konflikt – Einige erfahrungen mit dem Norwegische programm fur industrielle demokratie. *Gewerkschaftliche Monatshefte* 3/74, p. 193–199, 1974b.

Qvale, T.U. Comment: What about the foreman.? *Acta Sociologica, 19,* No. 1, p. 77–82, 1976.

Qvale, T.U. Bureaucracy or productivity? Experience with board level worker representation in Norway. *Human Futures.* Summer p. 1–5, 1978.

Qvale, T.U. *Safety and offshore working conditions.* Oslo: Universitetsforlaget, 1985.

Qvale, T.U. A new milestone in the development of industrial democracy in Norway? In C.J. Lammers and G. Szell (Eds.), *International handbook of participation in organizations.* Oxford: Oxford University Press, 1989.

Qvale, T.U. Design for safety and productivity in large scale industrial projects: The case of Norwegian offshore oil development. In B. Wilpert and T.U. Qvale (Eds.), *Reliability and safety in hazardous work dystems.* Hove: Lawrence Erlbaum, 1993.

Qvale, T.U. Direct participation in Scandinavia. From workers rights to economic necessity. In G. Kester and H. Pinaud (Eds.), *Trade unions and democratic participation. A scenario for the 21st century.* Vol. 2. Paris/The Hague: ISS/LERPSO, 1994.

Qvale, T.U. The role of research for the social shaping of new technologies: Designing a research strategy. *Artificial Intelligence and Society.* No. 1, 1995.

Qvale, T.U. and J. Hanssen-Bauer. Implementing QWL in large scale project organizations. Blue water site design in the Norwegian offshore oil industry. In H. Lee Meadow and M.J. Sirgy (Eds.), *Quality of life studies in marketing and management.* Proceedings from the 3rd Quality of Life/Marketing Conference, Blacksburg. Virginia: Omni Press, 1990.

Roggema, J. and E. Thorsrud. *Skipet i utvikling.* Oslo: Tanum, 1974.

Rogne, K. Redesigning the design process. *Applied Ergonomics,* 5 (4), p. 213–218, 1993.

SBA. *The Norwegian working life center: Styrets beretning til Rådet 1988–1993.* (The report from the board of directors to the council). Oslo: Work Research Institute, 1993.

Thorsrud, E. Job design in a wider context. In L.E. Davis and J.C. Taylor (Eds.), *Design of jobs.* Harmondsworth: Penguin Books, 1972.

Thorsrud, E. Complementary roles in collaborative action research. Paper presented at the arden house conference on the quality of working life. New York, 1972.

Thorsrud, E. Policymaking as a learning process. In B. Gardell and G. Johansson (Eds.), *Man and working life: A social science contribution to work reform.* Chichester: Wiley, 1976.

Thorsrud, E. and F.E. Emery. *Mot en ny bedriftsorganisasjon.* 2nd ed. Oslo: Tanum, 1970.

Trist, E.L. and K.W. Bamforth. Some social and psychological consequences of the Longwall method of coal-getting. *Human Relations,* 4 (1), 3–38, 1951.

Trist, E.L. G.W. Higgin, H. Murray and A.B. Pollock. *Organizational choice.* London: Tavistock, 1963.

Trist, E.L. A concept of organizational ecology. *National labour Institute Bulletin,* 12, 483–496, New Delhi, 1976.

Trist, E.L. Referent organization and the development of interorganizational domains. *Human Relations,* 36 (3), 269–284, 1983.

Walton, R.E. *Innovating to compete.* San Francisco/London: Jossey-Bass, 1987.

Ødegaard, L.A. Samarbeidsprosjektets fase B: Feltforsøk ved nobø fabrikker A/S. Trondheim: *Institutt for Industriell Miljøforskning,* NTH, 1967.

Thoralf U. Qvale is research director at the Work Research Institute, Oslo, Norway.

[37]

Human Relations, Vol. 51, No. 12, 1998

Influence at Work: A 25-Year Program of Research

Frank Heller[1,2]

Organization of any kind, from prehistoric hunting societies to companies working through the worldwide web, operate with a distribution of influence and power among their members. This distribution of influence has consequences at three levels: for the people working in the organization, for the organization itself, and, from time to time, for members of society outside the organization. A series of action- and policy-oriented projects on the distribution of influence were developed by or in collaboration with the Centre for Decision Making Studies of The Tavistock Institute over a quarter of a century. They started with a seven-country comparative research on top management decision making, followed by two 12-country studies on Industrial Democracy and a 5-year longitudinal program in seven companies in three countries. These and two longitudinal projects in Britian, one on a motor car manufacturer and the other on an airport, used a similar conceptual framework. The article draws on the evidence from this program of work, describes the evolving theoretical model and concludes that organizational influence sharing appears to have made only limited progress during the last 50 years. Four explanations are put forward: overidealistic expectations; a tendency to ignore the need for certain necessary antecedents, like competence; a tendency to act as if influence sharing is not subject to contingencies like the nature of tasks; and probably most importantly, the almost universal tendency to design influence sharing measures through uncoordinated mechanistic social engineering.

KEY WORDS: participation; organizational democracy; empowering; stakeholship; involvement; decision making.

INTRODUCTION

The article has four objectives. In the first place, I want to describe a series of applied research projects on various aspects of organizational

[1]The Tavistock Institute, 30 Tabernacle Street, London EC2A 4UE, England.
[2]Requests for reprints should be addressed to Frank Heller, The Tavistock Institute, 30 Tabernacle Street, London EC2A 4UE, England.

1425

0018-7267/98/1200-1425$15.00/1 © 1998 The Tavistock Institute

democracy carried out through the Centre of Decision Making Studies of The Tavistock Institute and its associates over the last 25 years. Secondly, the methodology and theoretical framework assumptions underlying these projects will be explained. Thirdly, the main results of the studies will be summarized and assessed against current developments. However, to judge whether we can be satisfied with what has been achieved so far, we start with a brief account of some historic events in the distribution of influence at work to show that, while some longstanding trends of power concentration have disappeared, others have transmuted and still play an important role in modern organizations.

HISTORIC ANTECEDENTS

A distribution of influence at work has always existed. In the term work we include all activities which sustain a person's material standard of life. Influence (which will be discussed in some detail later) is a way of describing the distribution of power-related activities between people. In prehistoric hunting societies, influence was based on skill and strength (Frazer, 1933). In medieval Europe, feudalism was the main form of social stratification. Like later systems, it was based on a hierarchy of authority and power from the apex of an inherited aristocracy to the lowly serf. The system involved an intricate sets of duties and obligations and, while serfs could not be sold, they were not allowed to leave their place of work. However, in return for services rendered to their lord, serfs were usually given a measure of autonomy over a portion of land which they could cultivate for their own benefit. Gradually feudalism became inconsistent with the growth of commerce, trade, and industry; in France it lasted until the eighteenth century and in Russia until 1861.

Various forms of slavery have been practiced since time immemorial. In Britain, it was formally ended with a law of 1833 and in the United States, where it led to a civil war, slavery became illegal with the victory of the northern states in 1865. However, some forms of slave labor are in evidence even in the last decade of the twentieth century; in Mauritania, it was outlawed in 1980, but has not been eradicated completely and bonded workers and child labor still exist in several low income countries (*The Economist*, 1996).

In the rapidly developing countries in eighteenth century Europe and the U.S., domestic industries flourished in weaving, pottery, and smithy work well into the nineteenth century. Influence was usually by arrangement and was, as in prehistoric hunting, based to some extent on strength and skill. The husband would run the smithy and the wife would concentrate on weaving (Toynbee, 1913).

When economies of scale and the use of power based on water, steam, and electricity led to the establishment of places of work away from the home in factories and offices, the distribution of influence at work became more complex as well as controversial. During the Industrial Revolution in England, formal power moved to the investor or shareholder and *de facto* power to the inventor of new machinery and later to managers. From a fairly early stage, the state also assumed some power in the shape of legislation to give a slight measure of self-determination, for instance to women and children of both sexes as young as 5 and 6 years old, who were forced to work underground 5 days a week for 15 hours a day and only slightly less on Saturday (Bland, Brown, & Tawney, 1914, p. 517).

These practices were justified on two grounds. One was competitiveness and is the same as used in 1996 by the British government to oppose European legislation to allow employees, if they choose, not to work more than 48 hours a week. The second argument also has echoes today and was put forward 200 years ago by Lord Lauderdale, who consistently opposed legislation and government interference in the textile industry with the request that their lordships should not "encroach upon that great principle of political economy, that labour ought to be left free" (Hammond & Hammond, 1925, p. 167).

Employees trying to improve their own conditions through association in trade unions were stopped by the Combination Laws of 1799 and 1800 and even limited collective bargaining rights had to wait another 70 years for some legislative support. Political freedom for unions in the U.K. was only granted in 1913.

Up to the end of the Second World War, the distribution of influence at work in most industrialized societies was set in a fairly rigid pattern of centralized hierarchies influenced by F. W. Taylor's scientific management, Adam Smith's analysis of the division of labor, and a belief in the economics of vertical integration producing large manufacturing units; workers tended to be treated as extensions of machines whose un-ergonomic design frequently caused unnecessary fatigue and pain.

POSTWAR DEVELOPMENTS

The end of the Second World War saw the defeat of three autocratic dictatorships demonstrating the evil as well as the weakness of centralized power. It is not unreasonable to see the trend toward a more democratic distribution of influence in postwar organizations, particularly in Western Europe, to be related to the lessons learned from the defeat of the dictatorships. J. B. Priestley, the playwright who broadcast regularly through the 1940s, expressed these sentiments well: "My own personal view, for what it's worth, is that we must stop thinking in terms of property and power and begin thinking in terms of community and creation . . . . And even already in the middle of this war, I can see that world shaping itself" (Priestley, 1940). Of course, there had been earlier attempts to democratize working life. Consumer cooperatives had started in Britain in 1844, and in Germany consultative and participative structures were legally sanctioned from early in the twentieth century. These tentative steps found little broad support although limited progress was made in some directions. The cooperative movement was successful in many parts of the world in spite of the well-documented difficulties of competing against more traditional hierarchically organized enterprises for access to finance, experienced management, and other support measures (Abell, 1983; Cornforth & Thomas, 1990). In Britain, worker cooperatives grew from 40 in 1968 to approximately 1200 in 1987, but then declined. During the First World War, production committees had been established and had successfully supported the war effort. The experience was incorporated in a recommendation to set up management–employee committees in public industries which became known as Whitley Councils. Having languished in the interwar years, they again came into prominence during the Second World War and then became either bargaining bodies or effete talking shops.

The cyclical nature of influence-sharing practices has led Ramsay (1977) to look at variations over a 100-year period and to conclude that participation flourishes when it suits management and when it helps to secure labor's compliance. A slightly different analysis of the distribution of influence is put forward by Brannen, Batstone, Fatchett, and White (1976) who describe two periods; one covers the first 20 years of the Twentieth Century, which included the rise of the shop steward movement, a worker control movement in engineering, syndicalism in mining and railways, guild socialism as a popular movement, and joint management–worker Whitley Committees. The second period covers the Second World War and reconstruction era which again brought on demands for worker control of industry (Coates & Topham, 1968; Robert, 1973) and led to a period of rapid growth of voluntarily established Joint Consultative Committees (Poole, 1975) which later registered a substantial decline (Milward, Stevens, Smart, & Hawes, 1992). In the 1970s, seeing the fairly successful example of the German codetermination system which had been in operation since 1952, the British Government set up a Committee of Inquiry on Industrial Democracy "accepting the need for a radical extension of industrial democracy in the control of companies by means of representation on boards of directors . . ." (Bullock, 1977, p. *v*). Several British unions and many industrial relations academics opposed boardroom representation, preferring to stay with traditional adversarial collective bargaining. Employers, too, believed that influence-sharing at any level had to be voluntary.

As we shall see later, the outcome of our research would not support either of these positions, but in any case, the Bullock report recommendations were never implemented. One of the most important aspects of the report, which received almost no publicity, was its analysis of very extensive training needs covering up to 11,000 representatives even in the first year of implementing the democratizing recommendations (Bullock, 1977, pp. 156-159). Using the term competence, we will later draw attention to widespread neglect of the need for training in relation to influence-sharing procedures at any level of organization.

In the 1950s and 1960s, European industry was weak and was being rebuilt; the strength and productivity of the United States was widely envied. Britain sent many sectorial teams of enquiry to the United States to discover the secrets of success and differences between U.S. and European organizations were closely investigated and analyzed to see whether America's high productivity was due to superior technology (OECD, 1968), greater inventiveness (Diebolt, 1968), higher capital investment (Servan Schreiber, 1968) or other macro economic indicators (Caves et al., 1968). However, none of these assumptions turned out to be convincing. Gradually, a considerable body of informed opinion came to believe that the difference in productivity was managerial and, in particular, that European industry operated with more centralized authoritarian methods than American industry (Servan Schreiber, 1968; Granick, 1962; Smith, 1968; Haenni, 1969).

The term "participation" came up frequently in these comparisons and social scientists and consultants in Europe were well aware of a major area of American research carried out in the University of Michigan which had come to the conclusion that participation was associated with higher employee satisfaction and greater productivity (Likert, 1961, 1967). It is interesting that 20 years later, a leading American academic in analyzing the relative weakness of American industry compared with Japan comes to the opposite conclusion: namely, that American management does not use "high-involvement practices" sufficiently (Lawler, 1986). Lawler quotes with approval an article by Reich (1985) who shows that "Since 1970 the net profits of America's largest corporations have declined 20 per cent when adjusted for inflation" and blames this on an excessive "concentration of power and rewards in the hands of top management" (Lawler, 1986, p. 10). These fluctuating judgments suggest that answers to challenging questions about reasons for economic growth are not yet available.

The authenticity of participatory practices has been challenged from time to time. Child, for instance, used Orwell's term "doublethink" to describe the use of catchwords by politicians and public figures, like "common citizenship," "partnership," and "the beliefs and loyalties we all share" which contradict "the reality of how people's lives and their relationships are being structured by institutions . . ." (Child, 1976, p. 431). Child examined the trends in the 1970s with their demands for an extension of participation in organizational decision making while, at the same time, organizations became ever bigger, more bureaucratic, and centralized.

Extensive and important reviews of the literature on the nature and distribution of power and influence accumulated after 1945 (for instance, Lowin, 1968; Bernstein, 1976; Loveridge, 1980; Lindenfeld & Rothschild-Whitt, 1982; Chell, 1985; Kochan & Osterman, 1994; Rogers & Streek, 1995), but it is not possible in a single article to trace the development of the distribution of influence at work systematically over large chunks of history. However, the preliminary evidence we have assembled suggests that there is no simple linear evolutionary trend. This is, in any case, the conclusion social philosophers usually come to when they attempt to order human activities over long cycles of history: "theories of social evolution are readily formed with the aid of some preconceived ideas and a few judicially selected corroborative facts" (Hobhouse & Westermarck, 1918, p. 1). The opposite is, of course, also true; the same process of combining values with a less sympathetic use of available data will refute any theory of progress.

THE PROGRAM OF RESEARCH

The concentration of evidence and argumentation based on the 1960 literature I have cited coincided with my move to Britain from the United States, where during 2 years' teaching and research at the University of California at Berkeley, I had carried out a project on participative leadership in 15 large American companies. It happens that Fred Emery, on sabbatical from The Tavistock Institute, was at that time a Fellow at the Center for Advanced Study in the Behavioral Sciences at Stanford. Emery was deeply concerned about the lack of democratic organizational practices and, with Einar Thorsrud and other Norwegians, had started some pioneering projects which soon snowballed into a series of programs in Norway as well as Sweden which have been influential to the present day (Emery & Thorsrud, 1969, 1976; Qvale, 1989, 1996).

Emery's interest at that time was concentrated on participation and work design at the shopfloor level following the successful demonstration in British coalmines that semi-autonomous work groups could be very productive (Trist, Higgin, Murray, & Pollock, 1963) My own preference, influenced by 6 years' consultancy in two South American countries, was to start by looking at the value system of senior management and their organizational practices on the assumption that values and democratic or autocratic practices would percolate down the hierarchy and set the pattern for the design of shopfloor work arrangements.

Emery accepted the potential of this approach and invited me to join The Tavistock Institute in 1969 to design an extension of the American research.

The distribution of influence and power in modern organizations was then and is today an important subject for enquiry. Stimulated by the claim that American managers' more democratic styles of decision making accounted to a large extent for their economic superiority, an eight-country comparative study of influence and power sharing among senior management was designed within The Tavistock Institute to test this assumption. The project is known as TMDM (top management decision making) and was followed by a policy-oriented research in 12 countries on Industrial Democracy in Europe (IDE, 1981). Ten years later, the project was repeated in the same companies (IDE, 1993).[3] The experience from these large scale projects was incorporated in a 4-year case study research on organizational decision making in seven companies in three countries (DIO, 1988). Another 4-year in-depth consultancy study was designed to help a major British car maker operate a newly introduced Employee Consultancy schema (BL, 1977).[4] The projects shared a common conceptualization of the nature of influence and power, but as the studies developed over two decades, the working assumptions, methodology, and emphasis changed to benefit from a rapidly escalating literature and a shift in role models from the U.S. to Scandinavia and Japan and, more recently, back again to the United States (after the economic collapse of Japan, 1997-1998).

Some of the studies were in the classical tradition of Action Research while the cross-national projects were more exploratory and heuristic and therefore what I have called "Research-Action" because new knowledge had to be accumulated before action or policy was capable of being implemented (Heller, 1986, 1993).

Several other studies by Tavistock Institute researchers and their Scandinavian colleagues are highly relevant for an understanding of the opportunities and limitations for participative organizational democracy (for instance, Jaques, 1951; Emery & Thorsrud, 1969; Herbst, 1976). The development of the sociotechnical model led to a recognition that decentralized influence to multiskilled semi-autonomous groups could prove to be more productive than hierarchically arranged work structures. The impor-

[3]This program of research was, in the U.K., supported by the Economic and Social Research Council and the Anglo-German Foundation.
[4]The company, British Leyland, now Rover had received massive government grants on condition that it introduced a new participative industrial relations structure. The project was supported by the National Enterprise Council the Nuffield Foundation and the Department of Employment (Heller & Varelidis, 1977).

tance of this shift led to resistance because, as Trist and Murray (1990) say: "Intensive socio-technical change threatens existing power systems and requires a redistribution of power" (p. 31). Resistance to changing power distributions through what are perceived to be zero-sum outcomes, is probably the major explanation for the perseverance of inequality of influence at work over history.[5]

The persistence of these historic trends has been described by the philosopher A. N. Whitehead, who sees it stretching as far into the future as it has into the past. He reminds us of the evolution from slavery to feudalism to business and argues that modern "big business involves a closer analogy to feudalism than does slavery. In fact, the modern social system with its variety of indispensable interlocked avocations necessitates such organisations." Whitehead sees the arguments about individualism and its alternatives as a debate "over the details of the neo-feudalism which modern industry requires." (Whitehead, 1942, p. 38). In the 1970s, we hoped that our program of research would refute Whitehead's pessimism.[6]

THEORETICAL CONSIDERATIONS

The main theoretical support for work on organizational democracy but also some relevant critique comes from philosophers and social scientists who are interested in investigating the idea of freedom and the relation between the state and citizens, with political obligation, and with what is classically called the paradox of self-government (Bosanquet, 1899, Chap. III). These theories will not be reviewed, but a few problems will be briefly noted. Popper (1945) writes about the difficulties faced by a civilization "which aims at humaneness and reasonableness, at equality and freedom" (p. 1). Berlin (1990) talks of liberty and equality as the primary goals of human beings but he is aware of the problems of pursuing such goals too fervently: "equality may demand the restraint of the liberty of those who wish to dominate . . ." (p. 12). Berlin is also conscious of a long line of critical assessment of human nature that would reduce the effectiveness of democratic processes. One line derives from Emmanuel Kant and is quoted by Berlin: "out of the crooked timber of humanity no straight thing was

---

[5]It is important to understand that, in general, resistance to change is the result of a basic need for predictability and equilibrium. This natural tendency has been carefully explained by Schön (1971).

[6]The five fairly integrated studies described above were carried out within the Centre for Decision Making Studies of The Tavistock Institute, which was also involved in several other projects with a bearing on influence and power. One was a seven-country comparative study on the Meaning of Working (MOW, 1987) which came to the conclusion that difference in the work ethic could be largely attributed to the nature of people's jobs and the degree of semi-autonomy in the job design was an important factor in this dimension.

ever made" (p. 48). Something like this negative assessment is incorporated in economic theory which contends that people have limited cognitive abilities (Martin, 1993) and major moral flaws which lead to cheating and unreliability in transactions (Williamson, 1980; Donaldson, 1990). A more recent and highly pessimistic account of managerial motivation is given by Korten (1996) who analyzes in some detail a range of inhuman forces driving modern corporations toward narrowly conceived and dysfunctional monetary objectives.

Then there is Foucault's work on the history of uneven power distributions. It is based, in part at least, on the suggestion that the best way to study power empirically is to use resistance as "a chemical catalyst to bring to light power relations, to locate their position, find out their point of application and the methods used" (Dreyfus & Rabinow, 1982, p. 211). As we shall see, there is extensive evidence of managerial resistance to the introduction of participative methods and resistance to change on a more general level has been attributed to a basic human need for security and equilibrium (Schön, 1971).

A much more positive and optimistic approach is taken by Pateman (1983) who tries to integrate philosophic ideals about political freedom and democracy with the severe constraints of hierarchically organized nonparticipative work systems. She argues that unless people are allowed to exercise influence and discretion in their work lives, their "political efficiency" will be diminished and their motivation and competence will be underused. She is also one of several observers who is aware that if the structure of hierarchical power is left unaltered, participation will be contrived and unreal, what Etzioni (1969) has called inauthentic participation.

Dahrendorf (1979) uses the term 'life chances' to describe "opportunities for individual growth, for the realization of talents, wishes and hopes . . ." (p. 30). He cites changes in universal suffrage as well as codetermination as examples of a development of life chances and although he is careful not to use history as a foil for assessing human progress, nevertheless believes that modern society has the opportunity of greatly increasing human life chances. The theoretical constraints on this growth of opportunities which he calls "ligatures" are all around us, and perhaps totalitarian power is a major inhibiting factor in reducing the opportunities people have to enlarge their personal potential.

Psychologists, starting perhaps with Allport (1945), have analyzed the individual's need for participation as a way of developing the psyche, a theory developed further by Wilpert (1989), who draws on various sources of evidence demonstrating that participation is a necessary human condition for psychological and social development and for achieving a feeling of self-worth. From the micro perspective of the mother–child relation,

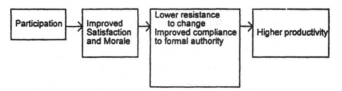

Fig. 1. The human relations model. Extended from the original by Miles (1965).

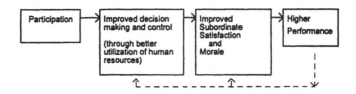

Fig. 2. The human resources model. Extended from the original by Miles (1965).

Winnicott (1950) makes a similar point when he develops the idea that democracy is unavoidably linked to the psychological health and maturity of its individual members.

Bowlby (1946) explores the relationship between democracy and psychoanalytic theory by drawing attention to the conflict between the desire for cooperation between individuals and the unavoidable acceptance of some sacrifice of individual needs. Another conflict arises from the development of in-group feelings as a result of successful cooperation which creates feelings of dependency, but also hostility, toward nongroup members. Bowlby was also one of the first scientists to see the limitation of democracy as due to an inequality of technical knowledge among people in organizations. I will come back to this important observation when I describe the outcomes of our program of research.

Among organizational scientists, theoretical preoccupation is incorporated in models which describe a postulated sequence of events, often without clarifying the dynamics within the schema. The Human Relations Model (Fig. 1) based on research evidence before the 1970s traces a sequence from participation, to increased satisfaction via lower resistance, to change, to superior productivity. The more recent Human Resources Model, based on a broader research base, suggests that participation leads to greater satisfaction at work, as a consequence to a better use of human resources, and consequently to superior productivity (Fig. 2). The important recognition in the Human Resources Model was the central role of skill and experience which are "liberated" by participative practices and would therefore be available to increase productivity.

WHAT IS INFLUENCE?

Organizational democracy, power, involvement, participation, and more recently empowerment are among the terms used to describe a variety of organizational practices in interpersonal and hierarchical relationships and other structural arrangements. A considerable number of theoretical schemas have evolved to describe and define these terms.[7] We have looked at this material[8] and decided to avoid the major prevailing conceptualization, derived from Max Weber, which describes the exercise of power as a struggle between individuals and the imposition of one person's preferences on another.[9] Instead we have taken a quasisystem process view of power. The process starts with access to the socioeconomic and personal sources of power, without which it is stillborn. The second requirement is information, and as we shall see later, competence to understand the information and use it. These conditions create the influence potential which can be achieved in various ways depending on conditions in the decision making system, for instance, the prevailing custom and practice. Using this theoretical framework, we were mainly concerned with operationalizing a description that could cover the range of practices described by the variety of terms in current use.[10] What emerged was the Influence and Power Continuum (IPC) that extended the four Likert styles of decision-making from authoritative to participative (Likert, 1961, Chap. 14) by adding delegation which I had found necessary to describe managerial behavior in the field.[11] The five range IPC was later refined and extended to six alternative degrees of influence and power sharing: (1) not involved (no or minimum amount of information is shared), (2) informed beforehand, (3) informed beforehand and can give opinion, (4) opinion is taken into consideration, (5) take part in decision with equal weight (decisions are made jointly or through consensus), and (6) decide on my own (a person or group is given a degree of autonomy or control). This influence power continuum was used in all the studies mentioned earlier (TMDM; IDE, 1981; IDE, 1993; DIO, 1988).

---

[7]Political scientists, philosophers, sociologists and, to a lesser extent, psychologists, have found it useful or necessary to make a contribution to this conceptual area, for instance, Adler (1925), Abell (1977), Bachrach and Baratz (1970), Boulding (1989), French and Raven (1959), March (1966), and Martin (1977).

[8]See, for instance, Ch. 2 (Heller, Drenth, Koopman, & Rus, 1988).

[9]This is not to deny that this form of power exists, but it is not the best way of analyzing organizational processes.

[10]Tannenbaum and Schmidt (1958) used a "Boss to subordinate centred" leadership behavior range which described seven styles, including one where a manager "sells" his decisions; another where he presents ideas and invites questions. The most participative style allows the subordinate to function "within limits defined by a superior."

[11]The extension of what in the American literature is called PDM (Participative Decision Making) to include delegation and autonomy takes account of research findings, including The Tavistock Institute studies in British coal mines, Scandinavian work on semi-autonomy, European codetermination legislation, and more generally, the trend toward team working.

Although the IPC attempts to assess an aspect of reality, we are very aware of its subjective nature. Influence is not sensibly treated from a structuralist perspective; the events underlying the language are not real in the sense that one can grasp the phenomenon like a maypole. Influence and power are fluid concepts that adjust themselves to new situational challenges. However, the situationally adjusted reality of the IPC is not poststructuralist in the sense that there is nothing behind the term that is not entirely socially constructed at the moment of delivery. The events describing influence and power are judgments by people embedded in the situation and are partly shaped by outside circumstances like hierarchy based on job definition and legal contracts. The translation of job definition backed by legality gives influence and power a transitionally constructed reality and quasi objectivity which decides who is expected to perform certain duties, who is promoted or deprived of work. Slavery from the time of ancient Greece, as well as serfdom, had clear legal foundations and constituted a very tangible reality to all the participants at the time the system operated.[12]

Of course, these transitional realities change and can be challenged, but adjustments are usually over long periods of time and this allows people to make subjectively-real judgments that have operational validity in the sense that they adequately explain current behavior as well as expectations, attitudes, satisfactions, and fears. One of the projects in the program had the aim of testing the assumption that legal power in the form of codetermination legislation acts as a determinant on socially constructed and subjectively assessed influence among different levels of organization (IDE, 1981; IDE, 1993).

A RANGE OF FIELDWORK DESIGNS

The studies in the policy and action program used a variety of methods which fall under the broad heading of applied research and each had a clear theoretical underpinning. All projects, at least in the U.K. sample, used a method called Group Feedback Analysis (GFA) which, in one of its various forms, confronts respondents with their own assessments and asks them to make appropriate interpretations of the data. The respondents must have suitable knowledge and experience of the field under enquiry and, consequently, their assessments are given equal status with the inter-

---

[12]Of course it can be argued that hierarchical structures, legal contracts and the institutions of slavery and serfdom are all socially constructed; that is not contested, but at the point at which these entities impinge on the behavior of people, they take on the appearance and substance of reality (transitionally constructed reality) and objectivity (quasi-objectivity). Laws and sanctioned structures like organizational hierarchies have a degree of immutability and must be distinguished from the constant flow of negotiable and subjective transactions between individuals which usually provide them with a range of options.

pretation of the researcher. The method, which will be explained more fully in the Appendix, can be used to combine quantitative with ethnographic data and by involving respondents, acts as a check on social scientists who may be tempted to give free rein to value judgments.

The eight-country study of senior management (TMDM) used small groups of 4–15 executives who spent an hour before lunch answering questions about how they go about carrying out 12 typical operations in their organizations. Their answers were combined and calculated into simple charts and frequency distributions and, after lunch, fed back to them as anonymous data. They could compare the group results with their own answers and were then invited to interpret how this material helps to explain how their organization operates and how it makes decisions. The discussions were tape-recorded and content analyzed (Heller & Wilpert, 1981).

The study used two levels: Level 1 operated directly under the chief executive; Level 2 were the immediate subordinates of Level 1 managers. Both levels knew that we would ask them identical questions which included an assessment of participative behavior. By using two closely interrelated levels, we expected, *inter alia*, to reduce social desirability distortions which are a frequent problem with enquiries of this kind. In some of the organizations, the feedback discussions led into an action research phase designed to facilitate changes in organizational structure and behavior (Heller, 1971, 1976).

The seven case studies, Decision in Organization (DIO, 1988) research were able to operate in some depth over a period of 4 years through informal meetings with staff at all levels, regular attendance at committee meetings, the use of Interview Schedules, and close contacts with trade unions. Group Feedback Analysis was used frequently to validate our observations and extend the interpretative range (Heller, Drenth, Koopman, & Rus, 1988; Brown & Heller, 1981). We observed 217 tactical and strategic decisions, including budget forecasting, new product development, the purchase of new equipment and the operation of consultative and safety committees and divided the decision process into four phases: initiation, development, finalization, and implementation. Over the 4 years it was possible to separate antecedents from consequences and thus arrive, at least tentatively, at cause–effect conclusions.

The two Industrial Democracy in Europe studies covered 12 countries. Field workers visited 134 companies and interviewed 9000 employees at all levels of the organization using interview schedules. The projects (IDE 1981a,b, 1993) were designed to engage with the European Commission's policy formation on harmonization. The Commission was attempting to persuade member states of the advantages of producing a "level playing field" in basic industrial relations structures for large European companies and multinationals operating in Europe. The main thrust of the IDE research was to see whether legislative or formal industrial democracy schemas had any impact on participative practices at various operation levels in companies.

The program of research described above, while only a part of the considerable literature on participation and related subjects that has been produced since the end of the Second World War, will be used, in conjunction with other evidence, to assess the present state of knowledge on the distribution of influence at work under three headings: one will describe findings on the amount of influence available to different levels of employees, another will attempt to answer questions about the utility of participative practices, and the third will describe the conditions under which influence sharing work designs can be expected to be effective.

HOW MUCH INFLUENCE IS SHARED?

I will start with the project discussed with Fred Emery and based on the 1960 literature cited earlier which claimed that participative styles of decision making were at least partially responsible for American industry's superior productivity. The results of our eight-country comparative study (TMDM) produced some significant and interesting results which we will discuss later, but the average participative styles used by our sample of American managers did not support the claim that their superior productivity can be related to their significantly greater use of democratic influence-sharing practices. Nevertheless, similar assumptions about the relation between participative decision styles and a country's economic performance continue to be made. Lawler (1986), for instance, claims that if American management wants to remain competitive with world class, particularly Japanese companies, it will have to adopt more extensive employee involvement practices. Two large-scale Norwegian and Swedish organizational democratization projects, particularly the former, also had as one of their main objectives to make their industries more competitive (Davies, Naschold, Pritchard, & Reve, 1993; Naschold, Cole, Gustavsen, & Beinum, 1993).

Each of the projects in our program of research assessed the distribution of participative practices on the Influence-Power-Continuum, sometimes by questionnaire, sometimes by interview and, in the DIO project, by observation. The results show that lower levels of organization have on average almost no influence on the decision process. Taking the range of six alternatives described above, the lowest level of employee does not quite achieve "being informed beforehand," and on strategic decisions like investment, they were close to "not involved at all." Even middle management barely reached the point where they can give an opinion (IDE, 1981b,

p. 186). The concentration of power at senior levels was very considerable (Heller & Wilpert, 1981; Heller, Pusic, Strauss, & Wilpert, 1998). Similar results have been found in other projects (Gill & Krieger, 1992; Gill, Beaupin, Fröhlich, & Krieger, 1993; Marchington, Goodman, Wilkinson, & Ackers, 1992; Gallie & White, 1993).

These average results hide the fact that, particularly at middle and senior levels, participative practices varied significantly for different types of decisions. This result derived from all our projects has important practical implications. Two factors account for this contingency: interest and competence. So, for instance, employees at workplace level are interested and able to participate in the resolution of problems close to their work but they are not very concerned with and lack competence in relation to strategic issues (see also Vroom & Yetton, 1973). Further support comes from our finding that participation varies significantly between the phases of a decision cycle. Lower level employees usually have more influence over implementation than over initiation or the process of development and alternative choices (Heller et al., 1988). Since interests and competency vary considerably between individuals, groups, and organizational level, one would not expect influence sharing to show uniform results. However, as we shall argue, although these contingencies explain differences, their significance for organizational practice and the design of participative schemata is rarely recognized.

WHY SHARE INFLUENCE?

Several reasons are generally put forward in support of participative practices. They are supposed to induce job satisfaction, increase employee loyalty, lead to higher productivity, and reduce resistance to change. Except for job satisfaction, the evidence in support of these contentions is not very strong (Wagner & Gooding, 1987; Wagner, 1994), and ever since the Bank Wiring Room experience in the Hawthorne studies, there is evidence that job satisfaction may be associated with complacency and low productivity.

Our projects take a different approach and find that high degrees of influence sharing are associated with a better quality and effectiveness of decisions and a significant reduction in the underutilization of people's experience and skills and therefore supports the Human Resources rather than the Human Relations model.

The evidence on the association between participation and the quality of outcome derives from two studies; firstly, from the TMDM research among senior managers where the "improved technical quality of decision" obtained first rank among five reasons for using participation in every country except France at the top level and first rank in six countries on the second senior management level (it came second in the remaining two countries; see Heller & Wilpert, 1981, p. 86). Discussion during Group Feedback Analysis (GFA) confirmed and elaborated this finding. The seven longitudinal case study project (DIO, 1988) used an assessment of the "effectiveness of decisions"[13] and "achievement feasibility"[14] as outcomes. Both were clearly a consequence of a variety of factors in the participation matrix (Heller et al., 1988, p. 220).

The data on the relation of participation to competence started with the surprising finding that there was a significant underutilization of experience and skill even among senior managers, and it was particularly strong among the younger as well as the more highly educated (Heller & Wilpert, 1981, pp. 116-122). However, the more participation, the lower was the extent of underutilization. Furthermore, subjective judgments about the competence of subordinates was related to the amount of influence sharing. Where a manager judged a subordinate to have low skills, even if this judgment was almost certainly mistaken,[15] he would allow little participation and *vice versa* (Heller & Wilpert, 1981; Heller et al., 1988). I conclude from this evidence that one of the principal consequences of appropriate influence sharing is a reduction in the extensive underutilization of human resources.

It should be noted that these outcome measures of quality and competence are fairly directly related to influence sharing while the more traditional measures of satisfaction, job loyalty, and bottom-line measures like higher productivity can be linked more easily to a variety of other conditions. Productivity, for instance, can frequently be shown to be a function of a variety of economic supply and demand variables, exchange rate variations, fiscal and monetary policy, or even to the weather in businesses selling cold drinks or ice cream products. No amount of participation, however successful, can make up for these external impingements.

Finally, following Wilpert (1989), I have already argued that an important sociopsychological reason for influence sharing is based on the assumption that participative activity among adults as well as children facilitates human development. Of course it is quite reasonable to go on and say that if participative decision making facilitates human development, leads to a liberation of existing competence (experience and skill), and improves the quality of decisions, then—other things being equal—it will also affect the bottom line. However, other things are not always equal and the

---

[13]This was described as the amount of energy, time, and other resources used in relation to the quality of the decision.
[14]The extent to which a solution to a given problem was achieved.
[15]We had some objective indicators of skill.

overidealistic expectations of some researchers and consultants have caused unnecessary disillusionment.

CONDITIONS FOR EFFECTIVE INFLUENCE SHARING

Experience with our own projects and acquaintance with some of the literature, for instance the six volumes of Year- and Handbooks on Participation,[16] confirms that among the necessary antecedent conditions for successful influence sharing two are particularly important: trust and competence. I start with competence, because this factor has just been described as an important outcome of participative behavior while now I am claiming that it is also a relevant though often neglected antecedent. In the section on theoretical considerations, I have argued that support for developments in democratic organizational practices has often come from philosophers or political theorists. This has meant that by analogy with citizenship rights in politics, participation can be treated as if it were a necessary condition for the fulfillment of democratic practices in modern organizations and available to everybody, like universal suffrage. However, this analogy neglects differences in structure and competence requirements. We have already seen that Bowlby (1946) has argued that it is difficult to sustain democracy when technical knowledge is unequally distributed and while there is a remote similarity between representative participation at work and the political system, there is none with direct informal participation. Other important differences between political and organizational democracy are in the complexity of concepts and the esoteric use of economic–financial language as well as the rate of change in technology, economic, and marketing expertise relevant for organizational decision making.

The cumulative evidence from various studies now shows that relevant experience and skill are a critical requirement for effective organizational participation (Heller, Pusic, Strauss, & Wilpert, 1998). However, the creation of experience and skill through training has been neglected. One of the causes of pseudoparticipation or inauthenticity is that employees are brought into a consultative process on topics with which they lack experience (TMDM & DIO). Furthermore, management's reluctance to give up influence in conditions which they believe to be a zero sum game, is another reason for pseudoparticipation which leads to distrust. We have found this to be openly admitted during the feedback procedure of GFA. Managers described what they were doing as "prior consultation" but then admitted

---

[16]*International Yearbook of Organizational Democracy* (Vols. I, II, and III published by Wiley and *International Handbook Of Participation In Organizations.* (Vols. I, II, and III) published by Oxford University Press. Editorial board: Frank Heller, Eugen Pusic, Jean Daniel Reynaud, George Strauss, and Bernhard Wilpert.

that the decision had been taken before the consultative procedure was used or they had already made up their mind but felt that employees had an expectation of being consulted anyway (TMDM & DIO)[17]

During GFA with two interlocked levels of management we found that subordinates are often fully aware of the deceptive techniques practiced by their seniors and this constituted an important reason for distrust. Differences in values between people and particularly between management and unions is a major source of distrust and an important reason for union opposition to formal as well as informal participative schemas. This was a major factor in the long drawn out and difficult negotiations that eventually led to British Leyland (BL) setting up a three-tier participative structure. Because the motor car industry has a long history of antagonism and distrust between management and unions, it is unlikely that such a structure would ever have been set up without government's insistence. The new Participation Councils worked well for 2 years and the chief executive attended every top-level council meeting and established good working relations with senior shop stewards. When the scheme disintegrated 3 years later, it was due to a revival of distrust based on noticeably different values. A new chief executive failed to attend the employee participation meetings, perhaps because he knew that this were incompatible with having to bring about widespread redundancies. However, as a consequence of his not attending council meetings, the economic justification for labor redundancies was never explained and the unions decided to pull out of the participation scheme (Heller & Varelidis, 1977). Trust is a feeling and perception; it takes a long time to build but is easily destroyed. Recent developments in management consultancy leading to a culture of abrupt structural changes and "downsizing" have made it difficult to retain trustful relations. Kay (1994), in his analysis of global economic competitiveness, has laid heavy emphasis on "social institutions which support trust relationships and the development of tacit knowledge . . ." (p. 9). In an extension of IDE (1981) among the British working population, we discovered that over a 15-year period, trust had substantially diminished (Heller, Wilders, Abell, & Warner, 1979).[18]

The model that emerges from the series of projects I have described, extends the central role of competence in the Human Resources Model by giving it a dual position both before and after influence-sharing practices and claims that prior relevant competence is a necessary motivating condition and requires an investment in the development of skill and experience. Improved performance is then a consequence of the superior utilization of the human potential (Fig. 3). The improved performance, often achieved by a better

---

[17]For one of many specific examples, see Heller (1971, pp. 63-64).
[18]The comparison was with identical questions asked in the 1963 Almond & Verba Civic Culture study.

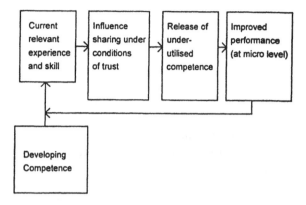

Fig. 3. The motivated competence model (adapted from Heller, 1992).

quality of decisions, is conceptually independent of productivity, which as we saw, can be a function of a variety of exogenous factors. The model also specifies that influence-sharing must be based on trust.

It is worth repeating that legal support measures, as used in most continental European countries, are indicative of *de facto* participative practices (IDE, 1981a, b; IDE, 1993). Formal schemata (Status Power in the DIO project) or policies enshrined in binding management–union contracts, as in some sectors of U.S. organizations, can achieve similar effects.

Finally, the longitudinal design in the DIO study and the division of decision-making events into four phases led to the discovery that the amount of influence different groups exercised over work activities varied significantly from phase to phase. Usually, this distribution of influence was functional and seen as appropriate by the participating employees. Variations in employee experience and competence was an important factor in the phase analysis of organizational behavior. Specialist middle managers often had most influence in the initiation and development phases of a process while lower levels had the experience to be particularly active in the implementation phase. Participative work designs that ignore such phase variations are unlikely to be successful.

BUT IT CAN WORK[19]

Our rapid gallop through several millennia of history at the beginning of this article did not provide us with a very positive developmental picture about a significant growth in the amount of influence given to people in

[19]This section contains some results not reported in the preceding sections, but derived from the Tavistock program of research.

their work activities. Furthermore, the results of the program of work I have just described do not amount to a paradigm shift toward organizational democracy. Apart from relatively isolated experiments, many of which have not lasted very long, employees at low organization levels do not, on average, even get information about decisions that could affect them and without information, no participation is practicable. Some students of organizational participation have claimed that at least over the last hundred years, changes in participative practices have been cyclical (Ramsay, 1977; Emery, 1993) and earlier we cited Hobhouse and Westermarck's view, fairly typical of the more cautious social scientists who do not wish to commit themselves to the value implications of an evolutionary view of human progress, Dahrendorf (1979) takes a similar circumspect approach.

While there may be no presumption of evolutionary progress, we have seen that many philosophers and social scientists believe that the exertion of influence through some form of democratic participation is important for human development, political maturity, and efficient productive organizations.

Reviewing our program of research, we can now ask whether there are experiences and findings that would justify a reasonable degree of optimism and allow us to conclude that, at some future date, a wider measure of organizational influence-sharing methods will be used.

I believe that a cautiously positive answer is justified on two counts; firstly, by summarizing our research evidence under four headings: expectations, contingencies, antecedents, and a structurally supported systems framework. Secondly, there are indications that some important trendsetters are beginning to think about pluralist organizational responsibility.

Firstly, our findings. Exaggerated expectations among some academics, miscellaneous well-wishers, and consultants, have inevitably led to disappointment (Strauss, 1963). They have also introduced unnecessary apprehension among managers. We find that while most employees want more influence at work than is currently available to them, their demands are very moderate and mainly confined to routine rather than tactical or strategic issues. By their nature, these expectations do not threaten the so-called managerial prerogative, though they may lead to fewer levels of management. Unrealistic and exaggerated expectations of the likely impact of participative practices on organizational productivity and therefore global competitiveness have ignored the obvious reality that the so-called "bottom line" is a function of many overlapping and competing external and internal circumstances among which democratic practices are only one ingredient. Nevertheless, we find that appropriate influence sharing leads to a high level of achievement and effectiveness of decision objectives accompanied by a substantial reduction in the pervasive underutilization of human capacity. It is this effect on the greater utilization of existing competence and motivation that is, in my view, the major outcome of democratic organizational practices (see Fig. 3). Under favorable conditions and the absence of exogenous detriments, this could lead to high productivity.

Successful influence-sharing is contingent on task and competence. Decisions that have critical personnel implications for work design or safety, for instance, require—and in our findings—achieve much higher levels of participation than issues concerned with narrow technological, legal, or financial considerations. Not all tasks are equally congenial or motivating to potential participants or are congruent with their current experience and skill.

Our research has identified two major antecedents for effective influence sharing in organizations: competence and trust. The former has already been mentioned as a contingent factor and while some experience and learning can be developed during the process of participation, most of it has to be acquired beforehand; this also increases the level of motivation and trust (see Fig. 3). An absence of the necessary learning and development opportunities for staff at all levels has been a major factor in the failure of participation schemes. The constantly increasing standards of education in most countries should reduce this obstacle unless it is neutralized by the rate of sophisticated technological change.

The literature of organizational democracy is littered with isolated idiosyncratic experiments and pseudo panaceas. Most operate at the lowest organizational level in the hope that by some strange law of osmosis the practice will percolate up to policymaking *fora*; some concentrate on senior management and boardroom level in the expectation, at one time shared by myself, that the initiative will gravitate through the organization. Very few have taken a systemic approach which argues for the need to integrate values and action in a holistic policy initiative endorsed throughout the organization and supported by appropriate incentives. Research evidence shows that success is a function of policies which introduce bundles of related participative measures throughout the organization (Heller et al., 1998) and the two IDE projects suggest that further support for lasting schemas of organizational democracy derive from formal, usually legally backed measures and thrive within a framework of collective representation. A further reason for optimism is the recent slowly growing advocacy for pluralist organizational responsibility.

TOWARDS PLURALIST ORGANIZATIONAL RESPONSIBILITY

The last decade of the twentieth century has witnessed a proliferation of economic and organizational ideas that have led to an increased speed of change, to greater pressure on individuals, to reduced organizational slack, and to a widening gap between the financial power exerted by people at the top and bottom of the organizational pyramid.

These developments have coincided with the demise of communist dictatorships in central and Eastern Europe leading some people to claim a new dawn in history based on the combined achievements of liberal democracy and modern capitalism (Fukuyama, 1993). However, these political changes did not obliterate economic cycles. Many economies have been seriously depressed, unemployment has grown in many parts of the world, the tenure of jobs has become unpredictable, global competition has increased, and stress has become a way of life at the same time as rewards have become more unequally distributed.

Some opinion leaders have begun to question the infallibility of the market as an "invisible hand" mechanism for regulating our lives.[20] In November 1993, the Pope was reported in the *La Stampa* newspaper to have condemned unbridled capitalism which in some parts of the world, he said, was almost as savage as 100 years ago and certainly excessively individualistic and in disregard of community needs. In the same year, the Royal Society of Arts started a business-led investigation into the shape of "Tomorrow's Company" initiated by the chief executives of 14 large enterprises. The enquiry team interviewed the Chairmen and CEOs of 48 companies and held a number of public meetings in different part of Britain. Altogether they claim to have debated the issues with over 8000 people. Their analysis, 3 years later, widely reported in the press, came to some startlingly untraditional conclusions.

As against the prevailing standard view that the overriding responsibility of directors is to maximize the returns to the current body of shareholders, they adopted the view of their legal advisers that companies have a much wider range of fiduciary responsibilities and that there is nothing in company law to prevent directors from having regard to the interest of other stakeholders including employees, suppliers, and customers. The responsibility of directors is to the long-term survival and economic effectiveness of their companies and this may require what they call "an inclusive" approach which has to pay close attention to the public's concerns (Cleaver, 1995). "Tomorrow's Company" report prefers the term "inclusive" to stakeholder to show their independence of political pressures, since the stakeholder concept, though derived from academic ideas in the United States (Ackoff, 1994) has recently been popularized and changed through adoption in political programs (Kelly, Kelly, & Gamble, 1997).

---

[20]Some of this critique dates back 100 years. See for instance Hobson's 1898 account of John Ruskin as a social reformer, quoting Ruskin's declaration that "there is no wealth but life" (p. 93).

The reassessment of concerns and responsibilities has been eloquently supported by Handy (1996) who looks at changes in public and organizational values. He starts with a critique of the ever-widening gap in remuneration which in America even in 1989 meant that the top 1% collectively earned more than the bottom 40%. Progress is now often identified with what he calls the "mercenary organization" which pays more attention to narrow measures of efficiency than to the broader assessment of effectiveness giving the example of a hospital which can increase its efficiency by turning away very sick people. He looks toward the future and a new decent capitalism which values freedom but is aware of Jean-Paul Sartre's view that we can also be condemned by freedom. With Rousseau he believes that we are born with the capacity for self-improvement, and he gives organizations the responsibility to help us develop our potential. He also sees the new-look capitalism as a preserver of our environment and presumably sees this as part of a re-orientation from a concentration of bottom-line efficiency and maximization toward a societal regard for long-term effectiveness.

Similar concerns have been expressed by Soros (1997), one of the most successful financiers of the twentieth century who starts his analysis with a reference to Hegel's philosophy of history, followed by a closely argued support for Henri Bergson and Karl Popper's views of the "Open Society" and its opposition to autocratic ideologies. Soros questions the validity of the basic equilibrium assumption of economic theory on the basis of re-flexivity feedback mechanisms, and he questions the magic of the market and the notion that the common good is best achieved by an uninhabited pursuit of self-interest. Like Handy, but from a more theoretical perspective, he criticizes the grossly uneven distribution of wealth and power and its market apologists. The pretentious and false assumptions of economic theory are, he says, the new enemy to the open society. Instead of *laissez faire* values that would support what he calls "robber capitalism," we need humility and a belief in our own fallibility. There have been several other similar critiques of economic doctrines (Etzioni, 1988, 1993; Ormerod, 1994; Nussbaum & Sen, 1993; Radin, 1996).

It is now appropriate to ask whether the Open Society concept should apply to organizations as well as to the wider community within which they operate. Neither George Soros nor Pope John Paul II address the distribution of influence at the micro level, but Charles Handy and the senior industrialists who support the ideas of "Tomorrow's Company," move quite close to contemplating such an extension. At the micro level, the Open Society concept would question the functional justification for steep hierarchies and the corollary that wisdom and good judgment should be monopolized at the apex. More generally, a micro Open Society view would recognize plurality of interests and values and would therefore organize representative as well as informal influence sharing structures to meet these legitimate aspirations and at the same time include employees as stakeholders.

The case for a micro level Open Society as a democratic norm is probably as strong as the case at the political level where the contrast is also between pluralism and monism, that is to say between a belief that diversity is not only equitable, but also functional in producing superior solutions compared with the imposition of a single authoritative regimen. A gradual movement in the public debate toward the concept of a pluralistic organizational responsibility is detectable beyond the few examples I have given, for instance, the current extensive debate and research on the "psychological contract" (Makin, Cooper, & Cox, 1996) and it is generally assumed that growing standards of education will support this movement, but it is, of course, also possible that we are only witnessing the upturn of another cycle of temporary idealism which has been identified by Ramsay and Emery and mentioned earlier.

DENOUEMENT

The outcome of the research program developed over two and a half decades by The Tavistock Institute's Centre for Decision Making Studies and its associates, can be interpreted in two ways. On the shadow side we find that, although there is now a very extensive scientific and popular literature on participation, employee involvement, and team working, the empirical evidence shows that on average very little influence percolates from the top to lower levels of organizations. There are of course quite a number of exceptions like the Glacier Metal company where an unusual organizational democracy schema lasted for over 30 years (Heller, 1986, pp. 131-134). In America, there was the Rushton coalmine experiment (Trist, Susman, & Brown, 1977) and a dozen others that have been written up extensively. Then there are a number of successful Scandinavian examples (Naschold, Cole, Gustavsen, & van Beinum, 1993) and organizations where participation and ownership is widely distributed as in the Scott Bader Commonwealth (Hoe, 1978) and the Spanish cooperative Mondragon (Whyte & Whyte, 1992). Our intention is not so much to make a balanced overall assessment of the situation, as to point out the contrast between what the 1960s promised and the 1990s delivered.

Similarly, our short excursion into the distribution of influence over time can be interpreted differently. The philosopher A. N. Whitehead, whom I quoted earlier, thought that big business still perpetuates the rigid inequalities of neofeudalism which modern systems of interlocked hierarchies seem to require, while an important group of British Chief Executives assembled by the Royal Society of Arts believe that some modern organizations already practice an influence-sharing "inclusive" approach based on a legal interpretation of shareholder vs. stakeholder responsiblities.

The stakeholder concept was anticipated by J. B. Priestley, who critiqued the world's preoccupation with distributing power through property rights. Property, he thought, was "an old fashioned way of thinking of a country (perhaps also an organization) as a thing instead of thinking of it as a living society and considering the welfare of that society, the community itself" (Priestley, 1940). However, the conflict between those who champion individual as against societal rights is likely to continue into the twenty-first century although I argue that recently, pluralist organizational responsibility thinking has been in the ascendancy.

On the narrower level of organizational influence sharing our research program, supported by other evidence, comes to the following four conclusions:

- Expectations about the extent and achievement of organizational democracy have frequently been unrealistic.
- There has been a tendency to ignore or minimize the need for certain necessary antecedents among which formal structural support measures, for instance laws, competence (experience and skill), and trust are the most important.
- There has been a tendency to believe and act as if influence sharing can operate universally, that is to say equally effectively in all or most situations. Findings show that this is not so. There are a number of contingencies: task, competence, motivation, and phase of the decision cycle that are particularly important.
- Most participation experiments are introduced through social engineering as isolated events. However, research evidence points toward the need for a holistic systems approach which cannot be confined to a single level or group, which cannot be used like a sticking plaster to hide a wound and which cannot derive from an *ad hoc* set of beliefs based on the short-term need for competition, higher productivity, a reduced exposure to trade unions, or a need to overcome resistance to change (Ichniowski et al., 1996; Heller et al., 1998).

Social engineering prescribes particularistic mechanical solutions to organizational problems while a systemic philosophy treats an enterprise like a complex social entity of interdependent parts operating within a wider sociopolitical economic life space sustained by humanistic values. Within an Open Society framework the main agents in that life-space, in particular, owners, employees, and customers, can be assigned an appropriate amount of influence commensurate with their long-term contribution to the socioeconomic well-being of the enterprise.

Looking at the cumulative results from the quarter century of research reported in this paper, I conclude that approaches grounded in this evidence are essential for a realistic appraisal of the potential that organizational democracy practices can achieve.

ACKNOWLEDGMENTS

Whenever The Tavistock Institute was involved in the projects described in this paper, the work was carried out in groups and responsibility was widely dispersed. Consequently, three of the books and several articles were published under acronyms rather than authors. We learned a great deal from each other and I gratefully acknowledge indebtedness to many colleagues. The Tavistock Institute's work on these projects was supported by the Economic and Social Research Council, the Anglo-German Foundation for the Study of Industrial Society, the Nuffield Foundation, the British Ministry of Labour, and the National Economic Development Council. Other funding bodies supported the overseas research teams; full acknowledgment is made in the various publications referred to in this article.

APPENDIX. GROUP FEEDBACK ANALYSIS (GFA)

While the method has been used in a variety of ways to accommodate different research requirements, it has one basic epistemological objective: to move from relatively simple uncomplicated, entropic, or superficial knowledge to a deeper idiographic heuristic. The method was originally devised to build a bridge between quantitative and ethnographic data collection (Heller, 1969). It was extended to harness the experience of the client system, that is to say the people who provide social science with information, to build up a reliable corpus of knowledge and to allow the accumulation of evidence, where appropriate, to facilitate self-motivated change processes (Heller, 1970). The learning or change element in the method is based on dissonance theory (Festinger, 1958) which postulates that if two psychological states are in conflict, then motivational forces will try to reduce the conflict (Zimbardo & Leippe, 1991). This is based on extensive evidence that, in general, people prefer a balanced cognitive state rather than one based on inconsistent attitudes, beliefs, values, or sets of data.

The method operates in a sequence of three steps. The first two are quite conventional; firstly, information is obtained from small groups by any appropriate method including short questionnaires, interviews, or a combination including participant observation and archive material. The second step is to make a preliminary brief analysis of the accumulated data for feedback presentation. The presentation can be made in writing or verbally, descriptively or quantitatively. The feedback session is the important part of the approach and is designed to achieve the objectives described earlier and in particular to see that the almost inevitable differences in judgment, values, and experiences exposed in the feedback material, are used—via dissonance reduction as a learning opportunity. The feedback establishes a dialogue between the people who supplied the information in the first place and are therefore assumed to be experienced and knowledgeable about the subject under scrutiny and the researcher(s). The opening phrase is usually something like: "This is the material we have obtained from you/your organization, can you please help us to interpret it. What does it mean to you, and is there something missing?" The ensuing dialogue is carefully noted (where possible tape-recorded) and serves as an essential part of the final analysis (Brown & Heller, 1978; Heller & Wilpert, 1981; Heller, Drenth, Koopman, & Rus, 1988; Heller & Brown, 1995). The clients or their representatives can collaborate with the researcher(s) in the data analysis and feedback presentation to achieve ownership of the process. When GFA is used as a part of Action Research or Research Action (Heller, 1993), the client becomes involved at a much earlier stage of the process, including the original formulation of the problem and approach.

The method is fairly flexible and can be slotted into a variety of research designs, including deconstructionism, in the sense that the interpretation of the data by the client system can be very critical of the traditional assumptions and preconceptions of the research community, by attempting to unravel hidden assumptions, internal contradictions, and repressed meanings (Gemmill & Oakley, 1992). In relation to a topic like leadership or power, the method would permit "us to question the limits that may have been imposed upon discourses of knowledge and (it) opens the possibility of enacting other, different discourses" (Calas & Smircich, 1991).

The method bears some resemblance to Search Conferences, as described by Emery (1981) and Weisbord (1992). Such a meeting "starts off by asking people to get off their hobbyhorse and suspend judgement about what specific outcomes will occur, until something like a shared overall picture emerges . . . . Values, ideals, and broadly based ideas are the main fare of search conferences and they are also the main feature of social change. Finally, in search conferences as in GFA there is a deliberate attempt to play down the role of the expert" (Emery, 1981, p. 467).

REFERENCES

ABELL, P. The many faces of power and liberty: Revealed preference, autonomy and teleological explanation. *Sociology*, 1977, *11*, 3-23.

ABELL, P. The viability of industrial producer cooperation. In C. Crouch and F. Heller (Eds.), *International yearbook of organizational democracy* (Vol. I). Chichester: John Wiley & Sons, 1983.

ACKOFF, R. L. *The democratic corporation: A radical prescription for recreating corporate America and rediscovering success.* New York: Oxford University Press, 1994.

ADLER, A. *The practice and theory of individual psychology.* London: Kegan Paul, Trench, Trubner & Co., 1925.

ALLPORT, G. The psychology of participation. *Psychological Reviews*, 1945, *53*, 117-132.

BACHRACH, P., & BARATZ, M. *Power and poverty: Theory and practice.* London: Oxford University Press, 1970.

BERLIN, I. *The crooked timber of humanity: Chapters in the history of ideas.* London: John Murray (Publisher) Ltd., 1990.

BERNSTEIN, P. Workplace democratization: Its internal dynamics. *Organization and Administrative Sciences* (special issue), 1976, *7*(3), 1-127.

BL (British Leyland). This was a 5-year field study in what was at the time the biggest U.K. car manufacturer employing 120,000 people. The action research was supported by top management and national as well as company unions. It was financed by the Nuffield Foundation, by the Department of Employment, and the National Enterprise Council. The project was negotiated by Frank Heller. Nikos Varelidis was the principal Research Assistant. The only detailed account is the Final Report to the funding bodies by Heller & Varelidis. References to this research have been made in various publications, 1977.

BLAND, A. F., BROWN, P. A., & TAWNEY, R. H. *English economic history select documents.* London: G. Bell & Sons, 1914.

BOSANQUET, B. *The philosophical theory of the state.* London: Macmillan & Co., 1899.

BOULDING, K. E. *Power: A general theory.* Boulder: University of Colorado, 1989.

BOWLBY, J. Psychology and democracy. *The Political Quarterly*, 1946, *xvii*, 61-76.

BRANNEN, P., BATSTONE, E., FATCHETT, D., & WHITE, P. *The worker directors: A sociology of participation.* London: Hutchinson, 1976.

BROWN, A., & HELLER, F. Usefulness of group feed-back analysis as a research method: Its application to a questionnaire study. *Human Relations*, 1981, *34*(2), 141-156.

BULLOCK. *Report of the Committee of Enquiry on Industrial Democracy.* Her Majesty's Stationery Office, Command Paper 6706, 1977.

CALAS, M., & SMIRCICH, L. Voicing seduction to silence leadership. *Organization Studies*, 1991, *12*(3), 567-601.

CAVES, R. (Ed.) *Britain's economic prospect.* London: Allen & Unwin, 1968.

CHELL, E. *Participation and organization: A social psychological approach.* London: The Macmillan Press Ltd., 1985.

CHILD, J. Participation, organization and social cohesion. *Human Relations*, 1976, *29*(5), 429-451.

CLEAVER, SIR A. Tomorrow's company. *Royal Society of Arts Journal*, December 1995, 21-32.

COATES, K., & TOPHAM, A. *Shop stewards and workers' control: A book of readings and witnesses for workers' control.* London: Spokesman Books, 1975.

CORNFORTH, C., & THOMAS, A. Cooperative development: Barriers, support structures and cultural factors. *Economic and Industrial Democracy*, 1990, *11*(4), 451-461.

DAHRENDORF, R. *Life chances: Approaches to social and political theory.* Chicago: University of Chicago Press, 1979.

DAVIES, A., NASCHOLD, F., PRITCHARD, W., & REVE, T. with the assistance of B. Olsen, T. Sørum, R. Saeveraas, and B. Willadssen. Evaluation Report, Commissioned by the Board of the SBA Programme, June, 1993.

DIEBOLT, J. Is the gap technological? *Foreign Affairs*, 1968, *46*(2), 276-291.

DIO (Decisions in Organization). This was an in-depth longitudinal (5-year) study in seven organizations; three in the Netherlands, two in Britain, and two in Yugoslavia (now Slovenia). The principal researchers were Frank Heller (coordinator), Pieter Drenth, Paul Koopman, and Veljko Rus. Field workers included Alan Brown, Miro Odar, F. B. M. Bus, A. J. Kruyswijk, and A. F. M. Wiersdma. The British funds came from the Social Science Research Council which also paid for some of the Yugoslav costs. The Netherland

Organization for the Advancement of Pure Research and the Research Community of the Republic of Slovenia supported their respective teams, 1988.

DONALDSON, L. The ethereal hand: Organizational economics and management theory. *Academy of Management Review,* 1990, *15*(3), 369-381.

DREYFUS, H. L., & RABINOW, P. *Michel Foucault: Beyond structuralism and hermeneutics.* Chicago: University of Chicago Press, 1982.

ECONOMIST, THE. The flourishing business of slavery, September 21, 1996.

EMERY, F. Searching for common ground. In F. Emery (Ed.), *Systems thinking* (Vol. 2). Harmondsworth: Penguin Books, 1981.

EMERY, F. Socio-technical foundations for a new social order. In E. Trist and H. Murray (Eds.), *The social engagement of social science* (Vol. 2). A Tavistock Anthology, Philadelphia: University of Pennsylvania Press, 1993.

EMERY, F. E., & THORSRUD, E. A New Look at Industrial Democracy. Symposium 15th International Congress of Applied Psychology, Ljubljana, August 1964. *Mimeographed,* The Tavistock Institute of Human Relations, London.

EMERY, F. E., & THORSRUD, E. *Form and content in industrial democracy: Some experiences from Norway and other European countries.* London: Tavistock Publications, 1969.

ETZIONI, A. Man and society: The inauthentic condition. *Human Relations,* 1969, *22,* 325-332.

ETZIONI, A. *The moral dimension: Toward a new economics.* New York: The Free Press, 1988.

ETZIONI, A. Normative-affective choices. *Human Relations,* 1993, *46*(9), 1053-1068.

FESTINGER, L. The motivating effect of cognitive dissonance. In Lindzey (Ed.), *Assessment of Human Motives.* New York: Rinehard & Co., 1958.

FRAZER, SIR J. *The golden bough: A study in magic and religion.* London: Macmillan, 1933.

FRENCH, J. R. P., & RAVEN, B. The bases of social power. In D. Cartwright (Ed.), *Studies in social power.* Ann Arbor, MI: Institute for Social Research, 1959.

FUKUYAMA, F. *The end of history and the last man.* Harmondsworth: Penguin, 1993.

GALLIE, D., & WHITE, M. *Employee commitment and the skills revolution.* London: Policy Studies Institute, 1993.

GEMMILL, G., & OAKLEY, J. Leadership: An alienating social myth. *Human Relations,* 1992, *45*(2), 113-129.

GILL, C., & KRIEGER, H. The diffusion of participation in new information technology in Europe: Survey results. *Economic and Industrial Democracy,* 1992, *13,* 331-358.

GILL, C., BEAUPIN, T., FRÖHLICH, D., & KRIEGER, H. *Workplace involvement in technological innovation in the European Community. Vol. II—Issues of Participation.* Dublin, Ireland: The European Foundation for the Improvement of Living and Working Conditions, 1993.

GRANICK, D. *The European executive.* London: Weidenfeld and Nicolson, 1962.

HAENNI, P. Management gap in a world context: A spectral analysis. *Progress, Unilever Quarterly,* 1969, No. 2, 106-114.

HAMMOND, J. L., & HAMMOND, B. *The town labourer 1760-1832: The new civilisation.* London: Longman Green & Co., 1925.

HANDY, C. What's it all for? Reinventing capitalism for the next century. *Royal Society of Arts Journal,* December 1996, 33-40.

HELLER, F. A. Group feed-back analysis: A method of field research. *Psychological Bulletin,* 1969, *72,* 108-117.

HELLER, F. A. Group feedback analysis as a change agent. *Human Relations,* 1970, *23,* 319-333 (German translation: *Gruppendynamik,* 1972, *3,* 175-191).

HELLER, F. A. *Managerial decision-making: A study of leadership styles and power sharing.* London, Tavistock Publications, 1971.

HELLER, F. A. Group feed-back analysis as a method of action research. In A. W. Clark (Ed.), *Experiences in action research.* New York: Plenum Press, 1975.

HELLER, F. A. Group feed-back analysis as a method of action research. In A. W. Clark (Ed.), *Experimenting with organizational life.* New York, London, Plenum Press, 197, pp. 209-222.

HELLER, F. (Ed.). *The use and abuse of social science.* London and Beverly Hills: Sage Publications, 1986.

HELLER, F. A. Another look at action research. *Human Relations,* 1993, *46*(10), 1235-1242.

HELLER, F., & BROWN, A. Group feedback analysis applied to longitudinal monitoring of the decision making process. *Human Relations,* 1995, *48*(7).

HELLER, F. A., & VARELIDIS, N. A Current British Development in Industrial Democracy. Paper to Second International Conference on Participation, Workers' Control and Self-Management, Paris, September 1977.

HELLER, F. A., & WILPERT, B. *Competence and power in managerial decision making.* Chichester: John Wiley & Sons, 1981.

HELLER, F. A., WILDERS, M., ABELL, P., & WARNER, M. What do the British want from participation and industrial democracy? London, Anglo-German Foundation for the Study of Industrial Society, 1979, 105 pp.

HELLER, F. A., DRENTH, P., KOOPMAN, P., & RUS. V. *Decisions in organizations: A three country study.* London: Sage Publications, 1988.

HELLER, F. A., PUSIC, E., STRAUSS, G., & WILPERT, B. *Organizational participation: Myth and reality.* Oxford University Press. 1998.

HERBST, P. G. *Alternatives to hierarchies.* Leiden: Martinus Nijhoff, 1976.

HOBHOUSE, L. T., & WESTERMARK, E. A. (Eds.). *The material culture and social institutions of simpler peoples.* Monograph No. 3 on Sociology, London School of Economics and Political Science, 1918.

HOBSON, J. A. *John Ruskin: Social reformer.* London: James Nisbet & Co., 1898.

HOE, S. *The man who gave his company away: A biography of Ernest Bader, Founder of the Scott Bader Commonwealth.* London: Heinemann, 1978.

ICHNIOWKSI, C., KOCHAN, T., LEVINE, D., OLSON, C., & STRAUSS, G. What works at work: Overview and assessment. *Industrial Relations,* 1996, *55*, 299-333.

IDE—Industrial Democracy in Europe Research. A cross-national study in 12 countries. IDE 1981 study covered Denmark, Finland, France, Italy, Israel, Netherlands, Norway, Sweden, U.K., West Germany, and Yugoslavia. The 1993 study in the same organizations also included Japan and Poland as new contributors. Thirty one researchers took part in both studies and are acknowledged in each publication. Bernhard Wilpert was the principal coordinator. The study was supported by various funding bodies in each country. Major coordinating funds came from the Ford Foundation, the Thyssen Foundation, from the Maison des Sciences de l'Homme and the Nuffield Foundation. The British fieldwork was financed by the Anglo-German Foundation. The British project was followed-up by a random survey of the working population which enquired into some of the issues of the field study and added questions on trust.

IDE (Industrial Democracy in Europe research group). *Industrial democracy in Europe.* Oxford University Press, 1981. (a)

IDE. *European industrial relations.* Oxford University Press, 1981. (b)

IDE. *Industrial democracy in Europe revisited.* Oxford University Press, 1993.

JAQUES, E. *The changing culture of a factory.* London: Tavistock Publications, 1951.

KAY, J. The Foundations of National Competitive Advantage: Is There Such a Thing as National Competitiveness? What Is the Nature of National Competitive Advantage? *The Fifth ESRC Annual Lecture,* ESRC, Swindon, 1994.

KELLY, G., KELLY, D., & GAMBLE, A. *Conclusion: Stakeholder capitalism.* University of Sheffield in Association with Political & Economic Research Centre, 1997.

KOCHAN, T., & OSTERMAN, P. *The mutual gains enterprise.* Boston: Harvard Business School Press, 1994.

KORTEN, D. *When corporations rule the world.* London: Earthscan, 1996.

LAWLER, E. *High involvement management: Participative strategies for improving organizational performance.* San Francisco: Jossey-Bass, 1986.

LIKERT, R. *New patterns of management.* New York: McGraw-Hill, 1961.

LIKERT, R. *The human organization.* New York: McGraw-Hill, 1967.

LINDENFELD, F., & ROTHSCHILD-WHITT, J. (Eds). *Workplace democracy and social change.* Boston: Porter Sargent Publishers, Inc., 1982.

LOVERIDGE, R. What is participation: A review of the literature and some methodological problems. *British Journal of Industrial Relations*, 1980, *XVIII*, 297-317.

LOWIN, A. Participatory decision making: A model, literature critique and prescription for research. *Organization Behavior and Human Performance*, 1968, *3*, 68-106.

MAKIN, P. J., COOPER, C. L., & COX, C. J. *Organizations and the psychological contract: Managing people at work.* Leicester: British Psychological Association, 1996.

MARCH, J. G. Power of power. In D. Easton (Ed.), *Varieties of political theory.* Englewood Cliffs, NJ: Prentice-Hall, 1966.

MARCHINGTON, M., GOODMAN, J., WILKINSON, A., & ACKERS, P. *New developments in employee involvement.* London: Manchester School of Management (UMIST), Department of Employment, 1992.

MARTIN, R. *The sociology of power.* London: Routledge & Kegan Paul, 1977.

MARTIN, R. The new behaviorism: A critique of economics and organization. *Human Relations*, 1993, *46*(9), 1085-1101.

MILES, R. E. Human relations or human resources? *Harvard Business Review*, 1965, *43*, 148-163.

MILLWARD, N., STEVENS, M., SMART, D., & HAWES, W. R. *Workplace industrial relations in transition: The ED/ESRC/PSI/ACAS surveys.* Aldershot: Dartmouth Publishing Company Limited, 1992.

MOW (Meaning of Working Research Team). *The meaning of working: An eight country comparative study.* London: Academic Press, 1987.

NASCHOLD, F., COLE, R., GUSTAVSEN, B., & VAN BEINUM, H. *Constructing the new industrial society.* Social Science for Social Action: Towards Organizational Renewal. Maastricht, Assen: van Gorcum, 1993.

NUSSBAUM, M., & SEN, A. (Eds). *The quality of life: A study prepared for the World Institute for Development Economics.* Oxford: Clarendon Press, 1993.

Organization for Economic Co-operation and Development (OECD). *Gaps in Technology: General Report.* Organization for Economic Co-operation and Development, Paris, 1968.

ORMEROD, P. *The death of economics.* London: Faber & Faber, 1994.

PATEMAN, C. Some reflections on participation and democratic theory. In C. Crouch and F. Heller (Eds.), *International yearbook of organizational democracy.* Chichester: John Wiley & Sons, 1983.

POOLE, M. *Workers' participation in industry.* London: Routledge & Kegan Paul, 1975.

POPPER, K. *The open society and its enemies* (Vols. 1 and 2). London: Routledge & Sons, 1945.

PRIESTLEY, J. B. Quotation taken from weekly wartime broadcasts and quoted in *An inspector calls*, 1940, Garrick Theatre Programme, December 1996.

QVALE, T. A new milestone in the development of industrial democracy in Norway. In C. Lammers and G. Széll (Eds.), *International handbook of participation in organizations.* Oxford: Oxford University Press, 1989.

QVALE, T. Local development and institutional change: Experience from a "Fifth Generation" National programme for the democratization of working life. In P. Drenth, P. Koopman, and B. Wilpert (Eds.), *Organizational decision making under different economic and political conditions.* Amsterdam: North Holland, 1996.

RADIN, M. J. *Contested commodities.* Cambridge, MA: Harvard University Press, 1996.

RAMSAY, H. Cycles of control. *Sociology*, September 1977, *11*(3), 481-506.

REICH, R. E. The executive's new clothes. *New Republic*, 1985, 23-28.

RIVERS, W. H. R. *Social organization.* London: Kegan Paul, 1924.

ROBERTS, E. *Workers' control.* London: George Allen & Unwin Ltd., 1973.

ROGERS, J., & STREEK, W. (Eds.). *Works councils, consultation, representation and cooperation in industrial relations.* Chicago: University of Chicago Press, 1995.

SCHÖN, D. A. *Beyond the stable state.* The 1970 Reith Lectures. London: Maurice Temple-Smith, 1971.

SERVAN SCHREIBER, J. *The American challenge.* London: Athenaeum, London: Hamish Hamilton, 1968 (French title: *Le Défi.* Editions Desroel), 1967.

SMITH, D. (May 1968) The "gap" that is a chasm. *International Management*, 1968.

SOROS, G. *The Guardian*, Saturday, January 18, 1997, headed "Capital Crimes."

STRAUSS, G. Some notes on power equalization. In H. J. Leavitt (Ed.), *The social science of organizations*. Englewood Cliffs, NJ: Prentice-Hall, 1963.

TANNENBAUM, R., & SCHMIDT, W. How to choose a leadership pattern. *Harvard Business Review*, March/April, 1958, 95-101.

TMDM. Top Management Decision Making was a programme of study in 129 large companies and interviews with 1500 senior managers in eight countries: Germany, Great Britain, Netherlands, France, Sweden, Spain, and Israel. The fieldwork was carried out by research teams in each country, including Peter Docherty, Jean Michel Foucarde, Pieter Fokkink, Bob Mays, Barto Roig, Theodore Weinshall, and W. t'Hooft. Frank Heller and Bernhard Wilpert were the coordinators. Several publications resulted; some are referred to in the present article. The study was financed by the Economic & Social Research Council.

TOYNBEE, A. *The industrial revolution of the eighteenth century in England.* London: Longmans, Green & Co., 1913.

TRIST, E., & MURRAY, H. *The social engagement of social science. A Tavistock anthology. Vol. 1: The socio-psychological perspective.* London: Free Association Press, 1990.

TRIST, E. L., HIGGIN, G. W., MURRAY, H., & POLLOCK, A. B. *Organizational choice.* London: Tavistock Publications, 1963.

TRIST, E., SUSMAN, G., & BROWN, G. An experiment in autonomous working in an American underground coal mine. *Human Relations*, 1977, *30*, 201-236

VROOM, V., & YETTON, P. *Leadership and decision-making.* University of Pittsburgh Press, 1973.

WAGNER, J. A. III (1994) Participation's effect on performance and satisfaction: A reconsideration of research evidence. *Academy of Management Review*, 1994, *19*(2), 312-330.

WAGNER, J. A., & GOODING, R. Effects of societal trends on participation research. *Administrative Science Quarterly*, 1987, *32*, 241-262.

WEISBORD, M., et al. *Discovering common ground.* San Francisco: Berrett-Koehler, 1992.

WHITEHEAD, A. N. *Adventures of ideas.* Harmondsworth: Pelican Books, 1942.

WHYTE, W. F., & WHYTE, K. K. Making Modragon: The growth and dynamics of the worker cooperative complex (2nd ed). Ithaca: ILR Press, 1992.

WILLIAMSON, O. E. The organization of work: A comparative institutional assessment. *Journal of Economic Behavior and Organization*, 1980, *1*, 5-38.

WILPERT, B. Participation behavior and personal growth. In E. Krau (Ed.), *Self realization, success and adjustment*. New York: Praeger, 1989.

WINNICOTT, D. W. Some thoughts on the meaning of the word Democracy. *Human Relations*, 1950, *4*, 171–185. Reprinted in E. Trist and H. Murray (Eds.), *The social engagement of social science* (Vol. 1), London: Free Association Books, 1990.

ZIMBARDO, P., & LEIPPE, M. *The psychology of attitude change and social influence.* Philadelphia: Temple University Press, 1991.

BIOGRAPHICAL NOTES

FRANK HELLER joined The Tavistock Institute in 1969 after 2 years as Visiting Professor at the University of California at Berkeley, a secondment to the Engineering School at Stanford and 6 years as consultant for the International Labour Office and the United Nations Special Programme in Argentina and Chile. Since the early 1970s, the Centre for Decision Making Studies at The Tavistock Institute, which he directs, has built up a network of associates and collaborators who have together conducted the various policy and action-oriented programs described in this article. He originally qualified as an engineer and worked in the motor car industry before taking a degree at the London School of Economics, and a doctorate at London University.

[38]

The future of industrial democracy

Velko Rus

Ambiguous trends and contradictory outlooks

Although there are many prospective studies on work, technology and unemployment, prospective studies on industrial democracy (ID) hardly exist. There are many good reasons for this: trends relevant to ID are ambiguous, and the prospects contradictory. This difficulty is, however, inherent in any social forecasting as already realized by Kahn (1967) many years ago. According to him, it is not clear whether it is better to extrapolate existing trends or rather to postulate reactions to these trends. The ambiguity of social trends is therefore unavoidable because of their dialectical nature.

Alongside this difficulty, another one, frequently stressed in more recent literature, is the discontinuity of the future. Drucker (1969) has described our time as an 'age of discontinuity'; certain other social scientists believe that discontinuity is not only characteristic of our time but is generally inherent in social history. It used to be possible to base technological forecasting on continuous trends, or on desired end states, but it is no longer possible to use

Velko Rus is senior research fellow at the Institute of Sociology of the University of Ljubljana, Yugoslavia, and chairman of the International Sociological Association's Research Committee on Participation, Workers' Control and Self-Management. He is the author or co-author of some ninety articles and ten books published in Yugoslavia and elsewhere and has conducted research in Sweden, Japan, the Federal Republic of Germany and the United States as well as in his own country.

surprise-free scenarios for social forecasting (Holroyd, 1978).

To overcome these difficulties another set of indicators for social forecasting has been suggested by Simmond (1975). According to him, objective and quantifying indicators like energy, technology, the educational qualifications of manpower, etc., are not sufficiently accurate for social forecasting. Instead behavioural patterns should serve as social indicators: 'It is high time, therefore, that industrial behaviour patterns were identified as a primary tools for forecasting and planning' (Simmond, 1975, p. 284).

The present article will attempt to accept this challenge. There is much risk in dealing with ID forecasting, but sociologists should move from descriptive studies of the past towards more future-oriented scenarios. Future studies are not only necessary for theoretical reasons but primarily for strategic ones. They should encourage us to move from participative and representative democracy towards the kind of 'anticipative democracy' described some years ago by Toffler (1971). In these times of turbulence caused not only by a great number of changes but also by their accelerated dissemination (Trist, 1980), participation in the future course of

Aspects of industrial discontinuity. *Above: Accident in a Machine Shop.* Drawing by the German artist Johann Bahr (1889). Caubove/Rapho *Right:* automated sawmill in Sweden. SCA's Arkiv, Sundsvall/L'usine nouvelle.

events becomes an increasingly urgent issue if we propose to bring down uncertainty to acceptable levels.

Professionalization versus industrialization

Here we postulate two theses. The first is that the contradiction between industrialization and professionalization is the most relevant cluster of behavioural patterns for the future of ID. The second is that the greater the de-industrialization of work and the repro-fessionalization of manpower, the better the prospects for ID. Let us begin with the definition of both industrialization and pro-fessionalization.

Fores (1983) warns that 'industry' is itself not clearly defined. It can be used at least in the following four different meanings; (a) a sector of employment, like mining or the automobile industry; (b) a pattern of production, i.e. industrial production or manufacturing; (c) a kind of arrangement, i.e. factory organization; and (d) a kind of global condition, i.e. industrial civilization as modernity. The greatest problem is that, for the majority of social scientists, these four dimensions are not mutually exclusive. Following Kerr (1960), they prefer to use multidimensional, cumulative definitions of industrialism which embrace highly technically educated manpower, a highly developed division of labour producing great specialization, an educational system subordinated to industry, high horizontal and vertical mobility, urbanization, mass culture based on science, technology, competitiveness, pluralism, pragmatism and materialism, a kind of corporatism, etc. Such definitions—though frequently quoted—have been criticized since they include many attributes that are not specific to industrial so-

cieties. A more comprehensive if still complex, definition of industrialism was developed by Feldmann and Moore (1969) by reference to the following three features: (a) a factory system of production and market economy which maintains mass production and mass consumption; (b) social stratification which conditions a complex division of labour; and (c) an educational system which supports the existing professional structure and stratification patterns.

This still seems too complex a notion and we prefer to follow Aron's definition of industrialism, which stresses the dominant role of technology and its structural correlates (Aron, 1967). Such domination of technology is not to be interpreted as the domination of machines, or as that of the means of production, but as the domination of the technical division of labour over the social division of labour. In our opinion, the technical division of labour is the microregulator that

conditions the rest of societal activity at the median and macro levels of industrial societies.

In more popular terminology the technical division of labour is called Taylorism. Industrialization therefore means the Taylorization of work, first in the manufacturing sector and later in other sectors of economic activity. Taylorization spreads from traditional branches, like textiles or automobiles, to new tertiary activities like tourism, education, medical care, etc. In all these endeavours similar task structures and corresponding organizational structures arise as an outcome of Taylorization. These structures can, with some modifications, be found in all countries: capitalist and socialist, developed and developing.

Professionalization is another trend that can be traced over decades in all contemporary societies. It does not only refer to the steadily increasing proportion of the active population with college and university degrees but also a specific type of socialization crystallized in professional ethics. These ethics display the following features: (a) a non-routine approach to work; (b) non-competitive co-operation with professional colleagues (Greenwood, 1962); (c) universalistic, non-discriminatory and non-utilitarian relations with clients (Parsons, 1939); and (d) cosmopolitan relationships with the wider social environment (Gouldner, 1957).

This type of socialization was generated in pre-industrial societies and clearly stands in opposition to Taylorism. However, some critics hold that professional ethics thus defined only constitute an approximative ideal-type, in reality sometimes reduced to mere privileges derived from the possession of university diplomas. They are certainly quite right (Gyarmati, 1975). However, this does not alter the fact that professional ethics are not only pre-industrial but even consist of anti-industrial sets of behavioural patterns which have been in steady conflict with the rules of industrial bureaucracy (Pavalko, 1971) from the early industrial age to the present. In recent times we can observe the rise of 'militant professionalism' (Corvin, 1970), a product of growing bureaucratization of organizational structures and growing professionalization of manpower.

The main features of conflict between professionals and management have been admirably described by McKelwey (1969), who distinguishes the following four types:

The identification of professionals with their professional communities which opposes the pressure of management for greater commitment to the goals of organization.

Non-routine and innovative professional aspirations collide with the pragmatic restrictions of organizations.

The long-term aspirations of professionals, striving for a meaningful professional career, and for continuous growth of competence, collide with the short-term needs of organizations to respond to current environmental demands.

Professionals evaluate their knowledge contributions, while organizations evaluate only their contributions to the organizational goals.

This describes the basic conflicts between the rationality of industrial organization and professional rationality. Industrial organizations try to control these conflicts by the reinforcement of Tayloristic task structures and executive hierarchies. They try to maximize the efficiency of organizations through the subordination of professional activity to existing 'technology'. However, the more efficient they are in this subordination, the more they destroy professional autonomy on which professional ethics is based; the result is the routinization or paralysis of professional activity. So long as the professionalization of manpower is low, the routinization of professional activity does not endanger the efficiency of the whole organization. But when professionalization of manpower increases, the domination of 'rationality' endangers organizational efficiency. Since this conflict cannot be avoided 'minimal rationality' is recommended to organizations as a kind of improvised resolution for inherent contradictions (Hedberg et al., 1976).

Micro effects of industrialization on industrial democracy

Having defined industrialization and professionalization, and provided a short description of the contradiction between these two processes, the implications of these contradictions for the future of ID must now be explored.

ID is a special case of political democracy implemented and modified in industrial organizations with Tayloristic task structures and corresponding hierarchical structures. As can be seen, ID is at its very outset a *contradictio in adjecto,* based on the following four principles (IDE Group, 1981):

1. Political equality—whereby all members of work organizations have the right to participate directly, on the basis of 'one person one vote' in all decisions affecting the organization.

2. Representation—according to which members have the right to delegate to chosen representatives some of their rights under (1) above.
3. Special competence—whereby it is recognized that certain decisions call for specialized professional skills and thus become the domain of specialists.
4. Efficiency—whereby it is recognized that the concept of goal fulfilment is a matter of survival for organizations.

The full and direct participation of all members in all decisions is thus conditioned by three constraints, i.e. the delegation of rights to representatives when an organization becomes large and complex, the delegation of decisions to professionals when such decisions demand expertise, and the accommodation of members' interests to the common goals of the organization. This definition of ID already highlights the privileged position of professionals and managers. They are 'more equal among equals', since they are by definition obliged to implement principles (3) and (4) above. Democracy is thus replaced by polyarchy which means a kind of balance of power between management (line), professionals (staff), workers and workers' representatives (Dahl, 1970).

Our question should consequently be rephrased as follows: To what extent is industrial democracy, as a polyarchic type of power structure, conditioned or limited by processes of industrialization? No direct answer to this question is yet available. Therefore we will start with a proxy, i.e. with empirical investigations of the social effects of technology. The most relevant among these are the ones demonstrating the skilling or deskilling effect of technological development. These investigations directly indicate the effects of the deprofessionalization or reprofessionalization of the labour force. On the other hand they indirectly suggest that, by deskilling or reskilling, human potential for greater or lower autonomy also varies. Of course, more skill does not necessarily mean more power, since certain other sources of power can be used. But for those who do not

possess legitimate power, coercive power or capital, skill is almost the only alternative to becoming less dependent or more powerful within organizations. This is even more true today when a steady decrease of trade-union power in developed as well as developing countries can be observed.

In discussing deskilling or reskilling, the situation during early industrialization will not be examined. It is widely known that the transition to mass production has had huge deskilling effects on the labour force. Our comments will be focused on the recent transition from mass production to semi-automated and automated production, computerization and the robotization of work processes. Early expectations concerning effects of automation and computerization were very optimistic. Faunce (1965), for instance, expected that the shift from mechanization towards automation would finally arrest the long-term trend of deskilling. In his opinion the assembly line causes anomie, while automation produces an organic society. Some years later he elaborated this vision of an emerging organic society, along the following lines (Faunce, 1968):

Automation of production will decrease the division of labour since workers will no longer service machines but only control and maintain them. These two functions, being more general, will lead to lower specialization at work in all branches.

Automation will create the need for engineers 'who are willing to get their hands dirty'.

Automation will transform work organizations into highly integrated systems in which even divisions between plant and office might be eliminated; the whole enterprise will be transformed into a single interconnected system.

Automation will have also long-term effects on the labour market: it will create less specialized occupations, thus increasing employment opportunities for the majority.

Similarly optimistic expectations were expressed by social scientists from Eastern European countries. According to Polzov (1966), for instance, automation should abolish the split between physical and intellectual labour thereby abolishing the alienation of work.

McLuhan (1964) broadens such optimistic expectations to all levels of social activity. According to him the automation of information will not only diminish fragmentation of jobs in the frame of production technology, but also diminish segmentation in the areas of learning. The automation of information should abolish the traditional division between culture and technology, between art and feeling, and between work and leisure time.

Over the past ten years such optimistic evaluations of automation have become more the exception than the rule. Evaluations of the social effects of automation are becoming increasingly critical: the most negative can be found in Braverman (1974) and Gorz (1973). Braverman thinks that workers today are less capable of managing their work than they were a century ago, that they are more dependent on machines than previously, and that they know their machines less well than they used to. The effects of automation are similar to those of mechanization: automation increases management control over workers, and lessens workers' needs for skills and education. Braverman tries to back this up with an empirical study by Bright (1966) who found that skill increases only between the first and fifth levels of automation, while it decreases from the sixth to the seventeenth levels.

Gorz (1973) makes a similar evaluation of the effects of new technologies. However, he believes that these negative effects are not conditioned by technology but by the 'scientific' organization of work, i.e. by Taylorism generating a scientific destruction of any chances of establishing workers' control. This 'scientific' organization of work has universal effects upon blue- and white-collar employees, upon highly skilled as well as unskilled workers. It also has very similar effects in capitalist and socialist countries; the 'scientific' organization of work under collective ownership might even be worse and could create greater dependence of workers on machines.

According to findings obtained by Shepard (1971) Gorz's conclusions may be too negative. He studied the automation of production and office work and discovered that the effects in both areas are quite similar. Through automation, alienation at work and especially meaninglessness decrease, which constitute certain positive effects of automation on the humanization of work. On the other hand, Shepard found that the automation of production and office work does not lessen employees' feeling of powerlessness, which remains constant or even increases. The introduction of automation does not decrease workers' dependence nor does it effect a more equitable distribution of power.

Based on these findings we can evaluate the optimistic expectations of Faunce and McLuhan, as well as the pessimistic ones of Braverman and Gorz as partially true and partially false. Automation makes work organizations more integrated wholes, which lessens fragmentation and therefore offers more meaningful work. At the same time such highly integrated wholes produce stronger feelings of dependence and powerlessness among employees.

The introduction of computerization seems to have similarly ambiguous effects. Glenday (1983) reports that case-studies demonstrate decreased requirements for craftsmen and tradesmen alongside an increase of 'bull work' and 'donkey work'. He states that, at each stage of technological change, mechanization and automation depress the skill levels of the work-force so that workers progressively lose control over the production process. The technical division of labour achieved by technological change subordinates labour while increasing management control over its labour force. Similar results have been obtained for office work by Sandkull (1980, 1983). He reports that progressive computerization of office tasks coincides with greater need for unskilled workers and more engineers as machines are substituted for much of the earlier know-how. 'After a couple of years most of the earlier competence residing in people had vanished.' It

Creative approach to work. Doisneau/Rapho.

seems that the position of Drucker (1962) regarding the nature of automation is still valid: it is not only equipment or engineering, but an overall structural concept of economic life which determines basic patterns of behaviour integrated into the balanced whole. Our survey regarding the micro-level effects of technology can thus be terminated by the tentative conclusion that it is not technology but the technical division of labour which, to a great extent, determines the skill levels as well as the power leverage of employees.

Macro effects of industrialization on industrial democracy

The effects of industrialization are not only limited to task structures or to the production subsystem of work organizations. While the predominant effects on ID have been established at micro levels, certain positive effects of industrialization may be found at median and macro levels of society. It is on this point that Braverman can be criticized. One of the most thorough critiques is one by Aronowitz (1978), who suggests the following objections to Braverman's analyses:

The increasing dependence of workers on capital, caused by the adoption of more complex technology, while observable in contemporary societies, is not the only trend to notice.

Together with trends towards increasing degradation of work, newly emerging knowledge and professions can be discerned.

At least part of the scientific endeavour maintains its autonomy, since the sciences can never be entirely subordinated to the technical division of labour.

Increasing division of labour steadily creates mutual functional dependence among workers, which stimulates their spontaneous solidarity.

Aronowitz's chief point, in our opinion is the third: it seems that no one can ever establish complete control over creative work. It is much easier to control repetitive work,

which is the main purpose of its 'scientific' organization as an attempt to transform creative work into more manageable and less skilled repetitive labour. While such deskilling effects of Taylorization are rather successful at plant and office levels, i.e. within work organizations, it seems that they are not so powerful at the level of society as a whole.

However, many studies point to the fact that deskilling within organizations coincides to some extent with processes of reskilling at overall levels. This was commented on by Rumberger and Russel (1981) and other researchers, who reported that not only the educational acquisitions of manpower but also the complexity and skill requirements of average jobs in the economy of the United States have steadily increased over past decades. Does this mean that Bell (1973) was correct in forecasting the start of a novel shift of technicians, engineers and managers in post-industrial society? According to Braverman this is an illusion since all these professional groups will remain the servants of power. Braverman (1974) actually forecast the proletarization of these new groups, arguing that engineering is becoming a mass profession subject to increased technical division of labour, simplified work, more routine operations, lower wages and higher unemployment.

Gorz (1973) adds segmentation between the technical and the humanistic intelligentsia. Such segmentation is also increasing among lower-level employees. In his longitudinal cross-cultural research Form (1976) finds that industrialization is followed by increasing sub-stratification of blue-collar workers: the more industrialization is developed, the greater the social distances between skilled and unskilled workers become. These processes of segmentation and differentiation can certainly not heighten the integrative power of unions: they are structural obstacles in the way of greater trade-union power.

But unionization is not the only possible form of power for employees. They can also increase their social power by reinforcing the role of professional associations. If such associations assumed the role of trade unions,

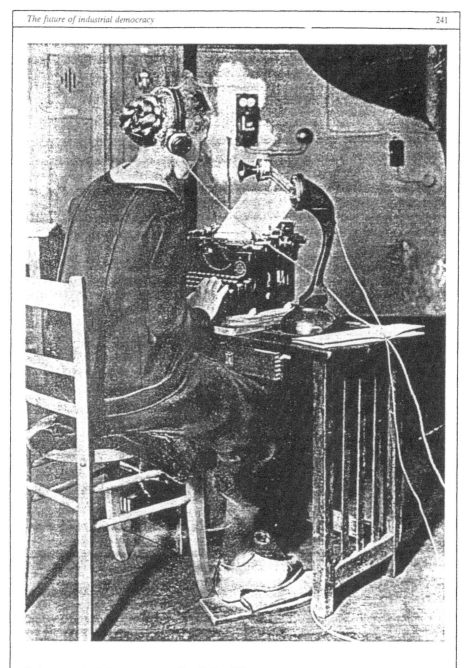

Early automation in the central post office, Berlin, 1931. Ullstein (*L'empire du bureau*, p. 27).

as has been suggested by Durkheim (1974), they would be able to enhance professional autonomy over work organization, and their intraorganizational roles as well. However, even this possibility seems to be endangered by the processes of reification of knowledge. Hennestad (1983) warns that current computer technology could transform the worker skills into reified knowledge, which might become part of technology. With the increasing role of computers previously autonomous, skilled activity could be preplanned and preprogrammed. With the introduction of the fifth generation of computers the preprogramming of organizational activity may increase, since computers will to a great extent become 'creative' and self-regulating. Although there will never be a complete reification of knowledge, increasing reification could endanger the existing autonomy of professionals, thus also endangering the bargaining power of their associations.

Apart from increasingly preprogrammed skills, increasingly predetermined stratification in work organizations can also be noted. Educational systems (the main regulators of the social division of labour) have to a great extent been industrialized over the past two centuries. Such industrialization implies subordination to the technical division of labour. By becoming industrialized, educational systems today represent the main reproducers of existing technical divisions of labour. They maintain predetermined occupational stratification structures, which, to a great extent, determine hierarchical relations within work organizations (Maurice et al., 1980).

The effects of professionalization

While the industrialization of work causes deskilling, alienation and powerlessness, reprofessionalization seems to be a no less strong, long-term trend in contemporary societies. Toffler (1971) reports on the emergence of new kinds of employees different from traditional 'organization men'. These employees

are increasingly poor company men. They are less committed to organization, less inclined to obey the organizational hierarchy, less interested in promotion across the organizational hierarchy and less satisfied with a secure and well-paid job. The typical employee is transforming himself from an organization man into an 'associative man' seeking self-fulfilment at work, greater autonomy, better co-operation with colleagues and a more meaningful career. An associative man is actually a more professionalized employee who is more committed to his profession and its ethics than to the organization and its goals.

With such increasing reprofessionalization, changes within organizational structures as well as in society will occur. Quite clear relations between organizational differentiation and professionalization have been established by Blau and Schoencher (1971): in departments having more skilled manpower and doing less routinized work, vertical as well as horizontal structural differentiation has been found to be narrower than in other departments. Obviously, more professionalized manpower co-ordinates tasks to a much greater extent than the less professionalized variety. Since less co-ordination is necessary, structural undifferentiation becomes possible. This finding has potentially a very great significance since organizational overcomplexity is becoming one of the greatest problems of contemporary societies.

Many omens support Toffler's (1971) thesis concerning the emergence of a new associative man. Yankelovich (1979) reports on the massive value re-orientation among younger generations in the United States, seeking more independent work, of a kind that offers greater opportunities for initiative, greater responsibility and more personal effort in small groups. According to Kerr and Rosow (1979), there is still high commitment to work among young educated people. They state that 80 per cent of a representative sample of American students agree with the statement 'hard work always pays off'. This value orientation is also confirmed by students' behaviour: more than half of American students work part-time during their studies. They are of course no longer prepared to take just any job, but are looking for jobs that offer opportunities for self-fulfilment, a good physical and social environment and reasonable remuneration.

The reason why many youngsters reject repetitive jobs is not a decaying work ethic but increasing work aesthetics, rooted in the fact that 'the workplace is in America among the most conservative of institutions' (Yankelovich, 1979, p. 20). If we propose to pursue these changed perspectives we should increase the autonomy of individual workers and decrease the autonomy of organizations. If nothing is changed at the work-place one must expect great flows away from work or great conflicts within the area of work.

These empirically based findings were predicted over a decade ago by C. Kerr and his colleagues, who defined the fundamental problem of industrialism in the following terms (Kerr et al., 1971, p. 604):

To adapt to the increased interdependence brought about by the new technology, society requires greater discipline; yet the new working class, better educated as it is, desires more individual freedom and scope for action within the professional setting as outside of it. Thus, technical society appears to harbour the germ of its own destruction, not because of class conflict but because of the contradiction between the discipline required by technology and the need for independence of the labour force which that society has itself helped to create.

Further, work autonomy is not only a personal need of professionals but also the necessary condition for the efficient use of skilled manpower.

These contradictions should sooner or later create open conflict between the coalitions maintaining the order of industrial societies and those acting as the main repositories of knowledge and professional ethics. Gouldner (1979) believes that in Western countries 'the old moneyed class is dying', while in Eastern European countries 'party officials and bureaucrats are even more of an obstacle to the new class'. Power passes from those whose incomes derive from financial investments to those with human capital, i.e. with relatively advanced education. The 'new class' is, according to Gouldner, a 'universal class' composed of humanistic intellectuals and the technological intelligentsia. Professionalism is one of the public ideologies of the new class, and a kind of collective consciousness. Professionalism is not only the source of its legitimacy; it also 'devalues the authority of the old class'.

According to Gouldner (1979, p. 20) it is the growth of this new class which is also decisive for ID. The new class, like the working class, earns its living through its labour. Aspiring to produce worthy objects and services, the new class must also be concerned with the control over its working environment. The new class thus embodies any future hope of working-class self-management.

Relations between economic and industrial democracy

Traditional forms of ownership are now being questioned again, not as an ideological alternative to capitalism or socialism but as a functional regulator at the micro level of everyday working life (Abrahamsson and Bröstrom, 1980). Existing forms are not contested in the old ideological way, since both private and state ownership represent an enormous dysfunction in the closer co-operation and greater participation of employees in integrated production systems: both state and private ownership are simply too exclusive, too impersonal and too rigid for contemporary working life.

The transition from a traditional industrial society to an information society requires new economic arrangements, new ownership, new markets, new flows of information, etc. The very character of information dictates new social arrangements because: (a) its rate of growth is fast; (b) there are not in principle growth limits for information; (c) it can to a great extent replace the use of physical and financial capital; and (d) it can save energy.

Finally, and this is the most relevant feature for ownership, it is sharable, so that any monopolization of information becomes dangerous, if not impossible (Cleveland, 1982). Monopolization of knowledge hinders the principal production processes in an information society: the continuous integration of facts into expertise, of expertise into scientific technology, and of the latter into an interdisciplinary whole. The increasing collectivization of work, therefore, forces contemporary societies to create alternative forms of ownership, less exclusive and more co-operative than private ownership, and less authoritarian and impersonal than state ownership. In this field great social innovations are needed in order to propel ID towards a polyarchic power structure.

The need for more inclusive forms of ownership are best expressed in co-operative movements where the most socialized form of ownership appears. It is known that co-operatives are decreasingly inclined to maintain shareholding arrangements. They are creating new profit-sharing systems in which employees' incomes are almost entirely based on their work contributions, and not on the number of shares they own (Jensen, 1981). As to decision-making, most new co-operative shares are no longer the criteria for participation in decision-making, i.e. they are not voting shares (Long, 1983). The socialization of shares goes even further: workers usually cannot buy more shares than other members of a co-operative, they cannot sell them before they leave it nor can they sell them to non-members of a co-operative.

It would seem that large entities such as corporations, industries, and states are too rigid to experiment with the innovations of co-operative movements. However, these large organizations might learn from small co-operatives how to survive in times of underfinancing by mobilizing hidden human resources through motivationally well-designed ownership schemes.

Since state and private capital does not support co-operatives, these lack the opportunity to become more than an alternative, participatory economy at the periphery of the 'mainstream' economy. Even if they received as much support from social-democratic parties and trade unions as they do in the United Kingdom, this would embrace no more than 5 per cent of the economy (Woodhouse, 1983).

Current trends in the United States are more promising. Rothschild-Witt (1983) reports:

Since tax incentives for Employee Stock Ownership Plans (ESOP) were passed into law in the mid-1970s, there has been a burgeoning of this type of organization in the US. Today there are an estimated 5,000 firms that are to some degree employee owned, involving an estimated 3 to 4 million employees.

Accordingly, it may be anticipated that the co-operative movement might go beyond marginal status in the mainstream economy. The growth of co-operatives would be in line with the dominant aspirations of United States citizens. A survey conducted by Hart Associates in 1975 showed that only 8 per cent of respondents would prefer to work in government agencies, 20 per cent in private enterprises with the great majority of 66 per cent in worker-owned enterprises. The time is ripe for change, though the structures are rigid and subject to great inertia.

Much greater financial potential for economic democracy is concealed in pension funds which in the United States total almost $1,000 billion and in the United Kingdom about £80 billion (Schuller, 1983). To date the nominal beneficiaries have had no control over these funds or any influence over investment policy which might support employment programmes or other kinds of alternative investment options. In Western countries these funds represent an enormous capital no longer in the hands of capitalists. With no employee participation in the investment decisions, no constructive investment policy and no efficient control over the management of

Computers: saviours or culprits? Leonard Freed/Magnum.

this 'anonymous' capital, a great opportunity to socialize such capital, and thereby strengthen economic democracy, is being lost. Certain social scientists are no doubt correct in claiming that new social arrangements might emerge from the growth of pension funds; a possibility that cannot be realized without the active participation and control of 'shareholders'. Representing a very broad base they could considerably increase economic democracy by taking control of management of these huge pension funds.

The phenomenon of 'anonymous' capital can also be observed in co-operatives often run exclusively by managers even though the capital is employee-owned. According to Long (1983, p. 11) its effects are more frequently negative than neutral:

The simple fact of ownership by employees will not automatically bring about this increased participation. Furthermore, it has been found that in cases where employee expectations about increased participation have been violated, employee ownership can actually lead to a decline in key job attitudes.

Long's (1978) empirical investigations proved that both share ownership and participation had significant effects on job attitudes. Studying three firms, Long (1980) also found that the most efficient was the one where there was the highest level of employee participation in decision-making and the greatest amount of employee ownership.

Similar findings have also been reported by Hammer and Stern (1980). Where neither job redesign nor an increased participation of employees in decision-making occurred, employee ownership had little effect on the day-today operation of the firm. However, when job redesign coincides with employee ownership and workers' participation in decision-making, a significant impact on productivity becomes evident. Therefore, co-operatives may be most competitive in those labour-intensive sectors where the high motivation of workers is an important factor of success (Russel, 1983). These labour-intensive sectors are not only traditional but also some knowledge-intensive branches like computer software, telecommunications, management, retailing, advertising, etc.

To summarize these findings, we can say that economic democracy based on any kind of employee ownership certainly facilitates industrial democracy. However, no causal link exists between economic and industrial democracy: if industrial democracy fails to progress, economic democracy will sooner or later degenerate.

The findings concerning co-operatives are equally relevant for Eastern European countries where state ownership contradicts ID. Recent trends—especially the new Soviet law concerning the greater role of workers in the joint management of their enterprises—convey the impression that, in the near future, these countries will also try to establish a closer connection between industrial and economic democracy.

In general terms this means that neither the technical division of labour nor private (or state) ownership should be treated in isolation. They both represent obstacles to industrial democracy, i.e. for the creation of a polyarchic power structure in work organizations. It is not only capitalism (or state-dominated socialism) but also industrialism which represents an obstacle to the further development of ID. The new societal arrangements which could be called post-industrial, post-capitalist and post-socialist societies will require both a new division of labour and more socialized schemes of ownership, schemes that will be more inclusive, which will offer closer contact between work and its outcomes, between work and ownership and which will therefore provide greater incentives and more responsibility. Novel schemes will be needed offering all these openings and at the same time preventing the domination and exploitation of man by man.

Certainly no single best way exists to achieve these goals. A wide variety of new ownership schemes should be promoted in the near future to satisfy emerging functional needs and to avoid ideological confrontation between traditional types of ownership. These are the criteria for the validation of new ownership schemes; they should be tested *a posteriori* not *a priori*, empirically not theoretically, experimentally not ideologically.

Unemployment and self-employment

We are all witnesses to the long-term transformation of welfare states into workless states (Sinfield, 1981). However, certain variations in policies exist among them: left-wing socialist and social-democratic governments give priority to solving the problem of unemployment, while right-wing governments give priority to solving inflation. For the future of ID this is certainly quite an important difference. According to Garraty (1978):

[Unemployment] strikes certain individuals down, while passing by others, no more skilful or hardworking; it focuses losses instead of distributing them. Inflation, on the other hand, attacks its victims gradually and erodes the worth of everyone's money equally.

Inflation has more egalitarian, unemployment more discriminative, effects. The first allows for a kind of solidarity among workers and facilitates trade-union activity, the second weakens unions and increases the gap between the employed and the unemployed. The first decreases the effects of substratification of blue-collar workers, the second increases them.

Trade-union leaders are afraid of unemployment while at the same time trying to ignore it. They are accustomed to calling for strikes over a few cents an hour wage increase, but rarely try to prevent reductions in the work-force. They are also traditionally against workers' solidarity as expressed by work-sharing. In the United States this idea was rejected during the Great Depression,

Macro effect of industrialization: *Manufacturing Town*, oil painting 1922, by the British artist L. S. Lowry (1887–1976) who specialized in scenes of industrial Lancashire. D.R.

i.e. at a time when public assistance for the unemployed was extremely niggardly. It is quite certain that unions will not adopt this idea now that unemployment benefits are much more generous.

Employers follow the same logic as do the unions. They try to avoid wage reductions because it means breach of contract and leads to conflicts with union leaders. Neither do they try to reduce working hours, since this could arouse unrest among the rank and file. For employers, lay-off is the best solution; thus they can avoid conflicts with organized labour, make a positive selection of employees and, through dismissals, externa-

lize internal problems. For employers unemployment has many desirable feed-back effects on the overall redistribution of power within and outside firms. Internally, employee dependence increases in relation to the shortage of work. When work becomes the main scarcity, its strategic value increases enormously. In such circumstances employers can raise the employment criteria: they can upgrade educational, personal and even political demands (Showler, 1981).

The next step is to increase job security for the employed, through which the gap between those employed and those out of work becomes greater: the more jobs are

Towards self-employment: do-it-yourself electronic components in a shop in Tokyo. Richard Kalvar/Magnum.

protected, the worse the chances of the unemployed. The constantly increasing proportion of skilled youth among the unemployed is perhaps the, most general and paradoxical outcome of employers' policies. However, employers here prefer social to economic rationality: they prefer to develop the internal labour market to increase the dependence of their employees to such an extent that the overcommitment of employees may offer extra economic returns.

The state of the internal labour market is conditioned by the split of the external labour market into primary and secondary segments most visible in Japan. On the primary segment skilled males prevail. They enjoy specially favourable industrial relations based on a seniority system, life-long employment, steady education, and company unions (Helwoort, 1979). More than a third of employees enjoy such job security, while the rest hold extremely precarious jobs, with hard work and low wages. The ratio between the average wage in the primary and in the secondary segments is 5:3, while the ratio between males and females is almost 2:1.

This system of industrial relations also plays a very important role, during the current restructuring of Japanese industry. The introduction of microelectronics and automation does not create unemployment among employees, nor arouse their resistance: on the contrary, Japanese industrial relations seem to be reinforced during the processes of industrial restructuring (Ishikawa, 1983). However, this Japanese model cannot avoid the externalization of social problems. Job insecurity is pushed out of the firm on to the national labour market, or even beyond it to the less developed countries (Kamibayashi, 1982).

For ID such an externalization of social problems certainly does not represent an optimal solution. What is the alternative? The dominant role of governmental planning as in Eastern European countries, or a more active employment policy as in Sweden and certain other Scandinavian countries? Compared with similar models developed in Western countries the Scandinavian model of active employment policy is certainly the best way to regulate the labour market, though it represents a huge bureaucratization of employment activity. Besides, it is very expensive and induces negative career patterns (Drambo, 1982).

Furthermore, there is no system of employment regulation that can prevent constantly increasing unemployment in Western Europe. To date, only two solutions have proved 'efficient'—totalitarian systems of the Nazi-fascist type, or war (Showler et al., 1981). Rejecting these two solutions, there is no way to solve the unemployment problem within existing systems. The same applies to the United States; as Yankelovich (1978, p. 17) states: 'There is no way to create 20 million new jobs through the business-as-usual approach, conservative or liberal.' And, it might be added, there is no way to create, using traditional methods, 1,000 million new jobs in the developing countries over the next twenty years.

The abolition of the labour market and the establishment of a planned economy is up to now the only known way to control unemployment. Yet, the abolition of the labour market does not solve unemployment, but transforms it into underemployment or, as Zeman (1980) calls it, 'unemployment of the employed'. It also increases the dependence of all employees on the state bureaucracy and creates a powerless population who cannot create any effective ID in-work organizations.

Bureaucratization and state regulation of employment being unacceptable, and given that we cannot return to the liberal economy, we should look for such new alternatives as may be appropriate to the overall restructuring of the world economy, and to ID demands

(Rus, 1982). Such new regulators of employment are not novel Utopias but spontaneously emerging schemes in many developed industrial countries. They are described by Heinze and Olk (1982), Woodhouse (1982), Robertson (1983), Cornforth (1983) and others. They might be called schemes for self-employment, individual or collective. They first postulate very flexible work-places and working hours: work might be carried out at home, in the neighbourhood, in co-operatives or in traditional plants. It could be arranged as part-time or full-time as temporary or continuous, or a combination of all these.

Such innovations need a social network. According to Heinze and Olk, a network model is a key to self-employment schemes. It is an alternative to the repressive strategy of 'Reaganomics' and also to a state-controlled strategy. Cornforth (1983) describes one possible network recently developed in the United Kingdom of forty local co-operative development agencies, which employ a small professional staff, usually of two to four people. They promote and support new co-operatives, offering them cheap financial, managerial, technical, organizational, educational and training assistance. Such networks might be an alternative to bureaucratic state employment agencies. They will certainly need support from many already institutionalized bodies and organizations like trade unions, local communities, special co-operative banks, professional associations, etc. The support of professional associations might be decisive, first, because such associations can prevent bureaucratization and state control of these emerging networks and, secondly, because they might be the most efficient instruments in combating structural unemployment (becoming increasingly dominant in the near future).

If these networks can build a new societal infrastructure they will be able to encourage self-employment. On the other hand, through them the traditional forms of work organization which were the core of industrial society—factories—will become increasingly obsolete. Instead of factories, more open, smaller, more flexible, more participative work units will emerge; they will correspond to the existence of more highly skilled manpower, as well as to the new technologies. This might create a meta-industrial world with a kind of populistic economy, different from existing capitalist and socialist economic systems.

Neocorporatism

Over the past decades a steady decline of traditional liberal political systems based on parliamentary democracy, opposed political parties and social consensus reached through parliamentary debate, can be noted everywhere (Lowi, 1969). Instead the rise of so-called neocorporatism based on bargaining between government bodies, employers' organizations and trade unions is in evidence. This neocorporatism resembles the former totalitarian corporatism by the extraparliamentary creation of social consensus but it nevertheless differs from it due to bargaining and conflict-resolution between the three main partners. The future of ID depends heavily on the power relations between these three partners. If unions were to hold a dominating position a switch from military or economist policy towards human-resource policy can be expected (Harbison, 1973). This would impose as a dominant goal the optimal development and use of human resources. Social development would no longer be measured by GNP, export ratios, etc., but by the growth of education, increased employment, an improved working and living environment, better public health and a reasonable control of population growth. For a human resource policy the development of ID itself would be one of the basic indicators of the quality of working life and, therefore, a basic indicator of social development.

Yet recent trends have not been favourable to ID. Trade unions, for reasons already mentioned, are losing their power. If unions remain unadaptable, as they are now, and are not supported by social currents, like peace women's, ecological, regional and consumers' movements, etc., it is quite possible that governments may become the dominant partners in tripartite neocorporatist political systems. In which case it is also quite possible that a politico-technocratic state may emerge (Krausse, 1971).

Increasing state control over total capital assets—which in most developed industrial states already approaches half (Kahn, 1982) —is another reason why states could play a decisive role in the near future. Without powerful states, it will be almost impossible to control 'stagflation', and to mediate between conflicting groups in societies. Heilbroner (1974) expects even more: a 'straitjacket economy' to redistribute the wealth of countries under conditions of zero growth. Under such circumstances it is difficult to imagine the unfolding of ID and the rise of alternative self-employment policies. They would perhaps appear only after the great crises or the breakdown of neocorporatist political systems.

Strategy implications

In the author's opinion, there are at the moment very few countries where ID could be efficiently promoted by legislation at the macro level or by a kind of bargaining at the median level. There are much better chances to develop ID at the micro level of daily work, for at this level the inertia of the megastructure is least burdensome, while new technologies and greater professionalization are the most influential agents of change.

However, even micro-level strategy should in these unfavourable times be highly selective in seeking an appropriate societal context which possesses great enough transformative potentials for work-place democratization. Should workplace democracy be developed within an incompatible milieu, the societal effects might be entirely opposite to those desired.

According to Lafferty (1983) the best transformative infrastructure for work-place democratization exists in the public sector, its main advantages being: (a) higher education of manpower; (b) lower level of industrialization, i.e. less advanced Taylorization of work; (c) more flexible technology; (d) non-market, client-oriented services; and (e) public ownership. An additional advantage might be that is is easier to introduce experimental changes into the public rather than into the private sector.

The implementation of work-place democracy also means that we prefer so-called 'microcorporatism' to the conflictual political model based on confrontation, bargaining and conflict resolution between employees' and employers' organizations Micro-level strategy should start by democratizing short-range, job-related decisions which are within the actual competence of each employee. This strategy assumes that no one partakes of anybody else's power, and that those who work possess power for the self-regulation of their work processes (Pusić, 1983).

Of course such a micro-strategy can succeed only where at least the following minimally necessary elements are present (Bernstein, 1980): (a) direct and representative participation in decision-making; (b) frequent feedback of economic results to all employees; (c) full sharing of management-level information and expertise with employees; (d) guaranteed individual rights including political ones; (e) an independent board of appeal to arbitrate disputes; and (f) a particular set of attitudes and values.

These minimally necessary elements have been even more selectively presented by Mulder (1971) along the following four dimensions: (a) participants should be motivated for participation; (b) knowledge differences among participants should not be too great; (c) the underprivileged should be specially protected; and (d) participation should be centred around work-place and profession. The more manpower is professionalized the broader the supportive environment for work-place democracy, since the new class of intellectuals—as submitted by Gouldner—strives for self-management of work processes.

The same might be said of the new technologies: the more they are introduced, the more work organizations will resemble the existing service sector. These then are the settings which—according to Lafferty—are most conducive to work-place democratization.

These two general micro-level trends are quite autonomous of the existing policy of megastructures. It is to be expected that they will be strong enough to promote a constant and gradual unfolding of ID at the level of everyday working life even if hindered by contrary trends at the median and macro levels of society.

References

ABRAHAMSSON, B.; BRÖSTROM, A. 1980. *The Rights of Labour*. London, Sage.

ARON, R. 1967. *Eighteen Lectures on Industrial Society*. London, Weidenfeld & Nicolson.

ARONOWITZ, S. 1978. Marx, Braverman, and the Logic of Capital. *The Insurgent Sociologist*, Vol. 8, No. 2/3.

BELL, D. 1973. *The Coming of Post-Industrial Society*. New York, Basic Books.

BERNSTEIN, P. 1970. *Workplace Democratization: Its Internal Dynamics*. New Brunswick, Transaction Books.

BLAU, P.; SCHOENCHER, R. 1971. *The Structure of Organizations*. New York, Basic Books.

BRAVERMAN, H. 1974. *Labor and Monopoly Capital*. New York, Monthly Review Press.

BRIGHT, R. 1966. *The Relationship of Increasing Automation and Skill Requirements*. Washington D.C., National Committee for Technology, Automation and Economic Development.

CLEVELAND, H. 1982. Information as a Resource. *The Futurist*, Vol. 16, No. 6, December.

CORNFORTH, C. 1983. Some Throughts on a Theory of Producer Co-operative Development in the Light of Experiences in the UK. Paper presented to international workshop: Future Perspectives of Economic and Industrial Democracy, Dubrovnik. (To be published in Vol. 4 of *The Yearbook of Organization Studies*.)

CORVIN, R. G. 1970. *Militant Professionalism*. New York,

Appleton-Century-Crofts.

DAHL, R. 1970. *After the Revolution; Authority in a Good Society*. New Haven, Yale University Press.

DRAMBO, L. 1982. *Spronget mot Frighetim*. Stockholm, Tragve Karlsson.

DRUCKER, P. 1962. *The New Society: The Anatomy of Industrial Order*. New York, Harper.

——. 1969. *The Age of Discontinuity*. New York, Harper.

DURKHEIM, E. 1974. *Division of Labor in Society*. Glencoe, Ill., Free Press.

FAUNCE, W. A., 1965. Automation and the Division of Labor. *Social Problems*, Vol. 13, No. 2, December.

——. 1968. *Problems of an Industrial Society*. New York, McGraw-Hill.

FELDMANN, S.; MOORE, W. 1969. Industrialization and Industrialism: Convergence and Differentiation. In: W. Faunce and W. Form (eds.), *Comparative Perspectives on Industrial Society*. New York, Little, Brown.

FORES, M. 1983. *New Information Technology as Another 'Industrial Revolution'*. Berlin, International Institute of Management. (Discussion Paper, LMP 82-6.)

FORM, W. H. 1976. *Blue Collar Stratification*. Princeton, N.J., Princeton University Press.

GARRATY, J. A. 1978. *Unemployment in History*. New York, Harper Colophon Books.

GORZ, A. 1973. *Critique de la division du travail*. Paris, Éditions du Seuil.

GOULDNER, A. 1957. Cosmopolitans and Locals: Toward an Analysis of Latent Social Roles. *Administration Science Quarterly*, Vol. 2, No. 2, June.

——. 1979. *The Future of Intellectuals and the Rise of the New Class*. New York, Macmillan Press.

GREENWOOD, E., 1962. Atributes of Profession. In: W. Form and S. Nosow (eds.), *Work and Society*. New York, Basic Books.

GYARMATI, G. 1975. The Doctrine of the Professions: Bases for a Power Structure, *International Social Science Journal*, Vol. XXVII, No. 4.

HAMMER, T.; STERN, R. N. 1980. Employee Ownership: Implications for the Organizational Distribution of Power. *Academy of Management Journal*, Vol. 23, No. 1.

HARBISON, F. H. 1973. *Human Resources as the Wealth of Nations*. London, Oxford University Press.

HEDBERG, B. L. T.; HYSTROM, P. C.; STARBUCK, W. H. 1976. Camping on Seesaws: Prescriptions for a Self-Designing Organization. *Administration Science Quarterly*, Vol. 21, No. 1, March.

HEILBRONER, R. L. 1974. *The Human Prospect*. Toronto, W. W. Norton.

HEINZE, R. G.; OLK, T., 1982. Development of the Informal Economy. *Futures*, Vol. 14, No. 3, June.

HELWOORT, E. 1979. *The Japanese Working Man*. Kent, Paul Norbury.

HENNESTAD, B. 1983.

Computer Technology, Work Organization and Industrial Democracy. *International Studies of Management and Organization*, Vol. 12, No. 3.

HOLROYD, P. 1978. Change and Discontinuity; Forecasting for the 1980s. *Futures*, Vol. 10, No. 1, February.

IDE GROUP. 1981. *Industrial Democracy in Europe*, Oxford, Clarendon Press.

ISHIKAWA, A. 1983. Microelectronics and Japanese Industrial Relations. Paper presented to international workshop: Future Perspectives of Economic and Industrial Democracy, Dubrovnik.

JENSEN, F. J. 1981. Producer Cooperatives as Change Strategy. Paper presented to International Conference on Producer Co-operatives, Copenhagen.

KAHN, H. 1967. *The Year 2000*. New York, Macmillan, 1967.

———. 1982. *The Coming Boom*. New York, Simon & Schuster.

KAMIBAYASHI, C. 1982. Economic Recession and Employment Adjustments in·the Textile Industry. In: V. Rus, A. Ishikawa, and T. Woodhouse (eds.), *Employment and Participation: Industrial Democracy in Crisis*. Tokyo, Chuo University Press.

KERR, C. 1960. *Industrialism and Industrial Man: The Problems of Labor and Management in Economic Growth*. Cambridge, Mass., Harvard University Press.

KERR, C.; DUNLOP, J. T.; HARBISON, F. H.; MYERS, C. A. 1971. Post-scriptum à l'industrialisme et le travailleur industriel. *Revue international du travail*, No. 6, June.

KERR, C.; ROSOW, J. M. 1979. *Work in America: The Decade*

Ahead. New York, Van Nostrand Reinhold.

KRAUSSE, E. 1971. *The Sociology of Occupations*. Boston, Mass., Little, Brown.

LAFFERTY, W. 1983. Workplace Democratization in Norway. Paper presented to international workshop: Future Perspectives of Economic and Industrial Democracy, Dubrovnik.

LONG, R. 1978. The Relative Effects of Share Ownership vs Control in an Employee Owned Company. *Human Relations*, Vol. 31, No. 9, September.

———. 1980. Job Attitudes and Organizational Performance Under Employee Ownership. *Academy of Management Journal*, Vol. 23, No. 4.

———. 1983. Employee Ownership: The North American Experience. Paper presented to international workshop: Future Perspectives of Economic and Industrial Democracy, Dubrovnik.

LOWI, T. J. 1969. *The End of Liberalism*. New York, W. W. Norton.

McKELWEY, W. W. 1969. Expectational Noncomplementarity and Style of Interactions Between Professionals and Organization. *Administration Science Quarterly*, Vol. 14, No. 1, March.

McLUHAN, M. 1964. *Understanding Media: The Extensions of Man*. New York, McGraw-Hill,

MAURICE, M.; SORGE, A.; WARNER, M. 1980. Societal Differences in Organizing Manufacturing Units. *Organization Studies*, Vol. 1, No. 1.

MULDER, M. 1971. Power Equalization Through Participation. *Administration*

Science Quarterly, Vol. 16, No. 1, March.

PARSONS, T. 1939. The Professions and the Social Structure. *Social Forces*, Vol. 17, No. 5, May.

PAVALKO, R. 1971. *Sociology of Occupations and Professions*. Itasca, Ill., Peacock.

POLZOV, V. R. 1966. Odpravljanje razlik med umskim in ročnim delom. *Teorija in praksa*, Vol. 3, No. 2, February.

PUSIĆ, V. 1973. Democracy and Self-Management. Paper presented to international workshop: Future Perspectives of Economic and Industrial Democracy, Dubrovnik.

ROBERTSON, J. 1983. If the Era of Full Employment is Over, What Will Come Next? *IFDA Dossier*, No. 35, May/June.

ROTHSCHILD-WITT, J. 1983. Worker Ownership as a Rorschach: How Competing Classes in the U.S. See It. Paper presented to international workshop: Future Perspectives of Economic and Industrial Democracy, Dubrovnik.

RUMBERGER, C.; RUSSEL, W. 1981. The Changing Skill Requirements of Jobs in U.S. Economy. *Industrial and Labor Relations Review*, Vol. 34, No. 4, July.

RUS, V. 1982. From Unemployment to Selfemployment. In: V. Rus, A. Ishikawa and T. Woodhouse (eds.), *Employment and Participation*. Tokyo, Chuo University Press.

RUSSEL, R. 1983. Employee Ownership in the Services. Paper presented to international workshop: Future Perspectives of Economic and Industrial Democracy, Dubrovnik.

SANDKULL, B. 1980. Practice of

Industry—Mismanagement of People. *Human Systems Management,* Vol. 1, No. 3, September.

——. 1983. Using New Technology to Prevent Economic and Industrial Democracy. Paper presented to international workshop: Future Perspectives of Economic and Industrial Democracy, Dubrovnik.

SCHULLER, T. 1983. Pension Funds and Economic Democracy; The UK Experience. Paper presented to international workshop: Future Perspectives of Economic and Industrial Democracy, Dubrovnik.

SHEPARD, J. M. 1971. *Automation and Alienation.*

Boston, Mass., MIT Press.

SHOWLER, B.; SINFIELD, A. 1981. *The Workless State.* Oxford, Martin Robertson.

SIMMOND, W. H. C. 1975. Industrial Behaviour Patterns, A New Dimension for Planners. *Futures,* Vol. 7, No. 4, August.

SINFIELD, A. 1981. *What Unemployment Means.* Oxford, Martin Robertson.

TOFFLER, A. 1971. *Future Shock.* London, Pan Books.

TRIST, E., 1980. The Environment and System Response Capability. *Futures,* Vol. 12, No. 2, April.

WOODHOUSE, T. 1982. Technological Change, Economic Recession and

Industrial Democracy. In: V. Rus, A, Ishikawa and T. Woodhouse (eds.), *Employment and Participation.* Tokyo, Chuo University Press.

——. 1983. Towards the Peaceful, Democratic Economy: Prospects in Britain. Paper presented to international workshop: Future Perspectives of Economic and Industrial Democracy, Dubrovnik.

YANKELOVICH, D. 1979. Work, Values, and the New Breed. In: C. Kerr and J. M. Rosow (eds.), *Work in America: The Decade Ahead.* New York, Van Nostrand Reinhold.

ZEMAN, Z. 1980. Manpower and Development in Eastern Europe. *Futures,* Vol. 12, No. 1, February.

What We Have Learned

What We Have Learned

The three interrelated programmes of research are about a central subject in the life of most people – namely, the influence they have over the half of their lives that is spent working. It is about the ubiquity of power and its distribution, which has not changed radically since the dawn of history (see Chapters 2, 37).

This final section concentrates on what I consider to be the principal theoretically interesting and action-relevant outcomes of each project area. Readers may already have made up their minds about what is most interesting for them; a broad picture was presented in the Introduction to the two volumes and each Part has its own overview. In these circumstances, an idosyncratic focused view may be permissible. I am aware that global generalizations, as in the previous paragraph, about the ubiquity of power and its relatively unchanging nature over time, invite criticism and may need to be adjusted in the light of explaining the concept of relativity. Of course, there have been changes in behaviour, sentiments, values and theoretical explanations relating to power, some of which are captured in these pages. At the same time there are aspects of hierarchy and dominance that reach back to our primate ancestors.

It is also worth noting that issues relating to the distribution of power in modern organizations have as many advocates as detractors. Advocates of organizational democracy speak with different voices, from the traditional practical claim that it increases organizational efficiency, or at least effectiveness (and therefore has competitive advantage), to the ideological position that it is a basic human right (see Chapter 1).

The position of most contributors to the projects reported here is somewhere in between these extremes. Influence-sharing in one form or another is seen as a requirement for human growth, maturity and skill development. Other things being reasonably equal, influence-sharing can therefore be seen as a competitive asset rather than a liability (see Chapters 1, 8 and 9). This position, and indeed the advocacy for organizational democracy, is not widely accepted, particularly by managers who believe that participative practices reduce their own influence and that this is sometimes associated with weak or indecisive leadership. Managers usually argue that power is a zero sum: one person's gain is another's loss.

Not everybody sees participation as a zero sum game (see Chapters 5 and 6). However, those who do are often prepared to ignore the evidence that even if there were a zero sum game situation, the impact on management is limited by the finding that, on average, employees want very little more influence than they have (see Chapter 20). Our findings also show quite clearly that lower-level employees, including even middle managers, have very little voice in the decision process (see Chapters 19, 20, 21). Furthermore, there are positive aspects to be considered – for instance, the finding that participation strengthens work motivation and liberates available employee competence (see Chapters 7, 29). More generally, one must be aware that there is always a gap between evidence and utilization even in biology and medicine – and more so in the social sciences. Thus, although the three programmes developed out of identified needs and had clear policy relevant focus, one should not expect social science findings to be implemented just because they appear to be statistically significant. The arguments about research utilization are complex and often acrimonious but one can detect a slowly emerging agreement that the relationship between the researcher and client (the people who supply the data) and the methodology of investigation has a great deal to do with the propensity to use the emerging conclusions.

There are many methodologies, including action research, that lay claim to facilitating utilization. In our programmes, the methods described in Chapters 10, 34 and 35 provide an example.

The Top Management Decision Making Programme (TMDM)

This research is based on eight countries, but the differences between them are less policy-relevant than the similarities. The main thrust of the six chapters and the recommended reading is to show that the distribution of power among top managers in large successful companies varies with the tasks they carry out and their judgement on the competence of their subordinates rather than with the personality of the executives. Although this is counter-intuitive for some people, it does not mean that personality is unimportant but, rather, that other contingencies are more prominent.

The practical implications of these findings are useful for management development and training. Managers have to be given an opportunity to develop a realistic appraisal of the competence of colleagues and subordinates. Our findings from all eight countries shows that this is frequently not the case and therefore has negative effects on their style of decision-making. Second, it is inappropriate to train managers in a 'one best' style of leadership; their interaction with colleagues and subordinates should adjust itself to the task in hand and to a correct assessment of the skill and experience of the available staff. Although participative methods are motivating and lead to a superior utilization of competence, the research shows that there are situations when a centralized style or delegation are more functional than sharing influence. There was virtual unanimity in all countries and at both senior levels that the most important reason for participation is the effect it has on improving the quality of decision-making.

Industrial Democracy in Europe (IDE)

The two large-scale projects described in 11 chapters and the recommended reading allow us to answer questions about the extent of participation in European companies (in manufacturing and service industry), the conditions under which democratic behaviour occurs and the consequences one can expect from it.

Perhaps the most important single finding is that, contrary to a widespread belief that legal and other formal support structures do not determine leadership behaviour in individual enterprises (which are thought to develop their own decision culture based on their own needs), the findings show that national laws affect behaviour even in small and medium-sized companies. Employees in countries that had legal and formal provisions for consultation had more influence over at least some decisions than employees in countries which had no such legal underpinning. This finding is robust, having emerged from two projects separated by ten years. It means that people and governments that advocate democratic practices only on a voluntary basis are unlikely to achieve their objectives.

At the same time these large-scale surveys in 12 European countries also demonstrate that very little real influence is given to lower levels of employees except over routine short-term rather than medium- or long-term decisions. Overall and on average, employees at the lowest level are rarely informed about decisions while foremen are informed but are not often asked to give an opinion. When staff were asked how much involvement they would like to have, the desired scores were moderately higher. For instance, at the lowest level they wanted to be able to give their opinion, but accepted that the opinion would not be taken into account. Foremen, on average, scored halfway between wanting to give their opinion and wanting to have it taken into account. The results show that employees in all countries accept the existence of hierarchy and an unequal distribution of influence, but want the inequality to be slightly reduced. As a consequence, it would seem that managerial fears of losing their decision-making prerogative are unrealistic.

Decisions in Organizations (DIO)

This longitudinal in-depth study in seven organizations in three countries complements the other two studies in content as well as methodology. One important outcome is therefore that the findings are congruent with TMDM and IDE I and II and consequently reinforce their conclusions.

One of the main thrusts of the nine chapters and recommended reading is to demonstrate the value of treating participation as a series of events over time. Time was divided into four phases and it emerged that the behaviour of managers – in particular the degree of participation with different levels of employees and the amount of conflict engendered by the decision process – varied significantly during these phases. This is the kind of finding which could not emerge from cross-sectional research and, since few studies are longitudinal, we are only beginning to understand the importance of looking at the distribution of influence over phases of events. There are indications that influence is exerted by employees in phases where they contribute experience and skill. This finding plus other evidence from the DIO study strongly reinforces the role of competence as a precondition for successful participation (see Part II especially Chapter 7).

The finding of IDE I and II that formal structures such as laws increase the amount of decision-making influence at lower levels is strongly reinforced by a variable called 'Status Power' (SP), defined in the DIO study as the formal influence of each organizational level as assessed from written records and the constitution of committees. This was conceived as similar – at the organizational level – to the national–legal support for organizational democracy called 'Power Structure' (PS). The results show that Status Power is a major predictor of the distribution of influence at all levels and, when SP is high for senior management, it leads to skill underutilization of lower levels.

Taken in conjunction with IDE, it seems that, like democratic practices in the political system, so democratic practices in enterprises need some formal support mechanism at national and/or organizational level.

Summing up

The second half of the twentieth century witnessed an increased appreciation of the role which employees can play in some aspects of the decision process in enterprises of all kinds. Social science research, including the three studies reported here, has played a part in clarifying the issues. Many of the findings are functional, have utility and do not constitute a threat to existing stakeholders. Can they help to speed up the slow process of organizational democratization in the 21st century?

Biographical Appendix

The following biographical material was supplied by authors of the articles and chapters published in these two volumes. However, the reader will be aware that several major contributions were published under acronyms like IDE and DIO. The reason for the use of acronyms was to avoid giving undue prominence to a name that would appear at the head of the list when all members of the group had contributed more or less equally to the collective research. Furthermore, the numbers involved were considerable: IDE I had 19 main authors, six Associates and three Corresponding members. Their names and affiliations appear in the Preface of the original book.

Professor Peter Abell
Director, Interdisciplinary Institute of Management
London School of Economics
Houghton St, Aldwych
LONDON WC2A 2AE
email: IIM@lse.ac.uk

Biographical statement for Peter Abell

Peter Abell is Director of the Interdisciplinary Institute of Management at the London School of Economics. His current interests include the nature of social theory, self-employment, entrepreneurship, and self-management.

Doctor Alan Brown
Principal Research Fellow
Institute for Employment Research
University of Warwick
COVENTRY CV4 7AL
email: alan.brown@warwick.ac.uk

Biographical statement for Alan Brown

Dr Alan Brown is a Principal Research Fellow in Education, Training and Employment at The Institute for Employment Research, University of Warwick.

Current research interests and major areas of work include (European) comparative vocational education and training, processes of skill formation, and development of occupational identities.

Professor Pieter Drenth
Vrije Universiteit Amsterdam
Dept. of Work & Organizational Psychology
van de Boechorststraat 1
1081 BT AMSTERDAM – Netherlands
pjd.drenth@psy.vu.nl

Biographical statement for Pieter Drenth

Pieter Drenth is Dean of the Faculty of Psychology and Education, Vrije Universiteit, Amsterdam, and Chairman of the Social Science Research Council, Royal Netherlands Academy of Arts and Sciences, Amsterdam. He has been professor of psychology (specializations: psychometrics, methodology and work- and organizational psychology) at the Vrije Universiteit since 1967.

His principal fields of interest and research have been test- and scale theory, intelligence theory, personality assessment, leadership and decision making, human resource management, and cross-cultural psychology. More recently his activities and publications have been concerned with science policy and science organization, and social and ethical questions in science. These interests grew from his administrative experience and responsibilities in science (Vice-Chancellor, Vrije Universiteit, 1982–1987; President Royal Netherlands Academy of Arts and Sciences, 1990–1996; and Chairman Social Science Research Council, 1999–).

Professor Peter Dachler
Hoogschule St Gallen
Guisanstrasse 11
CH-9010 ST GALLEN – Switzerland
email: Peter.Dachler@Psy.Unisg.Ch

Biographical statement for H. Peter Dachler

Peter Dachler is currently Professor of organizational psychology and Director of the Research Institute for Organizational Psychology at the University of St Gallen, Switzerland.

His research activities have covered a wide spectrum of areas from work motivation, leadership, participation, selection, organizational climate, assessment centres, women in leadership and management positions, to the current research projects that deal with the social processes of reality construction (relational theory).

Peter Dachler is a member of various US and European scientific associations and founding fellow of the American Psychological Society, as well as Fellow of the Society for Industrial and Organizational Psychology (SIOP) of the American Psychological Association. He was president of the Organizational Division of the International Association of Applied Psychology (IAAP) from 1994 to 1998 and is cofounder and served as the first president of the Swiss Society of Work and Organizational Psychology (SGAOP).

Doctor Frank Heller
The Tavistock Institute
30 Tabernacle Street
LONDON EC2A 4UE
Tel: +44(0)171 417 4573910 (Direct Line)
Fax: +44(0)171 417 0566
email: heller@tavinstitute.org

Biographical statement for Frank Heller

Dr Heller is the Director of the Centre for Decision Making Studies (CDMS) of The Tavistock Institute in London and a Visiting Professor at the University of Hangzhou, China and the University of Santiago in Chile.

His work has covered four main areas of social science: (i) the process of organizational decision making, (ii) the nature and distribution of power, (iii) the dynamics of change, and (iv) action orientated research methodology. Field research has tended to be longitudinal using feedback to encourage organizational learning and a recognition of resistance as a natural dynamic. Some of the most recent work has used the sociotechnical model and expanded its application at the macro level including the impact of technology on the environment. The under-utilization of the application of social science knowledge and the under-utilization of competence in organizations has been a *Leitmotif* throughout.

Professor Paul Koopman
Professor of Psychology of Management and Organization
Vrije Universiteit Amsterdam
Dept. of Work and Organizational Psychology
van de Boechorststraat 1
1081 BT AMSTERDAM – Netherlands
email: PL.Koopman@psy.vu.nl

Biographical statement for Paul Koopman

Paul Koopman is professor of the Psychology of Management and Organization at the Vrije Universiteit Amsterdam. In 1980 he finished his PhD study at the same university on the subject 'Decision making in organizations', a comparative research project in former Yugoslavia, UK and the Netherlands.

Since then he studied different types of processes of management and decision making on organizational level (industrial democracy, reorganization, turnaround management, privatization in Eastern Europe) and departmental level (leadership and motivation, works' consultation, quality circles, team work, automation, innovation management). For a few years he joined the Philips organization, where he was involved in complex reorganization processes. He is visiting professor of the Hangzhou University (People's Republic of China), and honorary associate of the Tavistock Institute (Centre for Decision Making Studies) in London. From 1995–1999 he was a member of the Executive committee of the European Association of Work and Organizational Psychology (EAWOP).

At this moment he is interested and actively involved in cross-cultural research, in particular in relation to issues of HRM, leadership and organizational culture. He is involved in international research projects with Robert House (culture and leadership in 65 countries), Michael West (reflexivity in teams) and Zhong-Ming Wang (differences in HRM-practices between China and the Netherlands). He was (co)author of books on decision making, charismatic leadership, organizational culture, and Human Resource Management.

Professor Oiva Laaksonen (Deceased)
Professor of Organization
Institute of Organization and Management
Helsinki School of Economics
HELSINKI – Finland

Professor William M. Lafferty
ProSus (Programme for Research and Documentation for a Sustainable Society)
Post Box 1097
0317 OSLO 3 – Norway
Tel: + 47 2 45 5181/82
email: Bill@PROSUS.nf.no

Biographical statement for William M. Lafferty

William M. Lafferty is currently Professor of Political Science, University of Oslo and Director of ProSus: Programme for Research and Documentation for a Sustainable Society, Research Council of Norway. His other appointments include Adjunct Professor, Western Norway Research Institute, Sogndal, Norway, and Adjunct Professor, CSTM, University of Twente, Enschede, The Netherlands.

Among his main current areas of work and/or interest are: Environment and Development, Sustainable Development, Democracy and the Environment, Participation and Change, and Democracy and policy implementation.

Professor Cornelis Lammers
Aert van Neslaan 612
2341 HV-OEGSTGEEST – Netherlands
email: lammers@rulfsw.leidenuniv.nl

Biographical statement for Cornelis Lammers

Cornelis J. Lammers is Professor Emeritus of the Sociology of Organization, University of Leiden, The Netherlands. He studied sociology at the Universities of Michigan, Ann-Arbor (USA) and Amsterdam (The Netherlands) where he obtained his PhD with a thesis on a comparison of the socialization of naval cadets and candidate reserve officers of the Royal

Dutch Navy (1963). His interest in comparative studies has continued ever since, for example in his activities as a member of the international IDE (Industrial Democracy in Europe) research team, in an anthology he edited with David J. Hickson, *Organizations alike and unlike* (London, 1979), in a treatise on the development and relevance of sociological thinking on organizations, *Organisaties Vergelijkenderwijs* (Organizations in Comparative Perspective, Utrecht, 1983) and last but not least, in his work in recent years on the sociology of occupation of conquered territories.

Professor Thoralf Qvale
Work Research Institute
P.O. Box 8171 Dep.
N-0034 OSLO – Norway
email: tq@afi-wri.no

Biographical statement for Thoralf Qvale

Thoralf Qvale, MSc is Research Director, Work Research Institute, Oslo and Professor, Technology Management, Department of Industrial Economics and Technology Management, The Norwegian University of Science and Technology, Trondheim.

He is currently leading the Institute group which is involved in action research in the private sector with the purpose of promoting productivity through participative procedures. The projects are all within the tri-partite research and development tradition which was started in collaboration between Einar Thorsrud and Fred Emery around 1960. Currently, focus is on developing long term collaborative relationships between research centres and groups of enterprises and institutions at the regional level. The institute, through a research group of circa 12 scientists, is participating in a national R&D programme developed in collaboration between the labour market organizations, the science foundation and seven applied research centres in Norway. Professor Qvale's main research interest for the time being is linked to what in earlier days was called the issue of 'diffusion' of participative forms of work organization. Today the challenge seems to be to work with large systems, across organizational boundaries with methods which secure human values like participation, learning and the quality of the working environment, a good fit between work and private life, learning and democracy. He is particularly interested in methods which can help educational and research institutions to develop new roles in this context. He is using his position as professor in the university in Trondheim for this purpose.

Professor Veljko Rus
Faculty of Social Sciences, Institute of Social Sciences
Kardeljeva ploščad 1
1000 LJUBLJANA – Slovenia

Biographical statement for Veljko Rus

Veljko Rus's current job title and other main affiliations are: Member of the Slovenian Academy of Science and Arts, Senior researcher, Coordinator of the Centre for Evaluation and Strategic Studies, and Member of the State Council.

Until the late 1980s Veljko Rus was involved in research on power, participation and responsibilities in work organizations. In the early 1990s he was mainly occupied with research on the welfare state and social services in Slovenia and in other Central European Countries. More recently his work has been focused on privatization of social services and issues which are part of New Public Management. His current interest is to participate in World Value Studies of 42 countries within which he would like to analyze Slovenian data.

Professor Bengt Stymne
The Economic Research Institute Stockholm
School of Economics
Box 6501
SE-11383 STOCKHOLM – Sweden
email: Bengt.Stymne@HHS.SE

Biographical statement for Bengt Stymne

At present Bengt Stymne is one of the leaders of a new programme called 'Fenix' that aims at developing the future leaders of Astra Zenia, Ericsson, Telia, and Volvo by running an executive PhD programme for successful managers of development projects in these companies. The PhD programme is linked to a research programme carried out jointly with industry. The research concerns the organizing of complexity, management of knowledge, and innovating stabilised structures. At present he is involved in research projects on organizational innovation, wage incentives for knowledge acquisition, corporate governance of public services, and organization of production in the globalized economy.

Professor Zhong-ming Wang
Vice-President, Hangzhou University
Professor and Dean, School of Management
University of Hangzhou
34 Tianmushan Road
HANGZHOU 310028
Zhejiang – China
email: zmwang@tiger.hzuniv.edu.cn

Biographical statement for Zhong-ming Wang

In addition to his position as Vice-President of Hangzhou University and Professor and Dean, School of Management, Hangzhou University, Zhong-ming Wang is Director of HRM Research Institute, President of Chinese SIOP; Vice-President of Chinese Ergonomics Society, and the Vice-President of the Chinese Personnel Assessment Committee. He is Associate editor of both the *Chinese Journal of Applied Psychology* and *Chinese Ergonomics*. He is an editorial board member of *International Journal of Human Resource Management, International Journal of Selection and Assessment, Applied Psychology, Journal of Cross-Cultural Psychology, Journal of Organizational Behavior and Human Decision Process, International Journal of Management Review, Journal of Management Development, Journal of Managerial Psychology, Journal of World Business,* and *Journal of Organizational Behavior.*

Professor Wang's main research areas and current interests include cross-cultural organizational behaviour, strategic human resource management, personnel selection, assessment and performance, organizational decision-making, leadership teams, and organization development.

Professor Malcolm Warner
Judge Institute of Management Studies
University of Cambridge
CAMBRIDGE CB2 1AG
email: Warner@dial.pipex.com

Biographical statement for Malcolm Warner

Malcolm Warner is Professor and Fellow of Wolfson College and the Judge Institute of Management Studies at the University of Cambridge. He is Editor-in-Chief of the International Encyclopedia of Business and Management (Thomson: London) 6 volumes, 1996.

His interests include human resource management, Asian management, cross-cultural management and virtual management.

Professor Bernhard Wilpert
Technische Universitat Berlin
Institut fur Psychologie
Franklinstr. 28, FR 3-8
10587 BERLIN – Germany

Biographical statement for Bernhard Wilpert

Since 1978 Bernhard Wilpert has been Professor of Work and Organizational Psychology at the Technical University, Berlin. He has made a number of international comparative studies in management and participation, and the introduction of new technologies. He was President of the International Association of Applied Psychology (1994–1998) and since 1990 has been Director of the Research Centre Systems Safety and, from 1993–98 was a member of the German Reactor Safety Commission and chairperson of its Work Group 'Man-Technology Organization'.

His present research interests include safety and reliability of complex socio-technical systems with high hazard potential.

Professor Gary Yukl
Management Department, School of Business
State University of NY at Albany
1400 Washington Avenue
ALBANY NY 12222 – USA

Biographical statement for Gary Yukl

Gary Yukl received a PhD in Industrial-Organizational Psychology from the University of California at Berkeley in 1967. He is currently a Professor in the Management Department, State University of New York at Albany.

Dr Yukl's current research interests include leadership, power and influence, management training, and change management. He has published many articles in professional journals, and he has received four best paper and best article awards for his research. Dr Yukl has written ten books, including *Leadership in Organizations* (Prentice-Hall, 1998).

Dr Yukl is a fellow of the American Psychological Association, the American Psychological Society, and the Academy of Management. He has served on the editorial board of several key professional journals and was an associate editor for the *Academy of Management Review*.

He has consulted with a variety of business and public sector organizations, and his management development programmes have been used in a number of large corporations. He has been invited to lecture about leadership at many universities, companies, and professional conferences.

Name Index

For Product Safety Concerns and Information please contact our EU
representative GPSR@taylorandfrancis.com Taylor & Francis Verlag GmbH,
Kaufingerstraße 24, 80331 München, Germany

Printed and bound by CPI Group (UK) Ltd, Croydon, CR0 4YY
08/05/2025
01864422-0004